THE TWENTIETH-CENTURY MIND
I
1900–1918

THE TWENTIETH-CENTURY MIND

in three volumes

THE
TWENTIETH-CENTURY
MIND

History, Ideas, and Literature in Britain

EDITED BY

C. B. Cox and A. E. Dyson

I
1900–1918

OXFORD UNIVERSITY PRESS

LONDON   OXFORD   NEW YORK

1972

Oxford University Press

LONDON OXFORD NEW YORK
GLASGOW TORONTO MELBOURNE WELLINGTON
CAPE TOWN IBADAN NAIROBI DAR ES SALAAM LUSAKA ADDIS ABABA
DELHI BOMBAY CALCUTTA MADRAS KARACHI LAHORE DACCA
KUALA LUMPUR SINGAPORE HONG KONG TOKYO

Clothbound edition ISBN 0 19 212191 X
Paperback edition ISBN 0 19 281118 5

© Oxford University Press 1972

First published as an Oxford University Press paperback,
and simultaneously in a clothbound edition, by
Oxford University Press, London, 1972

*Printed in Great Britain
by Richard Clay (The Chaucer Press), Ltd.,
Bungay, Suffolk*

CONTENTS

Introduction

This is not an encyclopaedia. If it were, it would have to include subjects such as South American history, Eastern mystical thought, and Arabic literature. We have asked a number of well-known scholars to write about developments in their own subject in the twentieth century. We have asked them to emphasize the climate of thought in Britain, but suggested that in certain cases major treatment should be given to developments overseas. The history chapters, and similarly the philosophy chapter, are mainly confined to Britain. In literature, too, we have restricted ourselves chiefly to British writers, though in the chapter on the novel Professor Friedman gives a brief account of European and American fiction. We have made a major exception in the case of drama, and encouraged Mr. Palmer to concentrate on Ibsen, Strindberg, Chekhov, Synge, and Shaw, as these are the main influences on the modern British theatre.

In psychology and the sciences, new discoveries become part of the international scene, and so in these chapters the authors give a general survey of the whole field. Our two chapters on social thought deal separately with the British and continental background. Mr. Raymond Plant's chapter gives an account of the influence of Marxism, obviously of vital importance in this period. We end with Mr. Edward Lucie-Smith's most comprehensive general survey of the other arts, whose forms also tend to be international.

Our idea is to provide the student with some sense of what has been going on in this century in some of the major disciplines of thought. For many years it has been fashionable to deplore the harmful effects of excessive specialization, and to assert the need for general or interdisciplinary studies. The famous text is C. P. Snow's *The Two Cultures*, in which he stresses how Arts people are often ignorant of the most important scientific discoveries, while scientists may know nothing of Wittgenstein or T. S. Eliot. But when we try to cope with this problem, we soon discover that to devise courses in general studies is very difficult. There is the danger that the student will know less and less about more and more, and that as he moves in one day from history to philosophy to physics he will fail to grasp the true nature of any of these disciplines. The sciences in particular have made their discoveries by creating special 'languages', and to understand these is no easy matter, to be picked up satisfactorily by an amateur through casual reading of paperbacks. Even the trained literary critic may be surprised to find that intelligent outsiders are mystified by his mode of discourse.

This situation has determined the form of our three volumes. We believe that one purpose of university study is to reveal to the student the extent of his own ignorance. The old idea of the cultivated gentleman, reasonably conversant with all major areas of thought, is impossibly out-of-date. In one lifetime no one individual has time to study all the major disciplines in depth. Therefore, as he tries to understand the bewildering variety of modern thought, each student must make a centre in one or two forms of specialist knowledge. He must become intimate with the detailed, rich climate of thought in a specific subject. From this centre he may push out into other disciplines, reading major works, relating ideas to the central areas of thought in which he is an expert, continually aware of his own ignorance. But no one can ever fill in all the gaps. World history is too huge for any one man to study the whole in any detail. Most of us can know only two or three languages, and in the sciences it is increasingly difficult to keep up to date with even the most narrow fields of research.

In our volumes, therefore, we have made a centre in Britain, and asked our authors to write in detail about specific events and ideas, rather than to provide only a superficial, encyclopaedic type of article. Such treatment inevitably causes major gaps, for with our approach we should need at least twenty-four volumes to give any comprehensive account of the twentieth-century mind. We believe, however, that by reading these chapters the student can gain some 'feel' of some of the major subjects, and that the brief reading lists may help him to extend his studies.

We have encouraged our contributors to select rigorously, and to concentrate on major ideas and writers. We have not rigidly adhered to the dates 1900 to 1918. Where there is a need to explain pre-1900 developments, or to take a trend to its logical conclusion after 1918, this has been done. Certain fields, such as theology and sociology, will be covered in a comprehensive chapter later.

In this first volume, the chapters concern the early years of this century. It is particularly fascinating to see experts in different fields describing their respective subjects in their own terms. Is it possible to make generalizations about the temper of the period? On the one hand, one could emphasize that this was the golden,

Edwardian period, supposedly serene, relaxed, complacent, before the devastating horror of 1914. Many writers were still imbued with the liberal faith in historical progress, individual freedom, tolerance, and the power of reason. In the chapter on historiography, Mr. Langhorne describes the influence of the liberal Catholic, Lord Acton, who was convinced that history showed progress towards general freedom of conscience. But on the other hand, the history chapters depict the turbulence of the social scene, and show that the period was one of tranquillity only for a privileged and possibly short-sighted élite. The social optimism of a Shaw or Wells must be balanced against ominous forebodings from the earliest years of the century in writers as different from each other as Conrad, Hardy, and Henry James. Mr. Plant's account of the development of Marxism points forward to the events of 1917.

Also, in various disciplines of thought changes were taking place which were to disrupt the optimists' faith that man's reason would gradually bring Utopia upon earth, and that reality was a harmonious whole tending towards perfection. Perhaps most important were the discoveries of the psychologists. The period begins with the publication in 1900 of Freud's *The Interpretation of Dreams*. Professor Hearnshaw tells us that at the centre of Freudian theory was the doctrine of two levels of mental functioning, primary and secondary processes:

Primary processes constitute a different and more basic type of thinking, best exemplified in dreams, but also in childhood fantasies, in the myths of primitive peoples, and in psychological disorders. Primary processes are symbolic and pictorial, lacking in objectivity or strict logic, and aimed not at truth but at pleasure and the expression of wishes and desires. By contrast, secondary processes, precariously developed in the course of civilization, are logical, objective, critical, rational, and directed towards reality. Psychoanalytical teaching shifted the balance of power in the human psyche from the secondary to the primary, and thus undermined the orthodox belief of western man, established since Greek times, in the priority of reason. The primitive mind, according to Freud, is imperishable, and not only openly dominates in dreams and disease, but subtly interpenetrates and distorts apparently rational processes. In the last resort it has the mastery. (P. 236.)

This undermining of the belief in the absolute value of reason can be seen in other changes of thought. In the philosophy chapter Mr. Bell describes the influence of G. E. Moore and Bertrand Russell, which induced in most philosophers a complete scepticism about the metaphysical–religious certainties of idealism:

Perhaps the most lasting effect of the comprehensive destructiveness of Moore's *Principia Ethica* was to replace philosophical debate *within* ethics, by philosophical debate about the whole enterprise and *logical* status of ethical enquiry. Scepticism about morality deriving from logical considerations could also ally itself with scepticism springing from the sociologist's and anthropologist's newly awakened interest in the widely different moral practices of peoples separated from us in time and space. (Pp. 177–8.)

The revolution in physics, which culminates in the publication of the special theory of relativity by Einstein in 1905, seemed to have solved the long-standing metaphysical question about whether space and time were absolute or relative:

While some surviving idealists greeted the demonstration of the relativity of space and time as a victory over materialism, more sophisticated philosophers such as Russell and Whitehead saw it as a triumph of the application of formal techniques to the definition of concepts. Furthermore, the point that according to Einstein two events are only simultaneous *for* a given observer was taken as justifying the relativism to an observer implicit in all empiricist epistemology. (P. 209.)

In the sciences themselves the old faith that rational inquiry could eventually solve all problems had been displaced by an awareness that absolute knowledge is unattainable, and that all scientific information is relative to the human observer. In his chapter on developments in physics, Professor Cole writes:

We are not dealing with the description of a universe in isolation from an observer; the observer is an essential part and his general (non-personal) characteristics influence his description of what he finds. The recognition of the central role of the observer is a characteristic feature of the physics of this century, and will continually emerge as an important constraint on our description of measured data. The idea that things are seen relative to a particular observer, rather than absolutely, is at the very root of modern physical thought, and contrasts markedly with the viewpoint of earlier centuries where the ultimate recognition of absolutes remained a possibility. (P. 250.)

The discoveries of Freud, Russell, and Einstein are reflected in all the arts. Professor Friedman points out how Henry James's technique has kinships with Einstein's relativity theory. In his great novels of the early 1900s, all values and measurements depend entirely on the selection of the 'point of view' of the observer. This parallels the development of the 'point of view' novel by Ford Madox Ford and Joseph Conrad.

The discoveries of Darwin also had long-term effects on the artist. In *The Disappearance of God*, J. Hillis Miller argues that for nineteenth-century writers such as Arnold and Tennyson, God seems to have withdrawn from the physical world. They try desperately to call him back, to find intimations of God in nature, society, and the soul. But Nietzsche's pronouncement that God is dead is the necessary conclusion—or so to many it seemed—of their uncertainties. Darwin's concepts of nature point towards the tragic worlds of Thomas Hardy, Ibsen, or Strindberg. The power of Christian belief was further weakened by the publication of Sir James Frazer's *The Golden Bough* in 1890, with the consequent awareness that Christian ideas of the dying god are paralleled in many primitive religions. The second edition of *The Golden Bough* came out in 1900, and in this Frazer first defined the relation of religion to magic, and speculated on the origins of the Christian religion.

Frazer was an armchair anthropologist who never engaged in field work. He was a man of the eighteenth century in his faith in reason, order, decorum, and good sense, and these virtues are exemplified in his prose style. His trust in the comparative method has been seriously questioned by modern anthropologists. He accepted that every society passes through the same stages, and this development is necessarily in the direction of progress and improvement. His contradictions typify the age. With his touching faith in reason and good sense he proved to the twentieth century how powerful are the irrational and savage elements in human civilizations. His influence on the artistic imagination, most obviously on T. S. Eliot's *The Waste Land*, has been immense.

Also of major importance were William James's Gifford Lectures at Edinburgh, published as *The Varieties of Religious Experience* (1902). Religion is considered as an area of psychological fact, and treated from the point of view of science and common sense. In *Pragmatism* (1907), also very influential, James argued that an idea has meaning only in relation to its consequences in the world of feeling and action.

All these developments, highly complicated and needing detailed treatment to be understood precisely, are part of a huge shift in the climate of opinion. The departure of God from ordinary social thinking is the starting-point for many twentieth-century writers. It was increasingly to be assumed, along with Comte, that theology and metaphysics belonged to earlier phases of human thought, and that the new 'positive' age—the age of pragmatism and sociology—

would study all moral and social questions without reference to, and without assumptions concerning, religious belief. 'God is dead' meant, of course, not that God really was dead and required an obituary, but that the idea of God was dead as a social power. Where, however, was man, without his creator? Was he more, or less, free on his own? If man knows only his own consciousness and lives without God, then what in fact does he know? The 'self' may prove isolated, locked in a prison, hearing, in T. S. Eliot's words, 'the key turn in the door once and turn once only'. In Conrad and James nothing exists except as it is seen by someone viewing the world from his own perspective. In Conrad the nihilism implicit in such attitudes is brought to the surface and shown for what it is. For him civilization is an illusion, an arbitrary set of rules and judgements, a house of cards built over an abyss. 'A man that is born', says Stein in *Lord Jim*, 'falls into a dream like a man who falls into the sea.' The pessimism of *Nostromo* (1904), in which purposive action seems always futile, foretells the dominating mood of much twentieth-century art.

Both Edward Lucie-Smith and John Wain feel that these under-currents of the pre-1914 world prefigure the horror that was to be realized in the Great War. Lucie-Smith suggests that if a single date be chosen to mark the birth of modern painting it must be 1905, when the artists who were immediately labelled the 'Fauves' or 'wild beasts' exhibited in Paris. In modernist painting there is 'a kind of will to barbarism, the feeling that the ground must be cleared with great sweeps of the axe if painting was to begin anew'. Of the pre-1914 styles, Lucie-Smith writes: 'They represent the exuberance, the fierce aggressiveness and nationalism, even the will to destruction, of those dizzying years. The ferocity and daring of much of the painting I have discussed may be thought of as a kind of pre-echo of political events.' (P. 497.) The vast technological changes of the nineteenth century, some of which are described in Mr. Wren-Lewis's chapter, had induced a restlessness, a sense of alienation, which expressed itself in the cult of violence typical of so much twentieth-century art.

John Wain similarly comments on the violent, disjointed, extravagant nature of modern literature, which led Thomas Mann to remark that in his lifetime the traditional categories of comedy and tragedy had disappeared, leaving the grotesque as the dominant literary mode. Wain puts forward the ineffective, death-in-life character, T. S. Eliot's Prufrock, as the figure who adequately sums up Western civilization in 1917:

For the tragedy of the years between, say, 1910 and 1918 is precisely that the highly-developed western nations had fallen into a trance. During the brief but golden epoch that we in England call 'Edwardian', progress seemed assured and civilization on an even keel. No one, or at any rate, no one who spoke for or to the 'average man', had any inkling of the forces of death that waited under the placid surface. Yet these forces must have been there, *in petto*; the four-year orgy of murder could not have suddenly descended on Europe like a cloud; it must have had latent causes in the very blood and nerves of the society that felt so sure of its reasonableness. And, after the slide into suicide of August 1914, the sleeper did not awake; he merely turned from a pleasing dream to a nightmare. (P. 410.)

We hope the individual chapters will stimulate students to read the original works of thinkers and artists for themselves. The bibliographies that follow the chapters offer guidance for further background reading in the various fields.

An excellent collection, *The Modern Tradition: Backgrounds of Modern Literature*, edited by Richard Ellmann and Charles Feidelson, Jr. (New York, 1965), traces cultural and intellectual history back to the eighteenth century. It includes selected texts by artists, philosophers, theologians, and psychologists, source material far more worth reading than a hundred commentaries. Other general surveys are *Edwardians and Late Victorians*, ed. Richard Ellmann (New York, 1960) and Samuel Hynes, *The Edwardian Turn of Mind* (Princeton, 1968). The latter is a richly documented examination of intellectual and social currents flowing in and out of the literature of England during the century's first decade. Useful reading lists for all the major British writers are to be found in *The Modern Age* (vol. VII of *The Pelican Guide to English Literature*), ed. B. Ford (1961). Several paperback series provide selections of famous essays on particular writers; see especially the Prentice-Hall *Twentieth-Century Views* series, ed. Maynard Mack, and the Macmillan *Casebooks*, ed. A. E. Dyson. Often it is best to read just one or two such essays, rather than to waste time with a glut of criticism.

C. B. Cox
A. E. Dyson

February 1971

History: Political and Diplomatic

DONALD READ

I

Queen Victoria died on 22 January 1901. On the next day young Winston Churchill (1874–1965) wrote to his mother with youthful flippancy more in anticipation of the future than in sorrow at the end of a long and notable reign. 'Edward the VIIth—gadzooks, what a long way that seems to take one back! I am glad he has got his innings at last, and am most interested to watch how he plays it.' Monarchs were changing, and so was the world around them, as monarchs themselves sometimes realized. Queen Mary agreed with her aunt in 1911 'about the ideas of the two centuries being so totally different, and it has come so rapidly too'. The Edwardian world, sometimes presented in retrospect as completely assured, unchanging as Queen Mary's toque, seemed to Edwardians themselves to be undergoing rapid alteration—political, social, economic, and technological. Rupert Brooke (1887–1915) was impressed in 1910 by the contrast between his own background and that of his Victorian uncle of seventy. 'The whole machinery of life, and the minds of every class and kind of men, change beyond recognition every generation. I don't know that "Progress" is certain,' admitted Brooke. 'All I know is that change is.' Change pressed upon the Edwardians, in the words of H. G. Wells (1866–1946), as upon a fine day in early October. 'One frost and the whole face of things will be bare.'

'Old-fashioned raptures about progress are voted middle-class—a dreadful thing to be—provincial, awful, vulgar, early-Victorian.' So complained Augustine Birrell (1850–1933), a Liberal Cabinet minister, man of letters, and himself a Victorian survival.[1] Edwardian young men (and women) viewed their Victorian inheritance with suspicion. Politics after 1901 were increasingly dominated by controversies about matters which most Victorians had not regarded as open to discussion. This Edwardian reaction against Victorian political certainties can be seen in six expressions:

(1) in the attack upon free trade, launched by the 'tariff reformers' from 1903;

(2) in the introduction of the 'social service state' by the Liberal Governments after 1906;
(3) in the unprecedented trade-union unrest of 1911–12;
(4) in the increasingly militant demand for 'votes for women', voiced by the suffragettes from 1905;
(5) in the resurgence of the Irish question, culminating in the threat of civil war in Ireland in 1914;
(6) in the acceptance of novel, even though vague, commitments towards France and Russia in their rivalry with Germany and Austria, underlying the British declaration of war on 4 August 1914.

II

The debate for and against these policies took place within a far from democratic electoral system: not simply 'one man one vote', not at all 'one woman one vote'. The compromise Franchise Act of 1884 had left an eccentric registration system unreformed. All women and over 40 per cent of men were without the vote in 1911. By contrast, of the 7,900,000 men (mostly householders) who did enjoy the franchise over half a million could cast plural votes.[2] Paradoxically, interest in politics was probably more continuous under this limited franchise than under the genuine democracy of later years. Meetings were often well attended, and they were fully reported in the newspapers. Nevertheless, sport watching and reporting, especially of association football, was competing increasingly for audiences and for space in the popular press. When payment of Members of Parliament (at £400 a year) was introduced in 1911, *Punch* showed a working man disdainfully pointing out his Member, speaking in the market-place, with the remark that 'we could 'ave two first-class 'arf-backs for the same money'. In Lord Northcliffe's (1865–1922) *Daily Mail*, started in 1896 and selling three-quarters of a million copies daily by the early 1900s, politics were freshly presented in terms of personalities and drama. 'We must get the *news* in politics,' explained Northcliffe, '. . . no long-winded columns of mere words and hackneyed speeches of corrupt solemnity. . . . Make the paper a happy one.' Winston Churchill, a favourite *Mail* personality, deliberately timed his evening speeches early enough to ensure full and friendly notice in the next morning's paper.[3]

Churchill had entered the Commons as a Conservative in 1900, crossing the floor of the House four years later to become a Liberal.

He wanted to make Liberalism 'the cause of the left-out millions'. Gladstone's (1809–98) Victorian Liberal party had concentrated upon setting the people free; but abstract liberty had left Victorian working men still exposed to sickness, unemployment, and hunger. 'That the world must be made a better place for the unprivileged many,' admitted the *Manchester Guardian*, a leading Liberal daily, in 1895, 'is a conviction which has come home to most of us, however little of socialists we may be.' Unfortunately, Gladstone's late preoccupation with Irish Home Rule had diverted the Liberals after 1895 into ten years of opposition; for the British electorate would not countenance Irish separation. But the Liberal return to power in 1905 was followed by a famous series of social reforms. In his 1911 Home University Library volume on *Liberalism* L. T. Hobhouse (1864–1929) now found no true opposition 'between liberty as such and control as such', only between 'the control that cramps the personal life and the spiritual order, and the control that is aimed at securing the external and material conditions of their free and unimpeded development'.[4]

In a companion volume on *The Socialist Movement* Ramsay MacDonald (1866–1937), leader of the Labour party, offered a personal interpretation of socialism which overlapped considerably with Hobhouse's Liberalism. Social re-organization, argued MacDonald, was 'the condition, not the antithesis of individual liberty'. MacDonald even took pains to emphasize how the Labour party was 'not socialist'. It was a federation of socialist societies, trade unions, trade councils, and local Labour parties 'for immediate political work'. The Independent Labour party, formed in 1893, was the largest truly socialist body. Its founder, Keir Hardie (1856–1915), had worked hard during the 1890s to win trade-union support for independent labour representation in Parliament. In 1900 he secured the formation of the Labour Representation Committee. At the 1906 general election 30 Labour Members of Parliament were returned. This breakthrough had been much assisted by a quiet electoral pact made with the Liberals in 1903. No longer could it be assumed, as *Iolanthe* had believed in 1882, that every boy and every girl would be born 'either a little Liberal or else a little Conservative'.[5]

Only a minority, however, of the 329,000 electors who voted Labour in 1906 were genuine socialists. This constrained Labour in Parliament between 1906 and 1914 to act with moderation. Yet this in turn made it difficult for the new party to project a separate identity. Paradoxically, this dilemma became more serious after the general elections of 1910 when the Liberals were able to continue in office only with Labour and Irish support. Hardie then complained that Labour had 'almost ceased to count'. In the first 1910 election not a single Labour candidate was returned against official Liberal opposition. No one could foresee in 1914 how four years of war would undermine Liberalism, and give Labour its chance to emerge as the major reform party.[6]

Conservative politicians, finding themselves in opposition after 1905, liked to exaggerate the danger of 'socialism'. There was, claimed Lord Hugh Cecil (1869–1956) in his 1912 Home University Library volume on *Conservatism*, 'a taint of jacobinism in socialist language'. In fact, as we shall show, the resistance of the Conservative party to the 1909 budget and to Irish Home Rule proved much more likely than the attitudes of the Labour party to produce political violence before 1914. Cecil presented the Conservative creed as support for the monarchy, the empire, the Established Church, and the rights of property. Conservatism, explained Cecil, had been formulated by Edmund Burke to defend these interests against the Jacobin principles of the French Revolution. It was 'plain that to take what one man has and give it to another is unjust, even though the first man be rich and the second man poor'. Cecil did admit both the Christianity and the expediency of paternalistic assistance for the poor. Paternalism, which strengthened property rights and class differences, was a traditional part of the Conservative philosophy. At the opening of the twentieth century Conservatives had yet to concede that paternalism was not enough.[7]

Cecil admitted that a critic 'might complain that selfishness, avarice, and an uncontrolled taste for alcoholic liquors were all elements that made for the success of Conservative politicians'. The party in Parliament was traditionally inclined towards the landed aristocracy and gentry, and increasingly towards the 'beerage' and high finance. In the December 1910 House of Commons equal numbers (272) of Liberal and Conservative/Liberal Unionist members were elected. Analysis of their occupational backgrounds shows that in banking, insurance, and finance the Liberals were outnumbered 92–124; Liberal landowners totalled only 38 against 123, brewers and distillers only 1 against 12.[8]

III

The Conservative leader and Prime Minister at the turn of the century was the Marquess of Salisbury (1830–1903), head of the

Cecil family, and one of the country's greatest magnates. When he retired in 1902 he was succeeded by his nephew, A. J. Balfour (1848–1930), who served as Prime Minister until 1905. Balfour was able as well as aristocratic, but his ability was of a cast which did not strengthen his party leadership. He was a keen amateur philosopher, the author of *A Defence of Philosophic Doubt*, published in 1879. When convinced about a course of action he could be tenacious, as in his advocacy of the 1902 Education Act. But where his refined intellect left him partly sympathetic to both sides of an argument, as in the controversy over 'tariff reform' which engulfed his Ministry in 1903, he was disinclined to give a lead:

> I'm not for Free Trade, and I'm not for Protection.
> I approve of them both, and to both have objection.

Balfour was a wit ('History never repeats itself: historians repeat each other'), knowledgeable about music, and enthusiastic about tennis even in old age. His talents made him a leading figure in Edwardian country-house life, an engaging host, 'an incomparable guest'. But to the public at large he was less appealing. 'He has no comprehension of the habits of thought of his countrymen,' remarked a colleague, 'and no idea of how things strike them.' He showed little understanding even of the new businessmen who were gradually taking control of the Conservative party in the constituencies from the aristocracy and gentry. In 1891 he condescendingly described his successor as Irish Chief Secretary, a worsted manufacturer, as 'that *rara avis*, a successful manufacturer who is fit for something besides manufacturing'. This lack of sympathy with the business middle classes contributed to his fall as party leader in 1911. His successor, Bonar Law (1858–1923), a Glasgow iron merchant, was a man of very different origins and temperament. 'I hate big houses, and the rich food and the chatter,' Law exclaimed soon after his appointment. For better and worse the Conservative party was to choose three businessmen leaders in succession between 1911 and 1940.[9]

Balfour was succeeded as Prime Minister in December 1905 by Sir Henry Campbell-Bannerman (1836–1908), the Liberal leader. But after little more than two years fatal illness compelled him to give way to H. H. Asquith (1852–1928), destined to be one of the longest-serving of all first ministers. Asquith was the son of a West Riding woollen manufacturer, but as a successful barrister he had made his way into the highest society. His second wife, Margot

Tennant, was a fellow-member with Balfour in the 1880s and '90s of a coterie known as 'the souls'. Both Balfour and Asquith adopted (in Asquith's phrase) 'a guise of lethargy' to reinforce an attitude which, according to circumstances, can be praised as constructive detachment or blamed as damaging aloofness. Asquith was never well known to the public, always stiffly described as 'H. H. Asquith'. On the outbreak of war in 1914 he complained of the crowds thronging Westminster. 'I have never been a popular character with the "man in the street", and in all this dark and dangerous business it gives me scant pleasure.' Yet he was an able speaker, in and out of Parliament, and during his peacetime premiership he gained an easy predominance in the Commons. 'Aloof in the House,' remembered a contemporary, he was 'yet recognised as its greatest member.' Asquith enjoyed a similar position within his pre-war Cabinet. He let his two brilliant but restless lieutenants, Lloyd George (1863–1945) and Churchill, have their heads, winning their respect (and asserting his primacy) by sometimes lending them support at critical moments. He chose these moments for intervention carefully, whether in public or in private. 'A sudden curve developed of which I took immediate advantage,' was his description of his adroit solution of a Cabinet clash in 1909. Unfortunately, these olympian methods did not qualify Asquith to be a successful war leader. A wartime Prime Minister must be continuously involved, otherwise his leadership will be doubted and the morale of both his colleagues and the country will suffer. 'Mr. Asquith, do you take an interest in the war?' asked a lady friend innocently but revealingly soon after its outbreak. As the war dragged on the newspapers began to complain. Asquith (again like Balfour, and quite unlike Lloyd George and Churchill) had never cultivated a newspaper connection, even with Liberal journals. His wife noted in 1915 how he was 'as indifferent to the press as St. Paul's Cathedral is to midges'. His phrase 'wait and see', used in a threatening sense during the 1910 budget debates, was now unfairly but tellingly presented as evidence of his preference for apathy and delay. Although his final ejection in December 1916 showed party intrigue at its most distasteful, Asquith's displacement by Lloyd George was clearly in the national interest.[10]

A different personality was needed at the top. David Lloyd George had proved himself both in peace and war as 'the man who gets things done'. Less than Asquith in intellect and character (he was an inveterate womanizer, Asquith merely a heavy drinker), Lloyd George was none the less much better qualified as a war leader. He was the first man springing directly from the people, the first Non-conformist (and the first Welshman) to become Prime Minister. His father, who came from farming stock, had died early, and the future politician was brought up by his maternal uncle, Richard Lloyd, a self-educated shoemaker and co-pastor of a strict Baptist chapel at Criccieth, Caernarvonshire. Lloyd George preached at this chapel as a young man. The local landowners were chiefly English-speaking Anglicans and Conservatives: uncle Lloyd and his nephew were Welsh-speaking Liberals. After gaining local prominence as a solicitor, Lloyd George was elected Member of Parliament for the Caernarvon Burghs in 1890, his seat for 55 years. During the 1890s he was very much the Welsh politician; then his courageous opposition to the Boer War (1899–1902) won him a national reputation, though at first a very unpopular one. In 1905 he became President of the Board of Trade, and in 1908 Chancellor of the Exchequer. In both offices he displayed great enterprise and industry, leading the Liberals through a succession of major social reforms. His 1909 'people's budget' precipitated a constitutional crisis of 'peers versus people'. In May 1915 he became Minister of Munitions, improvising a new department and overcoming a desperate shortage of arms and ammunition. In June 1916 he was appointed War Secretary, and six months later Prime Minister. Asquith had been reluctant to adopt a suggestion that he delegate direction of the war to a small committee presided over by Lloyd George; the Conservative leaders, and Lloyd George himself, had rightly decided that the Welshman's organizational talents must be given full scope for the sake of victory.

Lloyd George was both the best possible and almost the only possible Prime Minister at this time. Most Conservatives were refusing to continue support for Asquith: few Liberals would have countenanced Bonar Law. About 130 Liberals backed Lloyd George, rather more stayed with Asquith. Here was a split in the Liberal party which was to prove permanent. Lloyd George's Cabinet comprised fourteen Conservatives against only seven Liberals, plus one Labour member. The idea of a coalition with the Conservatives had long attracted him. First in peace, then in war, he had felt the need for radical action which transcended party politics. At the height of the 1910 constitutional crisis he had aired a plan for a coalition to tackle all urgent national problems. The party game for its own sake did not interest him. He expected real results from politics. In this spirit as soon as he became Prime Minister he created new Ministries of Labour, Food, Shipping, and Pensions.

Many of his wartime innovations were to become permanent parts of the machinery of government. At the centre he placed the War Cabinet, five or six politicians chosen for their capacity, not for their prominence in the party hierarchies. Churchill, discredited by his association with the Dardanelles failure, was not a member. Nevertheless, he learnt much from Lloyd George's example in these years which he was to remember as national leader in the Second World War. Both men were orators who raised wartime morale, but their talents here were very different. Churchill's studied manner was best on anticipated great occasions; Lloyd George was more spontaneous, able at will to inspire almost any audience. Peace finally came in November 1918, and Lloyd George was accepted by the voters at the ensuing general election as 'the man who had won the war'. His Government gained a huge majority. But he was really the prisoner of the Conservatives, and in less than four years he was to fall from power, never to take office again.[11]

One reason for Lloyd George's eventual fall was his deviousness. This does not mean that he was insincere, either in his desire for reform in peace or victory in war. But he was very ready to sacrifice individuals for the sake either of his policies or his own advantage. The civil servant who especially helped him to create the National Health Insurance scheme was afterwards quickly consigned to the obscurity of a commissioner for income tax. Christopher Addison (1869–1951), who played an important part in enlisting Liberal support in 1916, was ungraciously jettisoned five years later to ease pressure upon Lloyd George's own position. Asquith asserted plainly that, though Lloyd George possessed many qualities fitting him for the first place, 'he lacks the one thing needful—he does not inspire trust'.

The same was also said by Asquith and others about that other dynamic personality in the pre-war Liberal Cabinet, Winston Churchill. Asquith liked Churchill, but he did not foresee him reaching the top: 'to speak with the tongue of men and angels, and to spend laborious days and nights in administration, is no good if a man does not inspire trust.' Nevertheless, much of the distrust inspired by Churchill can now be seen as less damning than that provoked by Lloyd George. Churchill was never devious. Unlike Lloyd George, he had many friends. He was distrusted mainly for what was regarded as his instability. Lloyd George himself more than once expressed this view. 'A brilliant fellow without judgement which is adequate to his fiery impulse. His steering gear is too weak for his horsepower.' Churchill had been dogged by this opinion from his first entry into the Commons in 1900. He was welcomed there as a reminder of his dead father, the Tory radical Lord Randolph Churchill (1849–94). Lord Randolph had risen rapidly to the Chancellorship of the Exchequer in the 1880s, only to shatter his brilliant career by an impatient resignation. For forty years Winston was suspected of inheriting his father's brilliant recklessness. He certainly matched his father in ambition. A newspaperman, hearing him speak at the 1900 general election, commented upon young Churchill's self-assurance: 'He will never be content to be a back-bencher.' He was always full of schemes, some valuable, some wild, which his colleagues were expected to sift. But, unlike his father, Winston Churchill was capable of giving way (albeit reluctantly and loquaciously) and of learning from experience. In Asquith's Cabinet he was successively President of the Board of Trade (1908), Home Secretary (1910), and First Lord of the Admiralty (1911–15). At the Board of Trade he showed that he could be constructive as well as dashing, second only to Lloyd George in the promotion of social reform. At the Admiralty he supervised the continuing growth of the fleet to meet German naval competition. The conduct of the war, both at sea and on land, greatly excited his imagination. Trained as a soldier, he was fascinated by war, a fascination which (especially in the 1930s) caused him to be dubbed a warmonger. But in reality Churchill was horrified as well as fascinated by conflict. 'Much as war attracts me and fascinates my mind with its tremendous situations—I feel more deeply every year . . . what vile and wicked folly and barbarism it all is.' In 1915 he promoted the Dardanelles campaign, intended to eliminate Turkey and to open a Balkan front. The plan was good in itself, but it was never supported with sufficient vigour or resources of men and ships, and late in the year it was abandoned. Churchill had meanwhile been removed from the Admiralty as a scapegoat. This and later adversity in his own career was tempering his character in preparation for his 'finest hour' in 1940. Even in these early years Churchill sensed that he had been chosen for some great role. 'Winston may in your eyes and in those with whom he has to work have faults,' Mrs. Churchill told Asquith in 1915, 'but he has the supreme quality . . . the power, the imagination, the deadliness, to fight Germany.'[12]

The most important personality behind Britain's diplomatic commitment to war in the circumstances of 1914 was Sir Edward Grey (1862–1934), Foreign Secretary 1905–16. Born into a Northumberland landowning family with a tradition of public service, for

nine taxing years Grey forced his deep love of country pursuits into
second place. Gladstone never knew a man with 'such aptitude for
political life and such disinclination for it'. As a countryman Grey
consciously retained for himself (in Wordsworth's words, which
meant much to him) a 'central peace at the heart of endless agitation'. His judgement could not be disturbed by man-made crises.
Calm self-sufficiency was especially necessary in an Edwardian
Foreign Secretary, for, except at crisis periods, Parliament, press,
and public paid only spasmodic attention to foreign affairs. 'It has
become almost an impossibility in London to follow the trend of
foreign politics,' complained one writer only six months before the
outbreak of war. In the days of Gladstone and Disraeli foreign
policy had still been a matter of party disputation; but Grey
accepted and developed the policy of his Conservative predecessor,
Lord Lansdowne (1845–1927). This sought to extricate Britain
from her exposed diplomatic position. During the Boer War she
had been without the diplomatic support of any major power. The
term 'splendid isolation' had been coined in 1896 to describe a
situation in which the isolation had come to be felt more than the
splendour. An Anglo-Japanese alliance was hesitantly concluded in
1902 to protect British interests in the Far East, followed in 1904
by the Anglo-French *entente*, on paper simply the settlement of long-
standing colonial differences but increasingly in practice something
more. In 1907 Grey concluded a similar *entente* with Russia. This
was neither so successful nor so popular, but it meant that Britain
had come to terms with both partners (the Dual *Entente*) on one
side of the European balance, but not with the Triple Alliance of
Germany, Austria, and Italy on the other.

As early as 1906 Grey sanctioned secret military conversations
with France. Most members even of the Cabinet knew nothing of
these until 1912. Grey felt that conversations were necessary so that
Britain *could* (not necessarily *would*) support France effectively if
attacked by Germany. He always emphasized in public and in
private that there was no formal commitment: an *entente* was not an
alliance. But especially after naval discussions had led in 1913 to the
withdrawal of the French fleet to the Mediterranean, Britain's moral
obligation was hard to deny. During the 1906 Moroccan crisis provoked by Germany, Grey was already admitting how it would be
difficult for Britain to keep out of a Franco-German conflict. 'The
Entente and still more the constant and emphatic demonstrations of
affection (official, naval, political, commercial, municipal and in the
press), have created in France a belief that we should support her in

war.' Again in 1911, justifying further military conversations in response to the renewed Moroccan crisis, Grey told Asquith that 'no doubt these conversations and our speeches have given an expectation of support. I do not see how that can be helped.' We shall see later how in his famous speech on 3 August 1914 Grey successfully persuaded the Commons and the nation that Britain was bound to fight. Over the years the Foreign Secretary had committed the country very far, mainly upon his own initiative. By temperament Grey liked to act alone and in private. But it was the pressure of circumstances plain to all (German folly, Austrian disintegration, Balkan turbulence), which had forced his peace-seeking diplomacy to become also preparation for war.[13]

Before Britain concluded the *entente* with France she had first considered making some arrangement with Germany. Joseph Chamberlain (1836–1914), the most forceful personality in Lord Salisbury's Government, had asserted in 1899 that this was 'the natural alliance'. But the Germans had expected full British adhesion to the Triple Alliance, including commitments to war or neutrality in given circumstances, and Salisbury argued that no British Government could bind the British people in advance. By 1902 Chamberlain was warming to the idea of a settlement with France. He had also decided that no more time could be lost in fostering empire unity. Since his appointment as Colonial Secretary in 1895 he had become the leading exponent of 'the imperial idea'. He had begun his political career as a maker of opinion in the country, and he now decided to revert to this role. He resigned office in September 1903 to embark upon a campaign of speech-making. His aim was the bold one of persuading the Edwardian public to abandon free trade, the great article of Victorian commercial faith, secured by repeal of the Corn Laws and other measures some fifty years earlier. What was needed now, asserted Chamberlain, was 'tariff reform'.

He centred his campaign upon Birmingham, which he had represented in Parliament since 1876, and where his Unitarian family had become politically predominant. After making a fortune as a screw manufacturer, Chamberlain had retired from business and served as Mayor of the city from 1873 to 1876. He was probably the most successful civic head ever seen in Britain. Birmingham was, in his own words, 'parked, paved, assized, marketed, gas-and-watered and *improved*—all as the result of three years' active work'. After 1876 he set out as a Liberal M.P. to apply Birmingham methods in national politics. In 1880 he became President of the

Board of Trade under Gladstone. Five years later he propounded an 'unauthorized programme' for the Liberal party. This included manhood suffrage, payment of Members of Parliament, and moderate graduated taxation through death and house duties, plus taxation of unearned increment. But Gladstone preferred Home Rule. Chamberlain refused to go further than a form of federalism, 'Home-Rule-all-round'. He formed his own Liberal Unionist Party, and finally in 1895 he entered into coalition with the Conservatives. The epithet 'Judas' was hurled at him from the Gladstonian ranks, even though it was Gladstone, not Chamberlain, who had repudiated established party policy. In refusing to follow Gladstone, Chamberlain consciously sacrificed the almost certain succession to the Liberal leadership. Not surprisingly, he developed an increasingly hard exterior, sharp-featured, an eyeglass glinting in his right eye, an orchid always in his buttonhole. Private as well as public adversity had moulded him, two of his wives dying in childbirth. One was the mother of Austen Chamberlain (1863–1937), destined just to miss becoming Prime Minister, the other the mother of Neville Chamberlain (1869–1940), the Prime Minister of 'Munich'. Time always seemed to be working against Chamberlain. He was almost sixty before he gained a clear field for his talents. Balfour was said to have remarked that 'wanting to go too fast is Chamberlain's peculiarity'. Certainly, it was Chamberlain, in and out of office, at least as much as Balfour, the Prime Minister, who set the pace of British politics during the very first years of the twentieth century.[14]

IV

Opponents of Chamberlain's imperialism called the Boer War 'Chamberlain's war'. But Chamberlain had merely prepared for what he believed to be 'inevitable *at some time or another*'. He was unwilling to sacrifice British economic interests in the Transvaal to Boer nationalist and racial prejudice. After the end of the war he visited South Africa in a spirit of reconciliation. He was now seeking ways of uniting opinion both there and throughout the empire.[15] When he returned home he decided that it would be impossible to carry Balfour's Cabinet in favour of bold fiscal change. Some members were as staunch for free trade as the Liberals, the traditional free trade party. A corn registration duty, imposed in 1902 to help meet the cost of the war, had been abandoned in the 1903 budget contrary to Chamberlain's expectations. He had hoped that through remission to empire countries it might constitute the beginning of a system of imperial preference. The self-governing colonies were keen for this. Canada, for example, had given Britain a preference of 25 per cent in 1898 and 33 per cent in 1900. But all the self-governing territories still levied duties on British goods. They were determined to foster their own nationhood through protection of their infant industries; they rejected all imperial ideas which seemed to regard them merely as granaries feeding an industrial mother country. At the Colonial Conferences of 1897 and 1902 Chamberlain had found little support for an imperial customs union, or for closer political association through an Imperial Council. Disappointed at the attitude of the politicians, home and colonial, he resigned in September 1903 and turned to the British people.

Chamberlain outlined his tariff reform plans in a series of major speeches delivered during the next few weeks. He argued that Britain was not receiving the promised benefits of free trade because other countries had refused to trade with equal freedom. During the later nineteenth century protection had spread and intensified. Goods from countries such as Germany and the United States, whose protected industries now matched or surpassed those of Britain, were competing with British products in both home and foreign markets. Chamberlain proposed tariffs to defend home markets and for use as bargaining counters to force reductions of foreign tariffs. But he attached most importance to securing 'a greater development of trade within the empire and a nearer approach to a commercial union'. This, he believed, 'must precede or accompany closer political relations'. 'Our future history depends upon the extent to which we can weld the different parts of the empire together. What Washington did for the United States of America, what Bismarck did for Germany, it is our business to do for the British Empire.'

Chamberlain was a shrewd politician who realized that the British public would be more likely to respond to such rhetoric if it were linked with prospective benefits for specific occupations. He promised protection for work and wages. 'Agriculture, the greatest of all trades and industries, has been practically destroyed. . . . Sugar has gone, silk has gone, iron is threatened, wool is threatened; the turn of cotton will come. . . . At the present moment these industries and the working men who depend on them are like sheep in the field.' He argued that all the social progress of the nineteenth century was endangered through prospective unemployment. 'Free education, the Factory Acts, mining regulations, fair wage clauses, compensation for accidents, all these are good . . . but they are nothing in comparison with any policy or any legislation which would secure full employment, continuous employment at fair wages.' He promised that his new tariffs would increase empire trade by £26,000,000, giving new employment to 166,000 workers. This material aspect became an increasingly prominent part of Chamberlain's case, partly to attract working-class support, partly because his biggest financial backers were manufacturers in trades conscious of foreign competition. Protection for the empire's sake began to slip into protection for protection's sake. To the poorest classes Chamberlain offered the further inducement of old-age pensions, to be financed out of tariff revenue. He rejected universal pensions as damaging to thrift, but he wanted them for the deserving, such as those who had contributed for twenty years to a friendly society.

To publicize Chamberlain's ideas the Tariff Reform League was formed, soon followed by a Tariff Commission to supply facts and arguments. The League poured out pamphlets, leaflets, verses, and songs, while the *Daily Express* repeated day after day the cry 'Tariff reform means work for all'. Nevertheless, it quickly became clear that progress was going to be slow and uncertain. The promise of imperial strength or pensions counted for little with many people against the fear, carefully exploited by the free-traders, that tariff reform would mean dearer bread through the imposition of duties upon foreign corn. The contrast between the 'big and little loaf' was easily understood: Chamberlain's counter-arguments were not. He admitted that the price of bread might rise, but promised to balance this by reducing existing revenue duties upon tea, coffee, and cocoa. Chamberlain wanted to return, claimed the free-traders, coining an effective new phrase, to 'the hungry forties', to the starvation days before repeal of the Corn Laws. The 'little loaf' cry was especially influential in places where local industry seemed generally prosperous under free trade. Where trade was depressed, and foreign competition most noticed, tariff reform attracted more support, notably from the Birmingham and Sheffield metal trades. It attracted less backing from the wool towns, and very little from the cotton and coal-mining areas.[16]

Facts and figures exchanged in profusion by both sides probably went over the heads of most workmen. But many of them simply did not feel the shoe pinching hard or long enough. The year 1903 had been one of trade depression, but an international boom had begun by 1905. In December Balfour finally resigned, after more than two years of sinuous effort to hold his party and Government together. The Liberals took office, calling a general election for January 1906. The main issue was 'free trade versus protection'. In existing economic and political circumstances the verdict was not in doubt, only the size of the free trade Liberal majority. On the former Government side some candidates were tariff reformers, some were for free trade, some were Balfourites. In the jingoistic wartime election of 1900 the Conservative/Liberal Unionist coalition had won 402 seats and an overall majority of 134: now the Liberals won 400 seats, giving them a clear majority of 130, even counting the 83 Irish Nationalist and 30 Labour members against them.

Here was a famous Liberal victory. At the two elections, however, numbers of votes cast had not differed nearly so much as numbers of seats won:

	Cons./Lib. U.	Lib.	Lab.
1900	1,797,444	1,568,141	63,304
1906	2,451,454	2,757,883	329,748

Changes of voting allegiance cannot entirely explain the Liberals' 1906 success. They benefited from a new electoral register, from the greater willingness of agricultural labourers to vote in a winter election (an 82·6 per cent poll in 1906 against 74·6 per cent in 1900), and from improved party organization. Three hundred and ten new Members entered the Commons, 220 of them Liberals. Many of the latter were Nonconformist businessmen, uncommitted to established institutions, responsive to Lloyd George's radicalism. With the agricultural labourers voting strongly, and with the farmers disgruntled by the 1902 Education Act, which had increased their rates, the Conservatives did especially badly in the countryside. Their surviving areas of strength were mainly urban and suburban. According to one contemporary analysis, 102 tariff reformers (Conservative or Liberal Unionist) were elected, 43 from prosperous suburban London and the south-east (where the bogey of food taxation was less alarming to householders), 20 from Birmingham and the Midlands, 13 from Ireland (mainly Ulster), 5 from Liverpool (but only 1 from the Lancashire cotton district), and 2 from Sheffield (but none from the Yorkshire wool towns). Here was a revealing pattern of support and lack of support. Thirty-six Balfourites, 16 Unionist free traders, and 3 others completed the Opposition muster.[17]

V

Balfour himself lost his Manchester seat in 1906, though a safe one was soon found for him. He had resigned just in time to prevent party dissension developing into an outright split. His Government had not been successful judged overall, but it does deserve credit for three important reforms, with all of which Balfour himself was closely associated. At the turn of the century deficiencies in British education compared with the systems of foreign rivals were causing increasing concern. With the aim of raising standards Balfour promoted the 1902 Education Act, a measure which became the basis of twentieth-century progress in British education. It transferred control of publicly supported schools to local authorities, and encouraged a great increase in secondary education. At the same time it increased the financial help given to 'voluntary' denominational schools, insisting that all schools, municipal and sectarian, reach a satisfactory standard. The Act was well conceived in terms of education, but it aroused bitter religious opposition. Anglican schools greatly outnumbered those of the Nonconformists, who protested vociferously against increased state subsidization of the Established Church. Opposition, led by Lloyd George, was particularly loud in Wales. Hostility to the Education Act, followed in the next year by the rally in defence of free trade, did much to heal divisions within the Liberal ranks evident during the Boer War. Many Liberals had in varying degrees opposed the war, but the Liberal Imperialists (including Asquith and Grey) had supported it once begun. Yet by 1905 Campbell-Bannerman was able to form a strong Ministry embracing all shades of party opinion.

The Licensing Act of 1904 was another measure of Balfour's which angered Liberal Nonconformists. Drunkenness was a major Edwardian social problem, and the Act aimed gradually to reduce the excessive number of public houses. But it did not satisfy Nonconformist temperance enthusiasts who wanted local option, and the Conservatives were loudly denounced (not for the first time) as the brewers' friends. Less noticed at this time was Balfour's work in defence reorganization. The indifferent performance of the Army during the Boer War had shown the need for a supreme command, and between 1902 and 1904 he reformed the Committee of Imperial Defence, assuming its chairmanship *ex officio* and giving it a permanent secretariat.[18]

Balfour remained leader of the Opposition until 1911. In the

1906 Parliament tariff reformers were the largest group within his depleted following; but in July 1906 Chamberlain suffered a severe stroke and was never able again to take an active political part. Nevertheless, Austen Chamberlain and the Tariff Reform League continued to press the case, and in reply to Lloyd George's radical 1909 budget tariff reform came to recommend itself to the Unionists (a name increasingly adopted by the Conservatives and Liberal Unionists taken together) as a more constructive alternative than simple negation. Balfour now declared that the country must choose between 'the hopeful movement of tariff reform' and the 'downward track . . . to the bottomless confusion of socialist legislation'. He advised the Unionist majority in the Lords to reject the budget, so precipitating the general election held in January 1910. The Unionists tried to make tariff reform the election theme, but the Liberal cry 'the peers versus the people' rang louder. Though the Liberals lost their overall majority (and their majority of English seats), they remained comfortably in power with Labour and Irish support (L. 275, U. 273, Lab. 40, Irish Nat. 82). After a year of crisis the Liberals were confirmed in office at the general election of December 1910 (L. 272, U. 272, Lab. 42, Irish Nat. 84). During this second election Balfour had unexpectedly suggested that tariff reform might be withheld by a Unionist Government until after approval at a referendum. Some ardent tariff reformers, including Austen Chamberlain, were astonished at this move, and Balfour's leadership came increasingly under question during 1911. Right-wingers were also dissatisfied by his weakening resistance to the Parliament Bill. He retired in November, but Austen Chamberlain was unable to secure the leadership; the Chamberlains were still regarded as outsiders by the party rank and file. Bonar Law was chosen as a compromise leader, acceptable to all shades of Unionist opinion. He had been a strong tariff reformer, but during the excitement of the Home Rule and other crises of the immediate pre-war years fiscal reform became less prominent. Moreover, Law was conscious that the prospect of food taxation as part of the tariff reform programme had damaged his party's electoral appeal. In 1913, under pressure especially from Conservatives in Lancashire (where the Anti-Corn Law League had been based in the 1840s), he announced that the Unionists would develop imperial preference upon their return to power but would not adopt food taxes without a further election mandate.[19]

After ten years of tariff reform agitation Britain was still a free-trade country. The British people's attachment to free trade can now be seen as economically sound, even though most contemporary observers were unaware of the best reasons for this attachment. Economic circumstances had much changed since the adoption of unilateral free trade by the early Victorians. But in the Edwardian period Britain stood at the centre of a developing multilateral system of international payments. The great expansion of world production which took place during the later nineteenth century might have caused serious friction if payment for exchange of goods had continued on the old unilateral basis; for this would have required serious encroachments by new competitors upon established trade patterns. The new industrial powers, for example, needed to import additional food and raw materials from primary producing areas which were among Britain's best customers. Fortunately, these powers did not now need to concentrate their exports in direct competition with Britain. She did develop an increasingly adverse balance of visible trade, but this was compensated by steadily growing income from 'invisible' services which benefited the whole world economy. If Britain had attempted to raise tariff barriers and to extend imperial preference this new system would have been upset. Industrial Europe and the United States would have been forced either to intensify world competition in manufactured goods or to adjust their internal economies and to seek new sources of supply through the development of colonies and spheres of influence. Though the international economy of the early twentieth century was a curious mixture of British free trade and foreign protection, it worked well, allowing a great expansion of activity with a minimum of difficulty.[20]

Tariff reformers were, of course, influenced by imperial even more than by economic considerations. Though the Liberals rejected Chamberlain's economic ideas, they too were committed to maintaining and strengthening the empire. They aimed to achieve this not through fiscal policy but through conciliation of colonial peoples. Loyalty, Liberals believed, sprang from freedom, and unity from loyalty. In this spirit within a few weeks of taking office the Liberal Government decided to restore self-rule to the Transvaal and the Orange Free State, only four years after the end of the Boer War. One of the Boer generals, J. C. Smuts (1870–1950), visited England at the beginning of 1906. Given freedom, he assured Ministers that the Boers were willing to remain within the empire. 'You can choose to make them enemies, and possibly have another Ireland on your hands. If you do believe in liberty, it is also their faith and their religion.' Three years later the Liberals hoped that they were further promoting empire unity when they sanctioned the unification of South Africa, the linking of the former Boer republics with the British colonies of the Cape and Natal. Englishmen at home and in South Africa were confident that their language and liberal attitudes would gradually predominate within the union. Yet the 1909 Act involved the abandonment of the Cape Colony property qualification, which had allowed votes for some 22,000 non-whites. Liberty was being sacrificed for the sake of imperial unity. 'We must simply hope', concluded the Colonial Secretary feebly, 'for South Africans themselves to alter the matter in future.'[21]

In India during these same years, John Morley (1838–1923), the Secretary of State, and Lord Minto (1845–1914), the Viceroy, were attempting to counter emerging nationalist feeling by a series of limited concessions, culminating in the Indian Councils Act of 1909. Three hundred thousand whites in India were outnumbered over ten to one; but the Liberals hoped to overcome this by anglicizing at least the cream of the coloured majority, opening participation in government to 'a class of persons, Indian in blood and colour, but English in taste, in opinion, in morals, and in intellect'. Morley said plainly that full self-government was not in view; he was 'doing nothing to loosen the bolts', seeking only to recognize and to reconcile 'individual ability'. This Liberal policy of judicious concession to Hindu, Muslim, and Boer nationalism was fairly successful in encouraging imperial harmony in the short run. Morley seems not to have been looking further ahead in India. 'If we can hatch some plan and policy for half a generation that will be something.' But in South Africa the Liberals prided themselves that they had built well for much longer than this. The party traditionally concerned with individual liberty was trying to turn a blind eye to the prospects for liberty of the coloured majorities both in South Africa and India.[22]

VI

The period of Liberal rule before 1914 is rightly remembered for its social reforms. Yet such reform was not prominent as a 1906 election issue. Negatives predominated, notably opposition to tariff reform, also to the Education and Licensing Acts and to the importation of Chinese labour into the Rand gold mines on terms said to amount to slavery. Working-class electors greatly feared unemployment caused by tariff reform at home, or by cheap Chinese labour if they emigrated to South Africa. Yet they were slow to show interest in protecting themselves through insurance against the effects of loss of work. Unemployment and health insurance and other social reforms were introduced after 1906 with only a vague mandate from the electorate.[23]

It quickly became clear that several important Liberal proposals would meet total resistance from the House of Lords. During the late-Victorian years the upper house had acquired a large Conservative majority. Many Whig peers had left the Liberal party when Gladstone proposed Irish Home Rule. His 1893 Home Rule Bill had been overwhelmed in the Lords by 419 votes to 41. At that time the Liberal majority in the Commons was small, but after 1906 it was huge. Yet even before the new Parliament had met Balfour was declaring that 'the great Unionist Party should still control, whether in power or whether in opposition, the destinies of this great empire'. Unionists justified themselves by saying that they were acting to preserve the integrity of the constitution before the disruptive threat of (in Balfour's phrases) 'revolutionary changes', 'abominable revolutions', in other words 'socialism' and Home Rule. 'We are face to face', Balfour told the King, '(no doubt in a milder form) with the socialist difficulties which loom so large on the Continent.' The reckless manner in which between 1906 and 1914 the Unionist party pursued its opposition to 'socialism' in England and to nationalism in Ireland led it to threaten that very constitutional order which it claimed to guard. There was in these years, observes one political scientist, 'an apparent danger of the English political compromise collapsing, thanks to the folly of its chief beneficiaries'.[24]

In 1906 the Lords killed Liberal Education and Plural Voting Bills. In 1907 they mutilated English and Irish Land Bills, and rejected two for Scotland; in 1908 a Licensing Bill and two further Education Bills were negatived. Some of this opposition could be plausibly defended in detail, but not in general. It was the denial of measures for which the Government could claim a recent election mandate. By 1908 the Liberals clearly could not continue to allow their measures to be contemptuously dispatched. Using their Lords majority, the Unionists were discrediting the Government. 'They first make our work well nigh impossible,' complained Campbell-Bannerman, 'and then hold us up to the contempt of the country as impostors.'[25] The Liberals began to lose seats at by-elections, both to the Unionists and to Labour. These setbacks satisfied Asquith, Lloyd George, and Churchill that the Government must venture upon a bold new line. They hoped that this would both check

Labour progress and refute Unionist taunts about Liberal ineptitude in government. This new line was radical social reform.

Trade depression and falling real wages, concern for 'national efficiency' after Boer War failures, and increasingly precise knowledge of the miserable conditions forced upon many of the poor, had combined to give the 'condition of England question' a new prominence in the opening years of the twentieth century. Charles Booth's (1840–1916) *Life and Labour of the People in London* (1889–1903), and Seebohm Rowntree's (1871–1954) *Poverty, A Study of Town Life* (1901) had provided firm and disconcerting statistics. One in three or four of the urban population was living in poverty. The Victorian Poor Law, administered in a spirit of harsh deterrence by local guardians who were zealous stewards of ratepayer's money, was becoming discredited as a social instrument. It assumed that the poor were always responsible for their own poverty. Could this fairly be said of one whole third of the Edwardian population? Were they not the victims of the new urban industrial system, needing help not blame? Could society continue to tolerate that 'horizontal division between rich and poor' which the *Nation*, the leading radical weekly, compared with the 'vertical division between nation and nation armed to the teeth'? Both the Edwardian domestic and international scenes seemed dangerously poised. 'No civilisation can be sound or stable,' concluded Rowntree, 'which has at its base this mass of stunted human life.'[26]

Yet the Edwardians' first steps towards social improvement were very tentative. Balfour's Government had responded to a scare about the poor physical standard of recruits for the Army and Navy by appointing an Interdepartmental Committee on Physical Deterioration (1903–4). Its report helped to produce a Government Order requiring Poor Law guardians to undertake the feeding of necessitous schoolchildren (1905). Intense trade depression also led to the Unemployed Workmen Act of 1905. But this was a temporary and ineffectual relief measure. More important for the future was Balfour's promotion late in 1905 of a Royal Commission on the Poor Law and the Relief of Distress from Unemployment.[27]

The Poor Law guardians soon proved themselves unable to feed poor schoolchildren; and when the Liberals took office an Act allowing local authorities to undertake this work was passed, followed in 1907 by one authorizing school medical inspection. Though only permissive, these measures can be seen in retrospect as marking a new beginning in British social legislation. The state was now intervening in family matters which Victorians had assumed to stand outside its range, except under the stigma of the Poor Law. The authorities were offering *services* to the poor, no longer only and harshly correcting the poor's shortcomings. Intervention for the benefit of the young was soon logically extended to care for the old, in the form not of relief but of pensions (1908); and finally in 1911 the enactment of health and unemployment insurance recognized that the welfare of individuals of working age could now also concern the state.

At first the Liberals showed themselves almost as hesitant as their Unionist predecessors. The 1906 School Meals Act had been introduced upon Labour initiative; while only under back-bench pressure did Ministers sponsor the 1907 Medical Inspection Act. Many Unionists agreed about the need for medical inspection, but many also began to express alarm about the progress of state intervention.[28] Ignoring this, and under by-election pressure, the Liberals turned decisively in 1908 to the enactment of old-age pensions.

With a longer-living population the problem of the aged poor was assuming increasing significance. At least ten countries were already providing state pensions. Similar action in Britain had been under discussion for years, but the Liberal proposals still surprised by their boldness. Pensions of 5s. per week at seventy were provided for the poor without any attached stigma ('The receipt of an old-age pension under this Act shall not deprive the pensioner of any right, franchise or privilege'), and they were entirely non-contributory. Asquith, the sponsor of the pension scheme, fought hard to persuade Gladstonians in the Cabinet to relax their inherited ideas of financial stringency in government. As for opposition from the Lords, the Liberals astutely counted upon the custom whereby the upper house never rejected a money Bill. In the event, the Unionists decided that it would be electorally unwise to appear entirely hostile. Their tactic in the Commons was to try to extend the Bill beyond the limits of prudent finance, 'to overballast the ship so that it would sink,' as Lloyd George remarked. This manœuvre failed. The Lords did not dare to reject the measure, and thus the credibility of Liberal government was somewhat restored.[29]

'God bless that Lord George' was the cry at backwoods post offices when the first pensions were paid at the start of 1909. Lloyd George had inherited Parliamentary supervision of the Bill from Asquith on becoming Chancellor of the Exchequer; Churchill took his place at the Board of Trade. These two energetic men, who combined genuine concern for social improvement with shrewd political sense, quickly decided to continue the social advance. They agreed that the next major beneficiaries must be the unemployed. Revealingly, the very word 'unemployment' was still quite new. Before the late nineteenth century there had been no such concept. The assumption was that those without work were improvident; 'pauperism' was the only word needed to describe such a condition. Lloyd George and Churchill, flanked by experts such as Hubert Llewellyn Smith (1864–1945), William Beveridge (1879–1963), and W. J. Braithwaite (1875–1936), were venturing, in Churchill's phrase, upon an 'untrodden field'. Their innovations came upon a surprised Parliament and a confused public. What they proposed owed little to either the majority or minority reports of the Poor Law Commission, published in February 1909. Accepting the existence of the capitalist system with its fluctuating demand for labour, they argued that this gave the Government the responsibility not only to provide information about available jobs, but also to support financially those who still could not find work and those who could not work because of illness. Here, said Lloyd George, was 'the New Liberalism', more radical than Gladstonian Liberalism but less disruptive than socialism. Germany, which Lloyd George specially visited, had already provided social insurance. 'She is organised,' Churchill told Asquith, 'not only for war, but for peace. We are organised for nothing except party politics . . . the key class of legislation which is required is just the kind the House of Lords will dare not oppose.' Such legislation, claimed Churchill, would both 'benefit the state' and 'fortify the party'. His Labour Exchanges Act was passed without much dispute in 1909. It was followed by a Trade Boards Act establishing machinery for settling minimum wages in certain 'sweated' trades. This was a major innovation, assuming (however indirectly) that the state had an interest in ensuring a wage minimum. But the greatest innovation of all, social insurance, was to be delayed for two years by the constitutional crisis provoked by Lloyd George's 1909 budget.[30]

VII

Lloyd George deliberately set out to make his first budget a bold one. Despite the popularity of old-age pensions the Liberals were still losing by-elections. A 'people's budget' might restore them to electoral favour. Yet neither the Chancellor nor the Prime Minister schemed deliberately to produce a Finance Bill which the Lords would reject. Asquith's legal mind, in particular, could hardly conceive that the Lords would act against all constitutional custom. Lloyd George did remark that rejection of the budget by the peers would advance the Liberal cause still more than its acceptance. Some of his proposals were disliked even within the Liberal Cabinet, notably his land taxes. The Chancellor needed to find nearly £16,000,000 to meet the cost of old-age pensions and new battleship building. He also wanted fresh sources of revenue to finance social insurance. He decided that the rich must pay. While leaving rates of earned income tax unchanged up to £3,000, he raised the tax upon higher earned and all unearned incomes from 1s. to 1s. 2d. A £10 tax allowance was given to small income-tax payers earning under £500, but a maximum of 5d. super tax was introduced upon incomes over £5,000. By mid-twentieth century standards these rates seem Elysian, but they seemed very heavy in its first decade. Death duties and the tobacco and spirits duties were also increased, while taxes on cars and petrol were introduced. But the most contentious features of the budget were its new revenue taxes on land: 20 per cent on the unearned increment in land values, a capital tax of ½d. in the £ on the value of undeveloped land and minerals, and a 10 per cent reversion duty on any benefit which fell to a lessor at the end of a lease. Lloyd George was determined to extract money from those landowners who could make great profits with little effort simply because chance of nature had endowed their land with valuable minerals or because urban development had inflated site values. 'It is undoubtedly one of the worst evils of our present system of land tenure that instead of reaping the benefits of the common endeavour of its citizens a community has always to pay a heavy penalty to its ground landlords for putting up the value of their land.' The yield on these land taxes was to prove disappointing, but the Unionists concentrated their fiercest attacks upon them. They denounced such 'socialism' as 'the beginning of the end of the rights of property'. The taxes were made the more offensive by provision for an inquisitorial preliminary valuation of land. Lloyd George defended his proposals as a 'war budget . . . for raising money to wage implacable war against poverty and squalidness'. But before this war budget could be passed the country had to endure warfare on another front, party political conflict of remarkable bitterness.[31]

By July 1909 it was becoming clear that the Unionists might reject the budget in the upper house. In the Commons they resorted to delaying tactics, some seventy days of debate being needed to pass the Finance Bill, notwithstanding the Liberals' large majority. In the country a Budget Protest League was matched by a Liberal Budget League. As president of the latter body Churchill spoke with characteristic pugnacity up and down the country during the summer and autumn of 1909. Lloyd George himself was more tied to Parliament, but his few outside speeches had great effect. At Limehouse on 30 July he delivered a rousing defence of his land proposals, defining a landlord's 'sole function, his chief pride' as 'stately consumption of wealth produced by others'. The budget finally passed the Commons on 4 November, but by this date Balfour had decided to use the Unionist majority in the Lords to defeat the Government. On 30 November the Finance Bill was rejected there by 350 votes to 75. A general election was now bound to follow. This time the Lords had not simply rejected one measure, they had refused supply, without which no Government can rule. The peers had virtually claimed the right of deciding when a Parliament should end.

The Unionists tried hard to fix attention upon the allegedly dangerous character of the budget and upon the alternative merits of tariff reform, which Balfour was now inclined to support. Lord Lansdowne's rejection motion had attempted a show of democratic virtue: 'That this House is not justified in giving its consent to the [Finance] Bill until it has been submitted to the judgement of the country.' There never was an occasion, claimed Balfour, 'when the power, vested by the constitution in the second chamber, was more absolutely justified'. But the electors did not agree. In the general election of January 1910, as Austen Chamberlain admitted, 'they voted against the Lords and, above all, against the landlords'. Liberal and Labour candidates gained 51 per cent of the votes cast, against only 46·9 per cent for the Unionists. Here was a clear majority both over the Unionists and of the total electorate, even though the Liberals lost their overall lead in seats. The verdict was strengthened by the highest percentage turnout (86·6) in election history.

The Unionists had tried to minimize the constitutional aspect of the crisis and had failed. They could not submerge the Liberal cry of 'the peers versus the people'. Asquith announced that if his Government were re-elected acceptance of the budget by the Lords would not now be enough; the Liberals would insist upon a reduction of the powers of the upper house. Experience had shown this 'to be necessary for the legislative utility and the honour of the party of progress'. Lansdowne had argued that early acceptance of the budget by the peers against their known inclinations would have 'permanently impaired' their powers; they could never again have resisted, 'however outrageous the financial policy of a radical Government might be'. This was probably true. But either way the Lords were bound to lose, if the electorate remained firm behind the Government. Lansdowne himself foresaw this. He expected to be defeated at a first general election, but (rightly) anticipated the calling of a second one before the Lords question could be settled. Time, he believed, would cool feelings and work in favour of the Unionists, of the preservation of the powers of the Lords, and of tariff reform. But Lansdowne and Balfour were aristocrats, whose views about the role of the Lords were inappropriate for the twentieth century. They were congenitally unable to attune themselves to the majority of the electorate: and the electors had the final say.[32]

Nevertheless, the path from the election of January 1910 to the passing of the Parliament Act in August 1911 was to be long and difficult. At first Asquith seemed to be stumbling. The Cabinet wandered from the clear issue of the Lords veto to the much less clear question of reform of the composition of the upper house. But the Premier finally asserted himself, announcing on 18 March that the Government intended to proceed both with the budget and with a Bill limiting the powers of the Lords. He introduced the Parliament Bill on 14 April. The House of Lords was to lose all authority over money bills, but was to be left with power to delay legislation for two years. A measure (such as an Irish Home Rule Bill) sent up by the Commons in three successive sessions could become law on the third occasion regardless of the Lords' opposition. Asquith made it clear that if the peers rejected these proposals he would again appeal to the country, but only if the King were willing, as required, to create enough peers to muster a favourable majority, assuming the Liberals won the election. Without such a royal promise the Government would resign forthwith, and let Balfour (if he would) try to govern against the wishes of a majority of the Commons—with the King by implication condoning the attempt. On 28 April the Lords passed the budget in a few hours, Lansdowne accepting that the January election had settled the issue. The centre of dispute now shifted to the Parliament Bill.[33]

The culmination of the crisis was delayed, however, by the death of Edward VII on 6 May. Asquith felt that it would be unfair to expect the new King, George V, to be ready to honour his father's commitment until he had grown used to his new role and until one last effort at a settlement had been made. A constitutional conference was arranged between Government and Opposition leaders, which met during the summer of 1910 and again during October and November. Much ground was traversed both in relation to limitation of the power and to reform of the membership of the House of Lords. But the discussions finally foundered over Irish Home Rule, to which the Unionists were passionately opposed. They wanted such constitutional legislation, if twice rejected by the Lords, to be next submitted to a referendum. The Liberals refused to allow the Lords this new power to force an appeal to the country. On 15 November the Cabinet agreed to ask the King for a dissolution of Parliament on the terms announced by Asquith a year before. With great reluctance the King agreed, on the understanding that his promise would not be made public unless and until the need for creations was apparent.

So a second general election took place in December 1910, dominated by the Lords question, but without public knowledge that Asquith, if he won, would be able in the last resort to secure a massive creation of peers. The elections produced little overall change in the position of the parties, and the contest was said to be dull. None the less, the turnout was still high (82·6 per cent), and 56 seats changed hands. Asquith introduced the Parliament Bill to the new House of Commons on 21 February 1911. Churchill, who shared the Bill's management with the Prime Minister, urged his chief not to be afraid of making '500 peers if necessary'. Asquith and most members of the Cabinet hoped hard, however, that such action would not ultimately prove necessary. Everything depended upon the Unionists in the Lords. Logically, having rejected the 1909 budget for allegedly good reasons, they ought to reject a measure designed to prevent them acting in the same manner again. But the first move had proved a blunder, and Balfour, the party leader, now accepted that it would be an even greater blunder to force a dilution of the peerage in futile resistance to the Parliament Bill, 'so profoundly modifying the constitution of the second chamber that it would become with regard to some important measures a mere annexe to the present House of Commons'. If the Lords gave way on the Parliament Bill Balfour realized that they would still be able to delay a Home Rule Bill for two years: if the Liberals acquired a Lords majority Home Rule would be enacted at the first attempt. Lansdowne, leader of the Unionist peers, was more reluctant to surrender. In May 1911 as an alternative to the Parliament Bill he introduced an abortive scheme for comprehensive

reform of the membership of the upper house, which would nevertheless have perpetuated its Unionist majority. When early in July
the Lords began drastically to amend the Parliament Bill Asquith
asked George V to be ready to make a great creation of Liberal
peers. It now became known to the Unionists that the King was
firmly committed to such action. This destroyed the position of
those, including Lansdowne, who had kept up resistance in the
belief that Asquith was bluffing. Two hundred and forty-nine
candidates for ennoblement were now listed by the Government
Chief Whip, including Thomas Hardy (1840–1928), the novelist,
J. M. Barrie (1860–1937), the playwright, and Bertrand Russell
(1872–1970), the philosopher.

As July moved into August the Unionist peers were convulsed in
argument. 'Hedgers' prepared to give way under protest: 'ditchers',
led by the pre-Victorian Lord Halsbury (1823–1921), were ready to
die in the last ditch. During 9–10 August, with the temperature well
into the 90s, the final Lords debate took place. The result was in
doubt to the end. But Lansdowne and the bulk of his followers were
now for 'hedging'. They abstained; while 37 Unionists, urged on by
Lord Curzon (1859–1925) to avert 'pollution' of their order, actually
voted for the Bill. The Liberals mustered 81; 13 bishops supported
them. Here were 131 votes in all. The 'ditchers' could only total 114.
So the Parliament Bill was passed by 17 votes, thanks to substantial
Unionist voting for a measure which all Unionists abhorred. Into
such a paradoxical situation had Balfour and Lansdowne led the
Unionist Party. Balfour despondently left the country before the
final Lords debate began. Within three months he had resigned as
party leader.

The first part of the constitutional struggle was now over. But an
even fiercer dispute over Home Rule for Ireland was bound to
follow. In this second clash the Lords intended to use their remaining powers of delay to the full.[34]

VIII

The other major piece of legislation in 1911 was the National
Insurance Act. Social insurance, 'the magic of averages' as Churchill
called it, was a much greater innovation in social reform than old-
age pensions. 'We seek to substitute for the pressure of the forces
of nature, operating by classes on individuals, the pressures of the
laws of insurance, operating through averages with modifying and
mitigating effects in individual cases.' The Insurance Act provided

protection against both sickness and unemployment. The latter provoked little political debate. It was actuarily sound, being confined to certain trades exposed to cyclical unemployment but not chronically depressed, such as building, shipbuilding, and engineering. Employers and employees each paid 2½d. per head per week, the Treasury adding one-third. The Government was here feeling its way cautiously, though Lloyd George and the radicals expected this limited scheme to be gradually extended trade by trade until it became universal.[35]

The health insurance scheme was much bolder, and was passed and operated only after a struggle with powerful pressure groups. Both the friendly societies and the insurance companies had to be placated, for Lloyd George knew that their army of door-to-door collectors could exert great influence in the constituencies. They therefore became 'approved societies' through which much of the scheme operated. Insurance was made compulsory for all manual workers and voluntary for anyone earning less than £160 a year. The self-employed and non-employed were not covered. Workmen contributed 4d. weekly, employers 3d., and the state not quite 2d., making (in Lloyd George's phrase) 'ninepence for fourpence'. Ten shillings sickness benefit was provided for 26 weeks, backed by medical, maternity, and sanatorium care.

Yet health insurance was not popular. The Liberals lost three by-elections towards the end of 1911 while the Act was passing through its final stages. The Northcliffe press, and Unionist extremists, encouraged a short-lived but noisy agitation against sticking stamps upon insurance cards, especially by mistresses on behalf of domestic servants. More seriously, the scheme was presented to the working classes as an oppressive system of deduction from wages. Finally, after the Act had passed but before it came into operation in January 1913, extreme opinion tried to exploit the fears of the doctors. Throughout 1912 they grumbled about their prospects under the scheme. The president of the British Medical Association went so far as to describe Lloyd George as a 'national calamity'. But the Association's leaders overplayed their hand, and by making important concessions the Chancellor was able at the last moment to enlist most of the less well-to-do doctors. He took care not to seem to be creating a salaried state medical service. Nor did he break up the Poor Law, as demanded by the minority report of the Poor Law Commission. Throughout two years of difficult negotiations Lloyd George had prudently used conciliatory means to achieve radical ends.[36]

A 'social service state', in which certain minimum standards were assured, was now beginning to emerge, although this minimum was not universally available by 1914. The true 'welfare state', embracing the idea of the optimum rather than the minimum, lay another forty years in the future. But the principle of provision through insurance was already established. This contrasted with the socialist method, advocated by Keir Hardie in opposition to the 1911 scheme, of providing benefits entirely through graduated taxation. Ramsay MacDonald accepted the contributory principle in 1911, and the 1945 Labour Government followed MacDonald, not Hardie, when it created the present-day welfare state.[37]

With the enactment of health insurance the 'New Liberalism' had achieved all that it was destined to achieve in social improvement. Lloyd George, indeed, hoped to continue the advance by promoting comprehensive land reform. He discussed this question with See-bohm Rowntree, who in 1913 published *How the Labourer Lives*, a rural exposure complementary to his influential first book on urban poverty. Lloyd George wanted to create land tribunals to fix rents and wages, ending the misery of the rural labourers and enabling them to buy their cottages. In the autumn of 1913 he made a speech-making tour to publicize his land programme. 'Labourers had diminished, game had tripled. The landlord was no more necessary to agriculture than a gold chain to a watch.' These speeches failed, however, to achieve a major impact. Yet Lloyd George was still hoping to make land reform the dominant issue in a 1915 general election. 'Radicalism needs a great stimulus.' But in August 1914 his energies were to be suddenly diverted from making war against the landlords to making war against the Germans.[38]

IX

During 1911–12 noisy action by men on strike against economic underprivilege and by women suffragettes protesting against political underprivilege had attracted much more continuous notice than either the National Insurance or Parliament Bills. 'All political questions are thrust into the shade,' admitted Austen Chamberlain at the height of the 1912 coal strike. With danger threatening from both Europe and Ireland many Liberals as well as Unionists regarded the new trade-union militancy as a third possible menace to national security. The ideas of the syndicalists had come into circulation in Britain. These recommended pressure for workers' control of industry through 'direct action' and perhaps through violence. Yet outside South Wales it is now clear that the effective influences behind the strike wave were mainly material ones. During the Edwardian period the cost of living had risen steadily, 14 per cent in seven years according to a 1913 Board of Trade survey. But meanwhile capitalists had grown ostentatious in their wealth. This contrast was deeply resented. The cautious methods of the old trade union leaders had lost their appeal. Young workmen, explained H. G. Wells in the *Daily Mail*, had put the whole social system upon trial. 'The slack days for rulers and owners are over. . . . The supply of good-tempered, cheap labour—upon which the fabric of our contemporary ease and comfort is erected—is giving out.'

The feelings of the workers were further aggravated by the uncertain legal position of their unions. In 1906 the Labour party's Trade Disputes Act had been passed with Liberal support, allowing union funds total exemption from actions for tort. This reversed the Taff Vale decision of 1901, which had undermined the right to strike. But the courts remained suspicious of trade-union privileges, and the 1909 Osborne judgement held that it was illegal for unions to collect funds for political (Labour party) purposes. The 1913 Trade Union Act restored this power, though leaving members the right to opt out of payment.

The great strikes of 1911–12 were thus conducted against an unsettled legal background. The main protagonists were the railwaymen, the coal miners, and the port employees, well-organized workmen whose continuance in their jobs was vital to national life. A threatened national rail strike in 1907 had led to intervention by Lloyd George on behalf of the Government and to the formation of conciliation boards. In the next year the Government had conceded a statutory eight-hour day to the miners, a significant intervention by the state in industry. In addition, the miners wanted a statutory minimum wage. The year 1911 opened with a strike of South Wales miners, conducted under syndicalist influence and continued against the advice of the Miners' Federation leaders. During the hot summer of 1911 one strike followed another, seamen, dockers, railwaymen, and others. Never before had all the railways been stopped. Alarmists asked if this was the beginning of the syndicalist revolution. There was some violence and loss of life, and much more was feared. Lloyd George was again called to conciliate the railwaymen, who eventually secured employers' recognition of their unions and some wage rises. Early in 1912 it was the turn of the coal miners to declare a national strike. Ministers again tried conciliation, sponsoring legislation establishing district boards to fix wages. This was not the national minimum wage demanded, but it ended the strike. A bitter strike of London lightermen, dockers, and carters followed in the summer of 1912. Its failure emphasized the limitations of sectional action, and during 1913–14 the idea of a 'triple alliance' of miners, railwaymen, and port workers was under discussion. War came before this alliance had been formed, but it was destined to dominate industrial relations in the first years of peace.[39]

The suffragettes had added their shrill voices to the pre-war discord. The cry of 'Votes for women' within the Parliamentary franchise was an aspect of the wider demand for sex equality which had continued from mid-Victorian times. A woman's place was no longer only in the home. Women had entered the professions, and had come to play an essential part in offices and shops. Working-class women had provided factory labour from the earliest days of the Industrial Revolution. Women were already allowed to vote and to stand in local elections, on the ground that these impinged upon their domestic interests, But, emphasized the *Manchester Guardian* in 1910, 'almost every statute now directly or indirectly touches the home'.

Queen Victoria had been a sharp anti-feminist, asserting that one mid-Victorian enthusiast (the mother of Bertrand Russell) 'ought to get a *good whipping*'. For several years around 1870 the demand for women's suffrage had been quite strongly voiced in and out of Parliament; but it never looked like becoming practical politics. Many Liberals, though favourable in principle, were discouraged by the expected conservative bias of middle-class women voters. 'Gladstone spoke in favour, said he would vote against and ran away finally.' By the turn of the century, however, prospects were improving. Many self-governing colonies had given the vote to women. The new Independent Labour party was inclined to be sympathetic. In 1897 the National Union of Women's Suffrage Societies united all existing organizations. Finally, in 1903, the Women's Social and Political Union was founded by Mrs. Emmeline Pankhurst (1858–1928), widow of a radical Manchester barrister, supported by her daughters Christabel (1880–1958) and Sylvia (1882–1960). Mrs. Pankhurst was a remarkable woman, good-looking, an outstanding public speaker, and an able (though increasingly dictatorial) organizer. The *Daily Mail* dubbed her followers 'suffragettes' to distinguish them from the non-militant 'suffragists'. The W.S.P.U. raised the cry 'Votes for women', but left it vague whether this meant votes for all women or merely the franchise on the same (far from universal) terms as for men. The word 'social' in the W.S.P.U.

title probably reflected Mrs. Pankhurst's initial concern for the improvement of the lot of working-class women. But she later moved away from her early I.L.P. connections towards Conservatism. Though some working-class activists did emerge, notably Annie Kenney (1879–1953), a cotton worker, both the suffragette and suffragist organizations were predominantly middle-class, with a spicing of aristocratic supporters of both sexes.

For two years the W.S.P.U. attracted little attention. It was ignored by politicians and by the press. To win notice it therefore turned in 1905 to militant action, to the interruption of political meetings. Militancy began at a Liberal meeting in Manchester in October. Sir Edward Grey was asked if he would support votes for women, and when he refused to answer Christabel Pankhurst and Annie Kenney caused a disturbance and had to be forcibly ejected. They were later arrested for trying to hold a protest meeting outside the hall, refused to pay fines, and each spent seven days in prison.

The suffragettes wanted to know how much (or little) to expect from the new Liberal Government. Liberal and Conservative leaders and backbenchers were greatly divided on the question of female suffrage. Campbell-Bannerman was inclined to be favourable, Asquith to be hostile. The attitudes of Lloyd George and Churchill fluctuated. Balfour was friendly, Bonar Law rather less so. Even some Labour politicians hesitated, lest the grant of votes to some women damage the prospects of universal suffrage for men. Lloyd George concluded that the Liberals must either allow universal suffrage for both men and women or nothing, since enfranchisement of only middle-class women would strengthen the Conservative vote. Against this uncertain background it was not surprising that between 1907 and 1912 a succession of private members' bills came to nothing. In 1912 the Cabinet at last agreed to allow insertion of women's franchise, if the Commons accepted it on a free vote, into a Government Bill abolishing plural voting and extending the male franchise. But unexpectedly in January 1913 the Speaker ruled that such an insertion was inadmissible.

After this, suffragette militancy, which had already progressed from interruption of meetings to shop-window smashing, was further intensified. Systematic arson of churches, railway stations, and other public places continued through 1913 and into 1914. Cabinet ministers were assaulted. During the 1913 Derby a suffragette threw herself under the King's horse. Mrs. Pankhurst was sentenced to three years' imprisonment after accepting responsibility for a bomb explosion in a house being built for Lloyd George.

Suffragettes in prison had contrived to secure early release by going on hunger strikes. The Government now sponsored the 'Cat and Mouse' Act (1913), allowing release for recuperation followed by re-arrest. To such strange lengths had suffragette extremism driven the legislature. But this fanaticism had begun to disgust even many advocates of the women's cause. The *Manchester Guardian* denounced 'diseased emotionalism'. Defections had left the W.S.P.U. simply the tool of Mrs. Pankhurst. She claimed in her memoirs, published in 1914, that militancy had been proved right because it had gained notice for the agitation. The limited militancy of the early years can be so justified, but later excesses evoked anger not sympathy.

When war came in August 1914 the suffragettes patriotically stopped their agitation. This saved them from continuing along an increasingly dangerous and futile course. Gradually the contributions made by women to the war effort justified their claim to full citizenship. 'Time was', admitted the editor of *The Observer*, 'when I thought that men alone maintained the state. Now I know that men alone never could have maintained it.' The 1918 Representation of the People Act granted the vote to all men and to 8,500,000 women over thirty. In the same year women were also allowed to sit in the Commons. The 'flapper vote' for women between twenty-one and thirty had to wait until 1928, and plural voting survived until 1948. But substantially 1918 saw the beginning of electoral democracy in Britain. Since 1928 one fear of Mrs. Pankhurst's opponents has been realized—women voters have markedly outnumbered men.[40]

X

The Pankhursts justified their intensified militancy during 1913–14 by comparing its still limited character with the threats of civil war in Ireland being made by 'respectable' Unionist politicians. The cry 'Ulster will fight and Ulster will be right', coined by Lord Randolph Churchill in 1886 in opposition to the first Liberal Home Rule Bill, was now revived in opposition to the third Home Rule Bill of 1912–14.

The problem of the past, present, and future of Ireland had been transmitted unsolved from the Victorians to the Edwardians. Ireland had been bound to the rest of the United Kingdom by the Act of Union (1800). Preservation of this union, of the governmental integrity of the British Isles, meant so much to the Conservatives that they had adopted the alternative name of 'Unionists'. Gladstone, on the other hand, had persuaded the Liberal party to sponsor Home Rule. But twice, in 1886 and 1893, Gladstonian Home Rule Bills had failed to pass, and in the first years of the new century Liberals were inclined to varying degrees of caution over further attempts at Home Rule legislation. In the 1906 Parliament they pursued a 'step by step' policy (a phrase used by both Asquith and Grey), hoping temporarily to satisfy the Irish by lesser reforms while at the same time preparing the British public for the possibility of Home Rule in the future. In 1907 the Liberals promoted an Irish Council Bill, a modest measure of local government reorganization, so modest that Irish opinion repudiated it as derisory. More successful, however, were steps taken to end coercion, to protect evicted tenants, to improve housing and education, to encourage the Irish language, and to establish a national university.

The 1910 elections made the Liberal Government dependent upon Irish support in the Commons. Ministers now had to accept that a Home Rule Bill must follow once the Parliament Act had passed. The Lords could thereafter only delay the enactment of Home Rule; they could not negative it if three times passed by the Commons. Asquith introduced his Home Rule Bill in 1912; the Lords twice rejected it. Finally, in 1914 it went through without their sanction. But during these two years a real prospect of civil war developed in Ireland, centred round Ulster's refusal to be ruled by the South.

Ulster was Protestant, industrial as well as agricultural, and contented: the rest of Ireland was Catholic, agricultural, and discontented. The religious basis of Ulster's attitude came out strongly in Rudyard Kipling's (1865–1936) poem 'Ulster 1912':

> We know the war prepared
> On every peaceful home,
> We know the hells declared
> For such as serve not Rome—
> The terror, threats, and dread
> In market, hearth, and field—
> We know, when all is said,
> We perish if we yield.
>
> . . . .
>
> What answer from the North?
> One Law, one Land, one Throne.
> If England drives us forth
> We shall not fall alone.

Ulster's determination was firmly backed by the Unionists at Westminster. They seemed unwilling to abandon the claim to a Home Rule veto. During the Parliament Bill debates Churchill had complained to the King of 'their claim to govern the country whether in office or in opposition and to resort to disorder because they cannot have their way'. In 1912 Bonar Law ungrammatically but appallingly asserted in a public speech that he could 'imagine no length of resistance to which Ulster can go in which I should not be prepared to support them'. 'The veto of violence,' summed up Churchill in 1914, 'has replaced the veto of privilege.' The Unionists could not shed the belief that they were the 'natural' ruling party; yet by 1914 they had spent eight frustrating years in opposition. They convinced themselves that the Liberals had not been given a Home Rule mandate in 1910, and that therefore no such measure should be enacted unless and until a general election had shown public opinion to be favourable. The Liberals answered (with good reason) firstly, that Home Rule had indeed been under discussion during the 1910 elections; secondly, that to admit the Unionists' right to force another general election would be to admit their continuing right of veto; and thirdly, that even if the Government won a favourable election verdict Ulster would still threaten violent resistance to the enforcement of Home Rule. Around these arguments and counter-arguments language and feelings grew steadily higher during 1912–14. Social contact between Unionist and Liberal politicians became increasingly strained, in some cases to breaking point. The 'English political compromise' was disintegrating.

The strongest argument in Ulster's favour contended that under the unwritten modern British constitution majorities had generally respected significant minority rights. Unfortunately, both the Unionists and the Liberals began by assuming that, for economic reasons, respect for the rights of Ulster implied abandonment of Home Rule for the rest of Ireland. The Liberals therefore tried to ignore Ulster's claim for separate treatment, while the Unionists pressed Ulster's case not only on its own merits but also with the discreditable expectation of thereby preventing the introduction of Home Rule even in the rest of Ireland. A handful of southern Irish landlords were very influential within the Unionist ranks. Faced with such intransigent opposition, it was immaterial that the Home Rule Bill introduced by Asquith in April 1912 was extremely limited in its conception of Home Rule. Only restricted powers were conferred upon a Dublin Parliament, and much financial and other control was reserved to Westminster. In private, though not in public, Ministers were prepared to admit that Ulster might need 'special treatment', but they long hoped that the Ulstermen were only bluffing in their talk of civil war.

They were not bluffing, as the Government gradually realized. Sir Edward Carson (1854–1935), the Ulster leader, emphasized as early as 1911 in a private letter to Captain Craig (1871–1940), the chief organizer of resistance, how he was 'not for a mere game of bluff'. On 28 September 1912 at a public gathering in Belfast Carson's followers solemnly began signing the Covenant, a pledge to use 'all means which may be found necessary to defeat the setting up of a Home Rule Parliament in Ireland'. Almost a quarter of a million men signed this threat of armed resistance. By 1914 the Ulster Volunteers, Carson's army, were highly organized, and arms were being landed in only semi-secrecy from Germany. In England a British Covenant was published in March 1914, its first signatories including Kipling, the writer, Sir Edward Elgar (1857–1934), the composer (of 'Pomp and Circumstance'), and Lord Roberts (1832–1914), the most popular living British soldier. Like Roberts, many Army officers were Unionists with Irish connections. Early in 1914 Bonar Law even toyed with the disturbing idea of using his Lords majority to amend the annual Army Act, upon which all discipline depended, in order to prevent employment of troops against Ulster. In March the news that the Government had ordered military movements to meet possible violence in the North provoked a spate of resignations among Army officers. This so-called 'Curragh mutiny' was not a mutiny in the proper sense, but it did demonstrate the unreliability of the Army in the excited circumstances of the day.

After this, Asquith himself became War Secretary. He was still hoping to avoid a complete breakdown, either in Parliament or in Ulster. Moving on 9 March the second reading of the Home Rule Bill (now on its third circuit), he offered the Opposition an Amending Bill which would have postponed the application of Home Rule to Ulster for six years. This would have interposed two general elections between the beginning of Home Rule and its prospective application to the North. Carson dismissed this gesture as 'sentence of death with a stay of execution for six years'. Nevertheless, he and Bonar Law, though not all their followers, were now ready for some compromise. This was demonstrated in July when Carson, Craig, Bonar Law, and Lansdowne met Asquith and Lloyd George, plus John Redmond (1856–1918) and John Dillon (1851–1927), the Irish leaders, in a conference called under royal auspices at Buckingham Palace. The idea of exclusion was now accepted by both sides, but the conference still broke down over the exclusion or inclusion of two Ulster counties with almost equal Protestant/Catholic populations. The Unionists intended to insist upon the perpetual exclusion of Ulster, but the conference never reached discussion of this second problem.

Both sides had modified their positions since 1912, but because their remaining differences seemed intractable Ireland was on the brink of civil war by the last days of July 1914. The Catholics of the South were now armed and organized to match the Protestants of the North. Yet Asquith still confided to a friend his characteristic 'fixed belief that in politics the expected rarely happens'. And so, indeed, it turned out. Suddenly war erupted on the Continent. On 30 July Asquith and Bonar Law agreed that in the interests of national unity the Government's Amending Bill, which still only proposed the exclusion of Ulster for six years and which was certain to produce furious scenes in Parliament, should not proceed to a second reading. The Home Rule Bill itself was placed on the statute book in September, but its application was postponed for the duration of the war. By the time peace returned the 1916 Easter rising and its aftermath had added another bitter chapter to the history of Anglo-Irish discord, and such a limited measure of Home Rule could no longer satisfy southern Irish opinion.[41]

XI

'Ah 1914! "Oh! that a man might know the end of this year's business ere it come." I see not a patch of blue sky!' When at the year's opening a leading Liberal (Morley) wrote thus to a leading Unionist (Austen Chamberlain) all his fears were concentrated upon Ireland. A major European war, though always conceivable, did not seem especially likely in 1914. Relations between Britain and Germany were at least no worse than they had been for nearly a decade. On the other hand, real harmony in intercourse between the two countries seemed to have gone for ever. Certain fixed attitudes precluded this. At the heart of Anglo-German tension lay Germany's insistence from the time of her 1898 and 1900 Navy Laws upon building a large fleet. The Germans asserted their sovereign right to do so. They also argued that their commerce and colonies needed protection, a reasonable point but not one compatible with the short range of the new German fleet, which was clearly built to fight in the North Sea. In the early days of the new naval policy it was possible to justify this emphasis by an honest (if misguided) belief that the north German coast needed protection against a possible British attack. Another German line stressed the need to build a fleet so large that the British Navy would only be able to destroy it at prohibitive cost to itself; it was thought that this prospect could be used to influence British policy in favour of Germany and away from France and Russia. In reality, the only influence exerted by German fleet building was to make Britain counter-build. Traditionally Britannia had ruled the waves, and almost everyone in Britain, though there were differences over the mathematics of supremacy, agreed that this supremacy must be maintained. For Germany a fleet was (in Churchill's word) a 'luxury': for Britain, with her dependence upon imported food and raw materials and with her world empire, it was a necessity.

In a major speech to the empire delegates to the Committee of Imperial Defence in 1911 Grey linked the naval question to the balance of power. He emphasized how if Britain did not work to maintain that balance, if the Continent became dominated by one bloc, Britain would be isolated. To retain command of the seas in such circumstances she would need to build a navy large enough to match the fleets of all five European Great Powers together. Germany was already challenging Britain at sea; how much greater would be her challenge at the head of 'one great combination'. Did Germany plan 'to restore the Germanic Empire of Charlemagne in a modern form?' asked Balfour in 1912. Such a policy seemed 'almost incredible. And yet it is almost impossible to make sense of modern German policy without crediting it with this intention.' German policy may have been calculating; it was certainly blundering, its blunders proving disastrous for Europe.

By 1902 the British Admiralty was beginning to treat Germany rather than France or Russia as the chief naval rival. Sir John Fisher (1841–1920), the idiosyncratic but brilliant First Sea Lord (1904–10, 1914–15), mused at least half-seriously about a preventive strike upon the German fleet. Gradually, under the pressure of steady German battleship building, the two-power standard, under which the British fleet had been maintained at a strength more than equal to the combined strengths of the next two largest foreign navies, was replaced by a standard of 60 per cent superiority over the German Navy. From 1905 the construction of the *Dreadnought*, much more powerful than all previous battleships, compelled the rebuilding of all battle fleets from scratch. Britain led the way, but Germany was now not far behind. In 1909 a naval scare swept Britain, in the belief that the Germans had secretly accelerated their battleship building so that by 1912 they might have numerical superiority. 'We want eight and we won't wait,' voiced the popular clamour for the immediate construction of eight, rather than four, new capital ships. The Liberal Government, though reluctant to spend so heavily upon armaments, eventually did build the eight vessels, taking account of the entry of Austria and Italy into the dreadnought race. The fear of German acceleration was unfounded, but in the early stages of the war these four extra ships were to prove invaluable in maintaining British supremacy.

The Anglo-German naval race continued steadily up to 1914. On the outbreak of war 24 British dreadnoughts faced 16 German dreadnoughts across the North Sea. The Germans had been willing to halt the naval race only if Britain promised neutrality in a Franco-German war. Faced with the choice between expensive naval competition and the acceptance of political conditions which might lead to German hegemony on the Continent, the Liberal Government rightly chose the former course. As Grey had indicated, leaving aside all moral obligations, the abandonment of France would have cost much more in terms of naval expenditure in the long run. Already the price of outbuilding the Germans was distressingly high. Lloyd George, as Chancellor of the Exchequer, and Churchill, as First Lord of the Admiralty, fought a prolonged battle within the Cabinet over the cost of the 1914–15 naval estimates. The Germans were feeling the financial strain even more. Yet by 1914 their naval policy had plainly failed, both in naval and in diplomatic terms. Far from detaching Britain from France and Russia, it had driven her closer to them. The German fleet was a prime cause of this alignment, and yet it was still not strong enough either to protect German colonies and commerce in wartime, or to meet the British fleet in open battle at sea.[42]

Naval rivalry was much more important than economic competition as a cause of Anglo-German disharmony. Without this disharmony general war could probably have been avoided in 1914. Germany and Britain could have worked together for peace. 'If Germany would give the word,' declared Grey during the last days of peace, 'war would be averted.' The murder at Sarajevo on 28 June of the Austrian Archduke Franz Ferdinand by a Serbian nationalist, need not then have drawn the rival alliance systems into conflict. Britain was still not formally bound to fight in support of France and Russia, but her moral commitment was strong, even though half the Liberal Cabinet was reluctant to admit this. Grey was determined to resign if the Government refused to fight. The

German infringement of Belgian neutrality, guaranteed by the Powers in 1839, finally converted all but two Cabinet ministers to support the war. As Asquith wrote in his diary, 'this simplifies matters'. On the afternoon of 3 August Grey delivered a notable defence of his policy in the House of Commons. His speech, almost conversational in tone and rather ragged in form, none the less achieved the rare effect of making numerous converts, persuading the House to give retrospective sanction to the moral commitments—diplomatic, military, and naval—which he had quietly made since 1906. Grey summed up the purpose of his speech in his memoirs. 'The real reason for going into the war was that, if we did not stand by France and stand up for Belgium against this aggression, we should be isolated, discredited, and hated; and there would be before us nothing but a miserable and ignoble future.' The fear of isolation, which had led Britain into the *entente* policy, now logically led her into war. To draw back would have left her more dangerously isolated than ever she had been in 1904, with the not distant possibility of 'one great combination' formed in Europe against her, headed by Germany, united by a common hatred of 'perfidious Albion', possessing a huge combined army and able to build a great combined fleet.

Could Grey have done more during the final crisis to prevent war? Lloyd George argued in his memoirs (though not at the time) that if the Foreign Secretary had made it plain soon enough that Britain would fight for Belgium war might have been averted. Grey had anticipated this charge as early as 1915. 'The idea that one individual, sitting in a room in the Foreign Office, could pledge a great democracy definitely by his word in advance, either to take part in a great war or to abstain from taking part in it, is absurd.' Balfour in retrospect accepted that the Foreign Secretary could make no formal forecast, but he suggested that a personal opinion might have carried weight with the German Ambassador. 'I should not have said to him that she would come in *at once*, but I should have made perfectly clear my conviction that sooner or later she would do so.' It seems, however, that Germany would not have been stopped even if a blunt British threat of counter-intervention had been possible. 'Only if England went with us', declared Moltke (1848–1916), the Chief of the German General Staff, 'would a renunciation of the march through Belgium be possible. That, however, is inconceivable.' Germany ignored a British ultimatum demanding immediate withdrawal from Belgian territory, and at midnight on 4 August 1914 Britain entered the 'Great War'.[43]

The conflict immediately became known by this name. Its scale was clearly far beyond that of all previous contests. Once it had started its coming seemed to many to have been inevitable. It is less clear how many British people had felt this inevitability before the event. Some autobiographies written after 1914 describe their authors' strong sense of foreboding, but others explicitly deny having any such feeling. The international rivalries were of course well known, but by 1914 these had lasted for a generation without precipitating a major war. Perhaps a majority of British people vaguely held a middle position, fearing disaster some day but never expecting that day to be tomorrow. 'The great war that we have had in our innermost thoughts,' noted a leading journalist in his diary on 5 August, 'but have always kept in reserve, in the belief that it would be for our children or our children's children to go through is here, and *we* are to go through it.'[44]

XII

A short war was generally expected, 'over by Christmas'. To fight for 'little Belgium' was a satisfying moral cause. 'Beside the blatant vulgarity of the Boer War jingoism,' explained one writer, 'this war of 1914 is a religious crusade.' Only slowly was the enthusiastic mood of Rupert Brooke's highly popular war sonnets replaced by a more sober spirit, as it became realized that the conflict had settled into a prolonged war of attrition in the Flanders mud. The cry at home of 'business as usual' was gradually submerged by the need to fight 'total war' on the 'home front'. The *Times Literary Supplement* was among the first journals to show a revealing shift of attitude. On 20 August its editor was explaining how, with her allies fighting desperately for survival, Britain alone could retain some detachment. 'For the moment the conscience of the world is in our keeping.' But by 22 October its editorial was headed 'The Illusions of War'. 'It seemed easy not to hate the Germans when the war began, but it is less easy now that we have borne the strain of war for two months and a half.' A fortnight later a highly favourable review appeared of a short study of the Kaiser; the book's emotive title was *The Last of the Huns*.

By December 1914 Asquith was noting in his diary how deadlock had been reached in France. Were the British armies in Flanders to 'chew barbed wire' (in Churchill's phrase), or should an effort be made to turn the enemy flank via the Baltic or the Balkans? The outcome was the unsuccessful 1915 Dardanelles diversion. In May

1915 rather suddenly a coalition Government was formed, Asquith remaining Prime Minister. In France during 1915 the front nowhere moved more than three miles; yet the cost in casualties was sickening. After much Liberal heart-searching conscription was introduced in May 1916. The Battle of the Somme beginning in July was the first major action by a British army of continental size. The slaughter of this great volunteer force lasted until November. Over 20,000 men were killed or missing on the first day; well over 400,000 British casualties were suffered in all. Little was gained. Junior officers were outstanding for their bravery, generals for their lack of vision. Lloyd George, who became Prime Minister in December 1916, pressed hard for a major effort away from the vortex of the Western Front. But the generals thought otherwise. Sir William Robertson (1860–1933), Chief of the Imperial General Staff 1915–18, could scarcely justify the attrition policy, but he remained firmly attached to it. 'My views are known to you,' he wrote to Sir Douglas Haig (1861–1928), the British commander in France, after the collapse of the Russians in 1917. 'They have always been "defensive" in all theatres but the West. But the difficulty is to *prove* the wisdom of this now that Russia is out. I confess I stick to it more because I see nothing better, and because my instinct prompts me to stick to it, than because of any good argument by which I can support it.' Haig complained maliciously of Lloyd George's 'desire to gain ground in secondary theatres as if he did not believe in our ability to beat the Germans themselves': the Prime Minister (claimed Haig) wished 'to gain something with which to bargain at a peace conference'. In the end the Allies, from April 1917 including the Americans, won the war of attrition. On 11 November 1918 all fighting stopped. Three-quarters of a million men from the United Kingdom, and 200,000 from the empire, had died.[45]

This loss of life and diversion of resources was materially and psychologically very damaging for Britain. One recent American expert has concluded that concentration upon a mass army marked 'the beginning of the end of Britain's long preponderance as a world power'. Yet it would be wrong to assume that all the effects of the war were bad. It accelerated the pace of change, sometimes to advantage. We have noted the part played by the war in gaining 'votes for women'. The war also reduced the cleavage between the classes, a prominent feature of pre-war Britain. Taxation fell heavily upon the upper and middle classes. Income tax, only 1s. 2d. in 1914, had reached 6s. by the end of the war, and even in peace was never again to drop below 4s. Working-class employment remained steady during the war, and wages high. Labour was in demand as never before. The trade unions were now finally recognized as a necessary part of national life. Membership rose from over four millions in 1914 to nearly eight millions in 1919. Drunkenness, the scourge of Edwardian working men, was permanently reduced when licensing hours were restricted in the interests of the war effort and the specific gravity of beer progressively reduced. The war eroded class distinctions in dress, as middle- and upper-class clothes became more casual. The cinema boomed, losing its earlier proletarian associations and becoming a powerful instrument of all-class entertainment. Above all, a common cause and common suffering helped to pull classes together. It came to be accepted (even though more than fifty years later intention still outstrips practice) that the sacrifices made by working men in war entitled their families to adequate housing and education in peace. The 1918 Education Act and the 1919 Housing and Town Planning Act reflected an intensified readiness to act through legislation. The war had given the state a new prominence. Conscription, food rationing, control of employment, had all helped to bring victory. The bogey of state interference was not yet dead, but it was diminished.[46]

A Liberal Government had initiated this interventionist policy on patriotic grounds. But the fact of war and these war policies undermined the Liberal party as a major political force. 'War is fatal to Liberalism,' as Churchill had declared before 1914. The traditional Liberal slogan had been 'Peace, retrenchment and reform'. Now there was no peace, and the opposite of retrenchment. Free trade, the central Liberal economic creed, was sacrificed in 1915 when import duties were imposed, limited at first in range and duration but destined never again to disappear. The 1916 Asquith–Lloyd George split greatly added to Liberal difficulties, but the whole position of Liberalism was already weakened by this date. Perhaps it was already undermined even before the war. The social reforms of Lloyd George and Churchill had been improvisations, brilliant but uncertain in their intellectual ground, like the two men themselves. They had expressly repudiated 'socialism', but the rise of the wartime state made socialist methods of government credible. Before the war even the Labour party had not been explicitly committed to full socialism. By 1918 it was ready to offer a fully socialist programme and to become a fully organized national party. Its new 1918 constitution provided for party membership by individuals and for local party organization. *Labour and the New Social Order* committed the party to socialist objectives, even though the word 'socialism' was still avoided:

Today no man dares to say that anything is impracticable. The war, which has scared the old political parties right out of their dogmas, has taught every statesman and every Government official, to his enduring surprise, how very much more can be done along the lines that we have laid down than he had ever before thought possible.

Labour's four objectives were: (1) the enforcement of a 'national minimum', meaning full employment with a minimum wage for a maximum 48-hour week; (2) democratic control of industry through nationalization; (3) heavy taxation of the rich to subsidize social services, plus a capital levy to help pay for the war; (4) the use of the 'national surplus' to expand popular education and culture.

Both in organization and in policy the Labour leaders were seeking clearly to differentiate themselves from the Liberals, taking care at the same time to stand apart from the Bolsheviks, whose proclamation of world revolution had greatly alarmed the British middle class. Labour made it plain that it intended to work within the framework of Parliamentary government, and that it was content to wait upon the wishes of the now enlarged and democratic electorate. Labour membership in the War Cabinet had helped to prove that Labour's leaders were fit to rule. After the 1918 election, with Lloyd George's followers submerged in the mainly Unionist majority, and with the Asquithians reduced to only 26, Labour's 63 Members of Parliament constituted the official Opposition. In 1924 Ramsay MacDonald became the first Labour Prime Minister. Few even among Labour's most zealous pioneers had foreseen such rapid progress. Herbert Morrison (1888–1965), destined to become Deputy Prime Minister in C. R. Attlee's (1883–1967) notable 1945 Labour Government (the first with an overall majority), had started his political career in Edwardian London. 'That within my lifetime I should see Labour become the biggest and most powerful party in the state,' remembered Morrison, 'might have been beyond the imagination of any of us.'[47]

The political education of Morrison and Attlee was largely completed before 1914. Though they found much wrong with the Edwardian scene, Labour men as much as Conservatives had accepted it as the 'normal' world: 'a place full of evil, where only too often the wicked flourished like the green bay tree; but solid: a place which, by work and faith, we could and would make better.'[48] Politicians with an Edwardian background continued to dominate

British government until the retirement of Mr. Harold Macmillan (b. 1894) in 1963. Only now are British politics almost entirely in the hands of men with no Edwardian yardstick against which to measure changes in British society and British policy. Mr. Wilson and Mr. Heath, each born in 1916, are the first Prime Ministers not to have spent any of their formative years before the 'Great War'.

NOTES

[1] H. G. Wells, *Tono-Bungay* (1909), Bk. I, ch. i, sect. 3; A. Birrell, *Collected Essays and Addresses* (1922), I. 363; J. Pope-Hennessy, *Queen Mary* (1959), 384; C. Hassall, *Rupert Brooke* (1964), 238; R. S. Churchill, *Winston S. Churchill*, I (1966), 546.

[2] N. Blewett, 'The Franchise in the United Kingdom 1885–1918', *Past & Present*, No. 32 (1965).

[3] C. L. Graves, *Mr. Punch's History of Modern England* (n.d.), IV. 133; T. Clarke, *My Northcliffe Diary* (1931), 195–201; Lord Riddell, *More Pages from My Diary 1908–1914* (1934), 22; M. Marples, *History of Football* (1954), ch. xii; R. Pound and G. Harmsworth, *Northcliffe* (1959), 255–6, 419, 423–4; D. Read, *The English Provinces 1760–1960* (1964), 228–32.

[4] *Manchester Guardian*, 24 Dec. 1895; A. Bullock and M. Shock, *The Liberal Tradition* (1967), 190–217.

[5] J. R. MacDonald, *The Socialist Movement* (1911), xi, 235; F. Bealey and H. Pelling, *Labour and Politics 1900–1906* (1958); P. P. Poirier, *The Advent of the Labour Party* (1958); J. F. C. Harrison, *Society and Politics in England 1780–1960* (1965), 300–27; H. Pelling, *The Origins of the Labour Party*, 2nd ed. (1965).

[6] H. Pelling, *A Short History of the Labour Party* (1961), ch. ii; J. H. S. Reid, *The Origins of the British Labour Party* (1955), chs. ix, x, xi.

[7] Lord Hugh Cecil, *Conservatism* (1912), esp. chs. vi, ix; Riddell, *More Pages from My Diary*, 122; R. B. McDowell, *British Conservatism 1832–1914* (1959), chs. iii, iv.

[8] J. A. Thomas, *The House of Commons 1906–1911* (1958), esp. 28–9; W. L. Guttsman, *The British Political Elite* (1963), esp. ch. iv; J. P. Cornford, 'The Parliamentary Foundations of the Hotel Cecil', in R. Robson, ed., *Ideas and Institutions of Victorian Britain* (1967), 268–311.

[9] Riddell, *More Pages from My Diary*, 59, 69; Sir A. Chamberlain, *Politics from Inside* (1936), 464; Lucy Masterman, *C. F. G. Masterman* (1939), 218–19; Beatrice Webb, *Our Partnership* (1948), 248–9, 270–1, 309, 382; K. Young, *Arthur James Balfour* (1963), esp. xviii, xx, 126, 214, 314; Churchill, *Churchill*, II. 354; Robson, *Victorian Britain*, 296.

[10] W. S. Blunt, *My Diaries* (1932), 692; Riddell, *More Pages from My Diary*, 78–9, 85, 86, 87, 102, 106, 116–17, 118, 216; Masterman, *Masterman*, 137; W. S. Churchill, *Great Contemporaries* (1949), 103–17; Lord Beaverbrook, *Men and Power 1917–1918* (1956), x; Lord Beaverbrook, *Politicians and the War 1914–1916* (1960), 542; Margot Asquith, *Autobiography*, ed. M. Bonham Carter (1962),

306–8; R. Jenkins, *Asquith* (1964), esp. 13, 31, 91, 195, 208, 227–8, 279, 319, 330, ch. xxi, 415, 460–1, 462–3.

[11] *Slings and Arrows, Sayings chosen from the Speeches of the Rt. Hon. David Lloyd George*, ed. P. Guedalla (n.d.), 128–9; Riddell, *More Pages from My Diary*, 152, 155, and *passim*; D. Lloyd George, *War Memoirs* (1938), I. 21–3; Masterman, *Masterman*, 164–5, 170–2; Sir C. Petrie, *Life and Letters of the Right Hon. Sir Austen Chamberlain*, I (1939), 381–8; W. S. Churchill, *Thoughts and Adventures* (1949), 38–40; J. Ehrman, 'Lloyd George and Churchill as War Ministers', *Transactions of the Royal Historical Society*, 5th ser., 11 (1961); A. J. P. Taylor, *Politics in Wartime* (1964), chs. i, ix.

[12] R. D. Blumenfeld, *R.D.B.'s Diary* (1930), 74–5; T. Jones, *A Diary With Letters 1931–1950* (1954), 204; W. George, *My Brother and I* (1958), 253; Beaverbrook, *Politicians and the War*, 357; Jenkins, *Asquith*, 339–40, 361, 426; Churchill, *Churchill*, 11. 224–5, 451, 500–1, 574, 576–7, ch. xvii.

[13] S. Low, *The Governance of England* (1904), 297–303; *English Review*, Feb. 1914, 430; W. J. Harte, 'Fifty Years of British Foreign Policy', *History*, I (1916–17), 107; Sir E. Grey (Lord Grey of Fallodcn), *Twenty-Five Years* (1925), I. 95–6, and *passim*; Sir E. Grey, *Falloden Papers* (1926), 83, ch. vii; *British Documents on the Origins of the War*, ed. G. P. Gooch and H. Temperley, III (1928), No. 299; A. Birrell, *Things Past Redress* (1937), 225–6; G. M. Trevelyan, *Grey of Falloden* (1945), 40, 67, and *passim*; G. W. Monger, *The End of Isolation, British Foreign Policy 1900–1907* (1963), 233–5, chs. ix, x, xi, xii, 329–31, and *passim*; Bullock and Shock, *The Liberal Tradition*, 243–9; Churchill, *Churchill*, 11. 596–8; C. H. D. Howard, *Splendid Isolation* (1967); Zara Steiner, 'Grey, Hardinge and the Foreign Office 1906–1910', *Historical Journal*, x (1967).

[14] J. L. Garvin and J. Amery, *Life of Joseph Chamberlain* (1932–68), I. 202, and *passim*; Churchill, *Great Contemporaries*, 43–56; J. Joll, *Britain and Europe* (1950), 197–9; L. Mosley, *Curzon* (1960), 33; A. Briggs, *Victorian Cities* (1963), ch. v; Monger, *End of Isolation*, ch. ii, 68, 107–8; Read, *English Provinces*, ch. iv.

[15] R. H. Wilde, 'Joseph Chamberlain and the South African Republic 1895–1899', *Archives Year Book for South African History* (1956, vol. I), esp. ch. x; J. S. Marais, *The Fall of Kruger's Republic* (1961), 70, and *passim*; P. Fraser, *Joseph Chamberlain* (1966), ch. viii.

[16] Garvin and Amery, *Joseph Chamberlain*, III, IV, V; W. K. Hancock, *Survey of British Commonwealth Affairs*, vol. II, pt. I (1942), ch. i; B. Semmel, *Imperialism and Social Reform* (1960), chs. iv, v; Young, *Balfour*, 193–4, ch. x; Read, *English Provinces*, 184–90; A. Gollin, *Balfour's Burden, Arthur Balfour and Imperial Preference* (1965); W. H. B. Court, *British Economic History 1870–1914, Commentary and Documents* (1965), ch. ix; Fraser, *Chamberlain*, chs. vii, x, xi; Z. H. Zebel, 'Joseph Chamberlain and the Genesis of Tariff Reform', *Journal of British Studies*, VII (1967); J. E. Kendle, *The Colonial and Imperial Conferences 1887–1911* (1967).

[17] *The Times*, 30 Jan. 1906; E. Halévy, *History of the English People*, VI (2nd ed., 1952), 8–11; Thomas, *The House of Commons 1906–1911*, 6–8; P. Fraser, 'Unionism and Tariff Reform, The Crisis of 1906', *Historical Journal*, V (1962); D. Butler and Jennie Freeman, *British Political Facts 1900–1960* (1963), 122; Taylor, *Politics in Wartime*, 133–5; Fraser, *Chamberlain*, 273; H. Pelling, *Social Geography of British Elections 1885–1910* (1967), 19–20, 417, 426, 432; N. Blewett, 'Free Fooders, Balfourites, Whole Hoggers, Factionalism within the Unionist Party, 1906–10', *Historical Journal*, XI (1968).

[18] Sir A. Chamberlain, *Down the Years* (1935), 206–9; Halévy, *History of the*

English People, v. 139–210; Young, *Balfour*, 203–7, ch. xi; Gollin, *Balfour's Burden*, ch. xv; Marjorie Cruickshank, *Church and State in English Education 1870 to the Present Day* (1964), ch. iv; B. Simon, *Education and the Labour Movement 1870–1920* (1965), ch. vii.

[19] Chamberlain, *Politics from Inside, passim*; Thomas, *The House of Commons 1906–1911*, 8–12; R. Blake, *The Unknown Prime Minister, the Life and Times of Andrew Bonar Law* (1955), chs. iv, vi; R. S. Churchill, *Lord Derby, King of Lancashire* (1959), ch. viii; A. M. Gollin, *'The Observer' and J. L. Garvin 1908–1914* (1960), chs. viii, xi; Butler and Freeman, *British Political Facts*, 122, 125; Young, *Balfour*, chs. xii, xiii; Fraser, *Chamberlain*, ch. xii; Pelling, *Social Geography of British Elections*, 21–2.

[20] W. Ashworth, *A Short History of the International Economy 1850–1950* (1952), ch. vi; S. B. Saul, *Studies in British Overseas Trade* (1960), esp. chs. ii, iii, vi; F. Crouzet, 'Commerce et Empire: L'Expérience Britannique du Libre-Échange à la Première Guerre Mondiale', *Annales, Economies, Societés, Civilisations*, 19 (1964).

[21] *Speeches by the Rt. Hon. Sir Henry Campbell-Bannerman* (1908), 213–17, 232–5; Blunt, *Diaries*, 613; Riddell, *More Pages from My Diary*, 144–5; B. Williams, *Botha, Smuts and South Africa* (1946), ch. iv; G. B. Pyrah, *Imperial Policy and South Africa 1902–10* (1955), 122, and *passim*; L. M. Thompson, *The Unification of South Africa 1902–1910* (1960), ch. vii; W. K. Hancock, *Smuts, the Sanguine Years 1870–1919* (1962), chs. xi–xiii; R. Hyam, 'Smuts and the Decision of the Liberal Government to Grant Responsible Government to the Transvaal', *Historical Journal*, VIII (1965); B. B. Gilbert, 'The Grant of Responsible Government to the Transvaal: More Notes on a Myth', ibid., x (1967); Churchill, *Churchill*, II, ch. vi.

[22] Lord Morley, *Indian Speeches* (1909), esp. 91–2; Lord Morley, *Recollections* (1917), Bk. V; *New Cambridge Modern History*, XII (1960), ch. ix, esp. 212–14; S. R. Wasti, *Lord Minto and the Indian Nationalist Movement 1905 to 1910* (1964), 128, 191, and *passim*; M. N. Das, *India under Morley and Minto* (1964), 183, and *passim*; R. J. Moore, *Liberalism and Indian Politics 1872–1920* (1966), esp. ch. vi.

[23] Halévy, *History of the English People*, VI. 11–12; Pelling, *Social Geography of British Elections*, 19–20.

[24] *The Times*, 16 Jan. 1906; Lord Newton, *Lord Lansdowne* (1929), ch. xv; Blanche E. C. Dugdale, *Arthur James Balfour* (1939), II. 14–15; D. W. Brogan, *The English People* (1943), 20–1; R. Jenkins, *Mr. Balfour's Poodle* (1954), ch. ii; C. F. G. Masterman, *The Condition of England*, ed. J. T. Boulton (1960), xv, 52–3.

[25] Campbell–Bannerman, *Speeches*, 246–7; Cruickshank, *Church and State in English Education*, ch. v.

[26] *Nation*, 31 Oct. 1908; T. S. and M. B. Simey, *Charles Booth* (1960); A. Briggs, *Seebohm Rowntree* (1961), esp. chs. ii, iii; M. Bruce, *The Coming of the Welfare State*, 3rd ed. (1966), 133–46; B. B. Gilbert, *The Evolution of National Insurance in Great Britain* (1966), chs. i, ii.

[27] Gilbert, *National Insurance*, 81–101, 237–45.

[28] Ibid., ch. iii; J. St. L. Strachey, *The Manufacture of Paupers* (1907).

[29] Doreen Collins, 'The Introduction of Old Age Pension in Great Britain', *Historical Journal*, VIII (1965); Bruce, *Welfare State*, 147–56; Gilbert, *National Insurance*, ch. iv.

[30] *O.E.D.* under 'unemployed', 'unemployment'; W. H. Beveridge, *Unemployment, A Problem of Industry*, 2nd ed. (1930); Lord Beveridge, *Power and*

Influence (1953), 44–79; Bruce, *Welfare State*, 156–70; Gilbert, *National Insurance*, 233–65; Bullock and Shock, *The Liberal Tradition*, 212–13; Churchill, *Churchill*, II, ch. ix.

[31] *Parliamentary Debates*, IV (1909), 472–547; Blunt, *Diaries*, 689; Masterman, *Masterman*, ch. vi; Jenkins, *Balfour's Poodle*, 39–48; Jenkins, *Asquith*, 195–8.

[32] Newton, *Lansdowne*, ch. xvi; Lloyd George, *Slings and Arrows*, 93–150; Chamberlain, *Politics from Inside*, 196–200; Dugdale, *Balfour*, II. 40–2; Jenkins, *Balfour's Poodle*, 48–57, chs. v, vi; Gollin, '*The Observer*' *and J. L. Garvin*, ch. iv; Jenkins, *Asquith*, 198–204; Butler and Freeman, *Political Facts*, 122; Churchill, *Churchill*, II. 322–35.

[33] Jenkins, *Balfour's Poodle*, ch. vii; Jenkins, *Asquith*, 204–11.

[34] *The Times*, 11 Aug. 1911; Newton, *Lansdowne*, ch. xvii; Chamberlain, *Politics from Inside*, 200–345; Dugdale, *Balfour*, II. 45–61; Masterman, *Masterman*, 200–2; Jenkins, *Balfour's Poodle*, chs. viii–xiii, appendix C; Gollin, '*The Observer*' *and J. L. Garvin*, ch. x; Butler and Freeman, *Political Facts*, 122; Jenkins, *Asquith*, 212–32; Churchill, *Churchill*, II. 340–61.

[35] Beveridge, *Unemployment*, 263–72; Beveridge, *Power and Influence*, 80–92; Bruce, *Welfare State*, 171–4; Gilbert, *National Insurance*, ch. v.

[36] Masterman, *Masterman*, ch. ix; W. J. Braithwaite, *Lloyd George's Ambulance Waggon* (1957); P. Vaughan, *Doctor's Commons* (1959), 196–210; E. R. Turner, *What the Butler Saw* (1962), 254–60; Bruce, *Welfare State*, 183–9; Gilbert, *National Insurance*, ch. vi.

[37] P. Snowdon, *Autobiography* (1934), I. 228–9; Reid, *Origins of the British Labour Party*, 164–5; Pelling, *Short History of the Labour Party*, 27–8; A. Briggs, 'The Welfare State in Historical Perspective', *European Journal of Sociology*, II (1961), esp. 228–32; Gilbert, *National Insurance*, esp. 287–8, 451–2; A. Marwick, 'The Labour Party and the Welfare State in Britain, 1900–1948', *American Historical Review*, LXXIII (1967), 385–6.

[38] Riddell, *More Pages from My Diary*, esp. 63–4, 70, ch. xx; T. Jones, *Lloyd George* (1951), 45; Briggs, *Rowntree*, 66–78; Gilbert, *National Insurance*, 445–6; Bullock and Shock, *The Liberal Tradition*, 220–7.

[39] C. Watney and J. A. Little, *Industrial Warfare* (1912); C. Booth, *Industrial Unrest and Trade Union Policy* (1913), in *Charles Booth, A Memoir* (1918); Lord Askwith, *Industrial Problems and Disputes* (1920), esp. chs. ix–xxxiii; Chamberlain, *Politics from Inside*, esp. 443–5; W. B. Gwyn, *Democracy and the Cost of Politics in Britain* (1962), ch. vii; P. S. Bagwell, *The Railwaymen* (1963), chs. viii–xii; H. A. Clegg, A. Fox and A. F. Thompson, *A History of British Trade Unions since 1889*, I (1964); E. H. Phelps Brown, *The Growth of British Industrial Relations* (1965), esp. ch. vi; H. G. Wells, *Journalism and Prophecy 1893–1946*, ed. W. W. Wagar (1965), 43–53.

[40] *Manchester Guardian*, 12 July 1910, 9 June 1913; Halévy, *History of the English People*, VI. 490–527; R. Fulford, *Votes for Women* (1957), 75, 91, and *passim*; Christabel Pankhurst, *Unshackled, the Story of How We Won the Vote* (1959); Emmeline Pankhurst, *My Own Story* (1914), in A. Briggs, *They Saw it Happen* (1962), 113–19; D. E. Butler, *The Electoral System in Britain since 1918*, 2nd ed. (1963), 6–13, 38, 144–6; Jenkins, *Asquith*, 245–50; Blewett, 'The Franchise in the United Kingdom', 54–6; D. Mitchell, *Women on the Warpath, the Story of Women in the First World War* (1966); Constance Rover, *Women's Suffrage and Party Politics in Britain 1866–1914* (1967); A. Marwick, *Britain in the Century of Total War* (1968), 105–11.

[41] Halévy, *History of the English People*, VI. 527–66; Chamberlain, *Politics*

from Inside, 567–647; St. J. Ervine, *Craigavon, Ulsterman* (1949), esp. 185; Blake, *Bonar Law*, chs. vii, ix–xiii; Gollin, '*The Observer*' *and J. L. Garvin*, ch. xii; A. P. Ryan, *Mutiny at the Curragh* (1956); H. W. McCready, 'Home Rule and the Liberal Party, 1899–1906', *Irish Historical Studies*, XIII (1962–3); Sir J. Fergusson, *The Curragh Incident* (1964); N. Mansergh, *The Irish Question 1840–1921* (1965), esp. chs. v–viii; J. R. Fanning, 'The Unionist Party and Ireland, 1906–10', *Irish Historical Studies*, XV (1966–7); P. J. Buckland, 'The Southern Irish Unionists, the Irish Question, and British Politics, 1906–14', ibid.; A. T. Q. Stewart, *The Ulster Crisis* (1967); Churchill, *Churchill*, II. 431–2, chs. xii, xiii; F. S. L. Lyons, *John Dillon* (1968), chs. x–xii.

⁴² *British Documents on the Origins of the War*, VI (1930), 784; Chamberlain, *Politics from Inside*, 599; A. J. Marder, *From the Dreadnought to Scapa Flow, the Royal Navy in the Fisher Era 1904–1919*, I (1961); E. L. Woodward, *Great Britain and the German Navy* (1964); Churchill, *Churchill*, II, chs. xiv–xviii.

⁴³ B. J. Hendrick, *Life and Letters of Walter H. Page* (1923–5), III. 127; Grey, *Twenty-Five Years*, chs. xvii, xviii, xix; H. H. Asquith, *Memories and Reflections* (1928), II, chs. i, ii; Lloyd George, *War Memoirs*, ch. iii; Dugdale, *Balfour*, II. 88; Trevelyan, *Grey*, ch. vii; George, *My Brother and I*, 238–9; Jenkins, *Asquith*, ch. xx; Taylor, *Politics in Wartime*, 64.

⁴⁴ Clarke, *Northcliffe Diary*, ch. iv.

⁴⁵ G. R. Stirling Taylor, *The Psychology of the Great War* (1915), 182; Sir W. Robertson, *Soldiers and Statesmen* (1926), II, 255; Asquith, *Memories and Reflections*, II. 51–2; J. Terraine, *Douglas Haig* (1963), 354, 389; Jenkins, *Asquith*, ch. xxii; P. Guinn, *British Strategy and Politics 1914 to 1918* (1965); Sir L. Woodward, *Great Britain and the War of 1914–1918* (1967).

⁴⁶ S. J. Hurwitz, *State Intervention in Great Britain, a Study of Economic Control and Social Response 1914–1919* (1949); H. W. Baldwin, *World War I* (1962), 12, 73, 160; Jenkins, *Asquith*, 394–5; A. Marwick, *The Deluge, British Society and the First World War* (1965); A. Marwick, 'The Impact of the First World War on British Society', *Journal of Contemporary History*, 3 (1968); Marwick, *Britain in the Century of Total War*, ch. iii.

⁴⁷ W. S. Churchill, *Liberalism and the Social Problem* (1909), 67; J. Lawson, *A Man's Life* (1932), 148–9; G. D. H. Cole, *History of the Labour Party from 1914* (1948), chs. i, ii; Reid, *Origins of the British Labour Party*, chs. xiv, xv; H. Morrison, *Autobiography* (1960), 50; C. F. Brand, *The British Labour Party* (1964), chs. iii, iv; T. Wilson, *The Downfall of the Liberal Party 1914–1935* (1966), 15–131; B. McGill, 'Asquith's Predicament, 1914–1918', *Journal of Modern History*, 39 (1967).

⁴⁸ Mary Agnes Hamilton, *Remembering My Good Friends* (1944), 62–3.

FOR FURTHER READING

See the bibliography following chapter 2, at p. 96.

2

History: Economic and Social

T. C. BARKER

Half the people now alive have not known by effective experience the world before 1914, a world which, with all its injustices and evils, was in two ways better than the world is today. It was a world of many personal liberties now denied or diminished; Britons of my own age know what so many younger people have never known— what it was to travel freely everywhere without passports or visas or restrictions on currency . . . to build a house or start a business or place a lorry on the road if one so desired without a permit. It was a world in which peace rather than war and preparation for war appeared the normal state; there had been no general war for a hundred years; there had never been any total war at all.

LORD BEVERIDGE (1879–1963),
writing at the beginning of the 1950s

I think the main difference in the world before 1914 from the world after 1914 was in the sense of security and the growing belief that it was a supremely good thing for people to be communally and individually happy.

LEONARD WOOLF (1880–1969),
writing at the beginning of the 1960s[1]

I

For many of those who lived through it, and particularly for those in the middle classes, the Edwardian period seemed in retrospect to mark the end of an era—an era wistfully remembered, and significantly perhaps, for its several glorious summers. For these people it was a world of straw boaters and picture hats, garden parties, and bands on the pier. The nostalgic remember it, too, for its well-kept and punctual main-line trains and for its generous postal services.*

* In the main towns the G.P.O.s were open from 7 a.m. to 10 p.m. on weekdays, and on Sunday mornings. There were frequent collections and deliveries. At Manchester, for instance, on weekdays there were fourteen collections of letters (the first at 8.30 a.m. and the last at 12 midnight) and eight collections of parcels (the first at 8.30 a.m. and the last at 7 p.m.). On Sundays there were two letter collections, at 6 p.m. and 12 midnight. There were eight deliveries of both letters and parcels (one of which was restricted to the central area), the first delivery of letters starting at 7 a.m. and the last at 7 p.m. On Sundays there was one delivery of letters which began at 7 a.m. (*The Post Office Guide for Manchester and District*, April 1902; July 1907.) From the London East Central Office there were twelve deliveries every weekday and from the West Central Office fourteen (*Post Office Guide*, July 1907).

Above all, it was an age when those with possessions, whether small or large, still felt a great sense of security. The economy was anchored to gold, and golden sovereigns and half-sovereigns served as normal currency. (There were no Bank of England £1 or 10s. notes.) In the days when council housing was still in its very early infancy and the statutory control of rents unheard of, house property provided a safe and rewarding form of investment not only for Forsytes but also for men of much more modest means. Income tax, paid only on incomes above £160 a year, which virtually excluded members of the working classes, stood at only 1s. in the £1 for most of Edward VII's reign. It was actually reduced, in 1907, to 9d. on earned incomes up to £2,000; but in Lloyd George's famous 'people's budget' of 1909 the rate was increased from 1s. to 1s. 2d. for those earning above £3,000, with a small super tax (6d. in the £1) payable by those earning above £5,000.*2 Life for numbers of taxpayers, as Maynard Keynes (1883–1946) has vividly recalled,

offered, at low cost and with the least trouble, conveniences, comforts, and amenities beyond the compass of the richest and most powerful monarchs of other ages. The inhabitant of London could order by telephone, sipping his morning tea in bed, the various products of the whole earth, in such quantity as he might see fit, and reasonably expect their early delivery upon his doorstep; he could at the same moment and by the same means adventure his wealth in the natural resources and new enterprises of any quarter of the world, and share, without exertion or even trouble, in their prospective fruits and advantages; or he could decide to couple the security of his fortunes with the good faith of the townspeople of any substantial municipality in any continent that fancy or information might recommend. He could secure forthwith, if he wished it, cheap and comfortable means of transit to any country or climate without passport or other formality,† could despatch his servant to the neighbouring office of a bank for such supply of the precious metals as might seem convenient, and could then proceed abroad to foreign quarters, without knowledge of their religion, language or customs, bearing coined wealth upon his person,

* There is no satisfactory indicator of changes in the value of money over the past sixty years which is applicable to all income groups. It may, however, be worth noting that the price indicator for general consumers' expenditure has risen about sixfold during the period.

† The 11th edition of the *Encyclopaedia Britannica* (1911) described a passport as 'a document granted by a belligerent power to protect persons and property from the operation of hostilities. . . . Although most foreign countries may be entered without passports, the English foreign office recommends travellers to furnish themselves with them as affording a ready means of identification in case of need'. A passport then cost 2s. 'whatever number of persons may be named in it'.

and would consider himself greatly aggrieved and much surprised at the least interference. But, most important of all, he regarded this state of affairs as normal, certain and permanent, except in the direction of further improvement, and any deviation from it as aberrant, scandalous and avoidable.[3]

There is no doubt that the Edwardian years—which we shall take the liberty of stretching from 1900 to 1914—provided a growing minority of the population with great economic and social advantages. These were still the days of deference. Class distinctions remained firm and people's place in society could usually be guessed at once from the clothes they wore. Bright young men of ability were able to command remarkable salaries. One of them was the young William Beveridge whose understandably favourable verdict on the period has been quoted at the beginning of this chapter. In 1908 he ceased to be a leader writer on the *Morning Post* and exchanged what he described as an 'easy but risky' £600 a year in journalism for a steady £600 at the Board of Trade. He marked the move by buying a motor-car. Soon afterwards his salary was increased by £100 and he engaged a chauffeur.[4]

The lure of the civil service aroused comment at the time. 'Personally, I think it is most distressing the way the civil service swallows nearly all the best Cambridge men,' wrote G. M. Trevelyan (1876–1962) about 1904.[5] Arthur Salter (b. 1881), who entered the civil service then, felt, on reflection, that 'perhaps the State obtained too large a proportion of the best men available each year, and it might have been better if more had gone into industry'.[6] In fact, the country was soon to gain greatly from being able to call upon men of the calibre of Beveridge and Salter to help lay the foundations of state insurance. But did this social gain involve any economic loss in terms of inferior business leadership, as Salter suggested? There can be no doubt that Britain's industry was passing through a critical phase and concern was being expressed about the future health of the British economy. Already, in 1903, the distinguished Cambridge economist, Alfred Marshall (1842–1924), was warning the country that

England is at a steadily increasing relative disadvantage not merely with people like the Japanese, who can assimilate [*sic*] every part of the work of an advanced factory; but also with places where there are abundant supplies of low-grade labour, organised by a relatively small number of able and skilled men of higher race. This is already largely done in America, and it certainly will be done on an ever-increasing scale in other continents. Consequently England will not be able to hold her own against other nations by the mere sedulous practices of familiar processes. . . . England's place among the nations in the future must depend upon the extent to which she retains industrial leadership. She cannot be *the* leader, but she may be *a* leader.[7]

To this extent, the ardent devotees of Edwardian England do not receive any support at all from historians. Far from the period marking the end of an era, it should be seen rather as an early stage in a more competitive order of things in which Britain had to meet a growing economic challenge from abroad, particularly from America but also, though to a smaller extent, from Germany.

The real turning point in this sense was not 1914 but the 1870s. From then onwards British businessmen became more and more aware both of growing competition in developing countries abroad, often supported by rising tariffs, and of increasing imports of foreign manufactures into the home market. Particular anxiety was created by foreign, and especially American, success in the development of new products such as electrical goods, machine tools, and machinery for the large-scale production of consumer goods, for which there was to be a most promising future, at a time when Britain seemed content to go on increasing her output of traditional items such as coarse cottons and coal, for which future world demand was in the long run obviously to be much more limited. By the end of the century, books were appearing with titles like *Made in Germany* and *American Invaders*. The critical inquest into the state of the British economy had begun. It has been going on ever since.

Although historians agree that Britain's industrial production grew at a slower rate after the 1870s than it had done before, they take a much more favourable view of Britain's general economic performance in the later nineteenth century than contemporary critics used to do.[8] They point, for instance, to the expansion of consumer goods and services, to the great changes in retailing and the spread of multiple shops like the chain built up by Thomas Lipton (1850–1931). These greater shopping facilities accompanied and strengthened the remarkable rise in working-class purchasing power which was the outstanding feature of the last quarter of the nineteenth century. Business historians have also drawn attention to the new generation of industrial entrepreneurs, typified by W. H. Lever (1851–1925), who began to build up huge manufacturing complexes, while other larger business units were created by the amalgamation of older concerns.[9] The 1890s, indeed, saw the real beginnings of 'big business' in Britain. These thrusting newcomers swept into the twentieth century young and vigorous. One would expect their dynamic progress to have been maintained.

Those who have written about the Edwardian period in recent times, however, and especially writers who have based their work on statistical sources, have tended to confirm Marshall's gloomy diagnosis. In particular, Professor Matthews, who has studied the main trends in the British economy over the past hundred years as the background to a detailed investigation of Britain's performance since the Second World War, has reached the conclusion that the period between 1899 and 1913 saw a much slower peacetime rate of growth of gross domestic product than the years either before or since.[10] The denigrators have seized upon Britain's very large export of capital after 1906 which, it is claimed, starved home industry of up-to-date equipment and prevented new and promising products from being developed more rapidly. According to Professor Brinley Thomas, for instance:

At a time when productivity was being transformed in the United States and Germany under the influence of innovations in electricity and chemistry, British investors showed little interest in re-equipping industries at home. They preferred to indulge in an orgy of foreign investment in such things as gold, diamonds, rubber, Egyptian cotton, and Japanese and South American ventures. . . . It is not sufficiently realised that Britain lost a golden opportunity in the early years of this century when the craze for foreign securities led to a failure to take full advantage of contemporary technical innovations.[11]

This is a very widely held view of the Edwardian economy; but the statistical sources upon which it rests need to be tested and the interpretations placed upon them further considered. To what extent, for instance, were the British growth rates influenced by the need to use figures for the whole of the United Kingdom which, of course, then included sluggish southern Ireland? And to what extent may the use of 1899 as a base year influence the statistical verdict; and how much allowance should be made for the untimely setback in economic activity in 1908–9 which may have been induced by the financial crisis in the United States and not by usual trade cycle forces?[12] Again, was the capital exported from Britain in such quantity used to finance Britain's exports or those of her industrial rivals? Was this export of capital at the expense of investment in British industry or was it at the expense of other forms of home investment such as housebuilding? Or was it not at the expense of anything at home? (There is evidence that from 1907 home and foreign investment moved together.) Did the modernization of

British industry in fact require very large capital sums anyway? May it not have been a matter of quality rather than of quantity? Answers to these questions still await the results of further careful research. For the present, it may suffice to note that Sir Alec Cairncross, in his study of investment during the period, estimated that the value of machinery retained for use in the United Kingdom rose rapidly in the 1890s and then remained at this higher level throughout the Edwardian period, including most of the years of high capital export.[13]

Since the statistics are clearly in need of much further exploitation and study, it is necessary for the present to make the most of other evidence at our disposal. Does this reveal either serious weaknesses in existing businesses—less efficient labour and/or management— or an industrial spectrum which placed too much reliance upon slow-growing staples and not enough upon the more rapidly growing new products?

The performance of labour has been criticized in all countries and in all periods and Edwardian Britain was no exception. A German resident, for instance, claimed in 1905 that most British workmen were both thriftless and irresponsible:

So far as my own experience and observations go, the majority of your workers read little but the sporting press, and care for little but betting and sport. . . . If your men idle two or three days in the week, and do less than they ought to do in the other four, they cannot wonder that they do not hold their own. . . .[14]

Management also came in for its share of blame because it showed little interest in improving industrial relations. In 1902, for example, when a small party of trade unionists (the Moseley Commission) visited the United States, it returned most impressed by the contrast between American industrialists' willingness to listen to constructive suggestions from their employees and British business-men's lack of concern:

[In America] suggestions are welcomed (usually a box is provided for their reception), the more so because the American manufacturer has realized that it is not the man sitting in the counting-house or private office who is best able to judge where improvements can be made in machine or method, but he who attends that machine from morning to night. Hence, the employer asks for suggestions for the general conduct of business as well as for improvements in machinery. These are freely offered and periodically examined and, if entertained, the originator of them usually receives at once a small money gift, whilst for those found practical upon further trial and ultimately adopted, he is given handsome remuneration in the shape of a portion (or sometimes the whole) of the resulting profit, promotion, or purchase outright of the idea by his employer. . . . Has such a system ever been tried here? Except in quite isolated cases, I think not. As a rule, the British employer hardly knows his men, seldom leaves his office for the workshop, delegates the bulk of his authority to a foreman whose powers are arbitrary, and who, if any of the men under him show a particular initiative, immediately becomes jealous and fears that he may be supplanted. Hence as a rule a workman making a suggestion to the foreman (the proprietor himself is usually not accessible at all) is met with a snub, asked 'Are you running this shop or am I?' or told, 'If you know the business better than I do, you had better put on your coat and go'.[15]

Marshall, too, was critical of

many of the sons of manufacturers [who were] content to follow mechanically the lead given by their fathers. They worked shorter hours and they exerted themselves less to obtain new practical ideas than their fathers had done. . . . In the 'nineties it became clear that in future Englishmen must take business as seriously as their grandfathers had done, and as their American and German rivals were doing: that their training for business must be methodical, like that of their new rivals, and not merely practical, on lines that had sufficed for the simpler world of two generations ago; and lastly that the time had passed at which they could afford merely to teach foreigners and not learn from them in return.[16]

There is certainly no lack of examples of management's reluctance to move with the times. In 1903, for instance, in the works office of the Clyde Tube Works, belonging to the newly merged company of Stewarts and Lloyds, 'the only piece of modern equipment was the telephone, with a private line to the Glasgow office. . . . Everything was handwritten and the only duplication was by letterpress copy'.[17]

Britain's educational arrangements have also been held to blame for any backwardness that there may have been. More public money was being put into the grammar schools which, it was said, prepared men for the professions, not for business, and there was not enough technical training. Yet it is only fair to recall that some of the most remarkable businessmen—Henry Ford (1863–1947) included—received very little in the way of formal education. Others—again including Henry Ford—gained a great deal from their apprenticeship to a trade. Royce (1863–1933), Bentley (1888–1968), and A. V. Roe (1878–1949), for instance, all served their time in railway workshops, and Herbert Austin (1866–1941) was trained in engineering works in Melbourne. In any case, by the end of the nineteenth century, much more emphasis was in fact being placed on technical education: many technical colleges, which provided both day and evening courses, date either from the Edwardian period or from shortly before it. And an increasing number of science graduates, often the product of regional colleges which were granted university charters between 1900 and 1909, taught science in both secondary and elementary schools.[18] Professor Habakkuk, at the end of a searching study of British and American technology in the nineteenth century, reaches the conclusion that 'there is not much force in the argument that the English entrepreneur was hampered by the absence of the scientific skills required by the new technological developments'.[19]

Were any of these weaknesses fundamental ones? Did any shortcomings in management loom so large that they really impeded economic progress? There were, no doubt, inefficient businessmen then as now; but many examples may be cited of able ones, too. Since we are not yet in a position to count heads, it would be pointless to try to draw a conclusion either way. Certainly there would seem to be very little foundation for the view that entrepreneurial talent automatically declines with the generations.[20] Did an over-rigid social structure, such as the Moseley Commission described, discourage important innovation? Was not the really talented workman, if rebuffed by his own employer, in a position to interest a rival, or even to borrow the capital to set up on his own account if his ideas were of major importance and not just concerned with improvement of minor detail? Any profound and widespread weakness in existing business concerns would, surely, be very difficult to prove.

We need, therefore, to go on to consider the other possible cause of economic weakness: too much emphasis upon the manufacture of old staples and not enough upon that of new products. Here external forces were pulling in favour of the old staples while internal conditions tended to be less encouraging to the development of new products than were those in America. It is necessary, first of all, to consider the nature of Britain's export trade and then, after showing how new products were emerging from some of her old staples, to make a comparison between her home market and that of the United States.

Britain had grown great by the exporting of simple manufactures, notably coarse cottons, which a world with low purchasing power could afford. As other countries industrialized, they began to make these basic staples for themselves, but in the process of their industrialization greater purchasing power was generated and a new and growing market was created for more sophisticated manufactures, which Britain was well placed to supply.[21] Meanwhile, however, her exports of basic staples also continued to grow, for new primary producing areas were being opened up, in the East, for instance, and in Africa. And free-trade Britain's reliance for much of her food and raw materials on low-cost areas abroad, rather than upon British farms, assisted this process by providing these countries with purchasing power. Eventually the world demand for the basic staples was bound to fall away as these remaining primary producers followed the example of earlier industrializers; but there was no evidence of this happening, or being within sight of happening, before 1914. The wise course for Britain, therefore, was to continue to develop new markets while she still could for her basic staples, in which she was pre-eminent, and at the same time to put more emphasis upon the more sophisticated manufactures upon which she would have to rely increasingly in the longer run.

The process of developing trade with primary producing areas involved the sending abroad of capital as well as manufactures. The piling up of oversea investments, particularly in railways, had been going on throughout the nineteenth century. It gathered pace and, as we have noticed, after 1906 reached unprecedented heights. Perhaps more than one-half of the nation's savings went abroad in 1913, by which time Britain had committed overseas about as much as her entire industrial and commercial capital, excluding land.[22] Between 1900 and 1913 the total capital invested abroad grew from about £2,400 million to nearly £4,000 million.[23] Besides opening up new markets for Britain's staples, these investments greatly helped her capital goods industries. They also yielded dividends, amounting to one-tenth of the national income by 1914, and made a major contribution to her balance of payments.

This return upon capital invested abroad was important in helping Britain to bridge the gap between imports and exports. Ever since the early nineteenth century, Britain had imported goods to a greater value than she had exported. To meet the deficit, she looked to income from invisible items: to shipping (Britain then possessed the largest and most up-to-date merchant fleet in the world), insurance, banking, and other services, and above all by this time, to interest on capital investment. In 1900, when net imports totalled about £460m., the merchandise trade gap of about £170m. was more than offset by receipts on net invisibles of over £200m. Between 1900 and 1914, Britain's trade performance was very impressive and by 1913, although net imports had risen to nearly £660m., both domes-

tic exports and re-exports had risen at a faster rate. The trade gap
was reduced to just over £130m. at a time when the total net invisible income had reached over £350m.[24] Whatever may be our verdict
upon her manufacturing industry at this juncture or upon her long-
run prospects, there can be no doubt that Britain's international
position, already strong in 1900, was further strengthened. London was
still the unquestioned financial and business centre of the world.
'Great Britain for a short but vital period', as Professor Court has observed, 'was the centre of the economic development of the earth.'[25]

This highly satisfactory performance was achieved at a time when
Britain remained faithful to free trade in a growingly protectionist
world. While rival nations cocooned their new, infant industries,
Britain exposed hers to the full force of competition. Paradoxically,
however, the continued export of basic staples may well have acted
as a shield. As Professor Saul has shown,[26] in the years just before
1914, the U.S.A. and industrial Europe became increasingly
dependent upon the primary producing areas of the world for their
raw materials and certain foodstuffs and had adverse balance of
payments with these areas, particularly with India. Britain, however,
because of her export of basic staples, had a credit balance. If Britain
had not been prepared to run an adverse balance with the U.S.A.
and industrial Europe—which entailed the import of some of their
manufactures—those countries would not have been able to square
their debts with the primary producers. And, if that had happened,
they would either have had to seek alternative sources of supply
from within their own territories or to intensify their world trade
in manufactures. As Professor Saul concludes:

Undoubtedly British policy, however unconsciously, permitted the world
trading system to grow remarkably rapidly and peacefully. One is almost
inclined to think that it was this 'paradox of free trade' which was itself
one of Britain's most powerful safeguards against foreign competition in
the pre-war years.[27]

The growing export of basic staples to primary producing areas,
that is to say, was not only justified by its profitability; it also had
wider implications in the context of multilateral trade and international specialization. The further expansion of these old staples
made good economic sense so long as it was accompanied by the
growth of those newer products upon which the country was
ultimately to rely.

Newer products emerged from older staples as well as from new
industries. This was true, for instance, of the cotton industry which

exported three-quarters of its production and, just before the war, accounted for nearly a quarter of Britain's total exports. More than one-third of exports of cotton cloth went to India—the total reached 3,000 million yards out of 7,000 million yards in 1913, an unusually prosperous year there—thus helping to maintain Britain's crucial creditor position in that country. Yet at the same time, the industry was producing more yarn of higher count and cloth of better quality, and to this extent was manifesting the features of a newer industry with longer-term prospects. At the end of 1902, for instance, the secretary of the Manchester Chamber of Commerce compared the higher qualities then being produced in England with those of the United States and on the continent of Europe:

The yarn produced in English mills is by many degrees finer and of higher value per pound than that spun in the mills of the other two regions. For many years English cotton yarn has been growing finer and finer. This change has been brought about by two or three causes, but mainly as a consequence of the increase of machinery in countries to which our coarser yarns and piece-goods were formerly sent. These they now produce much more extensively for their own consumption, leaving to us the production of the finer descriptions.[28]

It was this greater emphasis upon quality which was one of the main reasons for Britain's continued reliance upon spinning mules, better suited for the production of medium and fine counts, when other countries were installing ring spindles.[29] The Americans certainly did not underestimate the strength of Lancashire cotton at this time. A U.S. government commercial agent, for instance, reported home in 1911 that, while Britain had lost some of her sales in coarser qualities, these losses had been more than offset by higher quality exports. He went on:

The great difficulty of keeping abreast of the tremendous increase in the cotton trade and holding their advanced position in the world's markets is recognised by Lancashire manufacturers, but no relaxation of effort to maintain and advance Lancashire's trade in every line will be permitted. . . . In view of the wonderful organization of the cotton industry in Lancashire, its vast extent, comprehensiveness and prestige, *it is very doubtful whether its presence and influence in the world markets can be seriously affected, at least for many years to come.*[30]

The building of 95 new cotton mills between 1905 and 1907 was by no means 'the real indictment of Lancashire';[31] the industry was very prosperous indeed, and remained so until the war.[32] And, depending upon a strong cotton industry, there had developed an equally strong, very resourceful and up-to-date textile engineering industry. In 1907 it was exporting 45 per cent of its output, including ring spindles to America.[33]

A similar, though more radical, instance of a new product emerging within an existing industry occurred when Courtaulds, old-established Essex silk weavers, under the new leadership of H. G. Tetley, who had been brought down from Yorkshire, set up in rayon (artificial silk) manufacture in Coventry. By 1908–9, in contrast to their floundering German rivals, they had managed to develop a tricky chemical process into a highly successful commercial proposition. Early in 1911, a transatlantic subsidiary soon to be highly profitable—the American Viscose Company—came into production and was the sole producer of viscose yarn in the United States until after the First World War.[34] This, however, was a rare British success inside America's tariff wall. With many other new products their home market and labour supply position encouraged the Americans themselves to pioneer and innovate.

In America, labour was the scarce factor of production. Despite the great, and mounting, waves of immigration into the United States and the rapid natural increase of the American population, labour remained scarce in relation to her apparently limitless natural resources. The American employer, therefore, had a much stronger incentive to adopt labour-saving methods than did his British rival and he had, during the nineteenth century, developed the habit of scrapping and buying new rather than keeping existing equipment going. Having been brought up to be most responsive to change by his need to save labour, he was encouraged to venture the more readily into new lines of manufacture not only by a home market which was very large in numbers (America had a population of 80,000,000 by 1900, to be compared with Britain's 37,000,000) but also by the relatively high purchasing power which each American working man could deploy, particularly after the 1890s. There was a much greater social depth of demand. The American market, that is to say, had a much larger potential appetite for the standardized product than had the British.[35]

The Americans' rich natural resources, which led, via relative labour scarcity and high earnings, to standardized production, were also, of course, a great asset in themselves. Britain had only one such rich natural resource, coal. Its vigorous exploitation was impressive—a profitable 287 million tons were mined in 1913, a record figure—and, we can now say in the light of the subsequent collapse of world demand, timely. The stepping up of production from 225 million tons in 1900 (and a mere 130 million tons in the 1870s) was achieved by a great increase in the labour force and a consequent fall in productivity. Nevertheless productivity in Britain was on a par with that in Germany and still well above that of any other European country in 1913.[36] Apart from coal, however, Britain lacked other resources in such abundance. Just as it was obviously impossible for her to rival America's oil industry, so it was very difficult for her, with limited supplies of iron ore, to compete with the Americans' rich mountains of ore in the Mesabi range south of Lake Superior. Even so, recent research suggests that there was no great difference in productivity in the British and American iron and steel industry before 1914. All in all, it was neither surprising nor reprehensible that Britain's output of crude steel grew at a much slower rate than that of the United States.[37] It would, however, have been a matter for concern if Britain had not specialized in the further processing of steel, in which she still possessed great technical advantages. As the free-traders put it:

By all means let us import cheap foreign angles and plates in order that we may build ships . . . let us import cheap foreign steel bars so that we may manufacture corrugated sheets for export . . . let us import cheap foreign billets so that we may manufacture the thousand and one articles of which they are the raw material, in order that we may export to the world.[38]

In steel processing, Britain continued to do well, and considerable economies were made at this time thanks to the activities of the Engineering Standards Committee, formed in 1901, the predecessor of the British Standards Institution.[39] In 1913 Britain was supplying the bulk of the iron and steel manufactures needed by the empire, excluding Canada.[40] Her shipbuilding industry was the largest in the world. She regularly produced half the world's tonnage and in 1913 a record of nearly 2,000,000 tons were launched. And the tin-plate industry, another steel user, made a remarkable recovery after having been hard hit in the 1890s by heavy United States tariffs.[41]

America clearly derived great advantages from her broad home market, her bounteous resources and, as Professor Habakkuk has emphasized, the very pace of her growth as she exploited these advantages. That Britain was not the first country to develop many new products on a commercial scale, does not necessarily reflect upon British enterprise. What is important, however, is the readiness with which British manufacturers were prepared to follow America's lead. The evidence suggests that the time-lag was usually quite a short one. In the manufacture of lighter machine tools, for instance, vital for the mass production of parts needed for large-scale manufacture of cycles and, later, motor-cars, a number of British concerns, notably that of Alfred Herbert (1866–1957) of Coventry, followed the Americans closely.[42] In the boot and shoe industry, British manufacturers were not slow to install American machines and use American methods, thereby stemming the rising tide of imported American-made shoes.[43] Electric tramways, which, despite pioneer ventures in Britain and continental Europe, first spread rapidly in America—thus giving American manufacturers all the advantages of large-scale production of generators, motors, and equipment— were soon being built in Britain.[44] Some of the equipment came from America, but much of it was made at home, and firms, such as Dick, Kerr and Co. of Preston, who engaged an American engineer, exploited to the full Britain's electric tramway boom in the early Edwardian period. At this time the two leading American electrical concerns, General Electric and Westinghouse, thought it worth their while to manufacture in England (as British Thomson-Houston, Rugby, and British Westinghouse, Trafford Park) rather than import their products duty-free from the United States. It was, however, Britain's performance in the motor industry, the great growth sector of the twentieth century, and of cycle manufacture with which it was often associated in its early days, which showed most clearly the readiness of the British economy to look to the future. Here again, the new was being resourcefully developed alongside the old. Mechanical engineering reveals the same symptoms as cotton.

Britain continued to be highly competitive in the older branches of mechanical engineering and, indeed, many workshops were re-equipped with modern machine tools during this period.[45] Textile machinery was still, in 1913, Britain's main export line among engineering products, three times as great as those of Germany, her next largest rival.[46] In the manufacture of locomotives and rolling stock, boilers and prime movers, British industry also continued to do well.[47] At the same time Britain had, particularly since the later 1890s, been developing a strong cycle industry, and, having standardized certain parts (such as chains and chain wheels) and introduced new machinery, had brought down costs and prices and gained world markets at the expense of the Americans from 1899 and of the Germans from 1907. Moreover, it was upon many of the manufacturing techniques acquired in cycle manufacture, and indeed upon many of the cycle manufacturing concerns, such as Rover, Humber, Singer, and Triumph, that her motor industry was to be based. Already, by 1907, the output of cycles, motor-cycles, and motor vehicles was worth as much as that of loco-motives.[48] So late as 1908 car ownership per head of population in Britain seems to have been nearly as high as that in the United States.[49] The motor-car market then was still a class market throughout the world; the customers for the early cars were those who had previously owned horse-drawn vehicles.[50] The point was made—in an extreme form—by C. S. Rolls himself, writing in about 1909:

Concurrently with its developing into a reliable, silent, odourless and smokeless power-driven vehicle, the motor car gradually came into more general use. . . . Its final triumph came when it began seriously to dis-place the horse vehicle, becoming the private carriage of the wealthier classes to be used on all occasions.[51]

The market was, however, about to enter a completely new phase: in 1908 Henry Ford began to produce his Model T. Large-scale production really began after he had moved to a new factory at Highland Park, Detroit, in 1910, and developed there first sub-assemblies and conveyors and then complete assembly-line produc-tion. Between the middle of 1910 and the middle of 1911, Fords made 34,000 cars. In the next two years production rose to 78,000 and 170,000 cars respectively and in 1913–14 (when the assembly line began to be moved by a continuous belt) to nearly 250,000. Meanwhile the price of the standard model in America was brought down from $900 (just under £190) to $550 (about £115).[52] (The pound was then worth about $4.80, twice its present dollar value.) This was the beginning of the mass market. Again, America had profited from her own favourable home market circumstances. As one of America's main car agents in Britain pointed out in 1911, 'the sale of cheap cars can never be as large in England as it is in the United States. The same class of people that find it difficult to pay $650 for a car in the United States, find it difficult to lay aside half that sum here.'[53] Yet there is evidence that, despite this handicap, British manufacturers were prepared to follow America's lead in this industry as they had done in the others, in this case modifying the vehicle to meet the pockets of the customer.

The pedal cycle makers had for a decade or so been manufactur-ing for quite a large market, but in 1908 and 1909, when Ford was about to move decisively ahead, both they and the motor manu-facturers were going through a critical phase, caught by a trade recession.[54] After 1909, however, the motor, but not the pedal cycle, market picked up well and a number of cycle makers turned their attention to the manufacture of motor-cars and motor-cycles.[55] The latter, particularly with side-cars, enjoyed considerable popularity, selling at between £30 and £60. The growing strength of the motor-cycle industry is also revealed in the trade figures, the value of exports exceeding those of imports for the first time in 1908. By 1911 they were seven times as great. Car exports also exceeded imports for the first time in 1910.

U.K. Imports and Exports of Motor-Cars and Motor-Cycles, 1908–1911
£'000

	Motor-Cars		Motor-Cycles	
	Net imports	Exports	Net imports	Exports
1908	1229	801	34	37
1909	1046	953	38	69
1910	1204	1377	41	122
1911	1410	1804	38	279

(Source: *The Economist*, 17 August 1912.)

Within these figures is concealed a fall in the number of cars imported from France and a sharp increase in imports of cheaper cars from America. Before 1910 never more than a few hundred cars had been imported annually from there, but in 1910 the figure jumped to over 4,000 and in 1911 to nearly 6,000. In that year Ford built an assembly plant at Trafford Park, Manchester. It is significant, however, that the American car agent, who has already been quoted, was emphatic that American cars, some of which were selling in Britain at just under £200 each, were not yet cheap enough to tap a new social level of demand. 'My experience has been', he wrote, 'that the cheaper cars sold in the English market do not supply a trade that can not afford an expensive car. . . . In other words, the manufacturers of low-priced cars are not creating a new buying public, but are doing the major part of their business with people who have already owned cars.'

The problem just before 1914, then, was to meet American competition in what was still quite a limited market. In 1912, the American consul in Birmingham reported that some British manufacturers had tried to put cars on the market at prices to compete with the Americans, but so far without success. He was, however, under no illusions about the British manufacturers' capacity to copy a good foreign idea:

The foreign manufacturers thus incur the expense of the introduction, and the British makers, after awaiting the results of such experiments, take advantage of the foreigners' experience, astutely modify the designs so as to more exactly meet the British ideas, and enter the market backed by the national preference for articles of domestic origin.[56]

Certainly some British manufacturers were already copying American methods of standardized production even though they could not as yet hope for great economies of scale. 'Some people seem to think', the American main agent reported home in 1911, 'that because the standardization of cars has not reached the perfection in this country that it has in the United States, therefore all English cars are roughly made. No bigger mistake could be made. Standardization has made rapid progress in this country in the past few years.'[57] By 1913 manufacturers were reducing the number of models they produced in an effort to secure greater economies of scale and, shortly after the war had broken out, the American consul in Glasgow reported that

Great activity prevailed in every branch of the motor car industry during the first seven months of 1914. All classes of motor vehicles, pleasure and commercial, were in demand and until the outbreak of war the year promised to be a record one. The factories in this district, and, in fact, throughout Great Britain, were well booked up with orders and fully employed. Manufacturers, aware of the growing demand within the past few years for a lighter and lower priced touring car, were prepared to turn out in quantity to meet all demands. . . . Anticipating an increased demand for cars, manufacturers had made considerable extensions to their works. . . .[58]

Herbert Austin, who had started to make his own cars at Longbridge in 1906 and had turned out a light, 7 h.p. model in 1910, was one of those manufacturers who had extended his works, and the company went public in February 1914.[59] His future rival, W. R. Morris (1877–1963), later Lord Nuffield, also entered the cheap car market at this time. Morris had recently acquired some disused premises at Cowley, outside Oxford, and these he extended in 1914. The standard version of his Morris Oxford sold in that year for £180, about the same price as the Model T, and a Morris Cowley, to be sold at £165 and made to some extent with imported American parts, was planned. But the war came and the Cowley works were soon devoted mainly to munitions production.[60] The *Economist* was justified in its sad comment that 'when war was declared . . . probably no British industry relying chiefly on home demand was more demoralised than the motor trade'.[61]

In one, often ignored, branch of the motor industry, however,

British producers were unchallenged from the outset: the manufacture of commercial vehicles. At the beginning of the century
these were usually steam driven,[62] and great efforts were made in
early Edwardian times to improve the efficiency of steam lorries.
As more efficient petrol engines came to be produced, however,
these became increasingly popular. The Post Office used motor
vehicles quite extensively not only for local services but also, in
some cases, for carrying mails between towns,[63] and the railway
companies were starting to use them, instead of horse-drawn
vehicles, for the collection and delivery of goods. Shops also used
light vans for delivery purposes. The Civil Service Stores, for
instance, by 1912 was providing a free delivery service within a
fifty-mile radius of London.[64] The heavier commercial vehicle also
found a passenger-carrying use from about 1904 onwards with the
development of the motor-bus which reached a reasonable level of
reliability by about 1910. A writer in the *Manchester Guardian* in
1913 even thought that Britain had been wise in concentrating upon
commercial vehicles,

when France, Germany and America were almost solely concerned with
the development of pleasure cars . . . hence British manufacturers of
steam and petrol wagons, vans and public service vehicles have kept well
in front. Lancashire set the pace more than twelve years ago and invaluable service was gained upon her set paved highways.[65]

There would seem to be some historical logic in the eventual
emergence of Leyland Motors as leader of the British-owned motor
industry.

There is, in fact, considerable evidence to indicate that the growth
in manufacture of newer products was not held back by the continued expansion of the older staples. (New and old products, not
new and old industries: the discussion in the past has all too often
been confused by thinking just in terms of industries and so
ignoring significant changes occurring within certain of the older
industries.) It is true that Britain lagged in the manufacture of
some of the new products: in three-phase electrical generators and
equipment, for instance, which caused her to lose the strong position
in the manufacture of generating plant which she had held in the
mid-1890s;[66] in her failure to make more of the Solvay ammonia
soda process or of zinc smelting; and in the almost complete neglect
of the manufacture of synthetic dyestuffs[67] (though it should be
remembered that the Americans were equally weak here).

Yet in both the electrical and chemical industries Britain could boast strong sectors; in both industries, taken as a whole, she had an export surplus.[68] In any case, nobody would suggest that, to be efficient and forward-looking, Britain needed to excel in all new products. Indeed, to do so would have been against the whole ethos of international specialization. All that was needed was for the new to be growing up alongside the old at such a pace that, when the markets for the old came to loom less important, the new would be in a position to continue to move ahead quickly to fill, and more than fill, the gap. There would seem to be abundant evidence for arguing that Britain was managing to do this before 1914, despite natural handicaps which placed her at a disadvantage to the United States. If this view is accepted, then it is difficult, if not impossible, to accept the two other, interrelated, interpretations of national economic development during this period. Britain's early start did not bias the economy with a deadweight of old ideas and equipment which arrested new developments—though one may find occasional examples of this happening, such as the adverse effects of the entrenched gas lighting interest upon the development of electric lighting or the discouraging attitude of local authorities to the spread of electricity supplies. Nor, as we have suggested, is there conclusive evidence that entrepreneurship was at fault, though the extreme self-assurance of cotton men before 1914 admittedly had its dangers. As one writer has persuasively put it: 'If the Lancashire of 1880 had been quietly proud, and the Lancashire of 1900 aloofly proud, the new Lancashire was arrogant.'[69]

There may, however, be some force in the argument that British businessmen, always keen for quick returns, had in the past perhaps been a little slow to invest in the kind of more costly, longer-term research and development increasingly needed for the successful manufacturing and marketing of more sophisticated products. Not the least merit of Edwardian business may have been its realization that in the newer and more complicated methods of industry and trade, quick returns were not always to be expected. In so far as the Edwardian period may reveal growth rates which compare unfavourably with those of earlier and later times, these may reflect to some extent not lack of resourcefulness but rather greater vision, heavier investment in education, technical and otherwise, at university, college, and school, and the laying of foundations in industries and branches of industries with better growth prospects which were to reap greater returns later.[70] Possibly the remarkable upswing in economic activity and increase in productivity after 1910 may have been the first indication of these greater returns.

Another explanation of the apparent stasis between 1900 and 1910 may be found, as has been recently urged,[71] in shorter hours and the economic effects of greater labour discontent. We must now consider the position of the working man at this time and the extent to which social changes were occurring which were to influence his living standards, changes not always readily perceived from the economic evidence alone.

II

Edwardian Britain—particularly during the years just before 1914—was marked by increasing social tension. The last quarter of the nineteenth century had seen a great and unprecedented rise in the real earnings of the working classes—so much as 40 per cent has been claimed—but from the middle of the 1890s rising import prices and reduced productivity halted this increase and even brought about a slight fall. The contemporary belief that the rich were in the meantime growing generally richer, does not, however, seem to be borne out by the evidence. Sir Arthur Bowley, having made a detailed study of the distribution of incomes, came to the conclusion that this view was a myth propagated by the press and supported by the numbers of costly new motor-cars which were dustily and noisily drawing attention to themselves on the as yet untarred roads; cars which were bought, in fact, by diverting expenditure from other purchases. 'A few motor cars', Bowley argued, 'can in a week give evidence of wasteful and arrogant expenditure over several counties while an equal sum spent on carriages and horses would have a much more limited effect.'[72] Another authority on the period has supported this view, calling the expensive cars of those days 'visible symbols of the selfishness of arrogant wealth'.[73] Certainly the income tax figures show that it was the total number of payers which was growing and not the total average sum declared.[74] This, however, still allows considerable scope for variation from the average within the tax-paying group. Those who invested abroad often did well for themselves at this time and the London season seemed more splendid than ever. Even if the gap between rich and poor was not widening, it still yawned alarmingly. In 1910, for instance, wage earners and others earning under £160 a year constituted 94·5 per cent of the population but together earned only 57 per cent of all incomes. Among them were the quarter or third of the population hovering on the poverty line or living below it whose deplorable existence has been clinically chronicled by Charles Booth (1840–1916), Seebohm Rowntree (1871–1954), and others, and more warmly and vividly described by Jack London (1876–1916) in *People of the Abyss* (1903) and Charlie Chaplin (b.1889) in the earlier pages of his *Autobiography*. At the other end of the scale and included among the 5·5 per cent who declared that they earned over £160 a year and paid income tax on the remaining 43 per cent of incomes were, at the very apex of society, 0·06 per cent who declared over £5,000 each and shared 8 per cent just among themselves.[75]

In the years immediately before the war, this great divide and the plight of the very poor, now widely publicized, were causing increasing disquiet among the more sensitive of the haves as well as growing resentment among the more militant of the have-nots. Charles Masterman (1873–1927) in his very successful book, *The Condition of England*, which came out in 1909 and quickly went through six editions, indicated the rather negative form which this disquiet took among the rich:

The whole standard of life has been sensibly raised, not so much in comfort as in ostentation . . . where one house sufficed, now two are demanded; where a dinner of a certain quality, now a dinner of a superior quality; where clothes or dresses or flowers, now more clothes, more dresses, more flowers. It is waste, not because fine flowers or rare flowers and pleasant food are in themselves undesirable, but because . . . additional expenditure in such directions fails to result in corresponding additions of happiness.[76]

For many of the middle classes there was no such heart-searching. Their problem was to make both ends meet as their way of life became increasingly more expensive. In 1911 Birmingham decorators were starting to complain that people were 'living more in hotels and on the roads' and neglecting the upkeep of their houses, and estate agents had noticed that some people were living in smaller houses in order to afford cars.[77] The trade unionists, for their part, tired of standing still amid all these signs of opulence, seized their opportunity during the revival in trade before 1914 to stage a series of impressive strikes. Over 10,000,000 working days were lost in 1911 (which saw the first national railway stoppage), nearly 41,000,000 in 1912 (three-quarters of them in the coal mines), and over 11,000,000 in 1913.

These immediate pre-war years, which brought more employment and overtime, came at the end of two separate fluctuations of the economy, and these ups and downs need to be borne in mind when considering working-class living standards in the period. From the

close of the Boer War down to the end of 1904 business declined
and unemployment rose. An improvement set in in 1905 and continued through 1906 to the middle of 1907, when trade again fell
off. The year 1908 was a bad one, but business began to pick up
once more in the course of 1909 and the years after that were
increasingly prosperous. There are no satisfactory unemployment
figures for the period, but the returns from some of the skilled
unions indicate a maximum rate of about 6 per cent in 1904 and
nearly 8 per cent in 1908 and 1909. On the other hand, it fell to a
little over 2 per cent in 1913. The pre-war boom and militancy was
a good time for trade-union recruitment. Total membership, about
2,000,000 at the beginning of the century (one-sixth of a total
labour force of over 16,000,000), had reached 2,500,000 by 1910.
By 1913, helped to some extent by trade union recognition as
approved societies for insurance purposes, it was over 4,000,000
(nearly a quarter of the total labour force, then over 18,000,000).[78]

Any attempt to relate these business fluctuations to the movement
of both retail prices and earnings during this period, and so gain
some idea by just how much actual purchasing power varied from
year to year, is a fearsome and hazardous task, for price and wage
statistics are even less reliable than those for unemployment.
According to an index of food, coal, and clothing prices compiled
by the Board of Trade, the main price increases occurred in
and after 1907 and particularly after 1909. Food prices, for
instance, seem to have risen only 2 or 3 per cent up to and including 1906, at which date clothing prices, after a brief fall,
were said to be only 4½ per cent higher than, and coal prices
about the same as, in 1901. From 1906, however, both food
and clothing prices moved up. In 1910 they were about 10 per cent
higher than in 1900 and in 1913 about 15 per cent.[79] A more recent
and detailed attempt to draw up a comprehensive price index for all
products, but not one related particularly to working-class expenditure, emphasizes even more the rapid upward movement just before
the war. According to this index, market prices in 1907 and 1908
were about 3 per cent above those of 1900, but by 1912 and 1913
they were approaching 9 per cent.[80] When earnings are also taken
into account—and here the estimator is being bold almost to the
point of foolhardiness—real earnings may have fallen by about 6
per cent between 1900 and 1905, regaining half of this loss by 1907,
but slipping back again to the 1904 level between 1911 and 1913
when prices, having once gone ahead of wages, stayed ahead. Only
in 1914, according to this estimate, did wage increases start to close

the gap, but even so real earnings may still have been some 3 per cent lower than they had been when the century began.[81] Professor Phelps Brown in a very thorough recent study has shown that the rise in real earnings was also virtually halted at this time, too, in Germany and France; but because of her earlier wage gains, the U.K. average earnings were 40 per cent or more above the German.[82] Clearly, the deterioration in British earnings in these years was not large in itself; but it did represent a grave setback when compared with the great progress of the previous quarter of a century. 'The wage earners', declared *The Economist* at the beginning of 1914, 'are increasingly dissatisfied with their position and increasingly aware of their dissatisfaction. This dissatisfaction has been accentuated by the increase in the cost of living.' The writer went on to remark, ominously perhaps, that 'there has been a marked tendency to break loose from the older trade union methods, to down tools without consultation of leaders'.[83]

Whether or not the gap between rich and poor was widening in terms of real incomes, there can be little doubt that family limitation was causing a greater disparity. In the middle of the nineteenth century the average family had consisted of between five and six children and there was little difference between classes; but when the birth rate began to fall, after the 1870s, it was the professional and managerial classes who were limiting their families rather than the working classes. By the early twentieth century, while the average family size had fallen to about four children, those of the middle classes tended to consist of four children or fewer while those of certain sections of the working classes, notably unskilled labourers and miners, were often still bringing up families of six. In some branches of industry, however—in the textile trades, for instance—the size of family was little different from that of the middle classes.[84]

Women who became mothers of the larger families continued to be engaged in bearing and rearing their children for much of their adult lives as their predecessors had done. Professor Titmuss has drawn attention to the fact that 'the typical working-class mother of the 1890s, married in her teens or early twenties and experiencing ten pregnancies [a number of children died in infancy], spent about fifteen years in a state of pregnancy and in nursing a child for the first year of its life'.[85] Although this situation may have been altered slightly in Edwardian times because of the fall in the infant mortality rate, it remained basically the same. On the other hand, mothers with smaller families were pregnant or rearing very young children for perhaps only a third of this length of time. These, no doubt, were the mothers whom *The Queen*, in 1910, remarked upon as looking 'as young as their daughters'. The writer went on to make the revealing journalistic point that 'in fact, the disappearance of the middle-aged woman is a marked sign of the period'.[86]

These demographic trends proved particularly costly to poorer families at a time when educational developments were making children much more of an economic liability than they had previously been. So long as schooling was not compulsory, quite young children could be counted upon to contribute to the family income. By the twentieth century, however, compulsory elementary schooling meant that most boys and girls up to the age of fourteen could earn little or nothing, yet still had to be fed and clothed. It is not surprising that in the textile districts where local authorities used their powers to allow children of twelve or thirteen to spend half their time at school and the other half at work, the system received strong support from cotton industry trade unions.[87] With the spread of secondary schools, and particularly after 1907 with the increased number of scholarships to these schools, the period of parental responsibility was extended still further. In 1900 there were 5,500 such scholarships and in 1912 over 52,500.[88] And beyond the secondary schools the education ladder extended to the universities, particularly the redbricks, the new universities of their day, to which a small but growing number of bright children of working-class parentage were finding their way.

There was, too, greater migration abroad as well as movement up the social scale at home. This was the time when more people than ever decided to emigrate from Britain and it was, as usual, mainly the young and vigorous adults and their families who left the country. The nineteenth century had been marked by waves of migration, part of a great transatlantic movement from Europe, mainly to the United States. The wave which rose again after 1900 towered to an even greater height than its predecessor of the 1880s. Total British emigration averaged 284,000 a year between 1901 and 1910, and 464,000 a year in the three years from 1911 to 1913; but by then most of the migrants were making for parts of the empire, and particularly for Canada.[89] A huge exodus of labour was accompanying the great export of capital. This, however, does not necessarily imply condemnation of social conditions in Britain, for many of the emigrants decided to move not because of unfavourable circumstances at home, but rather on account of the facility of travel and the lure of the more or less unknown, and very large numbers returned home again. One estimate would suggest that the net loss through migration between 1901 and 1911 was only about half the gross figure.[90]

The rather depressing picture of the lot of the mass of the British people at this time also requires qualification in a number of other respects. The considerable amount of upward social mobility needs to be borne in mind, for instance, when interpreting the real earnings data. The growth of businesses and the development of national and local government called for more executives and clerks, and with the spread of the typewriter and the telephone, retail trades and entertainment, there were greater opportunities for women as well as for men. The professions, too, were growing apace. The number of better-paid jobs was increasing much more rapidly than the number of poorly paid ones. Thousands of people, particularly young people, were moving up the social scale either into the lower ranks of the rapidly growing middle classes or to less laborious and better wage-earning jobs, many, no doubt, reaping the economic dividend of the increasing educational opportunities made possible by the sacrifices of their parents.

Another point which needs to be borne in mind in the interpretation of the real earnings data is that the consumption pattern was changing in a way which probably benefited the neediest sections of the population. The most striking change was the decline in alcohol consumption. Beer drinking had shown no definite decline in the United Kingdom before 1900, when about 36 million barrels were consumed, enough to allow one pint per day for every man and woman over fourteen.[91] Total consumption soon fell, however, to just over 32 million barrels in 1908, rising again to just over 35 million in 1913; but by then the population was 11 per cent greater than it had been in 1900. The fall in spirits drinking was even more remarkable: from just over 45 million proof gallons in 1900 to just over 31 millions in 1913. If the gin palace was the symbol of later Victorian times, the new teashop was becoming a prominent feature of the Edwardian era. The advocates of temperance could at last report some solid progress; and since the price of drink rose considerably less than prices generally—beer, for instance, remained at about $2\frac{1}{2}d$. a pint—presumably considerable amounts of purchasing power were released to be spent elsewhere. According to a recent calculation, two-thirds as much consumers' expenditure went on alcoholic drink as on food at the beginning of the century (18·3 per cent and 27·6 per cent respectively). By 1910–14 drink was down to 14·7 per cent and food up a little, to 28·6 per cent. It must be noted, however, that some of the purchasing power so released went on tobacco, consumption of which was nearly a third higher in 1913 than it had been in 1900. This is to be explained by the huge increase in cigarette smoking; expenditure upon this rose from £5,500,000 in 1900 to £21,500,000 in 1913. The Edwardians were drinking less and smoking more. If present surmises are confirmed, then the Edwardian period, which could boast a fall in alcoholism and cirrhosis of the liver,[92] also saw the real spread of a habit which was eventually to create a big increase in deaths from lung cancer.

There were other shifts of expenditure, too, which may have had some bearing on living standards. The Penny Bazaars were making available a wide range of goods, such as hardware, haberdashery, crockery, toys, stationery, and kitchen materials all at 1d. each. Marks and Spencer, the most famous of these companies, developed their business rapidly at this time. Between 1908 and 1914 their turnover was doubled and reached nearly £400,000 a year, representing, presumably, the purchase of nearly 100,000,000 articles. The food shops were also doing well. More chocolate and sugar confectionery were eaten per head, and more butter and (particularly) margarine, more milk and fish.[93] The big multiples, such as Liptons and the Home & Colonial Stores, which had been developed in the later nineteenth century expressly to meet the needs of working-class customers, were being further expanded, and new concerns, notably The Meadow and The Maypole, were growing rapidly, the latter chain opening a shop a week during much of this period.[94] By obtaining a large turnover of quite a small range of most-needed foods, such as bacon, eggs, butter, margarine, and tea, they were able to offer fresh produce at low prices in clean, attractive, and well-run shops. At the same time, other retailers were selling a wider range of fruit, and, thanks to increased supplies from abroad, fruit at seasons of the year when it had previously not been widely obtainable. Imports of apples rose by 50 per cent, while shipments of bananas, which became recognized as the fruit of the poor, increased fourfold.[95] Until a systematic study of working-class diets has been undertaken, we shall not know to what extent other foods, which were being consumed in larger quantities per head of population, were, in fact, being eaten by many poorer, as well as richer, people; and until these diets have been interpreted in the light of modern nutritional knowledge, it will be impossible to say to what extent the working classes may have really gained from such dietary changes.

There can be no such doubt, however, about increased working-class participation in the rapidly spreading leisure-time activities of the period. Expenditure on these grew by about 40 per cent between 1900 and 1913.[96] There was very widespread support for organized sport of all kinds on Saturday afternoons and for music hall performances on week-nights. And if the motor-car allowed the fortunate few to tear about the countryside like Mr. Toad (*Wind in the Willows* was published in 1908), the cheap bicycle—or, at least, a second-hand model[97]—a ticket on the new electric tramcar or on a railway excursion allowed most people to get out and about much more than before, particularly to attend sports fixtures. Lady Bell (1851–1930) says, in her account of life in Middlesbrough, that she was told by one of the local stationmasters

that it was quite amazing to see the number of workmen who were constantly travelling to and fro. . . . One man, who had 36s. a week, spent 17 of them on his expenses to a town some distance off to see a football match on which, according to his own showing, he did not even care to bet. . . . Thousands of spectators will watch these matches, the excitement of many of them, no doubt, whetted by having a bet on the result, but many of them watching out of sheer interest in the game.[98]

She went on to note that 'Moving Pictures . . . on the Cinematograph . . . have made an extraordinary difference to the leisure hours of the working class, adults, as well as children. . . .'[99] The early cinema in fact caught on very quickly in the years just before 1914. Sheffield, for instance, had seventeen 'cinematograph theatres' by 1912 and Bradford, in the following year, over thirty which together claimed a daily attendance of 30,000.[100] By 1914 Manchester had a cinema seat for every eight of its inhabitants and in Britain as a whole there were at least 3,500 cinemas.[101]

Those who preferred to stay at home and read had a wide choice of cheap national and local papers, notably the popular *Daily Mail*, started in 1896, which sold for $\frac{1}{2}d$. Lady Bell found that in Middlesbrough three-quarters of the workmen read a paper, and on Sunday, when they had the leisure to do so, 'many of the workmen . . . spend the day in bed reading and smoking'.[102] She found, too, that a quarter of them read books as well. Taking the country as a whole, the public was certainly much better served with libraries than it had been only a few years before, helped to some extent by the benevolence of Scots-born Andrew Carnegie (1837–1919) out of his American steelmaking profits. Between 1896 and 1911, the number of books issued by public libraries increased from 26 to 54 millions.[103] Those who wished to do so, could now buy many standard works very cheaply. Nelson's New Century Library (later known as Nelson's Classics) began to appear in 1900, The World's Classics in 1901, Collins's Classics in 1903, and the most famous series of all, Dent's Everyman's Library, in 1906. Many of these volumes could be obtained for 1s., and by 1909 reprints of books out of copyright could be bought for 7d. and (so it was said) any of Dickens's works, complete and unabridged, for as little as 1d.[104]

Medical and environmental improvements were also beginning to exercise a much more extensive influence throughout society. The fall in crude death rate, which had set in in the 1870s, continued. Between 1900 and 1913 it fell from about 17 per 1,000 population to 13½ in England and Wales and 15½ in Scotland. More important, the infant mortality rate (deaths of children under one year of age per 1,000 live births) *started* to fall after 1900 and went down from over 150 to less than 100 by 1913. It is true that better-off families still lost fewer of their very young children than poorer ones at the end of the period, as they had done at the beginning: in 1911, for instance, infant mortality rate averaged 76 for the upper and middle classes and 133 for wage earners. But among wage earners the spread was considerable, from the agricultural labourers (97) and the artisans (113) to the miners (163);[105] and even the high rate of the miners was little more than the national average had been only a decade earlier. All classes were losing fewer of their children.

Improvements in hospital provision at this time almost certainly made a greater contribution to the welfare of the poor than of the rich. Previously, hospitals, poorly equipped and staffed largely by ill- or untrained doctors and nurses, were places which catered mainly for the poorest sections of society. Those who could afford it, would not dream of entering an institution but were attended by doctors in their own homes and, if need be, operated on there. From the later nineteenth century, however, the quality of hospital provision and the calibre of their doctors and nurses were greatly improved. There was, in particular, a rapid expansion of poor law infirmaries, the best of which were up to the standard of good general hospitals, and these catered for many of the working classes who were far from being paupers. Between 1891 and 1911 the number of beds in the voluntary hospitals grew from 29,000 to 43,000 while those in public infirmaries increased from 83,000 to 154,000.[106] In all, the total number of beds per thousand of the population grew in these years from 3·9 to 5·5. Very few of them, however, were to be found in private wards; the better-off continued to receive treatment either at home or in the medically rather inferior nursing homes which were springing up. In an article entitled 'The Advantages of Poverty', *The Hospital* noted in 1903 that

Any arrangements that can possibly be made [for surgery] in a private house are at best makeshift, while it is doubtful if [with one exception] there is a single nursing home in existence in which conditions are not passed which, in a hospital, surgeons would not absolutely condemn. The rich man with all his wealth does not, and practically cannot, obtain the scientific advantage which the poor man can and does obtain for nothing.[107]

Moreover, the better-off sections of the workers were also members of friendly societies—sick clubs—and could call upon private medical care whenever it should be needed. It has even been suggested that at the end of the nineteenth century nearly half the adult male population possessed this cover.[108]

These hospital developments and a number of the other improvements, such as the better provision of schools, libraries, and parks, were made possible by the degree of urbanization which the country had then reached and the activities of enlightened local authorities, many of which, of quite recent origin, still maintained their initial enthusiasm and energy. Migration from the countryside to the towns, which had been such a prominent feature of the past century and a half, was ending; according to the census returns, 77 per cent of the population of England and Wales was urban in 1901 and 80 per cent in 1911. Councillors, now drawn from all sections of society and elected on a broad franchise, gave particular attention to the improvement of public services and the provision of more civic amenities. The 'gas and water socialism' of the later nineteenth century was extended, and a number of places also took an interest in electricity undertakings and in the building of electric tramways. In all, local government expenditure grew rapidly, from £76 million in 1900 to £140 million in 1913. Of this, the total devoted to social services had risen from £37 million in 1900 to £60 million by 1910. Central government expenditure on social services increased these totals from £51 million in 1900 to £89 million in 1910. They grew further to £101 million in 1913.[109]

Trains, electric trams, and, in due course, the motor-bus (and, in the case of London, the tubes, almost all of which were opened between 1900 and 1907) made it possible for towns to continue to spread outwards into more airy and less densely packed suburbs. The most rapidly growing districts were on the outskirts of towns. Most of the building, however, took place in early Edwardian times, for the building boom, which had started in the last years of the nineteenth century, fell away after 1905–6 and by 1911 building activity was a third, or less, of what it had been at its peak.[110] Capital was being exported, not invested in domestic housing. Nevertheless, more than 1,600,000 houses were built in Britain in the fifteen years from 1900 to 1914, some 200,000 more than in the previous fifteen years, and 100,000 more than were to be built in the next fifteen because of the First World War.[111] The Edwardian housing boom and better urban transport between them did much to improve working-class housing conditions. The effect upon the congested parts of London has been described by a leading historian of the period, who happened to be living in Poplar at the time. It was, he says,

like the draining of marshes. It is true that the movement went by layers, and when Poplar transferred to East Ham, Walworth to Wandsworth, or North Camberwell to Lewisham, the places left vacant might be filled from more central and crowded areas; true also, that the houses (except those built by municipalities or trusts)[112] took the best-off and not the neediest workers. Nevertheless, especially between 1905 and 1910, the net social gain was great.[113]

The Liberals' social reforms, carried out in an attempt both to establish a minimum standard of living and to improve physical efficiency—the high proportion of urban recruits rejected for the Boer War having assured the concern of imperialists as well as of social reformers[114]—loom relatively less important in the light of these other developments and in any case became effective only towards the end of the period: old age pensions did not begin to be paid until January 1909 and health and unemployment benefit not until January 1913. The circumstances under which these reforms came about have been described elsewhere in this volume (pp. 22, 28–9) by Dr. Read. By the end of March 1910, nearly 500,000 non-contributory old age pensions were being received by 45 per cent of all old people over seventy living in England and Wales and by 54 per cent of those in Scotland. (The Irish, whose needs were undoubtedly greatest, made the most of the new arrangements: 202,000 pensions were paid in Ireland but, according to the 1911 census, that country possessed only 192,000 men and women over seventy and no doubt some of these genuine septuagenarians were ineligible because they earned over 10s. a week.)[115] The compulsory health and unemployment schemes greatly extended the existing voluntary cover. Before 1913, perhaps about 4,000,000 among those in the working classes may have belonged to a sick club, and possibly about 950,000 could look to trade unions for some help, if only travelling benefit, when they were out of work.[116] Under the new state insurance scheme which, as Dr. Pelling has indicated, the working classes viewed with singular lack of enthusiasm and even suspicion,[117] more than 12,000,000 people, a quarter of them women, began to pay in to the sickness scheme when contributions began in July 1912; but only about 2,250,000 were then covered for unemployment in what was at first a trial run limited to a relatively safe range of trades and did not extend to the really needy employees working in unskilled and casual occupations. The unemployment scheme nevertheless did cause much more use to be made of the new labour exchanges set up in and after 1910.[118]

All this was just a beginning. These were measures of social insurance only, the foundations upon which the welfare state was eventually to be built rather than the true beginnings of the welfare state itself. Social investigators just before the war were still reporting high percentages of working-class households living below the minimum: 13 per cent in Warrington, for instance, in the autumn of 1913, and an alarming 23 per cent in Reading a year before.[119] Yet, together with the other economic changes which have been mentioned, the insurance provisions helped to make the social condition of Britain in 1914 considerably better, and the outlook considerably brighter, than they had been in 1900. And Lloyd George, advised by Rowntree, had plans for further social reforms at the expense of landed property.[120] 'The landslide in England towards social democracy', wrote Beatrice Webb (1858–1943) in February 1914, 'proceeds steadily, but it is the whole nation that is sliding, not the one class of manual workers.'[121] The war, however, halted the next round of reform as it was also to disturb the course of industrial development.

<h1 style="text-align:center">III</h1>

The war, which disrupted the existing trading arrangements, inevitably hit the world's greatest trading nation the hardest. The transition to a wartime footing was quite slow at the outset, for the authorities, thinking back to 1870 and unable to imagine anything but a short campaign, readily took up the shopkeepers' slogan 'business as usual'. But as the changeover to a war economy gathered pace, from 1915 onwards, exports and (particularly) re-exports fell while imports rose, despite efforts after 1916 to make the country more self-sufficient agriculturally.[122] And Britain had to sell perhaps 15 per cent of her long-term foreign assets and lost one-third of her shipping tonnage.[123] London ceased to be the unchallenged financial centre of the world as Wall Street grew in importance. America, from being a debtor nation, became a world creditor.

Most serious, however, was the imbalance which the war created in Britain's industrial structure both by encouraging the manufacture of basic staples abroad and by holding back the manufacture of newer products at home. As Britain's industries were switched to war production, shortages and higher prices in world markets gave advantages to her industrial competitors who were not so heavily committed. The United States, for instance, which did not declare war until April 1917, was quick to seize British markets in South America; and Japan, though an ally from 1914, was in a position to increase enormously her exports in the East, so much so that by 1918 she had blossomed into a fully fledged world power. According to one estimate, America's manufacturing production rose by 22 per cent between 1913 and 1920, and Japan's by 76 per cent. Britain's, in contrast, fell by $7\frac{1}{2}$ per cent.[124]

The effect of the curtailment of Britain's exports is well illustrated by her trade with India which, as we have seen, was before 1914 by far the most important market for cotton goods, her main export, and exercised a key role in the working of the international economy. Before the war India had already built up her own production of coarse yarns, and she and Japan had both developed an export trade in these in the East, particularly in China. But Britain still remained the main supplier of the finer counts and of cloth; while British exports to India of the coarser cloths had reached a plateau, trade in the better qualities was growing rapidly. During the war, however, Britain's total cotton exports were halved in volume and those to India fell by two-thirds. This gave India's mills the chance to gain a virtual monopoly of the coarse qualities and allowed the Japanese to secure a foothold.[125] While it may be true that Lancashire's post-war losses in the Indian market were 'clearly foreshadowed in the last three decades before the war',[126] the question still remains: how long were these shadows? It seems highly improbable that the collapse of this crucial market would have occurred so quickly without the wartime curtailment of Britain's exports. If this great benefit had not been bestowed on her competitors, Britain might have been able to maintain her hegemony in India for some time longer. And if that had been the case, the move to higher qualities in the Lancashire cotton industry could well have been allowed to continue smoothly along pre-war lines, accompanied by the switch to new fibres and other products with better long-term prospects. There would then not have been the large-scale dislocation, distress, and unemployment which in fact ensued.

Moreover, while the war lost irretrievably the markets for many of Britain's old staples, it also halted many important new developments, notably the expansion of the motor-car industry, which, as we have seen, was poised for promising progress in 1914. Production of cars for civilian use in America, however, went ahead fast and was never stopped by the war. In 1917 output there reached 1,750,000 (Ford's production itself being 730,000) and although it was halved in 1918, production returned quickly to 1,650,000 cars in 1919.[127] In 1917 Britain even had to go to America for tractors, urgently needed for the food production programme, because all British engineering works had by then been turned over to other forms of manufacture.[128]

It can, of course, be shown that some hopeful new developments in Britain were, in fact, encouraged by the war. The manufacture of motor lorries continued, for instance, and the British Army, which had only 100 of them when war broke out, were equipped with 60,000 by the time it ended. At the Walthamstow works of the A.E.C. a moving track assembly line was installed which made possible the production of a 3-ton lorry every half-hour.[129] Science was applied more extensively to industry, and the Department of Industrial and Scientific Research was set up in 1916. Dyes, previously made chiefly in Germany, had to be manufactured in Britain.[130] The steel industry was expanded and greater use was made of Britain's own phosphoric ores. Aircraft manufacture, barely established before 1914, was swiftly developed on the principle of standardized materials and parts. Output of electricity was doubled, almost all the increase in power being fed to industry and, to a certain extent, to transport (the railway electrification schemes in the London area were continued into the war). Some of this investment—additional electric power, for instance, and faster, more efficient suburban trains—was clearly of permanent value. But against this should be set the disadvantages. The railway system as a whole was run down during the war, for example, and the aircraft and iron and steel industries over-expanded. In order to pass a verdict upon the war's contribution to Britain's long-term industrial development, we require to know what growth there would have been had there been no war and development had continued to be directed solely to peacetime needs instead of being first geared to war production and then subsequently, and often painfully, adapted to peacetime needs. It is arguable that, taken as a whole, the manufacture of new products would have been in a much stronger position after 1918 if this had been the case. If this view can be accepted, then the war went far to determine the distress of the inter-war years by disturbing the expansion of the newer products as well as by accelerating the decline of the older ones.

The switch to a war footing inevitably entailed much greater public control over the economy. In 1914 the civil service numbered 168,000, 124,000 of whom were employed in the Post Office; by 1919 the total had been swollen to 393,000.[131] Public expenditure grew from £192m. in 1914 to £2,696m. in 1918. This greater state involvement occurred without any conscious planning: one step led inevitably to the next. The shell shortage of 1915, for example, led to the setting up of the Ministry of Munitions, to the commandeering of factories and the building of new ones, to the extension of controls back to the steel industry, and to iron ore production. Foreign orders had to be placed in bulk,[132] raw material and shipping space had to be carefully allocated; and the need to save shipping space and foreign currency led to the first significant departure from free trade: in the budget of September 1915 a duty of 33⅓ *ad valorem* was placed upon imports of cars, motor-cycles, cinema films, clocks, watches, and musical instruments. When the diversion of resources to war needs caused shortages and high prices on the home front, the Government had to intervene in an attempt to control prices and supplies, though the rationing of certain foods —sugar, fats, and meat—did not become fully effective until July 1918. New ministries were created: Labour, Shipping, and Food, in December 1916; Air, National Service, Pensions, and Reconstruction in 1917. By early in 1917 Beatrice Webb was reporting that the permanent civil servants were 'fighting desperately for the control of their departments, against invading "interests" and interloping amateurs'.[133] Among the latter was the future Lord Keynes, the Cambridge don who was drawn in to the Treasury to deal with Allied war loans and foreign exchange matters and who quickly became a leading authority on war debts. He also came into collision with the Bank of England, then ruled over by a man whom Montagu Norman (1871–1950), described as 'a dangerous and insane colleague'.[134] Among the invading interests were prominent men from the world of private enterprise and leading trade unionists, who were brought into government to control the branches of business with which they were familiar. As Beatrice Webb went on to observe:

The Insurance Commission is controlled by the great Industrial Companies; the Board of Trade is controlled by the Shipowners, the Food Controller is a wholesale Grocer; the Ministry of Munitions is largely managed by the representatives of the manufacturers of munitions, whilst a Duke's land-agent has been placed at the head of the Board of Agriculture. Finally, a Trade Union official is Minister of Labour and has been given, as the permanent head of his Department, an ex-Trade Union official.[135]

Greater government activity also led to more collaboration among businessmen within industry and to that extent it had the effect of curbing competition. Hitherto quiet and retiring trade associations came out more into the open and a number of new ones were formed in order to conduct negotiations with the Government. Indeed, during the war the Government encouraged their creation, for it was easier to deal with representative bodies than with a great maze of private concerns. And the Federation of British Industries itself came into being in 1916. The war also saw a great increase in the number of business amalgamations, often financed by money which would otherwise have had to be paid out in excess-profits duty.[136]

These larger units survived, together with some of the wartime ministries, and two new ones created in 1919: Health and Transport. But most of the wartime controls, hastily applied to meet particular emergencies, were as hastily removed when these emergencies were over. Researches into the papers of the Ministry of Reconstruction, recently opened to public inspection, suggest that useful inquiry and planning was being undertaken there.[137] Once the war was over, however, the climate of opinion was overwhelmingly in favour of reducing the power of central government in an attempt to return to a pre-war world which, as we now know, was gone for ever.

IV

The main social effects of the war resulted from its large-scale mobilization and wholesale slaughter. The armed services, some 500,000 strong at the beginning of the war, had been built up by volunteering, attesting, and conscribing to about 4,500,000 by the end of it. In all, 745,000 men from the United Kingdom were killed, about 9 per cent of the age group 20–45. A further 1,700,000 were wounded and of these 1,200,000 received disablement pensions.[138] The full meaning of these figures in terms of grief to relatives and friends, or experiences stamped indelibly on the memories of many of the survivors, wounded or not, must be left to the imagination of the reader, for, unlike the casualty figures themselves, it cannot be calculated. In coldly demographic terms, however, the losses were not so damaging; in total numbers they were probably fewer than the losses from permanent emigration which might have been expected if the flow of emigrants had not been stemmed by the outbreak of war. Whether in economic terms —in terms of business leadership—the losses in the fields of Flanders were greater than would have occurred by emigration, is, however, another matter.

The mobilization of such large numbers of men, at a time when great industrial effort was also called for, soon created an acute labour shortage. Unemployment among trade unions fell below 2 per cent early in 1915 and below 1 per cent later that year. In late 1916 and early 1917 it was down to 0·3 per cent for a short period.[139] For the first time within recorded memory the country enjoyed full employment. Labour was in a powerful bargaining position and it was able to withstand any suggestion of industrial conscription. The trade-union leaders chose to work closely with the Government. An industrial truce was declared when war broke out, and in 1915 the dilution of labour was agreed to for its duration. In that year, too, a scheme was introduced whereby men, although not liable for industrial conscription, could volunteer to be directed to munitions work anywhere in the country. Such close co-operation between trade unions and Government caused a growing division between the leaders and the rank and file, and this, in turn, led to the rise of the shop stewards' movement and a spate of industrial unrest into which a number of regional inquiries were carried out in 1917.[140] These divisions and dissensions did not, however, prevent the trade unions from gaining growing support: membership increased from 4,145,000 in 1914 to 6,533,000 in 1918. Many employers, who had previously refused to have any dealings with trade unions, were now obliged to recognize them; and, largely as a counterblast to syndicalist ideas, joint industrial councils, representing both sides of industry at national and local level, were advocated in 1917 by the Whitley Committee on the Relations of Employers and Employed. Meanwhile more canteens and welfare facilities made their appearance at work and, most important of all, earnings rose and the number of cases of low family incomes, which pre-war social surveys had shown to be one of the main causes of poverty, was very much reduced.

Rising earnings, were, however, inevitably offset to some extent by rising prices. Paper money poured from the printing presses and consumer goods became scarcer. £1 and 10s. currency notes, first issued by the Treasury after the monetary crisis at the outset of the war,[141] rapidly grew in volume. Gold sovereigns and half-sovereigns were quietly and unobtrusively removed from circulation; 'the abandonment of the gold standard which opened the way to inflation was not definitely announced or admitted, and was only realised some time after the fact had been accomplished in practice'.[142] The increase in prices was rapid up to the middle of 1917, but then, steadied by Government action, it became less severe. By the armistice, wholesale prices were about 140 per cent higher than they had been before war was declared. Retail prices did not rise so much: perhaps about twofold.[143]

Taxes rose, too, though the war was financed throughout mainly by loans: even in 1918 tax revenue yielded only about 30 per cent of national expenditure. (Among these loans were those raised on a broad, popular basis by means of war savings certificates and other activities of war savings committees from 1916.) Direct taxation, light though it may seem in retrospect, was nevertheless severe by pre-war standards. Moreover, in 1915 the working classes first began to pay income tax, for in that year, with earnings rising, the lower exemption limit was brought down from £160 to £130. Cards were introduced upon which weekly income tax stamps could be stuck, like insurance stamps, and handed over quarterly when the tax was collected.[144] Meanwhile, at the other end of the scale, the standard rate was gradually put up until in 1918 it reached 6s. in the £1 on earned incomes over £2,500 and unearned incomes over £2,000. On top of this was super tax, payable on a scale which rose to 4s. 6d. in the £1. Indirect taxes were also considerably increased, beer and spirits being singled out for particular attention. The Government was determined to see that the pre-war fall in alcohol consumption was continued; Lloyd George himself declared in 1915—in the best Liberal tradition—'We are fighting Germany, Austria and Drink'.[145] Opening hours and specific gravity were both reduced and the state itself acquired and ran licensed premises in certain areas. Consumption of beer fell from 36,000,000 barrels in 1914 to 21,300,000 more watery ones in 1918, and that of spirits even more steeply, from 31,000,000 gallons to 14,500,000, also of reduced strength.[146]

According to Sir Arthur Bowley, prices in general rose more rapidly than wage *rates* up to 1917 but then, in the last year of the war, wage rates caught up again. But wage rates for the lower-paid, unskilled workers rose more rapidly than those for the skilled, and, when the greater opportunities for overtime and the decline in unemployment are taken into account, there seems little doubt that real earnings ran ahead of prices for most wage earners throughout the war.[147] Moreover, since the number of female employees increased by about 1,000,000 and since they tended to move up from lower- to higher-paid jobs, the contribution of women, including married women, to the family income was very considerable. At the outbreak of war there had been 2,500,000 women working in overcrowded and badly paid occupations such as domestic service and dressmaking, and another 3,250,000 employed in industry and commerce. The former declined in number, while the latter grew by 1918 to 4,850,000, some of them replacing men and others taking up new jobs, particularly in the munitions factories.[148] Not all working-class families were better off, however. The real or imagined spending sprees of the 'canaries' working on munitions, for instance, were much resented by women with husbands in the forces who stayed at home and had to make do with meagre separation allowances. And for many of the middle classes, with taxation rising and domestic help more difficult to come by, times must have seemed harder, particularly if they had to rely to any extent on fixed incomes. But here again women made a contribution to family budgets, for in this section of society unmarried daughters in increasing numbers went out to earn their own living.[149]

In wartime, however, national fervour counts for more than purchasing power. The social upheaval of the period was to be of far greater significance in the long run than the economic effects of the brief heyday of full employment. Families were divided and scattered. Millions of men had their horizons broadened and their outlooks changed by travel, excitement, danger, and new companions. Women enjoyed greater freedom. Accepted norms came to be much more strongly challenged. The influence of Nonconformity and the principles and practices of Liberalism were weakened.[150] Many men in the Army began to doubt the capability of some of their leaders (and not without good reason); many workers demanded a greater stake in the running of their factories; and the revolutionary events in Russia in 1917 and 1918 did not pass unnoticed. Deference on the pre-war scale had gone for ever. Yet society was still prudish rather than permissive. Skirts came off the ground but they did not rise very far. New codes of behaviour were not passively accepted, though they were discussed with fervour and concern. If the old order of things was to be changed, what would take its place? One of the most discerning observers of the time, writing a few days before the armistice when victory was already assured, noticed 'the sombre looks of private persons' who were troubled about the future:

No citizen knows what is going to happen to himself or his children, or to his own social circle, or to the state or to the Empire. All that he does know is that the old order is seriously threatened with dissolution without any new order being in sight. What are the social ideals germinating in the minds of the five millions who will presently return from the battlefields and battle seas? What is the outlook of the millions of men and women who have been earning high wages and working long hours at the war trades, and will presently find themselves seeking work? What are the sympathies of the eight millions of new women voters? What has happened to the churches and the ten commandments? The Bolsheviks grin at us from a ruined Russia and their creed, like the plague of influenza, seems to be spreading westwards from one country to another. . . . Will western civilisation flare up in the flames of anarchic revolution? Individuals brood over these questions and wonder what will have happened this time next year.[151]

There was, in fact, no immediate cause for concern. The existing social order was far from finished, although higher taxation and death duties were beginning to bring more estates on to the market.[152] And the war had shown what could be achieved by better organization. Even the trade unions and the Labour party—both greatly strengthened, the latter fighting more seats and polling 2,374,000 to the Asquith Liberals' 1,299,000 in 1918—were beginning to perceive the value of research activities and were on the point of building up permanent advisory and administrative staffs. The time was ripe for the slow spread of new popular attitudes and more radical ideas. The extension of the franchise in 1918, increasing the electorate from 8,000,000 to nearly 22,000,000, was clear recognition of this. The distress which was soon to strike over a million of these voters was to subject the social order to severe strain but to leave it basically unchanged.

NOTES

[1] Lord Beveridge's introduction to *Beatrice Webb's Diaries, 1912–1924* (1952), xvii; L. Woolf, *Beginning Again: An Autobiography of the Years 1911–1918* (1964), 43–4.

[2] J. F. Rees, *A Short Fiscal and Financial History of England, 1815–1918* (1921), 192, 196–7; Sir Josiah Stamp, *Taxation During the War* (1932), 136.

[3] J. M. Keynes, *The Economic Consequences of the Peace* (1919), 9–10.

[4] Lord Beveridge, *Power and Influence* (1953), 101–2.

[5] R. F. Harrod, *The Life of John Maynard Keynes* (1951), 99.

[6] Lord Salter, *Memoirs of a Public Servant* (1961), 35.

[7] A. Marshall, 'Memorandum on Fiscal Policy of International Trade' (1903), in *Official Papers of Alfred Marshall* (1926), 404.

[8] See, for instance, Charles Wilson, 'Economy and Society in Late Victorian Britain', *Economic History Review*, XVIII (1965), 183–98; John Saville, ed., 'Studies in the British Economy, 1870–1914', *Yorkshire Bulletin of Economic and Social Research*, XVII (1965), 1–112; W. Ashworth, *An Economic History of England, 1870–1939* (1960), 260; S. B. Saul, *The Myth of the 'Great Depression', 1873–1896* (1969).

[9] P. L. Payne, 'The Emergence of the Large-Scale Company in Great Britain, 1870–1914', *Economic History Review*, XX (1967), 519–42. For Lever, see C. Wilson, *The History of Unilever* (1954).

[10] R. C. O. Matthews, 'Some Aspects of Post-War Growth in the British Economy in Relation to Historical Experience', *Transactions of the Manchester Statistical Society*, 1964/5, 3. See also H. W. Richardson, 'Retardation in Britain's Industrial Growth, 1870–1913', *Scottish Journal of Political Economy* (1965).

[11] Brinley Thomas, *Migration and Economic Growth* (1954), 229–30.

[12] N. J. Butlin, 'A New Plea for the Separation of Ireland', *Journal of Economic History*, XXVIII (1968), 274–91; N. K. Buxton, 'Economic Progress in Britain in the 1920s: A Reappraisal', *Scottish Journal of Political Economy*, XIV (1968), 183; D. H. Aldcroft and H. W. Richardson, *The British Economy, 1870–1939* (1969), 24–5.

[13] A. K. Cairncross, *Home and Foreign Investment, 1870–1913* (1953), 167.

[14] A. Shadwell, *Industrial Efficiency: A Comparative Study of Industrial Life in England, Germany and America* (1906), II. 455.

[15] Report of Moseley Commission (Manchester, 1903), 9. The party was taken over by the British businessman Alfred Moseley (1855–1917) at his own expense.

[16] Marshall, *Official Papers*, 406.

[17] Payne, 'Emergence of the Large-Scale Company', 534.

[18] D. S. L. Cardwell, *The Organisation of Science in England* (1957), 159–67. For attendance at evening schools of the London School Board and student hours at trade and science classes of the London Polytechnics, see S. F. Cotgrove, *Technical Education and Social Change* (1958), 54–6. For an interesting individual example relating to the later 1890s, see J. Rowland and Lord Cadman, *Ambassador for Oil* (1960), 19–22.

[19] H. J. Habakkuk, *American and British Technology in the Nineteenth Century* (1962), 216.

[20] S. B. Saul, 'The Engineering Industry', in D. H. Aldcroft, ed., *The Development of British Industry and Foreign Competition* (1968), 233–4; H. W. Richardson, 'Chemicals', ibid., 274; S. B. Saul, 'The Market and the Development of the Mechanical Engineering Industries in Britain, 1860–1914', *Economic History Review*, XX (1967), 111. For a careful study of the leaders in two of Britain's industries, see Charlotte Erickson, *British Industrialists: Steel and Hosiery, 1850–1950* (1959).

[21] For a full discussion of this argument, see the League of Nations report on *Industrialization and Foreign Trade* (Geneva, 1945).

[22] Cairncross, *Home and Foreign Investment*, 2–3. The estimates of Miss Phyllis Deane (*Review of Income and Wealth*, ser. 14, No. 2 (1968)) suggest this may have been nearly as high as two-thirds.

[23] A. H. Imlah, *Economic Elements in the Pax Britannica* (1958), ch. iii.

[24] Ibid. 74–5. I am grateful to Mr. D. A. Lury for his helpful comments upon the statistical references in this chapter.

[25] W. H. B. Court, *British Economic History, 1870–1914; Commentary and Documents* (1965), 178.

[26] S. B. Saul, *Studies in British Overseas Trade, 1870–1914* (1960), ch. iii.

[27] Ibid. 64.

[28] E. Helm, 'The British Cotton Industry', in W. J. Ashley, ed., *British Industries*, 2nd ed. (1907), 87. For similar improvements in the quality of cloth exports, see Lars G. Sandberg, 'Movement in the Quality of British Cotton Textile Exports, 1815–1913', *Journal of Economic History*, XXVIII (1968), 18–19.

[29] R. E. Tyson, 'The Cotton Industry', in Aldcroft, *British Industry*, 122.

[30] *U. S. Daily Consular and Trade Reports*, 14th Year, No. 15 (19 Jan. 1911), 232. My italics.

[31] P. Mathias, *The First Industrial Nation* (1969), 415. Cf. Saul, *Great Depression*, 46.

[32] See, for instance, the comments of B. Bowker, *Lancashire under the Hammer* (1928), Bk. I.

[33] S. B. Saul, 'The Market and the Development of the Mechanical Engineering Industries in Britain, 1860–1914', *Economic History Review*, XX (1967), 112.

[34] D. C. Coleman, *Courtaulds: An Economic and Social History* (1969), I. 181; II. 47–50, 111, 147.

[35] For a detailed study of the issues involved, see Habakkuk, *American and British Technology*.

[36] A. J. Taylor, 'Labour Productivity and Technological Innovation in the British Coal Industry, 1850–1914', *Economic History Review*, XIV (1961), 48–70; Saul, *Great Depression*, 44–5 n.

[37] Between 1900 and 1913, Britain's steel output grew from 4·9 million tons to 7·66 million tons, the United States' from 10·19 to 31·30, and Germany's from 6·36 to 17·32 (J. C. Carr and W. Taplin, *History of the British Steel Industry* (1962), 183, 230). For the latest research on this subject see Donald N. McCloskey's summary of his doctoral thesis on 'The British Iron and Steel Industry, 1870–1914: A Study of the Climacteric in Productivity', *Journal of Economic History*, XXIX (1969), 173–5.

[38] P. L. Payne, 'Iron and Steel Manufactures' in Aldcroft, *British Industry*, 87.

[39] Carr and Taplin, *British Steel Industry*, 228; D. S. Landes, 'Technological Change and Development in Western Europe' in H. J. Habakkuk and M. Postan, eds., *The Cambridge Economic History of Europe* (1965), VI. 542–3.

[40] Carr and Taplin, *British Steel Industry*, 84.

[41] W. E. Minchinton, *The British Tinplate Industry* (1957), 70, 74, 80.

[42] S. B. Saul, 'The Machine Tool Industry in Britain to 1914', *Business History*, X (1968).

[43] R. A. Church, 'The Effect of the American Export Invasion on the British Boot and Shoe Industry, 1885–1914', *Journal of Economic History*, XXVIII (1968); P. Head, 'Boots and Shoes' in Aldcroft, *British Industry*.

[44] J. A. Miller, *Fares Please!* (1960), chs. iv, vii; C. Klapper, *The Golden Age of Tramways* (1961).

[45] Saul, 'Machine Tool Industry', 40.

[46] Saul in Aldcroft, *British Industry*, 195, 227.

[47] Ibid. 227.

[48] Ibid. 192. For the cycle industry, see A. E. Harrison, 'The Competitiveness of the British Cycle Industry, 1890–1914', *Economic History Review*, XXII (1969), 287–303, and W. B. Stephens' brief but valuable contribution in the *Victoria County History of Warwick*, VIII (1969), 172–5.

[49] In that year 194,000 cars were registered in the U.S.A. and 71,000 in Great Britain, with 40 per cent of America's population. (*Historical Statistics of the United States* (U.S. Department of Commerce, 1960); C. S. Rolls, article on Motor Vehicles in *Encyclopaedia Britannica*, 11th ed. (1911).)

[50] A. P. Sloan, Jr., *My Years With General Motors* (1967), 173.

[51] Rolls, *Encyclopaedia Britannica*.

[52] A. Nevins, *Ford: The Times, The Man and The Company* (1954), 410, 489; C. Sorenson and S. T. Williamson, *Forty Years with Ford* (1957), ch. x.

[53] *U.S. Daily Consular and Trade Reports*, 14th Year, No. 44 (21 June 1911), 1269.

[54] *Economist*, 28 Nov. 1908; 27 Nov. 1909.

[55] *Economist*, 3 Dec. 1910; 9 Dec. 1911. Professor Prest has estimated that motor-cycle output may have increased from 3,500 (1909) to 13,300 (1910), 21,500 (1911), 29,000 (1912), and 32,000 (1913) (A. R. Prest, *Consumers' Expenditure in the United Kingdom, 1900–1919* (1954), 140).

[56] *U.S. Daily Consular and Trade Reports*, 15th Year, No. 192 (15 Aug. 1912), 828. See also R. D. Blumenfeld, *R.D.B's. Diary, 1887–1914* (1930), 237–8.

[57] On this point see, for instance, the account of the assembly line at the Sunbeam Motor Co., published in *Internal Combustion Engineering*, III (1913), 350, 379–80, and reprinted in Court, *British Economic History*, 156–60.

[58] *U.S. Department of Commerce, Supplement to Commerce Reports. Review of Industrial and Trade Conditions in Foreign Countries in 1914 by American Consular Officers*, I (Europe) 1916, No. 19, 8. The report was dated 11 Mar. 1915. For the development of light car manufacture at Coventry, see Stephens, *V.C.H. Warwick*, VIII, 181–2.

[59] Z. E. Lambert and R. J. Wyatt, *Lord Austin: The Man* (1968), 89, 99–102.

[60] P. W. S. Andrews and Elizabeth Brunner, *The Life of Lord Nuffield* (1955), chs. viii–x.

[61] *Economist*, 2 Jan. 1915.

[62] *Economist*, 22 Feb. 1902; 21 Feb. 1903.

[63] *U.S. Daily Consular and Trade Reports*, 14th Year, No. 64 (18 Mar. 1911), 1041; 15th Year, No. 198 (22 Aug. 1912), 957.

[64] Ibid., 15th Year, No. 130 (3 June 1912), 911.

[65] Quoted in ibid., 16th Year, No. 61 (15 Mar. 1913), 1299–1300.

[66] I. C. R. Byatt, 'Electrical Products' in Aldcroft, *British Industry*, 253–62.

[67] E. J. Cocks and B. Walters, *A History of the Zinc Smelting Industry in Britain* (1968), chs. ii, iii; H. W. Richardson, 'Chemicals', Aldcroft, *British Industry*, 286–8.

[68] Byatt, ibid. 257; Richardson, ibid. 293.

[69] Bowker, *Lancashire under the Hammer*, 19.

[70] This point is made by Richardson, 'Chemicals', 302–6, with special, but not exclusive, reference to the chemical industry.

[71] E. H. Phelps Brown with Margaret H. Browne, *A Century of Pay* (1968), 183–90.

[72] A. L. Bowley, *The Change in the Distribution of the National Income* (1920), 20–1.

[73] R. C. K. Ensor, *England 1870–1914* (1936), 510.

[74] Sir Josiah Stamp, *British Incomes and Property* (1920 ed.), 449.

[75] Bowley, *Distribution of the National Income*, 22.

[76] C. F. G. Masterman, *The Condition of England* (1960 ed.), 20–1.

[77] *U.S. Daily Consular and Trade Reports*, 14th Year, No. 201 (28 Aug. 1911), 919.

[78] B. R. Mitchell and Phyllis Deane, *Abstract of British Historical Statistics* (1962), 60, 65, 68. Beveridge has discussed unemployment rates before and after the First World War in his *Full Employment in a Free Society* (1944), 328–37. For trade unionism during this period, see H. A. Clegg, Alan Fox, and A. F. Thompson, *A History of Trade Unions Since 1889*, I (1964); E. H. Phelps Brown, *The Growth of British Industrial Relations: A Study From the Standpoint of 1906–14* (1959); and Henry Pelling, *A History of British Trade Unionism* (1963), ch. vii. For a vivid description of the life and work of a group of painters and decorators at Hastings *c.* 1906, see R. Tressell, *The Ragged Trousered Philanthropist* (Panther Books ed., 1965). Dr. Pelling discusses the rise in trade union membership in 1910–13 in his *Popular Politics and Society in Late Victorian Britain* (1968), 152–5.

[79] Mitchell and Deane, *British Historical Statistics*, 478; Consumption and Cost of Food in Workmen's Families, 1904 [Cd. 2337] LXXXIV; Board of Trade Enquiry, 1913 [Cd. 6955] LXVI. In 1912 the C.W.S. issued details of how what was described as an average grocery bill had gone up between 1898 and 1911. According to this, the increase was 5·37 per cent between 1898 and 1906 and 11·2 per cent between 1898 and 1911. (Report from the American vice-consul in Manchester, in *U.S. Daily Consular and Trade Reports*, 15th Year, No. 233 (3 Oct. 1912), 57.)

[80] Prest, *Consumers' Expenditure*, 175.

[81] A. L. Bowley, *Wages and Income in the United Kingdom Since 1860* (1937), 30.

[82] Phelps Brown, *Wages*, 159.

[83] *Economist*, 21 Feb. 1914.

[84] Report of the Royal Commission on Population (Cmd. 7695 of 1949), 24–30; Phelps Brown, *Industrial Relations*, 4–9; Ensor, *England 1870–1914*, 499.

[85] Richard M. Titmuss, *Essays on the Welfare State* (1958), 91.

[86] *Queen*, Feb. 1910, quoted by Cynthia L. White, 'Magazines For Women' (London Ph.D. 1968), 84.

[87] Phelps Brown, *Industrial Relations*, 58–9.

[88] D. S. L. Cardwell, *The Organisation of Science in England* (1957), 161.

[89] Brinley Thomas, *Migration and Economic Growth*, 57.

[90] Ibid. 52.

[91] The figures in this paragraph are from Prest, *Consumers' Expenditure*, and R. Stone and D. A. Rowe, *The Measurement of Consumers' Expenditure and Behaviour in the United Kingdom, 1920–1938*, II (1966), 125.

[92] Arthur Newsholme, *The Elements of Vital Statistics* (1923 ed.), 328.

[93] Goronwy Rees, *St. Michael: A History of Marks and Spencer* (1969), 26; Prest, *Consumers' Expenditure*, 7.

[94] Peter Mathias, *Retailing Revolution* (1967), 152, 171.

[95] Saul, *Overseas Trade*, 26; Angeliki Torode, 'Trends in Fruit Consumption' in T. C. Barker, J. C. McKenzie, and John Yudkin, eds., *Our Changing Fare* (1966), 126–8.

[96] Prest, *Consumers' Expenditure*, 133, 159.

[97] The socialist Clarion Cycling Clubs were very popular at this time. See, for examples, C. Stella Davies, *North Country Bred* (1963), 83–5, 117–21. Her second-hand bicycle cost her 30s. in 1914. The Premier Cycle Co. was advertising new machines from £5.5s. 0d. upwards in 1910. Cf. Compton Mackenzie's new Rover machine which he bought for 18 gns. in 1900 (*My Life and Times*, Octave 3 (1964), 35).

[98] Lady Bell, *At the Works* (1911 ed.), 182–3.

[99] Ibid. 185. For a succinct summary of the early development of the cinema in Britain, see A. Briggs, *Mass Entertainment: The Origins of a Modern Industry* (1960), 14–19.

[100] *U.S. Daily Consular and Trade Reports*, 15th Year, No. 142 (17 June 1912), 1153; 16th Year, No. 37 (13 Feb. 1913), 785.

[101] S. Nowell-Smith, ed., *Edwardian England, 1901–1914* (1964), 240; Briggs, *Mass Entertainment*, 16.

[102] Bell, *At the Works*, 206. Masterman (*The Condition of England*, 7) believed that, for 70 per cent of Englishmen, 'the sole picture they possess of the world outside their local lives' came from the Sunday paper.

[103] Derek Hudson, 'Reading', in Nowell-Smith, *Edwardian England*, 309.

[104] Ibid. 311–12; Marjorie Plant, *The English Book Trade*, 2nd ed. (1965), 415.

[105] Newsholme, *Vital Statistics*, 119–21; Phelps Brown, *Industrial Relations*, 39.

[106] This paragraph is chiefly based upon B. Abel-Smith, *The Hospitals, 1800–1949* (1964), 200.

[107] *The Hospital*, 28 Mar. 1903, quoted ibid. 192.

[108] B. B. Gilbert, *The Evolution of National Insurance in Great Britain* (1966), 167.

[109] Mitchell and Deane, *British Historical Statistics*, 416–7; Alan T. Peacock and Jack Wiseman, *The Growth of Public Expenditure in the United Kingdom* (1961), 106, 184.

[110] B. Weber, 'A New Index of Residential Construction, 1838–1950', *Scottish Journal of Political Economy*, II (1955), 130–1.

[111] Ibid.

[112] q.v. W. Ashworth, *The Genesis of Modern British Town Planning* (1954), chs. v and vi.

[113] Ensor, *England 1870–1914*, 509–10. See also Lucy Masterman, *C. F. G. Masterman* (1939), 82–3.

[114] Of 12,000 men examined for the Army in Manchester in 1899, 8,000 were rejected as virtual invalids and only 1,200 were found after service in the Army to be completely fit (Gilbert, *National Insurance*, 89). For the link between these warnings of physical deterioration and the beginnings of the boy scout movement, see Samuel Hynes, *The Edwardian Turn of Mind* (1968), 27.

[115] Gilbert, *National Insurance*, 227–8.

[116] Ibid. 167; Beveridge, *Unemployment*, 17.

[117] Pelling, *Popular Politics and Society in Late Victorian Britain*, ch. 1. See also Masterman, *The Condition of England*, 113.

[118] Gilbert, *National Insurance*, 261–2, 424; Beveridge, *Unemployment*, 270.

[119] A. L. Bowley and A. R. Burnett-Hurst, *Livelihood and Poverty* (1915), 237.

[120] A. Briggs, *Seebohm Rowntree* (1961), 62–78.

[121] Margaret I. Cole, ed., *Beatrice Webb's Diaries*, 1912–1924 (1952), 18.

[122] For agriculture during the First World War, see Lord Ernle, *English*

Farming Past and Present, 6th ed. (1961), ch. xix. The author, as R. E. Prothero, was President of the Board of Agriculture from the end of 1916.

[123] E. Victor Morgan, *Studies in British Financial Policy, 1914-1925* (1952), 329-31; Ashworth, *Economic History*, 288.

[124] *Industrialization and Foreign Trade*, 134.

[125] Britain's total exports of cotton piece goods fell from 7,075m. yds in 1913 to 3,699m. yds. in 1918 and her exports of twist and yarn from 210m. lb. to 102m. lb. To India, exports of piece goods fell from 3,104m. yds. in 1913-14 to 976m. yds. in 1919-20 and in the same period Japanese exports to India rose from 9m. yds. to 76m. yds. (Freda Utley, *Lancashire and the Far East* (1931), 253, 258.) See also articles on Cotton, India, and Japan in *Encyclopaedia Britannica*, 12th ed. (1922) [*E.B.* 1922], and Saul, *Overseas Trade*, 189-92. For the development of the cotton industry in Japan before 1914, see Landes, 'Technological Change', 467-8.

[126] Saul, *Overseas Trade*, 190.

[127] *Historical Abstract of the United States*; A. Nevins and F. E. Hill, *Ford: Expansion and Challenge, 1915-1933* (1957), 149.

[128] Ibid. 61-3; 'Agriculture' in *E.B.* 1922.

[129] W. K. Hancock and M. M. Gowing, *British War Economy* (1949), 14; *A.E.C. Fifty Years* (privately printed), 7.

[130] For succinct accounts of the wartime developments mentioned in this paragraph, often written by the leading participants, see the articles in *E.B.* 1922 on Aeronautics, Dyeing, Electricity Supply, Military Motor Transport, Munitions of War, and Railways. For iron and steel see also Carr and Taplin, *British Steel Industry*, chs. xxix-xxxii.

[131] G. A. Campbell, *The Civil Service in Britain* (1955), 73.

[132] See, for instance, on the need to ensure sugar, meat, and wheat supplies, Frank H. Coller, *A State Trading Adventure* (1925), 6-10, an account of the Ministry of Food by its Secretary. The official history of the Ministry is by Beveridge, *British Food Control* (1928).

[133] *Beatrice Webb's Diaries, 1912-1924*, 83.

[134] A. Boyle, *Montague Norman* (1967), 117, 123.

[135] *Diaries*, 83.

[136] John Hilton, *Memorandum on Combines and Trade Organisations* (1919), 47-9.

[137] See P. B. Johnson, *Land Fit For Heroes: The Planning of British Reconstruction, 1916-1919* (1968).

[138] Hancock and Gowing, *British War Economy*, 28; Ashworth, *Economic History*, 285.

[139] Morgan, *British Financial Policy*, 70.

[140] Humbert Wolfe, 'Labour Supply and Regulation', *E.B.* 1922; Pelling, *British Trade Unionism*, ch. viii; G. D. H. Cole, *A Short History of the British Working Class Movement, 1789-1927* (1932 ed.), III., ch. vi.

[141] For which see Morgan, *British Financial Policy*, ch. i.

[142] J. S. Nicholson, 'Inflation', *E.B.* 1922.

[143] A. L. Bowley, *Some Economic Consequences of the Great War* (1930), 69; *Prices and Wages in the United Kingdom, 1914-1920* (1921), 75.

[144] H. M. Sanders, Assistant Secretary to the Board of Inland Revenue, 'Income Tax', *E.B.*, 1922.

[145] Quoted in A. Marwick, *The Deluge* (1965), 65.

[146] Prest, *Consumers' Expenditure*, 76, 79; Newsholme, *Vital Statistics*, 327.

[147] Bowley, *Prices and Wages 1914-1920*, XIX, 75, 106-7.

148 'Women's Employment', *E.B.* 1922.
149 See, for instance, Davies, *North Country Bred*, 139–40.
150 Trevor Wilson, *The Downfall of the Liberal Party, 1914–1935* (Fontana ed., 1968), 24.
151 *Beatrice Webb's Diaries, 1912–1922*, 133–4.
152 F. M. L. Thompson, *English Society in the Nineteenth Century* (1963), 327–30.

FOR FURTHER READING: HISTORY *

The best one-volume textbook covering most of the period is R. C. K. Ensor, *England 1870–1914* (Oxford, 1936), written by a prominent Edwardian political journalist (1877–1958). Still the best longer general survey is E. Halévy, *History of the English People,* v (2nd ed., 1951), vi (2nd ed., 1952), the work of an anglophile Frenchman (1870–1937). For economic aspects, see W. Ashworth, *An Economic History of England, 1870–1939* (1960), Sir John Clapham, *An Economic History of Modern Britain,* iii (Cambridge, 1938), and, more briefly, R. S. Sayers, *A History of Economic Change 1880–1939* (Oxford, 1967). C. Cross, *The Liberals in Power* (1963) and R. Jenkins, *Mr. Balfour's Poodle* (1954) have the advantages and disadvantages of detachment, their authors not having lived through the period. *Edwardian England,* ed. S. Nowell-Smith (Oxford, 1964) comprises fifteen essays of varying quality on aspects of the time; the best is by Marghanita Laski on 'Domestic Life'. Margot Asquith, *Autobiography* (1920–2), new ed. by M. Bonham Carter (1962); Lord Riddell, *More Pages from My Diary 1908–1914* (1934) and *War Diary* (1933); Sir A. Chamberlain, *Politics from Inside* (1936); Lucy Masterman, *C. F. G. Masterman* (1939); Beatrice Webb, *Our Partnership* (1948) and Margaret I. Cole, ed., *Beatrice Webb's Diaries 1912–1924* (1952); and *Fear God and Dread Nought, The Correspondence of Admiral of the Fleet Lord Fisher of Kilverstone,* ed. A. J. Marder, ii (1956), all contain valuable material from contemporary diaries and/or letters bearing upon social and political life between 1901 and 1918, some of it colourful and idiosyncratic. C. F. G. Masterman, *The Condition of England* (1909), new ed. by J. T. Boulton (1960), is a lively and penetrating contemporary survey by a Liberal politician. Three notable autobiographies by young Edwardians are Vera Brittain, *Testament of Youth* (1933), Katharine Chorley, *Manchester Made Them* (1950), and L. E. Jones, *An Edwardian Youth* (1956). The 1914–18 war foreseen in fiction is usefully surveyed in I. F. Clarke, *Voices Prophesying War 1763–1984* (1966). The war in reality has been described many times by both participants and historians. J. Terraine, *The Western Front* (1964) is a recent British account (unfavourable to Lloyd George); H. W. Baldwin, *World War I* (New York, 1962), gives an American view. *Vain Glory,* ed. G. Chapman (2nd ed., 1968) is a powerful anthology of war experiences. Sir L. Woodward, *Great Britain and the War of 1914–1918* (1967) is comprehensive; P. Guinn, *British Strategy and Politics 1914 to 1918* (Oxford, 1965) is more penetrating within its narrower compass. W. S. Churchill, *The World Crisis* (rev. ed., 1938) is a masterly survey, half history, half self-justification; J. M. Keynes, *Essays in Biography* (1933) contains a useful review of the book. Lord Beaverbrook, *Politicians and the War 1914–1916* (new ed., 1960) and *Men and Power 1917–1918* (new ed., 1956) are

* Place of publication, in this and following reading lists, is London unless otherwise indicated.

depressingly but fascinatingly full of political intrigue. In contrast, R. Pound, *The Lost Generation* (1964) gives a sympathetic account of why so many young men willingly sacrificed their lives. The war on the home front is interestingly described in A. Marwick, *The Deluge, British Society and the First World War* (1965). A lively account of the war's course and effects opens A. J. P. Taylor, *English History 1914–1945* (Oxford, 1965).

Sir E. Grey (Lord Grey of Falloden), *Twenty-Five Years* (1925) introduces British foreign policy up to and into the war years. J. Joll, *Britain and Europe, Pitt to Churchill 1793–1940* (1950) prints some key documents in the history of foreign policy with a penetrating introduction. G. M. Trevelyan, *Grey of Falloden* (1937) is a readable defence, but much detailed work has appeared since Trevelyan wrote. Two notable examples are A. J. Marder, *From the Dreadnought to Scapa Flow, The Royal Navy in the Fisher Era 1904–1919*, I (1961); and G. Monger, *The End of Isolation, British Foreign Policy 1900–1907* (1963). C. H. D. Howard, *Splendid Isolation* (1967) provides a useful short discussion of a key expression. N. Angell, *The Great Illusion* (1909) won a large international audience, but its thesis (that modern war cannot pay) did not prevent recourse to war. This and other left-wing attitudes are discussed indulgently in A. J. P. Taylor, *The Trouble Makers, Dissent over Foreign Policy 1792–1939* (1957). A. J. P. Taylor, *The Struggle for Mastery in Europe 1848–1918* (Oxford 1954) outlines the European background. For the views of the United States ambassador in England before and during the war see B. J. Hendrick, *Life and Letters of Walter H. Page* (1923–5). Barbara W. Tuchman, *August 1914* (1962) concentrates readably upon the onset of war.

Biographies and autobiographies of contemporary British politicians abound, except that there is no satisfactory full-scale life of Lloyd George. C. L. Mowat, *Lloyd George* (1964) is a useful introduction. A. J. P. Taylor, 'Lloyd George, Rise and Fall', separately (1961) and in *Politics in Wartime* (1964) suggests a stimulating interpretation. For a comparison see J. Ehrman, 'Lloyd George and Churchill as War Ministers', *Transactions of the Royal Historical Society*, fifth series, II (1961). R. Lloyd George, *Lloyd George* (1960) contains his son's revelations of the human frailty behind the public man. R. Jenkins, *Asquith* (1964) is indulgent but usually persuasive. K. Young, *Arthur James Balfour* (1963) is also indulgent but less convincing. For a revealing sketch of Balfour (plus good accounts also of Asquith and Joseph Chamberlain) see W. S. Churchill, *Great Contemporaries* (1937). For Churchill himself R. S. Churchill, *Winston S. Churchill*, II (1967) displaces all previous accounts; it is elaborate but satisfying, containing much material not yet absorbed into the textbooks. J. L. Garvin and J. Amery, *Life of Joseph Chamberlain* (1932–68) is conceived on a similar large scale, and is likewise based upon a mass of private papers. For Chamberlain in his provincial setting see D. Read, *The English Provinces 1760–1960* (1964); and for the story of free trade versus protection from the point of view of the Victorian 'apostles of free trade' see D. Read, *Cobden and Bright* (1967). Bonar Law's career has been traced in detail but without adulation in R. Blake, *The Unknown Prime Minister, the Life and Times of Andrew Bonar Law* (1955). There is no satisfactory life of Keir Hardie, but Margaret Cole, *Makers of the Labour Movement* (1948) contains a good sketch.

The history of the Liberal party is outlined in R. B. McCallum, *The Liberal Party from Earl Grey to Asquith* (1963), and its collapse cogently analysed in T. Wilson, *The Downfall of the Liberal Party 1914–1935* (1966). For Liberal ideas see the anthology by A. Bullock and M. Shock, *The Liberal Tradition from Fox to Keynes* (1956). For an anthology of Conservatism see R. J. White, *The Conservative Tradition* (1950). The social history of labour is concisely outlined in G. D. H. Cole and R. Postgate, *The Common People 1746–1946* (3rd ed., 1949). H. Pelling, *The Origins of the Labour Party 1880–1900* (2nd ed., Oxford, 1965); F. Bealey and H. Pelling, *Labour and Politics 1900–1906* (1958); and P. P. Poirier, *The Advent of the Labour Party* (1958) together give a full account of Labour's earliest days. The story is continued in G. D. H. Cole, *History of the Labour Party from 1914* (1948). H. Pelling, *A Short History of the Labour Party* (1961) is *too* short, but his succinct *History of British Trade Unionism* (1963) is more successful. A fuller treatment will be found in H. A. Clegg, Alan Fox, and A. F. Thompson, *A History of Trade Unions Since 1889*, of which only the first volume, covering 1889–1910, has so far appeared (Oxford, 1964). E. H. Phelps Brown and Margaret H. Browne, *A Century of Pay* (1968) is a careful study of earnings, treated internationally, and A. R. Prest, *Consumers' Expenditure in the United Kingdom, 1900–1919* (Cambridge, 1954) examines how these earnings were spent. Dr. Pelling's *Social Geography of British Elections 1885–1910* (1967) is an indispensable guide to constituency politics and his *Popular Politics and Society in Late Victorian Britain* (1968) strays extensively into the Edwardian period. For statistics see D. Butler and Jennie Freeman, *British Political Facts 1900–1967* (2nd ed., 1968). R. Fulford, *Votes for Women* (1957) gives a lively but reliable account, to be supplemented by Constance Rover, *Women's Suffrage and Party Politics in Britain 1866–1914* (1967). D. Mitchell, *Women on the Warpath, the Story of Women in the First World War* (1966) completes the story rather journalistically. For further reading see O. R. McGregor, 'The Social Position of Women in England, 1851–1914, a Bibliography', *British Journal of Sociology*, VI (1955).

Edwardian industrial and social life have been penetratingly surveyed from two different angles in E. H. Phelps Brown, *The Growth of British Industrial Relations, a Study from the Standpoint of 1906–14* (1959); and A. Briggs, *Social Thought and Social Action: A Study of the Work of Seebohm Rowntree 1871–1954* (1961). A number of specialists have contributed chapters on a wide range of industries in Derek H. Aldcroft, ed., *The Development of British Industry and Foreign Investment 1875–1914* (1968). A valuable collection of extracts from contemporary sources is published in W. H. B. Court, *British Economic History 1870–1914: Commentary and Documents* (Cambridge, 1965). The evolution of Liberal social reform has been admirably revealed in B. B. Gilbert, *The Evolution of National Insurance in Great Britain* (1966) and the no less remarkable development in hospital provision in B. Abel-Smith, *The Hospitals, 1800–1949* (1964). W. Ashworth, *The Genesis of Modern British Town Planning* (1954) provides more of an outline of housing developments than its title would suggest. T. H. Marshall, *Social Policy* (1965) links Edwardian social reform with more recent developments, as (with more elaboration but less polish) does M. Bruce, *The Coming of the Welfare State* (3rd ed., 1966). Lord Beveridge, *Power and Influence* (1953) and W. J. Braithwaite, *Lloyd George's Ambulance Waggon* (1957) give the recollections of two key civil servants. The observations of a third will be found in Lord Salter, *Memoirs of a Public Servant* (1961).

B. R. Mitchell and Phyllis Deane, *Abstract of British Historical Statistics* (Cambridge, 1962) is an essential reference book. S. B. Saul, *Studies in British Overseas Trade, 1870–1914* (Liverpool, 1960) has become a standard authority on foreign trade and A. H. Imlah, *Economic Elements in the Pax Britannica* (Cambridge, Mass., 1958) should be consulted about capital exports, as should

C. K. Hobson, *Export of Capital* (1914) and H. Feis, *Europe, the World's Banker, 1870–1914* (1930). Brinley Thomas, *Migration and Economic Growth* (Cambridge, 1954) deals with the effects of transatlantic migration from the United Kingdom and A. K. Cairncross, *Home and Foreign Investment, 1870–1913* (Cambridge, 1953) is one of the most penetrating studies of the period.

On Ireland N. Mansergh, *The Irish Question 1840–1921* (1965) is a shrewd introduction. F. S. L. Lyons, *John Dillon* (1968) sees the scene from an Irish viewpoint in the light of much new material. A. T. Q. Stewart, *The Ulster Crisis* (1967) is a readable synthesis. The Edwardian empire is discussed with polish and penetration in W. K. Hancock, *Survey of British Commonwealth Affairs*, vol. II, pt. I (Oxford, 1942), ch. i. A. P. Thornton, *The Imperial Idea and Its Enemies* (1959) is stimulating. On South Africa G. B. Pyrah, *Imperial Policy and South Africa 1902–10* (Oxford, 1955) is comprehensive; and W. K. Hancock, *Smuts, the Sanguine Years 1870–1919* (1962) is indispensable. On India R. J. Moore, *Liberalism and Indian Politics 1872–1922* (1966) is a good introduction.

Links between Edwardian politics and journalism are elaborately explored in R. Pound and G. Harmsworth, *Northcliffe* (1959), and in A. M. Gollin, '*The Observer*' *and J. L. Garvin 1908–1914* (1960). For Liberal journalism see J. L. Hammond, *C. P. Scott of the 'Manchester Guardian'* (1934). A good selection of *Punch* cartoons for 1892–1914, plus a commentary, can be found in C. L. Graves, *Mr. Punch's History of Modern England* (n.d.), vol. IV. The man who gave his name to the age is rather ponderously described in P. Magnus, *King Edward the Seventh* (1964). His successor is more acutely portrayed in H. Nicolson, *King George the Fifth* (1952).

Since this bibliography was compiled in 1969, two further books have appeared which are of particular relevance to chapter 2. They are: Derek H. Aldcroft and Harry W. Richardson, *The British Economy 1870–1939* (1969), which also includes a guide to statistical sources and a bibliographical survey, and Robert Roberts, *The Classic Slum* (Manchester, 1971), which provides some very convincing recollections of life in a poor quarter of Salford before 1914.

3
Historiography

RICHARD LANGHORNE

The writing of history suffered the same dislocations and distortions as other human activities during the First World War, and the school of history which devoted itself to war propaganda is not worthy of the same attention as the very important expansion which occurred between about 1890 and 1914. The period is characterized by the appearance of an historiography which would now be recognized as familiar and valid, and by the prosecution of a vigorous debate on the nature of history itself. There is a surprisingly modern ring about this discussion and to those who are acquainted with similar more recent disputations, there is a strong sense of *déjà vue*.

The two developments were connected in that the very appearance of historical writing of an academic kind provoked the accusation that history was thereby debarred from seeking the appreciation of ordinary men, as it was also debarred, theoretically at least, from becoming the vehicle of political prejudice. It must therefore be a purely intellectual discipline, without point, unless all the research that was being undertaken in the records could in the end produce universal historical truths, comparable to the certainties that science—particularly biological science—was then thought to be establishing. Such a desire to describe human society and its past in analogies derived from the natural sciences was based upon a general acceptance of the laws of Newtonian physics and had been accelerated by the advance of Darwinism in the 1860s.

The intellectual revolution of the 1890s seemed to be trying to dislodge this positivist approach and to restore a rational, intellectual attitude to problems which had been shelved, because thinkers were resigned to the view that the accumulation of factual knowledge must of itself provide solutions. The expectation of what could be verifiably known was inevitably reduced, as new factors were admitted, particularly the psychological explanations of motive which flowed from the work of Freud, but areas of inquiry hitherto apparently locked in the grip of the positivist method were now released and the mind was free to speculate, to imagine and to create. The intellectual approach was restored, therefore, but by new means of inquiry; indeed, so alien were they to the existing intellectual framework that the change has sometimes confusingly been called anti-intellectualism. It is not surprising to find, in this atmosphere, that Wilhelm Dilthey (1833–1911), rooted in the Enlightenment, was hailed as a necessary antidote to the school of von Ranke, and that Benedetto Croce (1866–1952) was creating out of the work of Marx, Vico, and Hegel an independent view of history—as much of its content as of its methodology. Historians began to search for a way of looking at their subject which could insist upon the use of the scientific method, and admit the possibilities of insight drawn from novel sources: its claims could be reduced, while its range was widened.

Some attacks upon positivist history went too far, and academic history, far from succumbing, flourished. Scientific method has become indispensable, but it has become the handmaiden of men who believe in using the conclusions and methods of the social studies, as well as psychology, and who believe that there are practical lessons to be learnt from the knowledge of things, as von Ranke said, *Wie es eigentlich gewesen ist.*

However, the effect of the German school in England had been most marked. And because the Germans were interested in tracing the common origins of the Teutonic peoples, the first English historians to adopt the exact methodology and supposed impartiality of their continental colleagues tended to concentrate on the medieval period. They also shared a predilection for political history— 'History is past politics,' declared Freeman, 'and politics is present history'—and this view was the more likely to be taken, given that the sources which were becoming available were of an almost solely political kind. Stubbs's attitude to Parliament may be traced as much to the fact that he was largely dependent upon the Parliament Roll, as to the obvious primacy of the House of Commons in the 1860s and '70s. The construction of an accurate political narrative was the aim of William Stubbs (1825–1901), E. A. Freeman (1823–1892), and S. R. Gardiner (1829–1902); and it was significant that the authors of the *Constitutional History of Mediaeval England*, the *History of the Norman Conquest*, and the *History of the Great Civil War*, all used newly available resources, and all became university professors. The day of the private scholar was soon to be over; narrative histories even by academic historians were soon to come under a cloud.

The foundation of the *English Historical Review* in 1886 brought into being the third of the three great European journals of history, and thus the possibility of a monographic approach to the presentation of the results of historical research. The *Historische Zeitschrift* was founded nearly thirty years earlier, as was fitting in the country which had pioneered the new history, and its prospectus was revealing:

This periodical should be, above all, a scientific one. Its first task should, therefore, be to represent the true methods of historical research and to point out deviations therefrom. On this basis we plan a historical periodical not an antiquarian or a political one.[1]

In 1876, the foundation of the *Revue Historique* by Gabriel Monod (1844–1912) brought another prospectus, which echoed the words of von Sybel:

The *Revue* will accept only original contributions, based on original sources, which will enrich science either with their basic research, or with the results of their conclusions; but, while we demand from our contributors strictly scientific methods of exposition, with each assertion accompanied by proof by source references and quotations, while we severely exclude vague generalities and rhetoric, we shall preserve in the *Revue Historique*, that literary quality which scholars as well as French readers value so highly.[2]

By 1886, the *English Historical Review* had no need in its prospectus to make claims for its insistence upon exactitude and correct method. It had to decide what sort of history would be noticed, and disclaim any intention of being controversial—a disclaimer that would have seemed odd to Macaulay or Carlyle. But Mandell Creighton's (1843–1901) view of history itself is interesting: for by 1886 a paradox was becoming noticeable. History was in retreat from controversial politics, retiring to an academic ivory tower, but yet rising to a position of enormous esteem. From the later nineteenth century, the western world has lived in a supremely historical age, from which it is only now perhaps emerging into a new all-embracing culture of sociology. Lord Acton (1834–1902) never ceased to express his belief in 'historical thinking', and the prospectus of the *English Historical Review* took a similar line:

We believe that history, in an even greater degree than its votaries have as yet generally recognised is the central study among human studies, capable of enriching and illuminating all the rest. And this is one of the reasons why we desire, while pursuing it for its sake in a calm and scientific spirit, to make this review so far as possible a means of interesting thinking men in historical study, of accustoming them to its methods of inquiry and of showing them how to appropriate its large results.[3]

Before long it was clear that, as one historian has remarked, 'a tap on the knuckles in the *English Historical Review* came to be feared more than a cudgel blow on the head in the *Edinburgh*, or the *Quarterly*'.[4] The tap would be for an error in exactitude, never an expression of political *parti pris*.

The opportunity to write monographs, to approach the subject thematically, coincided with the availability in the Public Record Office of large new sources, throwing light on subjects other than the progress of politics. Into this world came Tout, Tait, and Maitland, and their history was the history of the law and of institutions. The great palaeographer A. G. Little (1863–1945) took his skills to Owens College in Manchester, where James Tait (1863–1944) and T. F. Tout (1855–1929) had already arrived respectively in 1887 and 1890. In Oxford, J. H. Round (1854–1928) pursued his genealogical studies, and in Cambridge F. W. Maitland (1850–1906), perhaps the foremost historian of the period, wrote beautifully and brilliantly about the history of English law in the Middle Ages. The efforts of the Manchester school, as it became known, and of its allies in other places, represent a remarkable redirection of research and amount to a marvellously successful anticipation of the work of Sir Lewis Namier (1888–1960), but in the earlier periods of British history. The work that was done and the devotion of its authors acquired an international reputation, and the history of the Manchester school was recognizably history of a modern kind. Unmoved by contemporary political divisions, wedded to the scientific method, cognizant of much wider fields than the exercise of political power, this was academic history for academic historians and it helped to provoke the debate mentioned at the outset.

One of the foremost historical publicists of the later nineteenth century was surely Lord Acton. A fascinating and many-sided figure, he was not typical of any school of history, despite his strong connections with the German tradition. Acton was a liberal Roman Catholic, whose greatest mentor had been Dr. Döllinger. He had acquired a great admiration for von Ranke, which did not take the form, as it did in his German successors, of a commitment to exact impartiality alone. Von Ranke had urged this method certainly, but he had also been himself inspired by preconceived convictions which contrary evidence did not dislodge. There were two contradictions in Acton, the second more apparent than real. His conviction that history showed progress towards general freedom of conscience, if not subject to historical evidence, nearly brought about a personal tragedy when confronted by the increasing absolutism of the church in the 1860s and '70s. It was an unhappy time for liberal churchmen. Secondly, he believed that history should be wholly impartial, studied in the spirit of the strictest scholarship. When this had been pursued diligently enough, all would be known, and then, apparently paradoxically, the impartial historian must proceed to severely moral judgements of the most damning kind—judgements which Acton had no hesitation in describing as sentences.

For all his readiness to amass facts and impartiality in the verification of them—for his predecessors as much as for the past [5]—Acton's idea of completing his evidence often sounds more like back-stairs gossip than the bubbling of a laboratory test tube. He recognized that his desire to judge was not the general view:

. . . the weight of opinion is against me when I exhort you never to debase the moral currency or to lower the standard of rectitude, but to try others by the final maxim that governs your own lives, and to suffer no man and no cause to escape the undying penalty which history has the power to inflict on wrong.[6]

He anticipated that others would continue it nevertheless: thus on the French Revolution: 'all will be known that ever can be known. . . . In that golden age historians will be sincere, and our history certain. The worst will be known and then sentence need not be deferred.'[7] This expectation was to be proved as misplaced as his determined clinging to an almost Whig view of history which saw a continuous pattern of progress—in his case the emergence of freedom of conscience.

The combination of rigorous impartiality based on complete evidence and his desire to conceive of long-term historical developments produced both his own relative silence, and the enterprise for which he is perhaps most famous. The *Cambridge Modern History* was published between 1902 and 1910 and Acton's instruction to the contributors shows him as an historicist depending upon the results of collaborative scientific history.

In our own time, within the last few years, most of the official collections in Europe have been made public, and nearly all the evidence that will ever appear is accessible now.

As archives are meant to be explored and are not meant to be printed, we approach the final stage in the conditions of historical learning. The long conspiracy against the knowledge of truth has been practically abandoned, and competing scholars all over the civilised world are taking advantage of the change. . . . The recent past contains the key to the present time. All forms of thought that influence it came before us in their turn, and we have to describe the ruling currents, to interpret the sovereign forces, that still govern and divide the world. . . .[8]

One of the earlier scientific historians, Fustel de Coulanges, declared that 'Patriotism is a virtue and history a science, and the two should not be confounded'[9], and although he was sensitive enough to appreciate that there could be no direct parallel with the natural sciences, he was followed by an increasingly vocal group. Frederick York Powell (1850–1904), Regius Professor of History in Oxford, wrote towards the end of the century that 'style and the needs of a popular audience have no more to do with history than with law or astronomy. . . . History, then . . . is a science; it must be worked on scientific methods or it becomes worthless gossip.' He actually took this view so far as to believe that historians 'must be employed by the State to work at the mass of materials that luckily exists for the study of national history. They must study and give us their results.'[10]

In 1902, when J. B. Bury (1861–1927) succeeded Acton in the Cambridge chair, he delivered an inaugural lecture on 'The Science of History', in which he insisted that, even though there had been a great advance in the last three generations of the nineteenth century, 'It has not yet become superfluous to insist that history is a science no less and no more; and some who admit it theoretically hesitate to enforce the consequences it involves'.[11] But it was superfluous; not because the doctrine was widely accepted, but because it was becoming widely rejected. For example, in 1907 A. F. Pollard (1869–1948) wrote in *Factors in Modern History* that:

history is not an exact science. Nothing that is real and concrete can be exact. Mathematics are exact, but only because they deal with abstractions. Two may be equal to two in arithmetic, but they are generally unequal in real life; no two men are exactly equal to two other men.[12]

C. H. Firth (1857–1936), writing in 1904, discussed the question differently and concluded that the collection of historical knowledge was a science, although the results could not be 'exact and certain', and its representation an art. But he was more impressed with the limitations of the historian.

Everywhere . . . the historian is made conscious of the limitations of his own knowledge about the past, and the limitations of men's possible knowledge. He feels that he moves in a little circle of light, seeing as far as his little candle throws its beams; and beyond that comes darkness.

Nor was this all. He was conscious also of the changing outline of the past as it became more remote, and the effect that this had on the questions that historians asked. Every age 'wants history written over again to suit itself'.[13]

These reactions were not alone. The side of Lord Acton which had demanded broad patterns and stern judgement was, though inherited from the past, something of a reaction, and the disturbing effects of academic, monographic history were to produce objections from at least two other quarters. There were those who objected to a practice of history which was neither genial nor useful, and those who objected because it concentrated too heavily upon political or quasi-political factors.

If Acton had wanted to use the new accuracy of history as a scourge, G. M. Trevelyan (1876–1961), an undergraduate at Cambridge while Acton was Regius Professor, reacted against both the emphasis on specialism and the desire to make strict judgements. He believed that men should be encouraged to learn the lessons of the past from histories in which the sympathy of the author and his polished prose style would combine to produce the after-effects of a sunlit evening. The result was a lifetime of historical acclaim and an ever-growing public regard for a thoroughly good and nice man. It has not always been historians, however, so much as the general public who have felt the charm of Trevelyan. For that public, such a wholesale reaction against the savagery of Macaulay or Acton, such a concern to maintain the readability of a Sir Walter Scott, produced history in which it is all too easy to wallow; history which, like its author, retired from academic life in 1903. By the time Trevelyan returned to Cambridge in 1928, it had established itself as an offshoot, like a Cornish branch line, carrying holiday traffic through pleasant scenery to agreeable resorts on the coast.

He was always at his best—and his best was very good indeed—when his sympathies were fully engaged by a drama, such as the struggle between Crown and Parliament during the seventeenth century or Garibaldi's career in Italy.[14] It was work of this kind which puts Trevelyan into the category so well defined by Sir Charles Firth:

Only those endure in which the matter is so solid and the form so perfect and both so harmoniously united, that they still satisfy and charm, and seem to triumph over time. Only those endure in which the individuality of the writer is so impressed upon the book that it seems 'to embalm and treasure the precious lifeblood of a master spirit', and becomes part of literature.[15]

Although he espoused the cause of social history, Trevelyan was fundamentally the heir of historians who had chronicled the political battle of the past: his concern with social history arose out of his great ability to re-people places with their former inhabitants. For this he felt a romantic excitement which emerges well from this passage:

The garden front of St. John's College, Oxford is beautiful to everyone; but for the lover of history its outward charm is blent with the intimate feelings of his own mind, with images of that same college as it was during the great civil war. Given over to the use of a Court whose days of royalty were numbered, its walks and quadrangles were filled as the end came near, with men and women learning to accept sorrow as their lot through life, the ambitious abandoning hope of power, the wealthy hardening themselves to accept poverty, those who loved England preparing to sail for foreign shores, and lovers to be parted for ever. . . .[16]

But it is not social history, as it was then becoming understood; nor was it influenced by skills learned or borrowed from other disciplines in the social sciences.

In 1904 (revised 1913), Trevelyan published an essay on history entitled 'Clio, a Muse', which had originally appeared in the *Independent Review*, as an attack on Bury's 1902 lecture 'The Science of History'. It was perhaps the most extreme reaction to scientific history to be produced, more extreme than the meticulous practice of its author suggests his real views to have been. Not Trevelyan's greatest work, it nevertheless contains many excellent observations —such as this definition of an historian: 'He will give the best interpretation who, having discovered and weighed all the important evidence available, has the largest grasp of intellect, the warmest human sympathy, the highest imaginative powers.'[17]

'Clio' also indicates that if others were not prepared to be polemical about it, historians of whom Seeley and Stubbs had so deeply disapproved were nevertheless again receiving attention. 'When no less an authority than Professor Firth thinks it worthwhile to edit Macaulay; when Mr. Gooch can give an admirable appreciation of Carlyle, times are evidently changing.'[18] He noted also that history had now become an academic discipline, threatening even the classics for primacy at Oxford and Cambridge, and showed a solicitude for the overworked dons of the day which must make their successors smile.

But, withal, he was not optimistic. However many men were now taking the Historical Tripos (established in 1873), history had lost its place as part of the national literature, and had lost its influence over the 'thought and feeling of the rising generation'. He thought that the change had come about because history itself had become the preserve of the specialist, dedicated to the use of the scientific method—'a sacred thing pinnacled afar on frozen heights of science, not to be approached save after a long novitiate'.[19] 'The qualities of mind and heart' had been driven out by German methodology and 'an attempt has been made to drill us into so many Potsdam guards of learning'.[20] Any other scientific aspect in history than that of accumulating and verifying facts, he denied, and while it is possible to feel the greatest sympathy for his refutation of the sillier claims that were made for scientific history, it is difficult to accept that historians should ignore the work of colleagues in other fields and regard highly only history that is 'delightful to read'. 'To read sustained and magnificent historical narrative educates the mind and character; some, even whose natures craving the definite, seldom respond to poetry, find in such writing the highest pleasure they know.'[21] But they may, if Trevelyan's rules are applied, be reading the work of a man who prefers to gain the feel of a period from its literature, rather than from the work of historians who have been concerned with more than just the literate or with those who have left at least a portrait behind them. 'Trevelyan', J. R. Hale has remarked, 'will remain a great name in the history of English historiography for his personality, his craftsmanship, and his success, but probably no famous historian has made a smaller contribution to the history of his subject'.[22]

The growth of a genuine economic and social history was strangely foreshadowed in the mid-nineteenth century by Henry Thomas Buckle, an historian who must have been more abused than almost any other, particularly from the pulpit. Buckle was a scientific historian who believed its most extreme form—all could be explained when all was known. But, alas, all around him quite unqualified men were working as historians and 'the most celebrated historians are manifestly inferior to the most successful cultivators of physical science'.[23] But this was not solely because historians had failed to recognize that they must elucidate the principles which underlay the development of civilization, although sadly, this was true, but because they failed to deal with the mainsprings of human action: climate, geography, and diet, and the shaping of men in the mass. If only the general laws which governed the operation of these factors could be discovered, then mankind could be helped to progress further. Buckle was clumsy and excited terrible rejoinders, but his theories now have a distinctly familiar ring, particularly when he regretted the appearance of two cultures and demanded the association of history with the social sciences. His way with statistics was alarmingly erratic, but it was nevertheless prophetic.

The view of history which would proceed from the revelations of the social sciences to the enunciation of general laws suffered the same fate that attended similar claims made once for political history. But in 1900 Henri Berr (1863–1954) founded in Paris a *Revue de Synthèse Historique*, in whose introductory prospectus may be found a last expression of such views. On historical study with social psychology, sociology, ethnology, anthropology depended 'not only our understanding of the past but our control of the future also'. Therefore 'let no one fear a return of the philosophy of history'.[24]

More fruitful developments were on the way however. If Croce's essay (1893) on history as an art, and Trevelyan's pleas for the Muse of history were not to achieve a great effect, the emergence in Germany of men such as Karl Lamprecht (1856–1915) and Dilthey, brought about both an effective attack upon the idea that history could be thought of as a physical science, ably assisted by Heinrich Rickert's (1863–1936) analysis of the logical and methodological differences between history and the natural sciences, and indicated something of the way history should move in relation to the social sciences—particularly psychology. Lamprecht had wanted a new sort of *Kulturgeschichte* which would bring socio-psychic methods to bear upon the collective units of history—societies or classes, and Dilthey insisted as Nietzsche had done in his essay of 1874,[25] that the historian must be psychologically involved in order to obtain an understanding of the past. He also sought to find a new way of describing the psychological complications of the task undertaken by individual historians when they interpreted the past—no matter of mere historical empiricism.

This development found its loudest echo in the United States, in the 'New History' of James Harvey Robinson (1863–1948) and Charles A. Beard (1874–1948), where it had in any case received the stimulus of a local precursor, F. J. Turner (1861–1932). 'History', he had declared, 'is all the remains that have come down to us from the past, studied with all the critical and interpretative power that the present can bring to the task.'[26] His own work on the American frontier, and C. A. Beard's on an economic interpretation of the Constitution, both broke new ground and revealed a profound dissatisfaction with the traditional political historiography. Robinson published his collection of essays, *The New History*, in 1912 and in them pleaded for a history which paid

attention to intellectual and social factors. 'It has,' he wrote in the
Preface to *The Development of Modern Europe*,

been a common defect in our historical manuals that however satisfactorily they have dealt with more or less remote periods, they have
ordinarily failed to connect the past with the present. And teachers still
pay a mysterious respect to the memory of Datis and Artaphernes which
they deny to gentlemen in frock coats, like Gladstone and Gambetta.[27]

This was a demand for history which was nearly contemporary,
which would be immediately useful, history which should add to
the traditional path of political development, by showing clearly
the social and intellectual trends of a particular period. In a Preface
to *An Introduction to the History of Western Europe*, Robinson and
Beard declared, what would now be regarded as essential, that
'more fundamental economic matters have been generously treated
—the Industrial revolution, commerce and colonies, the internal
reforms of the European states, even the advance of science have
all, so far as is possible been given their just due'.[28]

In the same year as *The New History*, the first major work of the
greatest of all historians who were the product of these years of
debate and changing historical methods was published in England.
A combination of literary ability, the widest sympathy and imagination, and a conviction that the sociological methods of the German
economic historians were right and necessary, produced an economic
historian who could write this of history: 'Whatever else the world
may contain man's relations with nature, his commerce with his
fellows, and the convictions, aspirations and emotions composing
his inner life, are for us, as for the poet, its capital constituents.'[29]
R. H. Tawney's (1880–1962) *The Agrarian Problem of the Sixteenth
Century* (1912), expressed the most modern kind of research leading
to a new conclusion, in prose which was as ardent as the author's
sympathy with the men—especially the underprivileged men—of
the sixteenth century. The years between 1540 and 1640 have come
in recent times to be called 'Tawney's century', and the respect
which he inspired in others came to be matched by their respect
for a mind and personality which found it impossible to turn
critics into enemies. Most of his work falls outside the scope of this
study, but in *The Agrarian Problem* can be seen two strands in
previous British historiography. The kind of questions that Tawney
asked echoed Maitland's sociological approach to the history of
law, and the methods of work employed by the Webbs (S. Webb,
1859–1947, and Beatrice Webb, 1858–1943), and, later, the Ham-

monds (J. Hammond, 1872–1949), in the service of social reform, strongly influenced Tawney, the social historian. It is therefore impossible to do more than note that *The Agrarian Problem* was the first of a series of studies by Tawney to have a galvanizing effect on whatever area of history he chose to take up. It seems to be the answer to Trevelyan, to Robinson, to Dilthey and Lamprecht, to Bury, if not to Acton; it seems to have been the product of all the theorizing and research which particularly mark the last generations of the nineteenth century, gathered up into history which was academic yet literary, scholarly yet readable, and instinct with the skills and sympathies of the social sciences. Much history from the end of the First World War until recent times was going to revolve round whichever controversy Tawney had most recently stimulated into life, and history after the First World War entered upon a great and fruitful period.

NOTES

[1] H. von Sybel, *Vorwort, Historische Zeitschrift* (1859).

[2] G. Monod and G. Fagniez, *Avant-propos, Revue Historique* (1876).

[3] M. Creighton, Prefatory Note, *English Historical Review* (1886).

[4] J. R. Hale, *The Evolution of British Historiography* (1967), 58.

[5] 'Teach to look behind historians, especially famous historians', quoted in H. Butterfield, *Man on his Past* (1955), 64.

[6] Lord Acton, *Inaugural Lecture* (Cambridge, 1895).

[7] Quoted in J. R. Hale, *British Historiography*, 70.

[8] Lord Acton, 'Letter to the Contributors to the *Cambridge Modern History*', in *Lectures in Modern History* (1952), 315–18.

[9] Quoted in F. Stern, *Varieties of History* (1957), 178

[10] F. York Powell, 'A General Survey of Modern History', printed in O. Elton, *Frederick York Powell* (1906), II. 1, 12.

[11] J. B. Bury, *Inaugural Lecture* (Cambridge, 1902). But see the qualification of this view in the Preface to his *Life of St. Patrick* (1905).

[12] A. F. Pollard, *Factors in Modern History* (1907), 35–6.

[13] C. H. Firth, *A Plea for the Historical Teaching of History* (1904), 5–10.

[14] G. M. Trevelyan, *England under the Stuarts* (1904); *Garibaldi's Defence of the Roman Republic* (1911).

[15] Firth, *Historical Teaching of History*, 10.

[16] G. M. Trevelyan, *Clio, a Muse, and other Essays* (1913), 156–7.

[17] Ibid. 144–5.

[18] Ibid. 141.

[19] Ibid. 175.

[20] Ibid. 142.

[21] Ibid. 176.

[22] Hale, *British Historiography*, 72.

[23] H. T. Buckle, *History of Civilisation*, I (1857).

[24] H. Berr, '*Sur Notre Programme*', *Revue de synthèse historique*, I (1900).

[25] F. Nietzsche, *The Use and Disadvantage of History* (trans. 1957).

[26] F. J. Turner, 'The Significance of History', in *The Early Writings of Frederick Jackson Turner* (1938), 43–67.

[27] J. H. Robinson and C. A. Beard, Preface, *The Development of Modern Europe*, I (1907).

[28] Robinson and Beard, Preface, *An Introduction to the History of Western Europe*, I (1902).

[29] R. H. Tawney, *Social History and Literature*, rev. ed. (1958), 5.

FOR FURTHER READING

Although historiographical works are numerous, there are relatively few which discuss this particular period. The most recent book to be published which contains relevant material is Arthur Marwick, *The Nature of History* (1970). It is not a profound work, but gives information clearly, and contains a good bibliography. *The Varieties of History: Voltaire to the Present*, ed. Fritz Stern (1957), is an excellent and most useful survey, containing both readings and commentary. Other works which might be helpful are J. R. Hale, *The Evolution of British Historiography: From Bacon to Namier* (1967); R. Hofstadter, *The Progressive Historians: Turner, Beard, Parrington* (1969); and Sir Herbert Butterfield, *Man on his Past: The Study of the History of Historical Writings* (Cambridge, 1955).

4
Social Thought in Britain

A. M. QUINTON

Five main streams of articulate social and political doctrine, which can be discerned in the Victorian period, still retained some vitality at the beginning of the new century. Each is associated with some large and persistent intellectual interest: one with the study of law and history, two with the main competing varieties of general philosophy, one with literature and art, and one with science, particularly biological science. Each stream persisted in the social thinking of the period between the death of Queen Victoria and the outbreak of the First World War. The social thought of this age is not wholly reducible in its content to these contributory factors, but a surprisingly large amount of what appears most original and characteristic in it can be understood as the result of combining them in varying degrees. Certainly the more pedestrian and forgettable productions of the Edwardian era in this domain can be seen as the direct continuation of earlier styles of thought.

Traditionalism

There is, first of all, the kind of conservative traditionalism whose leading Victorian exponents were Sir Henry Maine and Sir Fitzjames Stephen. In his *Ancient Law* (1861) Maine had insisted on the essentially customary and habitual nature of law throughout much the greater part of human history. In *Popular Government* (1884) he drew attention to the precariousness of democracy and to the dangers of the Hobbesian arrogation of state power, unrestrained by law because the creator of it, that was assumed by Benthamite liberals and progressives. Maine brought to bear on reformism a sense of its historical peculiarity and unprecedentedness. Fitzjames Stephen attacked it more directly and with its own weapons. *Liberty, Equality and Fraternity* (1873) is a criticism of the political doctrines of Mill, resting on a version of the principle that expediency is the touchstone of social action and institutions, which is more forthright and less qualified than Mill's own. There was also W. E. H. Lecky (1838–1903), whose *Democracy and Liberty* (1896) provided a full and melancholy elaboration of that disquiet about the likelihood in fully democratic states of a tyranny of the majority which had been voiced by Mill himself, the chief Victorian prophet of liberal democracy.

There was no straightforwardly conservative writer in the period from 1900 to 1914 whose thought achieved the kind of seriousness and thoroughness to be found in these three Victorian defenders of the established order. The most active polemicist for the traditional verities, in religion as well as in politics and social policy, was W. H. Mallock (1849–1929). At the age of twenty-seven Mallock had achieved notoriety with the publication of *The New Republic* (1876), a brilliant satirical dialogue in which thinly disguised representations of leading figures of the Victorian intellectual scene, such as Jowett, Arnold, Ruskin, and Pater were allowed to express themselves in a characteristic way. Mallock never recovered the wit and vivacity of this early work. In our period he was mainly active as a critic of socialism. He attempted to justify an élite by arguments of an economic order. Where Lecky had defended aristocracy as a safeguard for freedom, Mallock, true to the generally plutocratic spirit of his age, as symbolized by the new King's social circle of South African millionaires, defended an aristocracy of wealth on the ground that the differential rewards of the capitalist economy corresponded to the extent of the contributions made by their recipients to economic progress. In his *Critical Examination of Socialism* (1909) Mallock in effect stood Marx's labour theory of value on its head by contending that the productivity of pure labour power is not notably greater in an industrial society than it is in any more primitive economic system. The massive increase in productivity brought about by industrialism must be attributed to new instruments and methods of production which are the work of a small minority of people, the 'inventive classes', who are endowed with the relevant skill and energy. In Mallock's opinion Marx was a sentimentalist who tried to obscure the realities of economics by Teutonic bluster. The Fabians at least recognized differences of ability, but absurdly envisaged a social system devoid of the incentives without which that ability would not be put to effective use. Mallock condemned the provision of equal opportunities as well as the more visionary project of equal rewards. To provide the same facilities for advancement to all is inevitably wasteful, he said, since it involves social expenditure on the untalented majority who are unlikely to provide any compensating return for what has been lavished on them.

Mallock's crude defence of the capitalist mode of distributing wealth called forth an astringent criticism from George Bernard

Shaw (1856–1950): *Socialism and Superior Brains* (1910). Shaw
exploited an obviously weak point in Mallock's argument. It is not,
after all, those who invent new methods of production who usually
reap the financial reward for them, but rather the skilled financiers
who know how to take competitive advantage of them. *Laissez-faire*
economic theory, the most intellectually elaborate form of capitalist
apologetic, does not pretend that either invention or effort secures
the main reward: the profits of the entrepreneur are conceived by it
as a return for the taking of risks. More generally, Shaw found
morally objectionable the idea that individuals who have benefited
from natural inequalities in the distribution of talent should try to
monopolize the productive yield of their chance good fortune.
What economists call the rent of ability is no more imprescriptible
a natural right than the rent of land.

Mallock's memoirs make it clear that he was a reactionary snob
and there is an incongruity between this social attitude, which seeks
to defend the claims of long possession, however acquired and maintained, and the materially meritocratic point of view that underlies
his critique of socialism.

There is a less improvised and altogether more genuine air about
the defence of tradition to be found in the *Conservatism* (1912) of
Lord Hugh Cecil (1869–1956). He starts from the fact that men have
a natural sentiment of hostility to large and sudden changes: we
love the familiar and distrust the unknown. But to favour prudence
is not to endorse the ossification of imperial China. Conservatism
as a political doctrine is not opposed to change as such, only to the
kind of abrupt and inorganic change that, intoxicated by the delightful prospect of some innovation, fails to consider its less
obvious side-effects. Cecil's hero is naturally Burke, with his commitment to continuity and establishment in religion, law, property,
and the hierarchy of social stations. He felt a particular hostility to
the renegade conservative Sir Robert Peel, whom he regarded as an
opportunist administrator, devoid of general ideas and untouched
by any sense of the history of the country he so fatefully changed,
disturbing its religion by emancipating the Catholics and its general
social balance by repealing the Corn Laws. Imperialism, defined
rather nebulously as 'a feeling for the greatness of the country and
for that unity which makes its greatness', a sentiment that would
not seem to require colonial expansion to nourish it, is a third element in modern conservatism, in addition to men's instinctive suspicion of change and Toryism proper, 'the reverence for religion
and authority'. It was the French Revolution and the conflict of

Pitt and Fox that added this new element to conservatism. In the eighteenth century it was Chatham, the Whig, who created a British empire overseas and not the Tory Burke. Modern conservatism, for Cecil, was produced by the challenge of Jacobism. He saw the socialism of his age as a revived Jacobism and held its containment to be the main task of conservatism in the coming age.

An Anticipation of Fascism

Mallock's conservatism was that of the suburban villa and to that extent more novel than Cecil's which was rather that of the country house. But both were somewhat conventional prolongations of existing styles of thought. Before 1914, however, the first stirrings can be discerned of a harsher and more militant style of right-wing social theory. In terms of practical politics British Fascism never became more than a comparatively minor problem of public hygiene, an eruption of anti-Semitic hooliganism by means of which an upper-class outcast fed his wounded vanity. But its literary effects have been considerable. In different ways many of the leading imaginative writers of the period between the wars inclined towards Fascism or at least to a considerably more ruthless and unmitigated kind of authoritarianism than anything envisaged by traditional conservatives. Ezra Pound (b. 1885) lauded Mussolini (1883–1945) and Wyndham Lewis wrote in praise of Hitler (1889–1945). T. S. Eliot (1888–1965), in a more defeated and melancholy way, upbraided his juniors for their animus against the Fascist dictators of Europe whom he saw, with many conservatives, as the first line of defence against Bolshevism. W. B. Yeats (1865–1939) had a militant predilection for aristocracy in its most hierarchical form.

This whole style of thought has one of its main sources in that still insufficiently appreciated figure T. E. Hulme (1883–1917), who was killed in action in France and whose ideas had been fully formed and expressed by the outbreak of war. Hulme's influence, which was very large considering the small scale and fragmentary form of his writings, would appear to rest on three factors: his extremely forceful personality, impressed on the circle of his acquaintances by such things as the knuckle-duster made for him by the sculptor Gaudier-Brzeska, the irresistible lucidity of his style, and the fact that, for all their fragmentariness, his ideas did form a system with a broadly philosophical basis and with a host of significant applications to literature and art as well as in the field of social and political theory.

The firmness and clarity of Hulme's style does not conceal the fact that his ideas are often the result of incongruous borrowings. Henri Bergson's (1859–1941) scepticism about the intellect and Georges Sorel's (1847–1922) mythology of violence consort uneasily with a conviction derived from G. E. Moore (1873–1958) and Husserl about the absolute and objective character of value. But Hulme's fundamental principle is clear enough. He opts for a view of man which he describes as religious, in a highly non-devotional sense of the word, which insists on the finite and imperfect nature of human beings, as against the progressive, optimistic 'humanism' which believes that man is the measure of all things and that his eventual achievement of perfection is inevitable. In opposition to this kind of liberal Utopianism, Hulme maintains that men must acknowledge and be guided by values that are external to themselves and are not rooted merely in the desires they happen to have. This is as much the basis of his preference for an authoritarian organization of society as of his preference for classical, regulated, de-anthropomorphized art. Hulme's scattered writings do not descend to details and what he is opposed to is much more evident than what he would put in its place. But some form of élitism is plainly implied, one based on the recognition that some men have a clearer perception of absolute value and of the distance human achievements fall short of it than others, and, furthermore, that some men are distinguishable amid the general mass by reason of their capacity for heroic virtue, are relatively free from bondage to self-regarding desire. It is this latter, Sorelian, element that together with his personal aggressiveness gives some colour to the retrospective description of Hulme as a Fascist. But most of the characteristic features of Fascism are missing from his thought. He says nothing in support of semi-divine leaders, the deification of the nation-state, or militarily organized mass movements, and he left anti-Semitism to Belloc. Hulme's pessimism about automatic progress was timely. To many people the war in which he died was more than sufficient confirmation of it. Several of the survivors of the small circle of gifted people in which he was a dominating figure just before 1914, more especially Pound and Wyndham Lewis, may be seen as his disciples.

The Liberal Tradition

In 1900 Leslie Stephen (1832–1904) published his three-volume study *The English Utilitarians* and in the same year Henry Sidgwick (1838–1900), the last major figure in the direct utilitarian tradition stemming from Bentham, died. The political writings of John Stuart Mill, the most complex and many-sided of the utilitarians, formed then, as in a way they still do, the authoritative defence of democratic liberalism, the second stream of Victorian doctrine persisting into the new century. But in politics Mill's application of utilitarian principles, which was only moderately obstructed by his cultivated distaste for the cruder aspects of Benthamism, was hesitant and qualified. In the final result Mill was more a Whig in the tradition of Locke than a strict utilitarian like his father, James Mill, or Bentham. James Mill had converted Bentham from the idea that rational legislation should be introduced by an enlightened élite to democracy by the argument that only a democratic government could have a clear and automatic interest in measures designed to promote the utilitarian end of general welfare. J. S. Mill's attitude to democracy was somewhat more reserved. Sharing de Tocqueville's fear that democratic government would lead inevitably to majority tyranny, the imposition of a dull uniformity of opinion and style of life by the conformist and unenlightened masses, he recommended a form of representative government in which a special weight was given to the votes of the more highly educated citizens. His chief political enthusiasm was accorded to liberty, both in thought and personal conduct. The overriding aim of his great essay on the subject was the creation of conditions in which individuality and originality could flourish, unhindered by social interference. It is remarkable that the conclusions of this essay are nowhere supported by arguments of a specifically utilitarian kind. Mill did not favour liberty as a means to the general happiness but rather as a condition for the discovery of new truth and as something valuable in itself.

This kind of intellectual liberalism had no exponents in the period from 1900 to 1914 of anything like Mill's stature. It received practical expression in the political career of John Morley (1838–1923), the biographer of Gladstone, Cobden, and the major figures of the French Enlightenment, whose distaste for the frenzies of late-Victorian imperialism led him into opposition to the Boer War. But on the level of theory nothing very substantial was added. L. T. Hobhouse (1864–1929), whose main work was the inauguration of an academic tradition of evolutionary sociology in Britain, derived from the doctrines of Herbert Spencer (1820–1903) and Comte, presented a political theory in his *Liberalism* (1911) that was in all its fundamental respects derived from J. S. Mill. He favoured liberty as the indispensable condition for the growth and development of individual personality, and democracy only as the most reliable safeguard of liberty. At the same time he developed certain mildly socialistic intimations of Mill's *Principles of Political Economy* by proposing a considerable degree of restriction of economic liberty through redistributive taxation, welfare legislation, and a measure of workers' control of industry.

Even the mildest and most respectable of Edwardian liberals, Goldsworthy Lowes Dickinson (1863–1932), a gently avuncular Socrates who extolled the values of Greek civilization and the ideas of Plato, felt constrained to adapt the liberal inheritance to the social and economic problems of the age, above all the problem posed by the contrast between plutocratic excess and the poverty and insecurity of the industrial working class. His preferred method of expounding his political ideas was the Socratic dialogue, and in the most substantial of his writings in this form, *Justice and Liberty* (1908), he presents a debate between an aristocrat, a democratic socialist, and a practically-minded conformist. While taking it for granted that the preservation of individual liberty is the pre-eminent political value, he is prepared to admit the inescapability of some measure of collective interference with the economic life of society. Justice requires that income should be more closely proportioned to disagreeable effort than it is under *laissez-faire*. It is also important that some of society's wealth should be allocated to make possible the kind of leisure required for cultural achievement. Finally, he takes the view that the chief cause of most economic injustice is the institution of inheritance and he inquires how the distribution of wealth could be arranged so as to secure the rather unliberal end of the greatest productivity.

The most impressive bringing together of traditional liberal ideals with the need for collective effort to correct the injustices of an insufficiently controlled capitalist economy is to be found in the writings of J. A. Hobson (1858–1940). He first achieved notice in 1889 with the publication of *The Physiology of Industry*, in which he argued that a free-enterprise economy does not automatically make the most productive use of its resources. Unequal distribution of wealth leads to excessive saving by the rich and this reduces effective demand for the products of industry. Hobson was a consciously heretical economist and his ideas were curtly dismissed by conventional economic wisdom, as personified by F. Y. Edgeworth (1845–1926). Nearly half a century later John Maynard Keynes (1883–1946) was to redress the balance by singling out Hobson as by far the most perceptive anticipator of his own revolutionary ideas.

In *The Industrial System* (1909) Hobson distinguished three ends towards which the product of the economy could be distributed: to the simple maintenance of society's human resources, in other words to bare subsistence, to encouraging the growth and development of economic resources, and to mere surplus accumulation in the hands of the wealthy. Inspired by Ruskin, he was always insistent that economic science, by concentrating its attention on the straightforwardly measurable returns of economic activity to identifiable people and institutions, misleadingly ignored the general social effects of the workings of the economic system. He refused to divorce ethics and politics from economics and insisted that rational economic policy should also concern itself with the social costs that adversely influence the quality of life even if they do not figure in the balance sheets of accountants or directly influence the movement of prices. This side of his thought is most evident in *Work and Wealth* (1914). To counteract the wasteful and unjust fashion in which the economic surplus accrued to the rich in the prevailing scheme of distribution, he developed a set of proposals which constituted the essential economic policy of British Labour governments after 1945. He recommended steeply graduated taxation of income and inheritance, a large expansion of government financing for the social services, and the taking into public ownership both of monopolies and of the 'key industries', central control of which is required if there is to be effective national economic planning. It has been observed that Hobson was only in a position to develop his economic heresies in an atmosphere of total academic disapproval because he had a private income. The implementation of his proposals has made it hard for anyone like him to flourish.

Of equal or even greater influence were the ideas Hobson expounded in his *Imperialism* (1909). It was from this work, notoriously, that Lenin derived his own position about the colonial empires of advanced industrial societies. Hobson maintained that the imperial expansion of industrial nations was motivated by the desire of capitalists to secure markets for the production that the depressed demand of their own countries was insufficient to absorb. This view put the purely moralistic distaste of liberals for such imperialist adventures as the Boer War on a theoretical footing. Imperialism sought to secure an outlet for excess production and monopolistic control of sources of raw material supply. In order to achieve this nations were led, to advance the interests of a minute number of capitalists who were already unjustly rich, into the waste and danger of war. The problem of overproduction could be more justly, inexpensively, and efficiently solved by the internal redistribution of income and wealth.

A more Utopian use of economic reasoning to arrive at conclusions about policy is to be found in Norman Angell's (1874–1967) *The Great Illusion* (1910), which by demonstrating the absurdity of war from a rational, economic point of view suggested that war was in fact obsolete. His main point is that war does not bring economic gains but only the pointless destruction of wealth. The gains that might be hoped for from war conceived as a kind of piracy are in fact illusory. The basic sources of a conquered enemy's wealth, the land and its contents, the skill and energy of the population, cannot be taken away from it. What can be removed will serve only to disrupt the victor's economy. But the anticipated though unattainable profits of conquest can be secured by peaceful trade. The imperialism practised by Lenin's successors has shown that Angell underestimated the piratical determination of victorious military powers. The war of 1914 showed that he had overestimated the appeal of rational economic argument.

The Fabians

The liberal tradition, as was remarked in the last section, had deviated, under Mill's influence, from the strict utilitarianism of the early nineteenth century and had realigned itself with Whiggism, emphasizing the rights and liberties of individuals in the manner of Locke. But even comparatively orthodox liberalism as developed by such theorists as Hobhouse and Hobson could not stand simply on the primacy, among all political values, of the freedom of the individual. They had to accommodate their views to the obvious fact that remediable economic injustice followed from unrestricted freedom of economic activity. It is a natural response to this tension in the liberal outlook of the period to see it as corresponding on the level of theory to an evident tension within the Liberal party as an active political movement. This tension existed between the Whigs, whose defence of liberty had become at once traditional and to the advantage of established interests, and the radicals, like Lloyd George, who, far from wanting to circumscribe the sphere of state action, wanted to use the state's power to counteract the social effects of an unrestricted free-enterprise economy. After the 1914 war the remaining Whigs joined those who had earlier abandoned political liberalism over the issue of Irish Home Rule; the radicals came to be a substantial middle-class element in the Labour party.

The real continuators of strict, Benthamite utilitarianism in the early years of the century were the Fabians. This is made clear in the basic statement of principle to which the original Fabians agreed.

The members of the Society assert that the Competitive System assures the happiness and the comfort of the few at the expense of the suffering of the many and that society must be reconstituted in such a manner as to secure the general welfare and happiness.

The society had been founded in 1884, the year in which William Morris had broken away from Hyndman's Social Democratic Federation to found the Socialist League. In 1900 these organizations came together with Keir Hardie's (1856–1915) Independent Labour party, the political arm of militant trade unionism, to found the Labour party. The Fabian Society preserved its identity through this amalgamation of forces, for it regarded itself as having a special task to fulfil. The Society had developed out of an organization of libertarian idealists called the Fellowship of the New Life whose interests were moral rather than political. But under the intellectual leadership of Bernard Shaw and Sidney Webb (1859–1947) the Fabian Society became a consciously political organization. It did not aim to build up a mass movement. It conceived itself rather as an organization of experts who would articulate socialist policies on the basis of scholarly research into social and economic problems. In its early days it worked on much the same principle as Bentham had followed until he was converted to democracy by James Mill. Its preferred tactic was that of permeation, the winning over to specific socialist policies of people already in positions of power.

The fact-finding work of the Society was presided over by Sidney Webb and his wife Beatrice (1858–1943). Their main publications in the period were the massive *English Local Government* (from 1906) and their *Minority Report* on the Poor Law (1909). The latter, with its proposals for financing social security out of general taxation, was more directly in line with the preoccupations of the Society. It was, in a way, the culmination of a great deal of empirical study of the problems of poverty. In 1901 Seebohm Rowntree (1871–1954) had published his investigation into the conditions of the poor in York and in the following year Charles Booth (1840–1916) brought out his study *Life and Labour of the People in London*. This informed concern with the destitute condition of a large part of the population bore fruit in the social insurance proposals of the 1909 budget.

While the Webbs provided Fabianism with a foundation of detailed factual knowledge about social problems and also with the tactical method of permeation, it was left to others, in particular to Shaw, to work out its general ideas and values. These had been authoritatively expressed in 1889 in the collective volume *Fabian Essays in Socialism*. In the Edwardian period Shaw was still fully committed to these basic Fabian doctrines. Like many other British socialists he had been profoundly affected by the ideas set out in Henry George's *Progress and Poverty* (1879). George's main theme had been that the value of land is socially created, a by-product of the growth of population and public services, and is in no sense a result of the efforts of its owners. The rent by which they are rewarded is thus an unearned increment, for which credit should properly be attributed to the community as a whole. It followed that rent should be taxed, in respect of the large unearned element within it, to make possible expenditure advantageous to the community at large.

Shaw's chief theoretical contribution to Fabianism was to combine Henry George's moral attitude to the unearned increment on land with the economists' generalization of the concept of rent to cover, not just the returns to owners of land, but any return to fortuitous natural advantages. (His criticism of Mallock, mentioned earlier, applies this idea in maintaining that the rent of ability should not be monopolized by the ability's possessors.) The foundation of Fabian doctrine was the moral demand that a just society should return to the community the value that the community itself creates.

The Fabians, as the name they chose suggests, were gradualists, and rejected most of what distinguished Marx from other socialists. They dismissed the revolution whose inevitability he claimed to prove as both unlikely and undesirable. They were equally opposed to his insistence on class war. In their eyes, proletarianism, the idea derived from Marx's labour theory of value that all economic value is attributable to manual labour alone, was sentimental nonsense wrapped up in economic charlatanry. Accepting the marginalism of academic economists, they sought to produce a juster distribution of wealth through the taxation of all forms of unearned income. Webb, indeed, believed with Marx that socialism was inevitable, but only because it was the rational policy to adopt with the passing of the initial phase of capitalism. Modern large-scale industries divorce ownership from management, so that no element of profit can be regarded as a return for economic services rendered and their size makes them amenable to government control. The specific economic policy recommended by the Fabians contained the three elements already mentioned in the discussion of Hobhouse and Hobson: social legislation to enhance the welfare of the less fortunate, redistributive taxation, and the public ownership of industry.

Politically and constitutionally the position of the Fabians was fairly conventional. They regarded parliamentary government, rendered truly democratic as far as males were concerned by the three great Reform Acts of the nineteenth century, as an entirely adequate political instrument for carrying out the necessary reforms. Indeed they thought the existing political system quite democratic enough and had no sympathy for constitutional innovations like the plebiscite and referendum which were aimed at a more direct form of democracy. It was integral to the Society's conception of itself that public opinion should be guided by experts and that highly skilled administrators should translate into detailed policy the very broad aspirations which were all the populace at large was qualified to form. The working-class leaders of the Labour party, in particular Ramsay MacDonald (1866–1937), agreed with them that socialism implied representative government and not democracy of the theoretically purest kind. MacDonald, who was to be the first Labour Prime Minister, although in general agreement about policies, built his socialism on less self-consciously rationalistic foundations. In his books *Socialism and Society* (1905) and *Socialism* (1907) he supports the idea that it is the community which is the ultimate creator of wealth by biological analogies in which the idea of society as an organism is stressed.

The Fabians' conviction that intellectually adequate leadership was indispensable led them to deviate from much of radical opinion on the subject of imperialism. Indifferent to the emotions underlying nationalism, they saw the possession of colonies by advanced nations simply as an opportunity for those nations to confer the benefits of progress on their possessions. Thus the Fabians were not opposed to the Boer War. They saw it as a conflict between more or less enlightened colonialism and unenlightened Boer settlers. The Fabian view on this subject is applied to Ireland in Shaw's play *John Bull's Other Island* (1907).

The first signs of Shaw's subsequent deviations, not merely from Fabian orthodoxy, but from the whole Fabian order of priorities, are evident in this period. Certainly his eventual adoption of the principle of equal incomes for all and his unattractive predilection for the dictators of the inter-war period, whom he favoured as

rulers genuinely dedicated to efficiency, could be regarded as con-
tinuations of Fabian doctrine about unearned income and political
expertise. The contempt for democracy expressed in his play *The
Applecart* (1930), however, was something far beyond the only
moderate enthusiasm of the Fabians for popular government. This
line of thought is to some extent anticipated in *Major Barbara*
(1907). What was fundamental in Shaw's eventual transcendence of
Fabianism was his conversion to the idea that it is not really social
institutions which need to be reformed but rather human beings
themselves. The official Fabians, as much as Bentham, worked with
an assumption of the essential fixity of human nature. In *Man and
Superman* (1903), and in particular in the *Revolutionist's Handbook*
appended to it, Shaw makes it clear that in his view the main problem is to prevent the genuinely creative and original kind of man
from being smothered by the conventional demands of domesticity
and the pressures of existing society generally. Using ideas formed
from Nietzsche, Samuel Butler, and Bergson, Shaw was in the end to
develop a kind of religion of human self-transcendence which took
the achievement of human progress out of the arena of reformist
politics altogether.

Until 1908 H. G. Wells (1866–1946) was one of the more prominent members of the Fabian Society. His departure from it took
place after his proposal to turn it into a political movement on a
larger and more popular scale had been narrowly defeated by the
Webbs. Like Shaw, but for exactly opposite reasons, Wells was
hostile to the monogamous conventionality of the Victorian family.
The freer relations of the sexes that are always to be found in his
Utopias were something he strove for with unremitting vigour in
his private life. Where Shaw wanted to rescue men from cloying
entanglements with women, Wells wanted men, and particularly
himself, to be entangled with as many women as possible. The love
affair fictionally described in *Ann Veronica* (1909) was altogether too
much of a public scandal for the Webbs.

Wells's political views were set out in a series of books in which
the ideological message was made palatable to a large audience by
being mixed up with concrete Utopian fantasy. Wells had been
emancipated from a most unpromising initial position in the social
system through his contact with science, and it was not surprising
that he should recommend the same prescription for mankind as a
whole. There is nothing calculated about the way in which Wells's
books cater to the popular taste for marvels: his mind worked in the
same way as his readers', if more rapidly. *Anticipations* (1902) is the

most 'scientific' of these books, dwelling elaborately on the likely outcome of current trends of change influenced by science. Wells tried to work out the consequences for human beings of improved methods of transport and communication. But already in this book the outlines of a society something like Plato's ideal republic, though one in which natural science is the supreme intellectual activity, can be discerned. *Mankind in the Making* (1903) is a somewhat amorphous work, concerned with the problem of creating a new ruling class for the contemporary scientific state. In *A Modern Utopia* (1905) the traditional literary form of a voyage to a strange land is used to set out Wells's Platonic hierarchy in detail. Wells's *Samurai* make their first appearance in this book. In exactly the same way as Plato's ruling class they are to combine the highest measure of the mental abilities required for ruling with the disinterestedness without which such ability is a public danger. Wells proposes an openly meritocratic method of selection. *New Worlds for Old* (1908) is a more recognizably socialist work than any of the early ones. (It came out at the time Wells was attempting to reshape the Fabian Society.) Broadly speaking it is an appeal, addressed to rational public spirit, on behalf of collectivism.

Guild Socialism and Pluralism

Some socialists in the late nineteenth century were inspired by the sufferings of the less fortunate sections of society. Others, particularly the Fabians, reacted more strongly to the wastefulness and inefficiency of uncontrolled capitalism than to its cruelties. But of almost equal importance were those who were repelled by the simple ugliness of industrial society, not only by its degradation of the visible surface of the land with factories, railways, and cheap and congested housing, but more generally by its destructive influence on the true values of labour. This is the third stream of Victorian social philosophy that continued into the Edwardian age. Ruskin was the first and greatest of those who protested against the kind of economics which took the market price of the products of human work to be a measure of their real value, and which served, in the guise of science, as propaganda for soulless materialism. In the most concrete of his works on social issues, *Unto This Last* (1860), Ruskin called for state intervention to care for the destitute, to educate men in values higher than those of commercialism, and to maintain craftsmanly standards of work. Despite this leaning towards collectivism Ruskin was not a socialist, but he influenced many socialists, conspicuously Morris, who, fully embracing

Ruskin's ideals, believed that only through a socialist revolution could they be realized. Shaw, too, was influenced by Ruskin. Morris carried further Ruskin's ineffectual project of Saint George's Guild, a community to be governed by the true values of human work.

The chief revivers of this tradition after the turn of the century were the guild socialists. In 1906 A. J. Penty, an architect, published *The Restoration of the Gild System* which put forward the idea that work could be redeemed if it were carried on within the framework of self-governing organizations of craftsmen. This was a slightly humdrum application of Morris's nostalgic conception of the Middle Ages. But it was in accord with much of the more original social doctrine of its epoch in its revulsion from plutocracy. In late capitalism, the guild socialists contended, decisions about what should be produced and how it should be produced were not made by the producers themselves but by financiers, guided by starkly commercial principles. The inevitable result was inferior products, offensive to the standards of those who had to make them.

In the following year the weekly paper *The New Age* was started under the editorship of A. R. Orage (1873–1934), in some ways the most interesting figure to emerge in the Edwardian intellectual scene. Orage was an admirably pithy and adult writer, equally at home in the fields of politics and literature, and an extraordinarily gifted editor. He managed to elicit a great deal of first-class serious journalism from a very mixed bag of collaborators, and despite the somewhat *outré* character of his enthusiasms he introduced an unprecedented level of sophistication and metropolitan liveliness into periodical writing as well as setting an influential example with his forceful and uncircuitous style. Orage came to London from Leeds where he had been an elementary schoolmaster. At this time he was something of a Nietzschean and a leaning towards more or less mystical short-cuts to the perfection of humanity was always part of his nature. It came to the surface again when he left London in the 1920s to go into monastic seclusion for a while at Gurdjieff's establishment at Fontainebleau. But the main note that Orage struck was one of unremitting hostility to intellectual softness of any description, both to the long-winded and complacent pomposity of the established liberal tradition and to the amorphous romanticism and self-indulgence of many of that tradition's more radical critics. Nietzsche's unlimited readiness to criticize received ideas may have helped to foster in Orage a kind of European sensibility which in its astringency and freedom from genial and comforting illusions had a notably stimulating effect on the woolly and slack-gutted tone of English intellectual life.

Together with S. G. Hobson, Orage developed, in the columns of *The New Age*, a much more comprehensive and systematic version of guild socialist doctrine than anything envisaged by Penty. Their articles were brought together in 1914 in *National Guilds*. The basic principle they advanced was that labour should not be treated as a simply marketable commodity. Personal fulfilment through work and the production of honest and emotionally satisfying goods could be secured only by the abolition of 'wagery', the wage system in which men sold their labour power unconditionally, giving up all control over the manner and purpose of their work in doing so. Since work is not just an essential but distasteful means to life, but a fundamentally important part of life, the existing system was doubly intolerable: it frustrated men both as consumers and producers. The remedy offered was a thoroughgoing application of the democratic principle to economic life in place of competitive authoritarianism. This view implied that merely political democracy was ineffective and unreal. Its representation of the merely accidental territorial groupings of men made it trivial. What was needed was functional representation, based on the real and natural associations created by common work.

It is not necessary to enter into the detailed controversies that went on within the guild socialist movement about the ideal form that guild organization should take and about the place of the state within a society so organized. The predominant view was that the guilds should be national organizations of the whole of a given industry, that the state should serve as the ultimate arbiter in the system and as the representative of the people in its consumer aspect, and that control of industries by those who worked in them should be achieved by way of the trade unions. This last point, in its rejection of a straightforwardly political solution to the problem of social betterment, reveals a certain affinity between guild socialism and syndicalism. Both disliked bureaucrats almost as much as they disliked capitalists. But the guild socialists, although strongly critical of the Fabians' addiction to an all-powerful centralized state, shared the Fabians' distaste for revolutionary melodrama. One distinguished younger recruit to guild socialism, G. D. H. Cole (1889–1959), believed like Marx that eventually the state would wither away. Others sympathetic to guild socialist ideals were R. H. Tawney (1880–1962), who was later to take further the idea that property rights should be based on the fulfilment of a social purpose, not on the brute fact of acquisition, Bertrand Russell (1872–1970) and Major C. H. Douglas (1879–1952), the inventor of Social Credit, the redemptive nostrum to which Orage was eventually to attach himself after emerging from his period of seclusion with Gurdjieff.

Guild socialism was the most prominent and widely followed of a number of tendencies of an anti-centralizing kind in the period. By 1914, indeed, Cole was arguing that it must reconstitute itself as a mass movement to pursue the logic of its proposals of taking over the economy through the trade unions. But there were other, non-socialist, forms of opposition to the emerging shape of advanced industrial society in which individuals are absorbed into a featureless mass and their lives are wholly dominated by vast organizations, an ever more powerful state and immense business concerns run by financiers. The most lively of these was the distributivism of Hilaire Belloc (1870–1953). In the midst of a hectically active literary career Belloc found time to produce (with Cecil Chesterton) *The Party System* (1911), a vigorous attack on the manipulative character of parliamentary democracy, on the carefully articulated system of devices by which the political profession succeeded in frustrating the will of the people, and in 1912 *The Servile State*, in which he argued that individual freedom could be secured only by a wide diffusion of property giving each man a measure of economic security and independence, an anglicized version of French peasant proprietorship.

At a more literary level the first stirrings were evident of a hostility to the style of life in an urban mass to which industrial society condemned the great majority of the population. After the 1914 war this mood came to express itself as a fairly articulate agrarian ideology, which at its theoretical end traced the deficiencies of modern culture to the humanly distorting nature of urban life and expressed itself practically on behalf of the preservation of the countryside and the protection of agriculture. Before 1914 it was in works like George Bourne's attractive delineations of a vanishing style of rural life, *The Bettesworth Book* (1900) and *Memoirs of a Surrey Labourer* (1907), or the English writings of W. H. Hudson (1841–1922), such as *A Shepherd's Life* (1910), that this attitude of nostalgia for honest craftsmanship and a participating mode of recreation and leisure in the natural, rural setting 'where man belongs' is to be found.

These concrete rejections of a politically and economically

centralized form of social organization, guild socialist, distributivist and agrarian, were in harmony with a new line of thought in academic political theory: the doctrine of pluralism. For all their differences the idealist political thinkers who drew their ultimate inspiration from Hegel's *Philosophy of Right* and the Fabian inheritors of utilitarianism were in agreement about the supremacy of the state over all other social groups. The idealists regarded the state as the highest possible expression of social morality; utilitarian jurisprudence, following Hobbes in defining the sovereign as the indispensable source of all law, provided a foundation in theory for the view of Fabians and other radical reformers that the state must be the prime instrument of social change. The prevailing exaltation of the state was thus a complicated affair: partly a theme of metaphysical ethics, partly a thesis of abstract legal theory, partly a practical judgement about what was politically rational.

In the writings of the pluralists these logically disparate elements were not effectively distinguished. The idea of the moral supremacy of the state was an importation from Germany, inconsistent with the entire tradition of British political thought: even for Hobbes the state is a means to the end of individual self-preservation. The idea that law and the state are logically correlative is an analytical truism. The idea that the state would and should become increasingly dominant in the life of the individual combined a justified prediction with a highly controversial judgement of values.

Pluralism may be said to begin in this country with the publication in 1900 of F. W. Maitland's (1850–1906) translation as *Political Theories of the Middle Age* of a part of Otto von Gierke's *Das Deutsche Genossenschaftsrecht*, a German cure for a German disease. Maitland drew from Gierke the view that human groups and associations do not derive their existence as real social entities, and thus their rights, from the fact of legal recognition by the state. He invoked the legal conception of the personality of groups to justify regarding human associations as autonomous moral entities, in opposition to the view, prevalent in political theory since the seventeenth century, that individuals and the state were the sole moral beings and that the moral status of groups other than the state consisted entirely in the rights conferred on them by the state. On this view the function of the state with regard to law is not to create it but to ratify by legislative recognition rights and duties that have grown up independently of its initiative.

The Twilight of Idealism

Throughout this period the dominant academic social philosophy was that of idealism, derived ultimately from Hegel, but thoroughly anglicized in its first authoritative British expression: *The Principles of Political Obligation* (1885) of T. H. Green. This is the fourth stream of doctrine carried on from the Victorian period. Green shared some of Hegel's mistrust for the individual conscience that was the foundation of liberal political theory, and he elaborately criticized the instrumental theories of the state, based either on natural rights and social contract, or on the principle of utility, which took it to be simply a means for the realization of strictly individual ends. The fully developed human individual could not be understood in abstraction from the system of social relations in which he was placed. But where this conviction had led Hegel to accord an overriding moral authority to the state as the historically most advanced incarnation of social morality, in Green it took the form of an attribution of moral sovereignty to the community. In 1899 Bernard Bosanquet (1878–1923) published his *Philosophical Theory of the State*, which was more orthodox in its Hegelianism than Green's *Principles*, although Bosanquet envisaged a world state as the ultimate goal of historical development, something that Hegel, with his fierce nationalism, would have dismissed as sentimental Utopianism.

Bosanquet's book remained the standard text of academic political theory until the 1914 war brought it doubly into discredit: for the German origins of its ideas and for its somewhat bonelessly optimistic compliance with the verdict of history. In general, idealistic political theory came to seem a disreputable verbal device which provided a metaphysical justification for whatever distribution of power happened to exist, a kind of conceptual anaesthesia calculated to numb any impulse towards the rejection in principle of the existing order of things. The lesser idealists were content to repeat what their predecessors had already said in the typically amorphous and rhapsodic style of the movement. D. G. Ritchie (1853–1903), whose *Studies in Political and Social Ethics* appeared in 1902, at least took an independent step in endorsing Darwin, hitherto rejected by idealists for his mechanistic view of development, by saying that the theory of natural selection conformed with the Hegelian idea that the more rational is bound to supersede the less rational.

One doctrine that the idealists derived from Green rather than from Hegel and which was apt for the times in which they wrote was that of the propriety of interference by the state with economic life for the sake of the common good of the community. Their opposition to the concept of natural rights made them highly critical of established attitudes to property, which they conceived as held in trust for the community, and ready to endorse a substantial degree of state regulation of the conditions of work of the industrial population. Herbert Spencer, who defended unrestricted economic competition on evolutionary grounds, was a direct object of Green's polemics and the political theory of Green and his followers is certainly one of the sources of present-day assumptions about the proper sphere of state activity, of the conception of the welfare state introduced into political practice by the Labour party but now widely embraced by all but the most unbending adherents of inalienable natural rights.

The Science of Society

The fifth and final stream of Victorian social philosophy to show some signs of life in the new century was evolutionism, the application of the principles of Darwin's biology to social and political subject matter. From the publication of *The Origin of Species* in 1859, social applications of evolutionary theory had been numerous. As far as values and policy were concerned the same evolutionary premises led to very different conclusions. While Herbert Spencer argued that the process of evolution should be assisted in its work of improvement by the creation of conditions in which competition could flourish with unobstructed ruthlessness, T. H. Huxley maintained that the overriding moral task of society was to mitigate the cruelties of the natural struggle for existence. Others used evolutionary principles to interpret social change: Walter Bagehot in *Physics and Politics* (1869) and, predicting an unappetizing future, C. H. Pearson in his remarkable *National Life and Character* (1893). The last direct representative of this tradition was Benjamin Kidd (1858–1916). In his *Social Evolution* (1894) he put forward his highly idiosyncratic version of the social implications of the evolutionary principle and in *The Principles of Western Civilization* (1902) he applied his general doctrine to the actual course of human history with a special concern for the prospects of his own culture.

A more diffused influence of evolutionary ideas is to be found in many thinkers of the period. Shaw espoused them in the heretical form they were given by Samuel Butler, for whom primordial intelligence and foresight rather than chance variation were the crucial agents of change. Wells had been a pupil of Huxley's and the evolutionary point of view was deeply embedded in his general assumptions about the linear character of progress. Sociology had been inaugurated as a distinct discipline in Britain by Herbert Spencer and was made academically respectable by L. T. Hobhouse, who, while rejecting Spencer's endorsement of unmitigated competition, as we have seen, nevertheless developed a general theory of social change on an evolutionary basis. He did not transfer evolutionary ideas from biology to sociology in Spencer's uncritical fashion: in the order of rational beings change need not be the outcome simply of conflicts arising from chance variation; intelligent adjustment to changing conditions can take the place of blind mechanical response.

Perhaps the most fruitful new development in the study of society was the social psychology of William McDougall (1871–1938) (*Introduction to Social Psychology*, 1908) and the Fabian Graham Wallas (1858–1932) (*Human Nature in Politics*, 1908). In some respects McDougall was very much of his age, in others he continued an older British tradition of rather superficially empirical psychology. In any event his doctrines have not worn very well. The antiquated form of his inquiry, which seeks to derive the variety of human character and conduct from a small repertoire of basic data, in his case an array of innate instincts, associates him with abstract psychologists like James Mill from whose views in many important ways he dissents. What was modern about him, his rejection of 'intellectualism', in particular of the belief ascribed to Bentham that human behaviour is best understood as the outcome of rational endeavours to achieve the fullest possible satisfaction of desire, was to be found in an altogether more vigorous and memorable form in the work of such European contemporaries as Sorel, Pareto (1848–1923), and Bergson.

A more judicious kind of anti-intellectualism is expressed in Graham Wallas's *Human Nature in Politics*. Pre-eminently concerned with the application of psychology to actual political practice, Wallas did not try to lay more weight on the new science than, in its unfledged state, it could be expected to bear. His starting-point was the widespread disappointment experienced by those committed to representative democracy with the results actually achieved by the realization of their policies. Wallas drew attention to the very fitful and marginal character of the political rationality of the ordinary voter in a modern democracy, a weakness energetically exploited by professional politicians with the aid of the psychologically enriched art of publicity. The remoteness and complexity of the subject-matter of politics led to the currency in ordinary political reflection of oversimplified images of political entities—nations, classes, parties, and institutions. These carry a high emotional charge and are subjected to little rational criticism. But unlike most anti-intellectualists Wallas did not emphasize the non-rational character of public opinion in order to justify some kind of élitism. A convinced democrat and Fabian, he was anxious to devise methods of bringing the actual practice of democracy into closer conformity with its theoretical ideal.

Wallas's ideas may have had more influence in making political study more realistic than in improving the performance of professedly democratic institutions. Until this century 'political science' was a largely formalistic undertaking, mainly concerned with the constitutional structure of political institutions and only parenthetically with the real effectiveness of formal constitutional provisions in actual political life. As much as anyone Wallas prepared the way for a change of emphasis in political inquiry from form to content.

FOR FURTHER READING

The following works may be found to be of some interest in addition to those mentioned in the essay.

One aspect of Fitzjames Stephen's *Liberty, Equality and Fraternity*, namely the relationship between the law and morality, has received a good deal of attention recently, particularly after the publication of the Wolfenden Report in 1957. Central works in the current debate are Lord Devlin, *The Enforcement of Morals* (1965); H. L. A. Hart, *Law, Liberty, and Morality* (1963); and B. Mitchell, *Law, Morality, and Religion in a Secular Society* (1967). The present debate occasioned the publication of a new edition of Fitzjames Stephen's work, edited with a useful introduction by R. J. White (Cambridge, 1967).

The work of Mallock has not really received the attention which it perhaps deserves as a precursor in many respects of continental élite theorizing. There is, however, a short discussion in Raymond Williams's *Culture and Society* (1958). As Williams argues, '. . . the democratic idea needed its sceptics and Mallock, always, is shrewd enough to be attended to'.

Recent work on John Stuart Mill and the Liberal tradition in British politics includes J. M. Robson, *The Improvement of Mankind* (1968); A. Ryan, *The Philosophy of John Stuart Mill* (1970); and M. Cowling, *Mill and Liberalism* (Cambridge, 1963). A useful collection of essays dealing with various facets of Mill's work is *Mill*, ed. J. B. Schneewind (1969).

An interesting history of socialist thought is M. Beer, *A History of British Socialism* (1940). Margaret Cole has written a history of the Fabian Society, the development and ethos of which she knew intimately, *The Story of Fabian Socialism* (1961). The life of Beatrice Webb has been recorded by Kitty

Muggeridge and Ruth Adam in *Beatrice Webb* (1967). Again there is an interpretative discussion of the Fabian idea in the development of socialist consciousness in Raymond Williams, *Culture and Society*. S. T. Glass, *The Responsible Society* (1966), is a useful book on the history and development of the guild socialist movement. Other earlier works on guild socialism include G. C. Field, *Guild Socialism* (1920); Alexander Gray, *The Socialist Tradition* (1946); and the relevant parts of G. D. H. Cole's synoptic *A History of British Socialism*, 5 vols. (1953–60).

Idealist social and political thought is intelligible only against its Hegelian background. Recent books on Hegel include J. N. Findlay, *Hegel—A Re-examination* (1958), and R. Plant, *Hegel: through Philosophy to Community* (1971). On the British idealists, whose thought is now undergoing something of a revival, the reader may consult M. Richter, *The Politics of Conscience: T. H. Green and His Age* (1964); A. J. M. Milne, *The Social Philosophy of English Idealism* (1962); and Richard Wollheim, *F. H. Bradley* (1959). A more updated Idealist approach to politics is to be found in the work of Michael Oakeshott, particularly *Experience and Its Modes* (1933), and *Rationalism and Politics* (1962). For those who like their philosophy in literary form there is, of course, Mrs. H. Ward's *Robert Ellsmere* (1888), which deals in a rather intense way with the background and consequences of Green's work. The influence of Idealism on Asquith is discussed briefly in R. Jenkins, *Asquith* (1964).

5

Aspects of Continental Social and Political Thought

RAYMOND PLANT

O lasst uns endlich taten sehn
Verbrechen, blutig, Kolossal,
Nur diese satte Tugend nicht
Und zahlungsfahige Moral. *
            Heine.

I

The Spectre of Revisionism

Karl Marx died in 1883, Friedrich Engels in 1895, and by the turn of the century a bitter debate raged in Europe about the relevance of Marxian socialism to contemporary industrial society, a debate which found its most natural outlet in Germany where Marx's thought had received a fairly concrete articulation in the programme of the Social-Democratic Party (S.P.D.). The debate within this party between revisionists led by Eduard Bernstein (1850–1932)[1] and orthodox Marxists such as Karl Kautsky (1854–1938) and Rosa Luxemburg (1870–1919) was largely concerned with the issue of reform or revolution: whether socialism was to be achieved through a decisive, revolutionary break with the existing capitalist order—its economic relations, its institutions, its politics, and its law—or by working from within the system, by appropriating the means of production from the capitalists and socializing them in a democratic manner. The solution to this dilemma had to be an intellectual one, although of course it was quite central to both the political strategy and the tactics of the S.P.D. in Wilhelmine Germany. It was an intellectual problem in that the correct view depended upon the analysis of the existing social and economic system. Bernstein and the revisionists challenged the Marxian analysis of capitalism and rejected the consequent predictions about its future. Such a rejection, if persuasive, would clearly effect the political role of the S.P.D., and indeed Bernstein called on the party to jettison the

* 'O let us see deeds at last, crimes bloody and colossal, but not any more of this bland virtue and solvent morality.'

Marxian elements in its programme and to modify its revolutionary theory.

Before 1875, left-wing politics in Germany had been bedevilled by the rivalry between the Social-Democratic Workers' Party led by Wilhelm Liebknecht (1826–1900) and August Bebel (1840–1913), and the General Association of German Workers led by Hassen-clever, Hasselmann, and Tölcke, but dominated by the spirit of Ferdinand Lassalle. These parties differed significantly in matters of political doctrine. The former was largely Marxist in outlook, and indeed had been nurtured by both Marx and Engels since the time of the First International. It stressed the achievement of socialism through revolution, through a clear breach with the existing system. The General Association of German Workers on the other hand, drawing much of its inspiration from the Hegelian Lassalle, emphasized the need for change within the existing system, and the development of socialism through the democratic reform of bourgcois society. Lassalle was profoundly influenced by the Hegelian idea that the state was a moral entity which would have to be used to guide the masses to socialism, whereas the ortho-dox Marxist regarded it as a means of class repression. The rivalry between these parties was extreme, and they were fairly evenly balanced electorally as the Reichstag elections of 1874 showed. This election demonstrated how far the Left had dissipated its strength through this rivalry and what gains might follow if the socialists could present a united front. The realization of this led to the famous Gotha conferences of February and May 1875 which cemented a union between the parties under the name of the Socialist Workers' Party of Germany and led to the adoption of the Gotha programme which was a curious blend of Marxian analysis and Lassallian reformism—a fact which Marx trenchantly criticized in his *Critique of the Gotha Programme* (1875). Even in its inception therefore, the S.P.D. contained within itself the seeds of the future revisionist controversy in that it united revolutionaries who believed in the inevitable collapse of the capitalist system and the new order growing from the ashes of the old, and Lassallian reformists who sought to socialize the system through democratic means.

After 1878, and for the next twelve years, the party developed in a far more militant fashion following Bismarck's draconian anti-socialist legislation. The banning of most of the socialists' activities cast them in a somewhat false revolutionary light, but certainly their leaders moved to positions further to the left than they had occupied previously. In 1890, with the fall of Bismarck, this legislation was allowed to lapse, and the socialists adopted a new and more Marxist programme at the Erfurt conference in 1891. This programme removed the last vestiges of Lassalle's influence, and indeed so Marxist was it that Engels gave it his full support. It forecast the inevitable collapse of capitalism, the increasing misery, exploitation, and impoverishment of the proletariat, and a revolutionary break with the old order which would lead to the socialist promised land. At the very same time however, the socialist party was a parliamentary party seeking to maximize its power and influence in the Reichstag—theoretically committed to revolution and a root and branch rejection of the existing order, in practice it operated through parliamentary machinery. Indeed, the nearest the revolutionaries of the S.P.D. came to defying the system was the annual refusal to approve the Reich budget, an ineffectual, ritual gesture.

The party's theory was revolutionary, its practice reformist, and it was upon this bifurcation between theory and practice that Bernstein focused his attention. Before the Gotha conference and the unification of the Left, Bernstein had been a leading member of the Social-Democratic Workers' Party, and during the 'heroic' years of Bismarck's repression, he had been exiled first in Switzerland and afterwards in London. In Britain, Bernstein became acquainted not only with Engels, who in fact made him his literary executor, but also, and perhaps more importantly, with some of the founder members of the British Fabian Society. This acquaintance with a reformist brand of socialism was to affect profoundly Bernstein's view of the official doctrines of the S.P.D. of which he was a leading member. After the death of Engels in 1895, he began to attack some of the basic components of the Marxian analysis of capitalism, initially in the party newspaper *Neue Zeit*, but later in his work *The Underlying Assumptions of Socialism and the Tasks of Social Democracy*[2] (1899). It would be wrong however to attribute Bernstein's conversion to reformism solely to the urbane brand of socialism which was disseminated at the dinner tables of the Fabians. To some extent Engels himself had contributed to the atmosphere which made the questioning of the assumptions of revolutionary socialism respectable, in that in his Preface to the reissue of Marx's *The Class Struggles in France* (1895) he had suggested that since the achievement of socialism would depend on the support of the majority of the population, it might be necessary for socialists to concentrate on the parliamentary sphere, at least in the short run. This represented a very different emphasis to that of *The Communist Manifesto* (1848) in which one can almost hear the noise of the grapeshot and see the barricades. But the situation in 1895 was very different from that of 1848; the uniform collapse of the revolutions of that *annus mirabilis*, and the intervening tragedy of the Paris Commune, 1870–1, had undermined the prospects for a revolutionary overthrow of capitalism, at least in the short term.

What most impressed Bernstein, however, was that most of Marx's predictions about the development of capitalism just had not come true, and he argued that the failure of the predictive part of the theory indicated a weakness in the analysis on which the predictions were based. Since the foundation of the German Reich in 1870, a period of great prosperity had been experienced, a prosperity which, Bernstein argued, had benefited all classes, not just the capitalists and the leading members of the working class. Marxian theory could, of course, accommodate the view that at certain stages in its development capitalism could generate periods of relative prosperity, but such prosperity would always be restricted to the capitalists themselves, and perhaps to the élite of the proletariat whose revolutionary fervour was thus 'bought off'. It is clear in the mature analysis of *Capital* that Marx certainly did not envisage the possibility of a general and significant upward trend in real wages under the capitalist system, and in 1848, in *The Communist Manifesto*, he had in fact predicted a decline in the living standards of the proletariat. In Bernstein's view no such decline had taken place; quite to the contrary in fact, he believed that a modest upward trend could be discerned. This contention was both inconsistent with Marxian theory and with the morbid predictions of the Erfurt programme which, with the fervour of an Old Testament prophet, held that:

The number of proletarians is increasing all the time, the army of redundant workers is swelling, the differences between the exploiters and the exploited are becoming even sharper, the class struggle between the proletariat and the bourgeoisie is growing more embittered; it divides society into two hostile camps, and it is the common hallmark of all industrial societies [3]

Such a view as Bernstein's was controversial on the evidence available, but certainly his thesis was arguable.

It was not only in its account of economic changes that Bernstein found Marxian theory lacking. He argued that it could take no account of correlative changes in social structure. Marx had contended that as capitalism developed a polarization of classes would take place, between the oppressed and exploited proletariat on the one hand, and the exploiters, the capitalists, on the other. Such class polarization just had not occurred, Bernstein argued. Indeed, on the contrary, a greater differentiation in social structure had taken place in trade, industry, commerce, and in the bureaucracies middle-class occupations were on the increase.

The prediction of the polarization of classes and the greater and greater impoverishment of the working class were taken widely to be the two cornerstones of Marx's theory of revolution. The development of these two factors would exacerbate the tensions in capitalism to such a degree that the system would eventually collapse. As these predictions were not, in Bernstein's view, correct, the emphasis on revolution, he argued, could be dismissed. Furthermore the failure of the predictive part of the theory undermined the scientific pretensions of the analyses which underpinned the predictive element, and in his influential lecture *How is Scientific Socialism Possible* (1901), Bernstein broke with *scientific* socialism which was considered to be the major hallmark of the Marxian system. He argued that socialism was not an inevitable outcome of the development of capitalism, but rather a moral ideal for which those committed to it must struggle—one must not wait like some quietist saint for the gradual decline of the capitalist system, since no such decline could be discerned. Rosa Luxemburg, Bernstein's severest critic, conceded that Bernstein's position had a certain logic to it when she wrote that if one were to admit that capitalist development does not move in the direction of its own ruin then socialism ceases to be objectively necessary. Bernstein accepted the logic of his own position and formulated a conception of socialism based upon Kantian moral philosophy in which he envisaged a socialist society to be an ideal like the Kantian 'Kingdom of Ends'. In doing this he reverted to the tradition of Utopian socialism which Marx had criticized so stringently in the work of Fourier, Owen, and Saint-Simon.

Bernstein's critique very clearly had practical consequences. Revolution was not necessary, since the twin bases upon which the need for it had been predicated did not exist; rather the struggle for socialism had to be gradualist and reformist. Politically it would consist in the attempt to achieve full democracy; economically in the appropriation by the workers, both through political power and trade union pressure, of the means of production in society. The projected socialization of German economic power had in Bernstein's view been made easier by the development of cartels in the economy, thereby rendering the ownership of economic power less diffuse. The task was therefore to struggle for particular socialist objectives, not to wait for socialism to emerge fully complete from the womb of history.

It is important to remember that Bernstein was writing with the programme of the S.P.D. in mind. Committed to revolutionary theory, and yet involved in parliamentary practice, the S.P.D. was in a state of political schizophrenia. Bernstein's revisionism was a call to German Social Democrats to be theoretically faithful to their reformist practices, for a revision of the Marxist Erfurt programme in the face of the economic and social facts which he considered he had produced. His challenge to the party failed however in the short term. At its conference in Dresden in 1903, the party adopted the following resolution:

The Congress condemns emphatically the revisionist efforts to change our tactics based upon the class struggle which have been tested and crowned with success, in such a way as to replace the capture of political power by defeating our enemies by a policy of accommodating ourselves to the existing order. The result of these revisionist tactics would be to make the party one which is content with the reform of bourgeois society instead of one which is working for the quickest possible transformation of the existing bourgeois order into a socialist society.

The reaction of the party intellectuals too was hostile. Bebel rejected revisionism largely on pragmatic grounds because in his view the Erfurt programme was the only one able to hold the party together. Karl Kautsky and Rosa Luxemburg were opposed for more cogent reasons. Indeed Rosa Luxemburg was moved to produce her *Social Reform or Revolution* (1899), which was at once a superb piece of polemic against the revisionists and a brilliant attempt to deal with their arguments from a Marxian standpoint. At the same time Kautsky produced the more pedestrian but effective *Bernstein and the Programme of the Social Democrats* (1899).

Rosa Luxemburg attempted to dismantle each one of Bernstein's theses, in particular the denial of impoverishment and the assertion of greater social differentiation. She was willing to admit that capitalism did not undergo such frequent crises as had been the case in the past, and in consequence the lot of the proletariat might superficially seem to improve, but the basic facts of exploitation, the appropriation of surplus value and the growing contradictions between the relations of production and the means of production, were still present. She argued that what the crises had lost in frequency, they would make up for in intensity and severity. She also rejected Bernstein's theory of growing differentiation. In the long run with the development of the crisis in capitalism the middle classes would be forced into implicit identification with either the capitalists or the proletarians. They had no *sui generis* stake in the structure of the society in which there was a basic division between those who did and those who did not own the means of production. She also denied the possibility of any significant political reforms from within the structure of capitalism. In the first place the capitalists would allow only those changes, for example in welfare or conditions of labour, which would protect their interest and put off the development of revolutionary consciousness on the part of the proletariat: 'Reforms are not an interference with capitalist exploitation—they lend order and regularity to such exploitation.'[4] The second reason she gave for rejecting the possibility of social reform as a means of securing a socialist society was that the relationship between the capitalist and the proletarian was not primarily a *legal* relationship, for it was based upon the *economic* fact of exploitation. Only legal relationships could be changed by the exercise of political power; exploitation on the other hand could only be ended by the expropriation of the capitalist class. She argued in *Social Reform or Revolution* that the basic conditions of the capitalist class domination could not be altered by the reform of the law, since they had not themselves been brought about by such laws in the first place.[5]

Whereas Bernstein had looked to the trade unions in the hope of seeing them exert pressure for socialist objectives, in Luxemburg's view such a thesis was quite Utopian, for all that trade unions could do was to ward off the worst features of capitalist exploitation.[6] She did not think therefore that trade unions could be instruments for the transformation of society, and, as the debates in 1905 over the possibility of a politically motivated general strike showed, she was extremely sceptical of the socialist motivation of a great many union leaders.

Rosa Luxemburg's onslaught on Bernstein's views had no effect in dampening down the revisionist controversy, and the debate continued much on the lines indicated until the first attempted revolution in Russia in 1905. This event generated a threefold split in the ranks of the S.P.D., into the revisionists, led by Bernstein and the trade union leaders; the centre, occupied, as always, by Bebel, one of the few politicians to make pragmatism an ideology; and the extreme left, led by Kautsky and Rosa Luxemburg. The particular events which occasioned this split were connected with the view of the general strike and its role in precipitating a revolution and the downfall of capitalism. The trade union leaders disliked and disapproved of the offensive use of strikes and they were much perturbed by the spate of strikes in Germany during the early months of 1905. The attitudes of those on the right were crystallized at the Trade Union Congress at Cologne in May. The general feeling seemed to be that the offensive use of the general strike was an adventurist political weapon with no sure chance of success. No doubt this negative attitude was at least in part due to the passionate advocacy of the use of the strike for revolutionary purposes by Rosa Luxemburg; the trade union leaders were still smarting from her critique in *Social Reform or Revolution*, a critique which she resumed and enlarged in her *Mass Strike, Party and Trade Unions* (1906). At the S.P.D. conference at Jena in 1905, she was scathing about the revolutionary pretensions of the trade union leaders:

The trade unions must not become their own ultimate purpose and through that an obstacle to the workers' room for manœuvre. When will you finally learn from the Russian revolution? There the masses were driven into revolution with not a trace of union organization.[7]

This contempt for trade union leaders and for the pretensions of party leaders became a central feature of her Marxism as time wore on. She trusted the spontaneity of the proletarian masses, not the bureaucratic equivocations of the official leaders of the organized labour movement. It was largely because of her German experience that she was led to reject Lenin's attempt to bureaucratize the labour movement.

The dispute between the various factions of the S.P.D. continued until the outbreak of the First World War when the bitter controversy about its character broke old alignments and healed old wounds. Kautsky and Bernstein, once ideological enemies, took a stand against the war, which had originally been approved by the majority of socialist deputies in the Reichstag. Rosa Luxemburg and Karl Liebknecht too disapproved of the war, and the stand on the issue taken by the Social Democrats, and they founded the Spartacus League, the forerunner of the German Communist party. It must be said however that in the long term revisionism and reformism were triumphant within the German Social-Democratic party, a triumph which was crowned by the explicit adoption of gradualist principles at the Bad Godesberg congress in 1959.

Revisionism in Russia?

If revisionism is defined as the revision of basic Marxian tenets in the face of what appear to be recalcitrant facts, then some might well argue that the greatest and certainly the most influential revisionist of all was V. I. Lenin (1870–1924). The reason for such a view would be the apparent but controversial inconsistency between Lenin's theory of party organization set out in *What Is To Be Done?* (1902) and subsequently defended in *One Step Forward: Two Steps Back* (1905), and orthodox Marxist theory. Lenin was vitally concerned with two problems: what he considered to be the peculiar condition obtaining in Czarist Russia, which he believed inhibited the foundation of a mass political party representing the claims of the working class as for example the S.P.D. did in Germany, and the disadvantages connected with such a party, namely that it might be tempted to seek such wide-ranging support that its revolutionary impetus might be lost, as had arguably happened in Germany. His task was to formulate a conception of party and party organization which would be relevant to the peculiar conditions of Russia, and one which would preserve its revolutionary character and lead the working class to the overthrow of the Czarist system and towards socialism. The word 'lead' in the previous sentence is of vital importance, because in Lenin's view the working class had to be *led* to socialism; it could not by itself develop socialist consciousness, and engage spontaneously in revolutionary activity and the struggle for socialism. On the contrary, left to its own devices, the working class could develop only trade-union consciousness, and yet such a form of consciousness is bound by bourgeois conceptions and indeed is a legalized form of capitalist oppression:

The history of all countries shows that the working class exclusively by its own efforts is able to develop only trade union consciousness, i.e. the conviction that it is necessary to combine in unions to fight the employers. There is much talk of spontaneity, but the spontaneous development of the working class leads to its subordination to bourgeois ideology . . . for the spontaneous working-class movement is trade union consciousness, and trade union consciousness means the ideological enslavement of the workers to the bourgeoisie.[8]

It may seem surprising that Lenin regarded unions in this somewhat jaundiced light. But the rationale of the position appears to be that workers' organizations concern themselves only with petit-bourgeois points, for example seeking to get the best rewards for labour, and benefits in terms of welfare and so on for workers, leaving untouched the fundamental malaise of capitalist society: exploitation, the contradiction between the relations of production and the means of production, and the oppression of one class by another through the state structure. Unlike Rosa Luxemburg, Lenin was highly sceptical of the possibility of the working class spontaneously developing socialist consciousness, at least in so far as it was untutored and unled. The development of socialist consciousness on the part of the working class is, of course, quite fundamental for the Marxian theory of revolution. The proletariat can be defined objectively or 'in itself', to use the Hegelian terminology, by means of its relation to the means of production, but before a revolutionary situation can truly arise and the class struggle become explicit, the workers have to develop their own perception of their role in the capitalist system, and thus become members of the proletariat as a 'class for itself', conscious of its own role in society.

Marx seems to have argued that the development of this type of perception of the social and economic structure would arise naturally and inevitably out of the actual experience of the workers, as their economic conditions deteriorated, and as the class became more and more homogeneous as a result of workers being brought together to labour in factories, etc. Social existence determines man's perception of the world for Marx. Lenin however seems to hold an unorthodox view on this point. He argued correctly that socialist consciousness involves a *scientific* perception of the real nature of capitalist society, and as such, involves a grasp of the analysis of capitalism which Marx had provided; but, as he further pointed out, socialist analysis had always been the product of bourgeois intellectuals:

The theory of socialism however grew out of the philosophical, historical, and economic theories elaborated by members of the propertied classes—by intellectuals. By their social status the founders of modern scientific socialism Marx and Engels belonged to the bourgeois intelligentsia.[9]

The problem therefore presented itself to Lenin in this form: to secure socialism it was necessary to develop a socialist consciousness, for only then would the proletariat be ready, when the conditions arose, to make the decisive break with capitalism; left to itself it would develop only in a truncated manner, hidebound by bourgeois conceptions. The development of socialist consciousness was the task of a revolutionary party consisting mainly of intellectuals whose task was to be vigilant in trying to expose the proletariat to the class-oriented character of capitalist society:

Working-class consciousness cannot be genuine political consciousness unless the workers are trained to respond to all cases of tyranny, oppression, violence and abuse. . . . these comprehensive political exposures are an essential and fundamental condition for training the masses in revolutionary activity.[10]

Lenin's view was then that class political consciousness could only be brought to the workers from without by the efforts of a small élite band of revolutionaries who were able to penetrate the veneer of society to show the underlying repression and violence.

This was not, however, the only justification for the role of a vanguard party whose task it was to develop socialist consciousness among the workers—the other justification was more pragmatic and contextual. The conditions in Russia demanded it. The role of the police in keeping track of revolutionaries, the sheer size of Russia, the difficulties of communication made the creation of a mass democratic party impossible. The vanguard party had to be small to counteract the possibility of police infiltration and detection, and this small central committee of the party would control the revolutionary movement, deciding policy, strategy, and objectives. Those outside of this central committee would be able to engage in other activities, for example the distribution of literature and propaganda, but the content of such material would be decided by the inner revolutionary cadre. The basic criticism which could be levelled against Lenin's theory is its élitist and undemocratic nature, but in fact he anticipated this criticism by pointing to the peculiar conditions obtaining in Russia at the time. The prerequisites of democracy just did not exist in Russia, as they did for example in Germany. There was no possibility of publicity relating to party officials which would enable a sensible choice to be made between them for party office in an election; if there were such publicity it would leave the party wide open to police repression. Democracy had a value in Lenin's view, but it was not the only value to be taken into account. The overriding concern was the socialist revolution: 'Think it over a little', wrote Lenin in *What Is To Be Done?* 'and you will realize that broad democracy in a party organization amidst the darkness of autocracy and the domination of the police is nothing more than a useless and harmful toy.'[11] It was this work published in 1902 which laid the foundations for Lenin's particular conception of the dictatorship of the proletariat which he expounded in *State and Revolution* (1918) and which he used to justify the strict party dictatorship which he imposed on the Russian people.

On the face of it Lenin's theory seems to be inconsistent with some elements of orthodox Marxian theory. In the first place both Marx and Engels insisted that the emancipation of the working class was a task for the working class itself, whereas in Lenin's view the participation of *déclassé* intellectuals in the workers' struggle against capitalism is a *necessary* condition of the achievement of socialism. Moreover it is arguable that as this point appears in Lenin's work it is universally true and not just necessitated by conditions in Russia. He is quite explicit on the point: 'The history of *all countries* shows that the working class exclusively by its own efforts is able to develop only trade union consciousness. . . .' The role of intellectuals in the revolution is therefore vital in any revolutionary situation, be it in Russia or elsewhere. The only feature of Lenin's theory which seems to be relative only to the Russian situation is the non-democratic element in this relationship between intellectuals and the mass of the proletariat. In the *Preface to the Critique of Political Economy* (1859) Marx and Engels had argued that a man's consciousness is determined by his social existence, but Lenin's theory seems radically to undermine this view. A perceptive critic has made this point thus:

Lenin's class teleology (or the fact that socialist purposes and goals are instilled into the workers from outside) poses a troublesome issue that still remains unresolved in Marxist theory, for if the intellectuals create the socialist ideology while the workers left to themselves achieve only trade union consciousness, what then is the meaning of Marx's statement that existence determines consciousness and class fashions ideology.[12]

It is ironic that Marxist–Leninism should now constitute socialist orthodoxy whereas it is quite possible, although of course controversial, to argue that Leninism is a fundamental revision at a crucial point of this basic conception of Marx and Engels.

However the immediate effect of the theory at the time was to split the socialist movement in Russia in two at the Congress of the Socialist Party of Russia, held in London in 1903. One faction led by Martov wanted to open up the party to enlightened members of the bourgeoisie who might be in sympathy with the party's aims. Lenin naturally rejected this. The party in his view should admit only those who were deeply committed to the socialist revolution and were willing to act on the lines laid down in *What Is To Be Done?* Lenin despised 'beautiful souls'—fellow-travelling liberals with no real socialist motivation—and argued that conditions in Russia were difficult enough without the added difficulty of distinguishing between 'talkers and workers'. The dispute between Lenin and Martov was taken to a vote and the Lenin faction carried the day; they became the majority or the Bolsheviks, those in the minority the Mensheviks.

Although Lenin emerged from the Congress victorious, his intellectual victory had yet to be won. Plekhanov (1856–1918), the *doyen* of Russian Marxists, after supporting Lenin initially became a trenchant critic; so did Kautsky, the 'pope' of German Social Democracy and the guardian of Marxist orthodoxy, at least until the time when Lenin was in a position to define orthodoxy.[13] But it was Rosa Luxemburg and, at this stage of his development, Leon Trotsky (1879–1940) who formulated the clearest reply to Lenin.

In a series of articles published in *Neue Zeit* of 1903–4 and republished in *Organizational Problems of the Russian Social Democrats* Rosa Luxemburg formulated a critique of Lenin's theory of the role and the character of the party which she was to maintain consistently up to her death in 1919, and which she was to invoke against Lenin in the months following the October Revolution in 1917. The major dispute between the theorists was over the role of spontaneity. Rosa Luxemburg flatly rejected Lenin's ultra-centralism for a variety of reasons. Central committees of parties, she argued, tend to be dictatorial, self-perpetuating, and become unresponsive to the needs and wishes of the proletariat, and she pointed out that very often the spontaneous movements of the workers showed party bureaucrats to be both ill prepared and timid:

The most fruitful changes in the tactical policy of the Russian socialist movement during the last ten years have not been the inventions of several leaders and even less so of any central organizational organs. They have always been the spontaneous product of the movement in ferment.[14]

This she saw as being particularly the case with the 1905 uprising in Russia which she regarded as going far beyond mere trade union agitation, as the speech to the Party Congress in Jena quoted above (p. 143) shows. Furthermore, in Luxemburg's view, it was possible once the distinction between party and class had been drawn for the party to become estranged from the class, and the revolutionary élite which constituted the party could very easily turn into a Jacobin dictatorship, as in fact she argued later had happened in 1918 * when she criticized the type of dictatorship of the proletariat

* This criticism of Lenin, and Lenin's own views at the time, are discussed in chapter 4, vol. II of *The Twentieth-Century Mind*.

imposed by Lenin. Certainly there was some justice in her view that party and class might come to have divergent views and interests as the post-1917 experience in Russia demonstrated. In a speech in 1921, for example, Trotsky explicitly stated that the party was entitled to assert its dictatorship 'even if that dictatorship clashed with the passing moods of the workers' democracy'.[15] This is precisely what Rosa Luxemburg feared and foresaw in 1904.

However, the dispute between her and Lenin goes far deeper than this. As was argued earlier, Lenin regarded democracy as dispensable in particular contexts such as the Russian, in a way which Rosa Luxemburg did not. She regarded the active participation of the proletariat in political struggle as the only way to generate political consciousness; it could not be induced by the tutelage of bourgeois intellectuals, but arose out of the spontaneous struggle of the workers with their oppressors, a point which she made very explicit:

> ... the proletariat require a high degree of political education, of class consciousness and organization. All these conditions cannot be fulfilled by pamphlets and leaflets, but only by the living political school, by the fight and in the fight, in the continuous course of the revolution.[16]

Whereas Lenin regarded the generation of political consciousness as a prerequisite of revolution, Rosa Luxemburg regarded it as developing not only in the struggles preceding a revolution, but also in the revolution itself. No doubt the proletariat would often fail or make mistakes, but these would all contribute to the education of the class.

The position of Trotsky over this controversy falls some way between the views of Lenin and Rosa Luxemburg. He did not go so far with the latter as to trust implicitly in the spontaneity of the working class, but at this time (his views underwent several changes* subsequently) he also disagreed with Lenin and indeed split with him in the 1903 Congress. The point of disagreement was not the centralism of the party structure *per se*, but the *type* of centralism which Lenin advocated. It seemed to Trotsky that Lenin's views involved imposing a party structure and discipline from *above*, i.e. bourgeois intellectuals imposing it on the proletariat, but Trotsky thought that such a structure would have only a very formal and external link with the working class. The situation would be altered, however, if the working class could itself develop as it were from below, a centralized party organization which

* These changes are discussed in vol. II of this series.

would have its roots in the working class, and therefore be more sensitive to working-class aspirations.[17] However this disagreement seems more slight on the surface than it really was because Lenin's whole point was that the working class was not capable of developing such a socialist party—it could develop only trade union consciousness without the aid of intellectuals, and consequently Trotsky was implicitly denying Lenin's sceptical view of the possibility of the working class attaining socialist consciousness.

II

So far in this chapter, I have been concerned to indicate the attitude of convinced socialists to the legacy of Marx and Engels, and we have seen that these attitudes varied widely, from the revisionism of Bernstein to the orthodoxy of Kautsky, from the Jacobin élitism of Lenin to the revolutionary, but democratic fervour of Rosa Luxemburg. However not only had convinced socialists to come to terms with the heritage of Marx and Engels. Marxism was not only a doctrine of a political group, but also an over-arching theory of man, society, and the state, backed up with extraordinary erudition, and with claims to be *the* science of society. Consequently any social theorist working in the decades after the death of Marx and Engels had to make his own assessment of their work as a prelude to his own. This is particularly true of the 'founding fathers of social science' who worked at this time, writers such as Durkheim, Weber, Pareto, and Sorel, who were to bequeath to social science a legacy both of questions and method with which we have still adequately to come to terms.

Sorel, Pareto, and the Attack on Rationalism

Of the thinkers mentioned, Georges Sorel (1847–1923) possibly had the most complicated and idiosyncratic relationship to the body of Marxian theory, so much so that Fascist counter-revolutionaries and committed communists have regarded him as a spiritual ancestor. Sorel began as a Bernsteinian revisionist, but paradoxically drew revolutionary conclusions from the revisionist critique of Marx; he applied his Marxism to a variety of syndicalism,* toyed with Action Française, the incipient Fascist organization of which

---

* Syndicalism is a movement among industrial workers having as its object the transfer of the means of production and distribution from their present owners to unions of workers for the benefit of the workers, the method generally favoured for this being the general strike.

Charles Maurras was the chief ideologist, and finally, at the time of his death in 1923, wrote approvingly of Lenin, an approval which was based upon a complete misunderstanding of what was going on in Russia. However, Sorel was not concerned merely to write footnotes to Marx; rather his most distinctive contributions to social theory were developed out of his complex dialectical relationship to Marxism.

Most revisionists who regarded socialism as a moral ideal and not as something inevitable, turned away from revolutionary activity to concentrate on political and social reform, and certainly Sorel was so convinced by the revisionist critique of Marx that he was for some time a Social Democrat. In addition he was an ardent Dreyfusard and was an admirer, initially at least, of the alliance between the socialists and the enlightened members of the middle class which the Dreyfus case had produced, expressing optimism about the social reforms such an alliance might bring about. However the solidarity and idealism which the case had engendered soon evaporated and Sorel made no effort to conceal his contempt for the politicians who had used the idealism for their own or for party political advantage. The full extent of his bitterness is revealed in *La Révolution Dreyfusienne* (1909), and he went further and condemned the mediocre bourgeois virtues which democracy generates. Through all the tortuous windings of his political sympathies he never once came back to the approval of reformist politics, and he retained his hatred of politicians, a hatred which was perhaps made most explicit in *Matériaux pour une Théorie du Proletariat* (1919) in which he asserted that at least one thing in life was beyond question and that was that 'nothing great can come from workers' movements led by politicians'.

The experiences described led Sorel to see politics in a new light. Although he continued to regard Marxism as unscientific, he realized that the question of its logical status was very largely irrelevant. Scientific or not, it had a very strong hold over people's lives, it was able to engage men's capacities and powers for political struggle. Science could not do this, *myth* could, and Sorel came to the conclusion that Marxism was not so much a body of verifiable scientific doctrine as a political myth, a system of vague but appealing symbols, a form of social poetry which could move men to action. In *Reflections on Violence*, he defined a myth as 'a body of images which by intuition alone, and before any analyses are made, is capable of working as an undivided whole on the mass of sentiments.'[18] Consequently in Sorel's view those who were busily engaged in drawing up the balance sheet on the claims of Marxism to be the science of society were missing the point. It was the eschatological element in the theory, not the scientific value of the economic analysis, which was valuable—the picture of the proletariat, the despised and rejected of men competing with the powers of darkness in the shape of the capitalist, trying to inaugurate a truly human society to replace a system of exploitation and repression. It was a picture which Marx himself conjured up very vividly in the final sections of *The Poverty of Philosophy* in which he talked of the 'struggle of class against class, the shock of body against body'.[19] However, once a political myth had suffered the fate of intellectual dissection as Marxism had, then it lost its power, and this led Sorel to cast around for another myth which would galvanize the working classes into action. He found such a myth in the notion of the general strike propagated by the syndicalists. The role of the general strike in syndicalist theory functioned like that of the Last Judgment for Christian theology—the image of the heroic working class defying the capitalist order in a general strike which would precipitate the overthrow of the capitalist system and inaugurate a new socialist era. It was this commitment to revolutionary syndicalism which led Sorel to write the work for which he is perhaps most famous.

The *Reflections on Violence* (1908) deals with the role of violence in political life, and on the basis of his observations in this work Sorel has been taken, partly incorrectly, as an irrationalist who advocated the adoption of political myths and the achievement of the ends symbolized in those myths by violent means. There is no doubt a large element of truth in this picture; he certainly despised what he considered to be the supine virtues of political discussion and compromise—the very stuff of democracy. But on the other side of the coin he regarded himself as someone who could discern the *actual* role which violence and myth did play below the civilized rationalistic veneer of pre-war society. As far as myths were concerned, Sorel argued that revolutionary movements whether political, moral, or religious try to disseminate myths about the future, about the final state of human society in which happiness, brotherhood, and love are achieved, and as such, the myth is an attempt not to predict the actual course of development, although it may claim to do this, but rather to interfere with the probable course of development by seeking to induce people to accept the goals articulated in the myth and to change their behaviour accordingly. This would mean that the state of affairs symbolized in the myth might come about, not as the result of the inevitable development of society, but because people, once convinced of the truth of the myth, would work for its realization and thus alter the course of social development. Successful political, social, and religious doctrines are in a sense therefore self-validating. In Sorel's view nothing in political and social experience could be predicted; he agreed with Bergson that the future is open and can always be altered by human projects. Sorel therefore regarded his characterization of political myth as an attempt to draw attention to a set of social facts. What he did reject though is the failure of people to appreciate the mythical character of political creeds, and their propensity to treat them as intellectual constructions.

In his emphasis on the role of the myth and of non-rational elements in social and political life, Sorel cast doubt upon one of the central legacies of the Enlightenment, that there was some rational way of organizing social and political life based upon an insight into human nature and the laws of social development. In *Les Illusions du Progrès* (1908), Sorel was scathing about such shallow rationalism, and in particular showed his contempt for the greatest rationalist of all and the dominating figure in French thought, Descartes. In Sorel's view, Pascal was the counterpoise to Descartes. Whereas the latter had stressed the role of clear and distinct ideas, and the necessity of not going beyond what could be certainly known, Pascal was tormented by the fact that all crucial human activities depend upon wagers, commitments, and decisions and thereby go beyond the evidence. Such a view was in Sorel's mind much closer to the actual structure of social and political motivation.

In his discussion of violence several factors enter in. In the first place violent activity would lift men above the self-seeking bourgeois virtues which underpinned the unheroic character of French society; secondly he considered that the contemporary rationalistic abhorrence of violence was quite misplaced, in that it ignored both the fact that many of the great civilizing movements in the world had been the result of violence, and because its faith in the possibility of scientific solutions to political and social problems was quite Utopian, as all these problems had mythical elements in them. By violence, Sorel did not necessarily mean force, although its exercise could end in force; rather violence showed itself in the unwillingness to compromise. Understood in this sense, Sorel argued that violence has often been a civilizing process and pointed out that it was only the unwillingness of the early Christians to compromise their faith

that enabled Christianity to take up the burden of civilization after
the fall of the Roman Empire. Civilized men must acknowledge the
debt which their civilization owes to violence, and might well owe
again in the future.

Sorel's attack on political rationalism was coupled with a shifting
and ambiguous political commitment, but it articulated an attitude
which was shared by many other thinkers, particularly in France,
during this period whose political orientation was never really in
doubt. Charles Maurras (1868–1952), Maurice Barrès (1862–1923),
Eduard Drumont (1844–1917), and, to a lesser extent, the poet Paul
Claudel (1868–1955) shared an attitude of conservatism and extreme
nationalism. While all these thinkers owed something of a debt to
the leaders of reaction from previous generations, particularly Taine,
De Maistre, and De Bonald, each contributed a significant development of his own—developments which were partly crystallized by
the Dreyfus affair.

Barrès went much further than Taine in his attack on rationalism,
for whereas the latter had been concerned merely to point out the
limits of reason in social and political experience, Barrès attacked
the whole notion of political and moral rationality, particularly in
his novel Les Déracinés (1897). The particular form of rationalism
which he attacks most vigorously was Kantianism, which he
regarded as having an insidious hold over the French educational
system. Man is not the moral monarch of all that he surveys, as
Kant had argued, deciding in the cold light of reason his moral and
political principles; such a view ignores the fact that a man is the
product of a particular juncture of time, place, and circumstance—
the Nation.[20] His morality should be determined not by reflective
reason but by a felt empathy with the spirit of the community, both
past and present. The image of the continuity of the community for
Barrès was provided by the provincial graveyards of France which
contained the remains of those who had given their lives for the
nation—this was Barrès' myth: slightly more morbid than that of the
general strike! In Scènes et Doctrines du Nationalism (1925) he
contrasts vividly the attitudes of the political rationalist with those
of the person whose judgements are based upon empathy and feeling
for the tradition of the people in terms of attitudes of Creon and
Antigone in Sophocles' Antigone:

Creon was both master and stranger. He said 'I know the laws of the
country and I will apply them'. He judges with his intelligence; the intelligence, that insignificant thing which is only the surface of ourselves. How
difficult he is from Antigone who brings the depths of her ancestry to the

same question, whose inspiration comes from the regions of the unconscious. . . .[21]

The intellectual content of the works of Drumont was virtually nil. His work *La France Juive* bears a close relation to the views of Alfred Rosenberg and Julius Streicher. He displays fantastic and barbaric ingenuity in discerning the activities of the progeny of Abraham in most of the important political matters of the day, an ingenuity which was not merely confined to an occasional book but which unfortunately showed itself regularly in his newspaper *Libre Parole*. His example shows the truth of Goya's dictum that the sleep of reason brings forth monsters.

Of all these conservative thinkers perhaps the best known was Charles Maurras, initially because of his connection with Action Française,[22] which received such a boost from the Dreyfus affair, and latterly because of his role as the chief ideologist of Petain's Vichy regime (1940–4). Maurras was committed to a vision of France, a France which existed before the Revolution, a country both Catholic and classical. Indeed so strong was his commitment to this vision that along with Jean Moréas and Ernest Raynaud he developed the *École romane*, a literary group, in an attempt to explore and recapture the Graeco-Roman roots of French culture and therefore French identity. The Revolution of 1789, Maurras saw as the result of two influences, inward-looking German protestantism and Jewish influence,[23] a combination which made for political romanticism in contrast to the classicism which he so admired. His interpretation of the Revolution is somewhat eccentric, of course; the Revolution was profoundly influenced by the hard-headed rationalism of the *philosophes*, and also by the idealization of the experience of the Greek polis, an influence which can be found for example in the Jacobins, and particularly Robespierre and Saint-Just. A combination of royalism and Catholicism, the ancient religion of the French people, was the basic ingredient of Maurras's political attitude, an attitude which, incidentally, exercised a peculiar fascination over T. S. Eliot.[24] Maurras found the nearest practical articulation of this in Pétain's Vichy regime with its conscious rejection of the ideals of the Revolution, a rejection nicely expressed by Pétain's ideology of 'Work, Family, and Country' in direct juxtaposition to the ideals of 'Liberty, Equality, Fraternity' espoused by the revolutionaries. A return to blood and soil, an attempt to rebuild the *real* France, all perception of which had vanished in the public mind since the Revolution, was the political ideal of Maurras and Pétain, an ideal for which both paid the price of imprisonment and national disgrace and degradation after the Second World War.

This tendency to diminish the role of reason in political and social experience which we have just discerned in the writing of both Sorel and the French conservatives received a massive boost from the work of the Italian social and political theorist Vilfredo Pareto (1848–1923). There is considerable similarity between the works of Pareto and those of Sorel: both were tough-minded in their rejection of accepted social and political doctrines, and in particular about the desirability and the feasibility of parliamentary democracy, but more particularly they were both concerned to stress the role of non-rational and non-logical factors in social and political experience. It would however be wrong to press the analogy too far, for there are vast differences between them too. Sorel was never a systematic thinker, whereas Pareto was a system-builder par excellence. While Sorel never managed to produce a conceptual framework which would fully accommodate his views, Pareto constructed that vast conceptual edifice,[25] that 'house of theory', *The Mind and Society* (1916), a work which stands in sharp and vivid contrast to the rambling discursiveness of Sorel's work.

Pareto, like Sorel, was profoundly influenced by Marx, albeit in a negative fashion. He wanted to demonstrate the falsity of Marxian social, political, and economic analysis, and also to account for the hold which such an obviously false doctrine could have over the minds of so many intelligent people from his generation. The particular facet of Marxian theory which he selected for most telling criticism, a criticism whose effects transcend purely Marxian theory, was the sociology of political power and the prediction of the development of a classless society after a socialist revolution. In order to understand fully Pareto's reaction to Marx's theory of class, some salient points about the latter must be recounted. Marx's economic analyses had led him to the conclusion that the exercise of political power depended on the possession of economic power in the sense of the ownership of the means of production. The State, the embodiment of political power, was therefore basically an instrument for class domination and class repression: the domination of the capitalists who owned the means of production over the proletariat which did not. The exercise of political power had therefore, in Marx's view, to be explained in economic terms. His prediction, closely allied with this, was that the process of industrialization had developed a homogeneous proletariat which would, in the final phase of capitalism, confront the capitalist class face to face, and from this conflict revolution would follow. With the expropriation of the capitalist and the development of the common ownership of the means of production, the class basis of political power would disappear and 'the state would wither away', and with it all forms of political domination.

In the view of Pareto, Marx's class analysis, and consequently his sociology of political power, were false, as was the allied prediction of a society without classes and without political domination. Marx had explained political power in economic terms—the ownership of the means of production—but Pareto explained it in terms of irreducible psychological factors. He argued that the élite which governs a country at any one time is generated not by the relation of this élite to the means of production, but rather by its possession of certain psychological attributes. The psychological concept Pareto uses is that of a 'residue', of which he distinguishes four types, only two of which are really important. 'Residues' might be translated as 'basic qualities' and in Pareto's view they do not change over time, although the style in which these basic qualities are manifested—the 'derivations'—may differ significantly. What Pareto is arguing is that human nature can be understood in terms of two mutually exclusive sets of qualities which do not change. These two sets of residues are: Class I residues, which are characterized by the instinct for combination; and Class II residues, by the persistence of aggregates. Those who possess Class I residues are men of intelligence, guile, and cunning; those with Class II are dependable, men of honour, courage, and strength. Political power is exercised by élites which possess one or the other set of these residues, and the character and the style of the rule is governed by these residues. Politicians with Class I residues like to rule through consensus and consent, both of which they obtain by compromise, dissimulation, and through making concessions. They are, in Machiavelli's classification, the 'Foxes'. The typical politician with these residues is the liberal democrat. The trouble with the exercise of power by politicians of this sort is that the very nature of their political style involves corruption and compromise. They will not use force to stay in power, and they have therefore to appease conflicting and competing interest groups. In doing so though, they undermine their own position and when this situation becomes critical, politicians of the second class take over. A ruling élite with Class II residues, the 'Lions' of Machiavelli, are men of honour, incorruptible and with complete integrity, stressing ideals before consensus, and national pride before personal gain. The paradigm case of a

Class II élite would be the takeover of political power by a group of army officers who claim to stand above politics, and the equivocations of political life, and who dedicate themselves to clearing up the mess which liberal politicians have left behind. An élite of this kind, however, cannot manage for long without bringing back into its ranks some of the politicians which it is pledged to replace. It needs the skill and the financial expertise of the politicians, and eventually so many are absorbed that a Class I élite grows out of it.

Because these basic human characteristics are unchangeable, Pareto argued that there could be no justification for thinking that politics without an élite was possible, and he contended that Marx was wrong in thinking that the proletariat was struggling for the realization of some truly human essence in its struggle against capitalism; rather it was trying to replace one élite by another drawn from its own ranks, an élite which would not differ very significantly from any other.

So obviously false did Marxism seem to Pareto that he was led to inquire why it was that so many people accepted it. He agreed with Sorel that the acceptance of Marxism or any other political, moral, or religious doctrine was non-rational, or in Pareto's language, non-logical. Political principles are rationalizations of residues, or the rationalizations of particular qualities, instincts, and drives which people already have. Activities are the result of the operation of certain residues; principles are rationalizations, and have no intrinsic motive force at all—a point which Pareto made very vividly in his famous statement: 'a Chinese, a Moslem, a Calvinist, a Catholic, a Kantian, a Hegelian all refrain from stealing, but each gives a different explanation of his conduct.' People who refrain from stealing do not do so because they believe, for example, in the Kantian Categorical Imperative, but because they possess the appropriate residue which makes them strive to preserve their integrity.

The achievement of Pareto and Sorel was in many ways negative in that they both undermined the urbane rationalism of their time; Sorel with his emphasis on the role of myth and violence in human affairs, Pareto with his insistence upon the role of the non-logical. Human nature for Pareto, and in this he echoes many on the right, is both unchanged and unchangeable and therefore irredeemable politically, and in consequence all political creeds which are predicated upon the perfectibility of man are vain.

Although Pareto's actual analysis of the generation, rise, and fall of élites has not been widely accepted, largely because of his somewhat *simpliste* psychology, and the logical difficulties connected with the concept of a residue, in particular how a residue can be identified,[26] the élitist pattern of political analysis, which along with Mosca, Pareto can claim to have started, still exercises a profound influence over political theory. Subsequent élite theorists, for example Mosca, Michels, Burnham, and C. Wright Mills, have tended not to give a psychological interpretation of the possession of power by an élite, but have concentrated more on institutional factors. In the context of this chapter perhaps the theories of Robert Michels are the most interesting, in that in his study *Political Parties* (1911), which deals with the development of oligarchic organization in the German Social Democratic party, he went a long way towards supporting the views of Rosa Luxemburg over the estrangement between the leadership of proletarian movements and the rank and file. Where he would differ from Luxemburg however is in his assertion that oligarchy is endemic in any political movement of any duration however deeply committed that movement might be in theory to the value of participation and democratic party organization. Michels advanced many reasons for what he took to be the 'iron law of oligarchy' which is a feature of all organizations. The major reason, perhaps, is that any efficient organization has to make use of the services of full-time officials, and these officials soon develop experience and expertise which sets them apart from the ordinary rank and file membership. *Qua* full-time officials, they also have a financial stake in the continued existence and viability of the party, and as such they tend to be conservative; on this point Michels put forward the interesting hypothesis that the lack of revolutionary fervour among the leadership of the S.P.D. was a result of the party's having been banned by Bismarck for twelve years as a subversive organization—if the party moved too far to the left and was banned again then the full-time functionaries would have lost their livelihood! So far of course Michels's views give some substance to the scepticism of Rosa Luxemburg over the revolutionary motivation of the leaders of the labour movement, both in the S.P.D. and in the trade unions; but his analysis would have been of very little comfort to her in that the other reason why all political movements tend to oligarchy, he said, was that the masses are apathetic towards politics, they seek merely to, in Voltaire's phrase, cultivate their own gardens, and only become interested in politics when it interferes with or has a direct bearing upon their ability to pursue their own interests. Michels could therefore discern nothing in actual political experience which would justify Rosa Luxemburg's faith in the spontaneity of the proletarian masses. An apathetic general public coupled with the unceasingly specialized nature of the kind of knowledge required to make meaningful political decisions rendered the growth of oligarchy inevitable.

Élite theory of course was directed not only against the Marxist predictions concerning the possibility of a classless society with no political domination, but also against classical democratic theories, based upon some conception of rule by the people; indeed Mosca particularly cited his opposition to Rousseau's notions of popular sovereignty. If rule by some kind of élite is inevitable then classical democratic theory has either to be discarded or, alternatively, has to be rethought in such a way as to take account of élitist criticisms. This process of rethinking the conception of democracy was not undertaken in the period under discussion, but appeared much later, in fact in our own day, with the works of the American pluralists such as Robert A. Dahl in his major work *Who Governs?* (1961)— although it must be said that A. F. Bentley's work *The Process of Government* (1908), which interprets the political process in terms not of the imposition of decisions by a self-conscious élite but rather of the competition and interplay of interest groups, was an attempt to do this. Bentley's work was not, however, widely known in this period, and it is only recently, under the influence of both pluralist conceptions and such analyses of politics as *An Economic Theory of Democracy* (1957) by A. Downs and *The Calculus of Consent* (1967), by J. M. Buchanan and G. Tullock, that the real importance of his pioneering work in this field has come to be appreciated.

Max Weber: The Phenomenology of Bourgeois Society

The work of Max Weber (1864–1920) stands in close but complicated relationship to that of Marx, and he was certainly the only figure of this period who can match Marx in the breadth of his erudition and in the brilliance of his analysis of bourgeois society. He dealt with very similar problems to those which beset Marx, and although he often acknowledged the power and the plausibility of a great deal of Marxian analysis of capitalist society, he almost invariably dissented from the conclusions which such an analysis yields. To summarize Weber's attitude to Marx in very crude and superficial terms, one might say that he considered that Marx had very often simplified and falsified complex social and historical problems by taking one factor, in particular the economic, as basic, and by treating other factors as in some way parasitic upon this basic one. Weber conceded that an economic interpretation of history and social life was possible, but he was not willing to accept any mono-causal view in its entirety. Weber's work at many points complements rather than contradicts that of Marx; but to assert that Marxism needs to be complemented already implies that it cannot be considered to be *the* science of society. Against the monocausal theory of history and society, Weber counterpoised his great work *The Protestant Ethic and the Spirit of Capitalism* (1904), which stresses the complexity of the social and cultural, as well as economic, factors involved in accounting for the change from feudalism to capitalism; to complement the conflict model of society implicit in Marxian theory Weber stresses the way in which bureaucracy can be seen to articulate some kind of universal element in society; whereas Marx had seen history as a constant dialectic between the means of production and the relations of production, Weber saw it at least in part in terms of developing secularization and rationalization; and to counter the somewhat obscure Marxian methodology of the social sciences, Weber proposed a far more careful and complex relationship between values and social science.

Weber's *The Protestant Ethic and the Spirit of Capitalism* was recognized immediately as a vitally important contribution to the debate about the validity of the materialist conception of history. Marx had argued, at least (to say more is controversial), that within the orbit of Western European civilization the principal types of social and political orders could be distinguished in terms not of their religions or ideologies, but rather of their economic systems; and that furthermore, all significant changes in social structure, political structure, and cultural life could be explained in the final analysis by changes in the means of production. This point was somewhat crudely summed up by Marx when he said that the windmill generated society with the feudal lord, the steam mill society with the industrial capitalist. Changes in the means of production in society produce tensions with the predominant relations of production, and out of this tension and contradiction social changes emerge. Weber's thesis in *The Protestant Ethic* throws doubt upon even this modest interpretation of Marx, and there are more deterministic ways of reading the Marxian texts. Weber did not dispute that economic factors play an important part in social change generally and in the change to capitalism in particular, but he did want to argue that these changes are not the only ones and that changes in the forms of religious life, which Marx consigned to the impotence of the superstructure of society, could be crucial in accounting for social change. Weber made clear his relation to Marxian theory in the very last paragraph of *The Protestant Ethic*:

But it is, of course, not my aim to substitute for a one-sided materialist, an equally one-sided spiritualist causal interpretation of culture and history. Each is equally possible, but each, if it does not serve as a preparation, but equally as the conclusion of the investigation, accomplishes equally little in the quest for historical truth.[28]

In the work, Weber argues that the change from feudalism to capitalism could not have come about had it not been, at least in some measure, for a change in men's attitude to work and to the conception of wealth which developments in Calvinistic Protestantism had brought about. The psychological problems caused by the terrible doctrine of predestination led Calvinists to cast around for some evidence of their salvation. Such evidence was eventually found in the notion of success and achievement in one's worldly calling. To work hard and be successful could not procure salvation, since the fate of the individual had been decided since the foundation of the world, but it could, so it was argued, be interpreted as a *sign* of salvation. This premium on worldly success was tied however to a rigid puritan ethic which imposed draconian constraints on consumption, and the enjoyment of wealth, and as a result of this combination of factors, capital increased. Worldly success led to the accumulation of capital not as an end in itself but as a by-product of a religious attitude to work combined with a puritan ethic. The capital which was created in this way was used to finance the development of large-scale industrial enterprises which were essential to capitalism. Without this tremendous capital accumulation, the industrial changes which generated capitalist society could not have been financed. Religious changes also had an effect upon the social structure, effects which were also essential to the development of capitalism. The religious sanctification of the worldly calling provided some justification for the division of labour which had to become more and more acute as capitalism developed, and as a result, religion provided a transcendental justification for increasing social differentiation.[29] So too the repudiation of 'all idolatry of the flesh'[30] had its effect in facilitating the standardization of products which was necessary for the development of large-scale productive activity.

All these points, made with vast documentation, make Weber's work a valuable corrective to that of Marx, and the result of his analysis has been to make historians and social scientists aware of the role that ideological factors can play in social change. At the very least, ideological factors can either slow up or facilitate change even if they do not by themselves determine the course of such change.

One factor on which Weber insisted in understanding the history of European civilization was that of 'rationalization', a concept which in his work is very closely related to the process of secularization, intellectualization, and the attainment of mastery over the external world and over social forces. Whereas Marx had stressed the role of economic factors and in particular the class struggle in history, Weber argues that one feature which a great many significant social changes in Europe exhibit is what Schiller called 'the disenchantment of the world', the exorcising from reality, both natural and social, of all those forces, magical, religious, and supernatural, which were considered to be outside human control. Weber traced the growth of rationalization in most branches of human activity, political, legal, artistic, and economic. Although he denied that rationalization was any kind of Hegelian Reason in history, he very often comes near to this position, as for example when he says: 'The process of rationalization . . . must be pursued in every field as the motivating force in evolution.'[31] Rationalization means that the world is demythologized, but this is in fact only so in principle:

The increasing intellectualization and rationalization do not therefore indicate an increased and general knowledge of the conditions under which one lives. It means something else, namely the knowledge or the belief that if one but wished one could learn it at any time. Here it means that there are no incalculable forces which come into play, but rather that one can in principle master all things by calculation. This means that the world is disenchanted, this is above all what intellectualization means.[32]

Rationalization, secularization, intellectualization, were in Weber's view all central features of European social life for the past 1,000 years, and consequently central to any attempt to explain the course of history during that period. Possibly the clearest form of rationalization in political terms, in Weber's view, was the development of bureaucracy—perhaps the paradigm of the disenchantment of the world! In Weber's opinion, bureaucracy was developed hand in hand with democracy, understood not in the sense of the extension of the franchise, or the increasing accountability of the executive to parliament, but rather in the elimination of the power of arbitrary decisions by local notables whose position may derive from some accident of birth and wealth. Bureaucratic rationalization eliminates all such features in favour of some impersonal rule-governed system operated *sine ira et studio*. Such a creation was one of the major achievements of the European states, and was perhaps the greatest example in everyday experience of the power of rationalization. The development of bureaucracy was not an unmixed blessing in Weber's view, however, because with its organizational development goes a loss in individual freedom in many respects. Because he considered that socialism would involve submission to even more vast and more impersonal bureaucracies, he rejected it. Capitalism could to some extent at least allow freedom and rationalization to coexist, but this would not, Weber argued, be the case in a planned socialist economy. Rationalization is therefore closely related to domination by large-scale organizations, a fact which Weber regards as being in some sense the fate of modern man.

The counterpoint to secularization and rationalization is *charisma*, and in particular the exercise of charismatic authority by political leaders in certain contexts. Weber did not see the last 1,000 years of European history as a unilinear drive towards rationalization; there were on the contrary sharp breaks and discontinuities. Charismatic authority, or personal political authority usually comes into play when some crisis arises with which the system of legal rational authority cannot deal. In such a situation the system breaks down. A way out of the crisis is not possible in terms of the old order because the inadequacy of that order had generated the crisis. Charismatic authority is not therefore derived from an appeal to tradition, or to the existing legal rules, but from the personal character and capacities of the leader who exercises such authority. Charismatic authority, because it attaches to the person, depends for its maintenance on the success of the leader in coping with the crisis. With failure, authority dies away (such is not the case, Weber argues, with traditional or legal rational systems of authority). When the exercise of authority is successful in that the situation which occasioned the development is overcome, then the authority becomes routinized in terms of either tradition or the previously existing legal rational system. Charismatic authority cannot survive for long in a *sui generis* fashion, mainly because it is a break with the system of rationalization, and yet this latter process has to continue, for example in the economic life of the country. To resolve this contradiction, charismatic authority has to blend back with the previously existing system, although of course it may well involve a modification of that system.

Against the Marxist monocausal view of history therefore, Weber poses a far more complex picture. He accords the factors discovered by Marx a place, and an important place, in accounting for change, but he also insists on the autonomy and irreducibility of other factors, particularly religious ideas and rationalization. His other major contributions to social thought were largely methodological, but here again we can find him confronting the work of Marx. The latter had argued that the economic structure of society had a very central place in determining the nature and the content of the ideological superstructure of society, its art, politics, philosophy, etc. Included in ideology is social and political theory. All social and political thought is ideological and therefore to a greater or lesser degree distorted; it is shot through and through with the values of the society in which the theorist lives and works. Weber admitted that values have a place in social theory but he rejected Marx's account of this relationship. Weber insisted that the initial standpoint which a theorist adopts in his treatment of social phenomena is arbitrary and influenced by the values to which he subscribes, but he went on to argue that once this standpoint has been chosen and adopted, it is then possible to go on and conduct the investigation according to the standards of objective science—relating conclusions to available evidence, not fabricating or ignoring evidence, and not going beyond what is sanctioned by the evidence.

The other problem confronting the social scientist is his relation to social policy. Here Weber argued in terms of a means-ends analysis. The social scientist cannot *qua* scientist offer any guidance about social policy—that is a matter of evaluation, and for Weber, there was an unbridgeable gap between facts and values. Once the politician has decided on the ends of social policy, the scientist may then be able to help him decide how to implement his policy, and what are the most efficient ways of achieving his end. Social science is relevant to questions of value only in this sense; it can never help men to see how to live in society.

Émile Durkheim: Social Science and Social Cohesion

Émile Durkheim (1858–1917), however, had no such inhibitions. There was in his view a very close relationship between social science and social and political policy:

We would not consider our research to be worth one hour's trouble if it were only of speculative interest. If we carefully separate theoretical problems from practical aims, it is not in order to neglect the latter, but in order to solve them.[33]

The problems with which Durkheim was concerned were many: he wanted to discover what it was that held men together in society, not for purely academic reasons, but in order to go on to show how those bonds might be strengthened in order to maximize social cohesion; he was concerned with education, particularly after the introduction of compulsory secular education in state schools after the trauma of the Dreyfus affair—an action which, he believed, would have profound consequences for the moral fabric of society: 'In a word it is necessary to discover rational substitutes for the religious conceptions which have so long served for the vehicle of most common ideas of morality'; he was disturbed by the confrontation as he saw it between the individual and the state, and was concerned to emphasize the need for some kind of intermediary groups between the individual and the state so that the individual would not feel overshadowed by it.

Durkheim's first book, *The Division of Labour in Society* (1893), attacked the basic problem of social theory, the Kantian problem: how is society possible? He rejected the views of the utilitarians who had argued that society consisted of individuals who found it a convenient way of maximizing their own utilities, and in rejecting this theory Durkheim implicitly formulated a heuristic principle which he was to adhere to all his life, 'always explain social facts in social terms'. The way in which he answered his basic question was to draw a distinction between two forms of social solidarity—mechanical solidarity, which is characteristic of primitive societies where men differ very little one from another, and in which they have no conception of their own individuality, and organic solidarity which is the kind of solidarity found in advanced societies where differentiation of function and a consciousness of individuality had arisen. Differentiation of function, or the division of labour, is a central fact in ensuring human survival and avoiding anarchy in advanced societies because it mitigates the struggle for survival between people in conditions of material density, which results from the increasing number of people within a given geographical area. Division of labour inhibits competition and struggle by giving a man a function and a role to fulfil in such a way that he is not in competition with all the other men in society at any one time, but only with those who share his function. In an advanced society, therefore, the central bond which holds people together is the division of labour: this is the social cement.

Along with this differentiation of function goes collective consciousness. No society can exist without some form of agreement on values, and the collective consciousness articulates the values which are basic to the existence of a society. In a society such as in the first decade of the twentieth century, whose structures are being eaten away with the acid of individualism, the collective consciousness may come in for questioning; a man may accept only those things which he can 'prove on his own pulses', in Keats's phrase, and he may acquire ideals and conceptions of life which cannot in fact be satisfied within his society. In such a state—the consequence of individualism—a man may become morally rootless, or 'anomic' in Durkheim's terminology. This is the pathological element in modern society, and in his book *Suicide* (1897) he points out that in some cases suicides can be correlated with certain social problems; economic crises, political difficulties, and so on. Even suicide, that seemingly most personal of human acts, may be susceptible of a social explanation, and the explanation is in terms of *anomie*, or moral rootlessness resulting from some kind of breakdown between the individual and the society in which he lives in a period of crisis for that society. Durkheim's solution to this problem was greater social discipline based upon the differentiation of function. The way of helping an individual to identify more closely with the demands of his collectivity, with the values of his society, would be to make society more personal through occupational and professional groups based upon the division of labour. These groups, Durkheim argued, would provide a clear-cut social framework wherein the individual could receive discipline, support, and a greater awareness of the values of his society; they would, as it were, mediate the collective consciousness in a manageable form. In emphasizing the role of these groups, Durkheim was giving a sociological justification for something which had long been a tenet of idealist political philosophy.

Durkheim's prescription for binding individuals to the political structure was much the same. The major danger, he argued, in politics was the same development of *anomie*. Because of the progressive centralization of the state, 'a great gap', he argued, 'has been created between the state and the individual'. The smaller units through which political power had been exercised in the past had all lost their significance with the process of centralization. The solution to this political *anomie*, the feeling of being lost in the face of a vast institution, was the same—to develop occupational groups, corporations, professional associations, and so on, in order that, in Marcel Mauss's vivid description, 'the individual is not to be alone in the face of the state and to live in a kind of alternation between anarchy and servitude'. The trouble with such a theory was, as

Durkheim pointed out in *Professional Ethics and Civic Morals* (1957), that it would be very easy to find the individual totally submerged by *group* constraint, so that in avoiding the Scylla of *anomie*, he falls into the Charybdis of group oppression. Durkheim's solution to this problem was to suggest that the state should be able to hold the oppressive features of group constraint in check while at the same time the groups helped the individual to avoid the loneliness and rootlessness which he would feel if confronted only with the state structure. Out of this tension between the state and the secondary groups in society, individual liberty would be born.

The third facet of Durkheim's thought, his educational theory, ties in very closely with the considerations already advanced.[34] The basic social and political problem of the time was, as we have seen, in Durkheim's view the relation of the individual to society, and how to strengthen this relationship in a period of individualism. The content of education too had to be directed towards helping the individual to identify with the values of his society. One central factor involved in education therefore must be an emphasis on social discipline. Durkheim rejected any kind of overall Promethean view of the aims of education, that it should develop man's capacities and powers to their limits, and encourage them to be autonomous and self-directing. Such aims have a place, so long as the paramount importance of social discipline is recognized; otherwise education will contribute to social disintegration. Education, then, has to be made relative to man's nature and to the fact that he can live a truly human life only in society. A passage taken from his major work on socialism, *Socialism and Saint-Simon* (1928), illustrates very well the conception of human nature which underlies all of Durkheim's social thought and explains the emphasis which he places on social discipline:

What is necessary for the social order to prevail is that the generality of men be content with their lot. But what is necessary for them to be content is not that they should have more or less but that they should be convinced that they do not have the right to have more. And for this to be, it is absolutely necessary that there should be an authority whose superiority they acknowledge and which lays down the law. For never will the individual left to the pressure of his needs acknowledge that he has reached the extreme limit of his desires.[35]

Nothing could be further from the rigid distinction which Weber draws between facts and values, and nothing could be further from the emphasis of Marx and Engels, that only some societies are fit environments for human beings.

The Catholic Church and Modern Society

The growing awareness of the mechanics of advancing capitalist societies during this period, and the appalling conditions under which the working classes lived in the major European cities, compelled the Church both to update and to make more articulate its social philosophy. This task was performed most brilliantly by Pope Leo XIII in a series of encyclical letters which, although strictly speaking they fall outside the time-span of this chapter, are worth considering because they have largely determined the scope of Catholic social and political thinking to the present day. The encyclical *Populorum Progressio* of Paul VI, *Mater et Magistra* of John XXIII, *Quadragesimo Anno* and *Divini Redemptoris* of Pius XI, are all deeply indebted to the thought of Leo XIII, as of course they must be since encyclicals constitute *ex cathedra* pronouncements. Undoubtedly the most famous of Leo XIII's social encyclicals is *Rerum Novarum*, issued on 15 May 1891, but others preceding its publication are also notable, in particular *Arcanum* (1880) on the role of the family, *Diuturnum* (1881) on the origin of civil society, the nature of civil power, and the relations between church and state, the encyclical on Christian citizenship *Sapientiae Christianae* (1890), the anti-socialist encyclical *Quod Apostolici muneris* (1878), and that on human freedom, *Libertas* (1888). Even without the great *Rerum Novarum* these works would constitute a major contribution to Christian social and political thought.

In *Rerum Novarum* Leo XIII emphasized that the encyclical was occasioned by contemporary social, political, and economic developments and it was as much a philosophical and theological attempt to take account of these changes as were the theories and programmes which have been discussed so far. The changes which Leo XIII was interested in were those resulting from the

. . . vast expansion of industrial pursuits and the marvellous discoveries of science; the changed relations between masters and working men, the enormous fortunes of some few individuals and the utter poverty of the masses, the increased self-reliance and closer mutual combination of the working classes, and the prevailing moral degeneracy.[36]

The aim of the encyclical, briefly stated, was to find a *via media* between laissez-faire capitalism and socialism. Unrestricted laissez-faire was socially divisive and the poverty which resulted from its operation among large sections of the population was morally unacceptable. The result of such an economic system was that ' . . . a small number of very rich men have been able to lay upon the teeming masses of the labouring poor a yoke little better than that of slavery itself.'[37] Socialism too was unacceptable as a solution to the social, political, moral and religious crisis of developing capitalist societies. It was not acceptable largely because it involved the abolition of the ownership of property, a right which Leo XIII defended in the letter with a battery of arguments. The solution as Leo XIII saw it was in the permeation of society with Christian ideas and for this of course the Church was the agent. The Church teaches that there can be no earthly salvation, no perfect political and social order this side of eternity where all divisions cease and men live in harmony, brotherhood, and love. Inequalities of wealth and social position will endure, classes will continue to exist, but the Pope stressed that such inequalities need not lead to social conflict. In fact the contrary was the case: different people with different capacities, different classes with different interests all combined to make a unity within which differentiation existed. Once men realized their metaphysical equality as children of God, their political and social inequalities would cease to loom so large.

Nevertheless the condition of the working class needed to be alleviated and Leo XIII expounded what he took to be the correct attitude of the state in regulating the social and economic order. The state had to allow a large degree of autonomy to individuals, families, and institutions, and provide a framework of rules within which private interests could be pursued. The state was, however, justified in interfering with economic life if 'the general interest of any particular class suffers or is threatened with harm, which can in no other way be met or prevented'. In this it had a particular duty to interfere when the interests of the poorer classes were involved because the rich had ways of shielding themselves from the effects of economic and social change, whereas the poor, the wage earners, had no other means of protection other than the state. The interference of the state was justified for example in regulating the hours worked by people in very arduous occupations who, if the market were allowed to operate freely, might find themselves very much exploited. Similarly the state had an ultimate right to interfere if workers are not given a living wage since everyone has a natural, that is to say, God-given, right to procure what is required in order to live.

Finally the encyclical gave encouragement to the foundation of trade unions, although they seem to be envisaged more on the lines of medieval guilds than of socially and politically oriented interest groups. The combination of working men to further their own interests as a group was given biblical backing, and encouraged in so far as the ends to be attained were legally recognized because 'It is better that two should be together than one; for they have the advantage of their society. If one fail he shall be supported by another. Woe to him that is alone, for when he falleth he hath none to lift him up.'[38] This great encyclical with its manifest care for the poor and the exploited, for the material and the spiritual welfare of the working classes in Europe, became known as 'The Workers' Charter'.

NOTES

[1] A full account of Bernstein's life, thought, and role in the revisionist controversy may be found in P. Gay, *The Dilemma of Democratic Socialism* (1952).

[2] A literal translation of the German title, *Die Voraussetzungen des Sozialismus und die Aufgaben der Sozialdemokratie* (Stuttgart, 1899). The book was published in English under the title *Evolutionary Socialism* (1909).

[3] *Geschichteskalandar* (Berlin, 1891), 123.

[4] R. Luxemburg, *Social Reform or Revolution?*, trans. Integer (Colombo, 1966), 29.

[5] Ibid. 52.

[6] Ibid. 43.

[7] Quoted in P. Nettl, *Rosa Luxemburg* (1966), I. 309.

[8] V. I. Lenin, *What Is To Be Done?* (Moscow, 1967), 122.

[9] Ibid.

[10] Ibid. 154.

[11] For the arguments put forward by Lenin on these points see *What Is To Be Done?*, 208–15.

[12] D. Bell, 'The Debate on Alienation', in *Revisionism*, ed. L. Labedz (1962), 197. For the contrary view—that Lenin's views on the vanguard party are orthodox—see G. Lukàcs, *Lenin* (1970).

[13] *The Proletarian Revolution and the Renegade Kautsky*, in Lenin, *Selected Works*, VIII (Moscow, 1967), contains Lenin's polemic against Kautsky.

[14] Rosa Luxemburg in *Leninism or Marxism*, ed. B. Wolfe (1961), 92.

[15] Quoted in I. Deutscher, *The Prophet Armed* (1954), 508–9.

[16] R. Luxemburg, *The Mass Strike, Political Party and Trades Unions* (Colombo, 1964), 27.

[17] On these points the following work can usefully be consulted: *Our Political Tasks*, in J. Baechler, *Politique de Trotsky* (Paris, 1968).

[18] G. Sorel, *Reflections on Violence*, trans. T. E. Hulme (Glencoe, Ill., 1950), 61.

[19] K. Marx, *The Poverty of Philosophy* (Moscow, 1958), 167–8.

[20] As Barrès says, 'Kantian doctrine uproots him from the soil of his ancestors' (*Scènes et Doctrines du Nationalisme*, cited in J. S. McClelland, *The French Right* (1970), 178).

[21] Cited in McClelland, *The French Right*, 160.

²² There is an interesting discussion of Action Française in E. Nolte, *The Three Faces of Fascism* (1965).

²³ This argument is to be found in *Romantisme et Révolution* (Paris, 1922).

²⁴ The influence is to be found particularly in the Preface to *For Lancelot Andrewes* (1928), and to some extent in *The Idea of a Christian Society* (1939). In *The Criterion*, VII (March 1928) Eliot acknowledges a debt to Maurras in that he had enabled him to see the role of Christianity in cultural life generally.

²⁵ This is the English title of *Tratto di Sociologica Generale*, translated by A. Bongiorno and A. Livingstone (1935).

²⁶ For an interesting critique of Pareto's conceptual framework reference may be made to P. Winch, *The Idea of a Social Science* (1958).

²⁷ For a quite admirable discussion of the major problems in this area, see G. Parry, *Political Élites* (1969).

²⁸ M. Weber, *The Protestant Ethic and the Spirit of Capitalism*, trans. Talcott Parsons (1930), 183.

²⁹ Ibid. 163.

³⁰ Ibid. 169.

³¹ M. Weber, *Wirtschaft und Gesellschaft* (Tübingen, 1956), I. 195.

³² *From Max Weber*, ed. and trans. H. Gerth and C. W. Mills (1948), 139.

³³ E. Durkheim, *The Division of Labour in Society*, trans. G. Simpson (1947), Preface.

³⁴ Durkheim's educational theory is advanced in *Education and Sociology*, trans. S. D. Fox (Glencoe, Ill., 1956).

³⁵ E. Durkheim, *Socialism and Saint-Simon*, trans. A. W. Gouldner (1959), 201.

³⁶ *Rerum Novarum*, trans. Mgr. Parkinson (1960), 7.

³⁷ Ibid. 8.

³⁸ Ecclesiastes 4:9, 10.

FOR FURTHER READING

Useful general books on the social and political thought of the period are few. H. D. Hughes, *Consciousness and Society* (1967), deals with the reorientation of European social thought between 1890 and 1930, and interestingly relates developments in social theory to wider cultural changes. In *Main Currents in Sociological Thought* (1967), R. Aron, himself a distinguished sociologist and political scientist, expounds and criticizes the sociological writings of Pareto, Weber, and Durkheim. A necessarily much more superficial treatment is to be found in the appropriate essays in *The Founding Fathers of Social Science*, ed. T. Raison (1969). C. Antoni, *From History to Sociology* (1963), interprets the development of German sociology from purely historical preoccupations. R. A. Nisbet, *The Sociological Tradition* (1967), includes a discussion of most of the major writers.

There are, of course, any number of works elucidating the thought of Marx and Engels. G. Lichtheim, *Marxism* (1964), provides a synoptic view of the development of Marxist thought through to K. Kautsky, Lenin, Rosa Luxemburg, and Trotsky. On Marxist own writings the most notable recent works are S. Avineri, *The Social and Political Thought of Karl Marx* (Cambridge, 1968), H. Lefebvre, *The Sociology of Marx* (1968), and the interesting, although eccentric, R. Tucker, *Philosophy and Myth in Karl Marx* (Cambridge, 1961). Edmund Wilson in his well-known book *To the Finland Station* (1962) traces the intellectual development of Marx, Engels, and Lenin against a backcloth of social and political changes and events. In his *Lenin* (1970) G. Lukàcs argues for a view of Lenin which is contrary to the one advanced in the present essay; in particular he is concerned to demonstrate the orthodoxy of Lenin's Marxism. Lukàcs provides an interesting discussion of Rosa Luxemburg in the second study in *History and Class Consciousness* (1971). Although a review of Nettl's *Rosa Luxemburg*, the essay 'Rosa Luxemburg' in H. Arendt, *Men in Dark Times* (1970), has considerable interest. The definitive work on Trotsky is I. Deutscher's trilogy *The Prophet Unarmed, The Prophet Armed,* and *The Prophet Outcast* (1959–64). A semi-popular history of left-wing political thought of this period may be found in David Caute, *The Left in Europe* (1966).

The ambiguous work of Sorel has yet to receive the attention which it deserves from historians of political ideas. The reader may, however, usefully refer to R. D. Humphry, *Georges Sorel, a Prophet Without Honour* (1951), and G. Goricly, *Le Pluralisme dramatique de Georges Sorel* (Paris, 1962). E. Nolte in *The Three Faces of Fascism* (1965) deals in some considerable detail with French right-wing movements during this period. A very useful source book here is J. S. McClelland, *The French Right from De Maistre to Maurras* (1970).

The debate about political élites continues unabated, although not in Pareto's own terms, and the reader is well served by two fine synoptic discussions in T. Bottomore, *Élites and Society* (1964), and G. B. Parry, *Political Élites* (1969). The work of Max Weber has yet to receive the overall attention that it deserves. The staple work is R. Bendix, *Max Weber* (1966), while J. P. Mayer deals with the cultural and political background to his work in *Max Weber and German Politics* (1943). A recent treatment by a distinguished French sociologist is J. Freund, *The Sociology of Max Weber* (1968). There are interesting discussions of Weber, Pareto, and Durkheim in P. Winch, *The Idea of a Social Science* (1958). Talcott Parsons discusses most of the sociology of the period with a view to grinding a particular axe of his own in *The Structure of Social Action* (1949).

6

Philosophy

DAVID BELL

Philosophy stands in an intimate relationship to its own past. Just as one remark in a conversation or argument provokes a subsequent remark, fully intelligible only in the light of what provoked it, so the past state of philosophy illuminates its present state. But the continual dialectic between past philosophy and present philosophical thinking does not afford a series of crucial dates around which movements of opinion may be grouped. The year 1900 is a comparatively meaningless date in philosophy; the First World War did not provoke in philosophy profound changes which echo on in subsequent years. In short, the eddies and currents of philosophy's main stream bear no obvious relation to the stuff of history. The history of philosophy is more like an account of how a conversation went than like a straightforward narrative or, say, a road accident or a military campaign. In the present essay no attempt will be made to relate currents of thought in the period 1900–18 to major political and social events of that period. It may be that the xenophobia which induced worthy citizens to persecute dachshunds and German waiters in 1914 does have something to do with subsequent contempt in Anglo-Saxon philosophy for Hegelian idealism.* But it is easy enough to demonstrate that an argued philosophical basis for such contempt existed at least a decade before the outbreak of war in 1914. Indeed, the dates circumscribing the period 1900–18 will be transgressed, for they are largely arbitrary in the light of our material. The tenuous relationships between our subject matter and common-or-garden historical narrative may be regarded as an index of the rarefied atmosphere in which we shall be moving.

The most important transgression of our period's limits will be to go back beyond 1900 to identify and sketch currents of thought against which the developments of the period may be made intelligible. The currents distinguished are four in number and we shall be concerned with their significance in the British context, despite the cosmopolitan connections of at least two of them. Broadly, we

---

* The idealist J. H. Muirhead was moved in 1915 to a defence of the German tradition in philosophy in his *German Philosophy and the War*. He argued that German philosophers were not responsible for the Kaiser's national ambitions.

shall characterize them as follows. Firstly, we need to note the existence and continued vitality of that sober-headed empirical bias, originating in John Locke, which in the nineteenth century has John Stuart Mill as its many-sided and most influential representative. Secondly, we note the dominance in academic and ecclesiastical circles of idealism,* either of a home-grown or continental variety. Church connections need to be mentioned here because, as the following quotation indicates (with all of William James's pragmatic shrewdness concerning philosophical purposes), there is an intimate connection between the popularity of idealism and the attempts of worthy, intelligent, and well-educated believers to make sense of their faith in the light of modern philosophy and natural science. James said, 'It is a strange thing, this resurrection of Hegel in England and America after his burial in Germany. I think his philosophy will probably have an important influence on the development of our liberal form of Christianity. It gives a quasi-metaphysical backbone which theology has always been in need of.' Philosophical developments in Britain in the last decades of the nineteenth century are intimately linked with the theological crisis. James's observation is further illuminated when it is noted that 'the most prominent spokesmen for British Idealism were all sons of Evangelical clergymen within the Church of England'.[1] Thirdly, we shall need to recognize the increasing importance of experimental and theoretical advancement in the natural sciences. Darwin's evolutionary theories, Mach's radical empiricism and anticipations of relativity, and finally Einstein's re-examination of the nature of space and time in physical theory, all had repercussions in philosophy. By the time that our period opens there is a growing conviction among some philosophers that an intimate acquaintance with natural science is as important a weapon in the philosopher's armoury as the ability to illustrate an argument by reference to Plato and Aristotle. In our period and largely through the work of Russell, the dominant philosophical themes are expounded by philosophers who set out not to transcend the knowledge afforded by natural science but rather to justify it against sceptical attack. Russell said in 1914: 'There is not any superfine kind of knowledge, obtainable by the philosopher, which can give us a standpoint from which to criticise the whole of the knowledge of daily life. The most that can be done is to examine and purify our common knowledge

* Idealism: any system in which the object of external perception is held to consist, either in itself, or as perceived, of ideas. This philosophical meaning is *not* that of popular usage (i.e. idealism meaning aspiration towards an ideal).

by an internal scrutiny, assuming the canons by which it has been obtained.'[2]

Fourthly, we need to note the revival of formal studies stemming not only from researches into the foundations of mathematics by Bolzano, Dedekind, Peano, and Cantor but also from the writings of Sir William Hamilton, George Boole, and Augustus de Morgan.

So much then for general background. Does any general theme emerge from such a background for the interpretation of our period? There is one which relates to all the elements so far identified, namely the development of Russell's opinions. While it would be an exaggeration to say that the history of Anglo-Saxon philosophy in our period is largely the history of Russell's opinions, his standpoint is sufficiently comprehensive to deserve a principal position in any synoptic history. Let me briefly indicate why. Russell, a godson (if that is possible) of John Stuart Mill, early became an apostate from that powerful and original brand of British idealism concocted by F. H. Bradley. It was a dissatisfaction with the role accorded to scientific and mathematical knowledge which provided the stimulus for Russell's critique of Bradley's logic and metaphysics. The upshot of this is a refurbished and enhanced empiricism in the tradition of Hume and Mill, but carried forward by an assimilation and utilization of ideas thrown up in the course of the revolution of the formal sciences referred to above. It is this bulldozer of old empiricism and new mathematics which by the early 1930s had removed from the philosophical landscape almost every trace of the idealism which had dominated academic philosophy and much else in the last decades of the previous century. A thorough grasp of the arguments and issues at stake is indispensable to an understanding of our period.

Even though an exposition of Russell's central opinions formed and published during our period is the chief thread to guide us through the maze, it would be misleading not to emphasize in these preliminary strategic sketches two things.

Firstly, Russell's opinions not only owed a great deal to the elements in nineteenth-century British and continental philosophy already alluded to but also to the active co-operation and stimulation of three other figures, G. E. Moore, Ludwig Wittgenstein, and A. N. Whitehead. During the period of our survey Russell was actively co-operating in logical and philosophical projects with all three, even though their philosophical journeyings were subsequently to take each of them into different territory. The great single monument to this co-operation is the *Principia Mathematica* of

Russell and Whitehead of whose contents, despite its technicality, some account must be given.

Secondly, we must not forget the many able philosophers of this period who, for one reason or another, remained uninfluenced and unimpressed by the new movements of philosophical taste and opinion. The work of important thinkers of originality and abiding interest such as Alexander, and Bosanquet, testifies to a wide diversity of preoccupations on the British philosophical scene. The position taken by these thinkers deserves some expository mention.

Finally, a word should be said about philosophical ethics in our period. It was not a central preoccupation of philosophers, which perhaps reflected an absence of debate on fundamental issues bred by a monolithic Edwardian complacency and optimistic belief in gradual moral and political reform. The great moral issues of the public life of the period—the question of the condition of the people and its relation to the duties of the state—was not a widely debated issue among professional philosophers. The philosophically under-pinned moral commitment and earnestness of T. H. Green may be agreed to have had influence upon public life at some levels. But the moral issues which lay at the roots of the disputes between liberals, socialists, and traditionalists were not much debated by professional academic philosophers. The chief developments in moral philosophy were consequences of the decline of idealism. The new methods of philosophical discussion and approach were generalized to cover the traditional problems of ethics; the *Principia Ethica* of G. E. Moore stands beside the *Principia Mathematica* of Russell and Whitehead as a paradigm of method. In that work Moore puts his analytical knife not only to the ethic characteristic of idealism but also to the more sober-minded native-born utilitarianism of Bentham and Mill. Herbert Spencer's evolutionary ethics also does not escape, despite its widely appealing synthesis of Darwinian themes and *laissez-faire* industrial capitalist principle. One is justified then in regarding every significant philosophical basis of late Victorian moral optimism as being corroded if not dissolved away by the analytical reasoning of Moore's work. The resultant scepticism of anyone who was convinced by Moore's argument might reinforce and be reinforced by a corresponding scepticism induced by Russell about the comforting metaphysico-religious certainties of idealism. Perhaps the most lasting effect of the comprehensive destructiveness of Moore's *Principia Ethica* was to replace philosophical debate *within* ethics, by philosophical debate about the whole enterprise and *logical* status of ethical inquiry.

Scepticism about morality deriving from logical considerations could also ally itself with scepticism springing from the sociologist's and anthropologist's newly awakened interest in the widely different moral practices of peoples separated from us in time and space. Books such as Hobhouse's *Morals in Evolution* and Westermarck's *History and Origin of the Moral Ideas* were equally corrosive of moral certainty. However, it should be pointed out that although Moore's work in ethics ultimately resulted in a new variety of moral scepticism, Moore himself preached a positive if rarefied form of moral intuitionism, a doctrine perhaps only one step away from moral scepticism, as may be grasped by a study of an article by H. A. Prichard, an influential Oxford philosopher of the period. Prichard called his article 'Does Moral Philosophy Rest on a Mistake?', the suggested mistake being that of the very attempt to provide a rational foundation for morality. Prichard's positive conclusion is again intuitionistic; judgements of moral obligation are self-evidently valid and the whole enterprise of providing them with a foundation other than their intrinsic validity is misconceived.

A word should be said here about the restriction to British philosophers implicit throughout. This might be thought a manifestation of an insularity often held to be characteristic of British philosophy. We have already quoted William James's remark about the late arrival of Hegelian idealism on the British scene and this is an implicit admission of the importance of both Hegel and Kant as determinants of one important aspect of the nineteenth-century background. However, there are other claimants. The developments in logic and the foundations of mathematics were important evidence of the European nature of the scientific community. Bolzano, Weierstrass, Cantor, Dedekind, and Peano laid many of the foundations for Russell's early work, which on the logical side had been largely and brilliantly anticipated by the German mathematician Gottlob Frege (1848–1925). As one historian of the period has said: 'The logic of mathematics was a continental creation which yet achieved its classical form in Russell and Whitehead's *Principia Mathematica*'.[3] Also the logical and epistemological doctrines of Brentano and Meinong exercised an important influence upon the early Russell and Moore.

Other important foreign philosophical movements—important, that is, in their own right—are unimportant in comparison with these. Of them we might mention first Henri Bergson (1859–1941), then at the height of his fame in France. In 1911 Bergson gave the Huxley Lecture in Birmingham and J. H. Muirhead, who was present, noted the opposition of Bergson's thought to prevailing trends adding that, '. . . suspicion of it deepened when it received the enthusiastic approval of William James.' This rejection of Bergson by the professional philosophers is puzzling. William James and later Whitehead leant heavily upon Bergsonian insights. Bergson's own attempt to reconcile the realm of human consciousness with the material world studied by the non-biological sciences through his notion of creative evolution should have at least appealed to a generation familiar with evolutionary biology. It was perhaps the manner rather than the matter which repelled philosophers seeking ever sharper instruments to ply their trade. As a glance at *Creative Evolution* (1907) will confirm, Bergson's style is replete with striking metaphor and generates the suspicion that the superb literary façade hides a crumbling eclectic fabric. Russell certainly found it difficult to accept him as a truly scientific thinker, despite Bergson's constant recourse to scientific material to exemplify and support his philosophical doctrines.

James's philosophy of pragmatism had a lonely banner carried for it in Oxford by the lively F. C. S. Schiller but it took little or no hold upon British philosophers. Idealists regarded it as a corruption of their own philosophy while Russell and Moore took issue with it as corrupting logic. Either way it could only lose. Nevertheless, it ought to be said that William James's *Principles of Psychology* (1890) and his *Varieties of Religious Experience* (1902) exerted some influence, particularly the former. Its emphasis on the status of psychology as a humane discipline, its attack on Mill's idea that mathematical and logical principles are generalizations from experience, and the attack on the idealist insistence on the internality of relations, contributed to the new climate of opinion which was emerging in British as well as American philosophy. But despite this, James's own pragmatism remained a matter of scandal to most British philosophers. Of more importance is to notice a development in the United States which runs parallel to key changes initiated by Russell and Moore in Britain. This was the New Realism programmatically set forth by a group of American philosophers in a book of that title in 1912. This polemical work set out to turn a tendency of philosophical thought into a school, chiefly by insisting, against idealism, upon the independence of the knower and the object of knowledge as Moore and Russell had done some ten years before.

To sum up the general strategy of what follows as dictated by this preliminary discussion: we shall need to begin with a brief exposition of nineteenth-century British idealism and empiricism; we shall look at developments in the formal sciences of mathematics and mathematical logic. This background will place us in a position from which the attack upon idealism, spearheaded by Russell and Moore, can be understood and the impact of a refurbished empiricism and philosophical methodology appreciated. Before turning to philosophical ethics we shall mention major thinkers who fall outside the Russellian guiding thread we have chosen to follow. Finally, we shall consider, chiefly in connection with G. E. Moore, the new direction taken by philosophical ethics.

I

The Empirical Background

'Empirical', in common with most philosophical adjectives, is difficult to comprehend in a single definition. For our purposes we shall take it as connoting respect for the deliverances of ordinary sense-perception. Beyond this philosophical problems begin to emerge which mere definition cannot resolve. For nineteenth-century empiricists respect for experience was something which went along with respect for natural science. No better representative of this coupling can be found than John Stuart Mill. Mill was self-consciously aware of his inheritance from the empiricist estates of Locke, Berkeley, and Hume. In his major writings he appears as the systematizer and proponent of this tradition. His major philosophical writings neatly illustrate this. The *Examination of Sir William Hamilton's Philosophy* (1865) is an attempt to topple from its influential position a transcendental and intuitionist philosophy which Mill saw as internally inconsistent, obscurantist, and stultificatory of the progress of both science and philosophy. His *System of Logic* (1843), which went through eight editions in Mill's own lifetime, was an attempt to systematize 'the principles of evidence and the methods of scientific investigation' on an empiricist basis.

The very vigour, comprehensiveness, and judicially candid nature of Mill's attempt made the defects of a radical empiricism more obvious than they had perhaps hitherto been. The difficulties emerging by Mill's work are firstly, that of accounting for the certainty and truth of mathematics and logic; secondly, the difficulty, familiar since at least the time of Locke, of accounting for the common-sense belief in a natural world existing independently of our experience of it, on the supposition that our knowledge of it is derived from sense-experience. This difficulty, as old as Plato, arises mainly because sense-experience is fleeting and changing and hence appears to provide little basis for knowledge of a stable world of continuously existing material bodies which are there whether or not anyone is experiencing them. Both the idealist attempt to dispense altogether with the reality of anything independent of some experience of it and the rationalist attempt to give us access to knowledge of reality through reason alone are rejected by Mill. So on the one hand he is forced to explain mathematical and logical knowledge as being constituted by generalizations from experience and on the other to embrace a phenomenalism which makes our notion of a material object that of nothing more than 'a permanent possibility of sensation'. However, with regard to the first point, it is difficult to see how the truth of '$2 + 2 = 4$' could rest upon experience as distinct from finding exemplification within it. It seems that nothing could turn up in experience which might make this false. On the second point, Mill's extreme phenomenalism not only offends common sense but does so in a way which comes perilously close to Berkeley's idealist dictum that to exist is to be perceived. So it cannot really be said that Mill's *Logic* takes empiricism very far in the solution of its classic difficulties. Mill's empiricist successors inherited the joint problems of accounting for mathematical knowledge and avoiding a relapse into idealism in accounting for our knowledge of nature.

Despite these ultimate failures at the philosophical level Mill's philosophical thinking was widely influential. Whenever the German philosopher Nietzsche polemically characterizes the English philosophical climate he does so by reference to Mill and his scientific empiricism. Nevertheless, it must be said that Mill's followers were probably more numerous outside the English universities of his time than inside them. It takes an effort to see the obsession of mid-century Oxford with theological and spiritual niceties as co-existing with the hey-day of Mill's influence. But at the mid-century there was not, in England at least, any philosophical orthodoxy with a university base which could compare in scope and power with Mill's refurbished empiricism. However, in the course of the generation after 1850 one was constructed which was destined to have a grip on Oxford philosophy until well after the turn of the century, an orthodoxy moreover which was to exercise a wide influence upon public life. It self-consciously conceived its basic duty to be that of replacing by rebuttal the empiricist philosophy of mind associated with Mill's influence and that of followers such as Alexander Bain.

The chief opponents of Mill, F. H. Bradley (1846–1924) and T. H. Green (1836–1882), were both Oxford philosophers who had, somewhat tardily in continental terms, come to absorb something of the philosophies of Kant and Hegel. In addition they had strong moral interests and both considered that utilitarianism, which had been since Bentham the philosophical background of reformist politics, was a creed which did less than justice to man's spiritual and practical capacities. This attitude to Mill's moral philosophy was perhaps a little unfair; Mill's strong interest in the fundamental roots of social and political reform had led him to broaden the Benthamite emphasis on the harmonization of self-interest into something that appeared to be at least one step on the road to an ethics of self-realization. Nevertheless the attack on empiricism by Bradley and Green was forked, directed both against its philosophy of mind and against its account of morality. Bradley published his *Ethical Studies* in 1876 and his *Principles of Logic* in 1883. Green, returning to the fountainhead of modern radical empiricism in Hume, published a long critical introduction to Hume's *Treatise* in 1874 and a *Prolegomena to Ethics* in 1883. All four works made abundantly (and in Bradley's case scathingly) clear that the new idealism was forcefully hostile to empiricism, to natural science and its methods, to utilitarianism, and even to the evolutionary ethics of Mr. Herbert Spencer. The bland assumption of this passage from Bradley's Preface to the *Logic* conceals more than merely polemical irony: 'What we want at present is to clear the ground, so that English philosophy, if it rises, may not be choked. The ground cannot be cleared without a critical or, if you prefer it, a sceptical study of first principles. And this study must come short, if we neglect those views which, being foreign, seem most unlike our own.'

We should not leave the impression that the purport of the new idealism was negative and sceptical. The cast of Bradley's mind was deeply critical, that of Green less so. But in his *Logic* Bradley's unerring critical instinct had led him to place emphasis upon the fundamental weakness of the prevailing empiricism, namely its account of judgement and meaning. His treatment of this particular issue was to constitute a partial move towards the new foundations for logic which were to come to fruition in Russell's work. On the purely theoretical side Green's work has not the penetration of Bradley's. But in his teaching and published work he was, before his early death at forty-six, to contribute to a philosophical climate which motivated an earnest and dedicated devotion to social and personal improvement which went far beyond the confines of Oxford tutorials. Green and his pupils were even to end up advocating from the lofty pinnacles of their idealism measures of social and political change urged on a more mundane basis by the rapidly growing labour organizations and reformist movements of the later part of the century, something which perhaps reinforces the view of Oxford idealism as a secularized version of a rationally discredited Anglican orthodoxy. While the Bible could not perhaps be taken seriously by a well-trained philosopher, an attempt had to be made to avoid tossing out the moral baby with the revelatory bath water. Benjamin Jowett, master of Balliol and half a philosopher, tells us that 'Green wants to write a sermon in which the language of theology is omitted—a Christian discourse meaning the same thing in other words.' He added his own comment on the project: 'The attempt is worth making, but it requires great genius to execute it. The words will seem thin, moral, unitarian. . . . Yet something like this is what the better mind of the age is seeking—a religion independent of the accidents of time and place.'[4]

The new idealism set its course away from an interest in and a respect for natural science. In so doing it cut itself off from a salient intellectual movement of its period and more especially from the mathematical work which was to revivify logic. For Bradley, as for Hegel, the careful observational study of the natural world was a low-grade kind of thought and the philosophical auspices under whose guidance it was carried on were riddled with contradiction. Bradley had arguments to show that to suppose that existence of a reality consisting of material bodies independent of each other and of our perception of them but mutually interacting in a way traceable by natural sicence, was to suppose a mere abstraction. Still more, to suppose further that we have access to such a reality by means of sense-perception and sensation was to attempt an account of knowledge similarly based on an abstraction. The empiricist assumption that knowledge is based upon sensation and that uniformities among sensations are our clue to the uniformities among realities which science seeks in its laws to state, is wholly rejected by Bradley. To him the anatomy of knowledge is not the anatomy of sensations and the ways in which they are associated. Thought ought not to be regarded as a mechanical shuffling of acquired sensory images. Above all the conclusion which Bradley drew from his critique of sensationalism and associationism was that an idea was not to be regarded as a psychological entity mechanically associated with other entities of the same kind. For him the crucial thing about an idea is not its ontological status as an item of psychological furniture but its meaning: 'Judgement is neither the association of an idea with a sensation, nor the liveliness or strength of an idea or ideas. The ideas which they (sc. the associationists) speak of are psychical events, whereas judgement, we have seen, has to do with meaning, an ideal content which is universal, and which assuredly is not the mental fact.'

This insistence on the basic nature of 'ideal content', 'meaning', and the universal in logical theory had the effect of freeing logical study from the psychologism into which, on the empiricist view of the nature of thought, it had always been in danger of falling. Historically the view that man is the measure of all things and hence of logic stems from Protagoras, but in the modern period it was Hume who had set out to discover human nature at the root of the necessities of thought. Whatever else in Bradley was to be jettisoned by Russell and Moore, they were never to question Bradley's trenchant assertion of the independence of logic from any kind of psychology. It is worth mentioning that Bradley's insistence on the autonomy of logical science *vis-à-vis* psychology antedates the similar polemic conducted by Edmund Husserl (1859–1938), the founder of phenomenology, and parallels Frege's insistence that mathematical truth does not have a psychological explanation. Nevertheless, despite this step towards the new logic, Bradley remained an opponent of its development and when we come to the account of Russell's opinions we shall see why. In a broad sense it had to do with Bradley's monism, with his assumption that in the long run everything is not only connected with everything else but is one aspect of a single whole reality which thought, by its analytical activity, breaks up into apparent pluralities. The distinguishing, sifting, analytical activity of thought is presented by Bradley as something that takes us away from the concrete unity of reality into a world of abstractions. The new logic, in contrast, was conceived as an analytical tool appropriate for laying bare a pluralistic world of numbers and their relations.

The dominance of idealism at any time over the English philosophical scene was never complete. Bradley's own version of the creed was too much stamped with his own magnificently caustic polemical style to be wholly acceptable to others. T. H. Green's influence was exercised much more through his teaching than through writing markedly less trenchant than Bradley's. Even in Oxford, home of

English idealism, John Cook Wilson (1849–1915), Professor of Logic from 1899 to 1915, was arguing against both Bradley's logic and epistemology and for objective realism. He did so in part out of a conviction that accounts of the nature of thought and judgement pay too little attention to the actual forms which thoughts and judgements take when expressed in ordinary language. Cook Wilson's respect for the niceties of ordinary language as a preliminary to philosophical speculation is derived from Aristotle's habit of carefully surveying uses of expressions before theorizing about them. It also constitutes an anticipation of later so-called ordinary language philosophy. Cook Wilson, however, published little during his own lifetime and it is not his attack on idealism which discredited it.

Idealism was to some extent undermined from within. Like all influential schools of philosophy it developed controversy within itself. Many of the issues involved sprung from different assessments as to how far idealism in Bradley's form was adequate to play the role of a rational reconstruction of largely Christian insights. Bradley's absolute idealism seemed to make individual selves nothing but adjectives or aspects of the absolute. A school of personal idealists arose under the leadership of Andrew Seth (later A. S. Pringle-Pattison), intent on defending the unique reality of the self against the engulfing claims of the absolute. This reaction to Bradley can be seen as a British parallel to Kierkegaard's reaction to Hegel's idealism, a view reinforced by Seth's insistence that any idealism must be such as to accommodate as real the trinity of nature, God, and self, without which orthodox Christianity would be unthinkable.

But the *coup de grâce* to idealism was not to be delivered from within but from outside. To understand this we need to look towards the history of logic.

The Logical Renaissance of the Nineteenth Century

Modern philosophy is often regarded as starting with Descartes. One justification of this is to be found in Descartes's novel insistence on the paramount role of method in philosophical thinking. Descartes modelled his philosophical method on his own understanding of mathematical method. He was a mathematician himself and considered that of all the sciences mathematics provided clear and certain knowledge. Hence, to achieve clarity and certainty elsewhere, disciplines should model their method on that of mathematics. However, this emphasis on mathematical method came to be interpreted as the practical necessity of clarifying one's ideas.

Everyone who studies philosophy is familiar with the necessity of clear definitions and rigorous thinking, so this is unexceptional enough. But what was missing, despite all this emphasis on method, was an instrument for such clarification. Neither Descartes nor Locke, Berkeley, and Hume, saw the necessity of constructing an instrument for assisting in the clarification of ideas. The existing instrument was essentially the syllogistic of Aristotle, taught in a corrupt form. Descartes and Locke, for different reasons, were both contemptuous of this logic as an instrument of thought. Descartes paid little attention to it because it is incapable of throwing very much light on the nature of mathematics. Locke rejected it as a mere formal exercise connected with a scholasticism which he deplored and throwing no light upon how we acquire the content of our ideas in experience. Leibniz alone among his methodologically minded contemporaries had conceived the project of a universal grammar in which all necessary distinctions might be formulated. In addition he had divined and worked out certain similarities between reasoning with words and reasoning with numbers. While the project of a universal ideal language, which could be manipulated like a calculus and which would guarantee in formal terms the transmission of truth from true premises to true conclusions, never quite died out, it was scarcely a matter of debate among philosophers or logicians. Kant, despite the fact that his work bursts the bounds of the traditional formal logic, nevertheless expressed himself well satisfied with the view that Aristotelian logic enshrined all the differences of form among statements which logic needs to recognize. If one considers that syllogism cannot account for the obviously valid deduction of:

All who draw circles draw figures

from:

All circles are figures

the satisfaction is well-nigh staggering.

One should not in this picture of the logical dark ages from Aristotle to the nineteenth century get the impression of pitch darkness. The late medieval period and the Stoic successors of Aristotle had developed formal logic in a number of directions. But this was done piecemeal and not systematically. Above all these developments lacked the insight which we owe to the nineteenth century of the unity of formal methods in both mathematical and non-mathematical thinking. Given a predominantly mathematical natural science, and given also a demonstrated unity of logical and mathematical thinking, logic was bound to move back into a central role in any examination of the nature of knowledge. This is the significance of the nineteenth-century developments which we must now sketch.

The stimulus to the redevelopment of logic came in fact from the intuitionist and transcendentalist opponent of J. S. Mill, Sir William Hamilton. He suggested an extension of traditional syllogistic involving quantification of the predicate. This suggestion arises from the recognition that the Aristotelian form 'All A is B' is ambiguous as between 'All A is *some* B' and 'All A is *all* B'. While there was nothing especially new or of great intrinsic importance in this suggestion, it does suggest the further possibility of casting logical statements into an equational form like that found in algebra. To take our example, 'All A is some B' could be written as the equation, 'All A = Some B', while 'All A is all B' could be written as the equation, 'All A = All B'. These equational forms of logic were developed by Augustus de Morgan, who in his writings clearly demonstrated that logical rigour was not to be confined to the handling of the traditional forms of statement. It could be applied to other forms of statement as well and a calculus was constructible exhibiting the relations of these forms. Such a calculus was actually constructed by George Boole and presented in his *Mathematical Analysis of Logic* in 1847. The basis of Boole's system is the elective operation whereby a number of objects are selected from a larger group of objects, as when we pick out the class of whales from the class of mammals. Boole was then able to state general laws governing the results of such elective operations. For example, if the symbol x represents the result of selecting all the x's in the universe and y represents the result of selecting all the y things from the x's, then this result can be treated as analogous to algebraic multiplications and expressed x *Product* y i.e. the class of things which are both x and y. Furthermore, we can state as a theorem that it doesn't matter whether we first select the x's and then the y's or vice versa, that is we have:

$$xy = yx$$

Also performing the same election twice gives us $xx = x$ or $xz = x$. In this way Boole was able to demonstrate a hitherto not widely appreciated strong analogy between algebra and logic. As he put it in his introduction:

Every process (sc. of the calculus) will represent deduction, every mathematical consequence will express a logical inference. The generality of the method will even permit us to express arbitrary operations of the intellect, and thus lead to the demonstration of general theorems in logic analogous, in no slight degree, to the general theorems of ordinary mathematics.[5]

What we know today as Boolean algebra and utilize in the design of computing systems is, essentially, the system of Boole. Hence, he may be regarded as the founding father of modern symbolic logic. Boole's success in the construction of a logical calculus stimulated further work in all manner of directions. Charles Sanders Peirce (1839–1914), an American philosopher of undoubted genius, took up and systematically developed the insights of De Morgan and Boole. In particular he did two things: he refined the Boolean algebra, purging it of extra-logical elements, and he incorporated in its formal framework a logic of relations, which was to influence Russell through a report of Peirce's work in William James's *Principles of Psychology*. The inference noted earlier as incapable of expression in syllogistic logic of, 'All who draw circles, draw figures' from the premiss, 'All circles are figures' was now drawn into the ambit of systematic logic through an account of the formal properties of relations. To say of something that it is red is not to relate one thing to another thing. However, to say of one thing that it is to the left of another thing or of one person that he gives something to another person is to relate one thing to another thing. The traditional logic had neglected the study of relational statements, a type of statement obviously involved in the inference under discussion. For in moving from the premiss, 'All circles are figures' to the conclusion, what we appear to be doing is relating the class of persons to the class of geometrical figures by introducing the relation 'draws'. One of the reasons the traditional logic had neglected relational statements was its dogmatic assumption that every statement had to consist of a subject and predicate united by a copula. Clearly, it is only with some strain that 'A gives B to C' can be regarded as, 'A is *giver of B to C*'. As we shall see the whole topic of relations is of vital importance in Russell's arguments against idealism.

A logical development of a connected but different kind now requires notice. It was stimulated in part by developments in mathematical analysis itself. Since the time of Newton the differential calculus had proved an indispensable tool of physical theory. Despite the fact that it worked, that is gave the right answers, its formal foundations were obscure. Hence Bishop Berkeley's attack on the mathematicians of his day was entitled: 'The Analyst: or, a discourse addressed to an infidel mathematician. Wherein it is examined whether the object, principles, and inferences of the modern analysis are more distinctly conceived, or more evidently deduced, than religious mysteries and points of faith'. Scepticism about the rigour of mathematical deductions and the consistency of certain branches of mathematics had induced a series of attempts at foolproof formalization wherein all assumptions required for the development of a theory could be rigorously and clearly exposed. One impulse in this direction had come from the development of apparently consistent non-Euclidean geometries. This had two effects: one was to point up the dangers of relying on intuitions of self-evidence as many mathematicians and philosophers had done over the necessary truth of Euclid's parallel postulate; the other was to free mathematical systems and especially geometry from reliance upon the conclusions of visual experience. The question of geometrical truth was seen to rest not upon the self-evidence of geometrical axioms in terms of visual conceivability but solely upon the internal consistency of the geometrical system. So an interest in rigorous formalization of geometrical systems was bound to interest geometers. A medium was needed in which the formal structure of a mathematical system could be made clear and the deductions yielded from the axioms and postulates of the system tested for validity.

The work of Boole, De Morgan, Peirce, and a German mathematician F. W. E. Schroeder (1841–1902) had shown the way to a solution of this problem by developing a logical calculus. A group of Italian mathematicians under the leadership of G. Peano (1858–1932) set out to reconstruct mathematics on the basis of a few logical ideas and a small number of primitive mathematical ideas (zero, number, and the successor of a number). For this purpose Peano invented a symbolism which was more useful for this purpose than any developed previously, and it was essentially this symbolism that was to be adopted and adapted by Russell and Whitehead in their *Principia Mathematica*. Peano's work went farther than anything hitherto accomplished in showing that apparently autonomous mathematical ideas could be defined in terms of logical notions. It did not however go far enough nor as far as was possible in this direction. It was left to Russell and to the German mathematician Gottlob Frege to carry the reduction of mathematics to logic much farther and show how the whole of classical mathematics could be generated from a few logical notions together with a handful of not obviously mathematical assumptions. The demonstration, which we shall later examine in more detail, was achieved independently by Russell and Frege. It had two general consequences of great importance for philosophy. Firstly, it moved formal logic to the centre of methodological debate. Secondly, it provided a model of the *reduction* of one set of notions to another by rigorous analysis and formal definition of concepts. The method was too successful to resist generalization to fields other than that of mathematics.

The Work of Russell

To define Russell's philosophical achievement in a sentence is difficult and probably worthless. But one can say that it was a successful wedding of the new mathematical logic with the old empiricist tradition. Like all unions it has had its ups and downs but even today it ranks as one of the most successful and influential of twentieth-century philosophical movements. It is not the work of Russell alone as our previous discussion has made clear. But so much from other sources crystallizes in his work that he is a representative figure. In the course of expounding Russell's work we shall have to refer to two philosophical contemporaries to whom it owes much, G. E. Moore and Ludwig Wittgenstein.

Bertrand Russell (1872–1970) was born an English aristocrat and the speed with which he has always been able to change and develop his opinions reflects an aristocratic freedom.* Due to the early death of both parents he was brought up in the house of his grandfather, the radical prime minister and politician Lord John Russell. John Stuart Mill was his godfather, as Russell said, 'in so far as is possible in a non-religious sense'. He was never subjected to the conformist atmosphere of public-school education and was privately tutored until going up to Cambridge in 1890 to read mathematics, a subject in which he had evinced a lively interest since the age of eleven. The Cambridge of Russell's youth contained brilliant men and possessed an intellectual variety and freedom scarcely paralleled since. Victoria's reign was coming to its dignified but solid and optimistic close and a degree of social complacency in people of Russell's class made possible a pure devotion to things of the intellect. After completing the mathematics tripos Russell studied philosophy for a year and, under the influence of James Ward, G. F. Stout, and McTaggart, left Cambridge a convinced Bradleian idealist. This

* The writing of this essay preceded the publication of Russell's autobiography. Subsequent perusal of it has convinced me of the great light it sheds on the development of Russell's opinions. I have not however found anything importantly inconsistent with my interpretation.

Bradleian phase persisted at least until 1898. Writings of this period however still testify to Russell's interest in the natural sciences, although he treated scientific questions in an idealist way. This means that he played the Hegelian game of showing dialectically that the categories of natural science, even those of quantity and number, are necessarily contradictory and hence that the subject matter to which they apply, the world of concrete material bodies, cannot be ultimately real. As Russell has said of these writings: '. . . although they now seem to me to be misguided, I do not think they are any more so than the writings of Hegel'.

This idealist phase was not to last. In a paper read in 1898 and published in 1899, Moore roundly attacked the Bradleian and idealist account of judgement by arguing that facts are, in general, independent of experience. Bradley had argued that truth and falsity depend on the relation of our ideas to reality. Moore patiently argued for the conclusion that the truth or falsehood of a judgement cannot depend upon its relation to anything else whatever. Moore had never been especially impressed by the Cambridge idealism of his day and in his devotion to the deliverances of common sense he displayed a lucid indignation with bland idealist denials of the reality of space, of time, and of the material world. What Moore objected to in the Bradleian account of judgement was the assumption that when, for example, I say of a rose, 'This rose is red' I am attributing part of the content of my ideas to the rose. According to Moore the ideas involved in a judgement are not mental states or mental belongings of the person judging. Rather they are, so to speak, real existents. Consequently, the truth of 'This rose is red' depends not upon a coherence of *my* ideas but upon whether such a conjunction of redness and rosiness is existent. The curious feature of this robust realist account of truth, of great future significance, was the ontological open-handedness of it. By this I mean the readiness to postulate objectively existent concepts as the references or subject matters of statements and judgements. This had the consequence that even statements about imaginary things such as centaurs and chimeras had to have centaur and chimera concepts to be about. The readiness of Moore and Russell at this stage to countenance such things was an indication of their Platonism and was due in no small measure to the influence upon them of the writings of Alexius Meinong (1853–1920), a German philosopher who had revived and promulgated a modern version of scholastic realism which in one of its phases populated the universe not only with imaginary entities such as centaurs but even impossible entities such as square circles. No doubt the Platonism of Moore's theory was also reinforced by Russell's belief in the timeless and unchangeable reality of the cardinal numbers. If anything is timeless and unchangeable, then something like the number two would seem to be it. A good deal in Russell's subsequent work was to result from an attempt to do without the generous ontology of this extreme realism by a fierce application of a sophisticated new version of Occam's razor. If entities were not to be multiplied without necessity, then one had to demonstrate how apparent references to nonexistent things could be construed in terms of references to respectably existent things. The new symbolic logic was to be the instrument of this reconstruction.

Before turning to the vagaries of the realism embraced by Moore and Russell we must take a look at an additional ground of attack upon idealism mounted by Russell. Moore's attack in *The Nature of Judgement* (1899) had been an attack on idealism's epistemology. Russell mounted an attack upon the logical basis of its metaphysics and he was probably being unduly modest when he wrote in 1903:

On fundamental questions of philosophy, my position, in all its chief features, is derived from Mr. G. E. Moore. I have accepted from him the nonexistential nature of propositions (except such as happen to assert existence) and their independence of any knowing mind; also the pluralism which regards the world, both that of existents and that of entities, as composed of an infinite number of mutually independent entities with relations which are ultimate, and not reducible to adjectives of their terms or of the whole which these compose.[6]

It is the last point in this quotation we have now to understand. It has already been pointed out that idealism was a monistic doctrine, that is to say it believed, to use William James's phrase, in a 'block universe' where, ultimately, the plurality of individuals which ordinary experience presents are pronounced unreal. The logical basis of this view was to be found in the idealist account of relations. According to the traditional logic every statement had to consist of a subject and a predicate. This means that any relational statement asserting a relation between two or more things has to be reduced somehow to a statement attributing a predicate to some one subject. Thus an idealist would have said that 'A loves B' is really equivalent to a statement asserting of the complex AB a predicate, in this case 'loves'.

It is important to grasp how much follows from this view of

relations as internal. In the case taken it makes the relation 'loves' a part of the nature of A and of B, in exactly the same sense that A's being male, let us say, is part of the nature of A. From which it follows that if a relation ceases to hold between two things, this entails that their nature has changed. To take an example of Leibniz's: if a man living in Europe has a wife in India and the wife dies without his knowing it, the man undergoes an intrinsic change at the moment of her death. In this way a thing's nature is always a reflection of its relations to everything else whatsoever or, in Leibniz's formulation, each thing expresses the nature of the whole from its own point of view. It also follows from this doctrine that one cannot say anything absolutely true of any one thing without bringing in its relations to everything else, that is without bringing in everything else. So from this the idealistic doctrine about degrees of truth also follows. Short of a statement about the whole (and even according to Bradley short of that) no statement is absolutely true.

Russell brought a battery of arguments to bear against the doctrine of internal relations. One of the most telling derives from the new logic of relations previously mentioned. This had introduced a classification of relations in logical terms. A *transitive* relation is one which is inherited by each thing so related. For example, the relation 'ancestor of' is transitive, for if A is the ancestor of B and B of C, then A is the ancestor of C. *Intransitivity* is when this would not hold for A, B, and C. A *symmetrical* relation is one which holds, so to speak, 'both ways' among two things. For example, if A is a blood relative of B, then B is a blood relative of A. *Asymmetrical* relations are those for which this never holds, for example, 'father of'. Relations which are transitive and asymmetrical are of great importance in mathematics, for example in generating series. It was Russell's claim that the doctrine of internal relations could make no sense of asymmetrical relations. For example, consider the statement 'A is earlier than B' and attempt to express it as attributing a property to its terms. This might be done by means of dates, assigning one date to A and another to B. But now one will require it to be understood that A's date is earlier than B's date and one is back with the relation again. If you tried to find an adjective of the whole AB, you would still be left with the unordered whole AB, so one could not distinguish 'A is earlier than B' from 'B is earlier than A'. Yet these are very plainly different statements. These and many other examples clearly demonstrate that some relations at least cannot be analysed away into either characteristics of the related terms or characteristics of a whole composed of the related terms.

Hence, as Russell sometimes put it, some relations have to be accepted as ultimately real and this entails genuine and not apparent plurality in reality.

By this and similar arguments the logical foundations of the monolithic monism of absolute idealism were destroyed. Many consequences flowed from this, not least of which was that of taking for real the kind of related manifold of bodies in space and time supposed to exist by common sense and natural science. Kant had argued that space and time were forms of our sensibility of our way of experiencing the world, and did not belong to things in themselves. Russell's proof of the reality of relations and plurality meant that the move towards objectivity initiated by Moore's attack on Bradley could be extended to cover natural science. Indeed, Russell has himself told us how, in the first phase of his intoxication with realism, he accepted the objective reality not simply of bodies in space and time but also of numbers, points, instances, and even universals and logical notions such as disjunction and implication.

The break with idealism having been made, the new doctrine had on its hands the problems implicitly referred to just now—what we might call the problem of an over-inflated universe. As Russell has put it in his own account of his opinions: 'In my first rebellion against Hegel, I believed that a thing must exist if Hegel's proof that it cannot is invalid. Gradually Occam's razor gave me a more clean-shaven picture of reality.' [7] The cure for this ontological obesity was suggested by certain technical devices of the new logic and their use in indicating how mathematics could be derived from logic. Peano had reduced the essential notions needed for the development of mathematics to three, namely *zero*, *number*, and *successor of*. He had then laid down certain axioms involving these notions from which arithmetic could be derived with the help of certain logical operations. Two of the axioms were, 'o is a number' and 'The successor of o is a number'. One might think it difficult to go back behind the Peano axioms to things yet more fundamental. This is precisely what Russell did.

The essential step here was a definition of number in non-numerical terms. Clearly every cardinal number can be reduced to a series of 1's. So the problem is to define o and 1. This Russell did with the help of the new logical notation. Briefly, he used the notion of *class* in the following way. Classes have members and the members can be counted. In counting the members of various classes sometimes we shall get the same answer, sometimes a different answer. Where we get the same answer we have classes of the same number of members. If we can define equinumerosity without number we shall have done the trick. This could be done in the following way: two classes are equinumerous when each element of one corresponds to each element of the other. Given this idea it is possible to define a number, the number two say, as the class of all two-membered classes, the reference to the number two being construed in terms of equinumerosity as explained. It might be asked how you get the *different* numbers in this way. This can be indicated by looking at the definition of the number one. A class will be guaranteed to be one-numbered if the following condition holds, namely that if something is a member of that class, then anything else that is a member of that class is identical with that thing. The number one is then simply the class of all such classes. The number nought is simply the class of classes having no members. Notice the logical notions involved in these definitions: *if . . .*, *then . . .*, *something being a member of a class*; *anything else being a member of a class*; *nothing being a member of a class*; *identity*. Russell's logical symbolism provided a rigorous symbolic way of expressing statements involving these notions. For example, 'Something is a man' is read as '$(\exists x)Mx$' and 'All men are mortal' as '(x) if x is a man, then x is mortal' i.e. 'If anything is a man, then it is mortal'. Logical relations such as *if . . .* , *then . . .* , *or*, *and*, were symbolized respectively by ' $\supset$ ', 'v', and '.'.

So number, it appeared, was reduced to logic and to a logic furthermore which was more subtle and powerful than anything in the traditional logic which formed a subsection of it. The elimination of a Platonic realm of numbers in favour of the notions of *individual* and certain logical properties was to provide the model of reductive analysis in other fields.

Before leaving this brief sketch of Russell's mathematical achievements mention must be made of the stages in which this work appeared. In 1903 he published *Principles of Mathematics* in which he argued discursively for the reduction of mathematics to logic, indicated how it might be done, and dealt with certain philosophical issues affecting the new logic. However, just before publication of this work Russell discovered and communicated to Frege a contradiction in the system which could also be derived in Frege's system. Whitehead said in consoling Russell, 'never glad confident morning again'. More wounding was the comment of Henri Poincaré (1853–1913), the French scientist-philosopher and opponent of the new logic: 'Behold formal logic is not barren, it brings forth contradictions.' Russell, who had embarked with Whitehead upon the *Principia Mathematica** in which the whole of mathematics was actually to be deduced from logic, settled to devising means of avoiding his own and other antinomies. The device fixed upon was the *theory of types* which, it is fair to say, has been a centre of controversy in subsequent philosophical discussion of Russell's logic. This device was incorporated into *Principia* and numerous modifications have been made to it by other logicians. The significance of paradoxes, both formal and informal, in philosophy has always been great from the time of Zeno onwards. This indicates more than a taste for logical fun and word-play on the part of philosophers. Paradoxes are a crippling infection of the intellect in its search for consistency. To find them inherent in the foundations of logic as Russell did was something of a scandal. An ironist might reflect that while the Hegelian logician embraces dialectical contradiction at the outset of his inquiry, the analytical logician banishes it from the outset only to find it returning at the end.

Despite the fact that *Principia* had to be patched up by the theory of types it remains a profound achievement. It enshrines a clearly stated philosophy of mathematics and logic, called the logistic thesis, which has served as a paradigm ever since its publication. Many mathematicians and philosophers accept its central thesis of the reducibility of mathematics to logic but equally many reject it. Its competitors as a philosophy of mathematics are doctrines largely of continental origin, known as intuitionism and formalism. Intuitionism holds that mathematical thinking is *sui generis*, consisting in the construction by the mathematician of mathematical proofs and objects. Formalism holds that mathematics is simply a game played with written marks in accordance with chosen rules. Russell rejected intuitionism on the grounds that its concept of mathematical proof meant rejecting as unsound branches of mathematics he considered sound. Formalism he rejected partly on the ground that it makes of mathematics purely an intellectual game and partly on the ground that it cannot explain the application of numbers in counting objects in the world. Finally, as a full systematization of the new logic *Principia* acted as a stimulus to logical inquiry for its own sake and initiated a period of rapid growth in logical science.

It was certain tools of the new logic forged in the logical analysis of mathematics which were to be put to use in expounding the analytical realism initiated by Moore and Russell. In sketching the

* Volume I, 1910; Volume II, 1912; Volume III, 1913.

development of these opinions we shall deal with three issues: the use of the new logic in philosophical analysis both as tool and paradigm; the construction of a realist epistemology consistent with the approach to knowledge of the natural sciences; the emphasis in philosophy on questions of meaning which was an important by-product of these enterprises.

Russell's opinions on many matters changed rapidly during the period under consideration. We have already alluded to the discovery of Russell's paradox which involved extensions and modifications of the new logic. Many of these changes of opinion were matters of refinement in positions already established. But what Russell never lost sight of in this period was firstly, the insistence on realism and pluralism in philosophy, and secondly, an ideal of analysis made fruitful by the new logic as the key philosophical method. An important cause of changes in Russell's opinions was the eruption on to the English philosophical scene of the young Austrian, Ludwig Wittgenstein (1889–1951).* Russell himself has confessed that their collaboration during the period immediately preceding 1914 was so close as to make difficult any exercise in independent attribution of ideas. Even though Wittgenstein's first published work, *Tractatus Logico-Philosophicus*, was published after 1918, the revolutionary ideas it contained were worked out in close collaboration with Russell, as can be seen from Russell's *Lectures on Logical Atomism*, delivered in London in the early months of 1918. The title 'Logical Atomism' (a precursor of the style which later gives us 'Logical Positivism') testifies to a development of Russell's realism under the stimulus of Wittgenstein. It also testifies to a union of logic and natural science which held out the hope that philosophy was at last on the sure road to progress, as the natural sciences had seemed to be since the time of Kepler and Galileo. As Russell put it in 1914:

The old logic put thought in fetters, while the new logic gives it wings. It has, in my opinion, introduced the same kind of advance into philosophy as Galileo introduced into physics, making it possible at last to see what kinds of problems may be capable of solution, and what kinds must be abandoned as beyond human powers.[8]

Wittgenstein also noted in 1915 that 'Russell's method in his "Scien-

---

* The decision has been taken in the present chapter to treat the doctrines of Wittgenstein only as they seem especially relevant to bringing out the significance of Russell's views. Independent consideration of the fruits of his work in the present period will be reserved for a chapter in the succeeding volume.

tific method in philosophy" is simply a retrogression from the method of physics'.[9]

Bearing in mind these complexities I turn to a consideration of Russell's *theory of descriptions*, an aspect of the new philosophy which seemed to provide a decisive and elegant solution to one problem facing realism. The problem may be put as follows: realism had roundly asserted against idealism that judgements, thoughts, and propositions (we may take these as equivalent in this context) were about something independent of judgement, thought, or statement. This standpoint was equivalent to asserting that meaning and hence truth and falsehood depended upon a statement being *about* something. A problem immediately arises over those statements which while meaningful are patently not about anything, for example statements about mythical creatures or even impossible things like square circles. Rather than take the unrealistically heroic line which, following Meinong, Russell and Moore had at one time been inclined towards, of populating the universe with ghostly versions of non-existent things, Russell sought to show how such statements could be perfectly meaningful without presupposing the existence of patently non-existent things. Consider his own example of such a statement, 'The present King of France is bald'. Russell suggested that this statement should be regarded as a complex of three statements, namely:

(i) There is something which is King of France
(ii) Whatever else is King of France is identical with that thing
(iii) If anything is King of France, then it is bald.

The important thing to notice is that this analysis does not attempt to do the impossible by mentioning the non-existent. It is also fully translatable into symbolic logic in a rigorous way. Given this elegant piece of analysis, a point of great methodological importance follows. The suggested translation, if correct, makes it clear that the apparent grammatical form of a statement may be no clue to its real logical form. Russell's original statement on the face of it reveals none of the complexities brought out by (i), (ii), and (iii). This piece of analysis became a paradigm of philosophical analysis. Many philosophers came to believe that one had to get at the real meaning of statements which gave philosophical trouble by analysing them into forms expressible in the new logic. Hence, one name by which the new philosophical style became known was 'logical analysis'.

A further problem left unsolved by the theory of descriptions was that of assessing the results of such analysis. By using the theory of descriptions it is possible to avoid mentioning by name non-existent things. Unfortunately, it is also possible to eliminate in this way mention of actually existent things. So, despite the theory of descriptions, there remained a general problem of how to distinguish genuine mention of existing things from spurious mention of non-existent things. Just as on the Russellian definition of number, number breaks down into classes and class in turn into elements, so, it might be thought, tables break down into parts of tables and parts of tables into the molecules from which wood is made and these molecules into their constituent atoms and so on. In other words, the process of analysing judgements into their constituents in order to find what they are really about requires us to have some idea of what in general these constituents are.

It should be noted that the ideal of logical analysis is not as such a commitment to any particular account of the ultimate constituents of reality; it merely amounts to the assertion that for logical analysis to be possible there must be complexes and hence constituents. However, once one takes seriously the notion of reconstructing and clarifying what we can properly claim to know by means of the method of logical analysis, some suggestions as to the nature of the basic constituents of our knowledge and of reality are likely to be made. Russell was on the whole ready to do this and the way in which he did it reflects not only his respect for the method and results of natural science but also his place in the main stream of British empiricism. In this respect Russell differs from Wittgenstein. The *Tractatus Logico-Philosophicus*, while arguing for a rigorous form of logical atomism, does not argue that the atoms involved are of any particular kind. This should be said if only because there has been a persistent tendency to read Wittgenstein's early work as if it were the bible of a new empiricist logical atomism of the sort we associate with Russell and, later, with Carnap and other members of the Vienna circle.

Before coming to Russell's views on the basic constituents of reality it will be as well to mention the connection of this topic with a central issue in the theory of meaning. This issue is that of how language connects with the world. Another way to pose this issue is to ask what properties there are of any meaningful expression which enable it to mean something. For example, the statement, 'I have just written a complicated statement', says something about the world. What it says about the world is, roughly speaking, what it means. But how does it succeed in this task of meaning something?

The fundamental notion brought in by the new philosophy to answer this question was that of *reference* or *naming*. Russell believed that we are able to say things about the world only because the sentences which we use contain names of things in the world. It is the type of relation that holds between a name and its bearer which is the archetype of the relation between language and reality. Furthermore, this account is extended to cover also the relation between thought and what it is thought about. Russell, Wittgenstein, and to some extent Moore all treated thoughts as articulated thoughts. As Wittgenstein put it, 'the thought is the significant proposition'. This makes clear what an important role was played in the new philosophy by referring expressions and the technique for dealing with troublesome cases of them enshrined in the theory of descriptions. Names are a sub-class of expressions which refer, other examples of this type of expression being of the sort typified by 'the present King of France'. So an important task of the new philosophy was to sort out from referring expressions in general those expressions which are properly referring expressions in that they are first of all names and secondly names of genuine constituents of reality. The term which came to be used for this sort of referring expression was *logically proper name*.

In carrying out this task Russell invoked the traditional empiricist criterion for basic constituents of reality. To Russell it was obvious that 'the immediate facts perceived by sight or touch or hearing do not need to be proved by argument but are completely self-evident'. In taking up this stance on the question of the basic constituents of reality Russell was doing no more than returning to the philosophy of Mill. However, this return is made with a new armoury to tackle the logical issues involved, one which Mill and his empiricist precursors had not possessed. The new logic provided not only the tool of empiricist analysis to bridge the gaps between empiricism, common sense, and natural science; it also appeared to solve the problem bequeathed by Mill as to the nature of logical and mathematical truth. Thus a comprehensive and consistent empiricism at last seemed possible.

The reconstruction of the world of common sense and of natural science with the tools of logical empiricism was a task embarked upon by Russell in the published lectures *Our Knowledge of the External World* (1914). Here Russell tries to answer the question as to what we can properly be said to know concerning 'the external world'. The first thing to note about his approach is that the question is not posed in a Cartesian spirit. What I mean is that Russell is not looking for a certain and self-evident and unquestionable answer to this question fit to stand up to the epistemological deceptions of Descartes's evil demon who deceives me even when I think I know. Knowledge, for Russell, doesn't mean the un-assailable. It means the thing it is most reasonable to believe in the light of all the available evidence considered with a due respect for what already passes as systematic knowledge. 'Knowledge' for Russell is a term that covers degrees of certainty other than that of complete certainty. The second thing to note is that Russell makes it clear that there is no necessary connection between answering this question and deriving spiritual and ethical comfort from the answer. Indeed, Russell's view that a properly scientific philosophy cannot provide the sort of cosmic comfort afforded by idealism is in its own way a more mundane version of the view put forward by Wittgenstein in the *Tractatus* that the mystical standpoint only arises because when all scientific and philosophical questions have been answered, the basic problems of life still seem to be untouched. Also with this one can associate G. E. Moore's view that any attempt to define intrinsic value, the fundamental concept of ethics, in terms of facts of any sort is radically misconceived. These three stances, with their differing emphases, not only demonstrate the radical break with idealism in its Bradleian and Hegelian form; they also are the genesis of what nowadays people have come to regard as the radical distinction between fact and value.

Basic fact then for Russell meant what he often called 'the crude data of sense'. He saw his primary task as that of relating these data to the picture of the world presented by physics: 'The central problem by which I have sought to illustrate method is the problem of the relation between the crude data of sense and the space, time, and matter of mathematical physics.'[10]

In solving this problem Russell made use of an approach sug-gested in the work of his collaborator in *Principia Mathematica*, A. N. Whitehead (1861–1947). The fact that Whitehead's later work and interests diverged sharply from Russell's should not obscure the important influence upon Russell of Whitehead at this time. Briefly, Whitehead had indicated a way of treating the ideal points and instants of mathematical physics as formal *constructions* out of ordinary experiential data. Russell saw this method as changing the form of the problem concerning the reality of the world of which physics is supposed to give us knowledge. Hitherto, the problem had seemed to be one of justifying an *inference* from the immediate data of sense to a world of colourless atoms in geometric ritual dance. Russell replaced this problem with that of showing how, using the apparatus of the new logic, the conceptions of physical theory could be *constructed* out of the data of sense. From this is derived the emphasis of much philosophical work in the 1920s and 1930s on 'logical constructions' or 'logical fictions', as they came to be called. Russell also saw this approach to the problem of knowledge as overcoming the fruitless antinomian wrangles between realism and idealism, between the view that we can know a world of objects existing and persisting independently of human cognition and the view that all we can ever be said to know is something which depends for its existence on human cognition.

One problem implicit in Russell's acceptance of data of sense as the basic 'hard data' of knowledge is that raised by asking the questions, 'What has these data?' and, 'What can we know of what has these data?' Common sense would regard these questions as being answered by saying something like, 'Persons have experiences' or 'Minds have experiences'. But there are difficulties about these answers. Persons are themselves experienced so to say that persons have experiences looks like saying that experiences have experiences. Where minds are concerned there is a case for saying, as Hume suggested, that minds are never experienced at all despite or perhaps because it seems that all experience presupposes a mind. Russell's solution to these problems is a radical one, though it should be said that he arrived at it gradually over a period of some twenty years. What he came round to by 1918 was the view that it was a mistake to suppose that experiences are 'had' by anything at all. To suppose that they are 'had' by something is to suppose that experience is necessarily relational or, to put it in the customary way, that all experiences are related to some mind or consciousness or subject of experiences. The origin of Russell's final view on this topic goes as far back as William James's 1904 article, 'Does Consciousness Exist?'. By the time of the lectures on *Logical Atomism* in 1918 Russell has become an out-and-out defender of James's *neutral monism*, bringing to its defence further arguments from the armoury of the new logic.

The view lying at the basis of this theory is that there is only one kind of reality out of which by various techniques of logical construction the world of common sense and science can be constructed. The term 'science' here included for Russell not only physics and its associated disciplines but also psychological science. Psychological science had customarily been thought of as being differentiated from physical science in terms of its subject matter.

Physics was thought of as a set of theories about gross and less gross material bodies whereas the subject-matter of psychological science had been thought of as something not material or bodily, in short as mind or the *psyche*. The method appropriate to the study of psychical or mental phenomena was that of *introspection*, a method of observation partly the same but partly different from sensory observation. This view that physics and psychology were different because they had different subject-matters was denied by neutral monism. In its place was put the doctrine that physics and psychology have the same data and that the difference between them is to be found in the different sets of relations of these common data. In this way the subject which has experience was regarded as theoretically dispensable. To obtain an idea of what was meant by this consider the following example: a chair being observed by a number of people presents different appearances to each of them depending upon where they are situated in relation to it. If we take all these different appearances you get, as Russell put it, 'something that belongs to physics'. Suppose, however, one took the class of appearances that the different chairs in the room present to me at the moment, then this gives something belonging to psychology. This example, which is Russell's own, is crude and schematic but it conveys the general idea: 'That actual appearance that the chair is presenting to me now is a member of me and a member of the chair, I and the chair being logical fictions. . . . There is no simple entity that you can point to and say: this entity is physical and not mental.'[11]

What Russell stressed in his presentation of neutral monism was the crucial role of the constructive methods of the new logic in specifying the sets of data which, he held, corresponds to the objects in which common sense believes. He held that in order to test the theory of neutral monism you had 'to have at your finger's ends the theory of logic' because, 'You can never tell otherwise what can be done with a given material, whether you can concoct out of a given material the sort of logical fictions that will have the properties you want in psychology and physics.'[12]

Two observations about neutral monism are worth making before leaving the topic. The first is that the elimination of any metaphysical dualism of the mental and the physical coincided historically with the growth of the behaviourist standpoint in many of the cultural sciences and in psychology in particular. The philosophy of neutral monism appeared to provide a philosophical basis for a behaviourist methodology in the cultural sciences, a method of study which saw

men, so to speak, from the 'outside' only, so-called 'inner' mental
phenomena being complex ways of referring to observed outward
behaviour. Hence, the foundations were also laid for the view that
knowledge advances both in the natural scientific and the cultural
spheres through a method common to both spheres, namely that of
natural science. So in one sense it can be said that a result of Russell's philosophical work in our period was to set up natural science
and its procedures as the paradigm of method for all knowledge
whatsoever. This conclusion was stated most radically by Russell's
teacher and pupil Wittgenstein at the end of his *Tractatus Logico-
Philosophicus* when he said (my italics):

The right method of philosophy would be this. *To say nothing except what
can be said, i.e. the propositions of natural science,* i.e. something that has
nothing to do with philosophy: and then always, when someone else
wished to say something metaphysical, to demonstrate to him that he had
given no meaning to certain signs in his propositions.[13]

Here what is significant is that Wittgenstein speaks not simply of
knowledge, i.e. systematized truths, but of *Naturwissenschaft,* i.e.
natural science or systematized truths concerning the natural world.

The second remark on neutral monism follows on naturally from
the passage in Wittgenstein just quoted. This passage was used as
a trenchant expression of Russell's conviction that natural science
is the paradigm of all knowledge, a result which reversed the idealist
demonstration that compared with metaphysical knowledge natural
science was an inferior form of knowledge. But it should also be
remarked that Wittgenstein expresses this conviction as a thesis
about *what can be said.* Notice has already been taken of the important influence of Wittgenstein upon Russell but little has been said
independently of Wittgenstein's *Tractatus.* This is partly because
the publication dates of this work fall outside the period we are
considering; it appeared first in 1921 and was published as a book
in 1922. However, in the *Tractatus* a theme less explicit in Russell
and of crucial importance for the subsequent direction of philosophical speculation appears with impressive and gnostic force. In
that book Wittgenstein explicitly attempted to deduce the irrele-
vance of traditional philosophical concerns from a theory of meaning. This theory of meaning is an extreme form of the one adopted
by Russell, namely the denotative theory which explains the
connection between thought, language, and reality by invoking the
notion of naming. Wittgenstein developed this idea much further
than Russell, expressing, as we have noted, little interest in *what*

is named but great interest in *how* naming is connected with expressing anything at all. His concern was not, as Russell's was, that of reconstructing our knowledge on a secure foundation but rather that of charting the limits of the sayable or meaningful in order to show not only how little is sayable but how much that we feel to be of profound importance is not expressible in words at all.

Crudely, Wittgenstein took the view that naming enabled one to say something because a statement is to be regarded as a collection of names arranged in such a way as to form a logical picture of what the statement as a whole says. This theory is known today, for obvious reasons, as 'the picture theory of meaning'. From this *desideratum* of saying anything at all, Wittgenstein arrived at a whole series of conclusions akin to those to which Russell had come. The three most important were, firstly, the soul or self is not a possible subject of discourse; secondly, that the only possible mode of scientific discourse is that of natural science (and here Wittgenstein seemed always to think of mechanics as Russell thought of physics); thirdly, that philosophy does not consist in revealing to people truths other than those of natural science but consists in constantly reminding would-be philosophers that all which can be said belongs to natural science. Stated baldly these theses may sound bold but insupportable. This is not the place to sketch the argumentation of the *Tractatus* but it should be said that its arguments are profound and illuminating to all who have grappled with the problem of meaning in philosophy. Nowadays it is regarded as a classic error, as it came to be regarded by Wittgenstein himself; but as a classic error it illuminates the issues with which it deals.

For our present purposes it is the emphasis in the *Tractatus* upon the centrality of the problem of meaning and the limits of the meaningful that is important for future developments. It is not difficult to show how issues about meaning were bound to raise their heads in any assessment of neutral monism and in this way direct philosophical attention towards the central theme of the *Tractatus*. As we have seen Russell in 1918 conceived the task of philosophy to be that of utilizing the analytic apparatus of mathematical logic in order to show how the things of which common sense and natural science apparently speak can be shown to be logical fictions or constructions out of the data of sense. This amounts to a claim that all we say about the objects of natural science and common sense could be said in a language whose use presupposed only the reality of the data of sense and the formal apparatus of mathematical logic. Inevitably this raises a question as to whether the meaning of expressions in this language is adequate to convey all that is meant by the ordinary unreconstructed expressions of common sense and natural science. So the basic issue of neutral monism easily became the thorough investigation of the concept of meaning.

This direction of attention towards the concept of meaning was sharpened by the philosophical methods of Moore who tended in his work to a greater regard for common sense than Russell had. Russell was frequently content to regard common-sense assumptions about the nature of reality as crude, inaccurate, and dispensable and he saw the philosopher's task on occasion as the refining or even the replacement of common sense notions by logical constructions. Moore's procedures tended in the opposite direction, that is he tended to regard ordinary conceptions as irreplaceable and the philosophical task as that of clarifying their meaning. However, the full significance and treatment of these issues in the philosophy of meaning is a story that belongs to the post-1918 period.

These last remarks have implicit in them the question-begging view that the course upon which Russell had set philosophy was that which most English-speaking philosophers were going to follow after 1918. This would be an over-simplification and an error. However, one would be erring in the right direction. It is often the case that a philosopher is influential not because of the positive doctrines which he teaches but because he changes the way in which the perennial philosophical problems are discussed. While Russell's realism, pluralism, and neutral monism aroused much interest and gained many adherents, it is the way he changed the style of philosophical discussion that is more important. Analytical rigour, a preference for the rarefied discourse of theoretical physics, a utilization of the new mathematical logic as a basic philosophical tool, a piecemeal step-by-step approach to philosophical problem-solving, a respect for the methods and achievements of natural science, were all at the end of this period more characteristic of the tone of philosophical discussion than they had been at its outset. While other thinkers such as Moore, Wittgenstein, and Whitehead had contributed to this new climate and to the formation of Russell's own opinions, it was above all his own fresh, vigorous, irreverent and clear style which served to popularize the new positions and arouse interest in them. The portentous and comforting sobrieties of idealism had given way to a passionate intellectualism that had about it something of the radical hope and sceptical attitude to tradition of the Enlightenment.

II

It would be misleading to give the impression that the philosophical landscape 1900–18 contained only the figures of Moore, Russell, and Wittgenstein. While it has been argued that their concerns were setting the pace for the future it must now be indicated that competent and important work was being done by a number of people who it would be unfair to say are now of only historical interest. Roughly speaking the philosophical world had been divided by the new realism into opposite camps for which the two labels idealism and realism will do well enough, with the observation that such a nomenclature is so general as to accommodate warring factions within these respective standpoints. Within the realist camp, the highly original and independent metaphysical realism worked out by Samuel Alexander (1859–1938) most fully in his Gifford Lectures of 1916–18, *Space, Time and Deity*, deserves our attention.

Alexander was an Australian who had come to Oxford as a young mathematician from his native country. His work is characterized, as the title of his Gifford Lectures implies, by a respect for the categories of natural science and, unusually, a respectful concern with the religious issue. He attempted to work out in a realist spirit which held to the ultimate reality of space and time, a realist metaphysical system which would at the same time do justice to man's religious instincts and yearnings. It should be said that from the standpoint of Christian orthodoxy Alexander's deity is a strange creature. His realist position was fully developed in the published volumes of his Gifford Lectures, *Space, Time and Deity* (1920). The philosophical basis of his position is explained and defended in *The Basis of Realism* (1914). He makes it clear that he rejects, following Russell and others, the idealist doctrine of internal relations. This rejection is coupled with the positive assertion that he regards mind or spirit as 'an empirical character' of an organized body or nervous system. Beings with minds are descendants of lower forms of life and the capacity of conscious reflection and reaction to an environment is simply a special case of accommodation and adjustment to existing realities.

That mind and consciousness have a physical basis is not regarded by Alexander as meaning that mind can be reduced to matter: 'If anyone thinks this doctrine savours of materialism, he forgets that mind, though descended on its physical side from lower forms of existence, is, when it comes, a new quality in the world'.[14] For he insists that mind when it emerges as a function of organized matter is a genuinely new quality in the world, even though it could not exist independently of its physical basis. The standard dualist argument for the independence of mind, that in reflection I am conscious of myself as a consciousness, is dealt with interestingly. Alexander simply denies with Hume that we are ever conscious of ourselves as simply a consciousness or mental being. Rather, he asserts, we are always aware of something non-mental and the conscious mental aspect of all such awareness is its lived 'enjoyment'. While it is easy to see how this doctrine, if sound, is inconsistent with the existence of mind independently of its relation to something non-mental, it is more difficult to see just what it comes to. It is a doctrine similar in many ways to the 'no mind' theory of Russell and James discussed above. However, Alexander's insistence on the natural and material basis of mental life was widely influential especially in psychology, where his arguments tended to discredit a methodology resting on the idea of introspective access to the specifically mental. So according to Alexander mind emerges as one type of finite existence among others.

The use of the term 'emergent' to describe the genesis of mind is an indication of the influence upon Alexander of those late-nineteenth-century philosophers who had applied the Darwinian idea of evolution to account for the existence of mind. G. H. Lewes in *Problems of Life and Mind* (1875) and Lloyd Morgan later in a series of books one of which is entitled *Emergent Evolution* (1923), had attempted to transcend the dualism of mind and matter by claiming that mind was an evolutionary aspect of organized matter. The utilization of a biological and zoological theory in working out a philosophical theory was congenial to Alexander whose respect for natural science parallels a similar respect in Russell which we have already noted. This respect operates also in his insistence, against the general tendencies of idealist thought, on regarding space and time not as ultimately unreal but as the basic categories of experienced reality. The fundamental axiom in Alexander's general metaphysics is that reality is through and through temporal, an axiom that fits his evolutionary standpoint. He asserts that space and time are more fundamental than matter itself. This doctrine is difficult to understand but its general drift may become apparent if we reflect upon the observation that the macroscopic stabilities of ordinary tables and chairs can be seen in physics as resting upon a ceaseless dance and movement of fundamental particles. The basic reality for Alexander is motion which is to be regarded as the successive occupation of points each of which is successively present. Without this there could be no motion and no matter, for the possibility of matter depends upon the possibility of different points being simultaneously occupied. The characteristics of gross matter are the result of motions, that is of the activity of space/time.

This doctrine of qualities emerging from motions is applied by Alexander not only to the familiar gross properties of matter such as colour and shape but also to the emergence of mind as a quality of matter and, finally, Deity as a character of the whole of reality. Just as mind can be known to have evolved as a property of organized matter so, by extrapolation, Deity will emerge as a property of mindful matter. Such a god can scarcely be regarded as the eternal object or subject of ordinary religious attitudes. Indeed, it could be said that Alexander's religious thinking is a reduction to absurdity of the idea that a thorough naturalism can be consistently combined with the theological point of view. One effect of Alexander's metaphysical realism was to reinforce the naturalistic paganism of Russell and to hasten the decline of religious orthodoxy.

The naturalistic basis of Alexander's metaphysics and his desire to accommodate in philosophical constructions the results of scientific work is not just a reflection of enthusiasm for evolutionary ideas in biology, zoology, and botany. The revolution in physics, which had culminated in the publication of the special theory of relativity by Einstein in 1905, had apparently solved a long-standing metaphysical issue, namely whether space and time were absolute or relative. This achievement stood as an example both of the application of sophisticated formal and mathematical techniques to the solution of problems and of philosophical analysis. By digging into the logical conditions of saying of two events that they are or are not simultaneous and by reading Hume and Mach, Einstein had put mechanics on to a new and far-reaching basis. While some surviving idealists greeted the demonstration of the relativity of space and time as a victory over materialism, more sophisticated philosophers such as Russell and Whitehead saw it as a triumph of the application of formal techniques to the definition of concepts. Furthermore, the point that according to Einstein two events are only simultaneous *for* a given observer was taken as justifying the relativism to an observer implicit in all empiricist epistemology. In the same year, 1905, in which Einstein published the special theory, Whitehead produced a memoir for the Royal Society, *Mathematical Concepts of the Material World*, which was an attempt to use the techniques of *Principia Mathematica* to describe the physical world of matter in space. Throughout the subsequent period Whitehead was to continue not only his work on *Principia* but also his formal analysis of physics, culminating in 1922 in *The Principle of Relativity* in which an attempt is made to derive Einstein's relativity theory from first principles. Whitehead was later to extend his metaphysical interests beyond the field of scientific philosophy but his earlier work represents the same tendency noted in Alexander's case, to accommodate within philosophy the results and techniques of the natural sciences.

This tendency even crept into the idealist position, largely through the work of Bernard Bosanquet (1848–1923), the most influential and eclectic idealist thinker of the period. Idealism was certainly not without its defenders in 1900–18 but it was a rearguard action. Bradley in 1914 published *Essays in Truth and Reality*, in which he sought, with little success, to cross swords with Russell and defend the idealist logic and epistemology. Bosanquet's reaction was rather different: he attempted to include some of the new insights within an idealist perspective, as the title of one of his books, *The Meeting of Extremes in Contemporary Philosophy*, indicates. One of Bosanquet's obituaries described him as 'the central figure in British philosophy for a whole generation', a claim difficult to account for until one turns to the voluminous and cloudy writings on every philosophical topic which flowed so easily from his pen. His project was a reconciling one; he worked by taking from a philosophical position to which he was opposed always something of truth. It was difficult for a mind as eclectic as Bosanquet's to accept that some things might be plain false or hopelessly muddled. Bosanquet's charitable work on behalf of the poor extended even to his philosophical opponents.

The basis of all his work is the idealist emphasis on unity as the key to reality and the processes of thought whereby reality is grasped and known. The principle is laid down in the earliest of his writings, *Logic or the Morphology of Knowledge* (1888), and reiterated in his major work *The Principle of Individuality and Value* (1912). He there defines logic as 'the spirit of totality or effort to self-completion, which being the principle of individuality, is the key to reality, value and freedom'. Bosanquet could go some way towards admitting the truth of pluralism by the use of the idealist doctrine of degrees of knowledge: 'There is, of course, a dualism or rather a multiplicity, in our experience at first sight; but it is naive and hasty for philosophy to accept that appearance without an attempt to

overcome it.' The plurality of things which the new realists insisted
made up reality is an element in our experience but not in the last
analysis a real one. Diversity is merely apparent. To come
to understand something is to see it as part of an interrelated
whole.

Various modes of experience are treated in accordance with this
principle. Thus in his *Philosophical Theory of the State* (1899) what
is stressed is the intimate relationship of the individual person to
the whole of society which moralizes the bare individual person and
endows him with the capacity of creative and moral activity. The
power and value of a work of art reside, according to Bosanquet's
widely influential aesthetic ideas, in its capacity to suggest and
sustain coherences within our experience. He also follows the
principle of linking degree of coherence and system with degree of
value: 'When you have admitted the unity of the person with
himself, it is impossible to stop short of his unity with others, with
the world and with the universe; and the perfection by which he is
to be valued is his place in the perfection of these greater wholes.'[15]

He made an attempt to reconcile materialism and idealism which
provoked from McTaggart, in reviewing *The Principle of Individuality and Value*, the comment that, 'almost every word Professor
Bosanquet has written about the relations between mind and matter
in this chapter (Lecture 7) might have been written by a complete
materialist'. On this central point Bosanquet's metaphysic remains
impenetrably obscure, sustained by a combination of piety and
metaphor. Beside such refuge the sophisticated theory of neutral
monism had at least the virtues of courage and clarity.

III

Philosophical ethics is concerned with philosophical reflection upon
human conduct and the various standards in accordance with which
men judge the conduct of themselves and their fellows. Of course,
there are disputes among philosophers as to what philosophical
reflection is and what the rules of this particular game are. It is
clear that the application of different philosophical methods to the
subject-matter of ethics may lead to different philosophical conclusions as to the nature of the subject-matter and the validity
of some or all of the moral judgements which form part of it. In
the period immediately preceding 1900 we can distinguish in British
philosophy two traditions of ethical reflection which parallel in
important respects the dichotomy between empiricist naturalism

and idealism which we saw operating in the fields of epistemology and metaphysics. One tradition, the utilitarian, is represented by Bentham and John Stuart Mill and the other, the idealist, by F. H. Bradley and T. H. Green. The intellectual origins of these two traditions are to be found still farther back in Hume and in Kant and Hegel.

It will be convenient to begin our discussion by attempting a characterization of the utilitarian position for there is, especially in the case of Bentham, a no-nonsense clarity about its basic standpoint, while idealism of the variety we are concerned with is best understood as starting from a rejection of utilitarianism. Bentham, as a legal reformer, had been interested in laying down a clear standard in accordance with which one could be able to judge a piece of legislation beneficial or harmful. He suggested, not unreasonably, that it is beneficial when it contributes to the general happiness and harmful when it diminishes it. Implicit in the criterion is the standpoint that what is good in itself, *intrinsically good* in the jargon, is pleasure and that happiness which all men want and seek, consists in the maximum of pleasure and the minimum of pain. So conduct aimed at securing happiness or the ideal for man is conduct aimed at maximizing pleasure and minimizing pain. Such a view has the merits of simplicity and clarity but, apart from philosophical objections, is to many people repellent and destructive of the rich diversity of valued objects and activities. Carlyle, speaking of utilitarianism, referred to 'grinding in the Philistine Mills', a charge that might be levelled at J. S. Mill's father, if not at the son himself. Bentham devoted little trouble to proving his basic proposition, taking it, whenever he considered it might be doubted, as self-evidently true to all sensible men. The obscurities of the notion of pleasure never seriously worried him; he just forged ahead classifying pleasures.

Bentham's opponents were alarmed not so much by the master himself as by the fear that men of action and legislators in looking out on the diverse activities of men with this single standard in mind would fail to see the values implicit in activities in which pleasure in any ordinary sense is not an obvious factor. Thinkers as far apart as Coleridge and Marx expressed themselves in this sense. Also there was a strong tendency to cash Bentham's key notion of pleasure in terms of the pursuit of material goods and to take utilitarianism as the working philosophical basis for the dismal science of economics and the scramble for the accumulation of capital which could be usefully set to work, such capital being both a proof of and a source of utility. The maximization of pleasure was readily translated into the Gradgrind philosophy of the maximization of profit.

Some of these objections to the Benthamite standard were elaborated by J. S. Mill himself. On the whole Mill approved of the non-mystical anti-transcendentalist side of the Benthamite attitude. He approved of a moral standard set firmly in the sphere of things human. But Mill also expressed as strongly as any of Bentham's critics and from within the utilitarian fold strong objections to the levelling tendencies of Bentham's criterion. Speaking of Bentham he says: 'Nor is it only the moral part of man's nature, in the strict sense of the term—the desire of perfection, or the feeling of an approving or of an accusing conscience—that he overlooks; he but faintly recognises in human nature, the pursuit of any other ideal end for its own sake.'

J. S. Mill's correction of the levelling tendencies in Benthamite thought consisted in distinguishing between different kinds of pleasure and employing these differences as a standard for the worth of the associated activities. He observed in his essay *Utilitarianism* (1863) that it was more valuable, 'better', to be Socrates dissatisfied than a pig satisfied. He justified this departure from strict utilitarianism by the observation that, while this could be known to be true by a Socrates who has tasted both the pleasures of the flesh and those of dialectic, such wisdom must be taken on authority by those whose experience extends only to porcine delights. These élitist assertions testify to Mill's deep concern with the notion of self-improvement, almost to the extent of making him an intellectual Samuel Smiles. The standard of value that operates over and over again in Mill's writing is not the official Benthamite one of mere quantity of pleasure, but one deriving from the values of the intellect and of a cultivated sensibility. So it is fair to conclude that Mill is anything but a pure hedonist and utilitarian. This comes out in other ways too. In a chapter of *Utilitarianism* devoted to justice Mill struggles hard to give a utilitarian account of basic principles of natural justice such as the principle that all persons are deemed to have a right to equality of treatment. Mill attempts to account for the prominence of such principles in reflective moral experience not in terms of them being rational intuitions or self-evident truths but rather as being maxims of high social utility to which a peculiar sentiment attaches, this sentiment being 'the natural feeling of resentment moralised by being made co-extensive with the demands of social good'. Hence, Mill once more provides a psychological solution to what is properly speaking a logical problem. Mill's defence of utilitarianism and hedonism failed to satisfy critics as far apart as Herbert Spencer (1820–1903) and Henry Sidgwick (1838–1900). They both claimed that as presented by Mill the theory was internally incoherent. Sidgwick argued that one could only save utilitarianism by coupling it with the recognition that some principles of natural justice are self-evidently true and not defensible on Utilitarian grounds alone. In *The Methods of Ethics* (1875) Sidgwick put forward a doctrine which was a mixture of utilitarian hedonism and intuitionism. His book is still worth reading if only because his careful and patient analysis of the problems involved are a precursor and embryo of the later methods of G. E. Moore.

By far the strongest attack on the prevailing British style of naturalistic hedonism in moral philosophy came from the pen of F. H. Bradley in *Ethical Studies* (1876), a classic of British moral philosophy and a good introduction to Bradley's polemical style. As Bradley said in the Preface: 'These Essays may be dogmatic and one-sided. They were produced and are published because the writer knows no English moral philosophy which does not, rightly or wrongly, seem to him to be at least as one-sided and even more dogmatic.'

The dialectical counterweight to the prevailing ideas in England which Bradley introduces in the work is Hegel. This appeared heterodox to many of Bradley's contemporaries, especially to Sidgwick who referred in a review to the book's 'marked antagonism to current philosophical opinion'. Bradley begins from the general view that the only worthwhile end of action is self-realization. He then attempts to give a content to the idea of self-realization by successively considering prominent doctrines which, explicitly or by implication, do this. He first considers pleasure for the sake of pleasure and rejects it, holding that it is both inconsistent with morality as commonly understood and proffers an end of action which is illusory. He says of utilitarianism: 'The practical man hears of "the useful", and thinks he has got something solid, while he really is embracing (as I have shown) a wild theoretical fiction, from which he would shrink if he saw it apart from its false lights and colours.'[16]

Having disposed of pleasure for pleasure's sake Bradley turns to attack the idea of duty for duty's sake as the end of conduct. He has in mind Kant and the categorical imperative. While in the case of hedonism he had argued that it supplies morality with nothing but the arbitrary but real enough content of passing feelings, he argues that duty for duty's sake supplies no content at all to morality. Bradley then turns to what nowadays would be called sociological role theory and examines the view that morality consists in my station and its duties. To this view he is sympathetic and it stimulates him to an eloquence still worth experiencing. But even here the sceptic is not satisfied, for a man could on such a conception be only as good as his station in his society allows him to be: '. . . we must wrap ourselves in a virtue which is our own and not the world's, or seek a higher doctrine by which, through faith and through faith alone, self-suppression issues in a higher self-realisation.'[17]

The 'higher doctrine' which Bradley introduces at this point is one that sees morality itself as ultimately self-contradictory and incomplete requiring completion by reference to the religious standpoint: 'Reflection on morality leads us beyond it. It leads us, in short, to see the necessity of a religious point of view.'[18] Morality leads in this direction because man never experiences himself as fully capable of perfection yet feels strongly the need to believe in the reality of perfection.

In pursuing this line Bradley at one and the same time destroys the autonomy of morality and mounts an attack on the secular morality propounded with religious aids by Matthew Arnold. Speaking of Arnold's view that religion is properly only an aid to virtue and happiness Bradley says: 'When the literary varnish is removed, is there anything more? But the object of the religious consciousness must be a great deal more. It must be what is real, not only in the heads of this person or set of persons, nor again as this or that finite something or set of somethings.'[19] Here we see the attempt to make religion, metaphysically interpreted, the basis of morality. Bradley's stinging polemic in *Ethical Studies* sets the stage for the more tedious exercises in moral religiosity to be found in Green and Bosanquet.

T. H. Green possessed a less incisive and sceptical mind than Bradley. Furthermore, in his metaphysical thinking he was more interested in allowing a role for orthodox theological conceptions than was Bradley. For example, while Bradley was content to see the finite self eventually swallowed up in the one all-embracing absolute reality, Green clung, essentially for reasons having to do with Christian orthodoxy, to a conception of reality which included selves as real. In short, his absolute reality is not absolute at all in the required idealist sense, for it remains compatible with the existence of a plurality of real selves. However Green's systematic construction of an ethic of self-realization, coupled as it was with an interest in the social and political prerequisites of such realization, stamped itself on a whole generation of practical men who passed through the Oxford philosophy schools before 1882.

Green's philosophy originates in criticism of Hume. He opposed all forms of naturalism and therefore was an opponent of utilitarianism and also of the evolutionism of Herbert Spencer and G. H. Lewes. He began from the assumption that no naturalistic account of morality can be given. Moral experience can only be understood on the supposition that man is in some way a non-natural being. The gap between what is and what ought to be, between circumstance and aspiration, is one reflection of the dialectical tension between the natural and the supernatural in man. The spiritual principle in man is the condition of all knowledge, morality, and citizenship. Furthermore, it is clear that the conflict in man's nature between the natural and the spiritual is not a tragic one. Green's metaphysics are really a thinly disguised theodicy, expressing a belief in the moral government of the universe and a typical aspect of late Victorian educated pious optimism. The moral agent is the willing agent who attempts to realize some conception of himself in action. Actions having the end of self-realization are good in so far as they, firstly, seek to remove or mitigate an imperfection in the agent and secondly, in so far as they make possible further acts of the agent designed to remove yet further imperfections. So good action is what makes for self-perfection. This sort of view is also redolent of puritan and evangelical self-striving. In accordance with this conception Green's view of freedom is that of the positive ability to do something worth doing; freedom is submission to a moral end rather than absence of constraints upon action. In adopting this positive and Hegelian conception of freedom Green, despite his interests in improving social conditions to make self-realization possible, abandons the traditional liberal conception of freedom as absence of constraint. He abandons Bentham for Rousseau and his interest in social amelioration becomes an interest in removing obstacles in the way of men serving an imperative moral ideal of self-perfection. What lay in J. S. Mill's writings as a hope that ultimately rational social arrangements would produce a society of moral and responsible cultivated men, becomes in Green a metaphysically based assertion to the effect that this must and will happen.

There is one saving grace to his views which Mill would have

applauded. Green attempted to incorporate into his idealist framework the individualistic conception of natural rights. He accorded
to every citizen the right of judging whether any enactment of law
or sovereignty contributes to the moral good of society. This
apparent invitation to legislative anarchy does not appear as such
to Green, partly because of his complacent and characteristic faith
in the capacity of the British constitution for peaceful change and
reform and also because of his theodicean view that the common
good must be progressively realized in history. It is an ironic paradox
that Green's theoretical refusal to subscribe to any form of élitism
should in its influential exposition have inspired many members of
the English upper classes to take up his call to serve the common
good in the interests of their own self-perfection.

Bradley and Green then may be taken as typifying the idealist
style of moral philosophy which immediately preceded 1900. It was
a style found at its most acute in Bradley but practised by a host of
minor figures. As an ethic which defined the supreme moral end in
terms of self-realization it could satisfy feeling and moral striving
as well as the intellect. It was additionally comforting in that the
end of self-realization and the possibility of its achievement were
something deduced from the nature of reality conceived in the idealist
fashion as a single interrelated whole. However, one philosopher
was singularly unimpressed by this (and, one is inclined to add, any
other kind of moral philosophy), namely G. E. Moore (1873-1958).

We have already met Moore as an ally of Russell in the campaign
waged by realism against idealism. Moore's moral philosophy is a
combination of epistemological realism and the deployment of his
characteristic method of examining the nature of a philosophical
question rather than going straight ahead to answer it. His most
important ethical work *Principia Ethica* (1903) begins by insisting
that difficulties and disagreements in ethics are due to 'the attempt
to answer questions, without first discovering *what* question it is
you desire to answer'. Moore undertakes not only to lay bare the
nature of fundamental ethical questions but also to provide answers
to them. Because of this the book is less sceptical as a whole than
appears to be the case if one concentrates only on its methodological
aspects. Also the Preface makes clear how the argument employed
relates to realism in a philosophical sense. It will be recalled that a
central tenet of idealism is the notion that a thought or statement is
more true depending upon *how* it is thought, the *how* in question
having to do with thinking of something as constituting a coherent,
non-contradictory whole. Thus what is true (or perhaps we should

say for accuracy's sake 'the truth') is not independent of how we think for the idealist. There is a parallel idealist doctrine in ethics, which is best illustrated by reference to Kant. This doctrine is that the moral worth of an act is not something which depends upon or belongs to the act itself. It is rather a characteristic conferred upon the act by some relation it has to the agent whose act it is. In Kant's case the act had to be the product of a good will. In the cases of Bradley and Green it had to be an act aimed by the agent at self-realization. Moore, as a realist, rejected this doctrine. He held that the goodness or worth of anything which is good does not depend on its relation to an agent's willing or thinking at all. It is something the agent *discovers* and hence is something that is independent of anything thought or done by agents. Stated thus baldly the doctrine may not appear especially revolutionary or disruptive. To see that it is one needs to turn to the precise way in which Moore set the realistic standpoint to work in ethics.

He begins by laying down the dictum that the fundamental problem of ethics has to do with the application of the predicates 'good' and 'bad' both to conduct and to other things. We cannot answer properly questions as to what things are good without first knowing what goodness is. So Moore proceeds to the question of what goodness is. His answer is surprisingly simple. He denies that we can *say* what it is, largely on the ground that saying what something is consists in enumerating its parts and their relations. This one cannot do with goodness because, Moore holds, it is like yellow, a unique, simple object of thought. It has no parts. Henry Sidgwick, under whose influence at Cambridge Moore must certainly have fallen, said of the terms 'ought' and 'might' that 'the notion which these terms have in common is too elementary to admit of any formal definition'.[20] It is worth noting the extent to which this 'argument' depends upon a conception of analysis as breaking things down into their constituents. If then we cannot say what goodness is in the analytic sense, how can we know what things are good? Crudely stated Moore's answer is an application of the same point with regard to a sensory quality like yellow. It no more follows from the fact that goodness is simple and unanalysable that we can't know what things are good, than it does from the same point about yellow, namely that we cannot know what things are yellow, if we cannot define yellow. In the case of yellow we inspect them for the presence of the relevant property. So in order to know what things are good we need to inspect them for the presence of the simple and unanalysable property of goodness.

This argument by analogy with sensory qualities is not Moore's only argument for his view. It is clearly weak, if only because while we are prepared to admit that inspection of colours is possible because men characteristically possess an appropriate means, namely organs of sight, we may have hesitations about the existence of an organ, however rarefied, for the detection of goodness. Nevertheless, Moore himself had no doubts about his capacity in this regard and provides us with a list of invariable intrinsically good things. Also the pattern of analogical argument used accounts for the epithet of *intuitionism* usually attached to Moore's doctrine. The doctrine of our capacity for inspecting things and states of affairs for goodness (or its absence) and basing judgements upon it of apodictic* certainty and self-evidence was summed up by Bosanquet, an idealist critic, when, admitting the ingenuity of Moore's doctrine, he said that 'a false theory of judgement had effectively gagged the organ of ethical science'. Bosanquet was entirely correct in locating part of the origin of Moore's view in the realist epistemology.

In the greater part of *Principia Ethica* Moore proceeds to develop a number of startling irreverent and iconoclastic negative consequences. They are all directed at exposing something he calls, with scant accuracy in one so pedantic, the *naturalistic fallacy*. According to Moore this fallacy has been perpetrated by all or almost all his predecessors in the subject. To explain what it consists in one may refer to the motto of Moore's title-page, taken from Bishop Butler, 'Everything is what it is, and not another thing.' Essentially the naturalistic fallacy consists in suggesting explicitly or by implication that goodness is other than itself. In one way this can be regarded as a logical point and Moore probably owed it to Russell's insistence on distinguishing the 'is' of predication from the 'is' of identity. According to Moore it is in order to say of something other than goodness itself that it *has* goodness but not in order to *identify* such goodness with any other properties or property the thing possesses, for nothing can be identified *with* goodness as distinct from identifying it *as* good, except goodness itself. Russell's distinction between predicative and identical propositions is relevant here because commission of the naturalistic fallacy consists in sliding from a statement *predicating* goodness of, say, pleasure to a statement *identifying* goodness with pleasure. Such a slide is made more plausible by a failure to distinguish predicative and identical

* Apodictic: established incontrovertibly. By Kant applied to a judgement enouncing a necessary and hence absolute truth.

judgements, a failure which Russell constantly insisted was at the root of idealism's bad logic.

From this austere Platonistic view of the good, Moore attacks J. S. Mill for having identified the intrinsically good with the pleasurable and with happiness. These things may have goodness, Moore holds, but they are not goodness. The cutting edge of this dialectic does not stop short at the hedonists and naturalists, as Moore's title for this mistake suggests. In addition to disposing of Herbert Spencer's evolutionary ethics, Moore also goes on to slay the many-headed hydra of what he calls 'metaphysical ethics'. Moore begins with some curious observations about metaphysics, praising it for its constantly reminding us of 'the class of objects or properties, which certainly do not exist in time, are not therefore parts of Nature, and which, in fact, do not exist at all'. He makes it quite clear that his own property of goodness belongs in this class. However, the cardinal error of metaphysical thinkers in Moore's view is to define and describe goodness in terms of something supersensible. He cites Spinoza and his intellectual love of God, Kant and his 'kingdom of Ends', and 'modern writers who tell us that the perfect and final end is to realise our *true* selves'. Speaking of T. H. Green, Moore says: '. . . that any of his arguments are such as to give us any reason for holding that Green's convictions are more likely to be true than those of any other man, must be clearly denied. The *Prolegomena to Ethics* is quite as far as Mr. Spencer's *Data of Ethics*, from making the smallest contribution to the solution of ethical problems.'[21]

Two features of Moore's ethical thinking remain to be noticed. The first is that he remains a utilitarian, though not a hedonistic utilitarian. He holds that practical ethical propositions, as distinct from true statements about goodness and the things which have it, are statements about the course of action which is likely to have as a consequence the greatest amount of goodness in Moore's sense. Hence, the title 'ideal utilitarianism', often attached to Moore's doctrine. Secondly, Moore does offer us his self-evident intuitions concerning those classes of things which do have intrinsic worth. One interesting principle in terms of which Moore draws up his list is what can be termed his anti-Utopian principle. He holds that the possibility of making the relevant judgements of intrinsic goodness depends upon there being before our minds that of which we judge: 'We cannot judge of the comparative values of things, unless the things we judge are before our minds.'

This principle is to be seen as a dig at the all-inclusive but unimaginable perfect whole of the idealists. On its positive side it represents a prejudice in favour of the mundane here and now, as Moore's conclusions on the question of ultimate value make clear. He says 'that personal affections and aesthetic enjoyments include all the greatest, and by far the greatest, goods we can imagine'. Stress here should be laid upon the fact that it is not simply beautiful things themselves which are intrinsically good but rather the enjoyment and contemplation of them by persons. The aestheticism as a personal style of life which this view licences had an influence on the attitudes of writers such as Virginia Woolf and E. M. Forster and also influenced the aesthetic theories of T. E. Hulme. Indeed, Moore's emphasis on the objectivity of intrinsic value is a powerful influence behind the aristocratic classicism developed by Hulme, which would have no truck with the desires of men as furnishing a standard of value. Moore's passages on the other great class of intrinsic goods, human affections, reads like a denatured modern *Symposium*. There is an impressive Olympian detachment about Moore's discussion here which leads one to think that he is simply expressing and generalizing upon the intellectual companionship in beautiful surroundings which he enjoyed in the hey-day of Edwardian Cambridge. What he appears to speak of here is something far removed from the smelly warmth of an Edwardian slum or the sanguine comradeship of the trenches in 1914. Even J. M. Keynes, a disciple of Moore, spoke in reference to *Principia Ethica* of the 'undisturbed individualism which was the extraordinary achievement of the early Edwardian days'.

I have spoken of Moore's work as in part an application of the logical and epistemological assumptions of the new realism to the problems of ethics. The two-fold result of this was the initiation of a movement in moral philosophy not dominated by idealist assumptions and a certain vogue for moral intuitionism. An extreme form of intuitionism was argued for by the Oxford realist H. A. Prichard (1871–1947) in the article arrestingly called 'Does Moral Philosophy Rest on a Mistake?' (1912). Briefly, his view was that it is mistaken to suppose that discursive proofs can be offered of the view that some act or class of acts is a duty. He supposes that this has been the basic aim of moral philosophy. The customary reasons given as to why one ought to do something are either that doing it produces some good or contributes to the happiness of the agent. But Prichard observes that both these things can be the case with regard to some act and yet one can still ask 'Ought I to do it?' The upshot of this is the insistence on an unbridgeable gap between an act being obligatory and any other characteristics the act may have, a gap akin to that which Moore insisted upon between something's goodness and its other characteristics. Prichard's article was probably more shocking than influential, though it must be remembered that its positive side is the non-sceptical view that we do have a capacity to discern the obligatoriness or otherwise of actions.

Concentration on intuitionism as preached by Moore and Prichard should not blind us to other strains of thought in this period. Two in particular are worthy of mention: First of all, a range of moral speculation arising out of anthropological work and an evolutionary stance towards culture as well as nature. Secondly, and to some extent a generalization of this first strain, the impact of the idea that the only respectable form of knowledge is scientific knowledge upon the traditional idea that moral knowledge is possible.

This first current of thought is typified by Hobhouse's *Morals in Evolution* and Westermarck's *Growth and Origin of the Moral Ideal*, both published in 1906. They are worth mentioning in any survey of the period because they indicate a late phase in the consequences of Darwin and also a new interest in the social and political context of moral ideas. Both works draw heavily upon anthropological sources and Westermarck was a practising anthropologist. The evolutionary basis of Hobhouse's views is slight. It is not so much evolution of which he speaks in tracing the growth of moral ideas as of moral progress construed in a secular liberal sense. In considering 'how far there is an advance from lower to higher conceptions' in the history of ethics, Hobhouse concludes that in the 'slowly wrought out dominance of mind in things' there is 'a message of hope to the world, of suffering lessened and strife assuaged'. His conclusion here is reminiscent of T. H. Green's belief in moral progress though, if that were possible, there is even less of cogent argument in Hobhouse than in Green which supports this conclusion. What we have instead is a fair deal of speculation upon the different phases of moral thought as represented in anthropological and historical data. Beneath Hobhouse's optimism there can be discerned what it is not inaccurate to call a positivistic attitude to the data of ethics and a lessening of interest in questions of moral justification. Philosophical ethics in the traditional sense is on the way to being replaced by the scientific study of moral and practical attitudes.

This sceptical vein and 'scientific' approach to morality is still more obvious in Westermarck. He starts by making the Humean basis of his attitude to morality clear: moral judgements arise from an intellectual tendency to generalize and objectify tendencies in certain objects to call forth moral emotions. These emotions are broadly those of approval and disapproval. Properly speaking there are no general moral truths and hence the purpose of scientific ethics should not be that of justifying moral rules but rather that of 'studying the moral consciousness as a fact'. With these opinions Westermarck foreshadows the view that many philosophers were to take a generation later which held that so-called moral judgements were really expressions of emotion. His anthropological attitude re-echoes Durkheim's sociological determination 'to treat social facts as things', that is dispassionately, objectively, and scientifically. It is possible in this attitude to see a 'scientism', whose presence we have already noticed in the development of Russell's opinions, reaching out towards the sacred data of the moral consciousness.

This tendency was almost certain to be reinforced eventually by opinions already noted in connection with Wittgenstein. It will be recalled that the obsession shared by Russell and Wittgenstein with the question of the nature of meaningful discourse had tended towards the conclusion that the only respectable form of discourse was that of natural science. From this conclusion Wittgenstein had drawn the further conclusion that ethics does not consist of propositions, that ethics cannot be expressed, and that ethics are 'transcendental' i.e. belong to the inexpressible. It would be wrong to see this view of Wittgenstein's as simply a form of the emotivism mentioned in connection with Westermarck. But it shares with this view the supposition that ethical 'statements' do not belong to the true/false type of discourse characteristic of natural science. In Wittgenstein's case the conclusion that morality is not a field for cognitive discourse issues in a mysticism which owes something to Schopenhauer. Philosophy and the deepest problems of life pass one another by and one must see that this is necessarily so. In seeing this one will have grasped the limits of the expressible and so one will not be subject to that sickness of the intellect which consists in trying to solve the insoluble. The view of philosophy as a therapeutic technique directed to this end has something in common with Freud's therapeutic techniques developed to cure the sicknesses of the emotions. But other philosophers were to see in these aspects of the new philosophical tendencies little more than a justification for discarding the metaphysically based moral optimism of late-nineteenth-century philosophical idealism. Perhaps it is more than insignificant speculation to suggest that the blood-letting of 1914-18 really had made it difficult to take seriously the idea that reality was a harmonious whole tending towards perfection.

NOTES

[1] M. Richter, *The Politics of Conscience* (1964), 36.
[2] *The New Realism*, ed. E. B. Holt *et al.* (1912), esp. 36–42.
[3] J. A. Passmore, *A Hundred Years of Philosophy* (1957), 147.
[4] *Life and Letters of Benjamin Jowett*, ed. E. Abbott and L. Campbell (1897), II. 77.
[5] G. Boole, *The Mathematical Analysis of Logic* (1847), 6.
[6] B. A. W. Russell, *Principles of Mathematics* (1903), xviii.
[7] B. A. W. Russell, *My Philosophical Development* (1958), 62.
[8] B. A. W. Russell, *Our Knowledge of the External World* (Chicago, 1918), 59.
[9] L. Wittgenstein, *Notebooks, 1914–1916* (1961), 44e.
[10] Russell, *Our Knowledge of the External World*, Preface.
[11] B. A. W. Russell, *Lectures on Logical Atomism*, VIII, in *Logic and Knowledge*, ed. Marsh (1956), 279.
[12] Ibid.
[13] L. Wittgenstein, *Tractatus Logico-Philosophicus*, trans. Ogden and Ramsey (1922), 189.
[14] S. Alexander, *The Basis of Realism* (1914), 304.
[15] B. Bosanquet, *The Principle of Individuality and Value* (1912), 315.
[16] F. H. Bradley, *Ethical Studies* (1876), 140.
[17] Ibid. 204.
[18] Ibid. 314.
[19] Ibid. 318ff.
[20] H. Sidgwick, *The Methods of Ethics* (1875), 32.
[21] G. E. Moore, *Principia Ethica* (1903), 139.

FOR FURTHER READING

J. A. Passmore, *A Hundred Years of Philosophy* (1957), is the best general survey, although it covers a larger period than 1900–18; it is the most comprehensive and useful bibliographical guide to the period. M. Warnock, *Ethics since 1900* (1960), supplements Passmore, who does not deal with ethics. Another useful introduction is G. J. Warnock, *English Philosophy since 1900* (1958). Two other works which, while not strictly philosophical, are nevertheless able to furnish the inquirer with some idea of the social context in which idealism and Russell's early doctrines were worked out, are M. Richter, *The Politics of Conscience, T. H. Green and His Age* (1964) and B. A. W. Russell, *The Autobiography of Bertrand Russell*, I (1967), II (1968). B. A. W. Russell, *My Philosophical Development* (1958), is a fascinating work in the unusual genre of philosophical autobiography. R. Wollheim, *F. H. Bradley* (1959), sympathetic though not uncritical, is the best introduction to the doctrines of British idealism. David Pears, *Wittgenstein* (1971), in the Fontana Modern Masters series, provides a cogent analysis.

7

Psychology

L. S. HEARNSHAW

I

The last years of the nineteenth century and the early years of the twentieth century saw the birth of psychology as an independent scientific discipline. Man has speculated about his mind from primitive times; these speculations were systematized and critically elaborated by Greek, medieval, and modern philosophers, as well as by Oriental sages. In the eighteenth century the term 'psychology' became increasingly accepted, first in Europe, and then somewhat later in this country, to designate this field of study. 'There is,' wrote J. S. Mill in his *System of Logic* (1843), 'a distinct and separate Science of Mind', which, he added, may be termed 'Psychology'. By the middle of the nineteenth century textbooks of psychology began to be published, the first in this country being Herbert Spencer's *Principles of Psychology* (1855). Nevertheless 'psychology', though it now had a name of its own, and though sometimes spoken of as a science, was in reality neither emancipated nor scientific. It was still tied to philosophy, taught, in so far as it was taught, in departments of metaphysics, and lacking both its own techniques and its own practitioners.

The change came organizationally during the last quarter of the nineteenth century. In 1879 Wilhelm Wundt, Professor of Philosophy at Leipzig, founded his Psychologisches Institut, the world's first psychological laboratory. In America Stanley Hall followed in 1883 with the establishment of a laboratory at Johns Hopkins University. In England small laboratories were set up in Cambridge and at University College, London, in 1897. In the train of the laboratories came learned journals, Wundt's own journal in 1881, the *American Journal of Psychology* in 1887, the *British Journal of Psychology* in 1904; then learned societies like the American Psychological Association in 1892, and the British Psychological Society in 1901. The first international congress of psychology was held in Paris in 1889. These dry facts are important because they objectively establish the birth of psychology as an independent discipline with the apparatus and accoutrements of a science, laboratories, journals, learned societies, international congresses, and a breed of specialists. By the end of the century not only were psychologists eager and ready to assert their independence, their parents, the philosophers, were equally anxious to eject them from the philosophic fold, and to campaign against 'psychologism', the contamination of philosophy by psychological impurities.

As the twentieth century dawned the infant science came of age. The period under consideration in this chapter, 1900–18, was one of seminal importance in the development of psychology. It was richer in creative ideas and striking personalities than any other period in the history of psychology. A new continent of knowledge was beginning to be opened up to scientific exploration. It was an age of large vistas and pioneering enthusiasms, an age marked by controversy and confusion, but at the same time by lasting achievements. It saw the publication of such landmarks as Freud's *Interpretation of Dreams* (1900), William James's *Varieties of Religious Experience* (1902), Pavlov's early papers on conditioned reflexes (1903), Spearman's first paper on factor analysis (1904), Binet's intelligence tests (1905), Sherrington's *Integrative Action of the Nervous System* (1906), McDougall's *Social Psychology* (1908), the final volume of Havelock Ellis's *Studies in the Psychology of Sex* (1910), Wertheimer's experiments (1912) that led to the foundation of 'Gestalt' theory, and Watson's behaviouristic programme (1913). Indeed it would not be outrageous to claim that for psychology more substantial advances in techniques and in ideas were made between 1900 and 1914 than in all the 2,222 years between the death of Aristotle and the beginning of the twentieth century. In the years immediately prior to the outbreak of the First World War most of the main lines of development of modern psychology were laid down. A few years earlier, in 1892, William James in his famous lament had bewailed the pitiful condition of the 'new psychology'— 'a string of raw facts, a little gossip and wrangle about opinions, a little classification and generalization on the mere descriptive level; not a single law in the sense which physics shows us laws, not a single proposition from which any consequence can causally be deduced'. 'This,' he concluded, 'is no science, it is only the hope of a science.'[1] By 1914 to men of vision the outlines and trends of the new science were becoming more than a mere hope; they were beginning to be a reality. A new way of studying man and his mind had become established, which in its long-term promise and impact must surely count among the major landmarks of human intellectual development.

II

The birth of modern psychology towards the end of the nineteenth century was the result of the union of the older tradition of mental philosophy and the newer biological and social sciences. The harmonization of these two streams, themselves complex and diverse, was by no means easy, and the problems and controversies which marked the rise of psychology, and which still to some extent characterize it today, derive from this basic difficulty.

The philosophic heritage from which psychology sprang was essentially dualistic. Seventeenth-century Europe rejected Aristotle and his hylomorphic union of soul and body, and substituted the Cartesian doctrine of two incommensurable substances. In 1949 Professor Ryle could still describe this as 'the official theory',[2] and state that 'most philosophers, psychologists and religious teachers subscribe, with minor reservations, to its main articles'. The pioneers of psychology conceived their science as analogous to physics; but whereas physics analysed matter into particles and motion, psychology analysed consciousness into elementary 'ideas' and their succession. Corresponding to the basic physical laws of motion, it was suggested that psychology might discover (some even claimed, had discovered) equally basic laws of association. These were the fundamental philosophical preconceptions on to which experimental methodology was grafted in the second half of the nineteenth century.

Experimental psychology emerged from the physiological laboratories of the German universities. Until the nineteenth century accurate knowledge of the workings of the nervous system and of the sense organs was practically non-existent. Experimental investigations into sensory physiology early in the nineteenth century soon led naturally on to questions of sensory psychology, and it became clear that at least some problems of psychology were amenable to experimental, and indeed, quantitative treatment. Special methods were required to cope with the special problems raised by the subjective nature of psychological data; the so-called 'psychophysical methods' propounded by Fechner in the 1860s adapted numerical methods and measurement to psychology, and controlled 'introspection' was an attempt to remove some of the arbitrariness from the observation of psychological states and processes.

Soon other advances began to exert an influence on the development of psychology, and indeed on the very conception of its subject-matter. Evolutionary biology introduced a new way of looking at minds, as something functional and dynamic, subject to the laws of heredity and variation, and developing from simple to complex by stages. Considerable strides were made in the understanding of the structure and functions of the brain and nervous system. The long period of stagnation and superstition in the treatment of mental disorder was brought to an end early in the nineteenth century. The systematic study of abnormal and subnormal states of mind, together with new techniques, ranging from hypnosis to drugs, opened new territories for the psychologist. Finally the social sciences emerged with new data and new points of view. Comte, Marx, and the anthropologists had at least this in common, that they held that human nature was largely a product of society.

The most comprehensive of the early attempts to organize this new data was that of Wilhelm Wundt (1832–1920). Wundt's huge output (which ran to over 50,000 pages of print) was an immense collection of material rather than a closely integrated system. His principal psychological works were the *Physiologische Psychologie* (3 vols.) and the *Völkerpsychologie* (10 vols.), in which he attempted to organize respectively the experimental and physiological data, and the social and cultural data of psychology. There was no real guiding idea in the Wundtian corpus other than the ambition to make psychology scientific. The *Völkerpsychologie* did not blend with the *Physiologische Psychologie* in any meaningful way, and indeed the physiological and the psychological aspects of the *Physiologische Psychologie* ran in parallel rather than interacted. Wundt's preconceptions were dualistic, and he never questioned the assumption that the task of psychology was to analyse consciousness into its elements and to reveal the laws of their succession and composition. 'The whole task of psychology', he wrote in his short popular introduction, 'can be summed up in these two problems; (1) what are the elements of consciousness? (2) what combinations do these elements undergo, and what laws govern these combinations?'[3] The new data provided by evolutionary biology and by abnormal psychology found no adequate place in Wundt's scheme. The science which Wundt, together with his associates and rivals in the German universities, was creating was academic and philosophical in its inspiration. It had few links with the market-place, and few obvious applications to the daily lives of human beings. Though the importance of Wundt in the history of psychology cannot be questioned, his particular brand of psychology has died away in the twentieth century, and nearly all the vital developments of the period we are considering can be regarded as at once protests against the assumptions and limitations of Wundtian orthodoxy, and attempts to formulate a framework for psychology both more scientifically valid and more humanly meaningful.

III

In the English-speaking world the most influential of the protestors was the American psychologist, William James (1842–1910). His revolt against the Germans was partly temperamental. His warm and sensitive spirit could not abide the laboured detail of the German experimentalists and their 'brass instrument psychology'. Somehow in their meticulous analyses the colour and vitality of the human mind had got lost; all the ingredients which to James gave psychology its fascination had got left out. Their science, he maintained, could never have been undertaken in a country 'whose natives could be bored'. Wundt he rudely described as 'a Napoleon without genius and with no central idea. . . . Cut him up like a worm and each fragment crawls; there is no vital centre in his *medulla oblongata.*' Behind James's temperamental aversion were some solid disagreements on doctrine, and criticisms of the unreal fragmentation of the stream of consciousness. James's own two masterpieces, the *Principles of Psychology* (1890) and the *Varieties of Religious Experience* (1902) were written a little too early to do more than adumbrate the shape of things to come; their supreme importance was that they made psychology seem interesting to far more people than it had ever seemed so before. Among the interested in this country were two young men, William McDougall (1871–1938) and Charles Spearman (1863–1945), who were both to become leading figures in twentieth-century psychology, and to break away from the constrictions and artificialities of Wundtian orthodoxy.

Perhaps McDougall typified better than anyone else in Great Britain the new forces at work in psychology between 1900 and 1918. In 1900, after completing an extensive apprenticeship, scientific, medical, and anthropological, as well as psychological, McDougall was appointed to a part-time readership at University College, London. He later moved to Oxford. In 1920 he migrated, frustrated by the lack of opportunities for psychological research in British universities, to America, where he spent the remainder of his life. Though his heart was never perhaps wholly in experimental psychology McDougall showed himself in his early years a competent experimentalist. It was not long, however, before he was to sound the call of revolution against the basic presuppositions of Wundtian psychology. 'Psychologists,' he proclaimed, 'must cease to be content with the sterile and narrow conception of their science as the science of consciousness, and must boldly assert its claim to be the positive science of the mind in all its aspects and modes of functioning, or, as I would prefer to say, the positive science of conduct or behaviour.'[4] Other voices elsewhere had been proclaiming, or were about to proclaim, similar sentiments. Indeed they were to carry McDougall's points to conclusions which he was not prepared to accept.

Basically the protest was against the static, analytic, isolated study of consciousness, divorced from the matrix of nature and society. The demand was for a psychology that concerned itself with the behaviour and strivings of real individuals in the real world, not with mere abstractions and artifacts. McDougall, in making these points, was focusing protests which had been gathering strength for some time. In a more philosophic form they had been made by James Ward, the dominant figure in Cambridge psychology at the end of the nineteenth century, and author of the famous *Encyclopaedia Britannica* article (9th ed., 1885) which undermined the doctrines of British associationism and laid stress on the continuity and individuality of the mind. Ward's article, published in extended book form as *Psychological Principles* in 1918, was destined to exercise a powerful influence on British psychologists for almost half a century, partly because of Ward's strategic location in Cambridge, and partly because of his intellectual distinction. Many of his doctrines were taken up and developed by G. F. Stout, who was a Fellow of St. John's College, Cambridge, when McDougall was an undergraduate there and particularly influenced him. Activity, conation, effort, striving, will, attention—call it what you like—was of the essence of mind. All this tuned in not only with certain philosophical trends then in the air, and expressed by philosophers like Nietzsche and Bergson, but also with the teachings of evolutionary biology. Impulse, not reason, was king, or, according to McDougall, a cluster of basic instincts which we share with other members of the animal kingdom. The more elaborate superstructure of human mentality was in the end merely subservient to these same instinctive drives. The savagery of the 1914–18 War, the apparent breakdown of rational and civilized behaviour in the accepted sense, the revelations of Freudian psychoanalysis and of the new art forms, all seemed to confirm the basic rightness of

McDougall's viewpoint, and 'hormic psychology', as it was termed, became extremely fashionable. The speculative nature of many of its proposals was overlooked.

The demand that psychology should be dynamic was only one strand of McDougall's protest. He objected to the analytic search for elements, to what he called 'mosaic psychology', the attempt to reduce minds to conglomerations of simple and more basic units. Here again McDougall was voicing an objection that had been growing in strength. It had been powerfully made by Ward and Stout; it had been made by William James when he decried the 'domino psychology' which ignored the underlying unity and continuity of the stream of consciousness, ignored 'the self'. Then shortly afterwards it became a main plank of the important German school of 'Gestalt' psychologists, who were prominent in psychology between the wars. In a brilliant series of experiments, mainly in the fields of perception, learning, and memory, Wertheimer's experiments on the perception of movement (1912) being the first, they demonstrated that 'Gestalt' (i.e. form, organization, structure) dominated the perceptual process; that it was impossible to build up and construct what we perceive merely from a conglomeration of elements. To take a simple example, a melody is not just a conglomeration of notes; it is a 'Gestalt', a structure, which can in fact be transposed to an entirely different set of notes without substantial loss. Though disputing some features of their teaching, McDougall and many of his contemporaries found themselves in agreement with the 'Gestalt' criticisms of atomism in psychology. It seemed to tie in, too, with Sherrington's findings on the integrative action of the nervous system (1906) and the unity of organic functioning.

In human beings unity of organic functioning depended, according to McDougall, on the formation of character, on the building up on the foundation of the basic instincts of organized systems of emotional tendencies, or 'sentiments', as McDougall termed them, themselves harmoniously integrated under a master sentiment of self-regard, a largely social product closely linked with the development of self-consciousness and with the genesis of the idea of the empirical self. This whole area of character formation, obviously important in practical life, had been largely ignored by the early experimental psychologists, who focused their attention on elementary cognitive processes and simple motor reactions. For McDougall it became the most important area of psychology. Confronted with practical problems in schools, clinics, and workshops, many psychologists came to agree with him. Between the wars a new brand of psychology was born, the psychology of personality, wholistic in its presuppositions and subordinating all the special problems of psychology to the central theme of the person. William Stern in Germany and Gordon Allport in America were to become leading exponents of this viewpoint, the beginnings of which were clearly sketched by McDougall.

Another significant feature of the book in which McDougall first outlined his proposals for the reform of psychology was its title, *Social Psychology* (1908). According to J. S. Mill 'human beings in society have no properties but those which are derived from and may be resolved into the laws of the nature of individual man'.[5] This individualistic tradition was that from which experimental psychology emerged. Social psychology, and the full recognition by psychology of the social nature of many features of human mentality as we actually find it, did not finally emerge until the twentieth century. McDougall's book, and an American book by E. A. Ross published in the same year, were the first works actually entitled 'social psychology'. The intellectual precursors of social psychology go back, of course, a long way, at least to Plato. They were submerged by the Christian emphasis on the responsibility of the individual for his own deeds and his own salvation. But gradually the social viewpoint reasserted itself, in the social philosophy of some eighteenth-century thinkers, in German idealism, in the sociologies of Comte, of Marx, and of Durkheim, in the findings of the late-nineteenth-century social anthropologists (Tyler in England, Lévy-Bruhl in France) to emerge as social psychology in the twentieth century, and to receive perhaps the clearest formulation in the writings of John Dewey, the American philosopher-psychologist. McDougall in his *Social Psychology* was, therefore, swimming with the tide, though, in spite of his anthropological initiation in Borneo and New Guinea, he was not a particularly good social psychologist. His book was a prolegomena to, rather than a treatise on, social psychology, and his overwhelming emphasis on instinctive drives was biological rather than social. His sequel, *The Group Mind* (1920), was doctrinaire, prejudiced, and inadequately based on facts. In this country McDougall's contemporary, Graham Wallas, has a far greater claim to the title 'social psychologist'. Wallas's *Human Nature in Politics* (1908), while it owed a great deal to McDougall, was a brilliant analysis of the psychological forces at work in the political arena, based on much first-hand observation. There is no doubt, then, that during the first decade of the twentieth century social psychology was born as a recognized branch of psychology.

Finally we must note McDougall's significant definition of psychology as the science of behaviour. In 1900 Lloyd Morgan, then Principal of University College, Bristol, who was responsible for so many of the key concepts of modern psychology, introduced to psychology the technical term 'behaviour'. 'The term', he wrote, 'in all cases indicates and draws attention to the reaction of that which we speak of as behaving, in response to certain surrounding conditions or circumstances which evoke the behaviour.' [6] The term was adopted by McDougall and first employed in his brief *Physiological Psychology* (1905). Then it migrated across the Atlantic to become the central defining concept of psychology, ousting all earlier claimants, experience, consciousness, and mind. In this development McDougall could not follow the behaviourists, who, led by J. B. Watson, in 1913 rejected as futile the whole attempt to base a science on introspective observation of conscious phenomena, and maintained that objectively observable behaviour constituted the sole data of psychology. Similar proposals had been made more than once before. Comte in France, Maudsley in this country, and Sechenov in Russia had denied the value of subjective observation or introspection. The methodological and philosophical issues raised by the behaviourists have not yet been resolved, but at least we can agree with Professor Ryle, when he stated that 'the behaviourists' methodological programme has been of revolutionary importance to the programme of psychology'. [7] It involved to be sure a complete re-shaping of the psychology of the Wundtian period at the price, it now seems, of a too drastic simplification of the issues. Images, plans, concepts, decision processes, the self are not entirely otiose, and cannot as the behaviourists supposed be wholly reduced to stimulus-response terms. On-going central processes are somehow involved. McDougall grasped this, though his own particular formulations hardly stand up to critical scrutiny.

In McDougall we find most of the seeds of twentieth-century psychology, the seeds which after the 1914–18 War flowered in the various 'schools' of psychology, the succession states of the Wundtian empire. Hormic psychology, 'Gestalt' psychology, personality psychology, social psychology, behaviourism, all find some expression in McDougall's early writings, though McDougall himself remained obstinately uncommitted except to his own brand of hormic psychology, and indeed endeavoured to reconcile and embrace these new trends within the framework of traditional dualism, of which in *Body and Mind* (1911) he wrote a powerful defence.

IV

Spearman may be regarded as complementary to McDougall. Whereas McDougall's psychology developed the dynamic implications of Darwinism and culminated in a theory of character, Spearman's psychology derived from the Darwinian emphasis on individual differences between members of the same species and culminated in a theory of intelligence. By temperament Spearman was much less of a revolutionary than McDougall; he regarded his own work as supplementing rather than replacing Wundt, and for Wundt himself he always expressed a deep admiration. His researches on intelligence, however, were directly inspired by Francis Galton, and their effect was to lead psychology into areas far removed from Wundtian laboratory psychology.

The fact was that neither Wundt nor the older philosophical psychologists were interested in individual differences. They aimed at establishing general laws and descriptions. They were concerned with intellectual processes, but not with intelligence and its differential distribution. Interest in individual differences was a direct consequence of evolutionary theory. Herbert Spencer postulated a power he called 'intelligence', which was concerned with 'the establishment of correspondence' between organisms and their environment. Francis Galton, a cousin of Charles Darwin, attempted on the one hand to show the extent to which intelligence in human beings depended on inheritance, and on the other hand to devise techniques for measuring intelligence. These techniques were christened 'mental tests' by the American psychologist, J. M. Cattell, in 1890. They were developed and improved by a series of investigators (above all by Ebbinghaus in Germany, and by Binet in France), and by the time the Great War broke out were being used in a variety of practical contexts, educational, occupational, and clinical. In 1912 William Stern, who later built up a famous department in the University of Hamburg, coined the now notorious term 'I.Q.' (intelligence quotient).

The psychology of intelligence involved three main groups of problem: (1) What was the origin of intellectual differences? (2) What was the structure of human intelligence? (3) What was the nature of intelligence *per se*? To the first of these problems Spearman did not himself contribute. It was taken up, following Galton's lead, by Cyril Burt and other investigators into mental subnormality. Spearman's own contributions were to the second and third groups of problem. To the problem of the structure of human intelligence Spearman, who was a good mathematician, brought to bear original mathematical techniques, and came to conclusions which, though they have not entirely stood the test of time, nevertheless opened up new pathways, enabling what had been a largely speculative issue to be attacked by empirical and quantitative methods. On the third group of problems, the nature of intelligence, or as he would have preferred to say, the nature of the general factor in intelligence, Spearman contributed a powerful and erudite analysis, and though once again his theory of noegenesis, or creative intelligence, has not altogether stood up to subsequent scrutiny, it proved practically useful as a convenient simplification and a guide for test construction.

The importance of Spearman's work on intelligence, and the work of his pupils and disciples, lay not in the finality of their conclusions but in the opening up of new territory for psychological research, and the practical consequences that flowed from it. Here, to be sure, was an area of psychology that touched life at many points.

V

The most far-reaching developments, however, in twentieth-century psychology sprang from the work of two men who in the strict and narrow sense were not properly psychologists, Sigmund Freud (1856–1939) and I. P. Pavlov (1849–1936). Neither of them was greatly interested in academic psychology. The output of the Wundtian laboratories they simply ignored. They struck out independently on their own, formulating new concepts, and establishing new systems as their findings moved them. By very different routes, and using very different methods, towards the end of their long lives they had approached, though they did not know it, within hailing distance. Meanwhile on their diverse tracks they had profoundly modified both the foundations and the outlook of psychology.

Unquestionably Freudian psychoanalysis has had a greater impact on the twentieth century mind than any other system of psychology. Its influence has perhaps been greater on the general cultural outlook of the west than on academic psychology, where it has had to face both rivals and critics. We are here concerned mainly with the formative period and the theoretical platform of psychoanalysis. Its wider cultural impact occurred mainly after 1918.

In 1886 after a medical training in Vienna, a spell of neurological research, and a short visit to Charcot's psychiatric clinic in Paris, Sigmund Freud settled down in Vienna as a consultant in nervous disorders. Psychoanalysis was formulated partly to cope with the problems of his patients, partly to cope with his own personal problems. It was at once a method of investigation for unravelling psychic knots, a form of psychotherapy, a cult and organization (almost a medical sect), a body of psychological theory, and finally a general system of interpretation of human culture and society. At many points it borrowed from the scientific, philosophical, and literary milieu of the late nineteenth century, but as a synthesis it was original and uniquely powerful.

Perhaps the central doctrine of Freudian theory, and certainly the theoretical core of what Freud always regarded as his principal book, *The Interpretation of Dreams* (1900), was the doctrine of two levels of mental functioning, primary and secondary processes. Primary processes constitute a different and more basic type of thinking, best exemplified in dreams, but also in childhood fantasies, in the myths of primitive peoples, and in psychological disorders. Primary processes are symbolic and pictorial, lacking in objectivity or strict logic, and aimed not at truth but at pleasure and the expression of wishes and desires. By contrast, secondary processes, precariously developed in the course of civilization, are logical, objective, critical, rational, and directed towards reality. Psychoanalytic teaching shifted the balance of power in the human psyche from the secondary to the primary, and thus undermined the orthodox belief of western man, established since Greek times, in the priority of reason. The primitive mind, according to Freud, is imperishable, and not only openly dominates in dreams and disease, but subtly interpenetrates and distorts apparently rational processes. In the last resort it has the mastery.

Human beings have failed to recognize this owing to the repressive limitations of consciousness and conventionality. The concept of unconscious mind, which became another central tenet of psychoanalysis, went back nearly two hundred years to Leibniz, but Freud gave it a new significance, partly through his elucidation of the dynamic mechanisms which restrained it, and partly through his creation of techniques for exploring unconscious contents.

The revelation of the contents of the Freudian unconscious certainly startled early-twentieth-century society, when Freud's next major work, *Drei Abhandlungen zur Sexualtheorie* appeared in 1905.[8] Freud was not the first western sexologist. Krafft-Ebing in

Germany, and Havelock Ellis in Britain, to name but two, had deeply explored the functions and the pathology of sex, but their works were largely confined to medical readers. Freudian theories were more far-reaching in their implications, and Freud intended that they should circulate among a wider set of readers, as the publication of popular lectures makes clear.[9] Sex was no simple instinct, according to Freud, but soldered together from components, most of which were present in infancy, and could fall apart to constitute perversions. The apparently sexless infant was in fact 'polymorphously perverse', i.e. the infant showed a variety of sexual tendencies, which were they to persist into adult life would be regarded as perverted. But perhaps more important than this, human character was largely the result of how the component facets of sex had been handled in childhood.

What we describe as a person's 'character' is built up to a considerable extent from the material of sexual excitations and is composed of instincts that have been fixated since childhood, of constrictions achieved by means of sublimations, and of other constrictions, employed for effectively holding in check perverse impulses which have been recognised as being unutilizable.[10]

These findings were applied by Freud not merely to the treatment of neurotic disorders, but to the understanding of everyday behaviour (slips of the tongue, mistakes, jokes, and so on), to the customs and taboos of human societies, and to the elucidation of artistic productions and religious beliefs and practices. It looked as though most of the eternal values and verities were being brought down into the primeval slime.

After the 1914–18 War various modifications and additions were made to Freudian theory: to sexual 'libido' was added a destructive 'death instinct'; the psyche was differentiated into 'ego', 'id', and 'super-ego'; the nature of anxiety was redrawn: but its basic features remained, in spite of storms of controversy, to change the very presuppositions of man's image of himself.

The exclusive sect of pure Freudians who banded themselves together in the International Association of Psychoanalysis (founded in 1910) always remained small. In this country the London Society of Psycho-analysts, which was formed by Ernest Jones, a leading Freudian follower, in 1913, comprised at first only fifteen members. Moreover the Freudian strength was early weakened by defections. Alfred Adler broke away in 1911, largely because he could not subscribe to Freud's views on the role of the sexual impulses, and established his own school based on inferiority feelings. C. G. Jung also finally severed his connection with Freud in 1913 to set up a rival body of his own, more credulous of the revelations of the unconscious.

The influence of psychoanalysis, however, did not depend on the pure Freudians. Many features of Freudian teaching harmonized with contemporary viewpoints. Freud's theory, like McDougall's, was 'hormic' in that it emphasized innate drives. Psychoanalytic 'libido' bore at least some resemblance to Bergsonian '*élan vital*'. The Freudian unconscious had affinities with F. W. H. Myers's 'subliminal self' though its furnishings were rather different. The distinction between 'primary' and 'secondary' processes fitted neatly on to the doctrine of levels, propounded by Herbert Spencer, Hughlings Jackson, and the neurologists. Distinguished academic psychologists began to show an interest in Freud, and to give a qualified assent to some aspects of his theories. In England, for example, W. H. R. Rivers, who had helped to organize and run the first experimental laboratories in Cambridge and London in 1897, and who during the Great War acquired extensive experience in the treatment of war neuroses, pointed out that many of the doctrines of Freudian theory could be translated into a more acceptable biological language and harmonized with the findings of neurology. Though Freud's sexology continued to stick in the gullets of the prim, and his methodological looseness to worry the logical purists, by 1920 psychoanalysis had become a force to be reckoned with not only in psychology, but as a general influence on the twentieth-century mind. The gigantic figure of Freud, dispassionate, courageous, and utterly honest, was impossible to ignore.

VI

The initial approach of Pavlov, the physiologist, was wholly different. During the course of his twenty years' work on the digestive glands Pavlov had observed what he called 'psychic secretions'. The flow of gastric juice in the digestive systems of the dogs he was using as experimental animals would commence, not with the eating of the food, but at the sight of the attendant who brought the food. The flow, in other words, was an anticipatory one. In 1902 Pavlov, then fifty-three years of age and already a famous man, determined to investigate this phenomenon, which he was soon to term a 'conditioned reflex', or 'conditional reflex', as the Russian term might have been more accurately translated, and for the next

34 years it became the research focus of his St. Petersburg (Leningrad) laboratory. Pavlov considered, but rejected, a psychological approach to the problem. 'I decided finally,' he wrote, 'in regard to the so-called psychic stimulation to remain in the role of a pure physiologist, i.e. of an objective external observer and experimenter, having to do exclusively with external phenomena and their relations.'[11] The chief influence upon Pavlov in coming to this decision was the monograph of his Russian predecessor, Sechenov, on *The Reflexes of the Brain* (1863), which advocated a purely objective approach to the study of psychological processes.

The essential significance for psychology of Pavlov's work was that it provided an objective, precise, and quantifiable method for investigating the functions of the cerebral cortex and the higher nervous activity of animals. The conditioned reflex in itself was, of course, important in that it was an elementary form of learning, closely allied to the mechanisms of association proposed by British thinkers of the eighteenth and nineteenth centuries, by whom indeed Pavlov admits to having been influenced. Pavlov's work was one of the main factors which changed nineteenth-century associationism into twentieth-century learning theory. Pavlov's techniques, however, were even more important in that they opened the way to the precise investigation of many other cortical functions, to studies of the functions of the sensory 'analysers' in animals, of cortical time relations, of levels of vigilance or alertness, of the directional orienting reflex, of differences in types of nervous system and temperamental make-up, of conflict situations, and, when he came to human subjects, of the role of language, or as he termed it 'the second signal system' in modifying cortical functioning.

In Russia, where Pavlov's teaching eventually became one of the foundation stones of Soviet psychology, the derivatives of his work remained strongly tied to brain physiology. In the west the full significance of Pavlov's achievement was only slowly recognized, in spite of Pavlov's Huxley Lecture delivered at Charing Cross Medical School in 1906, largely because his principal work, *Conditioned Reflexes*, was not translated into English until 1927, and its fate was rather different. It obviously tuned in with, and hence was eagerly adopted by, American behaviourism. But behaviourism arose independently of Pavlov. Thorndike's experiments on animal learning were carried out several years before Pavlov switched his attention to conditioned reflexes. When J. B. Watson (1878–1958) formulated the behaviourist programme in 1913 and set out to write a psychology 'in terms of stimulus and response . . . habit formation, habit integrations and the like'[12] he made no reference to Pavlov's work. This was incorporated into behaviourism in 1916 in his article on 'The Place of the Conditioned Reflex in Psychology'.[13] From then onwards the theory of conditioning became one of the main planks of behaviourism, but it was adopted as a contribution to the psychology of learning, not to the physiology of higher nervous functioning. Pavlov's physiology receded into the background. The approach of most American behaviourists was frankly a 'black box' approach. They were interested in stimulus-response relations, and were quite prepared to ignore, or to invent, what went on inside the skull. Nor until quite recently were they impressed with the Pavlovian theory of the 'second signal system' and the importance of the part played by language in human behaviour. In contemporary Russian psychology it has for some time been recognized as one of the most significant parts of Pavlov's teaching. Certainly Pavlov regarded the 'second signal system' as a new attainment in evolution, 'a new principle of neural action' which differentiated man from the rest of the animal kingdom. We find, then, in Pavlovian theory a recognition of different levels of functioning, which links it not only with evolutionary theory generally, but, at least in this respect, to psychoanalysis. To psychoanalysis Pavlov's work on the effects of conflict situations and the production of 'experimental neuroses' constituted another bridge.

The implications and the applications of Pavlov's classical experiments are still, thirty years after his death, being worked out. One thing is certain—our approach to the study of the behaviour of organisms can never again be the same as it was before Pavlov.

VII

A further ingredient in the shaping of twentieth-century psychology, and a further feature of its impact on twentieth-century society, was the rise of applied psychology. If applied psychology had been merely a technology, merely the application in the field of methods and findings established in the laboratory, it would not deserve more than a mention. But theory and practice were not in fact related in this way. The findings the psychologist had at his disposal were thin and tentative except when linked to very small segments of behaviour. Amid the complexities of real life he was confronted with many unknowns, and was forced to undertake applied research. His new techniques were often designed in the first instance to deal with practical problems. Thus Ebbinghaus's completion test (1897), the first intelligence test of the modern type, was constructed to investigate fatigue in Breslau school-children resulting from continuous five-hour classroom sessions. And Binet's even more famous scale (1905) was the outcome of an inquiry into subnormal performance among Paris pupils. During this century the belief has gradually grown, perhaps at times over-optimistically, that the psychologist by his investigations can illuminate the practical human problems of society, and by the application of his technical 'know-how' do something to solve them. Upon the basis of this belief a psychological profession, with both medical and non-medical sectors, has grown up in most advanced societies.

Applied psychology began in the United States, where the earliest psychological clinic dates back to 1896. In Great Britain the first professional psychologist to receive an official appointment was Cyril Burt (b. 1883), who became educational psychologist to the London County Council in 1913, and who, during his tenure of office, not only carried out monumental investigations into sub-normality and delinquency, but also devoted himself to the construction and standardization of a number of mental and scholastic tests, and to investigating the interrelation of educational abilities. His pioneering work eventually led to the establishment and spread of child guidance clinics in this country, and it had a considerable influence upon the shaping of educational policy.

The Great War of 1914–18 accelerated the application of psychology in a variety of ways. In October 1914 Dr. C. S. Myers, director of the psychological laboratory at Cambridge, one of our most distinguished academic psychologists and also medically qualified, proceeded as a consultant to the British forces in France, where he was soon confronted with the problem of 'shell shock'. It eventually became clear that 'shell shock' was not a physical, but a psychological phenomenon, and that it could best be treated by psychotherapy. Psychotherapeutic clinics had already been started in a small way for treating neurotic disturbances before the out-break of the war. Wartime experiences were to result in a notable post-war efflorescence, in which W. H. R. Rivers, the Cambridge psychologist, who had devoted himself to psychotherapy during the war, played an important part.

It was the same in the new field of industrial psychology, which had been placed on the academic map in 1913 by Münsterberg with his book *Psychology and Industrial Efficiency*. The problems of wartime industry forced the British Government to undertake research on the human factor in production, and this led on to the postwar establishment of permanent research organizations, in particular the Industrial Fatigue Research Board, and the National Institute of Industrial Psychology.

By 1918 it had become apparent that psychology, as well as being a new branch of science, was also a new technology involving new areas of applied research. It is, after all, not surprising that in societies growing in technical complexity and changing with increasing speed, a branch of technology should be needed to cope with human adjustments and maladjustments; to guide, to counsel, and to rehabilitate the individual; and to assist in designing the fabric and furniture of society to fit human needs and limitations; and that to buttress this technology the psychologist should plunge into research covering a wide range of human and social problems. His efforts may possibly seem derisory when compared with the magnitude of the social dislocations and the violence of the social forces released in the twentieth-century world, but perhaps in the long run the way of the psychologist, and the social scientists with whom he collaborates, will win through and bring a mastery as striking as that which physical medicine has won over the epidemics and plagues of the past.

VIII

By 1918 most of the new trends and schools of thought which were to re-make psychology had emerged into the daylight. What had not emerged was any agreed conceptual framework or body of theory. Psychologists spoke not with one voice but with several conflicting voices. There were, it is true, 'middle of the road' psychologists content to accumulate facts and avoid commitments, and they were producing a growing volume of good, unspectacular, detailed work in an increasing number of psychological departments and laboratories in various parts of the world. The steady accumulation of silt, however, does not immediately form firm land. Solid foundations are needed, too, and these were lacking. The differences between psychologists involved fundamentally different presuppositions about the nature of their science, and fundamentally different methodologies. Until these differences were resolved, or at least harmonized, psychology could legitimately be criticized as 'a partly fortuitous federation of inquiries and techniques'.[14]

The 'two-worlds legend' has been the root of the trouble. Psychology's first bid to enter the common market of science was made without the relinquishment of this legend. Psychology strove to keep its special status as a study of the subjective, of consciousness, with unique introspective access to certainty. Even some of the new men who rejected Wundtian orthodoxy still clung to dualism. McDougall, as we have already seen, went so far as to write a lengthy defence of 'animism';[15] while the great physiologist, Sherrington, a good friend to psychology, saw no way to unite 'energy' and 'value'—the physical and the mental.

This was the knot that the behaviourists endeavoured to cut by an unreserved acceptance of the standpoint of the physical sciences. 'Psychology as the behaviorist views it is a purely objective experimental branch of natural science . . . (it) must discard all reference to consciousness . . . and never use the terms mental states, mind, imagery and the like.'[16] This radical programme, though salutory up to a point, was never wholly convincing; and it was opposed, particularly on the continent of Europe, by the philosophical trend towards phenomenology, which has gained continuously in strength since the publication in 1900 of Husserl's *Logische Untersuchungen*. Phenomenology, whatever else it entails, involves a subtle description of conscious experience and its acts, and its impact profoundly influenced the course of psychological development, particularly in Germany.

The tensions latent in psychology had indeed already led the philosopher, Wilhelm Dilthey (1833–1911), to propose that there were in fact two distinct sorts of psychology, scientific psychology which endeavoured to explain naturalistically and to formulate laws, and humanistic psychology which endeavoured to understand from within. Humanistic psychology was allied to the other humanistic disciplines, history, literary criticism, the arts, and involved similar interpretative and evaluative methods. Of the two sorts of psychology the latter, Dilthey and his followers made clear, was much the more significant, and alone capable of illuminating the deeper problems of human cultural life. The alignment of psychoanalysis, in spite of Freud's professed adherence to deterministic naturalism, was in effect with the humanists. Psychoanalysis was an exploration of symbolism, and its methods were not quantitative but interpretative. It has always appealed more strongly to the artistically imaginative than to the scientifically minded. The allegiance of Jung was even more markedly humanistic.

Dilthey's proposal aggravated rather than surmounted the difficulties for psychology arising from the two-worlds legend. The dividing fence was set no longer between the physical and the mental, but within the territory of psychology itself. On the one side there was *naturwissenschaftliche Psychologie* (scientific psychology), on the other *geisteswissenschaftliche Psychologie* (humanistic psychology). To take Dilthey's proposal seriously—and in Germany it was taken seriously—meant almost inevitably the division of psychologists into two hostile camps, speaking different languages, employing different methods, and sharing little in common except the name, psychologist.

But was there any third way, other than dualism or reductionism? Not long after the close of the period to which this chapter is devoted the Cambridge philosopher, Dr. C. D. Broad, undertook a review of the mind's place in nature in the Tarner Lectures, which he delivered in 1923.[17] In a subtle analysis of the problem, in which he distinguished seventeen possible theories of the mind-body relation, Broad came down, tentatively and with some qualifications, in favour of what he called 'emergent materialism' as providing the most acceptable solutions. According to this theory as matter becomes organized in more and more complex ways new properties emerge, including eventually mental properties. The theory began to take shape in the nineteenth century. It was proposed by J. S. Mill in his *Logic*; christened by Mill's contemporary, G. H. Lewes; made explicit by a number of early-twentieth-century thinkers, Bergson, Lloyd Morgan, Hobhouse, and Alexander. The weakness of the theory was that it never really explained the 'how' of emergence; its strength, that it descriptively seemed to fit the facts, particularly the evolutionary and developmental facts, and that it tied in with the doctrine of neurological levels expounded by Spencer and Hughlings Jackson. For the psychologist it appeared to provide the clearest hope of a way out of his difficulties, since it enabled him to escape from dualism without having recourse to reductionism. If emergence was a fact of nature, it was no longer necessary, indeed it was no longer justifiable, to 'reduce' mind to material terms alone. Though all mental processes necessarily have a material base, none is exclusively material. Moreover mental events themselves reveal emergent levels of complexity. So though the complex, or higher, are always rooted in the simpler, or lower, they can never be wholly reduced to the lower. The creative solution of an intellectual problem involves not just a set of reflexes, though it may rest on, and require the operation of, reflexes. Psychology, therefore, has two poles: one pole set in the physiology and the biochemistry of the organism, the other in the highest achievements and creations of human intelligence and personality. But this does not mean two psychologies, as Dilthey supposed, since there is a continuity of development, an emergent series of levels which link the two poles and which it is the psychologist's job among other things to study. The work of comparative and developmental psychologists, the findings of neurologists, and, in their different ways, the theories of Freud and of Pavlov, all seemed to point towards an emergence theory of the kind advocated by Broad.

As our period closed the emergence philosophy was to receive its most articulate expression in the Gifford Lectures of Samuel Alexander (1859–1938), delivered in Glasgow in the sessions 1916–18, and published as *Space, Time and Deity* in 1920. In Alexander's exposition mind was conceived as identical with neural processes of the requisite degree of complexity, qualitatively new, but not epiphenomenal or supernumerary, since mental quality was an essential, not an accidental, accompaniment of such processes. Mind, therefore, though in one sense wholly material, is not merely material. An analogy may make this clearer.[18] A lump of iron is a chemical entity; if the iron has the form of a poker, it is still analysable into iron, but cannot any longer be fully described in terms of chemical concepts. It now has an organization above the chemical level. It is not for the chemist to explain what makes it a poker. Similarly mind cannot exhaustively be described in physico-chemical terms in spite of its materiality. To describe mind psychological concepts must come in. Alexander accordingly held that 'there can be and is an independent science of psychology',[19] and acting on this belief he proceeded to persuade his own University of Manchester in 1919 to establish the first full-time chair of psychology in this country.

All psychologists would agree that the period 1900–18 laid the foundations for the extensive subsequent developments of psychology. The majority of psychologists would agree that it was among the most fertile and creative periods in the history of psychological thought. Even today we rely extensively on the seminal ideas and on the novel techniques which had their origin in the early years of this century. At the same time it was an era of conflict and controversy in psychology which inaugurated the phase of development often known as the period of 'the schools'. With the suggestion that in the philosophy of emergent evolution a way of reconciliation had also been provided by the thinkers of this period there would be much less agreement. Materialistic behaviourists and animistic phenomenologists are not so easily reconciled. Yet perhaps in the philosophy which Alexander and others expounded there was a framework large enough, and at the same time definite enough, to embrace everything the psychologist is interested in, from the firing of a single neuron to the contemplation of deity.

NOTES

[1] W. James, *Text Book of Psychology* (1892), 468.
[2] G. Ryle, *The Concept of Mind* (1949), 11.
[3] W. Wundt, *An Introduction to Psychology*, trans. R. Pintner (1912), 44.
[4] W. McDougall, *Social Psychology* (1908), 13.
[5] J. S. Mill, *System of Logic* (1843), Bk. VI, ch. vii.
[6] C. Lloyd Morgan, *Animal Behaviour* (1900), 2.
[7] Ryle, *Concept of Mind*, 328.
[8] Translated into English as *Three Contributions to the Theory of Sexuality* in 1910.
[9] Freud's lectures on *The Origin and Development of Psychoanalysis*, given at Clarke University in the U.S., were published in the *American Journal of Psychology*, XXI (1910). His more famous *Introductory Lectures on Psychoanalysis*, given in Vienna in 1915–17, appeared in English in 1922.
[10] S. Freud, *Three Essays on the Theory of Sexuality* (trans. 1949) 115–16.
[11] I. P. Pavlov, *Lectures on Conditioned Reflexes*, 1 (Eng. trans. 1928), 38.
[12] J. B. Watson, 'Psychology as a Behaviorist Views It', *Psychological Review*, XX (1913), 158–77.
[13] J. B. Watson, 'The Place of the Conditioned Reflex in Psychology', *Psychological Review*, XXIII (1916), 89–117.
[14] Ryle, *The Concept of Mind*, 323.
[15] W. McDougall, *Body and Mind* (1911).
[16] Watson, 'Psychology as a Behaviorist Views It'.
[17] C. D. Broad, *The Mind and its Place in Nature* (1925).
[18] I have borrowed this illustration from J. H. Woodger's *Biological Principles* (1929).
[19] S. Alexander, *Space, Time and Deity* (1920), II. 8.

FOR FURTHER READING

R. Thomson, *The Pelican History of Psychology* (1968), is a good and readily available introductory history with extensive bibliography. J. C. Flugel and D. J. West, *A Hundred Years of Psychology* (1964), is an excellent introductory history, covering the period from 1833. G. Murphy, *An Historical Introduction to Modern Psychology* (1949), commences in the seventeenth century and comes down to modern times. L. S. Hearnshaw, *A Short History of British Psychology, 1840–1940* (1964), contains an 18-page bibliography of works by and about British psychologists. G. S. Brett, *A History of Psychology*, ed. R. S. Peters (1953), is useful for the early history of psychology in particular. Originally this came out in three volumes in 1912. Peters has shortened the material, and added a chapter on contemporary developments. A very valuable work of reference, fairly detailed, is E. G. Boring's *A History of Experimental Psychology* (1950).

R. J. Herrnstein and E. G. Boring, *A Source Book in the History of Psychology* (1965), is mainly concerned with the period up to 1900, but contains some material relating to the period 1900–18. B. B. Wolman, *Contemporary Theories and Systems in Psychology* (1960), is learned, but wordy; nevertheless useful for reference and containing a very full bibliography.

A. A. Roback, *History of American Psychology* (1964) is the standard history of American psychology. R. S. Woodworth and Mary Sheehan, *Contemporary Schools of Psychology* (1965), offers essential reading for understanding the background of contemporary psychology. This is largely confined to American psychology, though the latest edition contains a rather weak chapter on Soviet psychology.

W. Dennis, *Readings in the History of Psychology* (1948), includes twelve extracts which relate to the period 1900–18; there are translations of Binet's papers on his intelligence tests. Among many writings on Freud, E. Jones's three-volume biography, *Sigmund Freud, Life and Works* (1953–1957), is magnificent. A shortened one-volume edition is available in the Pelican series. Margaret Knight, *William James* (1950), includes a selection from his writings on psychology together with a fifty-page introduction. Translated extracts from Dilthey's writings plus a commentary are to be found in H. A. Hodges, *Wilhelm Dilthey: An Introduction* (1944). Finally, in *History of Psychology in Autobiography* (1930–6), edited by C. Murchison in three volumes, many of the important figures in early-twentieth-century psychology contribute fascinating accounts of their life and work.

8

Physics

G. H. A. COLE

I. GENERAL APPROACH

Man appears always to have been overawed by his environment, and to have attempted to 'explain' it. The explanation has changed from time to time, but a constant feature has been a desire to generalize local experience and to unify it. Modern science is the latest technique of generalization and has proved to be a very powerful tool for increasing our knowledge and understanding of the physical world. Physics is the branch of science that is particularly concerned with the general principles and laws which can be supposed to underlie the behaviour of the material universe as we observe it. The last phrase emphasizes that the study of physics is fundamentally experimental. One of the central features of the study of physics during this century so far has been the according of a fundamental status to the recognition that science is experimental and is not exact and absolute in the true scholastic sense.

It has been found that theoretical discussion in physics can proceed more precisely if the language used is mathematical rather than verbal. In consequence, we have in physics a special mixture of experiment and mathematics. For convenience these two aspects are referred to as experimental and theoretical physics but this does not imply that there is a barrier between the two aspects; progress in science as a whole requires that workers in one aspect have an awareness of the techniques and difficulties of their colleagues in the other. Physics has come to be divided for reasons of convenience. Some divisions, like heat, sound, light, magnetism, electricity, and properties of matter, immediately suggest concepts familiar in everyday life. Other divisions, like atomic or nuclear physics, still retain some semblance of familiarity in their titles, but others, like field theory, or S-matrix theory, are clearly abstract. But the whole area of study is today isolated from purely human, non-quantitative, concepts in a much more thorough-going way than was the case at the beginning of the century.

The theoretical (mathematical) aspects of physics are intimately connected with the process of generalization and abstraction of the data provided by experiment. Experiment and observation provide the only ultimate source of information about the physical world. And when some generalization has been attempted, only experiment or observation can test finally its value and later validity by testing predictions made using the new theory.

We have talked of experiments and observations together, but a distinction between them must be recognized. In an observation we are able to watch only passively and are not able to influence the situation at all, or at least in any decisive way. In an experiment things are quite different. The system under test is now under complete, or at least very strong, control from outside, and can be deliberately changed in a specified and predetermined manner. The effect of the change on the system is measured in appropriate detail, and the effect can be repeated many times even though the time-scale may not be under our control. We might, for example, measure the behaviour of an internal combustion engine when it is working on different fuels and find its efficiency for each one. This can clearly be repeated: it is a trivial experiment, but it does show the high degree of control under such circumstances. This contrasts with the passivity of observation, for example, of an eclipse of the sun by the moon. Because experimental conditions are under our control but those associated with observations are not, experimental data are to be preferred as a basis for generalization and abstraction, even though observational data must be accepted as adequate when experiment is impossible or inappropriate.

The quality and detail of measured data are very important, because any isolated information can be generalized in an indefinitely large number of ways, if no other restrictive criteria are to be imposed. In physics it is necessary that generalizations that still apply to the physical world should be produced. For this purpose we assert that the universe with which we deal has a unity and uniqueness that make scientific discussion meaningful together with a simplicity that makes discussion practical. These assertions are not intuitively obvious and are far from trivial, for they introduce assumptions about the physical universe (or at least our appreciation of it) that are of the deepest significance. To begin with, it is by no means obvious a priori that all aspects of the universe are unique. (Even fingerprints must presumably repeat if enough people are involved, even though it may take thousands of years to amass them in the files.) And again, the universe need not be expected to present unity in all its aspects, except in the most trivial sense, and the fact that it appears to do so over a wide area is one of the most astonishing circumstances exploited by science. The meaning of these concepts will emerge further as we go on.

We are not dealing with the description of a universe in isolation from an observer; the observer is an essential part and his general (non-personal) characteristics influence his description of what he finds. The recognition of the central role of the observer is a characteristic feature of the physics of this century, and will continually emerge as an important constraint on our description of measured data. The idea that things are seen relative to a particular observer, rather than absolutely, is at the very root of modern physical thought, and contrasts markedly with the viewpoint of earlier centuries where the ultimate recognition of absolutes remained a possibility. An example of this idea that we shall see later is the Michelson–Morley experiment (of 1887) which laid the foundations for the epoch-making work of Albert Einstein (1879–1955).

Experimental and theoretical aspects of physics (and indeed of all science) are connected by a collection of abstract quantities called *physical concepts*. These physical concepts are a concise summary of our systematized knowledge of the physical universe at any given time, and are the result of the process of generalization which is the very nature of physics. The exact details, or even the number and complexity, of these physical concepts will generally change as our knowledge and understanding of the universe increases. The attitude in this matter has changed drastically so far during the present century. From the classical work of earlier scientists it appeared that physical concepts could be recognized that were indeed 'real' in some precise sense. But more than this; it seemed that our knowledge of them could be made exact if our skills of measurement were developed sufficiently. It is now recognized that this is not so, imprecision being an essential feature of the universe that must be explicitly accounted for in any description of it. This is stated in the well-known 'uncertainty principle' which expresses the idea that there are certain pairs of quantities, such as the position and momentum of a particle, that cannot both be known exactly. The more exactly the position of the particle is known, the less exactly its momentum can be known. This is because the observer, in trying to measure one quantity, disturbs the system as both he and his apparatus are a part of the system.

A system of physical concepts and quantities that describes the main features of a situation is known as a *model*. The fact that models are found to be useful in accounting for physical situations, although they ignore the contribution of the rest of the universe, is an illustration of our idea of the simplicity of the universe. Up to about the turn of this century it was accepted that the models were imperfect representations of restricted aspects of a unique reality, but now it must be doubted whether such a reality can be recognized as existing. The totality of our knowledge is lodged in the description that we can give our measurements and quantitative experience. The models we construct are the only backcloth that we can rely on with certainty; more than this is metaphysical hope which modern experience suggests is unfounded. This development (associated with the quantum theory and with statistical mechanics) will be explored later, but we can notice here that it is associated with a corresponding aspect of experimental physics, viz. the fact that all experimental measurements are subject to errors of measurement. The attitude to such errors has changed over the last fifty years owing to the uncertainty principle. The central role that must be accorded to errors of measurement means that the data available to the theoretician for generalization and discussion is not accurate beyond an accuracy that might be open to estimation. This limited vagueness is part of the fabric of modern physics, but was foreign to the exponents of the subject prior to 1900. The present century is characterized in physics by the abandonment of the absolute in its several guises.

The intimate link between theory and experiment is well illustrated by the often-performed task of relating a set of measured data, with specified experimental errors, graphically. We might think of plotting the dependence of the pressure of a gas on its volume, with the temperature held constant; this is one case of an unlimited number of examples of one quantity changing with another, with yet further variables held constant for the time being. The two quantities are plotted on a piece of paper (one along each axis—a three-dimensional construct could be made to plot three variables simultaneously), the results forming a series of measurements that are represented by a series of points on the piece of paper. We will suppose, from the unity of the world, that a single line will join each set of related points, and further that this line will be smooth and not discontinuous, of course unless the physical system itself shows discontinuity. Not all the measured points can be expected to lie on one single curve, and even if such a curve should be found we cannot place too much reliance on it because we have already seen that the measurements themselves are subject to errors of experiment. The accepted way of overcoming these difficulties is to select a smooth curve on the basis of a conventional criterion. Most often used is the 'least-squares fit', where the representative curve is chosen in such a way that it is continuous and the difference between the square of its value at each point (the square is used because then positive and negative errors give the same effect) and the square of the corresponding measured values is a minimum and of a value smaller than the square of the error associated with the measurement. Not all the actual measurements will lie on this curve (even though it is consistent with the errors of measurement), but yet the resulting information portrayed by the curve will be accepted by all physicists as deriving from experiment. We must accept generally that any experimental measurement must, in a very real sense, be corrected theoretically, on the basis of some criterion of simplicity and unity, before it can cease to be an isolated piece of information and join the corpus of what is accepted as being reliable experimental knowledge. Physics is thus an amalgam of experiment and theory in a vital sense, and it is not possible to separate the one aspect from the other, except as a temporary working emphasis.

To summarize, the measured values found in experiment are expressed theoretically as numbers derived from certain selected solutions of a set of appropriate mathematical equations. A wide variety of at first sight unrelated experimental data are linked by being taken as particular cases of the general solution of mathematical equations. These equations are based on premises expressing a theory, and involving physical concepts. The consequences of any theory are, therefore, open to experimental test, and often the premises themselves can also be tested in this way. The intermediate mathematical argument usually has an abstract form that does not relate directly to experiment. A good theory has many consequences and few premises; presumably the ideal theory has a very few premises (even only one) and many consequences. It is seen that a good theory for consequences of given accuracy or range of measurement may break down as the accuracy is improved, or the range is extended.

The universe is more complex and much more wonderful than we can imagine. For detailed description, therefore, we are forced to construct a conceptual universe chosen to contain only those special features of the actual world that appear directly relevant for our immediate purposes. Put another way, the real world is represented by a collection of models, each one chosen to account for a range of measured data of prescribed accuracy. The exact details of the model are important only in the relation of one component to another; they are of very little interest in themselves, being only convenient representations of some deeper statement.

II. THE CLASSICAL THEORY

Transferring Energy

The present century opened in the world of physics with a well-established order and structure, which had been built up steadily over the previous four hundred years. It is true that a few cracks and difficulties were discernible, but most physicists then felt that a final basis had been laid for the description of the physical world. Subsequent work has shown how utterly wrong that assessment was. The almost explosive development of physics during the twentieth century has been due in no small measure to technological applications of previously established physical principles; the link between fundamental discovery and practical application has stimulated the growth of both. Physics was found to be a hierarchical discipline of a form that was not realized before; the crucial element in the hierarchy has proved to be size. The experimental and observational data that were available for discussion before 1900 were almost entirely associated with the world of everyday experience (the macroscopic world); certainly the 'model' of the physical world and the associated physical concepts of that time were all derived from macroscopic experience. The great developments of the present century have arisen from the recognition that this is only one part of the world, and not even the most fundamental part. In 1900, the atom and the molecule were still hypotheses yet to be established in physical terms, and the structure of the atom was still entirely unknown.

The observational and experimental materials that provided the basis for the early construction of macroscopic physics were the large terrestrial features of everyday life and of the planets. This means that by modern standards the physical conditions from which the experimental data were to be obtained were moderate in every way. Thus the temperatures were neither high nor low (very roughly the temperature range of ice–water–steam), the pressures were centred broadly around that of the atmosphere, and the densities were in the range that is familiar in daily experience. This restriction to the circumstances of everyday experience allowed the theoretical discussion of experimental data to be in terms of a set of physical concepts that could immediately be accepted intuitively. Indeed, so intuitively obvious were these concepts that it was only recently realized that they *are* concepts, and not absolute properties of the world itself. They have played a central role in the development of physics during the sixteenth, seventeenth, eighteenth, and nineteenth centuries, and still play a central position even now. They are, after all, the result of an analysis of the real world at the everyday level and, at that level of discussion, must still be as valid today as they were in the past. They are in a definite sense classical and final within their limits of application; the macroscopic theory that is built on them is consequently called *classical*. Parts of the classical theory (e.g. in mechanics) appear so final and all-embracingly beautiful as to be designated canonical (I think particularly of 'the canonical equations of motion'). Medieval people did not realize that they lived in an age of faith and that an age of reason was to follow; they treated faith as reason. Just as the medieval world is part of our cultural heritage, so classical theory is a part of the development of physics that will always have some, even if decreasing, use in the future.

The problems of classical, as of modern, physics concern the passage of energy from one place to another. There are two broad ways in which energy can be transported, and this leads to two divisions in classical theory. One method is by the transference of matter from one place to another, like a projectile. For example, consider a cricket match. The bowler gives energy to the cricket ball when he bowls it down the pitch; the batsman redirects and supplements the energy when he hits the ball; if the ball is caught at the boundary, the fielder absorbs the energy when he catches the ball. The energy is transferred by a projectile. The understanding of such an energy-transfer system must involve the study of the trajectories of lumps of matter under various external influences and forces.

There is also the process of energy-transmission familiar in wave motion. You can easily let an angler know of your presence at the water's edge by stirring up waves in the water with your hand; the waves will move his float and he will know that someone is there, though no actual matter will have been transferred. And shouting to a person requires the passage of waves through the air without the net transfer of matter, even though energy has passed. Classical physics is thus concerned with the study of the trajectories of projectiles and with the study of wave motion.

The Mass-Point, Space, and Time

The motion of projectiles, which is the subject of mechanics, was systematized by Newton, building on earlier work. Newton and his predecessors were concerned on the one hand with terrestrial experiments with falling bodies, pendulums, and spheres colliding or running down planes, and on the other hand with observations on the motion of astronomical bodies, and in particular of the planets. The experiments with falling bodies were performed and analysed particularly by Galileo, who can have a very substantial claim to being the first modern scientist. The astronomer Tycho Brahe amassed over many years an enormous dossier of observational data of the motion of those planets that could be studied without a telescope. (The telescope had not been invented at that time: pure and applied science were as closely related then as now.) These data were subsequently studied by Kepler, who reduced them to three mathematical statements, which must remain a very remarkable précis operation.

Although Galileo and Kepler were considering different types of phenomena, their work showed the crucial common property that the main features of motion do not depend upon the shape and size of the bodies involved. This is seen by considering the results of these studies. Kepler's summary of Tycho's measurements is in three statements, referred to as Kepler's laws of planetary motion. These are: that each planet moves in a closed elliptical path with the sun located * at one of the foci; that the line joining the centre of each planet to the centre of the sun traverses equal areas in equal intervals of time; and that the square of the time for one single revolution round the sun (i.e. the year of the planet) is proportional to the cube of the major axis of the ellipse. (See figure, p. 256.) These laws are an excellent and very convenient restatement of Tycho's original observations; a few lines to be compared with many pages of numbers. But there is more than just a précis involved and this is true of any measured data. The observational (i.e. measured) data can be given only to a definite accuracy of measurement, and careful experiment is always accompanied by a quantitative estimate of the associated errors. But Kepler's laws make exact statements, like 'equal areas in equal times', and involve exact powers like 'square' and 'cube'. There is no room for error here; everything is exact. But

---

* We know now that it is the centre of gravity of the solar system that is located at a focus, but this is virtually the same thing as the centre of the sun.

the original data are not exact. Kepler's laws represent an essential generalization, and one that must be checked continually by methods of increasingly improved accuracy, for the replacement of measured data by mathematical formulae must always be made with the greatest caution. Actually, as will concern us later, better observations of the innermost planet Mercury have shown that in this case the orbit is not quite a closed ellipse, so that Kepler's laws are applicable there only as a first approximation, rather than as a good second approximation as is the case for the remaining planets.

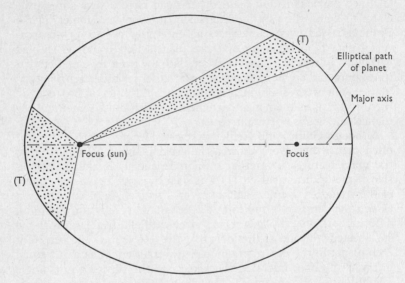

The shaded areas represent equal areas swept out in equal times (T) by the line joining the planet to the sun.

Would Kepler still have proposed his laws had he known of this discrepancy? We do not know, but we can see that one of the arts of making a précis is to separate what is of primary importance from what is of only secondary importance.

Kepler's laws are based on simplification. The exact physical nature or conditions of the sun and planets are not important for the description of the orbits, and neither is the size of the object nor its state of rotation, at least at this level of observational accuracy. Each planet and the sun can be visualized, for the description of orbits, as a point-like object in space. The position of each body can be fully specified independently of the location of the others, and the motion of the whole system can be specified instantaneously on a time-scale common to all, whatever the motion.

Galileo was able to demonstrate that all projected bodies trace out simple parabolic paths, irrespective of their shape, size, and physical nature, if the effect of the resistance of the air can be neglected. If dropped from a height, they all fall to the ground in the same way with the same acceleration. Here again, it seems that for many purposes the body in question can be represented as a single geometrical point in which all the ponderable mass is concentrated. There are limits, of course; this would not be sufficient if the effect of air resistance were of interest since the geometry of the surface could then be relevant; and the collision of bodies of complicated shape could in practice involve other factors. Nevertheless, the 'mass-point' arises as a central physical concept from these studies, as does the concept of an absolute system of locations (absolute space) and the concept of an absolute time, moving steadily forward.

Describing the Motion of a Particle

A mass-point is often conveniently referred to as a particle, and the question arises of the rules for calculating the trajectory of a particle. These rules for classical physics are contained in the three laws of Newton, to which I come next.

It was Galileo who first realized the value of the acceleration of a particle as a measure of its motion. The acceleration of a body is the rate with which its velocity changes with time, while the velocity itself is the rate with which the position of the body changes with time. It is quite proper to associate a velocity and an acceleration with each point of the trajectory of the particle. A particle in motion has a velocity; if the motion is changing, the particle is subject to an acceleration. Change of motion is caused by the action of a force; the motion does not change if forces do not act. This is the broad experimental content of the laws of Newton, summarized in the first and second laws.

The first law states that it is possible to find a set of co-ordinate axes (called a frame of reference) for the description of the motion of particles which are such that all mass-points not subjected to forces are unaccelerated, and so move in a straight line with constant speed or remain at rest (this is the so-called inertial frame of reference). It is interesting to see that this law provides a criterion for deciding whether a particle is acted on by a force or not. How do we know a particle is not accelerating? Well, if it is not it moves equal distances in equal time intervals (i.e. it has a constant velocity). These deductions assume that we can mark out equal distances (i.e. equal lengths), and measure equal times. That this is possible is part of the absolute classical background of space and of time, common to all observers independently of their motion. If a particle is moving in a constant direction at a constant speed (i.e. has constant velocity), then the observer can always move in a parallel direction with the same constant speed so that the particle appears to be at rest relative to the observer. Because acceleration is not involved we can express the first law slightly alternatively by saying that a body not acted on by a force either remains at rest or moves in a straight line with constant speed. Since an observer can always move so that he sees a particle moving with constant velocity as being at rest, all inertial frames of reference are equivalent in classical physics, a circumstance known to Galileo and often called the Galilean principle of relativity. The development of this principle into a major new branch of physics in the present century will be discussed later.

But what happens if a force is acting? Newton's second law of motion tells us that in this case the body has an acceleration and that in the subsequent motion the time rate of change of the momentum of the particle is equal to the measure of the force in magnitude and direction. In classical physics the mass of the particle is found to be independent of the motion of the particle, so that the time rate of change of momentum can, in this circumstance, be equated to the product of the particle mass and the particle acceleration. The negative value of this product is sometimes called the force of inertia. Mass is a permanent property of the matter and is additive in the sense that if two masses are put together the resultant mass is the sum of the component masses.

The Gravitational Force

An immediate development of the previous statements is to consider more than a single particle. In this way, the origin of the force on the particle of the last section can be given appropriate physical meaning. The most obvious macroscopic force with which one body can act on another body is that of the direct force of contact, such as in a collision between two bodies. The situation is covered by the third law of Newton, according to which each force exerted by one mass-point on another has a corresponding force exerted by the second on the first. The two forces are equal in magnitude but opposite in direction. Static equilibrium of rigid bodies can be accounted for by a suitable application of this empirical law. However, other types of force also arise between bodies not actually in contact. Both classical and non-classical physics are deeply concerned with forces acting at a distance and we shall have much to say about these things later. For the moment we follow a broadly historical pattern and consider the force between massive bodies separated by a distance—the gravitational force.

Newton showed that Kepler's summary of planetary motion is fully intelligible on the single hypothesis that every particle of matter in the solar system attracts every other particle of matter with an instantaneously-acting force which is inversely proportional to the square of the distance between them and is proportional to the products of the masses of the geometrical points that represent them; the direction of the force is along the line joining the two mass-points. This is the law of gravity.

What about the stars and the universe—is the gravitational law valid there as well? If we believe in the unity of the universe we would expect matter everywhere to be acting gravitationally. We can assert the universality of gravitation. The dynamics of star clusters then falls within our numerical study, and we might assume the galaxies themselves to be amenable for inclusion within the scheme. We find such a generalization is not in disagreement with the basic measured data summarized in Kepler's laws.

We must be careful to say that the law 'accounted for' rather than 'explained' the facts. Newton reduced a vast accumulation of apparently unrelated facts to a single association with the action of a single force. Further work in the eighteenth and nineteenth centuries brought more phenomena within the compass of action of the gravitational force, and the fall of a stone, the motion of a planet round the sun, the orbit of the moon round the earth, the motion of the sea tides, the air tides, and the earth tides, and over the last decade the trajectories of space vehicles, all combine as examples of the action of the gravitational force. But there is no explanation of the ultimate nature of the gravitational force—this is not part of the aim of the theory.

System of Particles: Conservation Laws

The concept of a physical point containing mass has been seen to evolve naturally from the study of projected bodies at the earth's surface and from the study of planetary motion. Although the mass-point is interesting from the point of view of mathematical simplicity, it hardly has a general physical relevance as it stands. But a gross gravitating body can be looked upon as being composed of an aggregate of mass-points and this leads us to consider the physical usefulness of the model of a large number of particles (mass-points) moving relative to each other. The gravitational force, acting instantaneously at a distance as it does independently of the motion of the gravitating masses, can act as a prototype for a general force with which one particle can affect another. Irrespective of any physical applications, there is a formal interest in treating the properties of many particles all in interaction one with the others. This study, originally encompassed in the study of analytical mechanics, is found to have a place at the very centre of the study of matter in bulk, for it is now well established that macroscopic matter is composed of an astronomically large number of particles (atoms and molecules) which can be approximated by mass-points, to a useful degree of approximation, for many practical purposes. The effect of the force is supposed not to be dependent on the particle speed, this being the simplest assumption to make. But this particularly simple assumption is not applicable to all cases, the speed being an important parameter in some (e.g. viscosity).

A collection of mass-points which exert forces on each other, possibly at a distance, and which move under the influence of the forces, is called a mechanical system. It is often of interest to consider a sub-group of interacting particles moving under the action of forces that are due to the presence of other mass-points not belonging to the sub-group. If it is accepted that a projectile moving near the surface of the earth is a collection of particles, then the force of external origin (called the external force) is due to the gravitational forces of the particles comprising the earth. The concept of a system of particles moving under the action of an external force other than gravitation will prove of great utility in our later arguments.

The laws of mechanics of Newton set down above (pp. 257–8) can be applied separately to each particle. The force that is equated to the time rate of change of momentum becomes the sum of external forces and the force between the particle under investigation and the remaining particles of the system. Both magnitude and direction of momentum and force must be accounted for in these calculations. It will be realized that the mathematical analysis of such a system of particles will be very difficult, or even impossible, unless special circumstances reduce the complexity of the calculations. One such special circumstance is when the force is associated with a potential energy. The work done by a particle against a force is equal to the product of the force and the distance in any chosen direction. Energy must be expended in doing this work, so that the movement of the particle against a force can be associated with an energy, technically written as a negative energy because energy is expended (i.e. lost to the particle) in overcoming the resistance of the force. This energy is a complete measure of the work done if it is the same regardless of the actual path of the particle. In this case only the location of the particle before and after a displacement is necessary to determine the work done in the movement: the associated (negative) energy is called the potential energy. Potential energy is as important a concept now as it was in the last two centuries. The kinetic energy of the particle is one half its mass multiplied by the square of its speed: the total energy of the particle is the sum of the kinetic and potential energies. A force that has an associated potential energy is called a conservative force, for reasons that will be clear in a moment. The gravitational force is conservative.

A mechanical system involving only conservative forces has special collective properties. For it is found that the total force arising from the action of all the *internal* forces vanishes and that the time rate of change of the sum of all the momenta of all the particles is equal to the sum of the externally-applied forces. This has the same form, for many particles, as the motion of a single particle. If there are no external forces acting, the time rate of change of momentum of the *total* system of particles vanishes, i.e. the total momentum of the system is constant. It is known that macroscopic matter does not spontaneously disappear so that the mass is constant also.

The energy also fits into this scheme. It is found that the time rate of change of energy is to be equated to the sum over all the particles of the product of the external force on each particle and the velocity of the particle. If the external forces all vanish (i.e. if there are no external forces) the total energy of the system remains constant in time. Finally, there is a corresponding constancy statement for the rotation characteristics of the system, i.e. the total angular momentum. Angular momentum is a particularly important concept in classical and quantum physics alike. It is the product of the linear momentum of a particle at a given point on its trajectory and the perpendicular distance from the particle to the point at which the angular momentum is to refer. We then have to talk about the angular momentum about some axis, and in classical theory we refer to a rotation of the total body of some kind.

If a quantity does not change in time it is conserved. What we have outlined above are the great conservation laws of classical physics, viz. the conservation of mass, momentum, and energy. The conservation of angular momentum is a by-product of the other laws. The acceptance of the conservation laws as elementary concepts is quite remarkable but is now commonplace in both classical and modern physics. They must always remain surprising in their generality and simplicity even though they are now well known.

The acceptance of conservation laws allows experimental observations to be expressed in a very compact form. As an example, consider Kepler's laws of planetary motion (p. 255). After a mathematical analysis it is found that the elliptical orbit, which is referred to in the first and third laws, is an immediate consequence of the conservation of energy, i.e. the conservation of the sum of the kinetic energy of the planet and the gravitational potential energy. The second law of Kepler can be re-expressed as the statement that the angular momentum of the plane orbit about a perpendicular axis through the sun is constant, i.e. angular momentum is conserved. But we can go further. An ellipse is only one member of a class of curves called conics; hyperbolae and parabolae are the remaining members. Many comets are known from observation to follow hyperbolic paths with the sun at a focus, and the conservation laws of energy and angular momentum are as fully compatible with hyperbolic as with elliptical orbits. The difference is in the relative importance of the kinetic and potential energies: the elliptic orbit arises when the initial potential energy predominates over the kinetic energy, whereas the hyperbolic orbit is associated with a predominance of the initial kinetic energy. A balance between the initial kinetic and potential energies leads to a parabolic orbit. The generalization involved in the passage to these statements from the original observational data of Tycho Brahe is enormous. And this provides a generalization of Kepler's laws themselves. For, if the solar system is regarded as a totally isolated system, then Kepler's laws refer to each separate planet-and-sun-system and this neglects the (admittedly very small) contribution of the energy of perturbation between the planets themselves. This can be accounted for by a small correction.

Matter in Bulk: Phenomenological Thermodynamics

The reduction of the description of the motion of a system of particles into the same form as that for a single particle is convenient if the motion of the total system is of interest, but is not helpful if we wish to explore the internal properties of the system itself. Consequently the general behaviour of macroscopic matter has been described in terms of models that ignore any microscopic properties of the system itself. Any treatment of macroscopic matter based on the study of the motion of the extraordinarily large number of constituent particles (molecules) presents almost insurmountable mathematical problems. Before the year 1900, the molecular structure of macroscopic matter was anyway not adequately known for these purposes. But even now, when more is known, the mathematical problems associated with any direct evaluation of the macroscopic properties in molecular terms are still too formidable for contemplation. It is both possible and necessary to relate the various measured properties of macroscopic matter in other ways. Consequently, the general behaviour of gross matter under various physical conditions has been described in terms of models that ignore any specific underlying structure altogether.

One theory that has had, and still continues to have, enormous utility is thermodynamics. It studies heat as a form of energy and is concerned with the relationship of heat as energy to all other forms of energy, such as mechanical, chemical, or electrical energy. Thermodynamics is concerned only with macroscopic everyday affairs and, being a highly practical and descriptive subject, is at home when dealing with highly-complicated systems, particularly those that the physicist would avoid but the chemist would revel in. Thermodynamics successfully avoids any discussion of the molecular structure of matter, and so is unaffected by improved knowledge of the molecular (microscopic) structure of matter. The relationship between thermodynamics and the molecular theories of matter has been very much a study of the present century and I shall refer to this in a later section when I discuss statistical physics. *Although developed during a period of absolutism in physics, thermodynamics contains the seeds of a relativity statement.* It is never concerned with absolute values but is always concerned with linking some final state to some initial state, i.e. with relative changes. This will be found to be important in later sections.

Matter in Bulk: Continuum Elastic Behaviour

In the last section we saw thermodynamics as a model for matter in bulk that almost disregarded the particular properties of the matter concerned, but that has proved of very great value in considering the transference of energy between different elements of a physical aggregation of matter that may be complex. The laws of thermodynamics are only tentative, even though they have every appearance of wide generality and total reliability. Thermodynamics involves the possibility of the performance of work by matter, but it is not directly concerned with the detailed configurations of the constituent parts of the matter while the work is being performed. This detailed concern is achieved by an alternative model for the treatment of bulk matter in which general elastic properties are introduced to account for the presence of internal forces of various kinds. We consider this model now. It comprises elasticity and fluid mechanics. Once again any possible or conceivable molecular internal structure of matter is totally and deliberately disregarded, the arguments involving macroscopic measured quantities and appropriate empirical information.

The arguments centre on the replacement of a real piece of macroscopic matter (such as a solid or a liquid) by a collection of mass-points, interacting one with another with an appropriate force that may not necessarily be conservative at the macroscopic level. With the real continuum of matter replaced by appropriate particles in this way, the Newtonian laws of mechanics can be applied directly and equations of motion for the system deduced. This work was very much the development of the last century where it was found that this programme could be carried through most effectively provided the interaction between a representative volume element and its contiguous environment were accounted for in a particular empirical way. For a solid, relative motion between its constituent parts will cause stresses and related strains within the body. We now know that the relation between them is to involve a knowledge of the arrangement of the constituent molecules in space, but these molecular features were not known then. Instead, at this level, the macroscopic stress is assumed to be related to the strain in an empirical way and the strain is determined by the actual deformation of the material. For simple solids it is sufficient to assume the stress to be directly proportional to the strain. More complicated solid material, however, requires a more complicated relation between stress and strain; this is of great interest in modern technology where new materials have been, and are being, developed for everyday use. An analogous approach is found useful for a liquid or a gas (liquids and gases are collectively called fluids) except that now the stress is dependent on the time rate of strain.

The important, and complicating, feature of these empirical forces is that they are not conservative and so cannot be associated with a potential energy function which is independent of the motion. In this they are unlike the gravitational force, which is conservative, and point the way towards the recognition of complicated forces as an integral part of the process of simplifying the description of the real world.

Electric Currents and Magnetism

One of the outstanding aspects of the last century was the study of the properties of electric charges and currents, and magnets. The central experiments, usually showing great skill and ingenuity, were performed to a great extent by Faraday, but other names like Oersted, G. Kirchhoff, and Ohm must also be mentioned. The impressive previous success of Newtonian mechanics (expressed in the three laws of motion) made it natural to suppose that the study of electricity and magnetism would involve the same descriptive structure. It was soon found, however, that this is not so: the modern era was about to dawn.

The experimental data were analysed successfully by Clerk Maxwell, in terms of the famous mathematical equations that are now named after him. Maxwell found that the experiments were not to be understood on the basis of an instantaneous interaction between moving particles acting at a distance (like the gravitational force), but that the interaction between charged particles is in fact to be expressed as an indirect effect which involves the co-operation of the intervening space itself. This indirect interaction, which is different from action-at-a-distance, allows one region of the medium to affect another region indirectly and continuously, through the action of the intermediate points of the medium. Before Maxwell's work this interaction had always involved a material medium: acting by analogy, where familiar concepts are utilized abstractly in place of truer concepts unfamiliar or yet unformulated, Maxwell found himself discussing this interaction by itself and without a material medium to support it. This is always a difficulty with arguments by analogy, for it is never clear where analogy stops and reality begins. But logical arguments are involved and mathematical equations are left: we are satisfied if we know that reality is there, even though we cannot describe it in detail.

Maxwell derived a set of mathematical equations which are able to account for all the experimental data that led to their construction, and which have led to new experimental verifications. The equations involve the physical concept of point-charged particles possessing inherent properties (fully analogous with the particles of mechanics) which accelerate when subjected to external influences, and which themselves affect their surroundings. But two point-charges separated by a distance do not influence each other directly, but only indirectly through the action of a separate entity called the electromagnetic field. While the charges and the electromagnetic field taken together form a fully deterministic system, the distribution of charges alone at some initial time is not sufficient information to predict the future behaviour of the system completely. Electromagnetic fields themselves must be treated as having a separate existence and must be ascribed linear and angular momentum, and even energy in empty space where there are no charges at all.

Maxwell found his equations to have solutions that describe a transverse wave disturbance, the wave motion being perpendicular to the direction of the passage of the associated energy. The appearance of a wave motion is not, in fact, surprising for it is an immediate consequence of the local interaction between the points of the medium. The same situation also applies to solids and fluids where wave motion is possible because of the continuous interaction between the contiguous elements. The highly significant feature for Maxwell was the recognition that the propagation speed is the same as that of light *in vacuo* (about 186,000 miles per second), and that the waves are transverse.

Light, studied through the development of optics, was by Maxwell's time a well-developed subject experimentally. Through the pioneering work of Newton, Young, Lloyd, and others, many of its properties were well documented. Its enormous speed had been a surprising feature; indeed it was not estimated until the classic experiment of Römer involving the observation of a moon of Jupiter.* Although the phenomena of polarization led Newton to suggest that light might have a corpuscular structure, the experiments involving interference and diffraction had been accepted as showing this to be quite wrong: light has a wave nature. This conclusion has been modified during the present century as we will see later, light often behaving as a wave but not always. But this was not known to Maxwell, and the experiments of Fresnel had apparently finally established the wave nature of light. Maxwell made the generalization of associating light with the electromagnetic wave field and linked the studies of optics and electromagnetism together for the first time. Optics is to be associated with electro-

---

* Galileo had tried to measure the speed, using lanterns on near-by hills, but this method was too crude. But he did not conclude that the speed was infinitely great—he said it was very great and his measurements were not good enough. Not for nothing is he quoted as the first scientist.

magnetic waves of a particular frequency range; other frequencies are associated with heat radiation, X-rays, and wireless waves. Such is the process of generalization in science.

The reality of the waves predicted by Maxwell can hardly be doubted if practical demonstration is the test, and yet their physical nature is not obvious. Surely, one might argue, the electromagnetic vibrations must be the vibration of something material, but we know now that this is not the case. The way this became recognized will be seen later (p. 268). The equations of electromagnetism are, in fact, as powerful in their way as is the Newtonian law of gravitation in accounting for measured phenomena, and must themselves be accepted as a fact of nature. There is no 'explanation' of the electromagnetic field here, but only a more ordered description in terms of some deeper reality, left at the moment unspecified.

Maxwell's theory has been seen to include the speed of light and the form of the equations leads to the conclusion that this will be recognized as numerically the same in any inertial frame of reference whatever. This result is contrary to the relativity concepts of Galileo already referred to (p. 258). The classical field-theory of Maxwell rejects instantaneous action-at-a-distance in electromagnetic circumstances and so stands in stark contrast to Newtonian gravitation theory, where the interaction is instantaneous. The difference between the two conclusions is not too important at the primitive everyday level of practical measurement because, at 186,000 miles per hour, the speed of light is virtually indefinitely great in these terms and the propagation of electromagnetic effects are virtually instantaneous. During the early years of the present century the essential difference lay in the structures of the underlying theories, which are diametrically different. Of course, with the advent of advanced modern electronic aids, the finite value of the speed of light is very readily demonstrated in the laboratory and outside.

III. SIMULTANEITY AND RELATIVITY

The advent of Maxwell's theory is of the greatest significance in providing a firmly experimentally-based theory of electromagnetism, of complete internal consistency, but which is incompatible with Newtonian mechanics and Galilean relativity. This incompatibility becomes the more apparent the more the experimental implications are explored.

The Ether

Maxwell's equations referring to free space involve only one speed of light and this is not linked to any particular inertial frame. They also describe the propagation of light in terms of certain (electro-magnetic) vibrations. The belief that mathematical structures deduced from experimental findings must be associated with an underlying tangible physical situation led physicists at the end of the last century to postulate a hypothetical ether as a 'material' within which light is propagated. Since only one speed of light *in vacuo* appears in the theory it is natural to associate the ether which carries it with the state of 'absolute rest'. It was presumed that the ether must be an all-pervading fluid-like material and, since light is transmitted on earth and within the solar system and beyond, it must exist everywhere in the real world if it exists at all. Assuming it exists, the light wave must be associated with stresses in the ether, by analogy with waves in a fluid or in a solid. Maxwell's theory assigns light a transverse form (vibrations perpendicular to the direction of motion) unlike sound waves, which are longitudinal (vibrations along the propagation direction). The classical wave theory shows that transverse waves can propagate only in a rigid material; a normal dielectric (non-electrically-conducting) fluid will not support a transverse wave structure (except possibly locally and heavily damped). To obtain a wave speed of the order of that of light the rigidity of the ether per unit mass density must be very high. But the motion of the planets shows no effect of such a rigid pervasive medium (it certainly doesn't appear in Kepler's laws or Newtonian gravitation theory).

The hypothesis of the existence of the ether is not without its difficulties, and observational or experimental help is required. We are looking for a fluid more rigid than steel! The measurements that led to the resolution of the problem had their beginnings in the experiment of Michelson and Morley (1887) and many variations of it have been performed since. The earth, moving in its orbit, must be expected to have a speed relative to the ether which is supposed to form the absolute background to the measurement of the trajectories of light beams. By comparing the measured speed of light in different directions at the earth's surface, the speed of the earth's absolute motion (relative to the ether) can be expected to follow. Using the most sensitive experimental optical arrangements, Michelson and Morley found no significant result; apparently the earth was absolutely at rest with respect to the ether when the measurements were made. Since it is known that the earth is moving in its orbit round the sun, a repeat of the experiment later might then show a positive result, but in fact it did not. Within very small experimental errors of measurement, the experiment failed to provide any evidence of motion of the earth relative to the ether. Expressed another way, these experiments failed to give experimental support for the reality of an ether. Because the ether, if it were found to exist, would form the natural condition of absolute rest, we can conclude that either the earth is at absolute rest, the remainder of the universe moving around it, or else there is no evidence in these experiments to support the physical existence of an absolute frame of reference. Even in 1900 the first alternative could scarcely be credited in serious discussion; the second one seems the only alternative, however remarkable and unexpected. It is often preferable to make a complete break with accepted theory than to stretch what is available to unrecognizable limits.

Special Relativity

The ether is needed if light propagation, described by Maxwell's theory, is to be reconciled with the concepts of the absolute space and time of classical mechanics summarized in the classical (Galilean) statement of the relativity of all motion. Classical mechanics has impressive experimental data to support it; but Maxwell's theory also is the result of a synthesis of different experimental data. The resolution of this paradox was found by Einstein, building on the work of H. Poincaré (1854–1912) and H. A. Lorentz (1853–1928), and involved a critical re-evaluation of the absolute character of space–time measurements. *Absolute motion of the earth was not detected for the simple reason that absolute motion does not exist; the concept of absolute simultaneity, which does not apply in optics, does not apply in mechanics either.* This was the sweeping assertion made by Einstein. Simultaneity and location are to have only a relative physical character which is dependent upon the frame of reference used. This is diametrically opposed to the classical ideas; the classical concepts of the previous centuries are to be abandoned. The immediate result is the breakdown of belief in the absolute nature of length and time, unexpected when first explored but now taken for granted. Each observer is to have a personal time and a personal view of the world, and comparisons between different observers must take account of their relative motion. In particular, it is now necessary to specify very clearly the technique of measurement in defining an observable quantity. As an illustration of this, consider the measurement of the length of a ruler. To measure its length it is necessary to compare it with some standard length scale (e.g. a set of inch measures or a set of centimetre measures) and count up the number of units of its extension on the standard length scale. The observer must mark first the position of one end of the ruler and then move himself to mark the position of the other end. There must be a time interval between the two marking processes (no one has yet found a way of being precisely in two places at once even if they are near together) and the motion of the ruler during this time interval will affect the details of the marking process. This is obvious now but seemed very strange when it was first realized. Of course, the effect is bigger the faster the ruler travels; classical ideas would really refer to the case when the ruler is at rest with respect to the observer and his standard length scale. Observers in motion relative to each other must be accounted for separately, and this special consideration of the relation between observers moving relative to each other is the new thing.

It is necessary in physics to make statements of experience in a precise form that can be translated into numerical terms. This was done by Einstein in 1905 in his theory of special (or better, 're-stricted') relativity, according to which the equations of physics are to remain unchanged in mathematical form in the transformation from the space co-ordinates, and the time, of one frame of inertia to another. The theory is of restricted validity in that it is concerned with inertial (unaccelerated) frames of reference; the general theory of the relativity of accelerated frames will be considered a little later.

The principle of restricted relativity is applied to practical cases by expressing it in the equivalent form, in two statements: the first is that the transformation law is to be *linear*, the space and the time co-ordinates of one inertial frame being a linear combination of (i.e. just multiples of, not powers of) the space and time co-ordinates of the other. The result is the set of Einstein–Lorentz transformation formulae, but there is no need to write them down explicitly here. The absolute nature of space co-ordinates and time co-ordinates (considered separately) is rejected by including both space and time co-ordinates in the transformation procedure for each component. We shall have more to say about this in a moment, but we can notice here that the transformation formulae involve the speed of light, and also that the formulae for the space co-ordinates and the separate formula for the time co-ordinate in one inertial frame of reference all involve both the space and time co-ordinates of the other inertial frame. The second statement is that a signal travelling with respect to one inertial reference frame with the speed of light will possess the same speed (when measured in the same units, such as miles an hour) in all inertial frames, whether the signal is emitted by a stationary or by a moving body. This accords the speed of light *in vacuo* a very special place in physical theory; it is the fastest speed with which anything (and hence information) can be passed from one observer to another. No influence can, accordingly, pass instantaneously, and the principle of restricted relativity is incompatible with the Newtonian theory of gravitation. It is also incompatible with the structure of classical mechanics. We can notice as one immediate consequence the impossibility in relativistic terms of ever having a completely rigid body. The evidence that a body is entirely rigid is that when one portion of it is moved then it all moves simultaneously. This is not possible if energy has a finite propagation speed, there being a time lag (extremely small, but not zero) between the movement of one portion and that of the others. The material must show elastic behaviour and the classical theory of rigid-body dynamics has no analogue in the relativistic theory.

Einstein was able to show that his principle of restricted relativity is entirely compatible with Maxwell's statement of the electromagnetic field, even though it was not compatible with Newtonian mechanics without modification of the underlying physical concepts. It was found that the form of the Newtonian equations could be maintained by regarding mass, momentum, force, and energy as having values dependent on the state of motion of the system in a special way. The mass of a body is no longer a simple classical constant, but depends upon the velocity of the body, increasing (non-linearly) with the speed. As the body approaches the speed of light, the mass becomes progressively larger until at the speed of light itself the body has an indefinitely large mass. The effect on mass of a low velocity is very small (of the second order of small quantities). This is fully compatible with Newtonian theory if errors of measurement are accounted for. Force again depends upon the speed of the body. Perhaps the most remarkable result of the new theory was the unexpected discovery (1905) of a relation between mass and energy. It appeared that even a body at rest was the seat of energy (the rest-energy as it is called), a mass m being associated with the energy mc^2 simply by existing (c is the velocity of light). Looking at this the other way round, potential energy (such as of elastic deformation) will also have an associated mass even though its magnitude will be very small (equal to energy divided by the square of the speed of light). Mass and energy are equivalent; the mass of a body is a measure of its energy content and it was really by accident that an empirical distinction has grown up between them. As a consequence, the three conservation laws of mass, momentum, and energy reduce in reality to two, one involving momentum and the other energy. The actual application of the conservation laws is now a somewhat technical matter which we can refer to a later volume.

One thing of classical Newtonian theory is lost; this is Newton's third law. Action and reaction are not instantaneously opposed except possibly in one particular inertial reference frame. The laws of physics are not, according to Einstein's principle, to be true in one frame and not any other—the third law must go.

The special theory of relativity has received every experimental verification and is now well established. It offers the essential generalization of accounting for high particle-speeds, close to that of light. Indeed, it amounts to a reformulation of the laws of the mechanics of a particle in terms of the laws describing the motion of light beams. When the speed becomes small compared with that of light it reduces to the usual Newtonian view of our direct perception. Revolutions in physics seldom produce the catastrophic consequences that one might expect, because the discussion is of restricted scope and is based firmly on experiment and observation—this is the secret and the only safeguard.

Generalization of the Theory

Classical Newtonian theory is a primitive approximation of the restricted (special) theory of relativity; Newtonian theory can account for gravitational effects at least at the level of Kepler's laws, but the special theory of relativity is incompatible with the simultaneity that is essential if the inverse-square law is to have any meaning. Since special relativity must specifically exclude gravitational phenomena it is, in this way, less complete than the corresponding Newtonian theory. We must ask, then, about the way in which the theory is to be generalized; we shall remember that any generalization must involve gravitation.

Generalization and abstraction go hand in hand. The great step forward for relativity, of absolutely enormous consequence for other branches of physics as well, was made by H. Minkowski in 1908: geometry is the key. You see, geometry enters mechanics through the notion of speed; speed is obtained by dividing the distance travelled by the time taken, and geometry is involved in specifying the distance. Minkowski realized the importance of the concise representation of the mathematical formulation of special relativity by making a four-dimensional representation of real events, built up from three space–co-ordinates and the time. This four-dimensional space–time has been the source of much mystic confusion in the past, but in fact is quite straightforward when it is accepted that the Euclidean three-dimensional space is not a pre-ordained unique means of describing the world. Lobatchewski had realized before this that the geometry of Euclid is only one possible form of geometrical structure, even though it had been accepted over the previous 2,000 years as uniquely self-evident. Later, Riemann had investigated the generalization of geometry to many dimensions, and had been particularly concerned with the curved geometry of the sphere. A small (i.e. 'elementary') area on a sphere is indistinguishable from a flat plane; the earth is a sphere but a garden might be flat to all intents and purposes. Minkowski used the four-dimensional flat form of Riemann's geometry, and so generalized the three-dimensional geometry of Euclid which also turns out to be a flat form of that of Ricmann.

The mathematical form of Minkowski's geometry involves the square root of minus one which is not a real number and so shows recognition of the fact that space and time are separate and different things, even though, in the real world, space changes always take a finite time. There is nothing basically more mysterious about time than about extension itself—both are equally mysterious! In mathematical terms, the path of an isolated particle is to be calculated as a geodesic line (a stationary path) of the flat space–time geometry, and the path of a light beam is a null-geodesic.* Nothing

---

* These are highly technical matters that it is inappropriate to pursue here, but I should perhaps say a little more about them. Quite independently of the number of dimensions, the 'shortest' distance between two points forms the geodesic line; in three-dimensional Euclidean space this is the straight line, and on a three-dimensional sphere it is the great circle. For spaces with more than three dimensions (which our mind cannot visualize in pictorial form but which can be specified mathematically nevertheless) the concept of the 'shortest distance' still applies even though the path is very complicated. In these cases the possibility exists of actual 'paths' of zero length existing which are associated with non-zero lengths in fewer dimensions. Thus, a path of zero length in four dimensions can be linked with a non-zero path in three dimensions. This possibility, which exists because of the complexity of the geometry, is expressed in mathematical terms by introducing the four-dimensional 'path' of zero length, i.e. a null-geodesic. A geodesic line in four-dimensional space need have no special properties in three dimensions. This verbal description will not be

new is added in terms of experimental results, but the theory is now ripe for extension. The generalization is clear and was made by Einstein in 1916: we ask what physical situation can be associated with the replacement of the flat form of space–time by the corresponding general full Riemannian form? In particular, we will associate the effects of gravitation with the non-Minkowski aspects of the geometry.

Newton's first law of motion, which carries over into special relativity, requires a body not acted on by a force to travel in a straight line with constant speed. Any deviation of a particle motion from this complete uniformity is to imply the action of a force on the particle. No particle is ever observed to travel with a fully uniform three-dimensional motion; Newton avoided contradiction with the first law of mechanics by appealing to the action of a gravitational force. Geometry allows us to avoid the introduction of the gravitational force as a real entity; the generalization of special relativity abolishes the force of gravitation altogether. To see how this is done, we assert that the intrinsic geometry of space near any material body has not a flat Euclidean form but a curved (non-flat) general Riemannian form. The radius of curvature will be supposed to become larger the further we go from the mass; at an indefinitely large distance away the radius of curvature is infinite, i.e. the space is 'flat'. In any case, the natural path of a particle is a geodesic line in the general four-dimensional geometry and the path of a light beam is a null-geodesic. We have no mathematical equations yet but already we have a new and unexpected physical phenomenon on our hands. A material body dictates the intrinsic geometry of the surrounding space and this geometry affects the path of a free, small particle moving nearby. The geometry which dictates the geodesic line will also dictate the form of the corresponding null-geodesic line associated with the path of a light beam. The presence of one body will not only affect the motion of a second body nearby, but will also deflect a light beam. The degree to which the beam is deflected will depend on the mass of the body; the earth is not a massive body in these terms but a star could be. The effect could have escaped terrestrial detection because the required level of experimental accuracy would need to be impossibly high. The corresponding astronomical effect may be observable with care. The proposed deflection of a light beam passing near a massive

clear to a reader not versed in the mathematical background—this is an example of the ability of mathematics to crystallize physical arguments in a way denied to words.

body is a matter of principle that must follow from any physically acceptable generalization of special relativity. The exact form and numerical value of the calculated deflection will depend upon the exact nature of the generalization, but the principle itself cannot be in doubt. Indeed, the presence of the effect has now received observational support for light grazing the sun although, as we will see in a moment, the actual numerical value is still a source of discussion. This is an example of the two levels of analysis in physics. The first level is that of qualitative prediction which must follow from the basic consistent structure of the body of theory itself; the second level is the separate quantitative prediction of the effect in a specific circumstance on the basis of a definite theoretical model involving definite mathematical equations. This distinction between the qualitative and quantitative description of the world is usually not sharp in practice, and it is not safe to argue on the basis of qualitative principle only.

General Relativity

The general theory of relativity is the name given to the general statement that the mathematical form of the laws of physics must be the same when referred to any co-ordinate frame whatsoever. There is no restriction here to inertial frames of reference, so that the restriction of the special theory is removed. Accelerated frames of reference can be used and in this way a particle showing a gravitational acceleration can be used as the centre of a frame of reference.

Relativity considers the relation between neighbouring observers in some form of contact (usually supposed to involve light sources, mirrors, and the passage of light beams). The general problem of the transformation of mathematical statements from one co-ordinate frame to another had already occupied the thoughts of mathematicians in the half-century before Einstein enunciated his principle of general relativity, even though there were no pressing physical problems to demand that the work be done. It was found possible to give this whole process a very precise and convenient mathematical formulation through tensor calculus. The local structure of interest to physics had once again been investigated by the abstract mathematicians and a tool (in the form of tensor calculus) was ready for the physicists to apply to their practical problems. This is an example of mathematics as a tool, the physics dictating the form of the mathematics used in any particular discussion of experimental data.

The setting up of the ten mathematical equations of general

relativity is an interesting story which, unfortunately, is too technical a matter to go into now. The observed equivalence between inertial and gravitational mass is a central assertion but the exact form of the equations is determined primarily by requirements of mathematical simplicity. The detailed consequences of the equations still remain very largely unexplored, only the simplest forms (corresponding to the least complicated physical situations) having been explored in any detail so far. The form of the equations is, however, interesting. By using as a boundary condition the empirical deduction that a uniform acceleration of a particle of matter is observationally indistinguishable from the effect of a uniform gravitational field (this is the principle of equivalence: Galileo essentially knew this for material particles but we now include light as well), the Einstein equations yield Newtonian gravitation theory as a zero-order approximation; in particular, stationary Kepler orbits are predicted.

Higher approximations of the Einstein theory predict effects not yielded by the Newtonian theory. Newtonian theory considers the motion of a mass particle in a gravitational field as the problem of calculating the complicated path of a particle acted on by a force and moving in a three-dimensional Euclidean space; the theory of Einstein considers the problem as one of the natural motion of a particle not acted on by a force but moving in a complicated four-dimensional space–time geometry. In the zero-order approximation these two views are equivalent in that each gives Kepler's laws of planetary motion; but they differ in the higher approximations and here is a method of distinguishing between them by invoking experimental or observation data.

The first approximation of the Einstein theory is important because it provides predictions that differ from those of Newtonian theory and that are open to observation even though the effects are small. Three such predictions were recognized early on (and were known as the three crucial tests). It is, perhaps, proper to anticipate later work and say that they are not necessarily to be regarded as being as crucial today as they were when they were first devised.

The first crucial test of general relativity relates to the orbits of the planets, where the zero-order approximation of the theory gives the Kepler orbits exactly, reducing to Newtonian gravitation theory. The next approximation predicts a movement, known as precession, of all the orbits (quite independently of perturbation effects between the planets), which is observationally significant only for Mercury. Newtonian theory could not account for this.

The second crucial test is associated with the deflection of a light beam by a heavy mass. This effect has been established observationally during eclipses of the sun. The light from a hidden star is bent as it passes very near to the surface of the sun and the star is actually seen during the eclipse period even though it would be expected, without the deflection effect, to be hidden behind the sun's disc. The deflection to be expected from the theory is small (about 1·75″ arc) and an effect has been found. The experimental values accepted now appear, after proper theoretical correction, to be about 10 per cent or more above the predicted value and the discrepancy may be real. The measurements are extremely difficult to make and it is a remarkable achievement that they have been possible at all. This effect is new; Newtonian theory did not predict it.* This must act in favour of the general theory of relativity.

The third crucial experiment uses the equivalence between energy and mass. The energy radiated from a heavy body (a star) has a very small, but still finite, associated mass. Work must therefore be done by the light beam in overcoming the gravitational pull of the body, and so the light beam will lose energy in the process: this will cause the light to be more red than it would be in the absence of the gravitational field. These two last effects will be considered again in a later volume.

Other results are difficult to come by and much more work is awaited. Problems of rotation (notoriously troublesome to discuss theoretically and considered often through Mach's principle in terms of individual motion relative to the totality of matter) have not yet been treated in any comprehensive way. The recognition that the equations of Einstein in their exact forms contain also a generalization of Newtonian hydrodynamics has also been largely ignored so far. General relativity, and so the quantitative representation of the physical principle of the invariance of the laws of physics, presents a picture today not unlike that of Newtonian theory at the end of the seventeenth century when the definitive work was still to come. Will there still be an analogous but more generalized situation two hundred years from now? This must be expected.

* Newtonian gravitational theory can be invoked to determine the deflection of the path of the mass associated with the energy in a light beam, but the calculated value is only about half of the value predicted from applying the general theory. There is also an internal inconsistency in the use of a theory involving a finite propagation speed (special relativity) for recognizing the relation between mass and energy while calculating the gravitational interaction from instantaneous action-at-a-distance.

IV. CLASSICAL STATISTICAL APPROACHES

It was realized during the last century that bulk macroscopic matter has an underlying molecular structure although virtually nothing was known for certain about the molecules themselves. Indeed, their existence had not been demonstrated directly experimentally although their reality appeared to be an inescapable deduction from indirect physical and chemical evidence. The exploration and elucidation of the microscopic (molecular) world has been very much a central issue for physics during this century. This study has had the most profound consequences and has led to a generalization of the concepts of causality and determinism; it has also introduced probabilistic arguments into the very heart of physics. During the first two decades of this century it was possible to treat the collective microscopic structure of matter in certain respects separately from the study of the molecular properties themselves. In particular, this has meant that a range of problems involving the collective microscopic structure of matter could be treated within the framework of non-relativistic classical physics even though a new non-classical (quantum) theory later proved necessary for the proper discussion of the properties of the molecules. We consider the classical arguments that are associated with the elucidation of the collective behaviour of molecules; the quantum developments then follow later in this chapter and in the two later volumes.

The Dilute Gas

Clerk Maxwell and Ludwig Boltzmann (1844–1906) were among the first to study the problems involved in explaining the properties of a dilute gas in terms of the motion of molecular constituents. The analysis relied on the concept of individual molecules colliding in pairs in the same way as two billiard balls collide, the real gas being supposed to be sufficiently dilute (i.e. to be at a sufficiently low density) for the direct encounters between more than two molecules to be so rare an event as to be neglected altogether. The actual physical gas is replaced by the model of an astronomically large number of particles in motion, moving freely and independently except for those very short times when they collide in pairs. The mechanical viewpoint is stressed here; the kinetic energy is dominant in the analysis, the speed being non-relativistic.

The important feature about the discussion is the way in which the trajectories of the particles are accounted for, and the way in which information about the trajectories is used to calculate those properties of bulk matter to be compared with experiment. Instead of attempting a detailed specification of the individual particle trajectories, each composed of free particle flight between closely analysed collisions, the particle flights are specified only statistically. A 'kinetic distribution-function' is defined which specifies the number of particles in an elementary volume of the gas centred at each point in the gas at any time, for a given particle velocity within a small range of velocities. Collisions between particles change the velocities of the particles involved. The total effect on the kinetic distribution is the summation over all dynamical collision-possibilities: it depends upon both the distribution of particles that can strike another particle and on the distribution of particles to be struck (in mathematical terms it is a non-linear effect). The collisions must actually proceed according to the laws of dynamics, and these describe entirely reversible processes. The equation devised by Boltzmann is remarkable in that, by the nature of the statistical form of the theory, it is linked to irreversible physical processes. The essential feature is the hypothesis of molecular chaos according to which the distribution of momenta among the particles in the gas is independent of the location of the particles; put another way, slow particles do not congregate together, nor do fast ones.

This theory is able to explain the collective movement of mass, momentum, and energy in the gas from regions of excess to those of deficiency. By averaging these fluxes over the entire gas, the Boltzmann equation can be combined with the conservation laws of mass, momentum, and energy to yield the previously-known equations of hydrodynamics for a macroscopic gas. But more than this, the analysis provided, for the first time, mathematical formulae linking the macroscopic transport coefficients like shear viscosity and thermal conductivity with the distribution of particle velocities. This links the macroscopic world to the microscopic world. And to make sure that the discussion is really concerned with a genuine non-equilibrium situation Boltzmann was able to define a function (the H-function) that can be linked with the macroscopic entropy (the degree of disorder of a system); it is demonstrated that the situation corresponds to an increase in entropy to a maximum value for equilibrium. The theory was developed by Enskog and by Chapman independently when, in 1917, they showed how Boltzmann's equation can be solved by a method of successive approximation. The analysis has since been applied to gas mixtures and more recently to plasmas; we shall have more to say about this later. This description of a dilute gas not in equilibrium has proved to be one of the most successful branches of statistical physics so far. It laid down the lines along which later developments could take place.

Statistical Mechanics

The kinetic theory of dilute gases outlined in the last section is statistical in the sense that the particle trajectories are specified in terms of the kinetic distribution-function involving the position and velocity of each particle. But this is only the first step towards a thoroughgoing statistical theory of macroscopic matter. Various attempts had been made to develop a full statistical theory of matter, but it was J. Willard Gibbs (1839–1903), in 1901, who laid the foundations for much of the modern development.

The full theory is not restricted to dilute gases, but applies to all states of aggregation of matter. In general, real macroscopic matter is represented by a number of particles, N say, in some macroscopic volume, V say. Each particle will be in continual motion and will interact with other particles within the volume. This interaction will be represented by a force that is conservative: the energy of each molecule can then be written as the simple sum of a kinetic and a potential term. To correspond to the real world the number of particles per unit volume (i.e. $N/V = n$) must be astronomically large: for a dilute gas under normal conditions $n \sim 10^{19}$; for a solid or a liquid, $n \sim 10^{22}$. These numbers are so large that we are led to consider the case when N and V are both indefinitely great (mathematically we would say that each separately approaches infinity) but with n, the ratio of them, remaining finite though very large in magnitude. With so many particles involved in a complicated interaction, a full dynamical specification of the time-evolution of the orbits is quite out of the question. It would be quite impossible to follow the details of 10^{20} particles because, quite apart from the sheer problem of writing down the information, the solution of this number of coupled differential equations would be involved. And again, the initial information about the particles could not be obtained from experiment for so large a number of particles. It is not possible for these practical reasons to deal with the full dynamics of the particles; there is no avoiding a probabilistic treatment. The mechanical system of particles representing the microscopic substratum of the molecules is to be specified by defining a probability distribution giving the number of particles in an elementary volume of space centred on a chosen location and having a momentum in an elementary region about a chosen momentum value. The fact that N and V are taken to be indefinitely large is vital here; because of this, the distribution functions can be regarded as continuous functions of time and the position and momentum of the particles. The continuum concept is retained even though we are dealing with discrete particles. There are, in this analysis, two important improvements over the analysis of Maxwell and Boltzmann. The first is the collective description of *all* the particles within a single continuum representation; the second is the use of position and momentum (called by Gibbs the 'phase') in place of the position and velocity. The value of the position and momentum in the treatment of dynamical problems of classical mechanics had earlier been shown by Hamilton and Jacobi, who reformulated the earlier mathematical analyses of Euler and of Lagrange.

The reasons outlined above for introducing probability arguments into physics have been really rather negative, relying on things we cannot do. But there is a very positive reason for doing this; it was exploited by Gibbs and had enormous consequence in the physics of this century. This positive analysis depends on clarifying the relation between the macroscopic and microscopic worlds in practice, and involves the concepts of the ensemble and the most probable behaviour, with the associated technique of representative sampling. These concepts can be introduced in the following way, referring to equilibrium conditions.

The measured macroscopic property of matter will be interpreted as the average of an appropriate molecular property (such as energy or momentum), averaged over all the phase available to the constituent particles. It is agreed that the number of particles is so large as to make it nonsensical to inquire of the precise phase (i.e. position and momentum) of each particle. A given value of the macroscopic property will be fully compatible with different complete phase specifications of the system, within the macroscopic accuracy of measurement. In the absence of precise information about the phase, it is natural to suppose the distribution of particles in phase to be uniform (equal *a priori* probabilities). This indefiniteness of the phase suggests a series of models, called an ensemble, the measured macroscopic property being a phase average over the total series of the ensemble. Consider a system of N particles with total energy E. The energy will be distributed among the constituent particles of the system, the particles assuming an appropriate distribution throughout the available phase. The same is true for each •system of the ensemble of systems, the total ensemble providing a measure of the distribution of phases of the particles compatible with a given value of the energy (which means the sum of the kinetic and potential energies of the particles). By making the ensemble consist of an indefinitely large number of individual systems all possible phases are included. The total ensemble can then be analysed to ascertain the proportion of systems in which a particular phase value for any arbitrary particle occurs, and this can be expressed as a probability. In this way the distribution of particles in phase for given energy E and number of particles N can be ascertained. What we have described here is the so-called microcanonical ensemble, but it can be generalized. In practice the energy of the system is not open to strict experimental control although the temperature of the physical system is, by the appropriate use of a heat reservoir. An ensemble of systems in which the energy is not fixed but can range over all possible values is more like the real world. For this purpose, the constituent systems must be supposed to be in weak thermal contact, weak enough, that is, to leave them effectively isolated, but nevertheless sufficiently strong to allow energy to pass from one to the other and so to allow an equilibrium distribution of energy over the systems to be set up, after a sufficient lapse of time. The ensemble that we have just described, in which the number of particles N and the temperature are specified, is called the canonical ensemble. It has proved of great importance in statistical physics. Finally, the actual number of particles N is not experimentally determinable to any precision, and the grand canonical ensemble is the logical final generalization in which each sub-system represents an energy distribution for a particular N, and the systems themselves represent the full range of N, from zero to an indefinitely large value.

The ensemble concept is vital in our discussion, for two reasons. First, it focuses attention on the distribution of energy over the individual members of a collection of particles—this has proved to be a central problem in modern physics and will be referred to in the next volume. Second, it allows all the possible initial phase-values for the system to be accounted for in the subsequent evolution of the system. This is extremely important, for in mathematical terms it means that we are able to deal with the most general solution to our problem. In this way the concept of the ensemble (using the phase) is a powerful generalization of the kinetic distribution first treated by Maxwell and Boltzmann. Of course, the arguments in this section have applied to uniform (equilibrium) physical systems whereas the analysis of Maxwell and Boltzmann applies to the non-uniform gas. The ensemble idea can be extended to non-uniform systems in principle, but in practice this problem is still unsolved, except for very special and restricted physical situations. We shall see why this is at p. 285, where we will have more to say about systems not in equilibrium.

One thing must be stressed here; the ensemble is an imaginative device and is not supposed to have physical reality. It is sufficient to be able to visualize the ensemble and so to discuss its properties mathematically; even though the ensemble is a fiction, the mathematics is real enough and is interesting because it allows deductions which are in agreement with experiment to be drawn about real physical systems.

Statistical Thermodynamics

The concept of the ensemble, devised by Gibbs, is of use in physics only because it provides a basis for the calculation of values of physical situations which agree, to acceptable limits of accuracy, with the corresponding experimental data. This has, in fact, proved to be the case for uniform systems and the statistical theory based on the ensemble concept has provided a molecular basis for macroscopic thermodynamics. It is, perhaps, rather surprising that the invariant laws and relationships of thermodynamics can be derived from statistical arguments involving average values rather than precise results. But is it surprising? Let us remember what an experimental measurement amounts to in this context. The macroscopic system is held under prescribed conditions for long enough for the required measurements to be made. These externally maintained conditions can be held at prescribed values only within certain limits of accuracy and the properties of the macroscopic system itself can only be measured within certain limits of error. Each measurement occupies a definite time interval, which may be small (a fraction of a second) but not indefinitely small. On a molecular time scale such a time is very large, since a molecule will undergo a very large number of interactions with neighbours in this sort of time interval. We can recognize that we are dealing with a time scale that may be macroscopically very small but it is certainly also microscopically very large. A repeat of the same macroscopic measurement made on different occasions will not yield precisely the same experimental value, due to the action of accidental errors of measurement. The numerical value of the property under investigation for different external conditions will also be subject to the same accidental errors, and interpolation between the measured points will itself be open to ambiguity.

But a numerical description of the world in unique and simple terms, such as is the aim of science, cannot be open to such accidental ambiguity: ambiguity is removed by accepting a standard procedure for its removal. For this purpose we accept that the total accidental error found in experimental observations is made up from an indefinitely large number of independent component errors. Further, each component error is equally likely to be positive or negative—there is no systematic error there. In these circumstances the accidental error of measurement and interpolation can be eradicated by using Gauss's law and the procedure of least squares. The statements of thermodynamics are then firm statements about the results of measurements corrected by procedure; they are definite relationships between macroscopic quantities whose numerical values are to be inferred by using arguments of probability. At the microscopic level, we have seen already that the molecular trajectories must be specified statistically, because we must account for all possible initial phases for the evolution of the system. Statistical mechanics is concerned with the link between the microscopic and macroscopic worlds in these terms; for equilibrium conditions of uniformity, the link is the concern of statistical thermodynamics. This theory achieved a great deal of formal completeness at the beginning of this century. The corresponding theory for non-equilibria is even today not properly established.

Statistical thermodynamics links the macroscopic to the microscopic worlds and allows the thermodynamic functions to be expressed in terms of molecular properties. If this were all, not a great deal would have been achieved, but in fact statistical thermodynamics is much more. Thermodynamics is concerned with the relationships between *changes* in some thermodynamic variables consequent upon *changes* in others. No absolute datum is involved, only values relative to some condition chosen as standard. Certainly, statistical thermodynamics can be expressed in these terms. But more than this, individual thermodynamic functions are expressed in molecular terms, so that numerical values for them can (at least in principle) be calculated quite independently of the values of other macroscopic functions. This is something quite new; it led, through other arguments that I shall develop below (p. 287f.), to the recognition of the general inadequacy of classical mechanics for the description of the structure of molecules and atoms.

The mathematical problems of evaluating the expressions for the thermodynamic functions to give numerical values has proved somewhat intractable. To begin with, multiple integrals must be evaluated and this can be done only for the simplest case of a dilute gas. Indeed, it is only very recently that firm progress can be claimed in this direction. Another aspect of a comparison between calculated and experimental values is the specification of the actual force acting between the constituent particles of matter. It is supposed that this force can be derived from a potential energy and the problem of specifying a realistic potential function is then of central importance. The first steps at defining an empirical expression for the potential energy as a function of the location of the constituent molecules were taken at this time. But the whole problem proved to be beyond the powers of classical mechanics; we shall need to defer it to a later volume.

Statistical thermodynamics allows for a further generalization of experience. If the macroscopic world is a manifestation of a microscopic structure, is it possible by careful measurement to obtain evidence of the molecular sub-structure? It is, and the study of this comes under the heading of fluctuation theory. The calculated values are to be mean values of the collective molecular properties, and the sharpness of the calculated values depends upon the number of particles present. The grand canonical ensemble is the appropriate starting point; because the number of particles in the actual physical system is indefinitely large it follows that almost all the systems in the ensemble have the same (mean) number of particles, and the same (mean) energy. Certainly, fluctuations about the mean can be recognized and can be related to macroscopic quantities such as compressibility and specific heat at constant volume. Fluctuation theory has become of great interest again recently in connection with the theory of non-equilibrium systems, and this will concern us in a later volume.

Irreversible Behaviour

Physical macroscopic systems explicitly showing the effects of molecular movement were the subject of intense theoretical and experimental study during the early years of this century. These studies were very successful and proved prophetic in paving the way for the recent work on non-equilibrium conditions which will be considered in a later volume. We can enter the discussion in one of two ways.

The first way involves the reversible features of classical mechanics. The mathematical equations of motion of classical physics are reversible in that they are unaffected if the sign of the time is systematically reversed throughout the equations. In physical terms, if the direction of all the motions of the constituent particles are reversed, the mechanical system will trace out the same motions as before but as a mirror-image of themselves. Indeed, because all the phenomena of the real world are to have an underlying molecular structure, and even dissipative phenomena (such as viscosity) are to be associated with molecular motions that are reversible, it is difficult at first sight to see how the micro- and macro-behaviour can be reconciled. If the underlying molecular motions are inherently reversible, where does macroscopic irreversibility have its origin? This is the problem that was raised by a number of scientists around the turn of the century, and Zermelo (1896) raised the question to the status of a paradox.

A particularly important contribution to the resolution of the paradox was made by Poincaré, who showed that a wide class of systems of particles of physical interest show a periodicity that is of relevance in the study of irreversibility. In particular, Poincaré showed that any initial conditions of the phase of the system will recur again to any desired accuracy if we are prepared, or are able, to wait long enough. The more exactly we require the initial conditions to recur, the longer we have to wait; if the initial conditions are markedly away from the mean we may have to wait for a very long time. If we do not (or cannot) wait long enough, the initial conditions will not recur; even though the arguments are based on classical mechanics (which show full reversibility), the net result is irreversible (initial conditions gone, never to come again). The time-scale to be associated with any particular physical situation showing irreversibility is vital in relation to the Poincaré analysis. Boltzmann estimated the recurrence time (often called the period of the Poincaré cycle) for a gas, for one case where the initial conditions are rather extreme. He found that the time for this initial state to recur would be orders of magnitude greater than the age of the universe (as known now but not then); the movement away from the initial state is to all intents and purposes entirely irreversible.

The quasi-periodic nature of collections of particles was studied in detail by von Smoluchowski in his theory of probability after-effects. This theory (these days very regrettably ignored) gives perspective to the nature of irreversibility, and has done much to clarify the essential statistical nature of the second law of thermodynamics. The theory is concerned with the time of recurrence of a particular molecular phase and the time for which any particular phase exists. For systems of macroscopic size, the irreversible behaviour shown by the work of Poincaré is found again. A state near the mean state is more likely to appear than one far away, and will have a longer life when it does appear. Pure size is important: on the microscopic scale the theory passes to the fluctuation theory of statistical mechanics, while on the macroscopic scale the recurrence characteristics show all the features of measured irreversibility. Smoluchowski's theory was put to experimental test by Smoluchowski himself and, in great detail, particularly by Svedberg (1911) and by Westgren (1916). The theory is now well established.

Brownian movement occupied many people at the turn of the century. This motion was first noticed by the eighteenth-century botanist Brown, who saw that small pollen grains floating in water were subject to a perpetual, irregular motion. This same effect is shown by all small grains or particles of colloidal (semi-macroscopic) size immersed in a fluid. It was realized at the turn of this century that this Brownian motion is owing to the bombardment of each semi-macroscopic particle by the molecules composing the fluid. The elucidation of this problem was an achievement of Einstein, and was important in providing the first direct method of studying molecular motion and molecular properties. In particular, the link between Brownian motion and mass diffusion in fluids, through the study of random flights, set the seal to the later studies of the motion of molecules. The theory of Brownian motion achieved a high level of sophistication through the work not only of Einstein, but also of Langevin, Fürth, von Smoluchowski, Fokker, and Planck. It showed the detailed workings of one statistical theory that could be studied in the greatest detail, and its success made certain the acceptance of statistical arguments at a fundamental level in physics.

The Ordering of Molecules in Space

X-rays were well known at the beginning of this century, and their power of penetration of matter had already set them apart from other radiation. The discovery of the diffraction and interference effects associated with the passage of X-rays through matter was quickly followed by the realization that this was a method capable of providing information about the molecular structure of matter. Starting from very simple beginnings, this X-ray technique has now become an established and indispensable technique for the study of the structure of matter, and has recently been developed to the stage where even the complex structure of vitamins can be elucidated with its aid. The early work was developed particularly by von Laue, Friedrich, Knipping, Debye, Scherrer, Menke, Zernicke, Prins, Keesom, and de Smedt.

The basis of the method is straightforward, although the detailed analysis is more complicated, both physically and mathematically. X-radiation falling on an atom or molecule causes the atom or molecule itself to emit radiation (characteristic of its own structure) in sympathy. If there are many molecules together, each will emit its own characteristic radiation. The secondary radiation of each molecule will interfere with that of the others. X-radiation incident on a sample of matter will then be diffracted by the constituent molecules and the diffracted beam will have a form characteristic of both the structure of the molecules themselves and of their relative ordering in space. We shall not go into details of this technique other than to say that the measurements involve the angle of scattering of the plane radiation incident on the specimen of matter.

The information about the arrangement of molecules in space, obtained in this way, has been of the greatest value in the development of our understanding of the structure of matter. Through its use, particularly, the highly-ordered long-range molecular crystal structure was recognized by the Braggs*; the short-range liquid structure was also ultimately recognized, as we shall see.

It is important to be clear about the nature of the information provided by X-ray diffraction techniques. The X-rays travel at the same speed as light in a medium, whereas the molecules themselves travel at about the speed of sound, which is some one million times slower than light. In the time it takes the X-ray beam to travel through the specimen and reach the photosensitive plate recording the pattern, the molecules will have moved only infinitesimal amounts; the molecules are virtually frozen. But a certain minimum amount of energy must collect on the photographic plate before an image can be recognized, i.e. the X-rays must pass through matter for a finite (non-zero) time before information about matter can be inferred. An overlapping series of consecutive 'frozen' pictures results, giving a smeared, i.e. average, picture of the molecular arrangement in space. The information derived from the X-ray diffraction technique is of the nature of an average; only very recently has the complementary neutron diffraction technique been introduced, which allows a more detailed time evolution of the molecular motion to be constructed. This has arisen with the avail-

---

* Sir William Bragg (1862–1942); Sir Laurence Bragg (1890–1971).

ability of neutron sources from nuclear reactors, and will be considered in a later volume.

From the X-ray data, a number of distribution functions can be obtained that specify the arrangement of molecules in space. For a crystalline solid, it is found that the molecules are highly ordered in space, a basic lattice arrangement being repeated, very much unchanged, over large volumes of the material. This is the long-range order, where the arrangement of molecules around any arbitrary one chosen as origin depends on direction. For a gas, the molecules are essentially disordered. A liquid falls midway between the two, the molecules being close together throughout the liquid but showing a spatial ordering only locally about any arbitrary molecule, chosen as origin. At larger distances there is no ordering; the spatial ordering is of short range.

In these ways classical physics was able to penetrate into the microscopic (molecular) background to macroscopic matter, at least to a limited extent. It will be noticed that no study has been made of the atom or the molecule itself; in this, classical theory proved totally inadequate. In generalizing physics to deal with these matters of very small size and very low mass, a totally new theory has needed to be developed (the quantum theory), which had its birth in the year 1900. We turn to this theory now.

V. ATOMS AND QUANTA

In part III we saw that Newtonian mechanics is not able to account for phenomena involving motion with a speed in any way comparable with that of light. Other difficulties of a fundamental nature arose also in connection with electromagnetic radiation. One was the difficulty of explaining the distribution of energy over the vibration frequencies (i.e. the modes) of an electromagnetic field in thermal equilibrium. The other was the inability of classical physics to account for the observed features of atomic spectra. These difficulties led to the development of a new physical theory, the quantum theory. This is a grand generalization of the classical theory and is a major achievement of physics during this century. Indeed, the present century is marked in physics by the development of the theories of relativity and of quantum mechanics.

In retrospect it might have been expected that the study of spectra would have been the area where the break with classical physics would have appeared first. This was not so; the first fundamental difficulties arose in the study of the thermodynamic properties of electromagnetic radiation in empty space, and we consider first the problems raised in this case. In science, as in other fields of life, a simpler path might have seemed better but a different, more complicated path was the only visible one at the time. This is an interesting point for it very much colours the impression the layman has about science and scientists. A new development may involve an imaginative leap, based on analogy, and its subsequent development may involve tentative physical analysis and clumsy mathematics. If the results compare favourably with experimental evidence, the analysis will be reworked, perhaps five or six times, until the physical arguments are tight and the mathematics elegant. It is this last form of the theory that is published. All the personal aspects are eliminated and the various chance circumstances that led to the work are disowned and suppressed. It is in this way that the impersonal veneer of science is established and maintained. This makes science appear, quite wrongly, lacking in humanity; but it also allows the subject to remain independent of purely personal conflicts.

Radiation in a Cavity

If a solid body is heated it gives off electromagnetic heat radiation, the effect becoming the more marked the higher the degree of heating. As the temperature is raised, it is found that the proportion of shorter wave-lengths in the radiation increases. This is found to be true for all substances under general conditions, the proportion of the various wave-lengths present being more dependent on the temperature than on the particular material of the emitter. The system is precisely prescribed if the emitter is enclosed in a large cavity. The temperature of the emitter and the cavity is dictated by the temperature of the walls enclosing the cavity (the whole system forming an oven): in this case the emitter is a source of electromagnetic radiation and the nature of this source is determined by the temperature of the oven alone. The emitter material is not now relevant if the oven temperature is held constant and enough time is allowed for the equilibrium condition to be reached. This equilibrium radiation is often called thermal radiation or black-body radiation, its characteristics being determined only by the temperature of the emitter. Such radiation is emitted independently of the existence of an enclosing oven and can be treated in discussion in this way. Its actual occurrence in real situations is perhaps rare and the inclusion of the oven here is for precision in the definition of the radiation we wish to discuss. This is no idle complication; it is always essential to define theoretical concepts and experimental conditions most meticulously, so as to be certain beyond any doubt that the theoretical discussion and experimental results are referring to exactly the same problem. It is of interest to describe this equilibrium situation in numerical terms using established physical theory: this amounts to calculating the distribution of energy in the electromagnetic radiation among the various wave-lengths present in the radiation (this is the energy spectrum).

This calculation was attempted towards the end of the last century. Classical theory gave the wrong answer and so started perhaps the most important single new development in physics, i.e. the development of the quantum theory. Situations of this type are of vital consequence in physics, but they do not occur very often. When one is found (and the Michelson–Morley experiment is another one) there is available a check on the range of validity of a group of basic physical concepts. Lest it be thought that such comparisons always show faults in established physical theory, we should notice that the measured equivalence of inertial and gravitational mass is now postulated as a basic relationship between these two physical concepts. This postulate is the basis of general relativity and all experimental checks on its validity have so far supported it entirely. The study of the equilibrium state of radiation in an isothermal cavity is a check that shows classical theory to be in error; it remains to see where classical theory breaks down in this case.

The experimental evidence is simple and clear. The wave-length spectrum of the radiation (i.e. the distribution of energy over the wave-lengths of the radiation) has been measured with great accuracy. Consider the energy of the very large wave-lengths first and then the energy in the progressively-shorter wave-lengths. The energy associated with the longest wave-lengths is very small, vanishing for infinite wave-length. As the wave-length decreases so the energy rises rapidly to a maximum value at a wave-length characteristic of the temperature of the emitter. Beyond this, at progressively smaller wave-lengths, the energy continuously decreases as the wave-length considered gets smaller, vanishing as the wave-length approaches zero. The maximum wave-length for a given temperature is found to be such that the product of this maximum value and the corresponding temperature is a constant, characteristic of thermal radiation. This is a statement of Wien's displacement law. As the temperature of the radiation increases, the maximum wave-length decreases correspondingly. Experiment gives definite information about the total radiation emitted by the body, over all wave-lengths. This is the Stefan radiation law, which states that the total energy emitted is proportional to the fourth power of the absolute temperature; the constant of proportionality is the Stefan radiation constant. These are the measured facts to be explained. In developing the theoretical description we will consider the classical theory first and so the way in which the theory breaks down. Then we will discuss the revolutionary hypothesis proposed by M. Planck to get agreement between theory and experiment.

The theory has three separate constituents. The first is that associated with the establishment of statistical equilibrium. This must involve the redistribution of energy over the vibration modes (i.e. the wave-lengths) of the radiation and so will centre around a loose coupling between all the wave-lengths present in the radiation. Such a coupling is of common occurrence in physical arguments. The coupling can come about in practice by allowing small particles of dust to be present in the radiation as an aid to the establishment of equilibrium. The arguments describing the setting up of equilibrium are of such generality, and have been so successful in other branches of physics, that we will not readily deny their validity in connection with thermal radiation. So far all seems safe.

The second part of the theory is concerned with the precise description of the electromagnetic field. This is centred on Maxwell's equations for the electromagnetic field. These equations involve the electric and magnetic wave vectors and are best transformed, for treating radiation, into the form involving the vector and scalar potential functions. We shall not enter into mathematical details here but shall use the result that the original equations can be replaced by a set of equations describing a system of simple harmonic motions covering all vibration frequencies. In physical terms, the electromagnetic field (which is a continuum) is replaced by a hypothetical set of simple harmonic oscillators (which is a mechanical system). The problem of distributing energy among the electromagnetic waves is replaced by that of distributing the energy among an equivalent system of oscillators. The replacement of one model (in this case the electromagnetic field) by another model (here the set of harmonic oscillators) is a commonly employed technique in physics. Which model is chosen for the detailed calculations is a matter of mathematical convenience, and physical preference. There is every evidence from other sources that Maxwell's equations are safe and there is no evidence for suggesting that they should be modified before being included in the discussion of thermal radiation. Again, the theory seems to be fully acceptable.

The third component of the theory concerns the energy itself. Classical theory is quite clear about the energy distribution under equilibrium conditions: each degree of freedom is associated with a mean energy proportional to the temperature. The constant of proportionality divided by two (a strange procedure but very sensible in the broad context that will become apparent from earlier and later remarks) is called the Boltzmann constant. It is a basic constant, and occurs very generally in classical and post-classical physics. For application to thermal radiation, each harmonic oscillator is to be associated with the same mean energy. There are an infinite number of oscillators in the field so that, on the basis of classical physics, the energy of the equilibrium electromagnetic field must be infinitely great. In physical terms this would need to be interpreted by the statement that equilibrium conditions could not be set up. Clearly there is something very wrong here, for we know from experiments that equilibrium can be established. It will be no surprise to learn that, if thermal equilibrium is assumed to be established, the predicted energy spectrum does not agree with experiment. The calculations were made mainly by Lord Rayleigh (1842–1919), Sir James Jeans (1877–1946), and W. Wien (1864–1928). The result is that the energy to be associated with a particular wave-length is inversely proportional to the fourth power of that wave-length. This expression has an infinite value when the wave-length is zero, and so predicts an infinite total energy for the radiation. On the other hand, this law (the Rayleigh law) agrees with experiment extremely well at very long wave-lengths. But the theory cannot account for the Wien displacement law. It would seem that the classical law for the equipartition of energy is at fault.

Although we can say this now without pain, it was a very serious matter in 1900. While scientists at that time were confused over these difficulties, Max Planck (1858–1947), in that year, made a revolutionary hypothesis designed to resolve the problem. This new hypothesis, which is strongly at variance with classical physics, was introduced rather apologetically as a temporary expedient—a stop-gap measure to get the right answer (as dictated by experiment). Although meant to be of only ephemeral use, this new hypothesis (the quantum hypothesis) is now an accepted and permanent aspect of physics. We can approach the arguments of Planck in the following general way.

To begin with, although the electromagnetic field is well described by specifying the component wave-lengths, the equivalent harmonic oscillators are characterized by their frequency of vibration. It is best, then, to replace the wave-length by the corresponding frequency (the frequency is obtained by dividing the speed of the wave, here the speed of light, by the wave-length). The classical law then is that the energy is proportional to the square of the frequency. In these terms the energy becomes infinite because of the massive contributions from the high-frequency oscillators. High-frequency radiation lies at the ultra violet end of the spectrum, so the classical dilemma is referred to as the 'ultra-violet catastrophe'. Planck pointed out that the catastrophe would be avoided if the high-frequency contributions could be suppressed.

From the classical point of view, the emission and absorption of radiation proceeds continuously and the equipartition law relies on just this point. The equipartition law does not arise if the emission and absorption of radiation are both discontinuous processes. Planck proposed that the ultra-violet catastrophe be avoided by asserting that the emission and absorption of radiation are discontinuous processes. This was a very revolutionary postulate, flying in the face of classical physics: it remains the very essence of the new theory, the quantum theory. We have still to specify the discontinuity precisely and it is in this way that experimental results are to be understood theoretically. In classical physics, the energy of each harmonic oscillator will continuously fluctuate as energy is emitted (decrease) or absorbed (increase). If the energy transfer is to be discontinuous, the energy of each harmonic oscillator will not fluctuate continuously but will have a definite value. In particular, Planck proposed that the important quantity should be the ratio of the energy divided by the frequency. Planck called this ratio the action. Classically the action can have any value: Planck asserted instead that the action for each oscillator can only have values which are an integral multiple of a new constant of nature, unknown in classical physics and now called the Planck constant. The value of this constant cannot be calculated from theory but must be found from experiment. As the result of many varied and refined measurements it is now known to have the value $6·624$ ($\pm$ $0·002$) $\times$ 10^{-27} erg sec. (the erg is a unit of energy), and is usually denoted by the symbol h. The dimensions of erg sec. are those of action. The emission and absorption of energy can involve only the energy associated with this unit of action. The integral multiples appearing with Planck's constant in the expression for the action are called quantum numbers. They range from unity upwards.

We can ask how this resolves the ultra-violet catastrophe. If the ratio of the energy divided by frequency is to be a constant, then, if the frequency is infinite, the energy exchanged must be essentially infinite also. If this amount of energy is not available (and it clearly isn't in any real system) then this exchange process cannot occur. Put another way, this particular oscillator remains inactive and makes no contribution to the distribution of energy in the equilibrium radiation field. The same will be true for the oscillators of sufficiently great energy, so that Planck's analysis avoids the appearance of infinite energy by freezing those oscillators that would cause it. The average energy of an oscillator, calculated on this basis, is not the same for all oscillators independent of the frequency (which is the classical result of equipartition): instead it is a function of the frequency itself. The mathematical expression for the energy as a function of the frequency is called the Planck radiation law. This law reproduces the experimental values in full detail and is now accepted as the proper expression to describe the experimental results. At low frequencies (long wave-lengths) it gives the expression derived by Rayleigh on classical arguments and referred to earlier. At high frequencies it predicts that the energy should decrease exponentially with the frequency.* It predicts fully the Wien displacement law and provides the correct value of the constant, in terms of the speed of light and Planck's constant of action. It also leads to the Stefan law of radiation, giving also the correct value of the radiation constant through a combination of the Planck and Boltzmann constants, and the speed of light. The quantum hypothesis has proved highly successful in accounting for experimental measurements and it is now well established, although in a rather modified form.

The relation between the new quantum theory and the older classical theory is rather closer than might appear at this stage. Thermodynamic arguments can be applied to the study of thermal radiation, and Wien showed (by this method) that the essential ratio in describing the radiation is the frequency divided by the temperature. This result is fully confirmed by Planck's detailed analysis, based on the quantum hypothesis. On this basis, an oscillator will become dormant if either the frequency is sufficiently high or the temperature is very low. On the other hand, an inoperative frequency will be brought into play if the temperature is high

* This result had earlier been obtained empirically by Wien.

enough. Alternatively, the discontinuous exchange of energy, characteristic of quantum theory, becomes continuous in the limit of Planck's constant being set equal to zero, provided the action remains finite and non-zero. This means that Planck's constant must be multiplied by a sufficiently large integer, i.e. a sufficiently large quantum number. Apparently, the results of the quantum calculations can be expected to reduce to a corresponding classical form in either limit of sufficiently high temperature or zero value of the Planck constant. In the latter limit, the action must remain finite and not itself go to zero; the energy levels approach ever closer together as the quantum numbers become larger, in the limit becoming continuous in conformity with classical ideas. The alternative first limit is particularly significant physically and will be referred to frequently later. We can see that the Maxwell theory of electromagnetism has proved very fruitful for the development of modern physics: it has been the starting point for a reassessment of our ideas of simultaneity and distance, and has been involved in the establishment of new rules for the study of radiation in equilibrium.

The Specific Heat of a Crystalline Solid

The study of the specific heat * of solids has been of great interest in the development of modern physics. It arose particularly because of the advances made, during the last century and early in this century, in reducing physical systems to lower and lower temperatures. This culminated, in 1908, in the liquefaction of helium by Kammerlingh Onnes in Leiden. The stage was set for the study of matter at the lowest temperatures available to a physical system. For our present purposes it is sufficient to notice that, whereas at ordinary temperatures the specific heat of all solids is essentially the same, and is independent of the temperature (this is the empirical law of Dulong and Petit), at low temperatures (well below room temperature) this is not so. At low temperatures the specific heat decreases with temperature, having every appearance (and as we now know from experiments) of vanishing in the limit of vanishing temperature. The explanation of these strange results was one of the early successes of the quantum theory of Planck.

Although the study of a solid crystal might appear to have nothing

* The specific heat of a specimen of material is the quantity of heat required to raise the temperature of unit mass of the material through one degree of temperature. Quite generally, this quantity of heat depends upon the initial temperature of the material, and on the conditions of the environment, e.g. whether the pressure is to be held constant, or the volume of the specimen to be kept constant, and so on.

to do with the study of equilibrium radiation, in fact Einstein showed that from the theoretical point of view they are very closely related. Just as the radiation can be represented by a set of harmonic oscillators, so also the crystal (through its ordered structure and acoustic wave properties) can also be represented by a system of harmonic oscillators. As for the radiation problem, the application of classical arguments will lead to the assignment of the same mean energy (proportional only to the temperature) to each of the oscillators of the solid. This result can be expected to apply at ordinary temperatures and does, indeed, provide a theoretical numerical understanding of the empirical law of Dulong and Petit. But at lower temperatures the contribution to the specific heat is less; apparently it is necessary to freeze the contribution of certain oscillators in this case. The problem in crystals at very low temperatures appears analogous to that met with in equilibrium radiation at high frequencies. The link becomes the stronger when we remember the result that the quantum effects for electromagnetic oscillators become the more marked the lower the temperature. Einstein developed the analogy in numerical terms and showed that the experimental results could be well represented in this way. The theory was later refined by Debye.

It is not our intention to develop this theory in detail here. It is sufficient to record it as providing early support for the general validity of the new quantum theory and also as an example of the treatment of one physical system by analogy with another, apparently unrelated at the strictly experimental level. The arguments were later extended to the treatment of the specific heat of gases.

Another unexpected property of metals at low temperatures involves their ohmic resistance to the passage of an electric current. As temperatures below some 20 degrees on the absolute scale were achieved, during the first decade of this century, it became clear that many metals lose their electrical resistance quite suddenly, at a temperature characteristic of the particular metal. This phenomenon, known as superconductivity, remained an experimental curiosity during the period that concerns the present volume. An understanding of superconductivity within the general field of physical concepts has been achieved only within fairly recent years, and so it will be considered in a later volume.

The Particle Structure of Light

It was seen above (p. 294) that Planck introduced the quantum hypothesis as a means of avoiding the ultra-violet catastrophe, and that the hypothesis amounted to a mechanism for controlling the number of high-frequency modes operative at any given temperature. The central feature of the quantum hypothesis is that the exchange of energy between matter and radiation is a discontinuous process. In the exchange, energy is to be treated in units, or quanta, and only discrete amounts of energy can be involved. Planck himself took the view that the continuum theory of Maxwell was to hold everywhere except in the immediate vicinity of an atom, and that there alone the mysterious discontinuous process of exchange is to occur. This rather makeshift approach is in keeping with Planck's earlier hopes that his quantum hypothesis was only interim and would be replaced in due course by a broader statement fully compatible with the classical theory. The hopes of scientists are not always fulfilled in their work; like the characters in a novel or a play, a hypothesis takes on its own life and works out its own destiny. The quantum hypothesis was not to be absorbed into classical physics however much it was felt at first that this must be achieved.

If the exchange of energy between matter and radiation is to be discontinuous we may ask whether the energy could remain quantized throughout the electromagnetic field, away from the atoms of matter. This possibility was raised by Einstein in 1905 when he proposed that the radiation could be regarded, at least under certain well-defined circumstances, as having a corpuscular structure. Einstein tested this hypothesis most carefully (by considering statistical fluctuations in the density of radiation (i.e. energy of the radiation per unit volume) under equilibrium conditions) and showed that the radiation described by Planck's law does indeed have a corpuscular nature. But the situation is not simple. Apparently the fluctuations in thermal radiation are composed of two quite distinct aspects. One is associated with a wave structure and is consistent with the continuum picture familiar in classical theory: these components of the fluctuations are concerned with the smaller frequencies of the thermal radiation. The other is not consistent with the continuum picture at all: it involves packets of energy, the quanta, each of energy equal to the Planck constant multiplied by the frequency of the radiation. The corpuscular nature of radiation is associated with the Planck constant so that we can regard the discrete nature of radiation as a characteristically quantum effect.

Radiation has a dual nature, part wave and part particle; it is not either one or the other, but both. Under some circumstances its properties appear overwhelmingly wave-like, whereas under other circumstances the properties appear overwhelmingly particle-like. The well-known wave properties of light (particularly the effects of interference and diffraction) still retain their place, but are enriched by the addition of other non-wave-like phenomena. It is worth noticing that Newton was inclined to assign light a corpuscular structure, particularly on the evidence of certain polarization experiments. To this extent, Planck's work was pre-dated by Newton. In classical physics, waves and particles represented alternative and different mechanisms for the transference of energy through space. The Planck hypothesis has joined them together as different limiting aspects of a single unified mechanism—but there is no attempt to visualize this single entity in physical terms.

The corpuscles of electromagnetic radiation are now called photons. They each move with the speed of light and have an energy equal to Planck's constant multiplied by the frequency of the radiation. The radiation has a momentum equal to the energy divided by the speed of light. Each photon must be assigned zero rest-mass, from energy considerations.

This extraordinary story can only be treated seriously if proper experimental support is found. Einstein drew attention to the experimental support provided by the photo-electric effect. It was discovered by Hertz, essentially accidentally, that a strip of metal emits electrons when irradiated by ultra-violet light. This phenomenon was studied in detail by Lenard. The experiments are not easy to perform, particularly because the surface of the metal readily becomes tarnished by the atmosphere if it has any chemical affinity with it.

The important general characteristics of these experiments is that the speed with which the electrons are ejected from the metal increases with the frequency of the incident radiation, but is independent of the intensity of the radiation. On classical theory it would be expected that the incident radiation would need to have enough energy to extract the electron from the metal, and any energy above this minimum would be available for conversion to kinetic energy of the electron. The available energy would then be measured by the intensity of the incident radiation. The quantum theory predicts a totally different story. The incident radiation arrives in quanta, each having an energy proportional to the frequency. The speed given to an emitted electron is then characteristic of the energy of each quantum: the energy of the electrons will depend upon the frequency. The intensity of the radiation is measured, on the quantum picture, by the number of photons per unit volume. The more photons, the more emitted electrons that can be expected. These conclusions are fully borne out by experiment. The energy in visible light is insufficient to cause the electrons to leave the metal, the effect being well displayed by ultra-violet light and spectacularly by X-radiation (having yet higher frequency).

The inverse effect is also observed, that is, photon emission from a metal surface bombarded by electrons. Indeed this is a well-established method of generating X-rays in the laboratory.

It is not necessary that the electron should be from a metal for the quantum effects to become manifest. A celebrated experiment involving free electrons was performed by A. H. Compton (b. 1892). The experiment involves the irradiation of free electrons by high-frequency radiation. The incident radiation shows a decrease in frequency through its interaction with the electrons and the incident radiation is also partially scattered. At the same time, the free electrons show effects that are compatible with them having suffered a collisional impact. These are the sort of results that one would expect from two sets of particles colliding, rather than waves and particles interacting, so while these experimental results are unintelligible in terms of the classical theory, they find a ready interpretation in terms of quanta. The incident radiation is represented as a shower of particles (the photons) which collide with the free electrons in the same way as billiard balls collide. The collisions scatter the photons (i.e. the incident radiation is scattered), and photons lose energy to the free electrons (so that the frequency of the radiation is reduced). The electrons which acquire energy move as a result of the impact. The collisions were treated quantitatively by applying the mechanical laws of the conservation of momentum and of energy to the photon–electron pair assuming that no energy is lost in the collision. The results of these calculations agreed well with the experimental measurements, and provided unambiguous support for the concept of photons in the radiation field.

These methods have been refined by later work but they allow the firm conclusion to be drawn that radiation does indeed have properties that can be discussed only in terms of a particle structure. The discrete form of the energy associated with radiation is not to be associated only with the immediate vicinity of interacting matter: the quantum of energy is of more general occurrence and the new constant of nature, the Planck constant, can be expected to be prominent in the calculations of the properties of radiation.

The linking of radiation with particle properties is of wider occurrence than in electromagnetism alone. It is, apparently, the inevitable logical result of describing a physical phenomena in local terms, i.e. of employing the structure of a field theory in the description of the physical world. We shall have much to say about this when considering developments later in the century, where we shall need to refer to the inverse concept, that is of material particles being associated with waves of a special type. It is, however, worth anticipating later discussion of this strange duality by noticing that the sound waves in a crystal, referred to above (p. 297), also have particulate associations when treated using quantum arguments. The 'particles' now are called phonons, and play a central role in modern solid-state physics. Other particulate entities will be introduced later. None of them are particles in the classical manner, as they have somewhat strange properties: for instance, their actual number is not conserved, so they cannot be treated even as hypothetical billiard balls in the usual sense.

Early Views about Atoms

Although positive information about atoms and molecules was obtained only during the present century, some inferences about their existence and properties were drawn before this. From chemical evidence, it became clear that molecules can be broken down into simpler units, viz. the atoms. Mendeleeff's periodic table had been established during the last century, and had been of definite value in the prediction of new chemical elements. Until about this century the stability and structure of the atoms was accepted passively and was not of scientific interest. Very little study of these topics was undertaken in consequence. Then the quantum hypothesis was applied and brought almost complete order to an otherwise (i.e. classically) unintelligible field of study.

The most basic experimental property of atoms is their extreme stability. Lord Kelvin (1824–1907) stressed the importance of this property and was the first person to attempt to explain it in theoretical terms. Kelvin used the idea of the stability of vortices in liquids to explain the existence and stability of atoms in terms of vortices in the luminiferous ether. The theory did not lead to new predictions of atomic properties and evaporated when Einstein used the results of the Michelson–Morley experiment as an authorization to abolish the idea of an ether altogether. This is an example of how changes in one aspect of physics have unexpected implications in another aspect.

The next attempt to impute a structure to the atom was made by J. J. Thomson (1856–1940), who recognized its essentially electrical nature. The first indication that electricity and matter might be intimately related followed from the recognition of the dielectric constant, the ratio observed by Faraday (1837) between the forces arising from electric charges in vacuo and the forces arising if the charges are inside matter. The existence of elementary charges in matter was established by Faraday's fundamental work on electrolysis, and the experiments of Millikan (1910), involving oil drops, established the magnitude of the elementary charge of electricity. Such elementary charges are known alternatively from the study of gases under low pressures, and maintained under a suitably strong potential difference. The existence of these same elementary charges in metals was demonstrated by Tolman in a series of very beautiful experiments. These studies showed the existence of a particle of negligible size, of mass about 9×10^{-28} grammes, and carrying an electric charge of about $4 \cdot 77 \times 10^{-10}$ electrostatic units. This is the electron, one of the essential basic concepts of modern physics. It is a matter of experimental observation that atoms in the real world are very often electrically neutral (in fact, when they are not neutral they are known as ions). With electrons being associated with matter, it is an obvious step to suppose that electrons are in some sense involved *in* the atom, so that the remainder of the atom must, on this basis, carry a positive charge of sufficient magnitude to balance exactly the charge on the electron. From the time of Proust (1815) it was realized that the hydrogen atom is the basic atomic unit and that in some way the hydrogen atom is the basic constituent of matter. With the experiments of Aston (1919), involving the mass spectrometer, it became clear that the masses of all atoms are roughly multiples of the mass of the hydrogen atom. On the assertion, later substantiated experimentally, that the hydrogen atom is a simple unit involving only one electron, it follows that the remainder of the hydrogen atom is a positively-charged particle unit, the positive charge having a magnitude equal to that of the negative electron charge. Measuring the mass of a hydrogen atom (strictly a representative hydrogen atom, since we cannot select one particular hydrogen atom in matter, extract it from its surroundings, and measure its properties alone) and deducing the electron mass, we obtain the mass of the positive elementary charge. This mass is found to be about $1 \cdot 7 \times 10^{-24}$ grammes, and the particle associated with it is called the proton. It is extraordinary that the proton has a mass about 1,840 times that of the electron. This imbalance between the electron and proton masses is a strange feature of our story, and will involve us in a later volume.

These ideas were behind the atomic model investigated by J. J. Thomson (1904), apparently first suggested by Lord Kelvin. According to this model, an atom is to be constructed from an equal number of electrons and protons. Although the electrons were regarded as corpuscular, Thomson supposed the positive charge to be a continuous fluid: we have a 'plum pudding' model in which electrons are embedded in a positive sphere of uniform electrification. The electrons are supposed to be in motion and the simplest paths are closed circles. An electron moving in a closed circular path is accelerating and will consequently radiate energy according to the laws of electromagnetism summarized in Maxwell's theory. In this way, the model atom will emit electromagnetic radiation and the attempt can be made to associate this with the observed light spectra.

Ingenious apparatus was constructed to obtain the results that are now commonplace but which then were often baffling. One piece of apparatus must be mentioned specifically, the cloud chamber devised by C. T. Wilson (1911). Damp air is expanded to near the condensation point of the water vapour, with the result that droplets form on any charges that may be present in the chamber. The air is expanded through a piston action and charges passing through the expanded gas cause ionization along their paths by collisions with the gas atoms. Deposition takes place on the ions still *in situ*, the track of the particle being visible, by suitable illumination, as a string of water beads, as the track of an aircraft can sometimes be seen as a trail of condensation. Technical improvements raised this method to a major procedure for the exploration of charged particles. It is said that Wilson got the idea of his expansion cloud chamber from his knowledge of a Scottish mist. Ideas in physics often emerge from the most unlikely sources.

The Rutherford Atom

The modern understanding of the relationship between the various constituents of an atom has been built up from the epoch-making 1911 experiments of Lord Ernest Rutherford (1871–1937). The information was obtained by Rutherford from a series of beautifully conceived, but simple, experiments in which a thin foil (particularly of gold) was bombarded by small fast positively charged particles. The measurements involved the study of the effect of the foil on the particles. The choice of particles was crucial. Rutherford was working before the days of the modern high-energy atom machines and his choice was quite limited. Indeed, he was very fortunate to be able to exploit the alpha particles given off by radio-active substances (we are not able to consider radioactivity in this chapter; for details reference should be made to the chapter on chemistry). These were later realized to be essentially the cores of helium atoms, but this realization was itself a result of the experiments. The important thing about the alpha particles is that they have, on the average, an energy sufficient to enable them to penetrate the gold foil and come out the other side, and that they are electrically charged. On bombarding the foil with the alpha particles, Rutherford found that the great majority passed through unaffected by the foil as far as could be measured. But a certain small proportion were affected and the effect was very marked: whereas most alpha particles passed straight through the foil undeflected, a small but definite proportion suffered large deflections. Because the mass of the alpha particle is very large in comparison with the mass of an electron, any deflection of the alpha particles must arise from the action of the net positive charge on the atoms of the foil. If this is smeared out uniformly over a sphere the average size of an atom the deflections of the alpha particles might be expected to be on the average small. An appreciable proportion of large deflections (as is observed) cannot be understood on this basis: the positive charge must be concentrated into a small radius if large deflections are to occur as often as is observed. Rutherford conducted a mathematical analysis of his observations and showed that the positive charge must be concentrated into a sphere of radius about 10^{-13} centimetres, called the nucleus. More than this, it proved possible to associate the hydrogen atom with a nucleus carrying a single positive charge and the way was set to associate the relationships set down in the periodic table of Mendeleeff with increasing (integral) nuclear charge. The explanation proved not to be quite as simple as just the elementary accumulation of protons in the nucleus, for this method of building would provide atoms that are too light. Instead it became necessary to construct a nucleus from protons and a smaller number of electrons, the whole having a net positive charge. There were to be about twice as many protons as electrons. The remaining electrons, necessary to assure electrical neutrality for the atom as a whole, must lie outside the nucleus.

The outer electrons could most properly be arranged in circular orbits of the type already envisaged in the Thomson atom. We are then presented with a picture of the atom that, while it has been modified in fundamental ways since 1911, is still recognizable as a not entirely unacceptable introductory glimpse. The model has a certain similarity with the planetary model of the solar system if we associate the nucleus with the sun and the electrons with the planets. The general size of an atom on this basis will need to be of the order of 10^{-8} centimetres. Remembering that the nucleus is some one hundred-thousandth as small as the atom, it is seen that the work of Rutherford reduces the atom to very largely empty space. Of course, it is empty in terms of material, but will be filled with electromagnetic interactions between the electrons and the nucleus, and between the electrons themselves. We are reminded of the analyses of the gravitational interactions of the solar system which occupied theoreticians during the eighteenth and nineteenth centuries, and may be excused if we think of adapting the solar work to the description of atomic problems.

We would be stepping a gulf in characteristic size of something like twenty million million million to one, an enormous scaling factor. In the event, the Rutherford atom represented an enormous advance over previous work in some directions, but was incapable of survival because of its total inability to explain the stability of the atoms known by experience to be an absolutely crucial feature. On the positive side, the arrangement of electrons in the orbits allowed for a systematic qualitative account to be constructed for the periodic table of the elements, among other things. It was also able to account for certain of the polarization properties of the radiation (light) given off by atoms when they are subjected to extraordinary conditions, like enhanced collision (such as at high temperatures), or when they are subjected to strong differences of electrical potential (such as a low gas pressure in a discharge tube). These conclusions show that the model contains at least a grain of truth, but the total lack of stability shows that much of the truth remains to be found. The instability arises from electromagnetic radiation effects.

The orbiting electrons are constantly accelerating (because they are constantly changing direction), and, according to the electromagnetic theory, are continually radiating electromagnetic energy in consequence. As the electron loses energy by radiation, energy conservation requires the kinetic energy to decrease correspondingly. The electron will then move away from the nucleus and the atom as a unit will disintegrate. Once again the consequences of radiation have caused trouble in a strictly classical model.

The Bohr Quantum Theory of the Atom

The Rutherford atom was given a more acceptable form by Niels H. D. Bohr (1885–1962) in 1913 when he modified it to account for the quantum conditions previously enunciated by Planck in connection with cavity radiation. Bohr recalled that the Kepler statements of planetary orbits can be expressed most concisely by requiring the planetary orbits to proceed under the general requirements of the conservation of the energy and the angular momentum of the planet in its orbit. The Rutherford atom can be treated in the same way, with the conservation restrictions applying to the electronic motions. The Planck statement of the discrete nature of the emission or absorption of radiation energy by matter can be applied to the Rutherford atom model by requiring the quantization of the energy and angular momentum of each electronic orbit, the unit of action again being the same constant (Planck's constant) as for cavity radiation. The introduction of this hypothesis accounts at once for the stability of the atom and further leads to new conclusions that can be checked experimentally.

Stability comes about in the following way. The electron orbits are supposed to correspond to allowed levels of the quantized energy, different levels being associated with different discrete energy levels, the energy being the smaller the further the level is from the nucleus (i.e. the higher the energy level). Because of the quantization condition, the electron in its orbit is associated with a constant energy: this means it cannot radiate and (by definition) its orbit is stable. But an electron may be induced to move from one orbit to another. If it moves from a lower to a higher orbit, there is an energy-excess equal to the simple difference between the energies associated with the two orbits in question. If energy is added to an electron, the electron can move nearer to the nucleus into a lower orbit if the energy added is of the correct quantized value. The quantized orbital angular momentum selects the spatial dimensions of the orbits open to the electrons, whereas the energy conservation condition dictates the magnitude of the energy emitted or absorbed in any transference of the electron from one orbit to another.

The simplest atom is that of hydrogen, which consists of a proton as the nucleus with one circulating electron. It was this atom that was chosen by Bohr for a detailed numerical test of his theory. The results were astounding, for the theory predicted a stable atom able to account for the known spectral lines of hydrogen with apparently complete precision. Let us denote the nearest orbit to the nucleus as the first orbit, the next nearest the second, and so on. With this notation, the theory leads immediately to the conclusion that the binding energies of the various states of the hydrogen atom (specified by the planetary electron being in an appropriate orbit) is proportional inversely to the square power of an integer. This result had previously been discovered empirically and was called the Rydberg formula. The highest binding energy is associated with the integer unity and is called the Rydberg constant. Bohr's theory expressed this constant in terms of the charge and mass of an electron and the constant of Planck, and gave for the Rydberg constant the numerical value 109677·76 cm^{-1}, virtually exactly the best measured value of that time. More than this, it predicts the wave-lengths of the known Balmer, Paschen, and Brackett series of the hydrogen spectrum with uncanny accuracy, through a mathematical formula which is an immediate consequence of the theory and which at the same time is precisely the combination principle propounded by Ritz in 1908, on empirical grounds after an inspired massive study of the wave-lengths of the known hydrogen spectral lines. To add to its plausibility, the theory predicts a radius for the inner electron orbit for hydrogen of about 0·5 × 10^{-8} centimetres, and so predicts a general atomic size of the same order of magnitude as that found experimentally. It has other successes to add to its credit, such as a successful numerical prediction of the effect on the spectral lines of the emitted radiation of immersing the atoms in a strong magnetic field (called the Zeeman effect after its discoverer).

Is this the final explanation of the structure of the atom? As impressive as these predictions are, many other questions remain to be answered. To begin with there are other elements to be accounted for, and here the predicted spectral lines are only broadly quantitatively correct, even for some of those atoms in which the radiation arises from the rearrangement of the outer electron only and in this sense are hydrogen-like. The theory certainly helps in understanding the profusion of spectral lines associated with more complex atoms, but needs to be augmented by further selection rules not furnished by the original theory if experimental data are to be given precisely. But more fundamental questions remain to be answered. The Bohr atom is in a sense a two-dimensional 'flat' atom and nothing is said about the known three-dimensional character of the atoms met with in the real world. And again, the electron-jumps from one orbit to another are not described in sufficient detail to be certain whether the jump is to be supposed to be an instantaneous event or not. Relativity theory makes us suspicious of instantaneous processes, and yet there is nothing within the original theory, without supplementary argument, to prescribe a time-characteristic of the electron-jump. Indeed, the requirements of the special theory of relativity have not been linked with the quantum theory in our arguments so far, even though the speed of the electron in its orbit (viewed in classical terms) will be a not insignificant fraction of the speed of light. There are other phenomena unaccounted for by the Bohr theory (such as the observed fine structure of spectral lines), and we must admit that it is not the end of the story. Historically, further developments began to take place about ten years after Bohr proposed his theory, and they will therefore be appropriate for study in the next volume.

The Principle of Correspondence

The new ideas involving the quantum of action (the Planck constant) are so different from the ideas of classical physics that it is not immediately clear how the classical theory relates to the newer quantum work. To be sure, the classical theory has had great triumphs and is still of the greatest value within a wide range of macroscopic physical situations. Planck's constant may well be of value as a battering ram for breaking into the citadel of classical theory, but the older classical theory still often has acceptably valid application. Since both theories are able to predict experimental data to high accuracy within their own spheres, it is natural to suppose that the one (the classical theory) can be regarded as in some sense a limiting form of the other. We have seen already (p. 296) that classical conditions for cavity radiation can be re-established if either the temperature is very high or, more formally, if the Planck constant is decreased to zero. These conditions will be found later to be applicable generally so that classical theory can properly be regarded as a limiting case of the quantum theory. This situation was formalized by Bohr in his correspondence principle, for the special case of the elucidation of spectral lines outlined in the last section.

Explicitly, the Bohr theory of the Rutherford atom has nothing to say about the probability of an electron making a particular jump between two given levels of energy, which might occur for example as the result of the direct collision between the atom in question and a neighbour. Again, the theory says nothing about the properties of polarization to be expected from the radiation. Bohr noticed, as a direct mathematical consequence of his theory, that the orbital characteristics of the electron become essentially classical if the quantum number describing the orbit becomes high enough. He therefore concluded that the polarizations and intensities of the radiation, although calculated using the quantum theory, are to be the same as those predicted by the classical theory. Apparently, the spectral frequencies are to be calculated according to the action arguments of Planck, whereas the amplitude and polarization of the frequencies are to follow from the classical theory. This has been said to be like using classical theory on Monday, Wednesday, and Friday, and quantum theory on Tuesday and Thursday. This is not a satisfactory position for a scientific discipline to find itself in. The theory must be generalized to obtain a description of the physical world acceptable on every day of the week. The mathematical expression for any physical concept in the non-classical range can be checked in at least a preliminary way if it has a corresponding classical form: the quantum form is to turn into the correct classical form when Planck's constant is set equal to zero, but with a non-zero value of the action. A succession of infinitesimal contributions of action add up together to provide a continuous, finite value of the action. The discontinuous interchange of energy becomes continuous in the limit of zero value of Planck's constant: the classical and quantum theories are reconciled in this way. Each has been constructed on the basis of firm experimental and observational measured values, and these remain true as the range and depth of the measurements continually increase.

Retrospect

In this chapter we have traced some aspects of the breakdown of the world order of classical physics. We have seen how mistaken was the belief, held at the end of the last century, that the key to a complete understanding of the physical world had been found. The concept of an absolute understanding of an absolute world has proved, in this century, to be naïve and the need to replace it with a concept of relative relationships between physical quantities has become clear. The new outlook in physics has come about solely because the range and accuracy of experiment and observation have both increased. This is very important, for the replacement of the old ideas has been necessary not because they are 'wrong' in any sense but simply because they are too restrictive to be able to encompass extended physical circumstances.

The Newtonian theory is roughly the theory of the everyday

world, and within this specific field it is as useful today as in the past. It demonstrates beyond doubt that a wide range of the properties of the physical world can be described consistently in logical, numerical terms. The inadequacy of Newtonian classical mechanics was recognized early in this century in its inability to describe high speeds. The post-Newtonian classical theory, developed by Einstein in his theories of relativity, abolished once and for all any hopes of an absolute world. The acceptance of the relative description as the only safe description entered physics; such was its power in that sphere that this notion has spread widely throughout human thought. But more followed. Through statistical physics it was recognized that errors of measurement play a fundamental role in the description of the world, and are not avoidable imperfections. It might even be that an exact description of the physical world was less than a dream—it might turn out to be an impossibility.

The detailed study of atoms and molecules provided more surprises. This study involves the very small and the very light in weight and here again classical physics proves totally inadequate. Not only do the laws lead to wrong calculated results, but the very concepts, such as particle and wave, seem to lose their unambiguous meaning, at least in connection with radiation, and reality apparently is concerned with something which is both particle and wave (a wavicle perhaps!) together. And this is not pure fancy—appropriate experimental data can be interpreted in no other way.

Such was the situation at about the time of the First World War. With the notion of 'back to normalcy' after the war it was possible to study these matters further. More discoveries of a fundamental nature were to be made and the early quantum theory itself was to be replaced by a more general theory.

FOR FURTHER READING

See the bibliography following chapter 10, at p. 357.

9

Chemistry

JOHN WREN-LEWIS

I. THE LANGUAGE OF CHEMISTRY

Chemistry is the business of transforming materials systematically, and hence is a crucial factor in the practical expression of human creativity. This seems to have been responsible for inhibiting the development of a real science of chemistry until relatively recent times, inasmuch as the whole subject was so surrounded by feelings of awe and mystery that exact, detached study was almost impossible. And this inhibition affected the whole development of man's scientific understanding, since, without some kind of language in which to break down the multiplicity of materials in the world and analyse them systematically, very little else can be understood. Without a science of chemistry, science is restricted to superficial classification, as in natural history, or to the applications of mathematical ingenuity to relatively simple observations, as in basic astronomy or elementary mechanics.

The fundamental importance of chemistry is reflected in the fact that the development of civilization can practically be dated from the period, about the fourth millennium B.C., when human beings first discovered the most primitive of all chemical skills, the hardening of clay by fire to make bricks and, later on, pots and tablets. For well over ten millennia prior to that we can trace back the existence of man as a distinctive species with unusual creative powers, but during the whole of this prehistoric period the practical skills of the new species were confined to making ingenious manipulations of the materials found in nature, the most important manipulations, utterly unknown in any other species, being the use of tools to conserve and pass on knowledge by making marks on stone and wood. With the discovery of the chemical transformation of clay, however, came the realization that it was possible to make entirely new materials in which human inventiveness could be expressed, and the subsequent development of civilization was paralleled by extensions of this discovery—the heating of certain rocks in fire to yield metals that could be worked or moulded in the same way as the gold or occasional lumps of iron that long before had been found lying around in the natural state; the slow burning of oil, crushed out of plants, to provide regular light in the dark; the fermentation of fruit juices to give intoxicating beverages; the production of glass by cooking sand and lime; the making of vivid new colours by mixing and heating various mineral and vegetable substances; and eventually, the making of papyrus for the first real spread of knowledge. Inevitably, a great deal of lore began to grow up around these crafts, and human ingenuity began to develop systematic theories about the transformation of materials, a study which came to be called alchemy. (Experts are still uncertain of the origin of the term, although it appears to be an Arabic term derived from the Greek word for pouring.)

The subject was overshadowed by a tremendous sense of awe and fascination, which had the effect of preventing alchemy from developing the really down-to-earth kind of thinking which is essential if progress is to be made. Hence although, over the centuries, a good many practical chemical skills like distillation, crystallization, fine grinding, and so on were developed to a high level in alchemical laboratories, and a substantial number of new materials were invented (notably mineral preparations with medicinal properties), theoretical understanding of the transformation of materials never really got started. The theories of alchemy represent a curious confusion of genuine scientific insights with emotional, artistic, and religious considerations.

For example, a typical alchemical theory was that gold might have been formed in the earth by the solidification of sunlight after it had been trapped by flowers and turned to nectar, then processed into honey by bees, then hardened by contact with the earth into sulphur. Similarly it was thought silver might have been formed from moonlight, trapped into dewdrops and then changed by contact with the earth into quicksilver, finally being solidified to silver by pressure. Theories like this reflected the fact that alchemists tended to see the preparations and combinations they were carrying out as processes involving not only the materials with which they were dealing in their flasks and crucibles but also the thoughts and feelings of their inner lives: the alchemical work or *opus* was as much a religious as a technical exercise, and this involvement of people's moral and aesthetic interests effectively prevented any detached understanding of what was going on.

Genuine scientific chemistry began during that extraordinary period about three hundred years ago when mankind's whole attitude to life and to nature seemed to change. For the first time in history the all-pervading atmosphere of awe and mystery began to recede from people's minds and to be replaced by a much more aggressive attitude, a willingness to try out new things on a much wider scale than had ever been thought permissible before, and to consider tearing things down to their component elements—in other words, a willingness to make experiment a central part of life, and in particular to make it the test of all speculation about nature's workings. Something of this approach to the study of the world had been advocated by a few scholars for some considerable time—it can certainly be traced back to Roger Bacon in the thirteenth century who, incidentally, is credited with having applied it on a practical scale by inventing gunpowder—but it was only in the sixteenth and seventeenth centuries that it really gained widespread support from scholars. British scholars played a notable part in formulating the new attitude, especially the founders of the Royal Society in Charles II's reign, who took their inspiration from the philosophical writings of Francis Bacon, Lord Verulam. He advocated the systematic development of 'experimental philosophy' as a means of restoring to mankind that dominion over nature which was regarded as proper by the Book of Genesis, which, he believed, subsequent religion had played down, even discouraged. His work was treated by the early experimentalists as something very like a revolutionary tract, a programme of action for changing the world.

It is customary to date the extension of the new approach from mechanics and astronomy into the field of chemical science from one of those early pioneers, Robert Boyle, who published a famous book called *The Skeptical Chymist* (1661). Among other things, he gave a crucial new twist to the ancient alchemical notion that all the multifarious substances in the world are combinations, in various proportions, of certain basic elements. In alchemy it had been assumed that the basic elements were spiritual principles corresponding to certain fundamental material qualities (earthiness, airiness, fieriness, and wateriness), and, equally, to certain human emotions. Boyle took a much more down-to-earth approach, by assuming that certain ordinary materials like iron, gold, carbon, sulphur, and phosphorus were elements, which under the right circumstances could combine or react with each other in varying proportions to make up the world's near-infinite variety. This opened the way for the exact study of the quantities in which elements react with one another to form compounds, and for the notion of tiny *atoms* of elements grouping themselves together to form the *molecules* which are the basic components of compound substances. The concept of the atom, which today is usually thought of in the province of the science of physics, began as an idea in the new language that was evolved during the eighteenth and nineteenth centuries for the science of chemistry.

Practically everyone today uses that language, even people who have no knowledge of chemistry at all, for even in common speech it is possible to refer to water as H_2O almost automatically. Behind this simple expression, however, lie a number of ideas which were sorted out from the confusions of traditional mystical-aesthetic thought only with great mental toil. In the first place, it took a large part of the eighteenth century to dispel the ancient notion that combustion is a mysterious process in which something escapes from the burning material, and to recognize that what really happens is that one element in the air, subsequently called oxygen, combines with the burning material to the accompaniment of heat and flame in the chemical reaction. It was the crystallization of this notion by Antoine Lavoisier which opened the way to the recognition by John Dalton that the atoms of different elements could be distinguished as having distinctive weights, and also for the development by Amedeo Avogadro of the idea that compound substances too are composed of basic particles analogous to the atoms of elements, 'molecules' which for any given compound are all alike; these may be imagined as 'corporate atoms', inasmuch as in each molecule of the same substance an exactly similar group of atoms is massed together in a characteristic fashion—for example, every basic particle of sulphuric acid contains two atoms of hydrogen, one of sulphur, and four of oxygen massed together. (The word 'molecule' derives from the Latin word for mass.) The decisive step of writing formulae like H_2O or H_2SO_4 to describe compounds was mainly the work of one of the greatest of all the pioneering chemists, the Swede Jöns Jacob Berzelius, who applied with this new precision the ancient alchemical idea of using symbols or letters to represent elements. He also developed the idea of representing reactions by *equations* of formulae; for example, the reaction of hydrochloric acid with caustic soda to give salt and water, which in our modernized version of Berzelius's terminology would be written:

NaOH	+	HCl	=	NaCl	+	H_2O,
Caustic soda or sodium hydroxide		Hydro-chloric acid		Common salt or sodium chloride		Water

where Na is the symbol for sodium (from the Latin, natrium) and Cl the symbol for chlorine.

A key feature of the syntax of this new language was the notion that atoms of a particular element have a characteristic *valency* for combining with other atoms. The valency of an atom is normally defined in terms of the number of atoms of hydrogen to which it will hold, since hydrogen is the simplest of all elements. Thus chlorine is said to be *monovalent* because the compound of hydrogen and chlorine (the gas from which hydrochloric acid is made) has the formula HCl, whereas oxygen is said to be *divalent* because its compound with hydrogen is water, H_2O. Some elements do not combine with hydrogen at all, but they can still be given a valency by reference to the compounds they form with elements whose valency in terms of combination with hydrogen is known: thus, sodium is monovalent because its chloride has the formula NaCl, and chlorine is monovalent. Carbon is said to have a basic valency of four because its normal compound with hydrogen is methane, CH_4, and this *quadrivalency* can equally be seen in its compound with divalent oxygen, which is carbon dioxide, CO_2. Some elements, however, are known to be capable of operating at, as it were, two or more quite distinct levels as far as valency is concerned: thus sulphur can have a valency of two, as in hydrogen sulphide, H_2S, or of four as in sulphur dioxide SO_2, or of six, as in sulphuric acid H_2SO_4, which should properly be drawn out something like this:

$$
\begin{array}{ccc}
O & & O-H \\
 & \diagdown & \diagup \\
 & S & \\
 & \diagup & \diagdown \\
O & & O-H
\end{array}
$$

The development of this language of chemistry in the nineteenth century was not just a matter of the intellectual pursuit of understanding. As the new knowledge developed—as more and more common substances were analysed into their elements, and more and more chemical reactions were explored in the laboratory— chemistry began to be practised on the industrial scale. It is customary to date the beginnings of the chemical industry from 1787, when Nicholas Leblanc, physician to the Duke of Orleans, won a prize from the French Academy for a large-scale process for making soda synthetically from chalk, salt, and lime, and the reason the French Academy offered the prize was that industrial processes were growing up (notably textile spinning and weaving, glass manufacture, and the boiling up of fat to make soap) on a scale which was beginning to exhaust natural soda supplies. By the middle of the nineteenth century chemical factories were taking their place alongside other industrial plants all over Europe, and when people in Lancashire objected to the pollution of the atmosphere by fumes of hydrochloric acid from the Leblanc alkali plants, ingenious inventors turned the manufacture of hydrochloric acid itself into a new business, for it was needed both in its own right as an agent for metal-work and also as a source of chlorine for bleaching. Then in the middle years of the nineteenth century a new leap forward was taken both in the development of the language of chemistry and in the growth of the chemical industry, when 'organic' chemistry began to emerge from the realm of mysticism into the realm of chemical science.

The term 'organic chemistry' is itself a survival from the ancient mystical way of thinking, which is expressed in the plaques on the walls of the baths at Buxton Spa giving a Victorian analysis of the waters to show their health-giving properties: after an impressive-looking list of mineral salts comes the punch line, a small percentage of 'substances unknown to science'. To even educated laymen at the beginning of the nineteenth century, it still seemed obvious that the principles of life and health must necessarily elude scientific analysis. Chemists had got beyond this, to the extent of recognizing that living materials could be analysed exactly into ordinary chemical elements just as thoroughly as minerals, but there still seemed to be something mysterious about living substances because their composition turned out to be very complex, even though most of them contained only a few constituent elements (mostly carbon, hydrogen, oxygen, and nitrogen, with other elements coming in very occasionally). Berzelius formulated the general opinion among chemists of the early nineteenth century that the science was likely to develop along two independent lines, 'inorganic' chemistry dealing with relatively simple combinations of elements capable of being carried out in the laboratory, and 'organic' chemistry dealing with the complex materials of the living world, like oils, fats, waxes, and sugars, which chemists might analyse but never synthesize for themselves. Then came the psychologically decisive moment, in 1828, when a young German chemist, Friedrich Wöhler, discovered that he could make urea (a compound which can be crystallized out of urine and had hitherto been known only as a product of animal metabolism) by a simple laboratory process starting with entirely mineral sources. 'I must tell you,' he wrote in a historic letter to Berzelius, 'that I can make urea without the need of kidneys or any animal whatever', and Berzelius had the wit to recognize that there was really no distinction of principle after all between the two branches of chemistry.

His term 'organic chemistry' survived, however, to mark off the very different kind of thought and practice that has to go into understanding the immense variety and complexity of compounds which can be made from the element carbon, by virtue of the unique ability of carbon atoms to hold on to each other in large numbers, with the atoms of other elements in attendance, in very big molecules. The processes of handling such complex combinations of a relatively small number of elements are so different, both in theory and in practice, from the processes of handling the relatively simple combinations that can take place between other elements, that it is convenient to think of the two fields of chemistry as more or less separate, and the names 'organic' and 'inorganic' have remained convenient labels for them to this day. The extension of chemical language to cover the organic field was based on two fundamental ideas. The first, developed mainly by Wöhler and another great German, Justus von Liebig, in discussion with the ageing Berzelius, was the notion that groups of atoms could for certain purposes be thought of as 'corporate atoms' even though they were not molecules that could exist on their own. For example, the simplest and most straightforward compound of carbon is methane or marsh-gas, CH_4, but it is possible to substitute other elements for one of the hydrogen atoms, for example, chlorine, giving CH_3Cl, and in the 1830s it began to become clear that the group CH_3 could for many purposes be treated as a 'compound element' capable of entering into all sorts of combinations in much the same way as sodium does—for instance 'wood alcohol', the poisonous principle of methylated spirits, has the formula H_4CO, but it makes more sense to write it $CH_3 \cdot OH$, with the CH_3 taking the place of one hydrogen atom in water or of the sodium atom in caustic soda, $NaOH$. Wöhler and Liebig coined the term *radical* for groups like CH_3, and the early development of organic chemistry consisted largely of the identification of more and more radicals of greater and greater complication, for example:

$$C_2H_5 \quad \text{as in} \quad C_2H_5OH$$

Ethyl   Ethyl alcohol
(ordinary alcohol)

$$CH_2 \quad \text{as in} \quad CH_2Cl_2$$

Methylene   Methylene chloride

$$CO_2H \left(\substack{\text{more commonly} \\ \text{written COOH}}\right) \quad \text{as in} \quad CH_3\cdot COOH$$

Carboxyl   Acetic acid

$$CHO\cdot \quad \text{as in} \quad H\cdot CHO$$

Aldehyde   Formaldehyde

Once formulated, the idea of radicals was extended backwards into non-carbon chemistry, so that OH is now described as a hydroxyl radical, SO_4 as a sulphate radical, and NH_4 as an ammonium radical.

The second major development in chemical language that was essential in understanding carbon compounds, and has since been extended back into non-carbon or 'inorganic' chemistry, is the notion of writing out formulae fully as diagrams in space. This becomes essential as soon as it is recognized that atoms can join together in chains. There are millions of quite different materials, for example, composed of carbon and hydrogen alone, and it becomes possible to see why if diagrams are drawn out thus:

Methane   Ethane   Propane   Butane

Now with the first three of these it is possible to 'collapse' the formulae, once you realize the basic principle that the carbon atoms are joining on to each other in chains, but with the fourth it is not, because there are two quite different materials with the collapsed formula C_4H_{10}, and it is possible to distinguish them *only* by writing the formulae out spatially:

'Normal' butane   'Iso'-butane

The man who takes most credit for making this development in chemical language was the German chemist Friedrich August

Kekulé, and his story is one of the most famous and astonishing in all science, for he made his great discoveries not just once, but twice, in dreams. On the first occasion he was working in London in the 1850s, and fell into a reverie on top of a bus, whereupon he saw carbon atoms dancing about before his eyes and suddenly observed that they were joining up in chains. On the second occasion, in Ghent in 1865, he was dozing in front of the fire when he had a dream of carbon chains as snakes, and suddenly saw one such snake swallowing its own tail. So he came upon the notion that it was possible to have not only chains (straight, branched, or wiggly) but rings too—especially the crucial six-membered ring of benzene, which today is practically the symbol of organic chemistry and is so familiar that it is often written as a pure diagram without bothering to fill in the atoms:

Benzene   Hydroxy-benzene   Benzaldehyde
            or phenol   ('oil of bitter almonds')

often
written

The double links between alternate carbon atoms in these rings indicate that these atoms can be considered as holding on to each other with two of their valency links, rather as carbon holds on to each of its two oxygens in carbon dioxide, $O=C=O$, and this is another important feature of the syntax of chemical language which needs special mention. Such 'double bonding' is not in any way stronger than ordinary single bonding—on the contrary, when it occurs between carbon atoms it normally indicates something of a strained situation, in which the atoms are constantly prone to pick up any stray elements there are about, as for example the simple hydrocarbon ethylene, found in coal gas, combines readily with chlorine to give ethylene dichloride:

$$\begin{array}{cc} H & H \\ \diagdown & \diagup \\ C=C \\ \diagup & \diagdown \\ H & H \end{array} \quad + 2Cl \quad = \quad \begin{array}{c} Cl\ Cl \\ |\ \ | \\ H-C-C-H \\ |\ \ | \\ H\ H \end{array}$$

or, more simply $CH_2=CH_2 + Cl_2 = CH_2\,Cl\cdot CH_2Cl$.

For this reason compounds containing double-bonded carbon atoms came to be referred to, in the middle years of the nineteenth century, as 'unsaturated' compounds, or sometimes 'olefinic' compounds, the latter term (meaning literally 'oil forming') being derived from the fact that ethylene dichloride was originally observed as an oily substance formed when ethylene reacted with chlorine. Nowadays olefinic hydrocarbons are produced in vast quantities from the 'cracking' of oil in refineries, and most industrial alcohol is now made by persuading ethylene from this source to satisfy its 'unsaturation' by combining with water:

$$CH_2=CH_2 + H_2O = C_2H_5OH$$

One vindication of Kekulé's idea about the ring-structure of benzene was the discovery that it could under certain circumstances take up chlorine or hydrogen to form, respectively, benzene hexa-chloride (nowadays used as an insecticide) or cyclohexane:

$$\begin{array}{cc} & CHCl \\ & \diagup\ \ \diagdown \\ ClHC & \quad CHCl \\ | & \quad\ | \\ ClHC & \quad CHCl \\ & \diagdown\ \ \diagup \\ & CHCl \end{array} \qquad\qquad \begin{array}{cc} & CH_2 \\ & \diagup\ \ \diagdown \\ H_2C & \quad CH_2 \\ H_2C & \quad CH_2 \\ & \diagdown\ \ \diagup \\ & CH_2 \end{array}$$

Benzene hexachloride   Cyclohexane

At the same time, however, benzene does not react with other elements nearly so readily as most ordinary unsaturated compounds like ethylene do: on the contrary, the great puzzle about it, prior to Kekulé's intuition, was precisely that it was known to be highly stable under most conditions, reacting with nitric acid, for example, to give nitrobenzene by the following equation:

$$C_6H_6 + HNO_3 = C_6H_5NO_2 + H_2O.$$

It clearly seemed, in fact, as if it was going to be necessary to think of benzene forming a radical, C_6H_5 (which came to be known as the *phenyl* radical, from the substance phenol or 'carbolic acid' known to be C_6H_5OH) that could persist through many different reactions in exactly the same way as the methyl radical (CH_3) derived from methane. This seemed paradoxical considering that the ratio of hydrogen to carbon atoms in the formula for benzene, C_6H_6, seemed to indicate a high degree of 'unsaturation', even perhaps the extreme form of unsaturation encountered in acetylene, C_2H_2, in which the carbon atoms are holding on to each other with no less than three of their valency links, thus:

$$HC{\equiv}CH$$

and which does indeed react very readily with chlorine, hydrogen, and many other things. Kekulé's intuition about the atoms being joined in a ring in benzene partly solved this puzzle, but only partly: why did reactions like the chlorination of benzene to benzene hexachloride not occur more often, instead of reactions like that with nitric acid? Eventually it came to be realized, towards the end of the nineteenth century, that the six-membered ring-structure does something very special to the bonding between the carbon atoms, which at that time chemists could think of only by thinking of the double linkages shifting continually round and round the ring, rather like a continuous game of musical chairs, creating a stable 'resonating system'. The full explanation of this phenomenon came only much later, when chemists learned to interpret valency in terms of the electronic structure of atoms, but in the meantime it was clear that the diagrammatic representation of benzene as a simple outline hexagon, far from being less accurate than the fully-drawn-out formula with double bonds, might actually be an advance as far as workable chemical language is concerned. Using this device, we nowadays write nitrobenzene like this:

where $-NO_2$ is called the *nitro* radical.

These ideas were worked out against a background of intense practical activity, both in the laboratory and on the industrial scale. Wöhler's discovery opened up the possibility not only of understanding and artificially synthesizing the 'organic' compounds of nature, but also of making entirely artificial carbon compounds of the same kind of complexity as natural ones. Chemists began to develop the art of ringing the changes on the various molecular structures discovered in nature, to create what came to be called, by the beginning of the twentieth century, 'the miracle of chemistry'.

II. THE SMALL MIRACLE

People judge things as miracles by their expectations. Looking back now from the perspective of the later twentieth century, the achievement of chemistry up to the First World War seems at best like a very small miracle: the discoveries which were really to revolutionize ordinary people's lives were still to come, most notably the revolution in materials made possible by modern plastics and synthetic fibres, and the revolution in health made possible by penicillin and similar 'wonder drugs'. Hints of both these possibilities had been given prior to 1918—indeed, prior to the end of the nineteenth century—and at the time these were no doubt enough to suggest the term 'miracle' in relation to chemistry, but looking back now we can see that they were no more than hints, and the really major developments in these fields depended upon intellectual revolutions in chemical science which were not forthcoming until the years between the wars.

The most impressive practical achievement of chemistry in the early years of the twentieth century was the flowering of industrial organic chemistry, which turned on the exploitation of the mineral that had already played a dominant role in the development of industrialization, namely coal. Because it was being mined so extensively for fuel—not just in its own right, but also for the production of coal gas for heating and lighting, which had already begun quite early in the nineteenth century—coal was available as an extremely cheap source of the carbon on which, as chemists now realized, the whole complexity of nature's life-processes was based. As early as 1820 chemists had begun to consider exploiting it, in particular by using the tar left behind in the gas-production process. Charles MacIntosh had given the first anticipation of the modern plastics industry by taking up the discovery of a Scottish surgeon that the 'naphtha' or liquid hydrocarbon spirit which could be obtained by distilling coal tar would dissolve rubber—MacIntosh used this to rubberize cloth for raincoats, and so turned his name into a household word. In Germany nitrobenzene (made by reacting nitric acid with benzene, which is also a coal-tar distillation product) was being made on an industrial scale and marketed as a soap-scent well before Kekulé had enabled chemists to understand what it really was. The real birth of the organic chemical industry, however, came in 1856, when W. H. Perkin (1838–1907) analysed quinine to the basic formula $C_{20}H_{24}N_2O_2$, and wondered if he could synthesize it from coal-tar compounds related to nitrobenzene, notably aniline, $C_6H_5NH_2$, which we should nowadays write:

where $^-NH_2$ is called the *amino* radical, derived from ammonia, NH_3. He failed, but instead obtained a mauve substance which he found would dye silk and would not fade with exposure either to washing or to light. He founded a flourishing industry, and the next few decades saw it expand enormously, with the production of a whole host of new artificial colouring materials. Chemists seized on Kekulé's recognition of the ring structure of benzene and began to play the game of seeing just what could be done by changing ring structures of various types, including very complicated ones such as those of the hydrocarbons naphthalene and anthracene (also both found in coal tar) in which the hexagon principle of benzene is multiplied in what have subsequently come to be known as 'fused ring systems':

Naphthalene

often drawn

Anthracene

often drawn

Another aspect of Perkin's idea which led to many further developments was its inclusion of the element nitrogen in among the carbon and hydrogen atoms. This is now known to be one of the key features of nature's most important materials, including the proteins which make up living tissues, and the chemists who followed up Perkin's discovery, both in academic laboratories and in the newly-developing industrial ones, notably in Germany, rang many changes on this aspect of Perkin's work too. One of the most important of these was the discovery of the *azo* radical consisting of two nitrogen atoms joined together, which to this day is still an important principle of a whole range of dyestuffs known as azo dyes:

−N=N−   as in the dye
Azo group   'Para red'
(1880)

Another important type of nitrogen compound has the nitrogen incorporated in a ring structure, as in the coal-tar distillation product pyridine:

often
written

Compounds of this general type came to be known as *heterocyclic compounds* (because they contained rings of non-uniform composition), and it gradually began to emerge that such compounds have a very important role in many natural processes. In particular the dye indigo, which has been extracted from plants for many thousands of years, was shown in the closing years of the nineteenth century to depend for its colour on a substance whose chemical structure is like this:

i.e. a structure with two identical complex ring-systems, each of them a 'fusion', as it were, of a benzene ring with a five-membered heterocyclic ring. The synthetic production of indigo and other ancient natural dyes served incidentally to scotch finally, at any rate for the educated public, any lingering thoughts that the more complex substances in nature might require a 'vital force' for their production—other, that is, than the vital force of the chemists' intelligence and laboratory skill.

By the beginning of the twentieth century the range of new dye-stuffs and colouring matters was so enormous that chemists' attention had begun to turn to trying to understand exactly why some substances are coloured and others not. It was obvious from the sheer diversity that colour could not be dependent upon any specific type of chemical structure, and chemists eventually came to recognize that the clue lay in the internal vibrations which take place in molecules of different kinds. This, however, is a subject which it will be more appropriate to explore a little later on.

Meanwhile the dyestuffs industry had begun to put out an off-shoot which was attracting even more human interest, the first major production of synthetic medicinals since the discovery of chloroform, $CHCl_3$, in the 1830s. Perkin's attempt to synthesize quinine had been a dramatic failure, but later chemists returned to the charge, and an important breakthrough occurred in the 1880s in Germany where Ludwig Knorr (1859–1921) followed up this work on quinine and other vegetable alkaloids (which like the work on indigo was throwing up the biological importance of heterocyclic compounds containing nitrogen) by making a number of synthetic substances that turned out to be useful for reducing fever symptoms. This led chemists to start exploring related chemical structures systematically, and although history books rarely mention it, one of the most notable features of the opening of the twentieth century, by any standards, must surely have been the first introduction, also from Germany, of the pain-killing drugs phenacetic and aspirin, both relatively simple benzene-ring compounds which could be made cheaply from coal tar by the kind of industrial processes that the dyestuffs chemists had begun to make familiar. Equally signifi-cant was the elucidation, in the late 1890s, of the chemical structure of cocaine. This too led to the systematic examination of related simpler compounds, and several synthetic local anaesthetics were introduced in the new century's first decade.

It seemed, in fact, that the key to health was at last being dis-covered by chemical science, but as yet the secret of quinine, which does not merely relieve symptoms but actually exerts a curative action, remained hidden, in two senses. The chemical structure of quinine eluded complete analysis until after 1918, although it was known to be based on heterocyclic rings. More important, however, quinine remained one of the few exceptions to the general rule that chemicals which were known to combat disease germs were assumed to be equally dangerous to the human organism. The man who set himself to find a way between the horns of this dilemma was the German physiologist Paul Erlich (1854–1915), who was struck by the fact that many dyestuffs were known to be highly selective in the staining of living tissues of various kinds, and conceived the notion of using this fact to find a 'magic bullet' that would hold on to and destroy bacterial tissue without harming other tissues. His work on this theme in the first decade of the twentieth century is commonly regarded as the foundation of the modern science of chemotherapy, and its most notable achievement was his discovery of salvarsan, a chemical which could be (and whose close relatives still are) used in the treatment of syphilis. Chemically this substance is interesting because it is not itself a dye but has a structure similar to that of an azo-dye, only with arsenic atoms (As) taking the place of the nitrogen atoms in the azo-group:

$$\text{HO} - \bigcirc - \text{As} = \text{As} - \bigcirc - \text{OH}$$

$$\begin{array}{cc} \text{H-N-Cl} & \text{Cl-N-H} \\ \diagup \diagdown & \diagup \diagdown \\ \text{H} \quad \text{H} & \text{H} \quad \text{H} \end{array}$$

The really significant thing about this drug, however, is something that Erlich never quite faced, namely, that although its structure is related to that of many dyestuffs, it is not itself a dye. Had he faced it, he might have recognized that the dilemma was really only a human assumption with no basis in chemical nature. There is really no necessary connection whatever between anti-bacterial activity and toxicity to human beings, even though most antiseptics do happen to be harmful to human tissue: but this was recognized only much later, in the 1930s, when chemists still pursuing Erlich's bullet found that the dyestuffs which *did* act against bacteria inside the body did not in fact do it by attaching themselves to bacterial tissue at all—the connection between their dyeing activity and their anti-bacterial activity was purely accidental.

Had this been realized sooner, the world might have had penicillin as a drug as soon as Fleming discovered its remarkable anti-bacterial action in 1929, or even earlier on the basis of old wives' tales about the beneficial effects of mould on wounds. As things happened, the real flowering of chemotherapy had to wait until just before the Second World War, when the mythical dilemma was finally shattered by, in effect, a series of largely accidental discoveries.

Nevertheless the work of Erlich and his contemporaries in the years before the First World War yielded (albeit often for the wrong reasons) sufficiently impressive medicinal achievements to give great impetus to organic chemistry, particularly to efforts to eluci-date the chemical structure of natural products. Many of the great achievements in this field too came from German laboratories. Emil Fischer (1852–1919), who started life as a pupil of Kekulé, had already, in the 1870s, laid the groundwork for an understanding of sugars and starches by showing them to be complex compounds based on five- or six-membercd chains of carbon atoms of the kind found in simple sugars like glucose or fructose (fruit-sugar):

$$
\begin{array}{cc}
H_2C\!\!-\!\!OH & H_2C\!\!-\!\!OH \\
| & | \\
H\!\!-\!\!C\!\!-\!\!OH & H\!\!-\!\!C\!\!-\!\!OH \\
| & | \\
H\!\!-\!\!C\!\!-\!\!OH & H\!\!-\!\!C\!\!-\!\!OH \\
| & | \\
H\!\!-\!\!C\!\!-\!\!OH & H\!\!-\!\!C\!\!-\!\!OH \\
| & | \\
H\!\!-\!\!C\!\!-\!\!OH & C\!\!=\!\!O \\
| & | \\
H\!\!-\!\!C\!\!=\!\!O & H_2C\!\!-\!\!OH \\
\text{Glucose} & \text{Fructose}
\end{array}
$$

(Later research was to show that in fact these chains are bent round on themselves to form rings of carbon and oxygen atoms.)

At the turn of the century Fischer turned his attention to two groups of natural products containing nitrogen. First, he showed that a whole range of plant products such as the caffeine of coffee, the theophylline and xanthine of tea, and the theobromine of cocoa were all complex derivatives of the heterocyclic compound *purine*:

$$
\begin{array}{c}
\text{CH} \\
N \diagup \quad \diagdown \text{C} \!-\!\!-\!\! NH \\
| \quad\quad \| \quad\quad | \\
HC \diagdown \quad\quad C \quad\quad CH \\
\diagdown N \quad\quad N \diagup
\end{array}
$$

This discovery led on to the elucidation of the structure of the *nucleic acids* extracted from the nuclei of living cells. Nucleic acids turned out to be complex compounds with ring-structures of the purine type attached to phosphorus atoms. In the middle years of the twentieth century these acids have been found to be the key factors in the transmission of heredity. They control the building-up of living tissue by controlling the immensely complicated synthesis of *proteins*, and this was the second important group of natural nitrogen-containing materials studied by Fischer in the century's first decade.

Although he could not at that time penetrate to the full complexity of these materials, he was able to show that they were built up from relatively simple substances known as *amino-acids*, substances whose molecules possess an amino radical ($-NH_2$) and a carboxyl radical ($-COOH$) with some kind of chain of carbon and hydrogen atoms (and sometimes other atoms as well) in between. One of the simplest amino-acids is *glycine*, H_2N-CH_2-COOH, and under the right conditions two molecules of this will react together to form a more complex amino-acid like this:

$$\begin{array}{c} H \\ \diagdown \\ \diagup \\ H \end{array} N-CH_2-CO\cdot OH \quad + \quad \begin{array}{c} H \\ \diagdown \\ \diagup \\ H \end{array} N-CH_2-COOH \; =$$

$$H_2O \; + \; \begin{array}{c} H \\ \diagdown \\ \diagup \\ H \end{array} N-CH_2-CO-NH\cdot CH_2-COOH$$

This reaction, known as *peptide* formation, can go on and on, and Fischer recognized that proteins were extremely complex poly-peptides. We now know that one of the simplest proteins, insulin, contains no less than fifty amino-acid groups in every molecule—not all the same, but twelve different ones combined in an almost bizarre order.

In Fischer's day there was an enormous intellectual inhibition about recognizing that molecules could ever be quite so complex as this: it seemed as if the very idea threatened to open the flood-gates to the mysticism and superstition that Dalton and his con-temporaries had so carefully and painfully excluded when they insisted on analysing all materials into more or less simple formulae so as to free scientific chemistry from the fantasies of the alchemists. This inhibition was not fully overcome until the 1920s, and in the early years of the century it not only helped to prevent the full understanding of nature's structural materials like starch, cellulose, and proteins but also prevented any really systematic progress in what had seemed, in the second half of the nineteenth century, to be a most promising third field of practical chemical miracles alongside the dyestuffs industry and the first ventures in chemo-therapy, namely, the synthesis of artificial substances for moulding, fibre-making, and surface coating.

The foundations for a chemical miracle here were laid in the middle of the nineteenth century in what might at first seem an unlikely realm, that of the explosives industry. Because traditional explosives like gunpowder had been found to produce their effects by extremely rapid combustion, made possible by the ready availability of oxygen in saltpetre (potassium nitrate, KNO_3, K being the symbol for potassium, from the Latin 'kalium'), chemists had begun, in the 1840s, to investigate the possibility of making better explosives by reacting nitric acid, HNO_3, with various cheap materials, and this led to the invention of nitro-glycerine (later made the basis of dynamite and blasting gelatine by Alfred Nobel), and guncotton (obtained by nitrating cotton waste). The same line of research led to the discovery of an even more powerful explosive in the years immediately preceding the First World War, namely trinitrotoluene, T.N.T., produced from a coal-tar hydrocarbon closely related to benzene, namely *toluene*:

Toluene   T.N.T.

A much more important development, however, was the discovery in the early 1860s that a slight variation of the process for producing guncotton would give a 'plastic' substance which could be softened with oil or camphor, shaped into many different forms and allowed to set. This substance, which later became known as celluloid, was only a modification of the natural structural material cellulose, but it inspired chemists to wonder if they could make purely synthetic ones (and in so doing avoid, if possible, the high inflammability of celluloid). Their attention was attracted by the resinous substances that had been found to form when formaldehyde, $H \cdot CO \cdot H$, reacted with various substances such as the proteinaceous casein of milk and, more interesting, the much simpler coal-tar product phenol. This last reaction was first exploited on the industrial scale in the early years of the twentieth century when Leo Bakeland (1863–1944) developed the process for making what he called 'Bakelite', but what is now called, more generally, pf resin.

With the outbreak of the First World War, this promise of synthetic materials was almost as important to the embattled nations as the new explosives, but the science of chemistry was not yet equal to its fulfilment. No one could understand what actually happened when phenol reacted with formaldehyde, and so no one knew how to start looking for new reactions that might yield new structural substances. In an attempt to crack this problem, great efforts were made to understand the precise chemical character of rubber, which seemed to be the simplest of nature's structural substances.

It had been established in the 1870s that rubber appeared to be related in some very close way to the doubly unsaturated hydrocarbon *isoprene* which is given off when rubber is gently heated and has the structure:

$$
\begin{array}{c}
CH_3 \\
| \\
CH_2{=}C{-}CH{=}CH_2
\end{array}
$$

Then at the turn of the century it had been found that this particular structure of atoms appeared to play a very large part in many plant products: for example, a great many natural oils turned out to be hydrocarbons whose molecules could be represented as two units of isoprene joined together in various ways, as with *limonene*, the main constituent of bitter orange oil, whose molecules have the ring-structure

which can be represented as two units of isoprene joined together with a little rearrangement of the hydrogen atoms thus:

and *pinene*, from pine oil, in which two units of isoprene can be thought of as joining up, with some rearrangement of hydrogen atoms, to make a double-ring structure thus:

$$CH_3$$
$$|$$
$$C$$

$$HC \diagup\!\!\!\diagup \qquad\qquad CH$$
$$| \qquad H_3C\text{-}C\text{-}CH_3 \qquad |$$
$$H_2C \diagdown \qquad\qquad \diagup CH_2$$
$$|$$
$$CH$$

Now the great Berzelius himself had, with his immense flair for inventing terminology, coined a word to describe the phenomenon whereby one organic compound can have a formula which is an exact multiple of the formula of another (as limonene and pinene both have the formula $C_{10}H_{16}$ and isoprene the formula C_5H_8): he called it *polymerism*. By the end of the nineteenth century many examples of it had been recorded, including cases where the simple compound would under the right conditions *polymerize* to form the more complicated one by intercombination of its molecules, as for example acetaldehyde, $CH_3 \cdot CHO$, will turn into a polymer which is the sleeping drug *paraldehyde*:

$$H\diagdown \quad O \quad \diagup H$$
$$\quad C \qquad C$$
$$CH_3 \diagup \quad | \qquad | \quad \diagdown CH_3$$
$$\quad O \diagdown \quad \diagup O$$
$$\qquad C$$
$$H \diagup \quad \diagdown CH_3$$

So in the early twentieth century chemists began to formulate the notion that rubber might be some kind of *polymer* of isoprene— but it was obviously a more complex polymer than limonene or pinene, which, because their molecules can be represented as combinations of two isoprene units, are known as *di*mers of isoprene. Indeed, immense research was being done at that time on this whole class of natural oils, which came to be known as *terpenes*, and the investigators, the most notable of whom was Otto Wallach (1847– 1931), who won the Nobel Prize in 1910, were able to show that some terpene-oils contains *tri*mers of isoprene with the formula $C_{15}H_{24}$, and even 'higher' polymers with formulae like $C_{20}H_{32}$ and $C_{30}H_{48}$—yet none of them was remotely like rubber.

Equally, efforts to persuade isoprene to turn back into rubber were at once encouraging and discouraging. Under some conditions a reaction that looked like polymerization did occur, and a rubbery mess was formed, which was encouraging to the general theory—but this mess was nothing like as good a material as rubber, which was discouraging from the practical point of view. As the First World War wore on, and both sides began to suffer from rubber shortage, chemists in desperation tried to see what could be done with other compounds related to isoprene, and some success was achieved with methyl isoprene or *dimethyl butadiene*, giving the so-called *buna*-rubbers. It was this work that laid the foundation for the eventual breakthrough to real understanding in the late 1920s, when it was finally recognized that the key to all structural materials is that they are *very* high polymers indeed, with enormous molecules containing many thousands or even hundreds of thousands of repeated units like isoprene.

Another effect of the war was to highlight the fourth field in which chemistry had promised over the previous decades to achieve a miracle, namely the field of nutrition. Conditions of shortage gave new impetus to the exploitation of the Nobel Prize-winning discovery of the French chemist Paul Sabatier (1854–1941) at the turn of the century, that treating vegetable oils with hydrogen would give a tolerable substitute for butter, namely margarine—and equally to the somewhat earlier accidental discovery by the American Constantin Fahlberg (1850–1910) of the artificial sweetener saccharin, a compound which is chemically interesting in that it has a hetero-cyclic ring containing sulphur as well as nitrogen:

Even more basically, war conditions increased the demand for intensive production of natural foods, which had the effect of giving a new and very practical twist to the growing chemical recognition of the importance of nitrogen in the life process, inasmuch as there was a great demand for nitrogen-containing substances to boost the primary food-producing process, agriculture. The use of cheap mineral materials containing nitrogen to fertilize the soil had been well established towards the end of the nineteenth century, but the war had the effect of cutting off the main source of such mineral nitrogen, namely sodium nitrate ($NaNO_3$) from the big natural deposits in Chile. This, combined with the need for nitrogen for explosives and other chemical products, gave an enormous boost to chemists' efforts to make use of the vast quantities of nitrogen in the air all around us as raw material for chemical manufacture, a possibility which had been under discussion for decades but had achieved practical realization only in the years just before the war. The difficulty had always been that native nitrogen does not react easily with anything, which may be put in another way by saying that processes to make use of it tended to be very expensive indeed—for example, a Norwegian process invented in 1903 made nitric acid by getting the nitrogen to combine with the oxygen of air under the energy-stimulus of electric arcs, but the electricity used was very expensive. The most effective way round this difficulty, which is still today the basis of the now enormous business of 'fixing' nitrogen for fertilizer and other chemical manufacture, was discovered by the German chemist Fritz Haber (1868–1934) in the years between 1905 and 1912: he found a relatively cheap method of persuading nitrogen to combine with hydrogen to give ammonia.

Of course, this process implied the availability of large quantities of reasonably cheap hydrogen, as did also the Sabatier process for making margarine, and in fact Haber's process was only one of several chemical inventions of a basic kind which provided what modern economic jargon would call the 'infra-structure' of the miracle of chemistry in the early twentieth century—inventions that made it possible to derive the elements needed for chemical manufacture cheaply on a vast scale from the cheapest possible raw materials. In the case of hydrogen the most important process was again developed in Germany just prior to the First World War, by the firm Badische Anilin und Sodafabrik. It was in essence an elegant adaptation of an idea which had originally been formulated by Lavoisier in the eighteenth century, namely that of extracting hydrogen from water by using carbon to take the oxygen out of steam:

$$H_2O + C = CO + H_2$$

The resultant mixture of carbon monoxide and hydrogen, known as 'water gas', had been widely used in the nineteenth century for enriching coal gas: B.A.S.F. found a way of making the reaction go further in various ways, either by getting the carbon monoxide to extract still more oxygen to give more hydrogen plus carbon dioxide (which can be used as a refrigerant), or else by making it recombine with hydrogen to give simple organic chemicals like methyl alcohol, CH_3OH.

The essential trick in all these processes, and indeed another essential part of the infra-structure of the whole miracle of chemistry, was the principle known as *catalysis*, whereby chemical reactions can be controlled by the presence of relatively small quantities of special substances—mostly metals, or metals oxides, in granular form—which do not themselves appear to take any part in the reaction at all. The term 'catalysis' was yet another coined by Berzelius, and the principle was given industrial application right from the first half of the nineteenth century, when it was found that the gas sulphur dioxide (SO_2) produced by burning sulphur or sulphur ores could be converted to sulphur trioxide (SO_3) for the production of sulphuric acid ($SO_3 + H_2O = H_2SO_4$) by passing a hot sulphur dioxide/oxygen mixture over finely-divided platinum, even though the two gases would hardly react at all on their own. Both in the laboratory and in industry, the expansion of chemistry during the subsequent century turned to a very considerable extent on the discovery of more and more catalysts to control more and more reactions—not just to speed things up, as with sulphur dioxide and oxygen, but also to select one particular reaction out of a whole range of possible ones. Today there is pretty big business in the manufacture of catalysts themselves, and a great deal of research is devoted to trying to understand how they achieve their effects, but no full systematic theory has yet been achieved, and there is still a good deal of hit-and-miss empiricism about the discovery of new catalysts. The essential groundwork for an understanding of catalyst action was, however, laid in the early years of the twentieth century, when chemistry began to draw upon the findings of the physicists to understand the whole business of chemical combination in terms of complex electrical forces inside atoms.

III. The Physics Underlying Chemistry

The language of science is full of paradoxes and ironies, arising from the fact that a term adopted in one context comes to find wider and wider application as knowledge grows, until instances occur where its scientific usage can be almost the opposite of the common-sense usage from which it was originally derived. For example, the modern scientist would deny the name 'crystal' to a fortune-teller's crystal ball or 'finest crystal' glassware, and even to the pendants on chandeliers with the same kind of shape as sugar crystals, yet would describe a formless lump of metal as crystalline and a nylon fibre as partially crystalline. Non-scientists coming upon this kind of thing often feel it is linguistic insensitivity carried to the point of perver-sity, but in fact it is simply the normal process of language-develop-ment taking place in a situation where the growth of experience is far faster than in most ordinary life-situations.

Thus the term 'crystalline' has come to have a special usage in science because it began to dawn on chemists around the beginning of our century that the regular external shape of natural crystals of substances like sugar, salt, quartz, alum, or copper sulphate was the outward and visible sign of an inner regularity of structure. In particular Sir William Bragg (1862–1942) and his son Laurence (later Sir Laurence) showed that the special effects obtained when X-rays are photographed after passing through a crystal could be explained only by recognizing that in a crystal the molecules are arranged in rows and columns in an absolutely regular fashion, so that the pattern of the atoms in each molecule is repeated regularly again and again like the pattern in a wallpaper (only in all three dimensions, not just in two), whereas in a non-crystalline material the molecules lie against each other in a merely higgledy-piggledy fashion. The Braggs went on to show how X-ray photographs of crystals of different substances could be interpreted so as to elucidate precisely how the atoms are arranged in each substance's molecules, even to the point of determining exactly the immensely small dis-tance (of the order of 0·00000001 centimetres) between the various atoms in each molecule, and this has proved a tool of such immense importance to chemical analysis that this remarkable father and son were awarded a Nobel Prize. Full use could not be made of their method until after the Second World War, when electronic com-puters became available to perform the enormous amount of com-plicated calculation necessary for the interpretation of the X-ray photographs, but since then it has helped to elucidate the chemical structure of substances like proteins and the nucleic acids which govern heredity, whose complexity puts them far beyond the reach of ordinary chemical methods of analysis. Meanwhile, it has become clear that glass does not have the regular structure of inter-molecular arrangement which scientists now regard as the defining characteristic of crystalline materials, so that the 'crystalline' character of certain kinds of glass is a purely artificial outward appearance, whereas metals do have it even when they are in formless masses, as do certain plastics.

One incidental effect of the Braggs' work was to underline the growing recognition among organic chemists that chemical structures written down on paper can sometimes be misleading because they are only two-dimensional, whereas molecules are three-dimensional objects. As long ago as the 1870s the Dutch chemist Jacobus van't Hoff (1852–1911) and the Alsacian Joseph le Bel (1847–1930) had independently put forward this notion to explain the already-observed fact that certain compounds that appear on paper to have the same chemical structure are nevertheless different in subtle ways; sometimes the differences are scarcely detectable in the ordinary laboratory except from certain optical properties of solutions of the compounds, but often these otherwise abstruse differences are accompanied by enormous differences in biological action. Van't Hoff and le Bel put forward the thesis that such differences were attributable to differences in the total three-dimensional shape of the molecules, and they suggested that a carbon atom should be envisaged as putting out its four 'valency-arms' in a symmetrical fashion in space, so that methane, for example, would have the shape of a regular tetrahedron with the carbon atom at the middle and the four hydrogens at the corners:

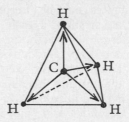

Methane, of course, is completely symmetrical, but if some of the hydrogen atoms are replaced by other groups a non-symmetrical shape is created, and if three different groups are put in then the three-dimensional model shows that two quite different versions of the resulting compound are possible, one the mirror image of the other:

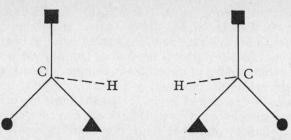

This particular trick was carried out in Britain in the early years of the twentieth century by W. J. Pope (1870–1939) and John Read (1884–1963), whose extensive researches helped to put the science of *stereo-chemistry* on a firm basis. They and other workers recognized that in very complicated molecules the differences in total three-dimensional shape might be vital in relation to biological action because the molecules were acting in the biological system by something like a lock-and-key mechanism, and this idea, now generally accepted throughout biochemistry, was given wide publicity with theological overtones in Dorothy L. Sayers's detective story *The Documents in the Case.*

The Braggs' work also, however, pointed in the opposite direction, namely towards the necessity for understanding not just the way atoms combine in spatial arrangements but also what they are like inside themselves. The behaviour of X-rays when sent through crystals is just one of many facts that made it impossible for chemists to go on thinking of atoms as simple solid lumps, for why *should* atoms interfere with X-rays? Another phenomenon which pointed in the same direction was that of radioactivity, investigated at the turn of the century by Marie Curie (1867–1934), who discovered that those unusual elements which happen to emit radiation will, as the result of this emission, turn into other elements in apparent defiance of the laws of chemistry (as when radium decays into lead without giving off anything except radiation). The following-up of facts like these in the early years of our century put the science of chemistry on an entirely new footing, but at the same time gave rise to one of the most remarkable of all anomalies of scientific language, the fact that the term 'atom', which derives from the Greek word meaning 'indivisible', is nowadays commonly used in the context of 'atom-smashing'.

This story is normally told in the context of the science of physics, and its great names are almost all British, notably Lord Rutherford

(1871–1937), Frederick Soddy (1877–1956), Sir William Ramsay (1852–1916), Charles Barkla (1877–1944), and Henry Moseley (1887–1915), but one of the most notable names of all is that of the Danish physicist Niels Bohr (1885–1962). Out of their work came the modern conception of the atom as a complex dynamic electrical system, something like a system of planets in spite of being only billionths of a centimetre across, a system consisting of a heavy nucleus of particles carrying a positive electric charge, known as *protons* (together sometimes with non-charged heavy particles called *neutrons*), surrounded by much lighter negatively-charged orbiting particles called *electrons*. On this model, every element has its distinctive number of protons in the nucleus and an exactly equal number of planetary electrons, and chemical combination is essentially a matter of the interaction of different atoms' electron-orbits. The phenomenon of chemical valency can be understood in terms of the fact that electrons seem to tend to arrange themselves in definite shells around the nucleus, and the outer shells (the effective ones from the chemical point of view) react with other atoms' outer shells in different ways according to the number of electrons in them.

This model made sense of the fact, observed long before by the Russian Dmitri Mendeleeff (1834–1907), that the elements of nature seem to fall into a few groups, the elements in each group displaying different versions of basically similar chemical properties: thus there is the group of *alkali metals*, all of valency one, consisting of lithium which is extremely light, sodium which is very similar but rather heavier and somewhat more 'sluggish' in its chemical behaviour, potassium which is also similar but more sluggish still, and so on, while in another group, the *alkaline earth metals*, the same kind of progression occurs with elements all showing a valency of two, including the very light beryllium, the slightly heavier magnesium, the still heavier calcium, and so on. The Rutherford–Bohr model of the atom made it possible to construct a complete list of the elements in the order of the number of protons in the nucleus, ranging from hydrogen, which has just one, right through to uranium, which has ninety-two, and to recognize that the list so constructed falls naturally into groups rather like the octaves of a musical scale. Thus the eight elements ranging from lithium with three protons, through beryllium with four, boron with five, carbon with six, nitrogen with seven, oxygen with eight, fluorine with nine, to neon with ten, are exactly matched in valencies and other chemical characteristics by the next group, sodium (11)

IA	IIA	IIIA	IVA	VA	VIA	VIIA	VIII			IB	IIB	IIIB	IVB	VB	VIB	VIIB	
1 H																	2 He
3 Li	4 Be											5 B	6 C	7 N	8 O	9 F	10 Ne
11 Na	12 Mg											13 Al	14 Si	15 P	16 S	17 Cl	18 Ar
19 K	20 Ca	21 Sc	22 Ti	23 V	24 Cr	25 Mn	26 Fe	27 Co	28 Ni	29 Cu	30 Zn	31 Ga	32 Ge	33 As	34 Se	35 Br	36 Kr
37 Rb	38 Sr	39 Y	40 Zr	41 Nb	42 Mo	43 Tc	44 Ru	45 Rh	46 Pd	47 Ag	48 Cd	49 In	50 Sn	51 Sb	52 Te	53 I	54 Xe
55 Cs	56 Ba	57 La	72 Hf	73 Ta	74 W	75 Re	76 Os	77 Ir	78 Pt	79 Au	80 Hg	81 Tl	82 Pb	83 Bi	84 Po	85 At	86 Rn
87 Fr	88 Ra	89 Ac															

IIIA

58 Ce	59 Pr	60 Nd	61 Pm	62 Sm	63 Eu	64 Gd	65 Tb	66 Dy	67 Ho	68 Er	69 Tm	70 Yb	71 Lu
90 Th	91 Pa	92 U	93 Np	94 Pu	95 Am	96 Cm	97 Bk	98 Cf	99 Es	100 Fm	101 Md	102 No	103

The periodic classification of the elements. The numbers in the boxes indicate the number of protons in the nuclei of the atoms of the element. Arranged in the order of these 'atomic numbers', the elements fall into 'octaves', the first two, hydrogen and helium, are odd. Then come two 'octaves' of eight elements each, then two of eighteen. The roman numerals indicate the 'groups' of elements with similar properties, like notes exactly one or more octaves apart on a piano.

which is like lithium, magnesium (12) which is like beryllium, aluminium (13) which is like boron, silicon (14) which is like a much less versatile carbon, phosphorus (15) which is in many ways like nitrogen, sulphur (16) which has similar valencies to oxygen, chlorine (17) which is like a slightly more sluggish fluorine, and argon, which like neon is a rare gas found in air and has almost no chemical reactivity at all. Things get more complicated after that, with 'octaves' of eighteen rather than eight, and the two lightest elements of all, hydrogen itself and the chemically inert gas helium (with two protons), form a kind of two-member octave on their own, but nevertheless the overall 'periodic classification of the elements' (p. 339) makes complete sense in the light of modern atomic physics.

This is not the only systematization made possible by the new view of the atom, however. It also becomes possible to understand such divers phenomena as colour, the chemical reactivity of different elements and compounds, and the control of chemical reactions by catalysts, all in terms of the dynamics of electron shells as they vibrate and interact. Such vibration can take place at many different frequencies, but every atom or molecule has several characteristic vibration-frequencies, and these correspond to the frequencies of the light-waves which are emitted by a glowing material or absorbed out of white light when it falls on a material. Hence it is possible not only to account for the colour-characteristics of a material but also to use them for identifying substances without chemical analysis: this is the technique of *spectroscopy*, originally invented by Sir Isaac Newton in the seventeenth century but systematically developed only towards the end of the nineteenth and at the beginning of the twentieth, its most triumphant vindication being the discovery by Lord Rayleigh (1842–1919) and others of the existence of tiny traces of hitherto unknown elements as betrayed by some unusual wavelengths of light emitted from glowing materials, including air. The technique could be used not only with visible light but also with other kinds of radiation whose existence can be detected only by instruments, including ultra-violet rays, infra-red rays, and X-rays.

Along the same lines, the chemical reactivity of materials came to be understood in terms of the behaviour of the electron shells of atoms and of the combined shells that are formed when groups of atoms hold together in a molecule: a particularly notable name in this field just before the First World War was the American chemist Gilbert Newton Lewis (1875–1946). It then became possible to understand catalysis in terms of the way in which certain materials (mostly materials involving metals) have particular configurations of electrons on their surfaces that will draw passing molecules of other substances together in ways that sensitize them to react with one another.

Still further phenomena that began to make new and more systematic sense in terms of the new 'physical chemistry' in these years were the special effects that take place at interfaces between solids and fluids, and the chemical effects of electric current. The stories of these developments are more properly told in relation to the even more dramatic developments of chemical science in the inter-war years, however, when revolutionary new discoveries began to make the earlier 'miracle of chemistry' seem rather small beer.

FOR FURTHER READING

See the bibliography following chapter 10, at p. 357.

10

Biology

C. H. WADDINGTON

I

Any attempt to trace the formation of the characteristic twentieth-century outlook on biology must inevitably be to some extent subjective. We are not far enough removed from the currents of thought which we shall have to discuss to see them in the perspective in which they are likely to appear to historians of the next century. Probably most people will agree that there has been some sort of revolution in biology during this century, but this revolution only gathered momentum rather slowly during the first few decades and is still in progress now when the century has run two-thirds of its course. An evaluation of the changes that have been going on must depend to some extent on an opinion about the direction the revolution will finally take. My discussion of the immediate past will, therefore, be coloured by my anticipations of what I think the near future is likely to hold in store. It is quite convenient to divide the period we have to deal with into three roughly equal sections, lasting about a quarter of a century each. It is the first of these that will be the subject of the present essay. It was essentially a period in which the late-nineteenth-century developments in biology became consolidated, while at the same time some of the characteristic features of twentieth-century biology made their first tentative appearances on the scene. The dominating aspects of biology, carrying on the traditions of the previous century, were classical biochemistry and physiology, while the newcomers destined to take the centre of the stage at a later period were genetics and causal embryology.

By the end of the nineteenth century the great excitement in biology which had been stimulated by the theory of evolution propounded by Darwin in *The Origin of Species* had to a large extent died down. The orthodox content of biology, exemplified by the courses given in university departments of zoology and botany, was indeed still dominated by a comparative anatomy firmly based on evolutionary principles. A typical biological textbook consisted largely of descriptions of the morphology of different groups of plants and animals and a discussion of the ways in which these morphologies illustrated evolutionary relations. Discussions of the mechanisms by which evolution is brought about were, however, somewhat in abeyance. The great lacuna in Darwin's theory—the lack of any understanding of heredity—had not yet been filled. There was no very convincing way to get round the difficulty, first raised by Fleem Jenkins, that the crossing of variant individuals in a population would over the generations lead to the disappearance of variation, and the production of a population so uniform that there would be nothing left for natural selection to work on. Darwin attempted to deal with this by finding some process which would continually engender new variation to replace that which had been smoothed out of existence by cross-breeding. He was for a time tempted to find such a source of new variation in the Lamarckian process, by which the varying environment would itself produce genetic variations, capable of being passed on to later generations. In the later years of the nineteenth century similar ideas were also vigorously propagated by a very effective writer, who does not quite rank as a professional scientist, namely Samuel Butler. His book on evolution, *Luck or Cunning*, has something of the character of a production by an *enfant terrible*. It was one of the influences which made many serious biologists feel that the problem of evolutionary mechanisms was a controversial and slightly disreputable subject which it would be as well to keep clear of; but the book also raised questions concerning the relevance of animal behaviour to evolutionary processes, which are only now, in the mid-twentieth century, coming back again into the forefront of biological thought.

The most definite contribution to evolutionary thinking in the closing years of the nineteenth century was the doctrine propounded by August Weismann (1834–1914), that there is an asymmetric relationship between what he called the germ and the soma. The germ, or 'germ line', is the hereditary constitution which is passed on from one generation to the next by means of the gametes. The germ controls the development of the gametes into the soma, that is to say the differentiated body of the adult organisms. The germ, therefore, influences the soma but, Weismann insisted, the soma cannot influence the germ. The soma during its development is subject to influences from the environment, which may cause the development to take unusual or even abnormal forms, but these changes in the soma have no effect on the germ which persists within the soma quite unchanged and which can be passed on unchanged to the next generation. This, of course, amounts to a radical rejection of Lamarckian ideas. Weismann produced a great deal of evidence in its support, but did not finally succeed in the perhaps impossible task of proving the negative, that alterations in the soma can never influence the germ. His ideas were widely accepted by biologists as what we have now learnt to call a dogma; that is to say, a statement that cannot be conclusively proved, but which one has every reason to believe and which one will only reject under the moxt extreme pressure of contrary evidence. Our biology of today is dominated by another rather similar doctrine—which Crick has christened the 'central dogma', which holds that DNA can affect the structure of proteins, but that the structure of a protein cannot alter the structure of DNA. This is, obviously, a restatement of Weismannism in mid-twentieth century, rather than late-nineteenth-century, terms.

The major current of biology at the beginning of the century was, however, not running in the field of evolutionary theory, but in that of the study of the workings of the living machine. Techniques of extracting chemical substances from living tissues, purifying them, and studying their behaviour and interactions *in vitro* had developed to the point where real progress could be made in understanding the chemical processes on which the phenomena of life depend. Pasteur's 'ferments' were beginning to be characterized as well-defined enzymes. It soon became apparent that these processes are of enormous complexity, and that their unravelling would take generations of hard and devoted analytical work. There were soon exciting discoveries, for instance of chemical messengers (hormones), of vitamins, of co-factors which influenced the activity of enzymes and so on. The study of these matters became the main stream of biology. If anyone had been asked in the first quarter of this century to name the most outstanding biologists, it is probable that he would have listed mainly biochemists and physiologists such as Gowland Hopkins, Keilin, Warburg, and their peers.

Even today this classical physiology and biochemistry would probably appear as the main stream of biology if one judged on sheer bulk alone. The chemical processes within a living cell are so complex and the control of them depends on such a subtle network of interaction, while their importance is so great in the practical applied fields of biology, such as medicine and agriculture, that they still call for the labour of probably the majority of biological research workers. However, one of the main characteristics of twentieth-century biology is that the most important problems, which offer the deepest insight into the nature of living systems, arise elsewhere —mainly in the area concerned with the nature of the genetic constitution, the means by which it becomes developed into the adult organism, and the means by which it undergoes evolution. In the early years of the century, however, the penetrating nature of these latter questions was not generally recognized. The orthodox view was that the best questions to ask about living systems were concerned with their methods of operation, and that genetics and development were relative sidelines. One of the classical statements of this point of view was made by the American biologist Jacques Loeb in his book *The Organism as a Whole* (1916): 'The constant synthesis, then, of specific material from simple compounds of a non-specific character is the chief feature by which living matter differs from non-living matter.' It was this point of view which led to the first revolution in the content of orthodox biology courses, at least in Britain (we shall see that things followed a rather different course in the United States, and Germany).

Just after the end of the First World War there arose a movement to renovate and bring up to date the content of zoology and botany courses at a few of the leading universities, particularly Cambridge. The 'revolutionaries' looked askance at the old emphasis on evolutionary comparative anatomy. They were anxious to change biology from a primarily descriptive to a primarily experimental subject. They founded a new *Journal of Experimental Biology*, from which a botanical section soon split off as the *New Phytologist*. The movement involved some mild flirtation with the subject of genetics, whose history we shall trace in a moment. The main emphasis, however, was on experimental studies of the physico-chemical functioning of organisms. Anatomy and morphology, in so far as they remained within the pale of respectability, were to be dealt with not in the context of evolution but as studies in the functional machinery of living things. Classical examples are the studies by J. Gray and his pupils of the anatomical mechanics involved in the swimming of fish, the crawling of snakes, the flight of birds and insects. More central to the new thinking, however, was an interest in the chemical and physiological functioning of cells and organs, in such processes as cell division, the secretion of urine, the control of the ionic concentration of body fluids, and so on. The classical statements of this point of view are perhaps J. Gray's *Experimental Cytology* (1931) and Lancelot Hogben's *The Nature of Living Matter* (1930).

II

Although the study of metabolism and physiological functioning held the centre of the biological stage during the first quarter of this century, those years also saw the birth and rapid growth to maturity of a branch of biology which in later years was to appear of even more profound importance. This was the science of heredity, for which Bateson coined the name genetics in 1906. Its early history is a most romantic one; born in what one must consider the almost disreputable periphery of the biological world, its meteoric 'rags to riches' rise to the centre of the biological stage was attended by perhaps more than its fair share of turmoil and barely respectable controversy.

At the end of the last century questions of biological inheritance were very peripheral indeed to the academically-accepted biology of the time. They tended to be left in the hands of such semi-academic hangers-on of the biological world as professional breeders of new agricultural and horticultural varieties of plants. One of the few students of such matters who was fully accepted by the respectable academic world was Sir Francis Galton (1822–1911), who dealt with questions of inheritance in the more aristocratic subject-matter of race horses, hounds, and the British aristocracy themselves. He used primarily statistical or biometrical methods, and was interested mainly, although not exclusively, in the inheritance of characteristics such as height, weight, coat colour, etc., which can be measured on a continuous or quasi-continuous scale. He propounded laws, which were mainly empirical with little basis in any theoretical model, by which one could use the statistics of such measurements among a group of ancestral individuals to deduce what would be the distribution of the measured character among a population of offspring. These biometrical laws of continuous variation formed the science of heredity of the time, as it was understood in orthodox academic circles.

The birth of a new outlook took place, however, among the practical plant breeders, many of whom were somewhat marginally connected with academic science. The time of the birth can be dated with extraordinary precision to the month of April 1900. It consisted of the independent discovery by three different plant breeders of the Mendelian 3:1 ratio of distinct types in the offspring from a crossing experiment, and the simultaneous discovery that Mendel had in 1865 (paper published in 1866) obtained the same experimental results and also provided an explanation for them.

It is salutary in these days, when we pride ourselves on the speed of communications of modern society, to realize how fast things moved in that month at the beginning of the century. On 26 March the Dutch botanist Hugo de Vries (1848–1935), who had been making hybridization experiments with the evening primrose *Oenothera*, made a preliminary report on his results in which he quoted several examples of segregation into a 3:1 ratio. A few days before a friend had sent him a reprint of Mendel's paper; this is not referred to in de Vries's preliminary account of the 26 March, but is fully acknowledged in a longer report on this work published on 25 April. Meanwhile Karl Correns, a German botanist, had been studying a number of peculiar phenomena reported to occur in connection with fertilization (e.g. effects of pollen on the fruit, as opposed to the embryo, or of the semen of a cock on the size and shape of the hen's eggs). His experiments had also involved considerable hybridization, in this case with peas. He had discovered a 3:1 ratio, and he describes how sometime in October 1899, the explanation of this dawned on him suddenly, 'like lightning', after a sleepless night. While he was preparing his results for publication he came across Mendel's paper and realized that his discovery had been made previously. On 21 April 1900, when his paper was almost ready, he received a reprint of de Vries's first publication. Although Mendel was not mentioned in this, it led Correns to speed up the submission of his own material, which he published under a title referring to Mendel's rule on the behaviour of the progenies of hybrids. He presented this to the German Botanical Society on 27 April, and it was published in the May issue of their journal. The third of the co-discoverers was the Austrian Erich Tschermak. He had been working in a commercial seed farm and also in a friend's garden. He discovered the 3:1 ratio (also in peas) in the autumn of 1899, and incorporated the result in a thesis submitted for a postgraduate degree on 17 January 1900. Before this was actually published he came across both de Vries's and Correns's papers. He was able to get his own manuscript back to insert references to these before it was printed, and he prepared an abstract which appeared in the June number of the journal of the German Botanical Society. How one wishes that present-day editors could emulate these feats of rapid publication!

There was no one in Britain who actually assisted at the parturition of genetics, but there was someone who was very ready for it when it arrived, and who was destined to play one of the most important roles in its early development. This was William Bateson

(1861–1926), a lecturer in zoology at Cambridge. He had for some years been studying as many examples of natural variation as he could lay hands on. He was moved by a feeling that evolution is the most important topic in the whole of biology, and that the nature of variation is a key factor in its consideration. He had been impressed by the number of cases in which variation within a population is not distributed over a continuous range, but takes the form of the appearance of definite 'sports' or 'mutations', which have a characteristic form distinctly different from the average of the species. In 1894 he published a large monograph under the title 'Materials for the Study of Variation, treated with a special regard to discontinuity in *The Origin of Species*'; and he continued to argue that the phenomena of heredity involve discontinuities which were not accounted for by the biometrical theories of continuous variation.

The most active champion of the biometricians at that time was W. F. R. Weldon (1860–1906), and controversy between him and Bateson began almost immediately after the publication of Bateson's book. By the spring of 1900 Bateson was already deeply involved in experiments on hybridization. He had not quite reached the 3:1 segregation—it was due to appear in his garden in about a year's time. In May 1900, he travelled by train from Cambridge to London to read a paper to the Royal Horticultural Society on his most recent experiments. Like so many of us he used the train journey to catch up with the accumulated reprints. Among these was Mendel's original paper of 1866, which had only just come to his notice. He immediately saw its importance and reformulated his whole lecture to incorporate Mendel's results. He then became Mendel's first and most enthusiastic advocate in the English-speaking world.

For the first two decades of the century Bateson was in fact the leading geneticist in the world. The three original rediscoverers of Mendel receded from the limelight. De Vries was singularly unlucky in his choice of experimental material; the evening primroses of the genus *Oenothera* have one of the most extraordinary and deceptive genetic systems known, with chromosomes that have suffered extensive reciprocal translocations, with the result that characters follow hereditary rules totally unlike those in more normally constituted organisms. Poor de Vries was led on an outlandish wild goose chase by the eccentricities of this peculiar genus, which were not cleared up until the early thirties. Correns continued to study interesting but rather special phenomena in plant genetics, such as the inheritance of variegation, which led him out of the central development of genetics and towards notions about non-chromosomal inheritance, which are only in the last few years coming back into prominence. Tschermak was too gentle a character, and too much on the periphery of the European scientific world, to make any very great impact on the scene in general. Bateson was left, therefore, as the main champion of the science of genetics. The word 'champion' is used advisedly. Bateson had not only to name the science, he had to fight a very bitter and tough battle on its behalf.

By 1900 Francis Galton, the founder of the biometrical school, had largely transferred his interests to the genetic improvement of the human population, a subject which still goes under the name 'eugenics', which he coined for it. The leaders of the biometricians were Weldon and Karl Pearson (1857–1936). They regarded Bateson's insistence on the importance of discontinuity in heredity as an upstart challenge to their academic pre-eminence. Bateson's acceptance of Mendelism infuriated them, since they believed that a Mendelian system of heredity was quite incompatible with the results of their studies on continuous variation. In this they were actually completely mistaken. As early as 1902, the statistician George Udny Yule (1871–1951), who was, like Bateson, a Fellow of St. John's College, Cambridge, showed that if a character were affected simultaneously by many Mendelian factors, its biometrical behaviour in a population would be exactly that which the biometricians had described. Unfortunately almost no attention was paid to this paper. Even Bateson made little reference to it, since his own interests were in phenomena in which discontinuity comes more obviously to the surface. He, therefore, replied with vigour to the polemic against Mendelian genetics which Weldon and Pearson began publishing in 1901. It was one of the most spectacular, bitter, and in many ways most disgraceful, battles in the history of biology. Weldon and Pearson were the senior men in the more established academic posts. They had founded and controlled the journal *Biometrika* in which they could publish their views. Somewhat later in the height of the battle they produced a journal with the revealing title *Questions of the Day and of the Fray*. Bateson had some of his experimental material printed in the *Report* of the Evolution Committee of the Royal Society, of which he was secretary, but this reached a very restricted public, and in the main he had to rely on the public scientific journals. Twice, however, the editor of *Nature* decided to terminate a series of controversial exchanges between Weldon and Bateson, and in both instances he brought the exchange to a close by refusing to print the latest contribution by

Bateson. In both instances this editorial support for the academic establishment was wrong; Bateson had been right and Weldon mistaken.

This battle cannot quite be dismissed as being of local interest only, since during the first years of the century Britain was probably the most productive source of new advances in genetics, particularly from the John Innes Horticultural Institution of which Bateson became Director in 1910. Genetics was, however, steadily growing in other countries also, and it was perhaps largely as a result of this unfortunate quarrel that in the second quarter of the twentieth century the lead definitely passed out of British hands into those of Germany and particularly America. For although Weldon died in 1906 the controversial atmosphere he had engendered had long-lasting effects. I have mentioned above the reconciliation in 1902 by Udny Yule of the facts of continuous variation with the theories of Mendel. For some years thereafter the subject was pursued mainly outside Great Britain, particularly by practical plant breeders such as Nilsson-Ehle, working on wheat in Scandinavia, and East and Emerson, working on maize in the United States. When an eminent British statistician, of the generation succeeding that of Karl Pearson, returned to the subject in 1918 he met with a very cold reception. In that year R. A. Fisher (1890–1962), submitted to the Royal Society of London a paper whose aim was to reconcile Mendelism with Galton's Laws of Inheritance. Fisher carried this out much more thoroughly, and with a much deeper analysis, than that provided in 1902 by Udny Yule, to whom Fisher does not refer. Nevertheless the endeavour was still considered too unorthodox to be tolerated by the citadel of the scientific establishment; the paper was rejected by the Royal Society of London, and later saw the light of day under the auspices of the more enlightened if less prestigious Royal Society of Edinburgh. Again, as I shall argue in discussing developments in later periods, it was the crusading zeal on behalf of the gene forced on the early Mendelians of England which led them to adopt a die-hard attitude of 'the gene and nothing but the gene', which paid off in the very early years, but became a considerable hindrance later.

In the closing years of the first decade of the century an event took place which was of far greater importance for the development of genetics than the noisy battle carried on in England between the Mendelians and the biometricians. This was the adoption by T. H. Morgan (1866–1945) of Columbia University, New York, of an experimental animal much more suited to genetic studies than anything that had been employed before. Morgan's colleague Castle was using, for physiological experiments not connected with genetics, a small, very fast-breeding fly, the fruit fly *Drosophila melanogaster*. Morgan realized that, because of its ease of handling in the laboratory and its rapid life-cycle and large number of offspring, the fruit fly would make ideal material for studying hereditary characters. As soon as they were looked for, abnormal mutant forms were discovered, and proved to follow the normal rules of Mendelian inheritance which were by that time becoming accepted as universally valid. Very soon so many mutant forms had been found, and their inheritance followed through so many generations, that the next major step forward could be taken—that of locating the Mendelian factors on material bodies visible in the cell. The great German cytologists at the end of the nineteenth century, such as Boveri and Weismann, had drawn attention to the complicated manoeuvres undergone by the chromosomes in the nucleus during the process of cell division, and had argued that their behaviour would make sense if they could be accepted as the carriers of the germ plasm which Weismann had distinguished from the soma.

At that time the behaviour of the chromosomes during gametogenesis and fertilization was still not fully understood. Very soon after the rediscovery of Mendelism, however, this subject was looked into in more detail. In 1902 the American McClung suggested that what were then known as 'accessory' chromosomes might act as sex determinants—they are of course now known as sex chromosomes. In the same year E. B. Wilson argued in a more general way that the chromosomes carry hereditary factors, and a detailed exposition of just how they might be fitted to do so was provided in the following year by another American, W. S. Sutton, at that time a young postgraduate student. These ideas were, however, at first not very generally accepted. Bateson, for instance, argued that there are not enough chromosomes to go round, since there was good reason to believe there are very many more hereditary factors than there are different kinds of chromosomes. This assumes, of course, that hereditary factors carried on the same chromosome would always segregate together as a single unit. This assumption was in fact at first also made by T. H. Morgan. Soon after he began working with *Drosophila* he published, in 1910 (*American Naturalist*, XLIV. 499), a paper in which he advanced this argument against the possibility that the chromosomes might carry the Mendelian factors. However, between submitting his paper for publication and its seeing the light of day, he had carried out further experiments which had convinced him that the so-called sex-linked factors are actually carried on the sex chromosome. The results of these experiments submitted to *Science* (XXXII. 120) actually appeared in print before the paper in the *American Naturalist*—a reversal of the true temporal order. This is not only evidence of how fast things were moving in those days, but is also a nice illustration of the fact that scientific advance is not always a smooth pedestrian shuffle along a well-laid-out road.

Once convinced of the idea that the hereditary factors postulated by Mendel are carried by the material chromosomes in the cell nucleus, Morgan and his group pursued the implications with vigour. The mention of 'his group' is not at all a mere politeness. Morgan was soon joined by perhaps the most brilliant trio of post-graduate students that any professor could hope for; A. H. Sturtevant (1892–1970), C. B. Bridges (1889–1938), and H. J. Muller (1890–1967). All three were indefatigable and precise experimentalists. All three were full of ideas, and all three extremely critical of the others' ideas and even of their own. Bridges was perhaps pre-eminent as an observer, Sturtevant as an experimentalist, and Muller as an inexhaustible source of new concepts and ideas.

The first triumph for Morgan and his group was to develop the theory that Mendelian factors—for which they coined the name 'gene'—which lie on the same chromosome, do not remain always together in heredity, but may undergo recombination; and that the frequency of this recombination is proportional to the distance which separates the genes. If this were so, estimates of the frequency of recombination between genes would make it possible to ascertain their relative positions along the length of a given chromosome. The Morgan group showed that all the predictions of this theory are fulfilled in practice. By the end of our period they had fully established the chromosome theory of heredity, including the linear order of the genes, and had made quite detailed maps of the chromosome of *Drosophila*. Bateson remained a sceptic for a considerable time. He clung as long as he could to the view that the Mendelian 'factor' should be regarded as an abstract logical entity, known only from the manner in which it behaves in the relations governing hereditary transmission between generations. But in 1921 he spent some days visiting Morgan at Columbia and was finally convinced that the 'factor' is a material particle, with a definable location. The publication of a monograph on *The Genetics of Drosophila* by Morgan, Bridges, and Sturtevant in 1925, and Morgan's *The Theory of the Gene* in 1928, showed that by the end of the first quarter-century the study of the passage of hereditary units from one generation to the next had been built up to an extensive, imposing, and unassailable edifice.

Considerably less progress had been made in understanding how these genetic factors operate. Morgan and Muller in particular were interested in this topic, but probably the most significant contributions in the first years of genetics were from the German geneticist, Richard Goldschmidt (b 1878). We shall return to this topic in discussing later periods, in which it attained much greater importance. Here it is only worth mentioning that Goldschmidt realized one of the main facts; namely, that genes act by influencing the enzymes on which the operations of the living system depend. He made, however, the mistake of supposing that genes always act by controlling simply the quantity, but not the kind, of enzymes. However, his book *Die physiologische Theorie der Vererbung* of 1927 is an indication that this aspect of genetics also had been launched by that time.

III

We must now turn to another field in which the endeavours of the first quarter of this century laid the foundations for what has since become a central issue in the mature twentieth-century outlook. This is the topic which in the early days was widely referred to as *Entwicklungsmechanik*, the name used in Germany, which can be regarded as the subject's original home ground. This was translated as 'developmental physiology' or 'experimental embryology'. Since its basic connection with genetics was established towards the end of the second quarter-century, it has gradually become customary to refer to it by the shorter title of epigenetics, a word which recalls the Aristotelian doctrine that during development new entities put in an appearance (a theory contrasted with the alternative, pre-formationism, which supposed that at the very beginning of development everything that will ever appear is already represented by some sort of germ).

In the later parts of the nineteenth century, several European (mainly German) biologists emphasized the importance of attaining some causal understanding of the processes of development. The most important of them was His, followed by Roux and Driesch. The mechanisms they discussed were perforce largely hypothetical, since it proved extraordinarily difficult to perform experiments which actually revealed any causal interactions. The experimental results obtained by the early authors remained for the most part only phenomenological. That is to say, they brought certain phenomena into the light of day, without giving much clue as to the causal processes by which they were brought about. For instance, both Driesch and Roux carried out experiments in which one of the first two blastomeres into which the fertilized egg cleaves is removed or killed. When Roux did this with a frog's egg, the remaining blastomere developed into a half embryo: exactly what it would have developed into if the experiment had never been conducted. It was not obvious that this told one anything one did not know already. Again, when Driesch performed a similar experiment with a sea-urchin egg, each half of the egg developed into a complete larva. This was a surprising new phenomenon, but again the bare fact presents a bland face which offers no hint as to how it is to be explained.

In the first few years of the new century there was a good deal of activity in this field, but not very much progress. There was a very flourishing American school of students of the early development of invertebrate eggs. Led by E. G. Conklin, they described in detail the 'cell lineages' through which the various parts of the cleaving egg come to form various organs of the larva. Further and more importantly, Conklin and his students described various identifiable regions of cytoplasm within the fertilized egg, which they showed to be necessary for the development of particular organs and tissues. There was little understanding of how these 'ooplasms' acted, or indeed of what were the really important operative characteristics of the regions, which were distinguishable by colour, or other superficial properties, under the microscope. However, one basically important insight was obtained. Boycott and Diver in Britain had studied the genetics of a snail, *Limnea peregra*, which exists in two different forms, one of which coils in a left-handed, and the other in a right-handed, spiral. They showed that these two topologically distinct forms could be recognized in the very early cleavage stages, and that the property almost certainly depends on the distribution of ooplasmic regions within the egg at the time of fertilization. Boycott and Diver found the inheritance very puzzling; but Sturtevant pointed out in 1933 that their results were easily interpretable, if one supposed that the direction of coiling depends on the structure of the egg cell from which an individual develops, and that this structure in turn is determined, not by the genes contained in that fertilized egg, but rather by the

genes in the maternal ovary in which the egg grew to maturity. This
case was taken by Morgan as conclusive evidence for the general
proposition, that the spatial arrangement of ooplasms within an egg
cell is in the last resort dependent on genes, namely the genes in the
maternal organism, and is not, as the opponents of genetics would
like to argue, an independent phenomenon which has to be added to
genetics before one obtains a full account of the basic factors on
which development depends.

Two other more isolated achievements of the time should be
mentioned. In 1907, Ross Harrison (1870–1960) in America succeeded for the first time in keeping isolated cells from higher
organisms alive outside the body, by cultivating them in a drop of
lymph. The technique was soon improved, for instance by Burrows,
and by Carrel, who used as a medium a drop of blood plasma clotted
by the addition of a saline extract of an embryo. With this technique
they succeeded in obtaining continuous growth and division of many
kinds of cells over indefinitely long periods—the technique of tissue
culture had been born. In itself, of course, it is not an experiment,
in the sense that it does not provide an answer to any particular
question. It is rather a technique, which makes it possible to carry
out further experiments if one can formulate them. Harrison used
the method to permit him to make certain important observations;
for instance, that the nerve processes grow out from the central
nerve cell, rather than originating elsewhere and growing in to
join it.

Harrison also made many experimental studies on embryos.
particularly on the questions of polarity. If one takes an early limb
bud, or ear vesicle, from an embryo and replaces it after rotation in
various planes, for instance so as to bring the original anterior end
towards the posterior, will the organ that develops exhibit the
polarity of the embryo as a whole, or only that of the rudiment that
has been rotated? His experiments revealed a wealth of phenomena;
for instance, of times before which the rotation was ineffective,
while if carried out later the resulting organ exhibited an abnormal
polarity corresponding to the rotation imposed on it. They did not,
however, provoke any questions about the possible causal sequences
that might be involved: all one could say was that up to a certain
stage the polarity of the rudiment was not fixed and after this stage
it was fixed. It was of considerable importance for the later development of biology that, under the influence of Conklin and Ross
Harrison, truly causal thinking almost dropped out of fashion
among Americans interested in development; T. H. Morgan kept

it alive, but he was too immersed in genetics to have much effect on the general climate of thought in American developmental biology.

Another, even more isolated piece of work which was, however, of great importance for the formation of the modern outlook in biology in later periods was the production by D'Arcy Thompson (1860–1948) of his book *On Growth and Form* (1917). In this he gave a very novel approach to the problems of morphology. He showed that the shapes of cells, and of some simple animals and plants, often closely resemble those of physical entities and can be described by the same mathematical symbolism. He was not so much concerned to argue that the organic and inorganic forms have been produced by the same physical processes. Indeed, when he compared the shape of a polyp with that of the splash formed when a drop falls into a pool of water, it is obvious that the physical forces involved are not the same, or even very similar. What is the same, however, is the mathematical description of the form. D'Arcy Thompson's work was important not for revealing new understanding about the processes which bring organic form into being, but rather for the more general point of the importance and possibility of applying mathematical treatment to types of biological processes which previously had been discussed only by common sense methods. His work did not have any very immediate consequences, but remained as a foundation which was taken up many years later.

The main centre of progress in developmental biology in the first quarter of the century was in Germany. The tradition of an experimental analysis of developmental processes had been firmly laid by authors such as Roux and Boveri. Around the turn of this century Hans Spemann (1869–1941) began to study the amphibian embryo. His great achievement was to formulate definite questions about causal mechanisms in terms of interactions between different parts of the developing system. The first success was to show that the development of the lens depends on an interaction between the eyecup, which grows out from the brain, and the overlying ectoderm. By transplanting the eyecup into other positions, it was shown that when it comes into contact with an ectoderm of a suitable age it may cause that ectoderm to develop into a lens, even though it would have developed in quite a different way if the contact had not been established. The eyecup was therefore said to 'induce' the lens.

By the end of the first quarter-century Spemann and his pupil Hilde Mangold had been able to generalize this concept, showing that it applies also to the first primary phase of differentiation of the amphibian egg, that in which the main axial organs (neural system, notochord, somites, etc.) make their appearance. They showed conclusively that the mesoderm can induce the appearance of the axial organs (neural plate) in any ectoderm of suitable age, even though this ectoderm would never have formed such an organ in the normal course of development. The importance of this result was that it provided the first experimentally-controllable causal process identified in the study of development. By placing an inducer into a suitable position in an embryo, one can control the way in which the surrounding tissues develop. This was the door that opened the way to the whole study of control processes in development.

Spemann himself, in the first phases of his work, defined his causal entities only in operational terms, without providing anything much in the way of a conceptual model as to how they worked. His inducers or 'organizers' were defined as those pieces of tissue which when transplanted into certain given situations produce certain given results, these results being described in terms of the histological and morphological characteristics of the organs produced. It was not until the second quarter-century that any serious attempts were made to analyse the causal sequences in more analytical terms, e.g. those of biochemistry or genetics.

FOR FURTHER READING: SCIENCE

There are an enormous number of books covering the sciences, and selection is not easy. Treatment of the sciences, of course, cannot be properly limited to the 1900–18 period.

The Origins and Growth of Physical Science, ed. D. L. Hurd and J. J. Kipling (1964), collects together a series of biographical essays of scientists in physics and chemistry. Both the man and his work are explored in detail; links between science and other human activities are made clear. Of especial interest are extracts from the original writings of the scientists themselves.

H. Margenau, *The Nature of Physical Reality* (New York, 1949), is a wide-ranging and full account of the fundamental background to physical theory. It is very readable and uses mathematics extremely sparingly. The fact that mathematics is used at all is a reflection of the necessity of such techniques in scientific discussion. M. Planck, *A Survey of Physics* (1925), is a collection of essays by one of the founders of modern physics. They make very penetrating reading. In P. W. Bridgman, *The Nature of Physical Theory* (Princeton, 1936), the use of mathematical models is explained and emphasis is placed on the logic of physical theory with relativity and wave mechanics as specific examples. J. H. Poincaré,

Science and Hypothesis (1905), is a most instructive contribution to the creative processes behind physical theory and explores thoroughly the links between theory and experiment. It is pre-quantum theory but Poincaré treats timeless problems in science in a non-mathematical way. It is interesting to see the essential features of relativity developing before the theory had been formally prescribed and solved. The exposition of the arguments is particularly clear. In M. Born, *Experiment and Theory in Physics* (Cambridge, 1943), the quantum aspects of physical science are used as a means of showing the balance between experiment and theory. This analysis is by one of the founders of quantum theory. B. Hoffmann, *The Strange Story of the Quantum* (1947), is an account, with the very minimum of mathematics, of the questions and answers, dating from about the year 1800, that have led to the modern quantum theory. E. Zimmer, *The Revolution in Physics* (1936), also describes the development of quantum theory but is of a broadly technical (though still non-mathematical) nature. Sir James Jeans, *The Mysterious Universe* (Cambridge, 1930), explores the implications of quantum theory and relativity for our description of the Universe as a whole. This is very readable. M. Born, *The Restless Universe* (1935), views the quantum theory in various forms from sub-atomic particles to the Universe at large.

L. S. Stebbings, *Philosophy and the Physicists* (1937), is a highly interesting attempt by a philosopher to probe carefully the philosophical background of physics. H. S. Lipson, *The Great Experiments in Physics* (Edinburgh, 1968), describes and discusses a range of the important experiments that have affected the development of physics in an historical context. Of especial importance is the personal comment of the author who is himself a well-known practising physicist. It is hard to think of a better introduction to mathematical thought and ideas than the two volumes by E. T. Bell, *Men of Mathematics* (1937). The great mathematicians are seen both at work and at play. Mathematics is the language of science and it is not possible to proceed very far in a detailed analysis of physical situations without the ability at least to follow a minimum of elementary mathematical manipulations. A general summary of this situation as it applies to physics is set down in a non-mathematical comment.

Popular and semi-popular accounts of astronomy and astrophysics are readily found on the library shelves, and it is not necessary to elaborate on these matters here except to notice the *Larousse Encyclopædia of Astronomy*. This is a very extensive and highly interesting book, containing a wealth of information very attractively set out and explained accurately in non-mathematical terms.

For advanced reading in physics the following books form a useful entry to the general field of physics. G. Joos, *Theoretical Physics* (1934), is a well-tried undergraduate survey of physical theory. P. G. Bergmann, *Basic Theories of Physics* (New York, 1949), is a very useful account by a well-known theoretician who was earlier involved particularly with the developments of the theory of relativity. A substantial survey of theoretical physics is the Pergamon Press seven-volume series by L. Landau and E. M. Lifschitz, *Theoretical Physics*.

A. Findlay, *A Hundred Years of Chemistry* (1965), provides a useful introduction. See also T. M. Lowry, *Historical Introduction to Chemistry* (1936). F. S. Taylor, *A History of Industrial Chemistry* (1957), charts the effects of new discoveries on society. Another good book on this subject is J. D. Bernal, *Science and Industry in the Nineteenth Century* (1953). B. C. Saunders and R. E. D. Clark, *Order and Chaos in the World of Atoms* (rev. ed., 1948), is a valuable descriptive textbook.

A Century of Darwin, ed. S. A. Barnett (1958) is a useful compilation, and the last chapter contains an excellent critique of evolutionary ethics. Nora Barlow has written a good book on Darwin: *Charles Darwin and the Voyage of the Beagle* (1945), and also edited *The Autobiography of Charles Darwin 1809–1882* (1958). W. Irvine, *Apes, Angels and Victorians* (1905) is a joint biography of Darwin and T. H. Huxley. H. Iltis, *Life of Mendel* (1932), is a fascinating account of this extraordinary man.

See also G. S. Carter, *A Hundred Years of Evolution* (1957), J. Huxley, *Soviet Genetics and World Science* (1949), T. H. Morgan, *The Theory of the Gene* (New Haven, Conn., 1926), and C. H. Waddington, *Science and Ethics* (1942).

11

Poetry

JOHN WAIN

I

What we know as 'modern poetry' was the invention of a brilliant generation of French poets and was born in Paris. It has also been much involved with the drama. So we may fittingly begin our story in a Paris theatre, the Théâtre de l'Œuvre, where one winter evening in 1896 the Irish poet W. B. Yeats (1865–1939) found himself staring in bewilderment at the harsh, splintering action of a strange charade called *Ubu Roi*. Its author, Alfred Jarry, was an utterly uncompromising rebel, as fierce as Rimbaud, as mocking as Corbière, and he filled his wild scenes with a desperate lyricism, an exultant savagery, foreshadowing a great deal of what we have in our time come to accept, with our curious mid-century complacency, as the 'Theatre of Cruelty'. Squabbling broke out among the audience, and the friend who had brought Yeats to the play said to him, 'There are often duels after these performances.' But Yeats, as he left the theatre, was not in a duelling mood. He was deeply discouraged and dissatisfied with himself and his achievements; he felt threatened.

Feeling bound to support the most spirited party, we have shouted for the play, but that night at the Hôtel Corneille I am very sad, for comedy, objectivity, has displayed its growing power once more. I say, 'After Stéphane Mallarmé, after Paul Verlaine, after Gustave Moreau, after Puvis de Chavannes, after our own verse, after all our subtle colour and nervous rhythm, after the faint mixed tints of Conder, what more is possible? After us the Savage God.'[1]

Yeats's insight here was perfectly accurate. For better or worse, *Ubu Roi* looked forward; the work of Yeats before the turn of the century, and of most men of his generation, looked backward. The violent, disjointed, extravagant nature of modern literature, which once led Thomas Mann to remark that in his lifetime the traditional categories of comedy and tragedy had disappeared, leaving the grotesque as the dominant literary mode, is perfectly seized by Jarry, whereas the characteristic poet of the late nineteenth century, in France or in England, drew back from the bruising contact; so that Verlaine, who died in the year that *Ubu Roi* was first performed, could say in his poem 'L'Art Poetique':

> Fuis de plus loin la Pointe assassine,
> L'Esprit cruel et le Rire impur,
> Qui font pleurer les yeux de l'Azur,
> Et tout cet ail de basse cuisine!*

For English poetry, the opening years of the nineteenth century had been a great age. In, say, 1820, when Wordsworth, Coleridge, Keats, Shelley, and Byron were all working, one could fairly say that the main current of English life was flowing through the work of English poets; that to read them was to be in contact with the national temper, to touch the 'spirit of the age': not in the journalistic sense, though there are topical elements in the work of several of these poets, but in the sense that they see the world of their time as Englishmen, in their moments of deepest perception and purest emotion, see it; that the rich, complex experience of the nation—both the accumulated experience in its bones and the immediate experience that claims its energies at that moment—is there in their work, in its rhythms, its imagery, its themes. But the nineteenth century wore on, and there was something in its air that was hostile to poets; they faltered and lost confidence, or perhaps it would be truer to say that they had the wrong kind of confidence; Tennyson and Browning, accepted as the major poets of the mid-century, were excellent writers, but they had a tendency to smother the pure flame of poetic imagination under an accumulation of detail and a fluency in moralization; to use T. S. Eliot's word, they 'ruminated'. So that by the end of the century it had become generally accepted that the poet was a minor artist; that he had a corner in those emotions that stern, practical men enjoy in their leisure hours when they are not being stern and practical: nostalgia, vague regret, dim yearning. The men of power, who actually control the world, have no objection to art as long as it ministers to their leisure; relaxed, gentle art, which spreads a mist of pleasant wistfulness over the hard outlines of experience, has always been much favoured by men of action, particularly if it transports them to a world remote from their real interests. Napoleon enjoyed Macpherson's Ossian so much that he read it over and over again; but if the Ossian poems had been set in Corsica rather than in the misty Highlands, and had contained concrete advice on how to deal with military adventurers, Napoleon

* Flee as far as possible from murderous gibe, cruel wit and impure laughter, that makes the eyes of Heaven weep, and all such garlic of the lowest kitchens!

would have thrown them aside, for all their attractive cadences and romantic magic. So, in the 1890s, English readers were enchanted by the sparse and haunting music of A. E. Housman's (1859–1936) *A Shropshire Lad*; not only the 'common reader', but the mighty of the land, adored Housman and quoted his delicately tuned verses to one another as insistently as their more leathery counterparts in mess, ward-room, and imperial outpost quoted the banjo music of Kipling. And the reason, apart from the undeniable attractiveness of the verse, was probably something to do with the pastoral nature of the subject-matter. Housman's rustics, fruit of a classical scholar's imagination and set in a landscape of the mind, live in a world of simple, violent action that has nothing in common with the world of the over-organized middle class who enjoyed reading about them.

> The sun burns on the half-mown hill,
> By now the blood has dried;
> And Maurice amongst the hay lies still
> And my knife is in his side.

By the end of the nineteenth century, England had become a fully industrialized country whose characteristic citizen lived in a large city and travelled every day to work in some huge complex enterprise in which his own part was often quite meaningless to him. His life was increasingly comfortable, but decreasingly simple and intelligible. Small wonder that he enjoyed reading about Housman's lads and chaps who suffer clear-cut individual fates like being hanged, or dying of unrequited love. And all this in a 'Shropshire' that never contrives to suggest the real Shropshire, at that time in the grip of an agricultural depression as a result of the invention of the steamship and the consequent bulk importation of cheap food from the Empire.

To talk in this strain is, of course, unfair to Housman, a poet with an exquisite sense of words who wrote many lyrics that recur to one's mind again and again. But the popularity of Housman's simplified view of life, his terse lyrics which dealt with a life so utterly remote from anything in his own experience as a Professor of Latin, is bound up with the reason for Yeats's despondency in his bedroom at the Hôtel Corneille. So is the vogue for Kipling; for all Kipling's reputation as a writer who dealt manfully with a man's experience, neither he nor the bulk of his readers were any closer to Danny Deever or Kim or Mowgli than they were to Housman's Ned and Dick. Their own lives were frustratingly complex and they liked to read about simple, usually tragic, certainties. Kipling and

Housman simplified life as drastically as Hemingway was to simplify it a generation later. Even Hardy, a poet of deeper resonance, taking account of more areas of life, appealed to the same taste in his novels. The predictable, clockwork tragedy of *Tess of the D'Urbervilles* was a satisfying blend of the small-scale (because it was about an individual) and the cosmic (because Hardy could pin the blame on 'the President of the Immortals'). In neither sphere was it at all intellectually complex.

There are a good many qualifications to be made here. Any generalization about a literary period can be proved wrong in numerous instances. Also, while poets like Housman and Kipling fit the pattern well enough, it is obvious that Hardy, in his verse, does not; and there is the strange and isolated case of Gerard Manley Hopkins, certainly a major poet. We shall revert to these poets later. But the generalization remains. The poet was tolerated, even substantially encouraged, as long as he lived in a haze of minor emotions or dealt with a pastoral world fenced off from the arena of real action. In that arena, the only writers who held their own were novelists and playwrights. Poetry had become a spare-time activity; the bustling, ambitious English of Victoria's latter years, building larger and larger systems and controlling more and more of the earth, seem to have valued it chiefly as an escape from workaday thoughts. Hence Yeats's shrinking fear of 'comedy, objectivity'. The poets of his generation, even when they inhabit Fleet Street, are instinctively poets of the cloister. Their art serves best as a vehicle for exquisite minor statements. The time was ripe for a poetic revolution; because the object of revolution in any art is to make that art into a vehicle for major statements.

The story of Yeats's life is the story of his search for a poetry that would be invulnerable to irony, capacious and strong enough to deal with the welter of discord that was modern life, indestructible even by the 'Savage God'. Yeats himself triumphantly broke out of the small pasture in which poetry had been put to graze; he evolved an art that was indeed the vehicle for major statements. Born in 1865, he formed a bridge between the first generation of modern poets (Verlaine, Corbière, Mallarmé, Hopkins were all born in the 1840s, Rimbaud in the '50s) and the second, Anglo-American generation (Ezra Pound and T. S. Eliot were born in the 1880s). His own personal struggle was parallel with, but not identical to, the struggle of his French seniors and his Anglo-American juniors. For these reasons, as well as because of his towering achievement, Yeats occupies the focal point of any account of modern poetry in

English. The story of his life and work is the cable along which its rich variety of shapes and sizes can be strung. For all his idiosyncrasies—and, as we shall see, they were many—he has the kind of centrality that makes us speak, in other connections, of 'the Age of Shakespeare' or 'the Age of Johnson'.

Yet if Johnson and Shakespeare were of provincial origin, Yeats's own background was more remote, more difficult to align with the main preoccupations of his age, than any mere provincialism could be. Ireland in the 1860s was a country with plenty of native talent but no workable tradition. The Irish language lived on only in the cottages of the west; all the business of Ireland, commercial, political, ecclesiastical, and intellectual, was conducted in English; yet no Irishman felt himself to be English in attitude or sensibility. Some nineteenth-century Irish writers had seen it as their business to produce patriotic work around which national sentiment might rally; but these writers, even the most respectable of them such as Thomas Davis, were incurably commonplace, and the effect of their vogue was to keep Ireland provincial in relation to England.

The Ireland into which Yeats was born consisted basically of three classes. There were the peasantry, brutally mulcted by their landlords, condemned to a life of poverty and with recent memories of such appalling disasters as the potato famine of the 1840s. There were the landowners, usually of Anglo-Irish Protestant stock, who had some social influence but little direct political power. And there were the Catholic middle class of the towns, hard-headed and narrow-minded, yet the only effective wielders of such power as was not wielded from England. With this middle class Yeats was born out of touch, and remained out of touch all his life. His father was an Anglo-Irish Protestant by family tradition, a painter by profession, and something of a bohemian by inclination. His mother, a Pollexfen, came of minor gentry in Sligo; she seems to have been a more purely Irish type, though 'Pollexfen' itself is a West Country English name. Yeats *père* moved his household many times, and William was educated in London or Dublin by fits and starts, with long spells at Sligo when shortage of funds made the family split up for a time.

Alien in England—where literary reputations were made—Yeats was only slightly less alien in Ireland. If he was remote from the power-holding Catholic middle class, he was not born into any relationship with the quasi-aristocratic life of the eighteenth-century country houses. The peasantry, as he met them on his grandfather's land in Sligo, were closer to him, being simple enough to talk directly to a child, and rooted enough to have a natural relationship with an employer's son. But of course there could be no close identification here either.

Yeats, in fact, was born with no real home. Wherever he went, he found himself on the fringes of life. Even in intellectual Dublin, where his father was well liked and had many acquaintances, William's place was a tangential one. Not academically inclined, he did not enter Trinity College, which had been his father's intention for him and where he might have been taught by his father's friend, the gifted and generous Edward Dowden, but went instead to the School of Art. His passion for a revival of the spirit of Ireland, for a renewed attention to Irish legend, Irish history, everything that could nourish the Irish consciousness, expressed itself in action, especially after the fall of Parnell in 1890 had disillusioned those Irishmen whose faith was in immediate practical action, and allowed a breathing-space in which the nation might lick its wounds and marshall its inward resources. Yet these years of involvement were bitter and exhausting, for Yeats found himself condemned to work with exactly that narrow and suspicious middle class which could never see Irish life, or any life, as he saw it. Looking back on these years in *The Trembling of the Veil* (1926), he regretted that the need to reject any compromise with the Unionists had made him difficult and aggressive towards the people of good family and education who might have been his friends and supporters. Later, he became finally disillusioned with the philistinism and narrowness of the people among whom he had tried to locate the new spirit of Ireland (the episode of Sir Charles Gavan Duffy, so wryly and with such brilliant reined-in humour recounted in Book II, 'Ireland After Parnell', gives the flavour of the whole bitter story).

This continual maladjustment to his surroundings was made more bitter by a deep personal disappointment. In 1888 Yeats met Maud Gonne, the daughter of an English colonel and therefore of much the same origins as himself. Miss Gonne, a statuesque and beautiful girl, was as deeply involved as Yeats with the dream of a revived Ireland, but in a more fire-eating way; she wanted action, overt and even violent. The two life-styles were at odds; Yeats tried to modify his to suit hers, but never succeeded in winning her love. Strained and embittered, he turned often to the consolations of the inner life; and the inner life, in his case, took a somewhat strange form.

If Paris, in the tumultuous person of Alfred Jarry, administered the shock that jolted Yeats from the groove of his life as a minor poet, this was emblematic of the whole situation of European poetry

at that time. Paris had witnessed the birth of the Symbolist movement in literature; it was also the European headquarters of occult
and magical studies, which at the time seemed closely entwined
with poetry and imaginative art generally. Yeats has put it on
record, in several places, that he found life unendurable without a
creed that would unite the scattered fragments of human experience
into one meaningful whole; and also that Victorian science had
rendered Christianity unconvincing to him. This scepticism towards
Christianity he may have partly acquired from his father, the painter
John Butler Yeats, who, though intended for the Church like his
father and grandfather, had become agnostic and refused to take
orders. But even without the example of his father, Yeats as a young
man in the 1880s and '90s might well have felt that Christianity had,
at any rate for the time being, exhausted its vital impulse. Materialism, especially in its frock-coated Victorian form, was equally unacceptable to him; and his solution was to seek the supernatural in
such places as it appeared to him with anything of majesty or
beauty.

The tale of Yeats's involvements with various forms of occult
study is one that continues all his life and leads the student into some
strange places. In 1885, while still living in Dublin, he formed the
Dublin Hermetic Society in association with two friends, George
Russell and Charles Johnston; they rented a small back room and
held meetings to study European magic and Eastern philosophy,
the fourth dimension, Odic force, *und so weiter*. On moving to
London in 1887, one of his first actions was to present himself with
a letter of introduction to Madame Blavatsky, the celebrated pro-
phetess of Theosophy, who had just returned from India and founded
a Blavatsky Lodge. In 1890, lured by the personal fascination of
MacGregor Mathers, he joined the Order of the Golden Dawn, an
esoteric society that seems to have had affiliations with Rosicrucian-
ism and perhaps with Masonry. Yeats saw Mathers as half lunatic,
half knave, and this indicates clearly enough the self-protective
irony and shrewdness he took with him into these adventures (see
his poem 'All Souls' Night').

The qualities in Madame Blavatsky that Yeats found attractive
were those that he might have found in some 'old Irish peasant
woman' who was half-feared, half-respected by the villagers for her
powers of intuition and clairvoyance. Her 'air of humour and
audacious power' was, at any rate, real; and it was something of this
air that Yeats himself, as he grew older and more authoritative,
began to take on. Two essential facets of his experience thus came

into a meaningful relationship: the unforced supernaturalism of the untutored West of Ireland cottagers, in whose tales he had found echoes of an ancient and lofty Ireland of king and bard; and the attempt to escape from the ennui of materialism by magic and ritual, symbol and contemplation.

MacGregor Mathers moved to Paris in 1894. In this he showed good judgement, since the kind of beliefs and practices represented by the Order of the Golden Dawn were taken far more seriously there than in London; Richard Ellmann writes in *Yeats: The Man and the Masks* that Mathers 'acquired considerable reputation in occult circles there, and for a time gave masses for the goddess Isis at the Théâtre Bodinière under the auspices of Jules Bois.' Though Yeats never made a long stay in Paris, he found it more stimulating than London to much the same extent that London was more stimulating than Dublin. In particular, the association of magical studies with poetry was, in Paris, an easy one to make. A number of poets were active in magical studies, and Yeats had no difficulty in finding his individual niche.

When he was not in Paris he was either in London or in Ireland; and in London his associates were the poets who belonged to the loose association known as the Rhymers' Club, and who were bookish, speculative, versed in ancient knowledge and strange lore; while Ireland to him meant partly the driving energy of Maud Gonne, partly the romantic intransigence of John O'Leary, and partly the twilight mystery of folk-tale and ancient myth. It is no surprise, then, to look at the three volumes of poems he published before 1900 and find that virtually every poem concerns itself with one of two themes: either Irish lore and legend, or the occult in some form or other. The general impression left by these volumes is that the two could effortlessly flow together, since both were at about the same remove from reality.

Yeats's real difficulty, at this time, was to align his imaginative vision with the harsh external objectivities of the 'real' world. The dream came so easily, the concrete experience was so hard and resistant. Maud Gonne did not return his love, Ireland moved no nearer to independence and dignity among the nations, nothing squared with 'the desires of the mind.' A poem like 'The Man Who Dreamed of Faeryland' in *The Rose* (1893) is a memorable, but almost entirely despairing, expression of the difficulty which Yeats, at this time, experienced in coming to terms with that 'reality' round which I cannot stop myself from putting inverted commas, but whose power I recognize as he recognized it. 'Reality' was Maud Gonne's refusal of him, and Ireland's subjection to England, and the wrangling of short-sighted Irish politicians, and the mediocrity of so many of the poets of the Rhymers' Club, and the ever-present poverty and shabbiness of his life in London. The lodgings he took at 18 Woburn Buildings, near St. Pancras Church (still standing, unspoilt, marvellously redolent of the period and an obligatory shrine for the Yeatsian pilgrim), were taken because he had despaired of Maud Gonne and decided after much hesitation to enter into an affair with an attractive married woman, with whom he solemnly went out—to Heal's, according to tradition—and chose a large bed. This was 'reality': and yet, as he wrote some twenty-five years later,

> I grow old among dreams,
> A weather-worn, marble triton
> Among the streams.

That image is worth pondering; Triton, son of Poseidon and Amphitrite, a sea deity usually shown as a fish-tailed merman, has his place in every formal garden adorned with lakes and fountains; he belongs to myth and symbol, whereas the stream is moving water, flowing and changing, full of unguessable life. Triton is dead marble beside the living stream; the image will recur, in another few years, in 'Easter 1916', and will be used for a very different purpose; while the image of marble holding its immobile shape amid the turmoil of a 'flood' that symbolizes the complexity of physical life will be central to one of the greatest poems of his final period, 'Byzantium'. One of the marks of Yeats's poetry is his power to strike out images that have this all-inclusive significance; his poems pivot on images that contain within themselves so much actuality, so much consciousness, that they can only be weakened by being described as 'symbols'. Nevertheless, 'symbol' is the best general term for them; and Yeats's concern for the living, all-inclusive symbol, for

> Those images that yet
> Fresh images beget,

has its root in these early years when magical symbol and poetic symbol could still be seen as one, when the Blavatsky Lodge and the Order of the Golden Dawn offered his developing mind a discipline in the techniques of meditation. Whatever reservations we have about Yeats's lifelong interest in the occult, however unreadable we find A Vision in any of its printed versions, we can still recognize that Yeats was right to undertake that discipline, that it gave him strength as a poet.

In the terminology of literary history, we may say baldly that Yeats, through his visits to Paris and through the generously shared erudition of his friend Arthur Symons, was able to relate himself to the European movement of Symbolism. Without losing his individual quality, he became, in the last years of the nineteenth century, a Symbolist poet. And it was the power generated by Symbolism that entered his work, strengthened it, and enabled it, at last, to defy the Savage God.

The doctrines of Symbolism are somewhat mysterious and liable to be interpreted differently by each observer who brings to them his own tastes and preoccupations. As a movement, however, Symbolism is not difficult to comprehend once we have placed it in its historical setting. It is one of the logical consequences of the fragmentation of belief which began in the Western world in the era of Descartes. From classical times until towards the end of the eighteenth century, the role of the poet—taking the word, as those ages did, to apply to any imaginative writer, any ποιητής or maker— had been to give imaginative and emotional flesh to the dry bones of abstract belief. Reality was expounded and systematized by philosophers or theologians; the poet imagined that reality afresh, clothed it in fitting language, made it vivid with apt figures, dramatized it, held it up for the contemplation of mankind. During most of the ages of which we have any record, it was thought perfectly normal that even the greatest poets should take some pre-existing view of the world and apply themselves to making it over into poetry, as Lucretius versified the system of Epicurus or Dante the system of St. Thomas Aquinas. This attitude disappeared in the west with the break-up of the stable intellectual order, and the chief distinguishing mark of European Romanticism is its discovery of the artist as an independent perceiver (some would say, creator) of truth. Instead of accepting a 'reality' handed to him from outside, the poet now makes the reality he contemplates. The poet's energizing metaphor, his 'image', his 'inscape', is the twitch of the water-diviner's twig.

This view was not entirely new; in a civilization as rich and complex as that of Europe, nothing is ever entirely new; the doctrine of demoniac possession of the poet, doubtless already old when Plato composed the *Ion*, implies that the poet's perceptions as well as his eloquence come to him from a source peculiar to him and that he is therefore holy among men, a vessel and seer. But this attitude was enormously dramatized and sharpened by the crisis in human attitudes that burst on the world with the approach of the nineteenth century. Now, each man must impose his own order on the universe, and the poet was the unacknowledged legislator.

Symbolism is to this extent the continuation of Romanticism. It takes over Romanticism's one basic tenet: that the imagination, no longer confined to the actualization of doctrine, is now the provider of material for doctrine. The imagination explores the world and reports back to the reason, which may or may not understand the message. Nevertheless, the later movement shows marked divergences from the earlier. It is much less trustful of personality, much more inclined to self-immolation, even to a kind of mysticism. The Romantic movement had glorified personality. It had begun with the explosion on to the European scene of huge, cloudy figures, impossibly larger than life, such as Macpherson's Ossian, or Werther, or the 'I' of Rousseau's immensely inflated *Confessions*; all of them supplanted by the supercharged ego of Byron, which swept Europe in the wake of the armies of Napoleon. The Romantic poet put his own ego at the centre of the universe; he saw himself as mankind, fulfilling his destiny by doing and suffering, colouring the universe with his joy and pain. Hence the stormy life-style of the typical Romantic megalomaniac, who had to go everywhere and do everything because his will, the instrument with which he brought the universe under the domination of man, had to be tested and fulfilled in action. For this reason, much of Romantic poetry has an interest that is mainly biographical. The poems of Shelley or Byron take on depth when read in conjunction with their personal histories; on their own, they often seem thin and crude.

Naturally this is not true of the greatest Romantic poets. Wordsworth and Keats managed to create an art which owes none of its importance to biographical colouring. And it is to the credit of the Symbolists that they followed this strand, took their cue from the greater Romantics rather than the lesser. To the Symbolist, the ego is an encumbrance and action a mere to-ing and fro-ing. His instrument is contemplation; he surrounds himself with stillness and non-event.

In essence, then, Symbolist poetry is a technique of meditation. It arises from the belief that the surface of life is a mere clutter, that reality lies deeper and can best be approached by training the mind to dwell on symbols which both express and embody it. These symbols are quite different from the one-to-one correspondences of the older allegorical writings. They cannot be cracked, like a code; they are irreducible; they do not 'stand for' something outside themselves. The power they have is the power to concentrate reality as with a burning-glass, to draw the scattered impressions of the human mind into a focus, so that when we see them in action in a work of art—on which, necessarily, they impose their own authority —we can at least say, as we contemplate this work of art, 'Order is imposed on chaos *here*.'

Symbolism has often been attacked as an unnecessarily arcane theory of art, but to me it seems like a very natural human impulse. It is not in our nature to accept life as a mere succession of impressions and sensations, each one replacing the last and replaced in turn by the next, with nothing to connect them. This may be how animals perceive the world (though there is evidence that the higher animals are aware of causality and so must have some kind of connected world-view), but the composition of the human mind is such that it *must* bind the scattered fragments of perception into a whole, or cease to function. We seek for the underlying pattern, the deeper level of reality, because to do so is a condition of our life. And in an age when various social and intellectual forces have combined to rob men of any generally accepted pattern in the carpet, they will naturally try to achieve their own independent vision of the pattern.

The symbols which the Symbolist poet so deeply contemplates, and which provide his means of contact with the interior reality of the universe, can be chosen from anywhere, so long as they are chosen for real reasons and not just picked up at random. The poet can make them up himself, like Rilke; he can assemble them from ancient and half-forgotten tradition, like Yeats; he can take them from a religious orthodoxy, like Eliot. In the end, all three methods come to the same thing, because, whether or not the poet's symbols are already known to the readers of his poetry, he has to re-invent them, to meditate on them so deeply that they become his own. Within the general landscape of modern poetry, the orthodox religious symbols of an Eliot or a Hopkins take their place easily beside the purely personal symbols invented or assembled by other poets. In practice, however, Symbolist poets have shown a tendency to take their symbols from myth and literature: naturally so, since artists are the priesthood of the Symbolist world, and great art is its collective Sacred Book. Thus, W. B. Yeats was writing as a good Symbolist when he recalled, in Book III of *The Trembling of the Veil*, how as a younger man

I had an unshakable conviction, arising how or whence I cannot tell, that invisible gates would open as they opened for Blake, as they opened for Swedenborg, as they opened for Boehme, and that this philosophy would find its manuals of devotion in all imaginative literature, and set before Irishmen for special manual an Irish literature which, though made by many minds, would seem the work of a single mind, and turn our places of beauty or legendary association into holy symbols. I did not think this philosophy would be altogether pagan, for it was plain that its symbols must be selected from all those things that had moved men most during many, mainly Christian, centuries.[2]

Yeats, as we shall see later, had his own idiosyncratic version of Symbolist doctrine, and some parts of the passage just quoted refer to specifically Yeatsian beliefs; but they bear the same relationship to the central Symbolist position as heresies do to an orthodoxy. All the Symbolists would have agreed with Yeats that we establish contact with the deepest truths by the contemplation of symbols, and *ipso facto* that what matters is not our restless differentiated selves but those still depths in which all mankind sees with one vision and speaks with one voice. In his very different idiom, T. S. Eliot was saying the same thing when in his first major critical pronounce-ment, 'Tradition and the Individual Talent', he declared, 'The progress of an artist is a continual self-sacrifice, a continual extinc-tion of personality': and again, that 'the poet has, not a "personality" to express, but a particular medium, which is only a medium and not a personality, in which impressions and experiences combine in peculiar and unexpected ways.'

Eliot also concurs with Yeats, and the Symbolists generally, in taking great imaginative literature as a Sacred Book; for in that same essay occurs one of his most often quoted *aperçus*: 'Someone said, "The dead writers are remote from us because we *know* so much more than they did." Precisely, and they are that which we know.'[3]

It follows that Symbolist literature concerns itself with the reality which is reached through imaginative literature and the great myths of mankind, and that many of its masterpieces are based on these things. To use an analogy from a different but related sphere, the Symbolist poet is Catholic, not Protestant; in approaching the supreme Essence he puts his trust in intermediaries, tutelary spirits who will clear the way and intercede for him. Poems like Mal-larmé's *L'Après-midi d'un faune* or Valéry's *La Jeune Parque* are stretched on a framework of classical mythology and thus gain an effect of double focus which, while greatly increasing the power of the poetry, also increases its imperviousness to explanation and analysis. Edmund Wilson, in his chapter on Valéry in *Axel's Castle*, has indicated very well the kind of difficulty we are likely to encounter in Symbolist poetry:

Is 'La Jeune Parque' the monologue of a young Fate, who has just been bitten by a snake? Is it the reverie of the poet himself, awakening early one morning in bed and lying more or less awake till dawn? Is it the voyage of the human consciousness testing out all its limitations, exploring all its horizons: love, solitary thought, action, sleep, death?—the drama of the mind which would withdraw from the world and rise superior to it but which is inevitably pulled back into life and involved in the processes of nature? It is all of these—yet the various strata, 'physical, psychological and esoteric,' as Francis de Miomandre describes them, are not overlaid one upon the other as in a conventional allegory or fable. They are confused and are always melting into one another—and it is this which makes the obscurity of the poem. The things that happen in 'La Jeune Parque' and in Paul Valéry's other mythological monologues—the Narcissus, the Pythoness and the Serpent of the rich period of poetic activity which followed immediately upon 'La Jeune Parque'—are never, on the one hand, quite imaginable as incidents which are actually taking place and never, on the other hand, quite reducible merely to thoughts in the poet's mind.[4]

The Symbolist poet, by the raptness with which he contemplates the chosen symbol, involves it both with his own mind and with the universe, so that analogy merges into a deep assimilation that can never again be separated out:

> O body swayed to music, O brightening glance,
> How can we know the dancer from the dance?

This symbiotic fusion of outer with inner landscape, this refusal to draw a line between subjective and objective reality, is the basis of the literary method of the Symbolists. Virtually all the important poetry of the early and middle twentieth century has this characteristic. It is the basis of the work of Eliot and Yeats, and of Pound's Cantos, and of the major European poets through Valéry, Éluard, Michaux, Ungaretti, Blok, Rilke, Gottfried Benn, Kazantzakis, and Seferis: and also of the great Symbolist novels, James Joyce's *Ulysses* and Pasternak's *Dr. Zhivago*. All these writers use the methods of Symbolism to break through the crust of everyday experience; they give to experience a mythical dimension by associating realistic observation with a landscape of traditional or newly-invented myth: James Joyce, a renegade Catholic, uses the *Odyssey* to indicate the giant shadow thrown on the screen of time by an insignificant advertisement canvasser in Dublin; Pasternak, a Jew, uses the New Testament for a similar purpose in telling the story of a man's death and resurrection; in Yeats's poetry, Cuchulain fights the ungovernable sea; in Eliot's, Tiresias foresuffers all. If these symbols cannot be unpacked into the language of explanation, neither can any of the central secrets of life; if by some intuition we were able to find out what life is and where it comes from, we should still not be able to explain our knowledge in workaday, non-metaphorical language.

When Yeats was dying in 1939, he wrote to a friend on the day after writing his last poem—that is, on 4 January—a letter in which he affirms the inner certainty to which his faith in this doctrine had brought him.

In two or three weeks—I am now idle that I may rest after writing much verse—I will begin to write my most fundamental thoughts and the arrangement of thought which I am convinced will complete my studies. I am happy, and I think full of an energy, of an energy I had despaired of. It seems to me that I have found what I wanted. When I try to put all into a phrase I say, 'Man can embody truth but he cannot know it.' I must embody it in the completion of my life. The abstract is not life and every-where draws out its contradictions.[5]

II

Modern poetry, indeed modern art in general, was invented by the French; Paris was the birthplace of Symbolism, the last great concerted movement in European letters; an Irish poet like Yeats, an Austrian poet like Rilke, an American poet like Eliot, had to leave their own countries and go to Paris to be baptized at the inter-national font of modernity. So runs the orthodoxy, and in large perspective it is certainly true. Yet in the history of any art there are unexpected eddies and tourbillions, since art is created in the deep recesses of the individual mind, where orthodoxy counts for nothing. Symbolism, variously interpreted by different poets in different places, channelled poetic energy into the task of making major statements. But some poets of importance can be found, especially in England, whose work would have been no different if inter-national Symbolism had never been heard of. Chief of these, without doubt, are Gerard Manley Hopkins (1844–1889) and Thomas Hardy (1840–1928). These poets are alike independent of Symbolism, but in opposite ways and for opposite reasons. Hardy, in many ways an archetypal English countryman, was content to draw in a literary tradition with the air he breathed and probably never in his life, except in mockery, used a word ending in 'ism'. Hopkins, a Jesuit priest, employed by his order mainly in teaching, had very little contact with the literary world of his day and was quite unaffected by what went on there; but, working in solitude, he evolved his own version of Symbolism, anticipated both the theory and the practice of the next fifty years, and produced a fully-developed 'modern' poetry which was immediately accepted as such when it was finally published in 1918.

Hardy was working as a poet before he took to writing fiction; indeed, he seems to have begun writing novels mainly because his poems were too often rejected by editors and he felt a very natural wish to reach a public. His first volume of verse, *Wessex Poems*, did not appear till 1898, by which time his career as a novelist was virtually over; but about a third of its contents had lain in his desk for thirty years. He went on to publish seven more volumes, the last appearing in the year of his death; his *Collected Poems* (1930) contains 918 poems, though his reputation as a poet probably rests on fifty or sixty.

Hardy's poems are better than his novels; they contain less that is contrived and melodramatic, and they go to their target more swiftly and memorably. A reader coming from the novels to the poems, as any reader in 1898 must have done, would find himself still in the same world of high Victorian atheism and pessimism, for Hardy resembles Housman in his conviction that (to use the words of the latter poet)

> The troubles of our proud and angry dust
> Are from eternity, and shall not fail;
> Bear them we can, and if we can we must.

But his sensibility is richer than Housman's, and more concrete; where Housman sees the countryside and its inhabitants through a veil of literature, Hardy speaks directly out of the experience of being a countryman; his poems are full of weather, stone, grass, animals, men and women. His way of bearing the troubles of our proud and angry dust is a peasant's way, compounded of irony, stoicism, and a dash of rural bloody-mindedness—there is satire and spite, though never petulance, in his poetry.

Any reader approaching the mighty *Collected Poems* might do worse than linger for a moment on the very threshold, the first poem in the volume.

THE TEMPORARY THE ALL
(Sapphics)

Change and chancefulness in my flowering youthtime,
Set me sun by sun near to one unchosen;
Wrought us fellowlike, and despite divergence,
   Fused us in friendship.

'Cherish him can I while the true one forthcome—
Come the rich fulfiller of my prevision;
Life is roomy yet, and the odds unbounded.'
   So self-communed I.

'Thwart my wistful way did a damsel saunter,
Fair, albeit unformed to be all-eclipsing;
'Maiden meet,' held I, 'till arise my forefelt
   Wonder of women.'

Long a visioned hermitage deep desiring,
Tenements uncouth I was fain to house in:
'Let such lodging be for a breath-while,' thought I,
   'Soon a more seemly.

'Then, high handiwork will I make my life-deed,
Truth and Light outshow; but the ripe time pending,
Intermissive aim at the thing sufficeth.'
   Thus I . . . But lo, me!

Mistress, friend, place, aims to be bettered straightway,
Bettered not has Fate or my hand's achievement;
Sole the showings those of my onward earthtrack—
   Never transcended![6]

At first glance this poem, with its classical metre, seems uncharacteristic. But in its own way it could help to prepare us for almost everything we shall meet in the crammed pages to come. The diction, for instance, is already fully Hardyesque; the Latin element in English was uncongenial to Hardy, whose sympathies lay with those English writers of the middle and later nineteenth century who made a conscious attempt to breed a language more consciously native. He admired William Barnes, the Dorset dialect poet, whose taste in linguistic flavours can be indicated by recalling that he wanted to replace the word *dormitory* by *sleepstow*; just as

William Morris, later, wanted to call a *perambulator* a *push-wain*. A line like

> Sole the showings those of my onward earthtrack

aligns Hardy squarely with the writers of that *echt*-English tradition (which also had its attraction, as we shall see, for Hopkins). Hardy varied his metres incessantly, his diction not at all; in the 1920s he was still using the same language as in the 1860s. Latinized English would not do; it had no soil clinging to it. Neither would the spare, monosyllabic, super-plain English often cultivated by scholarly writers; peasants do not value that kind of distilled plainness; Hardy's language, in its own way, is as fanciful as Synge's, and for much the same reasons.

In its content, in the attitude to life it expresses, the poem is equally characteristic of Hardy; this is Hardy's mood when it is not grandly tragic or piercingly elegiac. The wry story of how a man accepted a whole bundle of second-best expedients, to be discarded when life brought him something better, only to find that life never did bring him anything better—this, as Hardy sees it, is the story of anyone's life; anyone, that is, who is fortunate enough to have a life at all. Hardy's outlook was formed before 1860, and in those days rural poverty was grim and rural existence, for all the beauty of its setting, as harsh for the poor as urban, and much more monotonous. A poem like 'To an Unborn Pauper Child' reminds us that Hardy's life overlapped for two decades with that of Dickens; one thinks, on reading such a poem, of the little Dorset boy who, in Hardy's early days, was found dead of starvation and whose stomach, at the autopsy, turned out to contain nothing but raw turnip. Against this background, Hardy is too soberly realistic to welcome the arrival on earth of a pauper child; yet it is interesting to see that his honesty forbids any simple pitch-black colouring; he admits 'hope' into his picture; he knows that human beings are 'unreasoning, sanguine, visionary' and that it is because they are all these things that they can struggle on against all the odds.

There is very little more that need be said, in a survey such as this, about Hardy's poetry. It stands in no need of explanation or commentary. Anyone who will read with ordinary patience, ordinary alertness, will soon find himself deep in Hardy's mental world, responding to the exhilarating gloomy force of Hardy's art. In the novels, that world tends to be suffocating; the way is too long and dusty, the landscape too unrelieved; but in the poetry, Hardy's lyrical impulse gives an undertone of delight to his most discouraging comments on life. His ear was not infallible, but he knew what he wanted to achieve—an earthbound lyricism, like someone dancing lightly in heavy boots—and he kept on working, patiently, writing nearly a thousand poems that he thought good enough to publish, and no one knows how many that he did not: and his reward was to achieve that lyricism very often—sometimes uncertainly and intermittently, now and then gloriously throughout a whole poem.

Nearly all Hardy's poems are short, though he did try his hand at verse-drama in *The Queen of Cornwall* (1923) and the colossal 'epic-drama' *The Dynasts* (1904–8). Neither of these can rank with his best short poems; *The Dynasts* is worth reading for the highly cinematic visual sense displayed in the prose-directions and in the long visual descriptions which Hardy called 'Dumb Shows'; but the quality of its verse is generally below that in his shorter work. It was not, however, that he lacked the power to sustain large structures. Many of his shorter poems are sequences which stand together very well, notably in 'Time's Laughingstocks' and 'Satires of Circumstance'. Perhaps his finest sustained work, however, is held together by unity of subject and mood rather than formal intention. The death of his first wife, Emma Lavinia, in 1912 brought a rush of grief and nostalgia which found expression in poem after poem; the twenty-one 'Poems of 1912–13', in *Satires of Circumstance* (1914), can be read as a whole, and, so read, form a single elegy of great poignancy and beauty.

Gerard Manley Hopkins, the other major English poet to plough a lonely furrow, differs from Hardy in almost every respect. He was born into a typical Victorian middle-class family—eldest of nine children, father in the marine insurance business, living in a London suburb. Musical and artistic talent ran high in the family; two of his brothers became professional artists, and another, whose working life was spent in China, became an authority on the early Chinese written character. Gerard himself, after attending a grammar school at Highgate where one of his masters was R. W. (later Canon) Dixon, an accomplished minor poet, went on to Balliol College, Oxford, where he was in contact with such teachers as Jowett and Pater. An even more decisive influence on Hopkins's nascent mind was that of J. H. Newman, at one time a parish priest in Oxford, then at the Oratory in Birmingham. Hopkins became a convert to Roman Catholicism (largely, it would seem, through Newman's personal example), was received into the Roman Catholic Church in 1866 and entered the Order of Jesus in 1868, having in the meantime graduated with a 'Double First' as the term is understood at Oxford, i.e. a first in both 'mods' and 'greats', the two parts of Litterae Humaniores.

For the next seven years Hopkins's life was devoted entirely to his religious vocation; to his novitiate at Roehampton, to his theological studies at St. Mary's Hall, Stonyhurst, where in particular he made a delightedly intense study of the English medieval theologian, Duns Scotus. Not until 1874 did he renew contact with his college friend Robert Bridges, at that time a young poet with his reputation still to make. Bridges, a man without much mental pliancy, was nevertheless a good friend to Hopkins; his views on poetry were rigid and conventional, but they were the views of a civilized and well-read man; he never understood what Hopkins was trying to do as a poet, but he was at least someone to whom Hopkins could explain his aims and methods, and thus externalize the long creative struggle and get some relief from its tensions.

At the time of his renewed correspondence with Bridges, Hopkins had been silent as a poet since joining the Order; at that time, thinking poetry to be one of the things he must renounce, he had burnt his previous verse (a fair amount, happily, survived here and there). Unwittingly, however, during these years, he was gestating a new poetry, full of a new intensity and boldness, a new concentration and brilliance. In 1875 came the random external jar which caused the waiting machinery to shiver into motion, astonishing the poet as it has since astonished his readers. As Hopkins told the story in a letter to Dixon,

. . . when in the winter of '75 the Deutschland was wrecked in the mouth of the Thames and five Franciscan nuns, exiles from Germany by the Falck Laws, aboard of her were drowned I was affected by the account and happening to say so to my rector he said that he wished someone would write a poem on the subject. On this hint I set to work and, though my hand was out at first, produced one. I had long had haunting my ear the echo of a new rhythm which I now realised on paper.[7]

Hopkins goes on to say that the 'new rhythm' was not entirely new, but that 'no one has professedly used it and made it the principle throughout.' Later, he coined a name for his own distinctive prosody, 'Sprung Rhythm', and explained it to Bridges in detail; it is also the subject of his one semi-public pronouncement on his own poetry, the 'Author's Preface' at the beginning of a manuscript collection of his poems, later owned by Bridges. It was like Hopkins's modesty to play down the fierce originality of his work by describing that originality in terms of metre. In fact, his metrical innovations are the least of his departures from standard pre-modern practice. He takes liberties with conventional grammar and syntax; he coins new words; he telescopes images into one another; he uses the English language with a passionate grandeur and a brooding tenderness entirely beyond the range of any other English poet of the late nineteenth century. In his highly charged abruptness he reminds us of Donne; in his scholarly effrontery, of Milton; in his moments of pure lyricism he might be a poet of the singing voice like Campion; his vivid sensuousness is Keatsian; the catalogue, inevitably, leads nowhere, for he is always his own man and his own poet.

'The Wreck of the Deutschland' was refused by the Catholic paper, *The Month*; later, Hopkins tried them with another ship-wreck poem, 'The Loss of the Eurydice', and when they rejected that too, he gave up and never again sought publication. One can feel sympathy with the editor on whose desk the 'Deutschland' arrived; probably most editors at that date would have either rejected the poem or published it with a sense of their own daring as a confused mass of brilliant writing, a heap of unsorted diamonds. That it contains many obscure passages no one will deny; obviously one can 'explain' anything in poetry if one is willing to use enough ingenuity, but after twenty years of reading Hopkins I find several turns of phrase in the 'Deutschland' for which any explanation I could give would seem only tentative. Yet there is never, at any time, any doubt about the main structure of the meaning, and the difficulties nearly all occur in those ecstatic passages in which Hopkins is addressing the Godhead in a flight of adoration—and when has the language of mystical rapture been easy to decipher?

What must have puzzled the head-shaking editor of *The Month* was the absence of any concession to standard Victorian poetic convention. To begin with, the poem would have seemed to him impossible to scan. Nowadays, this difficulty has been removed by several factors: for one thing, metrical rules have in any case fallen into desuetude; for another, English departments in the universities have familiarized a wide public with the rudiments of Anglo-Saxon, so that a metric employing alliteration as well as rhyme and assonance is no longer puzzling to the ear; and most modern poets have tried, in various ways, to bring into their work the unceremonious immediacy which arises from the rhythm of speech rather than the rhythm of song. Quite early in his correspondence with Bridges, Hopkins was explaining his need to get away from the weakening effect of conventional metre:

Why do I employ sprung rhythm at all? Because it is the nearest to the rhythm of prose, that is the native and natural rhythm of speech, the least forced, the most rhetorical and emphatic of all possible rhythms, combining, as it seems to me, opposite and, one wd. have thought, incompatible excellences, markedness of rhythm—that is rhythm's self— and naturalness of expression—for why, if it is forcible in prose to say 'lashed: rod', am I obliged to weaken this in verse, which ought to be stronger, not weaker, into 'láshed birch-ród' or something?
My verse is less to be read than heard, as I have told you before; it is oratorical, that is the rhythm is so. I think if you will study what I have here said you will be much more pleased with it and may I say? converted to it.[8]

When Hopkins insists that verse 'ought to be stronger, not weaker,' than prose, he is foreshadowing much of the technical effort of the modern poet. Edward Thomas wrote approvingly of Robert Frost's early work, 'It is poetry because it is better than prose'; at about the same time, the young Eliot was remarking that 'poetry ought to be at least as well written as prose', and Pound was cautioning the neophyte not to 'retell in mediocre verse what has already been done in good prose. Don't think any intelligent person is going to be deceived when you try to shirk all the difficulties of the unspeakably difficult art of good prose by chopping your composition into line lengths.' All these men were in revolt against a period in which it was felt, at any rate by the weaker brethren, that poetry was the guaranteed result of obedience to certain rules, that any metrical composition was more poignant and dignified than mere prose. They united in feeling that verse-writing must begin again from bedrock, that all conventions were to be questioned. In this, Hopkins anticipated them, and one feels that it was this element in his work that really shocked Bridges, who was certainly a gifted man but who was 'literary' in a way that Hopkins was not. Bridges was very much aware of the rules; if he departed from them, he did so in a spirit of conscious experimentation; Hopkins, aloof from the institutional world of 'literature' both by temperament and through the circumstances of his life, made his own rules in perfect indifference.
To come back to 'The Wreck of the Deutschland', its form can be illustrated by quoting a stanza:

> Loathed for a love men knew in them,
> Banned by the land of their birth,
> Rhine refused them, Thames would ruin them;
> Surf, snow, river and earth
> Gnashed: but thou art above, thou Orion of light;
> Thy unchancelling poising palms were weighing the worth,
> Thou martyr-master: in thy sight
> Storm flakes were scroll-leaved flowers, lily showers—sweet
> heaven was astrew in them.[9]

The rhyme-scheme, a b a b c b c a, is adhered to throughout; it is an excellent framework, drawing the end of the stanza back to the beginning, and allowing the long, complex sentences to trail and wind about a firm structure. But rhyme alone will not contain the exuberance of Hopkins's language; alliteration and very strong assonance are needed as well; the first is obvious at a glance, the second occurs in phrases like 'Banned by the land' and 'scroll-leaved flowers, lily showers'. So much for pure sound. The rhythm, whether we call it 'sprung' or not, is obviously a matter of playing off a fixed and predictable number of heavy stresses against a variable lace-work of light, unemphatic syllables. This is most easily seen in the long final line of each stanza. If our idea of scansion is to count with a finger, we shall see a marked difference between the last line of stanza 11,

> The sour scythe cringe, and the blear share come

and that of stanza 25,

> The keener to come at the comfort for feeling the combating keen?

But if we simply listen, the ear will tell us that each of these lines contains six heavy beats, and the grouping of unstressed syllables is a way of achieving variety. In the stanza we have been examining, the last line seems at first sight to be impossibly longer than the norm Hopkins has established; but 'astrew in them' is a rhyme with 'ruin them' and 'knew in them', and so has the effect of only one beat; the line is certainly long, but not overbalancing. The rhythm of the 'Deutschland' stanza is that of an ode, balancing short lines with long, poising and steadying itself before soaring out on a long rhythmical spiral. It is finely adapted to the subject-matter of the poem: agony, terror, death, beatitude, immortality, are not to be spoken of cosily; the poem is intoning and chanting, not talking. Elsewhere, Hopkins shows himself a master of quieter rhythms; in 'Spring and Fall' the rhythm muses, in 'St. Alphonsus Rodriguez' it is like quiet, thoughtful soliloquy; in 'Felix Randal' it approaches plain-song.

To the editor of *The Month* in 1875, the stanza we have quoted must have seemed as baffling as all the others. While the reference to Orion would strike an agreeably classical note (one expected classical reference from poets), he would wonder what Hopkins meant by calling God's palms 'unchancelling'. To us, accustomed to the density of Hopkinsian language, it is plain that God's hands are not merely weighing but buffeting, driving the nuns forth from the shelter of their chancel to meet their fate so that they can know the joy of a martyr's crown, that He is not only a judge but a disciplinarian ('martyr-master') and also Orion the hunter. We see these things because we know that Hopkins deliberately packed his language with meaning, 'loaded every rift with ore', knowing that this rich complexity was the only way he could express his view of the world. This view owed much to Duns Scotus, who taught that, while the form of things is generic, the matter is individual; each individual being has not only a generic whatness, a *quidditas*, but also a thisness, a *haecceitas*.

To Hopkins, Scotus was 'of realty the rarest-veined unraveller'; the words are no idle compliment, for the poet was aware of external nature, of all creation indeed, as a subtle tissue of individual shapes and essences; to perceive at all was to 'unravel'. His own gift for patient and minute observation has never been surpassed; he would look at something until he had unravelled the complex strands of its being.

This faculty of close observation, in 'The Wreck of the Deutschland', would probably have struck its first readers as another proof of Hopkins's 'eccentricity'. As early as stanza 4, we find a fully-developed example.

> I am soft sift
>   In an hourglass—at the wall
> Fast, but mined with a motion, a drift,
>   And it crowds and it combs to the fall;
> I steady as a water in a well, to a poise, to a pane,
> But roped with, always, all the way down from the tall
>   Fells or flanks of the voel, a vein
> Of the gospel proffer, a pressure, a principle, Christ's gift.[10]

I suppose 'proffer', in the last line, could be taken either as a verb or a noun; if a noun, this would be one of those wrenchings to which Hopkins subjected the English language, but it would make better

sense grammatically; 'I am roped with a vein of the gospel's proffered offering.' Sand, as it falls through an hourglass, gives an
impression of smoothness and steadiness; the column of falling
grains appears to be standing still; it might be a rope, holding something in place, instead of the 'mine', the process of undermining that
leaves the steep cliffsides to tumble in one by one. The image of the
dedicated spirit is a precise one; on the surface as tranquil as the
surface of a well, or a pane of glass, it is steadily pouring through
the hourglass of its mortal life, and this very pouring is a 'rope', the
instrument of survival to the mountaineer who tackles the 'tall Fells
or flanks of the voel'—the Welsh word 'voel', meaning a bare hill,
reminds us that Hopkins wrote the poem 'on a pastoral forehead of
Wales'.

He had been studying Welsh, and finding delight in the intricate
power of forms such as the *cynghanedd*, until it struck him that his
Welsh studies might be a self-indulgence; he applied to his rector,
who told him that they were perfectly in place as long as they were
undertaken for the sake of ministering to the country people who
spoke no English. Hopkins could not find this certainty within his
conscience, and so he abandoned his Welsh studies; though a
Catholic, he had a scrupulosity which one normally might associate
with the extreme forms of Protestantism. Still, it is probable that
before giving up Welsh he had made enough progress, fine natural
scholar that he was, to be far more inward with it than many
subsequent poets have been with languages they have unblushingly
professed to know. Hopkins's Welsh (I cannot prove but dare
surmise) was firmer than Ezra Pound's Latin or Provençal.

In any case, Hopkins's attitude to language was as reverent and
subtle as his approach to experience generally. Words, for him, were
living things. He studied them with the delighted concentration with
which he studied trees, stones, clouds. This intimacy, this supple-
ness of give and take, protected him from the coarseness of Browning,
the empty cadences of Tennyson, or the undirected energy of
Swinburne. With Swinburne in particular, one feels that the form
is like a half-broken horse, fiery and unmanageable; the poet is a
rider clinging to the animal's back as it gallops along. Delicate
control is out of the question; the drumming hooves will go on until
the beast decides to stop. Hopkins had been an undergraduate at the
time of Swinburne's first vogue among the young, with the publication of *Poems and Ballads* in 1866, but he had been untouched by
the prevailing enthusiasm; Swinburne's handling of language
would have seemed to him thumping and unsubtle, even if the

subject-matter had been acceptable to him. Years later, in a letter to Bridges of 22 February 1879, he makes what seems to be a reference to Swinburne, with predictable distaste; briefly characterizing the kind of poetry he does not like, he calls it 'arrangements in vowel sounds . . . very thinly costuming a strain of conventional passion, kept up by stimulants, and crying always in a high head voice about flesh and flowers and democracy and damnation.'

Hopkins was aloof, then, from the contagion of Swinburne (and a glance at such minor poets as Kipling and Chesterton will remind us that this infection usually proved fatal). He formed his manner in isolation, from his own imaginative and scholarly resources. He was, of course, cut off from the taste of his own day by the circumstances of his life; he read only such books as the order had in its libraries, and naturally there was little money to spare for new volumes of poetry; if, in his letters, Hopkins quotes a contemporary poet, it is usually some fragment he has chanced on in a review; he had access to nothing else. But he would in any case have been isolated by his independence. His taste was as individual as his character. In music he had a special love for Purcell, in those days almost entirely unknown and unperformed. In poetry, he enjoyed Welsh and Anglo-Saxon, was fascinated by Milton, and rebuked Bridges for his failure to see anything in Dryden, a poet in whom he found 'naked thew', that strength he always looked for in art and achieved so fully in his own.

Indeed, Hopkins's liking for strong, massy, emphatic language provides the one link that joins him, tenuously, to the taste of his age. As we noted in connection with Hardy, the middle and later nineteenth century witnessed a movement, dictated partly by nationalism and partly by a genuine aesthetic impulse, towards the pruning back of the Latin element in our vocabulary and the re-emphasizing of the Anglo-Saxon groundwork. For some years, it looked as if there might be a possibility of a real change in idiom (*sleepstow* and *push-wain*); but this was an illusion, for the dual nature of English is too firmly established for the clock to be turned back. Hopkins sympathized with this movement, and though he saw the futility of its propaganda he embodied its finer spirit in his poetry.

This use of English has the effect of clearing away the clutter of abstraction and revealing the hard bones of concrete statement. Most of Hopkins's departures from orthodox syntactical usage are in the interests of strength and emphasis. The last line of 'The Wreck of the Deutschland', for instance, describes Christ as

Our hearts' charity's hearth's fire, our thoughts' chivalry's throng's Lord.

If we were writing these phrases in normal prose we should feel impelled to break up the tolling directness of these monosyllabic genitives by such locutions as, 'the fire of the hearth of our charity' or 'Lord of the throng of our chivalry'. This would not only weaken the driving force of the statement but would also betray it to one of the worst weaknesses of English, its proneness to clusters of little unemphatic sounds. To Bridges, such boldnesses were the outcome of 'a want of continuous literary decorum'; 'There is nothing stranger in these poems,' he wrote, 'than the mixture of passages of extreme delicacy and exquisite diction with passages where, in a jungle of rough root-words, emphasis seems to oust euphony; and both these qualities, emphasis and euphony, appear in their extreme forms.' As an objective description of Hopkins's poetry this is not without merit. But Bridges could hardly have guessed how 'the jungle of rough root-words' would answer so exactly to the need of a new generation of poets and readers when Hopkins, by Bridges's own agency, flung off his poetic tombstone in 1918.

Hopkins's later years were troubled by depression and physical weakness. In 1884 he was appointed Professor of Greek at University College, Dublin, and he appears to have found little in Irish life that was congenial. Inspiration as a poet came only fitfully, and his duties bore heavily on a constitution weakened by many years of selfless toil. But it would be a mistake to think of Hopkins, at any period of his life, as an unhappy man in any ordinary sense of the term. He was certain about his religious vocation; and if there was now and again a clash between his vocation as priest and as poet, so that he scrupled to spend time and energy on his writing, there was never any such conflict between his priestly dedication and his loving absorption in the *haecceitas* of each created thing. To him, rapt and devoted study of an object, or a landscape, or a word, or a work of art, was the equivalent of prayer. His version of the Scotist *haecceitas* he expressed by the word 'inscape', a coinage of his own which is found already in his early Journals. The Hopkinsian 'inscape' is the organizing principle which bestows identity; it is also an anticipation of the 'Image' of the Imagists, that Image which, as Ezra Pound said, 'presents an intellectual and emotional complex in an instant of time'. That the 'inscape' is not dependent on conscious artistry, but lives by mirroring itself in the perceiver's eye, is made clear by Hopkins's journal entry for 24 February 1873: 'All the world is full of inscape and chance left free to act falls into an order as well as purpose: looking out of my window I caught it in the random clods and broken heaps of snow made by the cast of a broom.'[11]

'All the world is full of inscape'; this recognition led Hopkins to put his powers of exact description at the service of the scientific fraternity in several letters to their journal *Nature*, the most remarkable being one of December 1883, describing one of the unusual sunsets which resulted from a volcanic explosion and the consequent accumulation of dust in the upper atmosphere. The passage is too long to quote here, but it will be found on pp. 165–6 of Hopkins's *Correspondence* with R. W. Dixon. It is safe to say that *haecceitas* has never been more memorably celebrated in a scientific journal.

Hopkins's poems were left in the sympathetic keeping of Bridges, who, after trying them out in anthologies, produced an edition in 1918. Bridges's notes and commentary reveal that he fell short of a complete understanding of Hopkins's poetry, but what matters is that he gave it to the world, and this alone makes 1918 an important date in the history of modern English poetry. Hopkins, working without aid or encouragement, had anticipated, by himself, the revolution in technique and attitudes that was to come after his death. The young poets who, in 1918, hailed this Victorian Jesuit as one of themselves may have been presumptuous, since very few of them were fit to stand anywhere near him; but at least they recognized that his achievement underwrote their own attempts; the very existence of his work gave 'modern' poetry a respectable ancestry.

Hopkins was once in the same room as Yeats, at some Dublin gathering, but the two poets held no converse, and Hopkins was nearing the end of his mortal existence by the evening when Yeats, returning from the first performance of *Ubu Roi*, suffered that fit of foreboding melancholy. From about this time, Yeats begins the long effort to strengthen his work, to free it from languid half-tones and indecisive rhythms. In practice this meant, as we have seen, a willingness to adopt the strategies of Symbolism: to make poetry a means of perceiving the inner truth of the human situation, not with the profuse documentation of the novelist or the socially conscious dramatist, but with the penetrating insight of the symbolic imagination. Yeats joined in this enterprise and finally emerged as one of its undisputed leaders. Not that his transformation was immediate or even rapid. His determination to claim a more central role for his work, to 'make it new', begins to take shape in the first volume he published after the *Ubu Roi* episode, *In the Seven Woods* (1904), where a number of the poems have a hard, realistic ring, a

firm rhythm and a general willingness to speak to the world in the
world's own terms, if only to berate it:

> We sat together at one summer's end,
> That beautiful mild woman, your close friend,
> And you and I, and talked of poetry.
> I said, 'A line will take us hours maybe;
> Yet if it does not seem a moment's thought,
> Our stitching and unstitching has been naught.
>
> Better go down upon your marrow-bones
> And scrub a kitchen pavement, or break stones
> Like an old pauper, in all kinds of weather;
> For to articulate sweet sounds together
> Is to work harder than all these, and yet
> Be thought an idler by the noisy set
> Of bankers, schoolmasters, and clergymen
> The martyrs call the world.'[12]

This note is strengthened in *The Green Helmet and Other Poems*
(1910), and rises at last to full power in *Responsibilities* (1914) and
The Wild Swans at Coole (1919). Yeats continued to grow as a poet
until his death at the age of seventy-three, though the trajectory of
his work was not entirely predictable. We have seen that he found a
renewal of energy and intensity by re-making his genius within the
broad area of Symbolism. But, owing to the accidents of history, the
waters of Symbolism do not run clear in Yeats's work for some
twenty years after that new beginning. From *Responsibilities*
onwards, all his volumes up to and including *The Tower* (1928) are
full of an urgent concern with the events being acted on the public
stage; with the clash of those personalities who offered rival solutions to the problems of Ireland, with the wave of violence that had
engulfed all Europe, with the crash of rifle-fire in the Post Office and
an Irish airman spinning downward to his death. Only in later
years, his own reputation settled, Ireland calmed, and the world
holding itself steady for a moment before the next plunge into
violence, does Yeats allow his mind to withdraw into itself and
produce, from a contemplation as rapt as Mallarmé's, the pure
distillation of his symbols. We must reserve our discussion of these
later poems, and of the mature development of Yeats's thought both
esoteric and social, for a further chapter in the volume dealing with
the appropriate time-span. But already during these middle years,
in which a life he had come to think of as a 'casual comedy' took on

suddenly the dimensions of heroism, outrage, and tragedy, Yeats is
the poet of a people and a civilization; the example of Homer is
never far from his mind; he celebrates the 'terrible beauty' of a
nation compelled into heroism.

Yeats's 'public' period, as we have seen, began long before the
armed uprising of the Irish Republicans in 1916. From the beginning, he had been active in London-Irish politics, forming societies
both there and in Dublin whose object was to foster those things in
which Irishmen might take a national pride and which might raise
them from an embittered province into a nation. All they had to
unite them, at that time, was a shared sense of grievance against
England, and Yeats saw that this was not enough; he dreamed of an
Ireland that would be fit for civilization, for great art and noble
lives. Deeply intertwined with these ideals was his passion for Maud
Gonne, who was for him a living symbol of the majesty that Irish
life could attain if it could only raise itself to that level.

These tumultuous early years are best described by Yeats himself
in *The Trembling of the Veil*, a superb autobiography that provides
the best commentary on his earlier poetry. This period was an
exhausting one for the poet; short of funds, his energy drained by
incessant journeys, meetings, arguments, feuds, and the public
speaking to which he had to nerve himself, and his emotions battered
by the unreciprocated nature of his love for Maud Gonne, he was
close to collapse when in 1896 he happened to meet Lady Gregory,
the widow of a landowner with an estate in Galway. Lady Gregory
immediately undertook the kind of healing and sustaining that Yeats
deeply needed; her house, Coole Park at Ballylee, became to Yeats
what Mrs. Thrale's house at Streatham was for Samuel Johnson;
in an effort to find some work that would interest his mind without
overtaxing it, she took him from cottage to cottage among her
tenantry, listening to those peasant folk-tales which he had begun
to explore, years before, in *The Celtic Twilight*. In this atmosphere
Yeats became calmer, and between cottage and great house he
developed that polarity of Irish values, the admiration which sang
the peasant and the aristocrat but consistently disdained the
politician and the 'huckster', and which became one of the main
themes of his verse.

Yeats had long cherished the dream of an Irish theatre. Unlike
the first-generation Symbolist poets, he wanted to bring his work
into the presence of a responsive audience and to witness the meeting. The project had never taken wing, but now, with the steady
support of Lady Gregory and a few other friends, the Abbey

Theatre was established in Dublin in 1904 with Yeats as its production manager, a post he held until 1910. These were the years of his
most strenuous involvement in Irish affairs, for the Abbey Theatre
offered itself to the world as an embodiment of the Irish mind, and
not all its offerings were acceptable to the prevailing Nationalist
sentiment. (This, we recall, was the epoch in which the youthful
James Joyce found his only possible programme in 'silence, exile
and cunning'; a little later, Joyce's collection of stories, *Dubliners*,
was refused by forty publishers and cost its author years of agonizing
struggle and frustration.) Slowly, with immense effort, the work of
creating an Irish literature went forward. Yeats had met in Paris a
diffident young writer named Synge, and on learning that Synge had
studied Gaelic at the university, he advised him to go to some
remote place in the west of Ireland, listen to the speech of the
people, and try to render it in English. Synge took the poet's advice,
and the result was his one undoubted masterpiece, *The Playboy of
the Western World*, which Yeats put on at the Abbey in 1907.
Popular sentiment, convinced that Irish manhood was being guyed
by a minority of artists and scoffers, rose in a storm; Yeats replied
with a magnificently lofty rebuke in his poem, 'On Those That
Hated "The Playboy of the Western World" ':

> Once, when midnight smote the air,
> Eunuchs ran through Hell and met
> On every crowded street to stare
> Upon great Juan riding by:
> Even like these to rail and sweat
> Staring upon his sinewy thigh.[13]

One does not altogether blame the Dublin audience who were
enraged by the *Playboy*, for these people were making a determined
effort to be taken seriously by the rest of the world, and the stage
Irishman was a great handicap to them; and Christy Mahon, however brilliantly he is portrayed, is certainly a stage Irishman. The
importance of this poem of Yeats's is not that it persuades us to be
unequivocally of his party but that it illustrates perfectly how
successfully he married the Symbolist poetic method to the demands
of a Homeric subject-matter, the need to speak in open language of
the struggle of a nation. The division between an artist like Synge
and the complacently stiff-necked Dublin middle-class is expressed
in terms of a symbolism drawn from legend, a legend in itself
refracted through much great art. And this should help us to get
into clearer focus the nature of Yeats's achievement during these

years of active participation. He satirized the philistinism of the
Irish public; he responded in his art to the violent and bitter
struggles of the Irish people towards freedom; he reflected the
savagery and desperation of the Black and Tan period; and always
his work has a universality that raises it above the merely local.
This poetry is intensely particular; it mentions names, it describes
specific events; yet always there is a grandeur of vision that intensi-
fies the particular into the universal. And this grandeur is directly
traceable to that side of Yeats's mind that made him responsive to
the doctrines of Symbolism, to the idea that meditation could pierce
the veil and touch the inner reality. For in Yeats's imagination,
everything is refined into its symbolic essence. O'Leary is not just
a brave and obstinate old Irish political leader, he is 'romantic
Ireland' that is 'dead and gone'. Major Robert Gregory is not merely
the son of his patroness and friend, who has given his life in a
quarrel not his own; he is the unifying symbol that brings together
the scattered elements of Yeats's life and the diverse men he has
known, so that 'In Memory of Major Robert Gregory' can be at
once a noble elegy and an exploration of the point to which Yeats's
experience as man and artist has brought him. As for Maud Gonne,
she is Helen, she is Pallas Athene, she is Ireland, she is the Countess
Cathleen, and all without ceasing to be that flesh-and-blood woman
to whom Yeats proposed marriage, and proposed again when her
estranged husband was among the sixteen leaders of the Rebellion
who were executed in 1916, and never succeeded in winning. Yeats
has the gift of seeing his own experience as part of some heroic
drama, and this gift is related to the imaginative power shown by
Pasternak when he makes the life of Yury Zhivago seem like the
three days spent by Christ in the sepulchre, or Joyce when he makes
Bloom into Ulysses. It is not a matter of inflating the commonplace;
it is the realization that nothing of human life *is* commonplace—not,
at any rate, from the standpoint of other human beings, for

> Whatever flames upon the night
> Man's own resinous heart has fed.

The poems in *Responsibilities*, which include that on the Synge
affair quoted above, are largely satiric in tone, with an earthy tang
and a strength that is often brutal. It is this volume that contains
the short poem 'A Coat', a splendidly truculent rhymed manifesto
in which the poet declares himself free of an old and hampering
convention and announces his decision to 'walk naked':

I made my song a coat
Covered with embroideries
Out of old mythologies
From heel to throat;
But the fools caught it,
Wore it in the world's eyes
As though they'd wrought it.
Song, let them take it,
For there's more enterprise
In walking naked.[14]

Since 'A Coat' is a poem and not a critical essay, there is no need to pin it down too literally; Yeats may have felt irritated at the imitation of his work by inferior poets, but this was in fact only a small part of his motive for his major change of style and procedure. Nor did 'walking naked' mean throwing away that accumulated store of 'old mythologies'; there is just as much mythology in Yeats's later poems as in his earlier. The difference is, as he acutely puts it, that the later poetry is 'naked'; the mythology is used as Symbolism uses it, as the exploratory thrust of life itself, not as a cloak which adorns and conceals.

During these years, when Yeats writes about the people whose life and struggles he shares, he raises them to the power of symbols. They inhabit the same dimension as those frankly symbolic figures, Owen Aherne and Michael Robartes, whom he introduced into both stories and poems as important embodiments of his thought. For that matter, Yeats mythologizes himself. It is during this period that he elaborates his doctrine of the Mask and the Anti-self, which he expounded in the prose work *Per Amica Silentia Lunae* (1917) and elsewhere. This doctrine maintains that any man who wins through to imaginative insight does so by using as instrument not his personality but an imagined personality which is its opposite. In this we can see the Symbolist demand for the abnegation of that personality which the Romantic poet had sent striding through every landscape he imagined. And we look ahead to Eliot's judgement that 'the more perfect the artist, the more completely separate in him will be the man who suffers and the mind which creates'.

Much has been made of Yeats's arrogance, as if he were some swaggering Ancient Pistol who claimed the right to act, look, and speak the role of Great Poet. Yet the doctrine of the Anti-self is at least as much the product of humility as of pride. Yeats wishes to attain to vision, and he knows that to do so he must transcend his limitations: and what better way than to live imaginatively in a self who is the antithesis of one's workaday self, so that in the tension between the two there may be room and scope for the full play of creative life?

> I call to the mysterious one who yet
> Shall walk the wet sands by the edge of the stream
> And look most like me, being indeed my double,
> And prove of all imaginable things
> The most unlike, being my anti-self,
> And, standing by these characters, disclose
> All that I seek; and whisper it as though
> He were afraid the birds, who cry aloud
> Their momentary cries before it is dawn,
> Would carry it away to blasphemous men.[15]

At all events, we can now establish that Yeats, having become a Symbolist poet, developed for twenty years in a way that finds very little precedent in previous Symbolist poetry, yet which seems natural in him, and perfectly achieved. Ireland is a small country, of no great importance on the world scene, and some of the people he writes about are not even very large figures in Ireland, yet because his imagination plays about them they have the mystery and power of Easter Island heads.

When we come to try to sum up the astonishing achievement of Yeats's lifetime, it may be that we shall find the greatest richness and power in these central years, when he is drawing strength from Symbolism and also from that turbulent active life from which Symbolism, in its earlier phase, had seemed to counsel a retreat. In the same volume, within a few pages of each other, we find a poem like 'Easter 1916', which seems a pure response to external event, and a visionary poem like 'The Second Coming', and when we examine them more closely we find that these two poems are drawn together not merely by proximity, not merely by belonging to the same phase of the poet's diction and style, but by the fact that the public poem draws strength from irreducible symbol, and the visionary poem seems a shrewd enough picture of the torn and blood-spattered world that the poet saw from his window.

III

If the problem of Ireland was to free herself from the dead hand of England, it is also true that during these years the English themselves were struggling with profound changes that threatened to overwhelm them. 'Easter, 1916' marks the point at which the wave of violence, washing over all Europe in the wake of that pistol-shot at Sarajevo, reached the streets of Dublin. By that time, many thousands of common Englishmen were dead, and in every English home it was obvious that the old days, for better or worse, would never come again. Yeats's attitude towards the First World War was, at first, aloof; he expressed it in his lines 'On Being Asked For a War Poem', which begin,

> I think it better that in times like these
> A poet's tongue be silent, for in truth
> We have no gift to set a statesman right.

But after the terrible beauty was born, after 'Pearse summoned Cuchulain to his side', Yeats realized that the whole nation was in it together, poets and all; he no longer felt any inclination to 'be silent' about the destiny of the nation, nor was he above trying, as occasion arose, to 'set a statesman right' here and there.

In England, the history of poetry from 1900 to 1918 is as obscure and troubled as the history of the national consciousness whose expression it was. When we stand back from the picture and try to get it into perspective, two things are obvious. First, of course, is the war. By killing off virtually an entire generation, by speeding up the technological and social changes that were already in progress, by imparting a widespread sense of betrayal and disillusion, that war ended a phase of English (and indeed of European) civilization and left the survivors to build a new one with such materials as they could find. The great pioneering generation of *circa* 1910, not only in literature but in every art, not only in the Anglo-Saxon world but in every highly developed society, had already announced a new era. The embattled forces of conservatism replied with destructive criticism of the new experimental work; the controversy was joined; but there is no means of knowing how the issues would have been settled, which path the community of sensitive and civilized people would have chosen to follow, and for two reaons: first, because the younger members of this community, the ones with the future in their hands, were taken out and butchered before they had a chance to make up their minds; second, because the world was so altered by the shock of the war that the terms of the discussion had to be redefined before any conclusion had been reached.

As far as English poetry is concerned, we can see that between 1900 and 1918 there were two separate reactions against the ruling convention, the 'Georgian' and the 'modern'. The convention itself was late-Victorian. In the early years of the century, English poetry was dominated, in terms both of popular acceptance and official recognition, by such trumpeters as Sir Henry Newbolt (1862–1938), Sir William Watson (1858–1935), and Rudyard Kipling (1865–1936), with some assistance, if that is the right word, from Chesterton and Belloc. All these writers were affirmers of simplicity. As literary technicians, none of them is to be despised. Kipling, in particular, was a coolly clever artificer who could learn from anything he chanced on in his reading; the poem in *Stalky & Co.* which begins 'There are, whose study is of smells' is an excellent semi-parody or irreverent reconstruction of the Horatian ode, and 'Danny Deever' uses the basic question-and-answer technique of the late medieval border ballad ('Why dois yir brand sae drap wi bluid', etc) to build up the same atmosphere of concentration and dramatization. Their fault, taken collectively, is that their work is too drastic a simplification of life, just as the literary tradition they maintain is too shrunken an inheritance from the full patrimony enjoyed by the Victorians.

That evening at the Hôtel Corneille, Yeats had chiefly feared the nervelessness of poetry, its assimilation to 'the faint mixed tints of Conder'; he had in mind his fellow-poets of the Rhymers' Club, Dowson, Johnson, O'Shaughnessy, and the rest. This danger was still present; but the trial of Oscar Wilde in 1895 had already started a rapid retreat from anything that looked like aestheticism, and the languor of the Rhymers was, for a few years at least, superseded by a beefy note that was even further from the possibility of an important statement about life. For ten years after Wilde's débâcle, Kipling and Newbolt had the big sales and the high reputation. Yeats, it is true, was steadily coming into his own (he published his first collected volume in 1909), but his unshakeable contempt for Edwardian heartiness set a gulf between him and conventional English taste, which he did nothing to narrow by such often-quoted asides as 'Chesterton and Belloc? Two buttocks of the same bum.'

Against this rowdy but inwardly nerveless poetry, the first attack was mounted when Edward Marsh, a gifted and generous civil servant whose talents were those of impresario and anthologist, rallied the younger men in a series of volumes, beginning in 1912, under the title *Georgian Poetry*. Since George V had come to the throne in 1910, the very word 'Georgian' was a banner, proclaiming an escape from the Victorian age and its deafening Edwardian climax. These newer poets favoured the woodwinds of the orchestra rather than the brass section so vigorously oompah'd by their seniors; they wrote of personal concerns, of individual feelings and perceptions, in language toned down almost to the level of conversation.

Georgian poetry was without doubt an improvement on what went before, and in its flexible and relaxed tone lay possibilities for a new broadening-out into experiment. It is the more unfortunate that the word 'Georgian' subsequently became a term of contempt, indiscriminately applied to all the poetry of the immediately pre-modern era and always linked with the weakest and least original work of that time. There are several reasons for this, the most prominent being the fact that the label 'Georgian' had two phases of life; in its first, pre-war phase, it was associated with Edward Marsh; in its second, in the early 1920s, it was revived in the *London Mercury* by the altogether less sensitive J. C. Squire and made into a roadblock against the advance of 'modern' poetry under Eliot and Pound. C. K. Stead in his interesting book *The New Poetic* (1964) does well to remind us that 'J. C. Squire's Georgians of the early 1920s—the "Squirearchy," as Osbert Sitwell called them—must not be confused with the group of liberal intellectuals which congregated around "Eddie" Marsh in 1911,' and that the work of this earlier group 'made possible both the war poetry of Wilfred Owen and the mature work of Robert Graves'. Nevertheless, the confusion persists. The fact is that if we are to do justice to Georgian poetry as sharply defined response to a particular historical situation, an attempt to let fresh air into a stifling drawing-room, we must first of all know what poems these men wrote and published; and if Georgianism made way for experiment, welcomed a free-verse writer like Lawrence, or the Isaac Rosenberg of 'Ah, koelue', then it is not for us to say that it oughtn't to have done.

Historical speculation on what *might* have happened is useless, but I believe that if the First World War had not happened, the new idiom in English poetry would have been a development of Georgianism. The seeds were there: the honesty, the dislike of cant, the 'selection from the real language of men', the dissatisfaction with a narrow tradition of poetry laid down by the literary Establishment and enforced by teachers and anthologists. It is interesting, in this connection, to note the distance travelled between Palgrave's *Golden Treasury* (1861) and Quiller-Couch's *Oxford Book of English Verse* (1900). Palgrave's book, which moulded the taste of the late-Victorian middle class, is a very partial selection from the wealth of English poetry, and Palgrave realized this perfectly well; the full title of his book is *The Golden Treasury of English Songs and Lyrics*, which acknowledges the existence of a mass of verse—satiric, narrative, epic, elegiac, abstruse—which must be looked for elsewhere. But by 1900, *The Golden Treasury* has done its work so well that Quiller-Couch, making very much the same kind of partial selection, can call his book *English Verse, tout court.* The Georgians were already breaking out of this mould, unlearning the literary influences that tended to make poetry an elegant amusement, bringing it closer to everyday speech and the actuality of life. By 1914, they had already done enough to serve as a workable foundation for a new major poetry. If England could have been left in peace, the work of the Georgians would have revealed itself as adequate to the needs of a new genius, as the crude but strong work of Kyd and Marlowe was adequate to Shakespeare, or the eighteenth-century tradition of fiction was ready for Jane Austen.

Two such geniuses did in fact appear. Both were Georgian poets in everything but name; both died in the war. Edward Thomas (1878–1917) and Wilfred Owen (1893–1918) are both major poets who take off from Georgianism. If their flight had been longer, there would have been no need of a modern poetic idiom imported from France via America. The Savage God, that *daimon* of a world without poetry, was already being challenged by Yeats; the seeds planted by Hopkins were still sleeping in the earth; Owen and Thomas, abetted by the excellent poets who survived the war, by Graves, by Blunden, by the older poets like Hodgson and De la Mare, would have made a living tradition out of English materials, arising naturally from English life. If they had, the Auden generation, coming into a healthier situation for English poetry, might have developed differently, and better.

But the war came, and nothing as moderate, or as sane, or as hopeful, as Georgian poetry could survive that Gadarene downrush of the nations. The lyricism of the early Pound, the Laforguian ironies of the early Eliot, might well have struck an alliance with a Georgian poetry strengthened by Owen, by Thomas, by the maturing Graves and Blunden; but when the Georgian tree was cut down, these neutrals had to stand alone, their roots in a poisoned soil, faced with the responsibility of devising a poetry that should ask the one remaining question:

> What are the roots that clutch, what branches grow
> Out of this stony rubbish?

Georgian poetry died with Thomas and Owen; its later form, under Squire, was not even a ghost. It died because its England died, and a new international poetry was all that could grow in the new international soil. Its epitaph might well be taken from the introductory essay written by Walter de la Mare for the first edition of Edward Thomas's *Collected Poems* in 1920.

There is nothing precious, elaborate, brilliant, esoteric, obscure in his work. The feeling is never 'fine', the thought never curious, or the word far-fetched. Loose-woven, monotonous, unrelieved, the verse, as verse, may appear to a careless reader accustomed to the customary. It must be read slowly, as naturally as if it were talk, without much emphasis; it will then surrender himself, his beautiful world, his compassionate and suffering heart, his fine, lucid, grave and sensitive mind. This is not a poetry that will drug or intoxicate, civicise or edify—in the usual meaning of the word, though it rebuilds reality. It ennobles by simplification.[16]

Edward Thomas is the last considerable poet to speak with an entirely English voice; to be, without programme or self-consciousness, the authentic utterance of the England he knew and of 'her sweet mother that died yesterday'. Since he was killed in 1917, he did not have to make the adaptation to the entirely different England that awaited those who came back from the war; nor is he in any danger of being labelled by thoughtless critics 'a war poet', as Rosenberg and Owen have been labelled, since, unlike them, he was already a mature man, fully formed in his attitudes and his sensibility by the time he enlisted at the age of thirty-seven. And yet, in one sense, Thomas is a war poet, for he began to write poetry after the war started, and all his poems, an astonishingly large output for some two years of work, came out in a rush of creativity as powers long dormant were liberated. Thomas had for years eked out a meagre living from literary hack-work; he had reviewed books, he had written the words for picture-book albums, he had knocked out critical, biographical, and topographical books to order, against pitifully small advances from publishers. For years, alternately sustained and depressed by his loyal wife and three children, who provided a domesticity which he needed and yet often hated, Thomas lived the simplest of existences in various country places, moving from cottage to cottage as it turned out that this one was insanitary and that one too expensive, choosing simplicity not only from poverty but because it was his natural way and he would have lived simply if he had been a millionaire. The countryside was his passion; he contemplated it with a calm yet visionary eye; he loved plant and animal, bird and fish, leaf and stalk; he loved digging and weeding and planting. A sad and troubled man, he knew that these things could never be to him a steady source of happiness, for he believed that no such source was possible in his case, but he needed them and

loved them. Deeply responsive to beauty, flashing out often into a
happiness that delighted his friends and could enchant women and
children, Thomas knew himself as one who never discovered any
rationale for these things, could never be confident that he knew
'what beauty is, and what I could have meant by happiness.' 'And
yet,' he wrote,

> And yet I still am half in love with pain,
> With what is imperfect, with both tears and mirth,
> With things that have an end, with life and earth,
> And this moon that leaves me dark within the door.

Harrassed by lack of money, stumbling under his load of literary
donkey-work (at one time he was reading four or five books a day,
and writing about them, and tormenting himself lest in his haste
he did injustice to some true artist still unrecognized), he came to
see himself as one to whom ordinary happiness was denied. 'Know,'
he wrote to Gordon Bottomley before the war, 'that only a revolution
or a catastrophe or an improbable development can ever make calm
or happiness possible for me.' And when the war came, he seems
to have seen in it the revolution, the catastrophe, the improbable
development, that would bring him calm and happiness. In the
unsettled state of everything, ordinary considerations of careers and
security went by the board; Thomas no longer cared that editors
were slow to employ him; he walked about the countryside, or went
on longer journeys by bicycle, putting up at the houses of friends,
and his mood seems to have been like that of Yury Zhivago at
Varykino, a man without a future rejoicing in the richness of life.
'I am sorry for nothing,' he wrote. The past was cut away.

True to his destiny as the voice of that England which was just
about to be cast into the fire, Thomas captured in poem after poem
the sense of being poised, in each precious moment, in a self-
justifying equilibrium. Already the past is gone, its values are strange
to us, we live by new laws not yet comprehended; but at least this
makes us see life as the strange miracle it is, stripped clean of
ordinariness. The poems Thomas wrote in this vein are entirely
English, yet they are like nothing else in English poetry. An example
would be 'As the Team's Head-Brass':

> As the team's head-brass flashed out on the turn
> The lovers disappeared into the wood.
> I sat among the boughs of the fallen elm
> That strewed the angle of the fallow, and
> Watched the plough narrowing a yellow square

Of charlock. Every time the horses turned
Instead of treading me down, the ploughman leaned
Upon the handles to say or ask a word,
About the weather, next about the war.
Scraping the share he faced towards the wood,
And screwed along the furrow till the brass flashed
Once more.
                    The blizzard felled the elm whose crest
I sat in, by a woodpecker's round hole,
The ploughman said. 'When will they take it away?'
'When the war's over.' So the talk began—
One minute and an interval of ten,
A minute more and the same interval.
'Have you been out?' 'No.' 'And don't want to, perhaps?'
'If I could only come back again, I should.
I could spare an arm. I shouldn't want to lose
A leg. If I should lose my head, why, so,
I should want nothing more. . . . Have many gone
From here?' 'Yes.' 'Many lost?' 'Yes, a good few.
Only two teams work on the farm this year.
One of my mates is dead. The second day
In France they killed him. It was back in March,
The very night of the blizzard, too. Now if
He had stayed here we should have moved the tree.'
'And I should not have sat here. Everything
Would have been different. For it would have been
Another world.' 'Ay, and a better, though
If we could see all all might seem good.' Then
The lovers came out of the wood again:
The horses started and for the last time
I watched the clods crumble and topple over
After the ploughshare and the stumbling team.[17]

Here, as naturally and inevitably as in any heightened moment of
life, fact and event, when contemplated with the eye of honesty and
simplicity, are raised to the power of symbol. The blizzard felled the
elm tree on the same night that the ploughman's mate, enlisted and
in France, was killed; the whole world, both the scene perceived and
the eye of the perceiver, were altered by this blizzard, this felling;
'I should not have sat here,' because even if the fallen tree had been
here, the man sitting on it would have been someone else. At the
same time, the lovers disappear into the wood, and come out again;
life and joy go on, humanity will not be quenched, even though it is
their destiny to be ploughed under. The great symbol with which
the poem ends, 'the ploughshare and the stumbling team', has

affinities with Hardy's 'man harrowing clods' in his poem 'In Time of "The Breaking of Nations",' and also with the Hopkinsian

> sheer plod makes plough down sillion
> Shine, and blue-bleak embers, ah my dear,
> Fall, gall themselves, and gash gold-vermilion.

At his best—and he rarely falls much below his best—Edward Thomas is worthy to be named with these great poets. Country-sentiment is common enough in English poetry, from the moment that towns grow large enough to be oppressive; but in his vision, the rural life is contemplated as *life*, with all its tragedy and harsh-ness, all its demand for stoical endurance, all its reminders of 'Soldiers and poor, unable to rejoice', as well as its lyricism, its 'cowslips wet with the dew of their birth', its 'sedge-warblers, clinging so light To willow-twigs'. Many writers have observed these things, but Thomas is one with the greatest of them, with Words-worth and Hopkins, because he conveyed the awareness that he and they were of one essence. As De la Mare put it, in the essay already quoted, 'One could learn and learn from him not the mere knowledge of the living things and scenes around us which were as familiar to him as his own handwriting, but of their life in himself.'

Edward Thomas must have been, at thirty-eight, one of the older men killed in fighting. Many of the poets who died were only just beginning to find their own voices; nor must we forget those who were potential poets, not yet aware of their gift and never living to be aware of it. (David Jones did not publish *In Parenthesis*, one of the finest of all poems about the war, till 1937; if he had been killed, the future possibility of this work would have been extinguished, and there must have been hundreds of such cases.) Charles Hamilton Sorley was killed when he was twenty. And perhaps the best way to approach the poetry of Wilfred Owen is to quote the first two stanzas of Sorley's poem, 'All the Hills and Vales Along':

> All the hills and vales along
> Earth is bursting into song,
> And the singers are the chaps
> Who are going to die perhaps.
> O sing, marching men,
> Till the valleys ring again.
> Give your gladness to earth's keeping,
> So be glad, when you are sleeping.
>
> Cast away regret and rue,
> Think what you are marching to.

> Little live, great pass,
> Jesus Christ and Barabbas
> Were found the same day,
> This died, that went his way.
>   So sing with joyful breath,
>   For why, you are going to death.
>   Teeming earth will surely store
>   All the gladness that you pour.[18]

Wilfred Owen was born of Anglo-Welsh parentage in Oswestry, Salop. His first five years were spent in the spacious comfort of his maternal grandfather's house, Plas Wilmot, but on the grandfather's death the house was sold, and from then onward Owen *père*, a hard-working but not very successful official on the railway, had to make what provision he could for the family, who moved with him to Shrewsbury, then to Birkenhead, where Wilfred began his education, then back to Shrewsbury. There was never quite enough money in the Owen household, with three boys and a girl to feed and educate, and from the beginning Wilfred had to show an iron determination to get for himself the essential training of a poet. He worked as a pupil-teacher in a Shrewsbury school; at eighteen, he accepted an unpaid post at a country vicarage, helping the vicar with various tasks connected with parochial administration, and receiving in return a certain amount of instruction. This place was near Reading, and Owen took the opportunity to attend classes at Reading University College, choosing with a poet's wise instinct a course in botany. In 1913, hungry for an enlargement of horizon and willing to suffer any drudgery and privation to get it, he went to Bordeaux, to teach English at the Berlitz school of languages. Though his pay was miserable and he seems at times to have been half-starved, Owen was right to make this move, for it brought him into contact with the European mind, at however humdrum a level, just before that mind ran insane; and through the good offices of a pupil, one Madame Leger, he spent a short time in the high Pyrenees, to whose beauty he was blissfully receptive. A week or so after this happy experience, the First World War broke out, and for Owen, as for every man of his generation, the sand began to run through the hour-glass. Young as he was, only four more years were left to him, and during these years he climbed to a sombre and tragic maturity in which his rigorous early self-training bore its fruit, abundant, bitter, and beautiful.

After joining the army in 1915, Owen had a prolonged experience of trench warfare at its most savage, on the Somme battlefield in the winter of 1916–17. In May 1917 he was invalided home with shell-shock, and spent some months at Craiglockhart War Hospital, near Edinburgh. These months of convalescence were very productive, for Owen was writing hard and also making the acquaintance of fellow-poets, notably Siegfried Sassoon, who gave him crucial encouragement. Hitherto, he had lived and worked in isolation from the world of letters; at Reading his gift had been recognized by that fine scholar and teacher Edith J. Morley, and during his time in France he had enjoyed the friendship of a French poet of an older generation, Laurent Tailhade, but these were fleeting contacts compared with the close and stimulating friendships he now enjoyed. Under the influence of Sassoon and of Robert Graves (who adjured him in a letter to 'Puff out your chest a little, Owen, and be big—for you've more right than most of us'), he felt his powers growing and gathering to a head. He also had literary contacts of a less essential but still cheerful kind, lunching and dining with such men as Robert Ross, Arnold Bennett, H. G. Wells, and Harold Munro.

Nevertheless, much as he enjoyed pleasant sociabilities with men whose writing he could respect, Owen never allowed his intention to wander from his principal objective, which was to tell the truth about the war from the soldier's point of view. In those days there was an impassable gulf between the serving soldier in his hell of mud, blood, and smashed bone, and the civilian at home who grumbled about rationing and exaggerated the danger from a few scattered Zeppelin raids. (For indispensable background here, see Robert Graves's *Goodbye to All That*, 1926.)

Owen's position was clear-cut. He believed that the war was an outrage against humanity and should be stopped immediately by a negotiated peace. All this time he was assembling a volume of poems which should, as Edmund Blunden put it in his *Memoir* of the poet, 'strike at the conscience of England in regard to the continuance of the war', and for this volume he began to rough out a Preface, which contains these sentences:

This book is not about heroes. English poetry is not yet fit to speak of them.

Nor is it about deeds, or lands, nor anything about glory, honour, might, majesty, dominion, or power, except War.

Above all I am not concerned with Poetry.

My subject is War, and the pity of War.

The Poetry is in the pity.

Yet these elegies are to this generation in no sense consolatory. They may be to the next. All a poet can do today is warn. That is why the true Poets must be truthful.[19]

Owen's determination to 'be truthful' and to 'warn' is perfectly embodied in the bareness and directness of his poetry. Yet he did not, as some later writers of 'engagement' have done, fall into the state of mind that rejects all art, all shaping and selection, as mere frivolous ornament, imagining that a naked shriek of pain or howl of rage will better convey 'truth'. Far from it; Owen's mature poems show that he had lost none of that loving care for artistry, that quick and lively response to the formal possibilities of language, which underlay his early efforts. He knew that a poet's way of saying something is to say it in poetry, and that poetry begins where the everyday use of language leaves off.

Rhythmically, Owen's poetry is superb: both strong and delicate. Perhaps his Welsh blood moved in him, for there is hardly a poet of such rhythmical *élan* in Britain until we come to Dylan Thomas. Nor one as little given to understatement. Owen describes his terrible subject in all its immensity, and to the task he summons every resource of lyricism and rhetoric.

> Heart, you were never hot
>   Nor large, nor full like hearts made great with shot;
> And though your hand be pale,
> Paler are all which trail
> Your cross through flame and hail:
>   Weep, you may weep, for you may touch them not.[20]

While never understating, always approaching his subject frontally, he could vary the texture of his language, sometimes achieving a sombre density that reminds us of Dante (in 'Spring Offensive' or 'The Show'), sometimes a harsh realism recalling Crabbe ('The Dead-Beat', 'Inspection', 'The Sentry'), and at other times a music as open-vowelled, as stately and unstinted, as that of Keats's Odes ('Anthem for Doomed Youth'); while a poem like 'Futility' challenges Hardy on his own ground. It is not that Owen ever slavishly follows these writers, merely that to mention their names is a rapid means of indicating his range. Technically, he was always moving on, impelled not by the wish to tinker with 'technique' but by the surging tide of his imagination. In the short time granted to him, he did not always manage to explore to its fullest extent every formal avenue he opened up. 'Spring Offensive', for instance, outlines an original and singularly effective rhyme-scheme which it does not quite manage to hold. Like so many of Owen's poems, it is a draft rather than an entirely finished work, and the wonder is that he managed to make these not-quite-completed poems sound so final and unalterable.

The form in which we read Owen's work owes much to the labours of successive editors, from Sassoon and Blunden in the early days to D. S. R. Welland and C. Day Lewis more recently. Many of the poems exist in several drafts and these have been conflated to make the versions we read. 'Strange Meeting', which many think his greatest single poem, appears to break off unfinished, and the moving, broken-off half line with which it ends ('Let us sleep now') was added tentatively. Finished or not, this dialogue between two dead soldiers is the most Dantesque writing to come out of the Inferno of those years of the great European self-murder. It begins:

> It seemed that out of battle I escaped
> Down some profound dull tunnel, long since scooped
> Through granites which titanic wars had groined.
> Yet also there encumbered sleepers groaned,
> Too fast in thought or death to be bestirred.
> Then, as I probed them, one sprang up, and stared
> With piteous recognition in fixed eyes,
> Lifting distressful hands as if to bless.
> And by his smile, I knew that sullen hall,
> By his dead smile I knew we stood in Hell . . .[21]

In such a context, it seems frivolous to talk of literary influences, of 'style', and all the other chessmen which critics of poetry push across the board. But, in speaking of a poet who cared as passionately for the body of his art as for its spirit, it cannot be irrelevant to point out that Owen was drawn to Dante in much the same way that Keats, at a similar stage of his development, was drawn (for Keats, too, shaped and strengthened his art within sound of the approaching footfall of death). But Owen's technical originality is the greater. In English neither blank verse nor *terza rima* will quite capture the majesty of Dante, and Owen has developed a form of the couplet which, rhythmically, might have been written by the mature Keats—the Keats who knew how to learn from Dryden—but, in rhyme, avoids the couplet chime which would have been, for these purposes, altogether too pat and predictable. These half-rhymes of Owen's (para-rhymes, off-rhymes, even meta-rhymes, as they have been variously dubbed) satisfy the ear while pushing away any suggestion of the patness and certainty that successive rhyme is apt to breed. Years later, when Owen's example had been thoroughly digested by English poets, such rhymes became standard form. Again and again one finds, in Owen, lines or stanzas that foreshadow the poetic strategies of ten and twenty years ahead. The poem we know as 'The Roads Also' (though it is actually untitled and put together by Edmund Blunden from two disparate drafts) might—but for its more unmistakable stamp of genius—have been written by the Auden of 1933–9.

Owen had every opportunity to opt out of the fighting side of the war, and take an honourable post as a non-combatant; the War Office were all ready to attach him to the Artists' Rifles as an instructor; but he chose to return to the front for two reasons. First, he felt strongly for his men, and wished to give them such help and comfort as he could; and second, he wanted his protest against the war to be uttered with the incontestable authority of the fighting soldier. He went back, and was killed exactly one week before the war ended, on the bank of the Oise-Sambre canal, near Ors, which his battalion had orders to cross in an assault at dawn on 4 November. Desperate, and in the end fruitless, attempts were made to construct a bridge across the canal, under heavy fire, and our last glimpse of the poet is as he moves among the men, encouraging them with 'Well done!' and 'You're doing very well, my boy.' Quite possibly these were his last words. He was lending a hand with some planks when a German bullet found him. On that accursed canal bank, 'Whereon the numbers could not try the cause', English poetry lost the second of the two men who could have guided it through the years of reappraisal and reshaping.

The gap had to be filled, and in fact the successor had already appeared. In June 1917, when attempts to halt the war had been repeatedly foiled, and Europe seemed to have settled down into a long and final night, a small volume of poems had been published in London under the title *Prufrock and Other Observations*. Its author was a young American, T. S. Eliot (1888–1965), who had spent the years immediately before the war in acquiring a solid education. At Harvard, he had studied under George Santayana and Irving Babbitt, and subsequently done graduate work on the philosophy of F. H. Bradley; in 1910 he had gone to Paris to study literature and philosophy at the Sorbonne; he had also attended the University of Heidelberg and Merton College, Oxford. His studies had given him a good grounding in the European literary and philosophical tradition, and in addition he had devoted a year's reading to Indian metaphysics.

Amid the uproar of war, *Prufrock* appeared quietly and attracted widespread neglect. Those who did chance on it, even when they responded to its strange attraction, seem to have misunderstood it more or less completely. Even to the approving eye, it appeared in 1917 to be merely escapist. E. M. Forster, in *Abinger Harvest*, has an essay in which he recalls the effect of coming across *Prufrock* in Cairo during the war. It won his heart, he tells us, by being 'innocent of public-spiritedness'; at such a time, 'he who could turn aside to complain of ladies and drawing-rooms preserved a tiny drop of our self-respect, he carried on the human heritage.' Some years later, in his essay 'Inside the Whale', George Orwell quoted Forster's judgement with approval, adding

> The truth is that in 1917 there was nothing that a thinking and sensitive person could do, except to remain human, if possible. And a gesture of helplessness, even of frivolity, might be the best way of doing that. If I had been a soldier fighting in the Great War, I would sooner have got hold of *Prufrock* than *The First Hundred Thousand* or Horatio Bottomley's *Letters to the Boys in the Trenches*. I should have felt, like Mr. Forster, that by simply standing aloof and keeping touch with pre-war emotions, Eliot was carrying on the human heritage. What a relief it would have been at such a time, to read about the hesitations of a middle-aged highbrow with a bald spot! So different from bayonet-drill![22]

Both these writers intend sincere praise of *Prufrock*. Yet both have radically misunderstood its nature. To praise Eliot for 'turning aside to complain of ladies and drawing-rooms', as if he were Lytton Strachey, or for 'standing aloof and keeping in touch with pre-war emotions', is to see his early work as its first readers saw it. Those readers might well misread the poems, even where they enjoyed them; they were battered and deafened by the war, and did not have, as we do, the advantage of hindsight. From where we stand today, it is easier to see the *Prufrock* volume as what it is—the first major utterance of a major poet: neither 'turning aside' nor 'standing aloof', but confronting the situation of 1917 at its frost-bitten heart.

The title poem of the collection, 'The Love Song of J. Alfred Prufrock', is indeed 'different from bayonet-drill', but it is a profound symbolic commentary on a world that found bayonet-drill necessary. In form, it is a dramatic monologue, not unlike those made familiar to Victorian readers of English poetry by Browning, and in fact 'Prufrock', as a satirically grotesque invented name to fit a man in a real situation, is the sort of detail Browning would have relished. Prufrock, accompanied by an un-named and unfocused companion, sets out on an autumn evening through city streets to pay a social call. The streets through which he passes are squalid, with an atmosphere of lonely futility, but the party he is going to exists on a different level: comfortable, cultured, at home where there is talk of the arts and of 'civilization'. Prufrock, poised between these two vividly realized worlds, is—we soon perceive— in a state of inner turmoil amounting to agony. There is something intolerably urgent which he both longs and dreads to utter, some spiritual burden which he cannot carry but dares not lay down. Lit by the glare of his torment, both halves of city life seem like the backdrop of some dramatized Inferno. The cultured chatter of the *salon* is summed up and rejected in the twice-repeated refrain,

> In the room the women come and go,
> Talking of Michelangelo.

The women 'come and go'; their lives are casual and unanchored, or anchored only in the thin dust of 'culture' that lies, an inch deep, over the world's capital cities; their talk drifts like

> the smoke that rises from the pipes
> Of lonely men in shirt-sleeves, leaning out of windows.

Both these lives seem insubstantial to Prufrock because he has something both terrible and splendid to communicate; he has broken through the paving on which they are all standing, and come upon the truth. As to what this truth is, various readers have come up with various answers. I have seen it argued that Prufrock is in love with one of the ladies at the *salon*, and wants to confess his love but dare not: again, that he has become aware that he, and the *salon*-frequenters, and the lonely men in shirt-sleeves, are all immortal souls, and is oppressed and overwhelmed by the knowledge that it does, after all, matter what they feel and think and do. The second of these conjectures seems to me more valid than the first. Yet, essentially, it does not matter what precisely is the content of the message which Prufrock dare not deliver. What the poem shows us is his situation, caught between two kinds of empty materialism, wandering through life with the knowledge that the people about him are somnambulists and that he, somehow or other, has broken through into reality. The world is asleep and poor Prufrock is awake, and, allowing for the very different idiom in which it is presented, his situation foreshadows the anguished questioning in Yeats's lines,

> What portion in the world can the artist have,
> Who has awakened from the common dream,
> But dissipation and despair?

Prufrock will not run into 'dissipation'; he is too timid and correct; he even has to screw up his courage before eating a peach, because peaches are notoriously difficult things to eat in a neat and dignified way, and Prufrock likes to be neat and dignified. If he did not, his knowledge would not be such agony to him. He hates to lose face because he is aware of having, on the social level, very little besides face to call his own. He is enclosed by the triviality of his milieu because there is so much in him that assents to triviality; like most of us, he is cowardly and attached to his comforts; and of course, once he has uttered his knowledge, there will never be comfort again.

> And the afternoon, the evening, sleeps so peacefully!
> Smoothed by long fingers,
> Asleep . . . tired . . . or it malingers,
> Stretched on the floor, here beside you and me.
> Should I, after tea and cakes and ices,
> Have the strength to force the moment to its crisis?
> But though I have wept and fasted, wept and prayed,
> Though I have seen my head (grown slightly bald) brought in
>   upon a platter,
> I am no prophet—and here's no great matter;
> I have seen the moment of my greatness flicker,
> And I have seen the eternal Footman hold my coat, and snicker,
> And in short, I was afraid.[23]

Small wonder that Prufrock has moments in which he savagely wishes to deny his humanity, of regretting that he is not free of its complexities and its choices.

> I should have been a pair of ragged claws
> Scuttling across the floors of silent seas.

The poem proceeds in a series of rhymed stanzas, formal and yet open to variation, which convey admirably the hesitations and questionings of Prufrock's mind. Then, at the end, it modulates into a romantic music, as haunting and suggestive as anything in Keats or Verlaine—Prufrock's love song at last, and the object of his love is

the mysterious mermaids, powerful symbols of a life unattainable
to him and a music he can hear but not join in. The mermaids are
sea creatures, and the sea is one of the great universal symbols of
life, where human arbitrariness and pettiness give way, as Byron
exclaimed in a famous passage of *Childe Harold*, to a deeper, unquestionable reality. Prufrock's fascination with the mermaids is the
measure of his awareness that a deeper level of truth and consciousness does exist and that he has seen it. The reason why 'we drown'
when 'human voices wake us' is because the element inhabited by
the sea-girls is in fact our true element, and we die of a spiritual
oxygen-shortage when dragged away to the level of 'the cups, the
marmalade, the tea', which is also the level of 'restless nights in
one-night cheap hotels' and, for that matter, of 'bayonet-drill'.

'Prufrock', in short, is about the burden of full human consciousness in a sleep-walking world. So far from merely 'complaining of
ladies in drawing-rooms', Eliot is here creating a major symbol
through which to explore the experience of those years. After all, if
we are looking for a figure which could adequately sum up western
civilization in 1917, it would be hard to find a better one than
Prufrock. For the tragedy of the years between, say, 1910 and 1918
is precisely that the highly-developed western nations had fallen
into a trance. During the brief but golden epoch that we in England
call 'Edwardian', progress seemed assured and civilization on an even
keel. No one, or at any rate, no one who spoke for or to the 'average
man', had any inkling of the forces of death that waited under the
placid surface. Yet these forces must have been there, *in petto*; the
four-year orgy of murder could not have suddenly descended on
Europe like a cloud; it must have had latent causes in the very blood
and nerves of the society that felt so sure of its reasonableness. And,
after the slide into suicide of August 1914, the sleeper did not awake;
he merely turned from a pleasing dream to a nightmare. In either
case, it was impossible to wake up. The misgivings, the profound
distrust of modern material civilization, which had led twenty years
earlier to the growth of Symbolist poetry, now had their tragic
justification. 'After us the Savage God', and the Savage God was
here, and as if in a dream the world's most progressive nations were
sending their young men marching, with polished boots, into his
maw.

When, at this distance of time, we read the infinitely touching
testimony of Owen, 'The Poetry is in the pity . . . All a poet can do
today is warn', we realize that J. Alfred Prufrock, wandering through
the unreality of the mean streets towards the unreality of the superior

salon, tortured by the knowledge within him, is the first major symbol of a major poet, for his impulse also is to 'warn',

> To say: 'I am Lazarus, come from the dead,
> Come back to tell you all, I shall tell you all.'

With this poem, and the handful of related pieces that accompanied it, Eliot's career was launched. How and to what heights it progressed is matter for a chapter in the succeeding volume.

NOTES

[1] W. B. Yeats, *Autobiographies* (1955), 430.

[2] Ibid., 314–15.

[3] T. S. Eliot, *Selected Essays* (3rd ed., 1951), 16–20.

[4] E. Wilson, *Axel's Castle* (1932).

[5] W. B. Yeats, *Letters*, ed. A. Wade (1954), 922.

[6] T. Hardy, *Collected Poems* (1930), 5. Quoted by permission of the Trustees of the Hardy Estate and Macmillan & Co. Ltd.

[7] *The Correspondence of G. M. Hopkins and R. W. Dixon*, ed. C. C. Abbott (2nd ed., 1955), 14.

[8] *The Letters of G. M. Hopkins to Robert Bridges*, ed. C. C. Abbott (rev. imp., 1955), 46.

[9] *The Poems of G. M. Hopkins*, ed. W. H. Gardner and N. H. MacKenzie (4th ed., 1967), 58.

[10] Ibid., 52.

[11] *The Journals and Papers of G. M. Hopkins*, ed. H. House and G. Storey (1959), 230.

[12] W. B. Yeats *Collected Poems* (2nd ed., 1950), 88–9. Quoted by permission of Mr. M. B. Yeats and Macmillan & Co. Ltd.

[13] Ibid., 124.

[14] Ibid., 142.

[15] Ibid., 182–3.

[16] Edward Thomas, *Collected Poems* (1936), 10. Quoted by permission of Mrs. Myfanwy Thomas.

[17] Ibid., 33–4.

[18] C. H. Sorley, *Marlborough and other Poems* (Cambridge, 1916), 57.

[19] *The Collected Poems of Wilfred Owen*, ed. C. Day Lewis (1963), 31. Quoted by permission of Mr. Harold Owen and Chatto & Windus Ltd.

[20] Ibid., 41.

[21] Ibid., 35.

[22] G. Orwell, *Collected Essays* (1961), 156.

[23] T. S. Eliot, *Collected Poems 1909–1962* (1964), 13–15. Quoted by permission of Faber & Faber Ltd.

FOR FURTHER READING

The standard biography of Yeats is J. Hone, *W. B. Yeats, 1865–1939* (1967). R. Ellmann, *Yeats: The Man and the Masks* (1949), and J. Masefield, *Some Memories of W. B. Yeats* (1940), also provide biographical information. Ellmann has written a further study, *The Identity of Yeats* (1954). Also useful are J. Unterecker, *A Reader's Guide to W. B. Yeats* (1959), and J. Stallworthy's two books, *Between the Lines: Yeats's Poetry in the Making* (1963) and *Vision and Revision in Yeats's Last Poems* (1969). U. Ellis-Fermor, *The Irish Dramatic Movement* (1939), is a brilliant study giving the whole background to Yeats's work as a dramatist.

The best concise, sensible treatment of the whole of Hardy's life and work in the one perspective is D. Brown, *Thomas Hardy* (1954). Biography is to be found in Florence Emily Hardy's two books, *The Early Life of Thomas Hardy* (1928) and *The Later Years of Thomas Hardy* (1930). Of great importance is Emma Hardy, *Some Recollections*, ed. by Evelyn Hardy and R. Gittings (1961), a manuscript discovered by Hardy among the papers of his first wife after her death, which makes interesting reading alongside the many poems which refer to their courtship and early life.

All the information on Hopkins, biographical and literary, essential and non-essential, is assembled in W. H. Gardner's enormous *Gerard Manley Hopkins*, 2 vols. (1944, rev. ed. 1958). For the rest, Hopkins has been too much written about, though there is an interesting essay by F. R. Leavis in *New Bearings in English Poetry* (1932) and Charles Williams's 1930 Preface has insight. See also J. Wain in *Preliminary Essays* (1957).

The essential criticism of the Georgians will be found in C. K. Stead's *The New Poetic* (1964) and J. Middleton Murry's essay 'The Present Condition of English Poetry' in *Aspects of Literature* (1920). Useful general books are S. K. Coffman, *Imagism* (Norman, Okl., 1951) and R. H. Ross, *The Georgian Revolt* (1967). War poetry is discussed in J. H. Johnston, *English Poetry of the First World War* (1964) and B. Bergonzi, *Heroes' Twilight* (1965).

I. M. Parsons's *Men Who March Away* (1965) is an excellent and comprehensive selection of poetry written about the First World War, much of it by serving soldiers. Students should browse through anthologies and individual collections, forming their own judgement, for there is no established canon of valuations of poets of this period.

Biography of Edward Thomas is to be found in Helen Thomas's two books, *As It Was* (1926) and *World without End* (1931), and in E. Farjeon, *Edward Thomas: The Last Four Years* (1958) and W. Cooke, *Edward Thomas: A Critical Biography, 1878–1917* (1970). J. Middleton Murry has an essay on Thomas in *Aspects of Literature* (1920); this is a brilliant pioneer study which makes all the essential points and largely undercuts subsequent criticism of Thomas. Walter de la Mare has an interesting Introduction to the collected edition of 1920.

Journey from Obscurity: Memoirs of the Owen Family, 3 vols. (1963–5), by Harold Owen, Wilfred Owen's younger brother, is a classic in its own right; it tells Owen's story as part of the wider narrative of his family and the times lived through. It is a mine of information about the social history of the early twentieth century as well as a skilful evocation of a number of creditable human beings. An adequate critical study is D. S. R. Welland, *Wilfred Owen* (1960).

W. H. Auden has edited *A Choice of De la Mare's Verse* (1963) with an introductory essay.

Most criticism of D. H. Lawrence's poems is unilluminating. A quicker way to understanding of Lawrence's mind is to read his letters, first edited by Aldous Huxley (1932), and in a more complete edition, ed. by H. T. Moore (1962).

Suggestions for further reading on T. S. Eliot will be found at the end of the chapter on poetry in the succeeding volume.

12

The Novel

ALAN FRIEDMAN

To understand what happened to fiction in the very first decades of the century, it will be useful to bear in mind two ideas, the first an image, the second an abstraction. First, the structure of the novel gradually underwent a change: from the structure of a ladder to the structure of a cobweb. Second, the energy of the novel shifted from a polar distribution between its two centres—the individual self and the social world—to an unbalanced concentration in the self.

It will be helpful to go back for a moment. From its beginnings in the eighteenth century, the moment-by-moment plot of the novel had portrayed the progress of characters who perceived very subjectively their passage through a highly objective social world. This polarity, this tension established between an objective pole and a subjective pole, was the source of the ladder-like narrative motion. Further, polarity had a meaning; polarity implies relationship, however quarrelsome. The form of the novel itself spelled out a cautious trust and wary partnership between the inner man and the outer world. When at the hands of its most restless and most perfect practitioners the modern novel underwent radical changes in form, its instabilities were not merely matters of literary tradition and technique. The sudden instabilities were psychological and sociological, epistemological and cosmological. The private self alert at the centre of the cobweb of the new novel, busily generating the fiction from within its own tissues, implied (by the form) a new and implacable mistrust of the public, outer world. The form implied a progressive estrangement from society and even at times a bewildering disaffiliation from any objective reality.

Now if the new imbalance—the central self—is kept in mind, a great deal else that happened to fiction in the twentieth century becomes readily comprehensible. First, as we shall see presently, the novelist's treatment of the inner dimension of character underwent a cumulative exploration. The focus of fiction gradually moved from a technical heightening of the treatment of awareness; through an investigation of the forces at work in the subconscious; to an attempt to render even the workings of the unconscious (James,

Conrad, Gide, Proust, Lawrence, Kafka, Joyce, Mann). Second, the mirroring surface of the novel slowly departed from a reasonably objective realism to the presentation of a daydream and even a nightmare world, that is, a world more and more responsive to the distortions of private awareness. Third, as the narrative centred (in effect, 'zeroed in') on the self, the rendering of time—the triumph of the story-teller's art in every age—underwent extraordinary modifications. The present moment together with the layers of the past, all of time buried in consciousness, all of time available there, became fair game for any degree of manipulation that might help to illuminate the new centre, the self. The fragmentation of the story-line which resulted from this unexampled freedom to move through time quickly became kaleidoscopic. The primary importance of plot ('the ladder') was called into question. Instead, the evocation of symbols to serve as centring nodes upon which meanings could condense, to give coherence and structure to the flux of the novel, became a useful but strange kind of network ('the cobweb', radiating from the self) that offered to replace the framework of plot. Plots that ended on a note of endlessness in order to give a deliberate sense of the incompleteness and irreducibly expanding complexity of private experience; extraordinary suspensions and final ambiguities in a novel's fundamental meaning; reliance on subjective and multiple interpretation rather than on public and coherent interpretation—all of these became commonplaces that readers found threatening and novelists found liberating. And most annoying, most bewildering of all, was the irreversible tendency of the novel in all those ways to become difficult in the simplest way—*hard to read*—a source of irritation and alienation between novelist and audience that no amount of theorizing has seemed able to soothe or smooth away.

This discussion will focus on practice, not theory. It will examine individual novels in some detail. But in doing so it will clarify the connection, point by point, between the practice of our novelists and the theoretical schema suggested above. The disruption of old forms, the struggle for new forms, was an unsteady, delicate, cumulative process. In the late summer or early fall of 1900, as his notebooks tell us, Henry James (1843–1916) put aside a novel he was never to finish and began work instead on *The Ambassadors*. That year in America Theodore Dreiser's *Sister Carrie* was suppressed, in Germany Thomas Mann's *Buddenbrooks* and Sigmund Freud's *The Interpretation of Dreams* were published; and in London where James was working, Joseph Conrad's *Lord Jim*

appeared: each of these had a curiously delayed effect on the
changing mood of fiction.

James was fifty-six years of age by the turn of the century.
American by birth, British by long residence, he was already an
acknowledged master of the profession of letters on both sides of
the Atlantic. And he was still on the verge of his last greatest years
as a novelist. The years 1902–4 saw the publication in astonishing
succession of *The Wings of the Dove*, *The Ambassadors* (the first of
the three to be written), and *The Golden Bowl*. What is equally
remarkable is that while James had always been peculiarly attentive
to inner awareness in his fiction, these last works brought his focus
on the private self—one by one—to unprecedented intensification
and elaboration.

The Ambassadors (1903), one of his most perfectly constructed
books, is a brilliant puzzle of consciousness. The principal private
ambassador referred to in the title is an emissary from the New
World to the Old: Lambert Strether, widower and editor, who has
lived for fifty-five years but who has not yet, as James conceives his
story, 'lived'. His personal mission to the French capital is to
persuade young Chadwick Newsome, at present mysteriously en-
snared, to abandon not only Paris but the woman who is detaining
him there. Strether's own future, dependent on Chad's mother,
hinges on the success of his efforts. His mission is to return Chad
forthwith to a worried mother, a secure fortune, and an unnamed
family business in Woollett, Mass. What happens instead is that
Strether goes over slowly to the enemy; to French ways and means;
even, in sympathy, to the ensnaring woman, Mme de Vionnet. The
gradual intrusion of the older man into the younger man's world,
into the artistic and aristocratic environment of the Parisian salon,
is the burden of James's tale: Strether's provincialism shattered, his
sensitivities engaged, his innocence sophisticated, his moral
understanding enlarged, and his capacity for life unleashed. 'Live,'
he passionately counsels a younger man part way through the story.
'Live all you can; it's a mistake not to.'

All of this narrative information, however, is not presented to us
directly by the author. Instead, like everything else in the novel, it
is presented as a puzzle: filtered elaborately, in successively unfolding stages, through the mind of one of the central characters. The
technique, crucial to James, has epistemological consequences. (In
passing, its kinship with relativity theory is noteworthy: in the
Jamesian technique, all values and measurement depend entirely,
and with startling results, on the selection of the point of view of

the observer.) James, who was given to analysing his craft, spoke at length and subtly of the way in which he used 'centres of consciousness' as the centre of his art. And only a few later writers—Joyce perhaps and Proust—have ever matched his gift for rendering the complexities of felt thought. It is therefore suggestive and significant that it was his brother, the philosopher and psychologist William James, who coined the phrase we have since come to associate primarily with James Joyce, the 'stream of consciousness'. And it is unfortunate that we cannot call the flow of fine apprehension in James's brother Henry's writing a 'stream of consciousness'. For while the difference between James Joyce's use of a 'stream' and Henry James's use of 'centres' is great, still the difference becomes negligible when contrasted with the rendering of the passage of consciousness in Samuel Richardson or Jane Austen or Henry Thackeray. It is true that the Joycean method, unlike the Jamesian, manages to convey the spontaneity and jumpiness of the thought process itself (and thereby to implicate areas of emotional life that lie beneath consciousness). And it is true that the Jamesian method is far more decorous and ponderous than the Joycean. Nevertheless, it is apparent that in James no less than Joyce (and quite unlike Richardson, Jane Austen, and Thackeray), the effect of each flow-of-awareness is to define everything in the novel by subjective perspectives exclusively—perspectives verifiable only by a succession of shifting angles of vision bearing on the world outside and the world within. The delineation of consciousness throughout a single work of magnitude celebrates subjectivity in still another way—by wedding the plot to the method. For the plot of *The Ambassadors* is not the intrigue of Chad and Mme de Vionnet, still less that of Strether and Maria Gostrey: it is the plot of the great flowering of Strether's mind.

The official reader for *Harper's*, therefore, who in 1900 turned down James's projected novel, *The Ambassadors*, for serialization, was extremely perceptive when he wrote of the book: 'It is subjective, fold within fold of a complex mental web, in which the reader is lost if his much-wearied attention falters.'[1] That is certainly the case, as is his careful distinction between the strenuous 'web' of the novel—'subjective'—and 'the story (in its mere plot).' Unhappily, he also wrote, 'I do not advise acceptance,' with the unfortunate clincher, 'We ought to do better.' But that was 1900.

The Wings of the Dove (1902) is a darker work. London and Venice are the settings; money and love, disease and life, covetousness and selflessness are the powers at work; and the story is a familiar, horrifying tale, the contamination of love. Two women, who are friends, are in love with the same man; the man, slow to understand the reality of his position, is disappointingly passive once he does. But it is the two women who drive the plot along and who disappoint in no respect whatever. Milly is rich, Kate is poor, Milly is American, Kate is English, and both are beautiful and clever. But to put the moral drama in James's terms—of Milly, Kate says, 'You're impossibly without sin, you know.' Of herself she says, 'My cleverness . . . has grown infernal.' The adjective is precise, the lines are drawn.

In the full knowledge that Milly is incurably ill and bound to die soon, the impecunious Kate conceives a subtle scheme. Without revealing her intent, she offers up her man in marriage—tacitly, not overtly—to the stricken heiress. 'We're making her want to live,' is what Kate *says*. But Densher finally grasps the full position: ' "I'm to marry her . . . and have money" . . . all along it had been only what she meant.'

And indeed Milly, when she dies, does leave Densher a fortune —though she has not married him. She has come instead to understand her friends' conspiracy: the knowledge of how she has been totally betrayed precipitates her decline and decease. But in the end, a paradox of love and guilt, Milly's unflinching bequest, dictated by generosity, comes as a vengeance. Kate's greed, though continually moved by practical considerations and managed by a clear-eyed, hard will, is finally at the mercy of love. Not hers: Milly's and Densher's. Densher, touched to the quick by Milly's posthumous 'gift' of the means to marry his Kate, cannot bring himself to touch the money. Kate, unable to have both Densher and the money, and unwilling to take the man without the money, turns her back on him.

But with that ending James set the mark—as well as the tone and style—for generations of novelists to come. The suspended novel: a last chapter, a last page, even a last line that draws the wide-eyed reader to an end while leaving him with extraordinary doubts about the entire meaning, especially the moral significance, of the novel he thought he had just finished reading. The last eight words of *The Wings of the Dove*, Kate's 'We shall never be again as we were', have never been equalled for their mingled sense of finality and suspension, for resolute, absolute clarity and studied, haunting ambiguity. Closing the back cover of the book opens the door, and the final *exeunt* adumbrates further experience, not only uncertain but irreducible.

A more ambitious and still more painful novel is *The Golden Bowl* (1904). The rustle and crackle of large bills, an audible million dollars, accompanies the rustle of the text as the reader turns pages from first to last. 'Silver and gold' and 'precious stones' on page one, and the image of a 'money-bag' on the last page: but there is no sense of the grounding of this wealth in any sort of enterprise, private or public, commercial or social. Middle-aged Adam Verver, so bland, so featureless now, that one wonders how he ever had the energy to emerge with a fortune from the modern industrial world, does, however, collect works of art. As the book opens he has just bought a marriage present for his daughter Maggie—that is, a husband—without a flaw and without funds, the Italian Prince Amerigo. Soon he collects another 'great' addition for himself, a wife—his daughter's dearest friend Charlotte, who 'has, in every way, a great attitude'. Two couples then, living in England and utterly freed of the necessity of *doing* anything: the novel slowly studies them, stubbornly contemplates *only* their intensely private condition, against a background of incestuous affection and healthy reiterated adultery, punctuated by a procession of card-parties, tea-parties, and garden parties. The effect is both languorous and terrifying.

For both the Prince and Charlotte are flawed, however valuable, and being flawed, they are fragile. They have had, before their respective marriages, a quiet affair, of which the Ververs, father and daughter, know not a thing. Left continually alone together by the continuing preference of father and daughter for each other's company, the Prince and Charlotte become lovers again, reasonably.

Used as a symbol, the novel's title is built heavily into the book. It is true that the ways in which James manages to use the symbol of a crystal bowl, once flawless, now slightly cracked, yet covered over and resplendent with gilt, are ingenious and complicated, but they are very far from subtle. 'Does one make a present', Charlotte asks, 'of an object that contains, to one's knowledge, a flaw?' Elsewhere Mr. Verver actually tells the Prince, 'You're a pure and perfect crystal.' Maggie and a friend indulge unabashedly in this:

'I want a happiness without a hole in it big enough to poke in your finger.'
'A brilliant, perfect surface—to begin with at least. I see.'
'The golden bowl—as it *was* to have been. . . . The bowl with all our happiness in it. The bowl without the crack.'

And beneath the shining symbol, a hazy, quieter mythology of the golden age, of Paradise, Innocence, and the Fall. Charlotte and the bowl's present owner discuss its age:

'But of what time then is the whole thing?'
'Well, say also of a lost time.'

The name Adam, echoes of Milton ('we watch them with their fate all before them'), and the chorus of friends who comment on Maggie ('Her sense will have to open. . . . To what's called Evil—with a very big E: for the first time in her life')—all of this underlies not only this particular novel, but in a wider sense all of James. And James's great theme, the exposure of American innocence to the dubious corruptions of Europe, goes back continuously and coherently—through the vanity of Jane Austen's Emma and the imprudence of Fielding's Tom Jones—to Bunyan's Christian, the first picaresque hero with a pack of sin on his back.

When Maggie's innocent eyes are finally opened to everyone's nakedness, she makes a brilliant attempt to resurrect them all, especially her Prince, an attempt whose brilliance lies in her maintaining, after a few words to her husband, a nearly total silence on the sore issue—to preserve the Prince's dignity and her own, to allow the next decision to be his, to keep her father from suspecting Charlotte's infidelity, and to force Charlotte to surrender without understanding that she has been forced. The inward agony of the suspense that follows makes arduous reading. But Maggie's strategy works. When Charlotte and Adam Verver depart permanently for 'American City', the ending of the novel predicates a new and permanent felicity for the Prince and Princess. But the 'flaw' of the novel extends through the ending, and there are symbolic signs everywhere that Charlotte's and Adam's lives from here on out will be lives of protracted emptiness and captive anguish.

The novel's reliance on symbolism is often awkward, especially when compared to the graceful, restrained touches with which James had recently rendered Milly's dovelike wings, covering Densher and Kate with her love and money in *The Wings of the Dove*. But the reiteration and heaviness of James's underlining suggest irresistibly that he is reaching out for solid ground, in myth, in symbol, somewhere, anywhere, outside his web of consciousness. In *The Wings of the Dove* there was a powerfully consolidated and powerfully articulated society, centred in the home of Mrs. Lowder, but extending outward from there. In *The Golden Bowl*, the last of his long novels, James seems unwilling or unable to evoke anything so solid—perhaps because he sensed that already in the new century there was no longer a meaningful and coherent social world outside his characters in which they could relevantly be anchored for his fiction.[2] There was only their mutual awareness—quite perfect, but desperately private.

James's last three novels, labyrinths of perception and labyrinths of style, had only a small critical success. They received an annoyed, heavily qualified respect. But the novelist remained an influential critic himself for the next decade. And one result of his effort to exhort, scold, examine, and mould the fledgling novelists of the new century was an illuminating literary quarrel. The rising, irresistible force of H. G. Wells (1866–1946) collided with the immovable subtlety of James.

Their discussions, carried on personally, respectfully, and tactfully, slowly grew bitter as they became public. The argument, as James saw it, was between the discipline of art and the admirable but undisciplined energy he saw embodied in Wells (and notably also in Arnold Bennett). It was an argument, on the one hand, between painstaking selection and care in the 'treatment' of the central, inner theme of a novel, and on the other, mere 'saturation', a thoroughgoing immersion in the handiest details of the social scene, the shell alone, the outer life of fiction. But Wells saw the matter otherwise. He argued impatiently that 'perceiving the discordant things [in life, James] tries to get rid of them. He sets himself to pick the straws out of the hair of Life before he paints her. But without the straws she is no longer the mad woman we love.'[3]

Late in his career, quoting his own early ambition, Wells ruefully admitted, 'I never got "all life within the scope of the novel".' He added '(What a phrase! Who could?)'[4] Looking back, we can see clearly that the old novel's transformation into, in James's phrase, 'the New Novel'[5] had little to do with anyone's attempt to catch 'all life' within its covers, but was instead everyone's attempt to redefine the word 'life' for our century. James's tag, 'the New Novel', offers us a helpful redundancy: if a novel is not in some sense novel, newly phrasing the sense of life for the reader's imagination, then it is in that sense not a novel at all.

On these grounds, Wells's haunting scientific fantasies and his appealing, free-wheeling novels are worth attention; but not a great deal. His novels are spurred on by modern concepts of the utility of engineering and the futility of the past, but while informed, his books are not in fact formed by these ideas. On the contrary his novels have the form of the past—stale grounds percolating with fresh notions. Now it is of the essence of the present critical argument that if an ostensibly original vision is to be brewed successfully in art, a special technique must be devised to do so. But as a writer, Wells has greater affinities with the nineteenth-century novelist than with the twentieth. He has no grasp of the new technical resources that made a genuine and fresh vision possible in fiction. When his novels persuade, they persuade by sheer verve and high spirits; when they fail to persuade, the failure is often due to a didactic impulse. Still, quite apart from his early science fiction, which remains classic in its realm, *Kipps* (1905) and *Tono-Bungay* (1910) both continue to possess a certain spunky power and even charm in picturing the formative ideas of the rational, practical world of that first decade.

Arnold Bennett (1867–1931) is by contrast a far greater craftsman. Moreover, the novels of the 'Five Towns', tracing in detail the disconcerting rise of the new industrial society, have a great, almost a documentary solidity. If old-fashioned, still *The Old Wives' Tale* (1908) remains an admirable work of long narrative scope. And yet . . .

'The Old Wives' Tale' is the history of two sisters, daughters of a prosperous draper in a Staffordshire town, who, separating early in life, through the flight of one of them to Paris with an ill-chosen husband and the confirmed and prolonged local pitch of the career of the other, are reunited, conclusively, by the return of the fugitive after much Parisian experience and by her gradually pacified acceptance of the conditions of her birthplace. The divided current flows together again, and the chronicle closes with the simple drying up determined by the death of the sisters. That is all; the canvas is covered, ever so closely and vividly covered, by the exhibition of innumerable small facts and aspects. . . .[6]

Henry James here catches the trouble with Bennett precisely. Later on it was phrased more bitterly by Virginia Woolf, who attacked Bennett, Wells, and Galsworthy together for taking a trivial and 'materialist' approach to the mysteries of personality and experience.[7] But the paradox—the greater Bennett's artistry, the greater the reader's dissatisfaction—was immediately apparent to James, who wrote at the time that our confidence 'in the solidity of every appearance [in Bennett's work] may be said to represent our whole relation to the work and completely to exhaust our relation upon it'.[8] Allowing for an exhaustion magnified by a more ambitious study of a family and a society, and allowing for the differences of another temperament—John Galsworthy's (1867–1933)—the same thing may be said of *The Forsyte Saga* (1906–22). From the first, and best, volume of the saga, *The Man of Property*, to the last, Galsworthy's constant irony falls rapidly into a mere stance—'. . . like every Forsyte, he could be a thorough optimist when there was anything to be had out of it' or 'The Forsyte in him said: "Think, feel, and you're done for!" '—it is an irony that palls almost before each sentence has had time to conclude. One reads these monumental, documentary, chronicle novels with a sense of deprivation: dark frustration blended with pale admiration.

A writer more driving, more exciting, and more experimental than these, Joseph Conrad (1857–1924) published his first large novel, *Lord Jim*, at the turn of the century. He was then forty-three. Fluent in Polish and French, he spoke English always with a heavy accent, but wrote with a style so pure that George Bernard Shaw called it no English at all: too impossibly free of local idiosyncrasies. Born in Poland, Conrad had run off to sea as a young man and had already become, before he turned to fiction, a master seaman in the British merchant marine. His early tales were so exclusively of ships and seas and archipelagos that later on he struggled with only partial success to break the public's happy but destructive instinct to strangle his work by putting it in a class with the sea romances of Robert Louis Stevenson and Frederick Marryat. Yet *The Nigger of the 'Narcissus'* (1897), a grimly symbolic short novel of a voyage home, of a ship studied closely in the process of nihilistic moral corruption, had already given evidence of a remarkable and unfamiliar voice in fiction. By 1900 with *Lord Jim* (and in the shorter 'Heart of Darkness', written while he was still at work on the former), the voice of Conrad had modulated to the tones of his favourite narrator, Marlow.

Marlow tells the story of Jim, a perfectly conscientious young seaman caught off guard by a 'burlesque disaster', who destroys in an instant his self-esteem and his capacity for life by abandoning his ship, the *Patna*, with 800 passengers aboard—a jump, an unwilled reflex of cowardice. In the long-delayed ending Jim is again caught off guard by the trickery of 'Gentleman Brown', a diabolic and symbolic mirror of his weakness. Along the way there are several shining passages of consummate interest; one especially has fascinated generations of readers, Chapter XX, in which the entomologist and merchant Stein counsels: 'to the destructive element submit yourself'. Nevertheless, between its perfect dramatic prelude —symbolic—and its nearly perfect finale—allegoric—there are unmistakable *longueurs* where nothing happens except the ingenuities of the narrator's meditations. Partly on Marlow's account therefore, *Lord Jim* is an extended story too big for its breaches of story-telling conventions. And yet for Conrad, Marlow was crucial.

Taken at the smallest estimate, Marlow is the author's British *persona*, the necessary mask through which the foreign voice can speak with virtuoso ease, a mouth capable of transmuting not merely language, but by the same alchemy the entire fabric of Conrad's foreign assumptions into threads of the Union Jack—into a pledge of allegiance to the moral codes of the Empire's readers. Yet Marlow is more than this. He allows Conrad to transform fiction along lines similar to James's, to transform the old sea romance into the 'New Novel'. It is fundamental here that everything we are allowed to see, to think, to feel, every interpretation of every event, is filtered before it comes to us, as in James, through the consciousness of someone other than the author: through the mind of Marlow. Events— melodramatic, romantic, or commonplace—bent through the refractions of his energetic monologue, take on the suggestive shapes, the spectral colours, and the concealed darkness which by now have come to seem elementary to the configuration of the self in the modern world. Because and *only* because the intonations of Marlow's voice oblige his readers and his author to assume the posture of salute—absurdly, deceptively; because and *only* because his voice remains reassuring though bewildered, pipe-smoking even when probing—Marlow permits Conrad to confront the implacable forces of the psyche at a depth of anxiety and ambiguity, of crack-up and redemption, that makes Conrad's work at its best the strained and straining experience it is. Marlow's voice functions in fact like a Jamesian 'reflector' or 'centre' of consciousness. The voice allows Conrad to move the novel inward, in the direction that Joyce and Virginia Woolf were soon to push it with the stream of conscious-ness; and to move it downward, as D. H. Lawrence was soon to do with the voice continually descending into the inward darkness. That is, Conrad shifts the balance of self and society in the novel heavily in upon the self. His modern subjective deployment of 'voice', of the ancient convention of story-telling which employs a setting and a narrator to frame the tale, has a kinship with the strategies of Joyce and Virginia Woolf. Their methods have often been called techniques of 'interior monologue'; Conrad's technique, exterior monologue, works more at the surface, but to many of the same ends.

Nostromo (1904) is the greatest of Conrad's novels, epic in its design, range, and implications. *Nostromo* is also much simpler than that, a kind of modern morality play set in Latin America. Its hero, instead of bearing the name Everyman, is called Ourman. (*Nostr'uomo* is 'our man' in Italian.) The moral theme of the action is human corruption. And if something is wrong with the book, as even its greatest admirers have been ready to admit, the trouble lies with the hero and his corruption. As a character in fiction, Nostromo is unsatisfying, his story melodramatic. If, however, Nostromo is taken as an emblem, and his career as symbolic—he and it enacting and showing forth starkly the fate of a new small country, as nineteenth-century 'Costaguana' enacts and starkly reveals the fate of the emerging industrial economy of the twentieth century—the role of Nostromo takes on the character, and the novel assumes the force, of allegory. Even his oversimplified love story (as later Heyst's and Lena's in *Victory*) has a heavily representative function; it is a coda of corruption.

The story covers a period of more than fifteen years of revolution and counter-revolution in Costaguana. Conrad is immensely successful in creating the complex, felt reality of his hypothetical country, not only 'history, geography, politics, finance', but every detail of the land's visual immediacy, together with dozens of characters whose lives are focused in the glare of history. None of these elements, however, is treated head-on: they are presented indirectly and a-chronologically. They shift as they come and bounce off each other at odd angles. The running 'story' resembles a cable of twisted threads, interlocked but separate. The reader's attention, with no regard whatever for the actual passage of time, is not only shunted rapidly, without warning, from one thread to another; it is pressed constantly forward by a dazzling display of new narrative viewpoints, one mind after another, views which slowly gather the story into a single whole.

In the emergency of an imminent invasion, acting on instructions, Nostromo, the captain of a waterfront gang, puts to sea with a cargo of silver and only two passengers, Hirsch and Decoud. Hirsch vanishes—Decoud vanishes—the silver vanishes—Nostromo returns. Hirsch is found and accounted for; Decoud never. Foul play? But Nostromo's reputation places him above investigation. The perfectly evident possibility that he has actually hidden a stupendous hoard of silver (which he has) and conveniently murdered (he has not) the only witness to the theft, causes not a tremor of suspicion. No one investigates his version of the story. (There is circumstantial evidence to confirm his story, but only one person, Dr. Monygham, 'whose short, hopeless laugh expressed somehow an immense mistrust of mankind', suspects some flaw in the truth; and he is obliged to keep his doubts to himself.) Nostromo, publicly and privately, is known as the Incorruptible. Given the sheer unthinkableness of his corruption, the fact that he is indeed inevitably rotted by his experience is the energy of the book's conception and design. Nostromo as a character is one-dimensional, but he is a central point in a cross-section of personages; his story is central, or coaxial if you will, to every thread in the cable of events; and mindless as his views remain in a book of complex theories of the psyche, ethics, and economics, he nevertheless remains the pattern for the national experience and the experience of everyman.

The technique by which Conrad makes Nostromo an emblem is perhaps as old as Homer—the technique of Hephaestus in forging the shield of Achilles. But Conrad works at his method until by a fine extravagance, he achieves a detailed and microcosmic set of symbolic correspondences, a net of analogies that suggests irresistibly the still more elaborate grid of symbolic correspondences in Joyce's *Ulysses*. For a couple of hundred pages we see Nostromo only in bits, moments so arranged that words and images begin to function as motifs and, later, symbols. The lover of a 'pretty Moreñita girl', but without any funds at first, Nostromo gives her instead a 'hoard' of 'silver buttons'. We hear that 'the fate of national honesty trembles in the balance'; later, 'thrown off his balance', we learn that Nostromo has become the slave of the very silver he has concealed. When he embarks with his cargo of silver ingots, he says darkly of the treasure and of himself, 'It has been tied for safety round Nostromo's neck.' Decoud replies, 'I see it.' And the hero who cannot understand that he will certainly drown, by a series of dramatic efforts 'saves' the silver, 'saves' all the major characters, and 'saves' the country—always in the same darkly ironic sense: 'There is no peace and no rest in the development of material interests,' Dr. Monygham explicates. Like the country as a whole, whose economy is based on the mine, Nostromo decides to 'grow rich slowly' by expending and yet concealing his treasure. As the silver mine enslaves the country—'more soulless than any tyrant, more pitiless and autocratic than the worst Government: ready to crush innumerable lives in the expansion of its greatness'— so the silver he has concealed makes Nostromo too a 'slave' with 'full self-knowledge'.

Nostromo had lost his peace; the genuineness of all his qualities was destroyed. . . . His courage, his magnificence, his leisure, his work, everything was as before, only everything was sham.

To liken Nostromo ironically to the imperishable metal he serves, Conrad's epithet is 'incorruptible'. For the silver mine's owner, Charles Gould—whom Conrad deliberately contrasts with Nostromo 'racially and socially' and who stands at the peak of the social order as Nostromo near the bottom—the repeated epithet is 'incorrigible'. They are 'both captured by the silver'; like the social order, their lives are possessed, consumed, and burned away.

Not a ladder but a web: Conrad's treatment at all points characteristically denies and flagrantly defies the steps of causation and chronology we call plot. Time flies and cause has effect but neither determines his structure. Instead, his construction is radial, an explosive fantasia of symbols leading in every direction from (and back to) Nostromo, the emblematic centre of corruption—a web that displays to best advantage the links of symbolic correspondence. The weaving of Nostromo's moral ruin into the ruin of other characters and into the thicker, more theoretical texture of the novel is continuous and subtle. When a Jewish merchant named Hirsch is tortured, he is suspended physically in the position of the 'estrapadc', precisely the position in which Decoud finds himself unwillingly self-tortured into suicide by the unbearable solipsism of his isolation—a figurative, spiritual suspension:

The solitude appeared like a great void, and the silence of the gulf like a tense, thin cord to which he hung suspended by both hands.

The rendering of Decoud's last days on the island—the tension of the sceptical mind locked to itself in the void—is a high point in Conrad's originality and artistry. When Nostromo comes to Decoud's beach, he sits 'in nearly the same pose, in the same place' as Decoud, and he lives through a night 'as tormenting as any known to Decoud'. Decoud, literally weighted down with silver ingots, had drowned himself in the gulf. All this happens to Nostromo figuratively. Shot while crawling to his treasure, he embraces his Giselle, and

weighted with silver, the magnificent Capataz clasped her white neck in the darkness of the gulf as a drowning man clutches at a straw.

He dies self-confessed as 'Nostromo the thief. . . . I have said the word', a thief not only of silver, but of passion: having stolen the love of his fiancée's sister *because* she was more corrupt. And the rotting of Nostromo's love runs parallel to the disintegration of love within the Gould family; and again runs parallel, within the nation, to the continuing corruption of political loyalties and of patriotic love.

The casual reader of novels will be put off by the book—and was from the start, for after the more popular success of the much looser, indeed limper, *Lord Jim*, *Nostromo* was not enthusiastically received. The reader must be willing to work for his pleasure. In this ulterior demand the book is characteristically modern, as are its experiments with fragmentation and symbolism, its concern with isolation, extreme distortion, and subconscious determinants in the actions of its characters. Nostromo, Decoud, Gould, Monygham— each is separately consumed by the cancerous growth of invisible energies within himself: a will for death. The progress of that will is hidden, subconscious. Its progress is in fact built into the book's construction, an organic model that tends to proliferate unpredictable, disturbing rearrangements of its elements. The form is more than formal. Only a portent of more disturbing patterns to come, the tale of the novel, rather than unfolding, keeps erupting. The reader discovers that he has been asked to abandon reliance on orderly sequence, in favour of courses of seeming unreason, to follow a pattern in fiction that reflects the play and progression of irrational forces.

Tracing that progression still further—to nihilism bordering on madness—*The Secret Agent* (1907) is a study of violence set this time in London itself, rather than in Malaysia or Latin America. The city's underworld and its characters have a kind of Dickensian grotesqueness, made harsh by the loathing of the author. Everything in the book seems to Conrad a 'senseless outrage', starting with the king-pin in the plot, the proposed bombing of the Greenwich Observatory: an attack on time (Greenwich Mean) and space (Greenwich Meridian). Bug-eyed anarchists, longing to strike a terrifying blow against order itself, accidentally cause the death of the feeble-minded Stevie, and the accident provides a clue—a cloth fragment. And the clue sets off a train of suspicions, investigations, other deaths. But Conrad's irony is heavy and fuming, his seigneurial distance from his madmen, morons, simpletons, fiends, parasites, and perverts—that is, from 'revolutionaries' and 'anarchists'—is woefully great. In consequence, the thrust of his attack on the anarchy he senses not merely in them, but in the wider social order, loses its force. Lathering at the mouth, the triumphant sneering author shadow-boxes with demons of straw.

Perhaps to keep his sense of perspective for another, more intellectual account of revolutionary activity and violence, this time in Czarist Russia, Conrad employed the device of a narrator in *Under Western Eyes* (1911). An Englishman, a teacher, views through distant 'western eyes' the Russian (conspiratorial, tyrannical, barbaric) scene in St. Petersburg and Geneva. On the whole, Conrad's choice proves an advantage; Razumov is seen more closely, more humanly, than any character in *The Secret Agent*. But this study in assassination, betrayal, misery, confession, and final vengeance through the deliberate maiming of Razumov, is exceptionally grim, even for Conrad. It remains not merely brutal and cynical but cumbersome and sketchy: embarrassing, as if its author were unable or unwilling to integrate its cruelties and his despair.

But despair yielded. In *Chance* (1914) as in *Victory*, published in the following year, Conrad held out some hope of 'trust in life'. In the last three works discussed above, the setting was land and the spectre was revolution. In *Chance* (1914) Conrad moved out to sea and returned to his neglected narrator, Marlow. All of these changes and more—his sentimental love story, his rambling and jocular humour, his lush and serene rhetoric—helped make the book Conrad's greatest popular success. And yet for sheer complexity of narrative method, not even *Nostromo* can match the intricacies of *Chance*. We move back and forth through time, which suddenly telescopes for dizzying effects; there are several narrators, one within another, like Chinese nesting-boxes; there are even two separate endings. Wretched, inferior Flora de Barral, her self-confidence destroyed by a lifetime of oppression, after four hundred pages finally discovers trust with her husband, heroic Captain Anthony. And at once, on the next page, Captain Anthony goes down with his ship in a wreck (though time has elapsed between those two pages). The End? But as we make our way through narrator after narrator we discover a traditional marriage ending: years and years after the shipwreck, the mate, one of the narrators, will marry the widowed Flora after all. The ending ('Breathing the dreamless peace around the picturesque cottage I was approaching . . .') is unbelievably banal.

Victory (1915) is another matter. Clipped, ingenious, yet not pretentious, the story of Heyst and Lena mounts to a climax of 'trust in life' that remains impressive—even hallucinatory—and yet ambiguous. The ending has built-in defences against a too-easy, sentimental reading. Events rise to the final holocaust on the island of Samburan with a nerve-reaching intensity. Heyst, for all his lifelong nihilism and 'infernal mistrust of life', has unexpectedly rescued a helpless cockney girl named Lena, carried her off to his island, and achieved with her a greater sense of reality and trust than he has ever known before. The couple are pursued to the island by a trio, a gang in search of loot: by deathlike Mr. Jones, catlike Ricardo, and apelike Pedro. Disarmed, Heyst watches Lena (who is only trying to get Ricardo's knife) *apparently* betray him with Ricardo. His trust is not great enough yet for this vision. Hideous doubt, the equivalent of death, 'seemed to spread itself all over him, enter his limbs, and lodge in his entrails. He stopped suddenly, with a thought that he who experienced such a feeling had no business to live—or perhaps was no longer living'. Moments later Lena is shot— sacrificially, Heyst realizes—in protecting him; she dies in the 'Victory' of her perfect innocence and trust. But Heyst? Heyst is crucial. 'Woe to the man,' he says to Davidson, the narrator of the final, telescoping pages, 'whose heart has not learned while young . . . to put its trust in life!' This is remorse. But trust? All we are allowed to learn from Davidson is the ambiguous news of a con- flagration: Heyst has burned himself, Lena's corpse, and their bungalow. Is this funeral pyre, as one reading holds, 'a triumphant victory, a victory over his own cold heart—a noble prince at the last, in tragic death with his beloved'?[9] Or is it, as another holds, the revulsion of despair rather than rebirth: 'The very opposite of it, Heyst's flaming suicide, is not "trust in life".'[10]

Victory was published during the war; its title, which had nothing to do with the war, helped to sell copies. Conrad continued to publish for almost a decade, but nothing so fine. *Victory* is short, it is moving, it is realistic in its detail, it is allegorical in its simplicity and power; it is, however, far from patent or clear in its ending. The doubleness of the ending, the cunning of a positive affirmation in a context that suggests its opposite, is masterly. Its controlled ambiguity, together with Heyst's isolation from the world, his lack of genuine connection with anyone or anything, the haunting suggestion that eery Mr. Jones embodies the nihilism in Heyst's own head—an unconscious pursuit by death, as Heyst has pursued death in life—and the ultimate irruption of the subconscious world of nightmare into reality—all of this brings us closer by 1915 to the world of the modern novel as we have since known it.

To turn from the works of Conrad to those of E. M. Forster (1879–1970) may cause a momentary wrench. We turn from a brooding, portentous, voluminous production to something rela- tively slender and apparently inconsequential. Except for *A Passage to India*, a work of acknowledged power but written much later

(1924), Forster's novels—there are only four others, and they
appeared quickly, between 1905 and 1910—have a gracefulness that
belies their consequence. It is an undeniable fact of literary taste
and criticism that since the Second World War even Forster's
earliest books have attracted and aroused admiration in a puzzlingly
large number of readers and critics—why Forster and not, say,
Bennett? It has sometimes seemed hard to say why. But it is
possible to say why, and important to do so. Forster shares something—it is more than artistry—with James and with Conrad. What
he shares can be suggested by quoting Conrad on James. Conrad
once described what struck him as 'a certain lack of finality' in
James.

One is never set at rest by Mr Henry James's novels. His books end as an
episode in life ends. You remain with the sense of the life still going
on. . . .[11]

While it is not always clear that Conrad himself achieves that
sense of 'the life still going on' (he does so in *Nostromo*, he certainly
doesn't in *Lord Jim*), it is clear that he was impressed by the
necessity and beauty of doing just that, of avoiding the tradition of
finality and rest. Alongside Conrad's comment we may set a remark
of Forster's:

Expansion. That is the idea the novelist must cling to. Not completion.
Not rounding off but opening out.[12]

The similarity in these remarks goes beyond structure, beyond
endings. It is far from clear that Forster's conclusions ever avoid
the tidiness and convenience of traditional conclusions; but it is
evident that his endings lead his characters (and his readers) invariably outward: at the end he sets their lives (readers' and characters')
into motion rather than at rest. In Forster, the conflict between the
developing self of personality and the inhibiting mould of society is
explicit; it is always decided in favour of the self; moreover, what is
noteworthy is the special definition of the self that Forster insists on.
He is devoted—however shyly—to symbolism: and more specifically,
to symbolic geography. Italy and India, Sawston and Monteriano,
are not merely places, but congeries of mysterious notions and
values. To some extent all novelists write a shorthand form of
symbolic geography: Defoe's island, Fielding's London, even
Arnold Bennett's Paris—these are more than places. But what
makes Forster's relatively quaint, almost sentimental rendering of
Italy partake of a common aura with the more menacing symbolic

renderings of Italy given us by James, Gide, Mann, and Lawrence is the character and content of the symbolism, *what* it suggests: the subconscious. That is precisely what leaps out startlingly into the light of his characters' consciousness when Forster packs them off to Italy—the subconscious life of bodily feeling. (And later on, what emerges in Forster's India emerges from still further down in the self and further back in history: from the unconscious.) This is the self of which Forster writes. And its expansion is the method by which he achieves an 'opening out'.

In *Where Angels Fear to Tread* (1905) Caroline Abbott is at first 'appallingly narrow'. But in Italy, she begins to think, feel, and respond as the Italians do—she becomes frightened—she cries, 'Help me!' and she promptly 'shut the window as if there was magic in the encircling air'. The hero Philip too at first seems 'fated to pass through the world without colliding with it or moving it . . . if other people die or fall in love they always do it when I'm just not there.' The action of the novel concerns the efforts of the Herritons—Philip Herriton, his sister Harriet, and his mother Mrs. Herriton (who stays at home)—to bring back from Italy to England a small child who is half-English, half-Italian. (He is the son of Philip's sister-in-law, now deceased.) The boy's father, the Italian Gino Carella, refuses to give the child up; so priggish, obtuse Harriet finally precipitates a violent crisis of kidnapping, death, torture, and love. In the process of these adventures—and this is the main goal for Forster—their awareness changes greatly. When Gino finally gets a devilish grip on Philip's broken arm, when Philip awakes from a faint during his torture to see Caroline holding Gino in her arms, both Caroline and Philip emerge with a 'consciousness of wider things'.

Her eyes were open, full of infinite pity and full of majesty, as if they discerned the boundaries of sorrow, and saw unimaginable tracts beyond.

In love with Gino, whom she sees she cannot marry, she confesses to Philip, '. . . if I mayn't speak about him to you sometimes, I shall die.' And loveless, friendless Philip finds that he has 'reached love' for Caroline and 'perfect friendship', even 'alarming intimacy', with Gino. The erotic implications in both directions are delicate but clear. Of the three who set out from England, only spinsterish Harriet fails to expand in Italy.

A similar heroine—Lucy Honeychurch—and a chaperone who reminds one of Harriet—the frozen Miss Charlotte Bartlett—go off to Italy together in Forster's *A Room with a View* (1908). Lucy at first responds to Italy, aesthetically, erotically, and otherwise; and then refuses to respond.

> 'Oh goodness!' her mother flushed. 'How you do remind me of Charlotte Bartlett!'
>
> '*Charlotte*?' flashed Lucy, pierced at last by a vivid pain.

Lucy is pained not only because Charlotte Bartlett is an old maid, but because unlike Charlotte, Lucy has begun to glimpse an existence beyond the closed circle of her life. 'Life, so far as Lucy had until then troubled to conceive it, was a circle of rich, pleasant people, with identical interests and identical foes. In this circle, one thought, married, and died.' To her fiancé Cecil Vyse, she admits, 'When I think of you it's always in a room. How funny!'

> To her surprise, he seemed annoyed.
>
> 'A drawing-room, pray? With no view?'
>
> 'Yes, with no view, I fancy. Why not?'
>
> 'I'd rather,' he said reproachfully, 'that you connected me with the open air.'

Even at their best the English have only views. Italy offers vistas— the twin truths of human feeling and bodily love. Lucy Honeychurch is finally seduced and saved by panoramas. The American Mr. Emerson 'made her see the whole of everything at once'. And she marries George, the boyish and passionate son of Mr. Emerson, acknowledging thereby that 'love is of the body; not the body, but of the body'.

A more complex novel, a novel of a very different sort, is Forster's *Howards End* (1910) which, while avoiding all suggestion of a documentary approach, nevertheless attempts head-on a full rendering of the contemporary social scene in and about London— the new commercial, political, and cultural world—and *succeeds* in documenting that world with passages of great dramatic, and even poetic, gusto. Hints of melodrama, caricature, and exaggeration now and again spoil the achievement, but despite these weaknesses, the novel manages to hold its own by its lively comedy, its persuasive, nearly prophetic tone, and by its remarkable suggestion that Howards End—the name of the country house in which the action is symbolically centred—is a microcosm of the new century's inescapable fate. 'Only connect' is the book's epigraph. It is also its structure. The plot, and finally the house, connect in symbolic fashion a multitude of things, but principally bring together materialists and idealists: two families known as the Wilcoxes and the Schlegels. The Wilcoxes, especially Henry and his son Charles, are businessmen, robust, conservative, organized, practical yea-sayers who lead lives of 'telegrams and anger'; they are above all masculine, the guardians of English rare-roast-beef no-nonsense character. The Schlegels, their foils, are two sisters named Margaret and Helen, literary liberals of the sensitive Bloomsbury stamp, who lead busy lives of concert seats, bookcases, and discussion groups; they are feminine, they are intuitive, they are too talkative; but they are the guardians of 'the light within'. The decision to connect these spiritual antagonists required all the author's will power (one senses his anxieties throughout), ingenuity, and sympathy. Complicating their uneasy union, there is a third force, the Bast family, the new aspiring proletarians—hopeless Leonard who 'knew he was poor', and his still more pathetic wife Jacky. And then there is, or was, Ruth Wilcox, Henry's wife. She appears early in the story with handfuls of hay, she dies near its beginning, and she is intended by the author as his representative of the natural world and of England's countryside tradition: Howards End is not only *the* country house, it is the country itself—the nation. And this older, pre-modern England is spiritually Ruth's, though all her Henrys and her Charleses come to inherit it technically and legally.

Bristling with these antitheses, the realistic seams of the story often burst under the pressure of symbolic statement. That Ruth Wilcox, in dying, should actually attempt to leave the Wilcox house to Margaret Schlegel makes perfect symbolic sense, but little more than that. That Margaret Schlegel, for all the poetry of her com-passion, should actually marry Henry Wilcox, with all his athletic commercialism! Yes, a fascinating idea, but unconvincing. That Henry in the past has actually had an affair with futile, frowzy Jacky! No. Tender credulity refuses this rough coincidence. On the other hand, that Helen should be impregnated with the seed of the Basts—not quite so unexpected—is one of Forster's best touches. That suddenly—death in a subordinate clause—'they laid Leonard, who was dead, on the gravel'! The sentence remains a stunning *tour de force.* That the survivors of all these sordid comedies should reside together at the ending under a single roof, Howards End—all these extravagances alternately delight and tax the imagination. It is a flawed book. It is a blatantly plotted book. But despite strains and weaknesses it achieves an 'expansion', an echoing of symbols beyond the paradigm of plot, the kind of 'opening out' in the reader's mind that Forster desired [13] and which he was to achieve again much later and much more perfectly after the war in *A Passage to India.*

The single greatest master of the novel in this period seems unquestionably to have been D. H. Lawrence (1885–1930). Possessed—to an extraordinary degree—of conviction in himself, faith in the novel, and genius, he directed his attention less to the morals and manners of his time—though both of these figure handsomely in his work—than to something at once more elemental and more tenuous, the inward conditions of human existence. Setting his earliest novels in the mining and agricultural region of England he knew best, Nottinghamshire, he gradually moved his characters outward from English rural and industrial scenes to Switzerland, Italy, Australia, Mexico. Conventional at first, his work gradually became radical. Aspiring to be at once a philosophical novelist, a political novelist, an apocalyptic novelist, and a psychological novelist, Lawrence was driven to experiment with the texture and form of fiction. The reader is apt to feel alternately disturbed by a roughness of style—whatever the integrity of the novelist—and disturbed as well by an illumination that goes beyond what the art of the novel can normally give. However he may respond, it is clear that Lawrence's novels, like the modern novel generally, gradually move from an appeal to his readers to direct assault, from poetry to politics, from naturalism to nature myths, from social relations to sexual relations, from plot and theme to symbol and dream, from transparent meaning to opaque complexity, from the delineation of character to the exploration of the psyche.

Sons and Lovers (1914), Lawrence's third novel, shows all these elements, not yet visibly precipitated and explicitly developed as in his later fiction they were to become, but present everywhere under the surface, held in solution. On its surface the story is told in a familiar pattern, it is the novel of a young man's development: his rise out of and beyond his family origins and limited circumstances to incipient adulthood and the promise of life as a painter. On that level, his mother's and father's marriage and their intimate tormented life, the economic and social life of the miners, the nurture of the Morel children, the adolescence of William and especially of Paul, Paul's schooling, his jobs, his happiness in the countryside, his struggle for vocation, his bond to his family, his troubled courtship of Miriam, his heated affair with Clara, his mother's death, his concluding despair—all this is recounted in grainy, almost documentary fullness of detail. The author's method is naturalistic, his eye painterly, his intent psychological. But beneath this crowded human surface the novel has a whole other life, elemental and symbolic. The reader is taken along on an extraordinary expedition, a search for a new map of the human condition, a map which shall be other than human, at once less and more than human—extra-human. The goal of that search, in *Sons and Lovers,* must probably be judged a failure. But the search itself—the novel—is maintained at such a pressure that its power becomes almost that of a natural force.

The course of the entire action is projected by Mrs. Morel's need to find in her two sons, one after another, a lover to replace her own husband, whom she has found intolerable as a husband and whom she destroys as a man. Soon after its publication, understandably, the Freudian parallels (which Lawrence had arrived at on his own, more or less intuitively) were pounced upon by a world excited by the new depth psychology. The biographical parallels with his own life (which Lawrence was never much at pains to conceal) were pounced on with equal lust by an audience enamoured of the aura of new sexual frankness. But *Sons and Lovers* is more than a psychological portrait, and more than an autobiographical confrontation, just as it is more than a stern story of trapped sexual passion. The trap, maternal love, remains throughout a mystical blend of selfishness, fulfillment, and sacrifice, and the long, slow shuttling of passions back and forth among Paul, his mother, and the two young women produces a psychological context that in the long run is not satisfactorily presented in psychological terms—despite the author's lengthy expository efforts—but is in fact generated and comprehended by non-rational vision and by physical details. Moonlight and coal dust, the wind in the ash tree, the drop of mother's blood that falls on a baby's hair, William's coffin and Paul's pneumonia, the plucking of flowers, the dancing of a 'big red beast' of a stallion, the 'blind and ruthless' hot blood bath of sex—these are not merely symbols in the usual sense, not merely embodiments and not merely vehicles of meaning, but agents of the drama. They are the terms of the fate that drives Lawrence's people and his plot—physical terms, finally, rather than psychological terms—a startling attitude towards the human psyche which, by the time he came to write *The Rainbow,* he made fully explicit.

The Rainbow (1915) was originally conceived together with *Women in Love* (written in 1916, published in 1920) as a single novel about two sisters, Ursula and Gudrun. Later Lawrence split the story into twin volumes. The twins are non-identical. But although different—the first a good deal more conventional than the second—both form parts of a single experiment, an experiment that simply grew more complex as Lawrence continued to write.

To put the matter briefly: before James Joyce and by a different avenue, Lawrence attempted a direct literary rendering of his characters' unconscious.

The attempt did not help him with the censor, any more than it helped to reconcile the censor to Joyce in the following decade. *Something* was unconventional about Lawrence, all right—and the police and the courts decided it was sexual frankness. In a decision that now seems nearly inexplicable, *The Rainbow* was adjudged obscene and the entire printing suppressed because a pregnant wife dances nakedly and triumphantly before her hypnotized husband. Now there is no doubt that Lawrence fought a running and continuing battle for years against a centuries-old tradition of literary prudery. But it is not always understood that his fight against literary suppression was part and parcel of his effort to find a literary method that would clear the channels to the unconscious.

The conventional elements of *The Rainbow* are quickly enumerated. Lawrence presents in a leisurely narrative three generations of a single family; the book's kinship with such large-scale chronicle novels as Thomas Mann's *Buddenbrooks* (1900) is easy to recognize. Moreover *The Rainbow* has a strong affinity with the familiar pattern of *Sons and Lovers*, the novel of a sensitive young man's development—here a girl's. Her name is Ursula: to arrive at her, Lawrence takes a running leap. He begins with her grandparents (as in *Sons and Lovers* he begins with parents), and the leap he here takes is appropriately longer—Ursula's history continues into the second volume. *The Rainbow* is a novel of landscapes and kitchens, motherhood and fatherhood, childhood and adolescence. But throughout, what Lawrence does with conventions is unconventional. From the first character on the first page who is 'aware of something standing above him and beyond him in the distance', to Ursula and her communion with a rainbow on the last page—precisely as in the startling scene of a pregnant woman's naked dancing—what Lawrence is trying to evoke everywhere is the unconscious—directly. Not only its manifestations and its ceremonies, but its content—as starkly as he could imagine or express it.

Readers familiar with Joyce's method—of pulverizing *verbal* consciousness in order to render preconscious and unconscious material—are often puzzled by Lawrence's technique. Lawrence utilizes another kind of distortion, the distortion of emotional awareness, and thereby takes us into another region of the unconscious. It is an easy error to assume, despite constant clear evidences to the contrary, that all the strange passages in Lawrence are wild descriptions of feelings—

Terribly, shocks ran over her body, like shocks of electricity, as if many volts of electricity suddenly struck her down—

metaphors for an emotion. And as emotion, such descriptions are understandably felt to be exaggerated, bizarre, absurd, embarrassing. But in fact Lawrence is trying to get away from—beyond and behind—feeling; and away from—beyond and behind—consciousness. From the beginning, in each of the three generations, the entire significance of very extended narrative passages condenses on moments which function as cores or nodes: in the first generation, that of the grandparents—

And he remained himself. he saved himself from crashing down into nothingness, from being squandered into fragments, by sheer tension, sheer backward resistance

—in the second, that of the parents—

The strangeness, the power of her in her dancing consumed him, he was burned, he could not grasp, he could not understand. He waited obliterated

—and in the third, that of the contemporaries—

He was afraid of the great moon-conflagration of the cornstacks rising above him. His heart grew smaller, and it began to fuse like a bead. He knew he would die.

In each generation, these moments are visionary, impersonal, demonic, physical.

This commitment to a new concept and a new approach was deliberate; Lawrence knew what he was doing. In a famous letter to his editor, he wrote explicitly that in creating a character in fiction, what now fascinated him was a part of the human self that was 'non-human'—'that which is physic'—a region of the psyche which functioned apart from the moral, consistent, stable, individual ego, a level of character at which 'the individual is unrecognizable'.[14]

In *Women in Love* this strange approach to character (impersonal, physical, demonic, visionary) grows more intense and extends its hegemony to include not merely the characters, but plot, structure, themes, and meaning. Deliberately, Lawrence's characters seem more and more like nuclear patterns, shimmering arrangements of physical and psychic forces, and though they often act in the daylight as visible, polite, sensuous, sexual, and social beings, even then they seem less like characters than like crystals—intricate, hard, and flashing.

The structure of the novel is built less on the plotting of action than on the plotting of symbols—pistil and stamen, the moon in a lake, a mare and a freight train, the Marsh and the Alps, ancient African sculpture and contemporary industrial sculpture. And the rhythmic forward motion depends on the permutation of couples, lovers, and friends: the psychologically possible number of combinations in pairs among the sisters Ursula and Gudrun, the friends Birkin and Gerald, and two outsiders, Hermione and Loerke. Their constant attempt (as they are driven by the plot and drawn into its meaning) is to find in each possible pair 'a final, almost extra-human relationship'. Only Birkin and Ursula manage to succeed—'a consummation of my being and of her being in a new one, a new paradisal unit regained from the duality'—though even their success remains unstable. The interweaving of relationships reaches its crisis in the death grip Gerald takes on Gudrun's throat. When he lets go, Gudrun goes off with her 'mud-child' Loerke, and Gerald freezes to death in the ice of the Alps. He becomes 'cold, mute Matter'. But mere Matter—never genuinely alive—he all along was anyhow. The industrialist in Gerald stands for a new and special kind of perverse mastery, mental, mechanical, life-destroying, the sickness of an entire industrial society (though admittedly one can't help feeling that it's especially Gerald's money that irritates Lawrence). Together, Gerald and Gudrun have perverted Lawrence's living mysteries. And so the novel ends appropriately in the watch over Gerald's corpse when Birkin cries, shaken, 'He should have loved me.' Ursula replies with an understandable denial, insisting that Birkin cannot have two kinds of love 'because it's false, impossible'. The novel ends by posing this problem and refusing to solve it. Like *The Rainbow*, *Women in Love* ends on a suspension, rather than a resolution, in both cases deliberately suggesting the continuance and expansion of the book's complex meanings after the close of the final paragraph.

Part of the interest in Lawrence's fiction was, and still is (though less so now), the excitement of his restless theorizing—a rhetoric of notions that flooded out over the novels into essays, tracts, and utopian schemes. But beneath every notion and every analysis, underpinning even his irrational politics, lay his intuitive psychological theory whose implications were religious—his belief in

blood-consciousness with the sexual connection holding the same relation as the eye, in seeing, holds to the mental consciousness. One lives, knows, and has one's being in the blood, without any reference to nerves and brain. This is one half of life, belonging to the darkness.[15]

For Lawrence tragedy is in effect the tyranny of consciousness. Through history, through civilization, through every political and social institution it could create, the human mind has worked to cut itself off from its own inner chaos. Increasingly successful, increasingly separated, and therefore increasingly afraid of that chaos, consciousness has suppressed the unconscious roots of its being. His novels are an effort to render the fear and the conflict; if possible, to rectify the balance. And though neither his vision nor his methods, neither his style nor his awareness, can be counted on to work for everyone, Lawrence remains a novelist of remarkable authenticity and power.

For perspective, the middle years of the First World War provide a convenient place to pause for a look backward and forward, in and out of England. Since Sigmund Freud's important and seminal work, *The Interpretation of Dreams*, appeared in Germany in 1900 (translated into English in 1913), it has always been tempting to assert a direct connection between depth psychology and the psychological deepening of the novel: as it is tantalizing to see a connection between Max Planck's quantum mechanics (1900 again) and methods of discontinuous, fragmented presentation in the novel; or between Albert Einstein's later theory of relativity and the novel's increasing ambiguity (regularly produced by a point of view which is fixed, arbitrary, and not reliable); or between cosmological theories of a limitlessly expanding universe and novels written in limitlessly expanding forms. Connection there undoubtedly is, but direct influence is another and more complex matter. The data seem to suggest rather that everyone had begun to move at the same general time in the same general direction. *Buddenbrooks*, for example (again, 1900), by Thomas Mann (1875–1955), falls clearly in the tradition of that nineteenth-century partnership between society and character which distinguishes earlier fiction. But what distinguishes Mann from such other contemporary practitioners of solid social realism as Grazia Deledda in Italy or Arnold Bennett in England is—even in that early first novel—his clearly developed sense of the inner connections between psychological sickness, physical disease, and death (young Hanno); between society and sublimation, between personality and what we should now call libido (Thomas and Christian). Yet *Buddenbrooks* is in no sense whatever Freudian. The Thomas Mann who later delighted in the ironies of introspection and of depth analysis, who wrote *Tonio Kröger* in 1903 and *Death in Venice* in 1911 (in the latter, the unleashing of repressed forces from the unconscious into consciousness destroys the protagonist), was impelled early in his career to contemplate the ambiguities of abnormal mental processes. An interest in these processes was more than 'in the air'; it was already in the novel.

In France André Gide (1869–1951) as early as 1902 in *The Immoralist*, and later in *Strait Is the Gate* (1909) and *Lafcadio's Adventures* (*Les Caves du Vatican*, 1914), had begun to write novels in which the attention of the reader is directed subtly away from the claims of the social and objective world to the still more imperative claims of inward upheavals—'immoral', liberating, threatening —to the wilful separation of conscience from consciousness and (as in Mann) to the unleashing of sexual repressions. By 1913 Marcel Proust's (1871–1922) *Swann's Way* had appeared, the first of a series of volumes whose publication remained stalled till after the Armistice and which finally constituted the vast *Remembrance of Things Past*. When complete, Proust's work as a whole (though not Freudian) was to constitute an incessant tracking down of time in the labyrinths of consciousness: the encirclement by fiction of a great continent of the psyche. There is an evident relation here not only to James Joyce's doubling of other continents in *Ulysses* (1921), but even to Joyce's first novel (for which see below).

In the United States a novelist of another sort entirely, Theodore Dreiser (1871–1945), tackled the art of the novel, and the relation between the psyche and society, with less subtlety than main force. In 1900 Dreiser's *Sister Carrie* was suppressed before distribution by its own publisher; and then, when it was published after a delay of twelve years, condemned by the critics on moral grounds. Not, however, for its sexual frankness, but for its amorality: its frank view that 'immorality' may indeed not fail to prosper in the end. In the 'Titan' trilogy and *The American Tragedy* (1925), Dreiser kept up his onslaught against received beliefs—social, sexual, and philosophical—and against institutionalized stupidities. But much of Dreiser is crude: his style, his structural heavy-handedness, his deterministic philosophy (which struggles to present characters in terms of 'chemisms' and 'magnetisms'). Despite his fervent amassing of details, and partly on account of it, the world he paints remains flat. A very different American writer, Edith Wharton (1862–1937), a friend and admirer of Henry James, had followed the master's lead in novels of considerable technical adroitness, psychological perception, and social awareness. These works are not quite so intense nor quite so challenging as the novels of James; nevertheless *The House of Mirth* (1905) and *The Age of Innocence* (1920) are more than novels of manners and morals, however astute. They evoke 'a society of irresponsible pleasure-seekers' with an art that conveys a sense of tragedy. And technically, as in James, the careful focus is less on society itself than on its moral reflections through the central consciousness of characters.

After James, more effectively than any other novelist in English, together with Proust in France (and later, each in his own way, Kafka in Germany and Faulkner in America), James Joyce (1882–1941) pushed the highly wrought social surface of the novel inward. He opened it wide to the exploration of a self so private that even characters who think before the reader's eyes are themselves continually caught unawares by the fertility of their imagination. Consciousness in Joyce leads at once downwards—through unusual psychological penetration—and outwards—through increasingly vast erudition—into the opacities and ambiguities, the symbols and distortions, of an unconscious self that threatens to assert its quasi-divine independence of any verifiable reality, indeed to engulf reality. Even his first novel, *A Portrait of the Artist as a Young Man* (1916), despite resemblances to other novels which portray the growth of a sensibility, is about the development of a young mind rather than a young man. Partly the result of a scrupulous technique, this emphasis of Joyce's, however relative it may seem, was so crucial in its effects on literature that in the *Portrait* and in *Ulysses* (1922) Joyce rewrote for the modern novel generally the definition of a man.

In tracing his hero's growth, Joyce fragmented the usual stream of events to produce a pattern that was irregular, discontinuous, corresponding to the inward man alone. And through this uneven rhythm of events runs a pattern of images as complex and fluently stitched as the structure of a poem: birds and roses, eyes and hands, air and water, flying and falling. Reiterated through varying contexts of the action, these images take on a rich incantatory force. They become symbols of a meaning that defies explanation finally because every symbol seems to have two diametrically opposed meanings. This practice was deliberate. The greatest virtuoso of prose in English fiction, Joyce had already evolved a subtle control of his medium by the time of his first novel, a control which he had once disastrously lacked. In an earlier version of the novel (published posthumously in fragmentary form as *Stephen Hero* in 1944), he had written unambiguously of his hero:

He desired for himself the life of an artist. Well! And he feared that the Church would obstruct his desire.

This sentence, which comes near to summing up a good deal of the later *Portrait*, does so in the characteristic brassy, slovenly, expository style for which the later Joyce would not have wished to accept responsibility. By the time he came to write the *Portrait* he could write of a Stephen who proposes to become

a priest of eternal imagination, transmuting the daily bread of experience into the radiant body of everliving life.

Here the style is gorgeous and subtle—so subtly gorgeous that we are at a loss to know whether or not the author is making his adolescent hero the target of grim adult mockery. In *Stephen Hero*, the hero advised his mother to go 'tell the priest he was making a torpedo'. In the *Portrait* he chooses quieter weapons—'silence, exile, and cunning'—against the same enemies—'home . . . fatherland . . . church'—and delivers the great refusal of Lucifer—'I will not serve.' But the question remains whether we are to view Stephen as grand, rightful, and creative, as Stephen tells us himself —or whether we are to understand him as damned, spiteful, and infertile, as some of Joyce's images and symbols suggest—for example, those of flying and falling. Here, as in *Ulysses*, Joyce has not only already begun to deploy a mythic background—an ancient time set against his present moment, informing both his plot and his characters' minds—but also, as in *Ulysses*, mythic correspondences that are distressingly double. Is Stephen Dedalus to be contemplated against the shadow of the ancient Daedalus, the artificer who flew, escaped, and triumphed? Or is Stephen to be measured against the shadow of Icarus, as the son of Dedalus, the prideful son who flew and fell and was drowned? The only answer the novel will support seems to be: both. In his first novel Joyce concludes with an unstable fusion of opposites. It is one of the first but not the last novel of this century to end indeterminately, in a state of ambiguous suspension.

One could hardly wish to end otherwise here. In 1918 the war was 'over'. Freudian doctrine had gained grim acceptance through the use of psychoanalytic technique in shell-shock cases, the U.S.A. set up air-mail service, the Royal Flying Corps became the R.A.F., and Gerard Manley Hopkins's *Poems* were published posthumously.

In the following year Adolf Hitler founded the Nazi party, Mussolini formed his *Fascia di combattimento*, the Soviet Republic was established in Russia, and Virginia Woolf began burying Arnold Bennett in the pages of *The Times Literary Supplement*.[16] It was an end and a beginning.

NOTES

[1] *The Notebooks of Henry James*, ed. F. O. Matthiessen and Kenneth Murdock (1947), 372.

[2] F. W. Dupee, *Henry James* (rev. ed., 1956), 267ff.

[3] *Henry James and H. G. Wells*, ed. Leon Edel and Gordon N. Ray (Urbana, Ill., 1958), 246.

[4] Ibid. 223.

[5] *The Times Literary Supplement*, 19 Mar. 1914, 133.

[6] Ibid. 186f.

[7] V. Woolf, 'Mr. Bennett and Mrs. Brown', *The Captain's Death Bed* (1950).

[8] *Henry James and H. G. Wells*, 187.

[9] R. F. Haugh, *Joseph Conrad: Discovery in Design* (Norman, Okla., 1957), 116.

[10] K. Widmer, 'Conrad's Pyrrhic *Victory*', *Twentieth Century Literature* (Oct. 1959), 129.

[11] J. Conrad, 'Henry James, An Appreciation', *Notes on Life and Letters* (1924), 18f.

[12] E. M. Forster, *Aspects of the Novel* (1927), 241.

[13] Ibid.

[14] *The Letters of D. H. Lawrence*, ed. Aldous Huxley (1932), 199f.

[15] D. H. Lawrence, *Letters to Bertrand Russell* (1948), 63.

[16] *The Times Literary Supplement*, 10 Apr. 1919, 189.

FOR FURTHER READING

There are several notable books which examine critical approaches to fiction. E. M. Forster's *Aspects of the Novel* (1927), designed for the general reader, asks fundamental questions in an acute, illuminating and entertaining manner. F. R. Leavis, *The Great Tradition* (1952), argues that Jane Austen, George Eliot, Henry James, Joseph Conrad (and D. H. Lawrence, examined in a later book) constitute the great English tradition of the novel. D. Van Ghent, *The English Novel: Form and Function* (New York, 1953) provides short perceptive studies of major novels, including three on Conrad, Lawrence, and Joyce. W. C. Booth, *The Rhetoric of Fiction* (1961), carefully inquires into the techniques, assumptions, morality, and methods of persuasion explicit and implicit in all fiction. L. Trilling's *The Liberal Imagination* (1951) collects together illuminating essays on the connections between imaginative expression and social and political realities.

Among general studies of the twentieth-century novel, W. Allen's *Tradition and Dream: The English Novel from the Twenties to Our Time* (1964) provides one of the most balanced and intelligent surveys. D. Daiches, *The Novel and the Modern World* (rev. ed., Cambridge, 1960), views the relation between changes in modern civilization and changes in the modern novel through studies in the work of major novelists. L. Edel, *The Psychological Novel, 1900–1950* (1955), studies the novel's special attention to the flow of mental experience; especially focused on the psychological techniques of James, Proust, and Joyce. S. Spender, *The Destructive Element* (1935), explores the relations between modern literature and social decay, and includes perceptive essays on the late novels of Henry James and on D. H. Lawrence. Other good surveys are G. S. Fraser, *The Modern Writer and his World* (New York, 1953), and R. Humphrey, *Stream of Consciousness in the Modern Novel* (1954).

Henry James and H. G. Wells: A Record of their Friendship, their Debate on the Art of Fiction, and their Quarrel, ed. L. Edel and G. N. Ray (1958) collects documents valuable for an understanding of the literary temper of the pre-First World War era. J. K. Johnstone, *The Bloomsbury Group: A Study of E. M. Forster, Lytton Strachey, Virginia Woolf and Their Circle* (1954), gives an informative and scholarly account of literary relationships, with particular insights into the personalities of the writers. A. Friedman, *The Turn of the Novel* (1966), studies the novel's structure during the period of transition between Hardy and Lawrence, emphasizing a shift from a closed form of experience in fiction to a suspended form.

There are countless books on the major novelists, and new ones appear every year. J. Baines, *Joseph Conrad: A Critical Biography* (1960), is a comprehensive biography, with critical assessment of Conrad's works. M. C. Bradbrook, *Joseph Conrad: Poland's English Genius* (Cambridge, 1942), offers a concise study of Conrad and his major works in chronological order. D. Hewitt, *Conrad: A Reassessment* (Cambridge, 1952), is a useful introduction to Conrad's methods and preoccupations. A. J. Guérard, *Conrad the Novelist* (Cambridge, Mass., 1958), is particularly thorough and perceptive in interpretations of major works. In T. Moser, *Joseph Conrad: Achievement and Decline* (Cambridge, Mass., 1957), an attempt is made to account for the unevenness of Conrad's work and the decline of his powers after *The Shadow Line*. E. W. Said, *Joseph Conrad and the Fiction of Autobiography* (Cambridge, Mass., 1966), examines Conrad's inner world through the letters and short fiction: the links in consciousness between the seaman and the man of letters.

L. Trilling, *E. M. Forster* (1944), is still perhaps the most enlightening treatment of the novelist. W. Stone, *The Cave and the Mountain: A Study of E. M. Forster* (1966), interprets Forster's symbols as the evolution of a personal mythology. Other recent critical books are J. Beer, *The Achievement of E. M. Forster* (1961), J. McConkey, *The Novels of E. M. Forster* (New York, 1957), and D. Shusterman, *The Quest for Certitude in E. M. Forster's Fiction* (Bloomington, Ind., 1965). For a contrary view, see C. B. Cox, *The Free Spirit: A Study of Liberal Humanists in the Novels of George Eliot, Henry James, E. M. Forster, Virginia Woolf and Angus Wilson* (1963).

L. Edel's six-volume biography of Henry James has been appearing in 'serial' form since 1953. The volumes are *The Untried Years, 1843–1870* (1953), *The Conquest of London, 1870–1881* (1962), *The Middle Years, 1882–1895* (1963), and *The Treacherous Years, 1895–1900* (1969), with a final volume, *The Master, 1900–1916*, to appear shortly. F. W. Dupee, *Henry James* (rev. ed., New York

1956), provides a penetrating biographical and literary study in one volume. *Henry James: The Critical Heritage*, ed. R. Gard (1968), gathers together contemporary letters, reviews, and articles to show the reception of his work up to his death in 1916.

F. O. Matthiessen, *Henry James: The Major Phase* (1944) sensitively explores James's moral consciousness and technical craftsmanship in the final novels. D. Krook, *The Ordeal of Consciousness in Henry James* (Cambridge, 1962), examines complex and intense states of consciousness in James's fiction. Good criticism is also to be found in F. C. Crews, *The Tragedy of Manners: Moral Drama in the Later Novels of Henry James* (New Haven, Conn., 1957), J. A. Clair, *The Ironic Dimension in the Fiction of Henry James* (Pittsburgh, Pa., 1965), and L. B. Holland, *The Expense of Vision: Essays on the Craft of Henry James* (Princeton, N.J., 1964).

R. Ellmann, *James Joyce* (1959), is the definitive biography, comprehensive and invaluable. *James Joyce: The Critical Heritage*, ed. R. H. Deming (1970), includes in two volumes a diverse collection of critical responses to Joyce. S. L. Goldberg, *Joyce* (Edinburgh, 1965), a brief but illuminating survey, synthesizes many of the most important critical judgements of recent years. Another good introduction is H. Levin, *James Joyce: A Critical Introduction* (rev. ed., Norfolk, Conn., 1960). Other useful studies are H. Kenner, *Dublin's Joyce* (1955), and J. M. Morse, *The Sympathetic Alien: James Joyce and Catholicism* (New York, 1959). *Joyce's 'Portrait': Criticisms and Critiques*, ed. T. E. Connolly (New York, 1962), is designed as a companion for readers of *A Portrait*. This collection includes both general essays on the work, and studies of such special topics as the aesthetic theory expounded in the novel.

R. P. Draper, *D. H. Lawrence: The Critical Heritage* (1970), gathers together a fascinating group of contemporary reactions. F. R. Leavis, *D. H. Lawrence: Novelist* (1955), remains probably the most influential assessment of Lawrence's achievement. Leavis places him in 'the great' English tradition as 'incomparably the greatest creative writer in English of our time'. G. Hough, *The Dark Sun: A Study of D. H. Lawrence* (1956), sets Lawrence's work in the perspective of his attempts to find satisfaction for the religious impulse. Two good studies are H. M. Daleski, *The Forked Flame* (1965), and M. Jarrett-Kerr, *D. H. Lawrence and Human Existence* (1951). G. A. Ford, *Double Measure: A Study of the Novels and Stories of D. H. Lawrence* (New York, 1965), is a recent work with new views of Lawrence now increasingly influential, and changing the emphasis on Lawrence's 'wholeness' as interpreted by F. R. Leavis.

13
Drama

D. J. PALMER

... In my opinion the theatre of today is in a rut, and full of prejudices and conventions. When I see the curtain rise on a room with three walls, when I watch these great and talented people, these high priests of a sacred art depicting the way people eat, drink, make love, walk about and wear their clothes, in the artificial light of the stage; when I hear them trying to squeeze a moral out of the tritest words and emptiest scenes—some petty little moral that's easy to understand and suitable for use in the home; when I'm presented with a thousand variations of the same old thing again and again—well, I just have to escape, I run away as Maupassant ran away from the Eiffel Tower, which so oppressed him with its vulgarity. . . . We need new art forms. New forms are wanted, and if they aren't available, we might as well have nothing at all.

Chekhov, *The Seagull*

The young Trepliov's passionate denunciation of conventional theatrical standards is too closely bound up with his own abortive aspirations as a playwright, and too much a part of his anguished relationship with his mother, Arkadina, who is a celebrated popular actress, for us to receive this speech simply as a direct expression of Chekhov's own views on the state of Russian drama in 1896. Nevertheless, the interdependence of art and life is a central concern of *The Seagull*, and Trepliov's rejection of the false and trite image of reality presented on the commercial stage of his day anticipates a course of events in which his own vision of truth is deepened and his callow idealism outgrown. In the complex dramatic function of the speech, therefore, Chekhov is endorsing his character's condemnation of a theatre impoverished by the superficial and artificial treatment of reality. The call for a greater truth to life is not only a criticism of stale and threadbare dramatic methods; it is also by implication an attack on the false conventions and hollow pretences encountered in life itself. The 'new art forms' demanded by Trepliov, although he does not yet understand this himself, involve a more genuine awareness of both the inner and the outer realities, of the self and its relationships. New art forms must express new perceptions of truth, not merely recast the old ideas in new ways.

Trepliov's speech in this sense may be taken to characterize the spirit of the progressive movement in European drama during the last quarter of the nineteenth century, a movement which, in its search for new forms to articulate new apprehensions of reality, deserves to be called 'modern'. Trepliov echoes most of the major dramatists of this period in their complaints about the prevailing conditions of the commercial theatre and, indeed, the more significant developments in the drama were introduced to the public not on the ordinary professional stages but in the small 'independent theatres' that were founded in the capitals of Europe towards the end of the century. Of these, Antoine's Théâtre Libre, established in Paris in 1887, was one of the most famous; it was followed in 1889 by the Freie Bühne in Berlin, both theatres being particularly associated with the avant-garde naturalism which outraged more conventional audiences. J. T. Grein's Independent Theatre Society, founded in 1891, was London's equivalent, while the subsequent establishment of the Moscow Art Theatre (1897) and of the Irish Literary Theatre (1899) in the same tradition, suggests how much the 'modern' movement in the drama of the period was a phenomenon of European culture as a whole. Indeed, dramatists who formulated their attitudes in terms similar to those which Chekhov put in the mouth of Trepliov, expressing the need to emancipate themselves from outworn conventions, shared a quality of more radical significance than the differences between them, differences of generation, nationality, and imaginative vision. In the period of forty years, say, between Zola's attempt to introduce scientific naturalism to the stage in *Thérèse Raquin* (1893) and the outbreak of the First World War, European drama witnessed many new developments, but the variety of innovations is in itself less important than the fundamental persistence of the spirit of 'modernism'. The sense of a need for change, the constant urge towards new frontiers, are the distinctive features of all the major achievements in drama throughout this period, in which a distinction between the modern and the merely contemporary (to use Stephen Spender's terms) is fully in evidence. It is the merely contemporary that Trepliov finds so inadequate.

This spirit of 'modernism' not only cuts across the chronology of the period, it also embraces the divergent theories of naturalism and symbolism alike, and both pessimistic and optimistic philosophies, relating Ibsen and Chekhov, Strindberg and Shaw, each in his own way concerned to discard the conventional and false, in values as in art. Alongside Trepliov's speech from *The Seagull*, for instance, we may put the famous lines of Mrs. Alving in Ibsen's *Ghosts* (1881):

But I'm inclined to think that we're all ghosts, Pastor Manders; it's not only the things that we've inherited from our fathers and mothers that live on in us, but all sorts of old dead ideas and old dead beliefs, and things of that sort. They're not actually alive in us, but they're rooted there all the same, and we can't rid ourselves of them.[1]

Trepliov protests against the 'prejudices and conventions' of the theatre, while Mrs. Alving is aware of the fossilized attitudes that cramp life itself, but clearly their points of view are parallel and akin to each other. 'Modernism' presupposes that self-consciousness and introspectiveness which make an age acutely aware of its own identity, and of the direction in which it moves, of becoming as well as of being. The developments in dramatic form during this period are often closely related to the progressive movements in political, ethical, and spiritual thought, to whatever guides prompt social or personal life to realize itself. Self-realization on the social or personal plane, emancipation from the inert and moribund forms in art and life, are the burden of the drama we are considering in this chapter. Nevertheless, this is not an ideological drama, nor even, in any important sense, a drama of ideas. For the authenticity of the playwright's work depends, not upon the relevance or usefulness of the message which may be abstracted, but upon that imaginative power which alone makes an image of life truthful and meaningful.

The idea of 'emancipation', therefore, in the form and the subject-matter of drama, will be the main theme of this chapter. Instead of attempting a comprehensive survey of the many-sided developments in drama throughout this period, I have chosen to focus attention on the five playwrights who, above all others, are of most enduring significance, namely, Ibsen, Strindberg, Chekhov, Synge, and Shaw.

I

To many of his contemporaries, Henrik Ibsen (1828–1906) was the figurehead and inspiration of the modern movement in drama. But his reputation as a dramatist of social realism, a champion of progressive causes and reforms, was based on a misconception of his art, and Ibsen was constantly dissociating himself from many of the claims made by admirers who regarded his work as propaganda and the age as his platform. The growth of his reputation, first in Germany and later in England, certainly emphasizes the European nature of the modern drama, which acknowledged no national barriers, but misunderstanding, through translation and through such polemics as Shaw's *Quintessence of Ibsenism* (1891), is also reflected in J. M. Synge's reference in 1907 to 'Ibsen and Zola dealing with the reality of life in joyless and pallid words'.

Ibsen's boldness in broaching on the stage such indelicate subjects as hereditary syphilis and euthanasia (both in *Ghosts*), in treating controversial moral questions that conventional decorum (in the theatre, at least) preferred to avoid, and in introducing plots that concerned such prosaic matters as public sanitation (in *An Enemy of the People*), filled his first audiences with alarm, disgust, or exhilaration, according to their cultural allegiances. In the excitement of encountering advanced opinions and realistic 'modern' situations in the theatre, Ibsen's real preoccupations as a dramatist were obscured by the novelty of his material. It is small wonder, for instance, that *A Doll's House* (1879) was originally received as a play about female emancipation, a burning issue of the day. Nora is treated by her husband as a pampered little pet without a mind of her own, and through her ignorance of the law and her child-like irresponsibility, she forges a cheque which leaves her exposed to blackmail. The situation is developed to bring Nora to full recognition of her plight and of the false role she has been forced to play by her husband's desire for a wife who is no more than a pretty ornament. At the end of the play the moment of choice is reached when Nora, her eyes opened to the kind of life she has been leading, decides to leave her husband and children:

HELMER. Is this the way you neglect your most sacred duties?

NORA. What do you consider is my most sacred duty?

HELMER. Do I have to tell you that? Isn't it your duty to your husband and children?

NORA. I have another duty, just as sacred.

HELMER. You can't have. What duty do you mean?

NORA. My duty to myself.

HELMER. Before everything else, you're a wife and a mother.

NORA. I don't believe that any longer. I believe that before everything else I'm a human being—just as much as you are . . . or at any rate I shall try to become one. I know quite well that most people would agree with you, Torvald, and that you have warrant for it in books; but I can't be satisfied any longer with what most people say, and with what's in books. I must think things out for myself and try to understand them.[2]

Emancipation is certainly the theme of *A Doll's House*, and marriages like that of Nora and Helmer may well have been common enough in the middle-class households of the time, but Ibsen is not preaching the cause of feminism. As Nora's speech implies, the abstractions and collective attitudes of general causes, such as feminism, actually stand in the way of individual self-recognition, and Ibsen's concern is with the individual. Nora has won through to an honest realization, while her husband is left still in self-deception; she has taken the moral initiative, and in this reversal of their original roles the deception underlying the marriage itself is exposed. It is not social justice that is on Nora's side at the end of the play, but her own superior moral awareness, which she has earned through the crisis that has shattered her complacencies and delusions one by one. As Nora leaves the false marriage behind, she can say, in the words of Stockmann at the end of *An Enemy of the People*, 'the strongest man in the world is the man who stands alone'.

Although Ibsen's contemporary admirers and critics were inclined to interpret his work in terms of the naturalist drama that presented modern social problems on the stage in as authentic and realistic a manner as possible, *A Doll's House* also reveals Ibsen's unashamed use of theatrical artifice and plot-mechanism of a kind that any true naturalist would have eschewed. The devices upon which the action is hinged, the guilty secret and the web of circumstances in which Nora is trapped, the suspense derived from the unopened letters, and so on, all indicate Ibsen's debt to the old-fashioned conventions of the 'well-made play', in which skilful contrivance of the twists and turns in the action was of greater concern than psychological probability or the development of a serious theme. Nora's swift growth to maturity is psychologically unconvincing within the scope of the action. But Ibsen's achievement lies in the new use to which he has put the machinery of the 'well-made play': the mutual deceptions and the menace of exposure are given a deeper moral significance. In fact, the threat of blackmail is called off before Nora decides to allow her husband to know the truth, and 'the truth' in this case refers not merely to the secret of the forged cheque but to the very basis of the relationship between herself and Helmer, just as the falsity of Nora's 'situation' as it is unfolded is not merely that of the conventionally guilty wife. That Nora is the one who makes the central discovery of the play, a moral discovery about herself, not a simple piece of factual information, shows how far Ibsen has transformed the purposes of the 'well-made play' while retaining the theatrical effectiveness of its smooth and workmanlike design.

The convention of the 'guilty secret' recurs throughout Ibsen's work as a means of dramatizing the progress of his central characters towards the goal of self-realization, and it is particularly associated with his fondness for retrospective actions, plots in which the true events have already happened in the past and await the discoveries that clarify the destinies of his characters. *Ghosts* (1881) is probably the most perfect piece of dramatic construction along these lines, moving with a remorseless and ironic logic like that of Sophocles' *Oedipus Rex*. In this tragedy, the theme of emancipation is only superficially present in the conflict between Pastor Manders's rigidly conventional point of view and the 'advanced' liberal ideas of Mrs. Alving and her artist son Osvald. The play's central theme, which this 'drama of ideas' only serves to reflect, is the tragic futility of the struggle of mother and son to liberate themselves from the past. Mrs. Alving is determined that her son should not inherit anything from his dissolute and depraved father, now dead; to protect her son from knowing the truth about his father, she has sent him abroad since his early childhood. He now brings home with him a secret of his own that ironically exposes his mother's sacrifice as vain and useless: he has inherited venereal disease from his father, and now awaits the final onset of the madness from which he knows he will never recover. There can be no escape from this situation, but it is Mrs. Alving who comes to the central realization of the play: the dead father, whom Osvald so closely resembles, was no monster of evil, but a man pining desperately, like Osvald now, for that 'joy of living' which the bleak and frigid moral climate, represented by Pastor Manders, denied to him:

Your poor father could never find any outlet for this overwhelming joy of living that was in him. And I didn't bring any sunshine into his life, either. . . . They'd taught me a lot about duty and so forth, and I'd long ago come to believe it. So everything was based on duty—my duty and his duty . . . and I'm afraid I made his home unbearable for your poor father, Osvald.[3]

This compassionate awareness which Mrs. Alving reaches embraces them all, and in the face of the horrific catastrophe they confront, hers is a heroic acknowledgement of their betrayal by life itself.

The Wild Duck (1884) presents a very different approach to this theme of the buried past. Here the idealist, Gregers Werle, who is determined to expose his father's deception of the Ekdals, is a misguided instrument of destruction. The Ekdals are happy in their illusions; the old man, who was framed by Werle senior and has served a prison sentence, potters about in his fantasy world of the attic, imagining he is once more Lieutenant Ekdal, the great hunter in the forests; Hjalmar Ekdal indulges his illusions of being the great inventor, and the family is held together in Hjalmar's ignorance that the woman he has married is old Werle's former mistress. Gregers explodes the falsehoods and disintegrates the family's happiness; his attempts to remedy the situation result in Hedvig's shooting herself.

It seems as though Ibsen has here reversed his treatment of the theme of emancipation from all that is false and delusory, and declared a retreat into the refuge of the necessary lie. But there is a further level of irony on which the theme is enacted: Gregers himself is not the free agent of disinterested truth that he supposes himself to be. His own motives rise obscurely from his hatred of his father, instilled in him by his mother; and therefore, like his father, albeit unconsciously, he is merely using the Ekdals for his own ends, although on the surface he (again like his father) seems to be acting out of pure good will. The disabusing of Gregers is therefore the central revelation of the play: as much as the Ekdals, he stands in the light cast by the symbol of the wild duck, which 'dives down to the bottom' and 'bites hold of the weeds and the tangle—and all the rotten stuff down there'.

Rosmersholm (1886) also employs a retrospective action to dramatize the theme of self-realization. In this play Ibsen returns to the heroic world for his central figures. While the confrontation with reality shattered the fragile characters in *The Wild Duck*, Rebecca West and Rosmer choose to destroy themselves, and by so doing emancipate themselves from the situation which has made it morally impossible for them to continue living together. A double discovery precipitates this situation: they gradually learn that Rosmer's wife had committed suicide because she had thought that he and Rebecca were in love, and Rebecca confesses that their belief in a free intellectual companionship is really an illusion, since her true feeling for Rosmer, despite herself, has become a passionate sexual desire. Rosmer's attempt to liberate himself from the traditions of his ancestors, which he is accused of betraying by his conservative brother-in-law Dr. Kroll, is ironically defeated by 'the dead that cling to Rosmersholm so long', the old superstition that becomes a reality. The progressive and enlightened views that he and Rebecca share are apparently belied by the real nature of their relationship, which they are compelled to recognize; yet paradoxically in their deaths they release themselves from the power of the dead even as it seems to claim them. In *Rosmersholm*, therefore, the 'drama of ideas' between the emancipated Rosmer and the staunch traditionalist Kroll gives an inverted reflection of the tragic progress towards the self-realization in the final catastrophe.

The ironies and ambivalences of Ibsen's dramatic methods make it clear that he was not writing thesis-drama, or the kind of play which dealt directly with contemporary social problems. Just as he turned to his own purposes the conventional devices of the 'well-made play', so too he adapted the intellectual and social awareness of the 'problem play' in order to articulate the particular consciousness and self-recognition of his characters. The movement of an Ibsen play is always inwards, towards the will of the individual, and not a reference outwards towards the total situation, or, beyond that, towards the conditions of social reality. Even the naturalistic domestic interiors of these prose dramas serve to suggest more than the mere illusion of contemporary authenticity: the cramping, repressive presence of the physical settings is part of the dramatic meaning in *A Doll's House*, *Ghosts*, *Rosmersholm*, and in *Hedda Gabler*. Ibsen's realism is modern, not primarily in the sense that it reflects the ideologies and attitudes of the contemporary social scene, but more significantly in its capacity to express in terms of the contemporary world an impulse towards an ultimate reality emancipated from the merely contemporary. In Ibsen, as in Strindberg, Chekhov, and Synge, the naturalistic reflection of contemporary life is an image of the provincialism from which the characters strive to liberate themselves. 'The spirit of truth and the spirit of freedom, they are the pillars of society.'

The unity and continuity of Ibsen's work, throughout a career that almost exactly spans the second half of the century, declare themselves in his exploration of this theme of spiritual freedom and self-realization. It is at the core of *Peer Gynt* (1867), the poetic odyssey of a hero who plays many parts but is never truly himself, because he is self-regarding and afraid to commit himself fully to life. The truth that Peer lives for is that of the Trolls' existence, 'To thyself be enough', and in the course of his adventures he is therefore selected Emperor of the Madmen, for reasons that are explained to him in the asylum:

> here man is himself to the uttermost limit—
> himself, and nothing beside whatsoever.
> As himself, he progresses full steam ahead;

he encloses himself in a barrel of self;
in self-fermentation he steeps himself,
hermetically sealed with the bung of self,
between staves that were seasoned in self's own spring.
No one sheds tears for another's sorrows,
no one considers another's ideas.
We're ourselves in thought, and word, and deed—
Ourselves to the springboard's uttermost edge . . .
so if we're enthroning an Emperor here,
it's obvious you are the very man![4]

Peer is spiritually too negative even to be damned as a sinner, and he is only saved from being thrown into the Button-moulder's melting-pot by the authentic identity conferred on him through Solveig's love. *Hedda Gabler* (1890) contains a heroine who is, like Peer, afraid of life, 'an awful coward', but who longs to experience, even at second hand, 'a feeling of release, in knowing that there really can be such a thing in the world as free and fearless action'. The sequence of prose dramas that followed *Peer Gynt* were the result of Ibsen's conscious renunciation of poetry as a dramatic medium, but nothing could be further from the truth than the image of a prosaic and literal-minded playwright sometimes suggested by Ibsen's reputation as a social realist. The poet in him is apparent in his exploration of the spiritual realities that determine the lives of his characters, in his desire to make them confront the imperatives of their own natures, and so to emancipate themselves. 'To be a poet means essentially to see,' he wrote in 1874, and twenty years later, when he turned to a dramatic form that was different again, to the intensely personal vision of his last plays, his lifelong theme of the emancipation of the self is still not exhausted. In *The Master Builder* (1892), Solness tells how the fire which destroyed his domestic happiness enabled him to find a newly liberated self as an artist:

I'd never before been able to climb up, free and high in the air. But that day I could. . . . And when I stood right up on the top there and hung the wreath over the weather-vane, then I said to him: Hear me, now, Thou Almighty! In future I too will be a free master builder. In my own sphere. As Thou in Thine.[5]

Now, through the inspiration of the strange girl Hilde, Solness will once again attempt the impossible, and climb to the top of the tower he has built, achieving his purpose although he falls to his death in doing so. *The Master Builder* is so close to an allegory of the artistic life of its creator that in one sense it is a play about its own composition, the strenuous effort, the triumph, and the human cost.

Ibsen's final play, *When We Dead Awaken* (1900), is indeed a visionary meditation on the life of the artist, the sacrifice of human fulfilment for the sake of creative achievement. The sculptor Rubek in his old age encounters Irena, the ghostlike figure of his former model, whose love for him he refused to accept, destroying her life while creating their 'child' in his masterpiece. It is a play filled with the bitterness of regret for a life not realized, a reality denied:

IRENA. We see the irreparable only when . . .
RUBEK. When?
IRENA. When we dead wake.
RUBEK. What do we really see then?
IRENA. We see that we have never lived.[6]

Rubek and Irena celebrate their strange 'marriage-feast' out on the mountain-side, while Rubek's young wife Maia goes off with the hunter Ulfheim. We catch our final glimpse of the sculptor and his companion as they climb towards 'the topmost peak gleaming in the sunrise', and just before the avalanche overwhelms them, the refrain of Maia's song rises from below:

> I am free, I am free, I am free!
> No longer the prison I'll see!
> I am free as a bird, I am free!

II

The secret of modern literature lies precisely in this matter of experiences that are lived through. All that I have written these last ten years, I have lived through spiritually. . . . I have been inspired by that which, so to speak, has stood higher than my everyday self, and I have been inspired by this because I wanted to confront it and make it part of myself. But I have also been inspired by the opposite, by what appears on introspection as the dregs and sediment of one's own nature. Writing has in this case been to me like a bath from which I have risen feeling cleaner, healthier, and freer. Yes, gentlemen, nobody can picture poetically anything for which he himself has not to a certain degree and at least at times served as a model.

The words are Ibsen's, from an address given in 1874, but they apply with particular force to his younger Swedish contemporary, August Strindberg (1849–1912), whose creative processes were to an even greater degree controlled by his deepest emotional and personal experience. Compared with the distanced and objectified clarity of

Ibsen's drama, with its impulse towards a new and courageous wholeness of being, Strindberg's plays are the product of a mind too urgently involved in the crisis, a sensibility too irreparably damaged by its suffering, for the achievement of an artistic poise and calm. Instead of the almost classical lucidity and sense of form that characterizes Ibsen's work, therefore, Strindberg's art is informed by energies that ultimately of their very nature are not amenable to the kind of ordering and full objectivity which require greater rational and self-critical powers than he possessed. His drama, in fact, like the rest of his prolific literary output, is the result of his life-long effort to understand and come to terms with the irreconcilable inner conflicts that were, for him, reality itself. The comparison with Ibsen does not imply an adverse judgement on Strindberg's achievement; on the contrary, the articulation of his tormented and disturbed vision constantly extends the expressive resources of the dramatic medium into new and unexplored territories. In the apparent formlessness of Strindberg's plays, in terms of conventional plot-construction, lies their great strength, not their limitation.

The subjective and experimental qualities of Strindberg's work make it difficult and sometimes obscure, and it is not surprising that his reputation as a major dramatist was slow to emerge. While Ibsen enjoyed immense fame, or notoriety, in his lifetime (even though often for the wrong reasons), Strindberg's influence was only beginning to be felt in the period after the First World War, when the Expressionist and Surrealist movements could claim him for their own. Curiously, as if to suggest how little meaning such labels sometimes have with respect to the truly great artist, Strindberg conceived his own early plays to be in accord with the ideals of Naturalism, although in an essay written in 1889 he reinterpreted those ideals, to reject the 'photography which includes everything, even the grain of dust on the lens of the camera':

This is realism, a working method elevated to art, or the little art which does not see the forest for the trees. This is the misunderstood naturalism which holds that art merely consists of drawing a piece of nature in a natural way; it is not the great naturalism which seeks out the points where the great battles are fought, which loves to see what you do not see every day, which delights in the struggle between natural forces, whether these forces are called love and hate, rebellious or social instincts, which finds the beautiful or ugly unimportant if only it is great.

It was in this spirit that Strindberg conceived *Miss Julie* (1888), which he described as 'a naturalistic play'. The action of the play, which is presented as one unbroken sequence, concerns the relationship between the aristocratic Miss Julie and her father's manservant Jean. 'The struggle between natural forces', represented in their coming together, concerns not only the class war and the battle of the sexes, twin concepts of nineteenth-century evolutionary thought. It is a Nietzschean conflict of elemental wills, the will to self-immolation and the will to power, in which hatred and love are inseparably and necessarily a part of each other. The characters are not personalities in the conventional sense, but expressions of instinctual and sub-rational drives, as their dreams reveal them in their inner reality. Miss Julie dreams of her desire to fall down from a high pillar, 'deeper and deeper into the earth', while Jean's dream concerns his aspiration to climb to the top of a tree and 'rob the nest that holds the golden egg'. Mutual contempt as well as fascination, repulsion and attraction ambivalently mingled, lead them to seduce each other, and then to plan an elopement; but their attempt is foiled by the return of Miss Julie's father. At the end of the play, Miss Julie leaves the stage under the hypnotic influence of Jean, to cut her throat, while Jean himself trembles like a coward at the bell which summons him to her father upstairs. Together they realize the power for a heroic and decisive act which neither of them is capable of alone. This nihilistic gesture is their emancipation from a life which, as Miss Julie says, is 'just scum floating round and round on the top of the water—till it finally sinks'.

'The great naturalism which seeks out the points where the great battles are fought' is also exemplified in *The Father* (1887). Here also the two principal characters are a man and a woman, the Captain and his wife Laura, who are locked in mortal combat. The issue for which they contend with ruthless ferocity is ostensibly the control of their daughter Judith, but the child is only a pawn in this 'life and death' struggle, or rather she embodies the marriage itself, the expression of a union that can only be dissolved by the total defeat of one partner. From the very start, Laura's superior strength is apparent, not because she is more intelligent, or more aggressive, than the Captain, whose military rank suggests that outwardly he possesses the authority and experience of the world proper to his sex. But Laura's victory over her husband is determined by her intuitive, even naïve, sense of purpose, as she sets about undermining his trust in her, in his own manhood, and eventually in his reason. As he says of women at the beginning of the play, 'That's what's so dangerous—that their innate dishonesty is quite unconscious.' The Captain fights his campaign as an open, frank, and rational protagonist; his very candour and reason are his undoing, for Laura's strategy is opportunist, almost accidental, as she recognizes when finally she has him strapped in the straitjacket:

I don't know that the thoughts and motives that you're suggesting ever entered my head. It's possible that I was swayed by an obscure desire to be rid of you, as something that stood in my way; if you see some plan behind my actions—well, there may have been one, but I knew nothing about it. I've never considered them, they've simply run on the lines that you yourself have laid down, and, before God and my conscience, I feel myself innocent even if I am not. Your existence has been like a stone on my heart, weighing and weighing it down till the heart struggled to throw off the burden that oppressed it.[7]

There is a terrible irony in these words, but Laura is not being disingenuous. Her own drives are blindly instinctual, and she succeeds in the struggle because she reduces her husband to her own level of primal existence, destroying his rational equilibrium until he reverts to an infantile helplessness. Strindberg's depiction of mental torment in this play and in *The Dance of Death* (1901), his sense of the insecurity of the male and his fear of the female will, may be derived from his own unhappy experiences of marriage, but the theme he is exploring is a profounder one: the liberation of the destructive forces of the unconscious.

In his later work, Strindberg turned away from naturalism towards an overtly symbolist mode. Yet the change was not as fundamental as this might suggest. The exploration of the irrational in dramas such as *A Dream Play* (1902) and *Ghost Sonata* (1907) is really a continuation of the fluid and freely-moving rhythms typical of his earlier work. The hypertensions and distorted sensibilities presented in *The Father* and *Miss Julie* demanded a highly volatile and flexible dramatic momentum, an electrically charged atmosphere in which the progressive revelation of the darker face of reality pursues its own logic. The fantasy conventions of the later plays represent Strindberg's continued attempts to apprehend and articulate planes of consciousness that are almost beyond the reach of formal expression.

Ghost Sonata, as its title implies, was one of Strindberg's 'chamber plays', constructed on the analogy of musical form. Its fluidity and delicacy of movement almost defy analysis, as we follow the Student into the house of strange figures whose buried past is brought back to life, and, with their ghastly secrets exposed, we pass on to the Hyacinth Room, where the Young Lady awaits him. There, in the final scene, the Student is overcome by the futility of hoping that he might release her from the hell, the madhouse, which poisons and corrupts the air around her. His despair kills her, although the play ends, not in horror and distress, but with his gentle, elegiac benediction:

You poor little child, you child of this world of illusion, guilt, suffering and death; this world of eternal change, disappointment, and pain! May the Lord of Heaven have mercy on you in your journey.

[*The whole room disappears, and in its place appears 'The Island of the Dead' by Böcklin as background. Soft music, very quiet and pleasantly sad, is heard from the distant island.*][8]

Compassion and reconciliation are also the final realities of *A Dream Play*, in which the Daughter of Indra descends to the world of men to share their miseries and bafflement. The play is a series of shifting episodes, melting into each other in a way that creates a pattern of universal hopelessness and disillusion. The dream technique distances the tragic cycle enacted by each group of characters whose situations are interwoven one with another by free association, in a curiously remote but beautiful transmutation of suffering. This is Strindberg's ultimate and visionary statement of the human situation, from a transcendental point of view beyond tragedy itself: 'Here you have suffering as the liberator'.

III

Although naturalism is often regarded as an essentially prosaic view of reality, and contrasted with the poetic view of life, the antithesis is false. Throughout this period, the real converse of naturalism is the conventional idiom of the theatre, and this is well illustrated by the conception of plot in the work of Ibsen and Strindberg. While the conventional plot is constructed from a succession of events occurring during the course of the play, naturalism, in its tendency to present a 'slice of life' rather than a story, calls for an action much less dependent upon sensational and contrived events. 'People don't do such things': the curtain-line of *Hedda Gabler*, in its mordantly ironic comment on Hedda's life and death, suggests how Ibsen is able to have his cake and eat it, retaining the narrative kind of plot while adapting its conventions to the point of view of naturalism. Ibsen's use of retrospective action, particularly, enables him to bring the whole lives of his characters into critical perspectives, while nothing much happens outwardly until the final moments of the play. *Rosmersholm* is a fine example of this method, which progresses not along the chronological plane of events, but according to the inner dynamic which brings the central figures to self-realization. Strindberg is even more economical in his use of external event, and his actions are not built on narrative principles at all.

In the liberation of the drama from dead forms and the exploration of new dimensions of experience, naturalism makes common cause with the symbolist drama. It was the contemporary poetic playwright Maeterlinck (1862–1949), for instance, who in 'The Tragical in Daily Life' (1896) took to its furthest extreme the conception of an action without narrative progression:

I have grown to believe that an old man, seated in his armchair, waiting patiently, with his lamp beside him; giving unconscious ear to all the eternal laws that reign about his house, interpreting, without comprehending, the silence of doors and windows and the quivering voice of the light, submitting with bent head to the presence of his soul and his destiny— an old man, who conceives not that all the powers of this world, like so many heedful servants, are mingling and keeping vigil in his room, who suspects not that the very sun itself is supporting in space the little table against which he leans, or that every star in heaven and every fibre of the soul are directly concerned in the movement of an eyelid that closes, or a thought that springs to birth—I have grown to believe that he, motionless as he is, does yet live in reality a deeper, more human, and more universal life than the lover who strangles his mistress, the captain who conquers in battle, or 'the husband who avenges his honour'.

Such a scenario has more in common with Trepliov's visionary drama of the World Soul in *The Seagull*, than with Anton Chekhov's (1860–1904) own kind of poetic realism, but Chekhov's plays do seem to represent an advanced stage of naturalism, in which the dramatist is more concerned with his scrupulous fidelity to the random flux of reality than with the forward progression of a chain of events. The action of a Chekhov play typically gives an impression of inactivity, of a delight in registering inconsequential detail and fragmentariness, with the dramatic interest diffused over a loosely-organized group of characters, instead of being concentrated upon the fortunes of one or two central figures. The earliest of his full-length plays, *Ivanov* (1887), is in fact more conventional in focusing upon the titular hero, and a story of sorts is told about his neglect of his sick wife, and, after her death, his betrothal to Sasha and eventual suicide. But, significantly, Ivanov continually protests that there is 'nothing remarkable' about him, although the doctor Lvov dramatizes him as a heartless villain, and Sasha idealizes him as another Hamlet. In *The Seagull*, similarly, melodramatic or sentimental views of life are exposed, when the stage-struck Nina is dazzled by the famous actress, Arkadina, and her lover, the celebrated novelist Trigorin, whose lives are shown to be really frustrated and empty. The seagull, with which Nina self-consciously identifies herself, does not function as an obvious piece of symbolism on Chekhov's part, but rather as an exposure of Nina's naïvely 'theatrical' behaviour in the first part of the play. As Ivanov says, 'we all have too many wheels, and screws, and valves inside of us to be judged by first impressions or by a few external traits. I don't understand you, you don't understand me, and we don't understand ourselves'.

This impression of the uneventfulness and formlessness of ordinary life is of course only part of the truth about Chekhov's naturalism; the real action goes on below the surface, and his dramatic method is essentially one of obliquity:

Let the things that happen on the stage be as complex and yet just as simple as they are in life. For instance, people are having a meal at the table, just having a meal, but at the same time their happiness is being created, or their lives are being smashed up.

The apparently inconsequential diffuseness of his scenes, the unobtrusiveness of the progression from one situation to the next, are not merely naturalistic techniques to create the illusion of 'a slice of real life'. They express the quality of that particular area of experience he has chosen to explore, in which life is aimless and stagnant. Nothing positive seems to happen in Chekhov's plays because his characters are inconclusive and incapable of taking a firmer hold on life. The pistol shots that are fired at the ends of *Ivanov* and *The Seagull* are final gestures of self-realization, but in the later plays even this moment of truth is blurred: Uncle Vanya's marksmanship proves mercifully unreliable, and although Tuzenbakh is shot in a duel at the end of *The Three Sisters*, his death makes no real difference to the empty life Irina shares with her sisters. Chekhov himself pointed out that in his last play, *The Cherry Orchard*, he had managed to dispense altogether with pistol shots, a removal of the final recourse to definite and conclusive action in the Chekhovian world: instead, the strange and melancholy sound of a wire snapping in a distant mine shaft emphasizes the silence of the deserted house.

Baffled and ineffectual though his characters often are, Chekhov's drama is not static, but shifting and fluid in pursuing the rudderless course of their lives. The famous obliquity of Chekhov's dialogue, in which trivial small-talk, inarticulacy, or even silence, may be power-fully expressive of the undercurrent of feeling in which they participate, is one aspect of his highly sensitive and complex art, which gains its effects by nuance, irony, and evasiveness. His characters are often charming in their indolence, and sympathetic in their suffering or their bewildered search for meaning and purpose in their lives; and yet, while he is too objective to assume the role of the moralist, there is evidence that Chekhov wanted to do more than merely offer to us a compassionate, half-humorous, half-pathetic view of life. He wrote to a correspondent: 'All I wanted was to say honestly to people: "Have a look at yourselves and see how bad and dreary your lives are." '

It is certainly possible to interpret Chekhov's drama as a reflection of the state of contemporary society, the decadent upper-class society of pre-revolutionary Russia. His two last and greatest plays, *The Three Sisters* (1901) and *The Cherry Orchard* (1904), both concern members of this class, refined but simple people who attract affection easily, and who are being gradually pushed aside by forces they do not understand, until their very existence seems meaningless and superfluous. Both plays treat the theme of dispossession; in the first, the three Prozorov sisters and their brother are by almost imperceptible degrees being turned out of their own home by the vulgar and selfish Natasha, and in the other play Madame Ranevsky is forced to sell the beloved orchard from her estate, and to see it pass into the hands of Lopakhin, whose father was once a serf on the same estate. In an important sense, the dispossession which occurs in each play only reflects a condition already existing, and therefore changes nothing. The Prozorovs are really homeless from the very beginning of the play, aliens in this provincial town, and sharing with their fellow-exiles, the army officers from the garrison, their nostalgia for Moscow. Madame Ranevsky similarly spends most of her life abroad, and the old estate is no longer her real home. The state of exile is a restless spiritual condition: Ivanov, Nina, and Arkadina, in Chekhov's earlier plays, also find their homes impossible to live in. The sociological interpretation, which sees these plays in terms of the transitional state between a disintegrating past and a new society as yet to be realized, can readily find support from speeches in the plays themselves, like Trofimov's declaration in *The Cherry Orchard*:

Humanity is perpetually advancing, always seeking to perfect its own powers. One day all the things that are beyond our grasp at present are going to fall within our reach, only to achieve this we've got to work with all our might, to help the people who are seeking after truth. Here, in Russia, very few people have started to work, so far. Nearly all the members of the intelligentsia that I know care for nothing, do nothing and are still incapable of work. . . .[9]

No doubt Chekhov himself speaks through Trofimov, but this is no 'key' to the play, but merely one point of view, one note that reverberates through this and the other plays. They are too complex, and too artistically disinterested, to be reduced to a single 'meaning' of this kind. Chekhov's characters inhabit a temporal dimension in which the retrospect is filled with a sense of loss, and the prospect is a dream of hope and renewed purpose. But Chekhov's plays are not, any more than Ibsen's, in their deepest sense a reflection of the spirit of the age or contemporary social problems. The emancipation with which Chekhov is concerned is not liberation from a transitional or maladjusted present, for both past and future are no more than shadows cast by the present. It is the present his characters must live with (this is Trofimov's point), and to come to terms with the present they must emancipate themselves from the spiritual malaise with saps their energies and wastes their lives. As Masha says in *The Three Sisters*:

I think a human being has got to have some faith, or at least he's got to seek faith. Otherwise his life will be empty, empty. . . .

IV

The Irish dramatic movement which arose in the 1890s was a rebellion against the domination of the contemporary English social-problem drama, as much as Irish nationalism in the political sphere sought independence from English rule. That the new Irish drama managed to exist as something more than a mouthpiece for the nationalist cause was due mainly to the firm guidance and artistic standards of its chief architects, W. B. Yeats and Lady Gregory, whose Irish Literary Theatre, founded in 1899, became the Irish National Theatre in 1902, and the Abbey Theatre Company in 1904. Yeats's ambition was to foster a drama that was distinctively Irish in character, yet neither provincial in quality nor propagandist in spirit, and he wrote in 1903, 'if we are to do this we must learn that beauty and truth are always justified of themselves, and that their creation is a greater service to our country than writing that compromises either in the seeming service of a cause'. They were brave words, for the greatest opposition to his purpose, not stopping

short at physical violence, was to come from the nationalists who
wanted a theatre that would directly reflect their own non-artistic
aims. But Yeats was the leader of a different kind of revolution,
which brought verse back to the English-speaking stage, in the
living idiom of contemporary speech rather than the literary pastiche
of pseudo-Shakespearian rhetoric:

That idiom of the Irish-thinking people of the west . . . is the only good
English spoken by any large number of Irish people today, and we must
found good literature on a living speech, see 'the difference between dead
and living words, between words that meant something years ago and
words that have the only thing that gives literary quality—personality,
the breath of men's mouths.'

The Irish drama was therefore essentially a poetic drama, in reaction
to the intellectual prose plays then being written for the London
stage by Henry Arthur Jones, Arthur Wing Pinero, and George
Bernard Shaw. The Abbey Theatre itself was the latest in a distinguished tradition of small 'independent' theatres which had
promoted the modern dramatic movement throughout Europe.

The one dramatist of European stature produced by the Irish
theatre in this period was John Millington Synge (1871–1909).
Again, it was Yeats who turned Synge into a dramatist, persuading
him to return to Ireland from Paris, where they had met in or
about 1897, and to visit the west of Ireland, where Synge studied the
speech of the peasants from which he fashioned his own rhythmic
and poetic style. 'In a good play every speech should be as fully
flavoured as a nut or apple,' he wrote in the Preface to *The Playboy
of the Western World* (1907), 'and such speeches cannot be written
by anyone who works among people who have shut their lips on
poetry.' The danger of transplanting the rustic idiom of folk-speech
to the stage is that of a sentimentalized degeneration into the merely
'quaint', and some of Synge's Irish contemporaries and successors
did not always avoid this pitfall; but in Synge's own work there is no
trace of such debasement. The language in his plays retains its
natural authority, its eloquent capacity for humour and for tragic
dignity, because Synge exploits its characteristics as a speech of
people who live close to the elements, to the primal realities of life
and death, of nature and the supernatural. It is in many ways a
fulfilment of Wordsworth's conception of poetic diction, in another
century and another country:

Come along with me now, lady of the house, and it's not my blather you'll
be hearing only, but you'll be hearing the herons crying out over the

black lakes, and you'll be hearing the grouse and the owls with them, and
the larks and the big thrushes when the days are warm, and it's not from
the like of them you'll be hearing a tale of getting old like Peggy Cavanagh,
and losing the hair off you, and the light of your eyes, but it's fine songs
you'll be hearing when the sun goes up, and there'll be no old fellow
wheezing the like of a sick sheep close to your ear.[10]

So speaks the Tramp at the end of Synge's one-act play, *The
Shadow of the Glen*. The brief action, like much in Synge's work, is
based on a tale he had heard, about a husband who feigns death to
catch his wife with her lover. In the play, the Tramp witnesses all
that takes place, and when the young lover turns out to be more
interested in running off with the husband's flock than with his
wife, it is the Tramp who offers to share his life with her, and they
leave together. Typical of Synge's genius is his ability to blend the
farcical potentialities of the situation with real compassion for the
wife's betrayal, her bitterness a reflection of her wretched and loveless existence in that remote, desolate countryside. The Tramp
cannot promise her even those pitifully few creature-comforts of the
cottage for which her lover renounces her, but he describes for her a
new life that will release her from the cruelty and insecurity she has
suffered.

The *Shadow of the Glen* was Synge's first play for the National
Theatre Society. It was followed in 1904 by *Riders to the Sea*,
another one-act play in which the lives of the characters are intimately related to the natural world. Here it is the sea that governs
human life, in a tragic drama that is no less powerful for its brevity.
Maurya has lost all her sons at sea, except Bartley, and when at the
end of the play his drowned body is brought home, the bitterness
and heart-sick fear turn into a calm resignation, as though this final
loss were a kind of release from the sea's power: 'They're all gone
now, and there isn't anything more the sea can do to me.' As in this
line, the play's profoundly moving effects reside in its simplicity,
its purity of language and feeling. The situation is universalized, as
though the sea signified the inexorability of Fate itself.

Riders to the Sea is the clearest example of the tendency in
Synge's drama towards the archetypal; as though his peasant characters live in such close communion with the elements that the very
form of their existence, like the language they speak, is shaped into
those primordial patterns that are the stuff of mythology. Characters
like the Tramp from *The Shadow of the Glen*, old Mary in *The
Tinker's Wedding*, and the blind beggars Martin and Mary Doul in
The Well of the Saints, have the timeless quality of figures in ancient

folklore. Synge therefore has no need of allegory or metaphor to create a dimension of universality; his characters are as individual and vital as their language is concrete, literal, and direct. In *The Well of the Saints* (1905), Martin and Mary Doul miraculously receive their sight at the hands of a wandering holy man: a theme that might have been taken from some saint's legend, and presented from the point of view of the humble recipients instead of that of the hagiographer. For their newly-bestowed vision destroys their illusions in each other, and they see themselves and the world for the first time and know it all to be unbearably ugly and painful. Thus when their sight fades and they become blind once more, they refuse with apparent ungraciousness the proffered restoration of sight. For all its rather brutal comedy, this is a pessimistic play about the necessity of illusion: human kind cannot bear very much reality. As Martin says, 'I'm thinking by the mercy of God it's few sees anything but them is blind for a space.'

It is a similar theme that finds expression in Synge's one undoubted masterpiece, *The Playboy of the Western World* (1907). Christy, believing he has killed his father, is on the run, and reaches the village in which the action of the play takes place in a state of terror and despair. When his story is told, however, he is treated as a hero, and even comes to believe in the image of himself as a legendary giant-killer that is created by the villagers' glorification of his deed. His father's arrival in the same village destroys the basis of his fragile glory, until he strikes down his father once more, in the presence of the villagers. This time, however, instead of confirming his heroic status, they try to hand him over to justice. For the villagers, apparently, there is a world of difference between the deed reported and the same deed actually witnessed, or, in Pegeen's words, 'there's a great gap between a gallous story and a dirty deed'. But Christy's father achieves a second resurrection, and the two of them go off together with contempt for the villagers' folly. Here, as in *The Well of the Saints*, it seems that humanity prefers illusion to reality.

But *The Playboy* is a more complex play than such a simple interpretation suggests. Synge is now writing from a point of view outside the mythopœic consciousness of the folk which elsewhere framed his dramatic vision, but which in this play is represented by the way the villagers turn Christy into a living legend. Their need for a legend, for a mythological hero to give meaning to their own lives, is treated with the ironic sophistication of a modern, critical mind. Christy and the villagers are victims of each other, but at the end of the play, while the villagers return disillusioned to their ordinary, frustrated lives, Christy really has been transformed. Through the imagined experience of a heroic role, into which he is seduced by the villagers, Christy discovers a new faith and confidence in himself: the true myth which informs his progress through the play is the modern, Freudian version of the Oedipal wish to murder the father. The play celebrates the power of the imagination, not to deceive, but to express a hidden, ultimate reality; and Christy achieves the truth, not by rejecting the illusion, but by finding that it has emancipated his formerly inhibited self:

Ten thousand blessings upon all that's here, for you've turned me a likely gaffer in the end of all, the way I'll go romancing through a romping lifetime from this hour to the dawning of the judgment day.[11]

V

George Bernard Shaw (1856–1950) was not the only playwright campaigning for a reform of English drama at the end of the nineteenth century. But the fact that his dramatic aims were an integral part of his systematic analysis of the very structure of society made him the most radical and most controversial champion of the 'new drama'. He prepared for his own arrival as a dramatist by writing *The Quintessence of Ibsenism* (1891), which in its immediate context was a retort to the abuse and sense of outrage provoked by the appearance of five Ibsen plays that year in London. Shaw's misrepresentation of Ibsen as essentially a dramatist of social problems and advanced ideas is less to the point than his polemical call for a serious intellectual drama; 'Ibsenism' is a rallying-point for reformist action rather than a dispassionate exposition of particular plays. Prominent among the characteristics of the 'new drama' was to be the discussion of ideas relevant to the world of the spectator:

. . . the introduction of the discussion and its development until it so overspreads and interpenetrates the action that it finally assimilates it, making play and discussion practically identical; and, second, as a consequence of making the spectators themselves the persons of the drama and the incidents of their own lives its incidents, the disuse of the old stage tricks by which audiences had to be induced to take an interest in unreal people and improbable circumstances, and the substitution of a forensic technique of recrimination, disillusion, and penetration through ideals to the truth, with a free use of all the rhetorical and lyrical arts of the orator, the preacher, the pleader, and the rhapsodist.

Shaw's first play, *Widowers' Houses* (1892), fulfilled most of these requirements. But instead of discarding 'the old stage tricks', he retained them and put them to new purposes. The plot, in which a young man calls off his marriage on discovering that his fiancée's dowry is tainted money, her father being a slum landlord, belongs to a 'well-made play' of the very kind that Shaw was deploring. But instead of resolving the situation so that honour and love are both finally triumphant, Shaw twists the story to reveal that the young man himself unwittingly derives his income from the same shameful source. The marriage can therefore take place after all, since no individual can free himself from a corruption that exists in the very heart of the social system. The 'forensic technique of re-crimination' is directed in these early 'Plays Unpleasant' not by one character at another, but by the dramatist at the society which the audience recognizes as its own.

This method of inverting the conventional theatrical expectations remains a feature of Shaw's work as characteristic as his recourse to the explicit discussion of ideas. In *Arms and the Man* and *Candida* (both performed in 1894), Shaw seems to have acknowledged that his own dramatic bent was for comedy rather than for the realistic drama he admired in Ibsen. But his plays are not so much comedies as exploitations of the comic mode as the most effective vehicle for his own subversive activity. The burlesque of melodrama in *Arms and the Man* and *The Devil's Disciple*, and his ironic treatment of the conventional 'moral' ending in *Candida*, where the wife chooses loyalty to her husband instead of adultery with the poet, suggest that the shallower illusion of comedy best suited Shaw's desire to turn inside out the complacencies and false assumptions entrenched in the world around him. His cavalier attitude to the usual dramatic proprieties is not simply the inartistic carelessness of a dramatist more concerned with haranguing his audiences than with construct-ing a plot they can believe in. By treating the flimsiness of his comic plots with the contempt they deserve, Shaw was also exposing the flimsiness of conventional thinking: the shattering of the theatrical illusion becomes a means of shattering illusions outside the theatre.

Shaw has often been criticized for the 'impurity' of his art, by those who object to receiving lectures in the theatre; he has also been criticized for squandering his gifts as a polemicist and thinker in trifling with stage-plays. It has been held against him that he needed to write prefaces and long stage-directions for the printed versions of his plays because his dramatic skill was inadequate to express his meaning fully, and conversely that his message is sadly diluted by the demands of dramatic craftsmanship. The truth is that if the plays are unashamedly polemical, the polemics are also highly theatrical. Shaw's basic strategy is always to involve the audience, or the reader, by teasing, provoking, or outraging them. In the theatre his characters are only the indirect victims of his fondness for turning things inside out (this is why Shaw is careful to prevent us from becoming too closely involved in the plot): it is the audience that is really on the receiving end of his irony and use of surprise. In his prefaces, the element of deliberate perverseness, the paradoxes and half-truths, are employed in anticipation of the reader's known or suspected assumptions on the subject, and whatever the topic under discussion it is approached from an angle calculated to test the reader's own alertness and considered position. In this sense, Shaw does not always mean quite what he appears to be saying, though he is never without a serious point, and at the same time he never ceases, as it were, to play the reader or spectator on the hook at the end of his line. Unfortunately, his work is therefore constantly subject to two contrary sources of misunderstanding, and Shaw has commonly been treated either as a man of profound and original vision or as a licensed buffoon, eccentric but harmless, who wrote good prose.

Although his career spans the first half of the present century, Shaw's best work was written by 1923, when *Saint Joan* appeared. In his convictions and outlook, in fact, he belongs to the late Victorian and Edwardian age, to the heyday of the British Imperialism which he so detested (being an Irishman lent a particular intensity to his views on this subject), and to the infancy of British socialism. Above all, his confidence in the power of reason to provide the answers to the problems of the contemporary world, his relentless application of logic to the absurdities and abuses of life, remind us of the period to which he belongs. Shaw's particular adherence to the Nietzschean idea of the Superman, or to the quasi-religious, quasi-scientific concept of the Life Force, might be supposed to date him even more strictly, if not disastrously; but oddly enough the play which gives these doctrines their most explicit treatment, *Man and Superman* (1901), has survived rather better than most of his less ambitious work. The play is both romantic and antiromantic, conventional notions of love, morality, and decorum between the sexes being exploded by the conception of the blind, instinctive operation of the Life Force which impels woman to use man to fulfil its demands. By making Jack Tanner first the philosopher of the Life Force and then its victim, Shaw manages to suggest in the helplessness of intellect against instinct both that the business of the Life Force is a comic screen for a simple love story, and that what we call love is indeed an unscrupulous, unsentimental biological principle, no respecter of persons. Tanner's philosophy is both shattered and verified by events. But Shaw's deepest convictions are reserved for the most fantastic and paradoxical part of the play, the interlude of Don Juan in Hell. Juan is Tanner in another dimension, the intellect raised to the level of heroic legend; the hero-philosopher is the Life Force raised to consciousness of itself, moving on from Hell to Heaven, just as humanity itself is evolving towards higher forms of being:

I tell you that as long as I can conceive something better than myself I cannot be easy unless I am striving to bring it into existence or clearing the way for it. That is the law of my life. That is the working within me of life's incessant aspiration to higher organization, wider, deeper, intenser self-consciousness, and clearer self-understanding.

But the Devil speaks with Shaw's other self:

An epoch is but a swing of the pendulum; and each generation thinks the world is progressing because it is always moving. But when you are as old as I am; when you have a thousand times wearied of heaven, like myself and the Commander, and a thousand times wearied of hell, as you are wearied now, you will no longer imagine that every swing from heaven to hell is an emancipation, every swing from hell to heaven an evolution. Where you now see reform, progress, fulfilment of upward tendency, continual ascent by Man on the stepping stones of his dead selves to higher things, you will see nothing but an infinite comedy of illusion.[12]

The theme of emancipation or self-realization, which in *Man and Superman* is a metaphysical issue involving the whole human race, is treated in *Pygmalion* (1912) in moral and individual terms. The ancient myth undergoes a characteristic Shavian inversion, so that Higgins first tries to turn a living creature into a dummy, until Eliza rebels and asserts her independence, in another contest between masculine knowledge and feminine power. *Pygmalion* echoes from the earlier play Shaw's confidence in the 'fulfilment of upward tendency', but in *Heartbreak House* (1913–16) the Devil seems to have had the upper hand. Heartbreak House is Hell, the home of love and beauty; it represents, in the words of Shaw's preface, 'cultured, leisured Europe before the war', and, echoing the nautical metaphor of the Hell in *Man and Superman* (where one drifts instead of steering), the stage set has the appearance of a ship.

Although Shaw's presentation of the aimless and futile life of Heartbreak House is reminiscent of Chekhov (the play is sub-titled 'A Fantasia in the Russian Manner'), it is really 'an infinite comedy of illusion', in which the only progress is towards disillusion. It is a return to the subject of contemporary society, which, incapable of regenerating itself, awaits an unknown end:

Either out of that darkness some new creation will come to supplant us as we have supplanted the animals, or the heavens will fall in thunder and destroy us.

Eventually the bombs fall from the sky, killing Mangan the industrialist, and so accomplishing what Captain Shotover and his dynamite would never have done. The advent of war, so incomprehensible and mysteriously exciting to these people, will be their longed-for emancipation from the old, frustrated life—or is their hysterical joy at the end of the play that final illusion which the bombs will shatter?

MRS. HUSHABYE. But what a glorious experience! I hope they'll come again tomorrow night.
ELLIE (*radiant at the prospect*). Oh, I hope so.
[*Randall at last succeeds in keeping the home fires burning on his flute.*] [13]

With this apocalyptic vision of catastrophe in the Great War, the first wave of modern drama, its forces spent, makes way for its successor.

NOTES

[1] H. Ibsen, *Ghosts and Other Plays*, trans. P. Watts (Penguin Classics, 1964), 61.

[2] H. Ibsen, *A Doll's House and Other Plays*, trans. P. Watts (Penguin Classics, 1965), 227–8.

[3] Ibsen, *Ghosts*, 92.

[4] H. Ibsen, *Peer Gynt*, trans. P. Watts (Penguin Classics, 1966), 157.

[5] H. Ibsen, *The Master Builder and Other Plays*, trans. U. Ellis-Fermor (Penguin Classics, 1958), 205.

[6] H. Ibsen, *When We Dead Awaken*, in *Ghosts and Other Plays*, trans. Watts, 278.

[7] A. Strindberg, *The Father*, in *Three Plays*, trans. P. Watt (Penguin Classics, 1958), 71.

[8] A. Strindberg, *Ghost Sonata*, in *Six Plays of Strindberg*, trans. E. Sprigge (Anchor Books, 1955), 304.

[9] A. Chekhov, *The Cherry Orchard*, in *Plays*, trans. E. Fen (Penguin Classics, 1959), 363–4.

[10] J. M. Synge, *The Shadow of the Glen*, in *The Plays and Poems of J. M. Synge*, ed. T. R. Henn (1963), 93–4.

[11] Synge, *The Playboy of the Western World*, in *Plays and Poems*, ed. Henn, 229.

[12] G. B. Shaw, *Man and Superman*, in *Complete Plays* (1931), 387.

[13] Shaw, *Heartbreak House*, in *Complete Plays*, 802.

FOR FURTHER READING

Among the general surveys of drama in this period, Allardyce Nicoll's compendious *World Drama from Aeschylus to Anouilh* (1949) is probably the most readable introduction, although its scope is broad rather than deep. Two brilliant and influential critical approaches to the major dramatists of this period are to be found in Eric Bentley's *The Playwright as Thinker* (New York, 1946) and in Francis Fergusson's *The Idea of a Theater* (Princeton, 1949). Both these studies, which have become classics of dramatic criticism, focus upon the development in this period from naturalism towards the forms of modern drama. This is also the theme of Raymond Williams's *Drama from Ibsen to Eliot* (1950), which is particularly concerned with naturalism and the problems of language and style; much influenced by an admiration for T. S. Eliot in this respect, the book adopts a point of view which does less than justice to the earlier dramatists, and seriously underestimates Chekhov in particular. A different conception of the continuity of European drama since Ibsen is offered by Robert Brustein in *The Theatre of Revolt* (1965), which shifts attention away from the traditional stylistic distinctions between naturalism, symbolism, and expressionism, to consider the major dramatists each as manifesting and evolving an expression of revolt against conditions of modern life. In Brustein's view, the attitude of protest or rebellion, romantic, social, metaphysical, or spiritual, is the unifying feature of drama in this and later periods.

In a period when so many of the major dramatists came from the fringes of the European tradition, from Scandinavia, Russia, and Ireland, studies of their individual work and careers give importance to the national as well as the biographical background. Correcting the earlier conception of Ibsen as essentially a social realist, M. C. Bradbrook's *Ibsen the Norwegian* (1946) brings out the poet and visionary behind the plays, and tries to give a somewhat impressionistic picture of the specifically Norwegian qualities in his work. This cultural context is given in greater depth in J. W. McFarlane's *Ibsen and the Temper of Norwegian Literature* (1960). *Strindberg: An Introduction to his Life and Work*, by B. M. E. Mortensen and B. W. Downs (Cambridge, 1949) is informative on the life but does not penetrate very far into the work. Ronald Hingley's *Chekhov* (1950) is a biographical and critical account which, like the more recent and more detailed study by David Magarshack, *Chekhov the Dramatist* (1960), examines Chekhov's relations with the Moscow Arts Theatre and the traditions being then established by Stanislavsky, in their bearing on the plays. Una Ellis-Fermor's *The Irish Dramatic Movement* (1939) still holds its place as a standard historical and critical work, although Alan Price's *Synge and Anglo-Irish Drama* (1961) supplements it in several respects. Shaw's reputation as a dramatist has fallen in recent years, but he receives able and sympathetic treatment in E. Bentley's *Bernard Shaw* (1957), and in A. Henderson's *George Bernard Shaw: Man of the Century* (1956), while the measure of his contribution to the drama of his day is assessed in M. Meisel's excellent *Shaw and the Nineteenth-Century Theater* (Princeton, 1963).

A number of the statements by playwrights quoted in the above chapter are from *Playwrights on Playwriting*, ed. T. Cole (1960).

14

English Criticism

GRAHAM HOUGH

I

The earlier years of the twentieth century are not a period with any very distinct literary characteristics. The High Victorian synthesis had pretty well come to an end by 1880. The new poetics and the new critical outlook that we associate with Eliot, Pound, Joyce, and Wyndham Lewis hardly began to make itself felt until after the First World War. The period from 1900 to 1918 is a sort of interregnum, subject to various influences, but with no overmastering purpose. It will be noticed that there is a gap of twenty years in this skeleton chronology—the years from 1880 to 1900. This is of course the celebrated *fin de siècle*; the period of Walter Pater, of aestheticism and decadence, Ibsenism and Wagnerism. It would be a great mistake to dismiss it as an era of green carnations and ethical eccentricity. It was in fact the time when the major influences of continental European thought began to make their impact on England, and the early part of the new century is still busy adjusting itself to them. But after 1900 they seem to be experienced with a good deal more caution than in the immediately preceding years. There had been set-backs. The trial and condemnation of Oscar Wilde in 1895 caused something of a revulsion, not to say a panic. Beardsley disappeared from *The Yellow Book*, and greenery-yallery young men tended to revert to a more customary colouration. As Yeats put it in the Preface to his *Oxford Book of Modern Verse* (1936):

Then in 1900 everybody got down off his stilts; henceforth nobody drank absinthe with his black coffee; nobody went mad; nobody joined the Catholic Church; or if they did I have forgotten.

In many quarters the reaction was quite conscious; not a panic-stricken reflex but a deliberate choice. G. K. Chesterton's *Heretics* (1905) and *Orthodoxy* (1909), Hilaire Belloc's *The Path to Rome* (1902) are purposeful, polemical returns to traditional moral and social standards, from a Catholic point of view very different from the aesthetic Catholicism of the nineties. It was an earthy, populist

Catholicism, eager above all to show its community with the native temper of England, old England, that dreamland old England that had haunted the imagination of Dickens and Cobbett, and was still, under the name of the organic society, to cast a dying glow on the pages of *Scrutiny*. From another direction the aesthetic mists and cobwebs were to be blown away by Bernard Shaw and H. G. Wells, campaigning for a fresh acceptance of the modern world and a changed social organization. In fact English thought in this period was a muddle, as it has been ever since; and, as it has been ever since, a muddle that rarely sorted itself out into sharp and committed oppositions. The concept of pre-1914 England as a long summer afternoon is quite false; it was filled with conflict, political, social, and ideological. But it is true that the fabric of high bourgeois culture was as yet unbroken, and it managed to hold all together in a precarious fusion until the war blew it away for ever.

As far as strictly literary thought is concerned the years from 1900 to 1918 were chiefly a time of absorption. Two great continental movements, Symbolism and Realism, had already been much discussed in the 1880s and 1890s. They were now to lose the air of mystery and scandal that had vaguely hung about them, and were beginning to be absorbed into the general literary consciousness. At the threshold of our period comes a celebrated book, a landmark and an influence for many years to come, Arthur Symons's *The Symbolist Movement in Literature* (1899). It is dedicated to W. B. Yeats as 'a perfectly sympathetic reader'; and it is an accompaniment to Yeats's own contributions to the Symbolist aesthetic in England. Symons's book offers to introduce to the English reader the chief Symbolist writers of France—Gérard de Nerval, Villiers de l'Isle Adam, Rimbaud, Verlaine, Laforgue, Mallarmé, Huysmans, and Maeterlinck. Several of these had been names to conjure with for some years, but they had been mentioned in an allusive and esoteric fashion, rather than discussed. They are not easy writers (Rimbaud, Laforgue, Mallarmé, and Huysmans all in their different ways present notable difficulties), and it may be doubted whether most of the English men of letters who were willing enough to cite them had enough real understanding of the French literary scene to know what was going on. Symons (1865-1945) was a genuine French scholar; he had a deep sympathy with contemporary French literature; and his role in this book is that of the unveiler of a mystery. He was personally acquainted with Verlaine and Mallarmé; he gives glimpses of the lives of most of the writers he discusses, and some of them have become exemplary. Villiers, willing to abandon the business of living to servants as long as he was left alone to pursue a proud interior dream; Verlaine, exalting music above all things, through alternations of debauchery and devotion; Rimbaud, the miraculous boy who recreated French poetry at the age of eighteen and then abandoned it for ever; Mallarmé, a life almost without incident, devoted to the utmost refinement of a verbal art in which all science, all religion, all experience were to be contained: these have contributed so richly to the image of the alienated artist in the twentieth century that it is hard to imagine subsequent literary history without them. It was Symons who revealed them to the English. His criticism of their work is not profound or searching by modern standards; but he is a truthful guide as far as he goes. He offers sympathetic descriptive notices of the chief works of his authors, gives generous quotations, and above all transmits the atmosphere of a literature that sets itself up, in delicacy, mystery, and pride, against the bourgeois world of commerce, administration, and affairs. An onslaught against bourgeois society, or a mere evasion of it? The question never occurs to Symons for a moment. He works entirely from within the ethos that he describes.

Yeats's (1865–1939) essays are essentially a creative and personal adaptation of Symbolist ideas, though they are partly derived from different sources and developed in a highly individual way. The two volumes in our period are *Ideas of Good and Evil* (1896–1903) and *The Cutting of an Agate* (1903–15). Yeats did not know French well, and his knowledge of French Symbolist thinking was mostly derived from Symons. But there are currents of thought and feeling that have an almost independent life, and Yeats was by temperament and conviction a natural member of the international Symbolist movement. His literary concerns are given a special direction by his Irishness. He found, or thought he found, in the spirit of his own country a deep affinity with what was emerging in contemporary poetry, and on this basis he elaborated a literary mythology of his own. Like all the Symbolists he wished to fuse poetry and religion, or absorb religion in poetry; like Rimbaud he believed in magic and the occult; like Villiers he felt an aristocratic disdain for the common business of living; like Verlaine he wanted to wring the neck of rhetoric—meaning by rhetoric all the expository, hortatory, political, and social side of literature; like Mallarmé, although more inter- mittently, he saw the mystique of art as the unifying factor of a whole life. But this complex of ideas is given quite a different turn by Yeats's concern with the popular and traditional roots of poetry, perpetually brought before his mind by his concern with the nature of Irish culture. The essay 'What is "Popular Poetry" ' distinguishes between poets who have been popular, like Longfellow and Mrs. Hemans, because they produce a middle-class version of the literary tradition, and poets who are authentic products of a pre-literary national life. Yeats liked to think that poetry of his own kind could recapture these ancient sources of strength, and that his own esoteric religious interests were simply a return to an ancient and universal tradition. Like all active-minded men who want to change the course of things he thought the world was going his way. It was not, as he later perhaps discovered; but it is notable that his apparently anachronistic ideas were able to give to poetry a greater vitality and depth than any others current in his time. Neither the concern with technical innovation that we find in Pound and Eliot nor the political and social preoccupations of later writers have been able to do as much for poetry as the thought of Yeats, on the face of it so blankly hostile to actual contemporary developments. This seems to show that the history of poetry has its own logic, at least partly independent of social and ideological history—a conclusion that Yeats would have entirely approved.

Yeats is quite capable of writing straightforward and sensitive critical essays, like those on the philosophy of Shelley's poetry and Edmund Spenser. But they always draw their strength from deeper currents of thought and feeling, which are not merely 'critical'. We do not feel, as we often do with Eliot, that he is making propaganda for his own kind of poetry, but that his critical thinking springs from the same source as his poetry. It is not the kind of criticism that is poetry in disguise, for all the beauty and distinction of its expression. Yeats had an extremely clear analytical mind, and was even, as we see in other parts of his work, a great system-builder. His writing on the drama, collected in *Plays and Controversies* (1923), is often precisely detailed and practical. Yet his critical work has not, or not yet, become absorbed into the accepted canon of English critical thought, which seems in general to leap blindly from Arnold to Eliot. His criticism is far more than a by-product of his own poetry, and a recognition of this is long overdue.

II

An excited controversy about 'realism' had been a prominent feature of literary life in the 1880s. A battle for the recognition of Zola was fought; Flaubert too was under discussion; and George

Moore was active both as a propagandist and a practitioner of realist fiction. The point at issue was the treatment of 'unpleasant' subjects, and the dominance in England of prudish circulating-library standards. With the arrival of Ibsen in the 1890s the field extended to the drama, and the turn of the century was deeply engaged with extending the range of English literature to social and sexual areas that had formerly been taboo. There are parallels to this situation at the present time, but they are not complete. The fascinated devotion to pornography shown by the Sunday papers today had not yet manifested itself, and most of the campaigners for the new fiction were interested in freedom, not the dirty-book trade. However, then as now, most discussion of the novel was on a sub-literary level, and it might have remained so if it were not for the work of Henry James (1843–1916).

James's status as a novelist is assured: it is less often realized that he is one of the greatest of all critics of the novel. He writes of his immediate predecessors and contemporaries, and even more extensively of his own work. Much of his novel-criticism is early and so outside our period. (The best of it is collected in *The House of Fiction*, ed. Leon Edel, 1957.) He comes into our view chiefly by reason of the Prefaces to the New York Edition of his own works (1907–9). These are ruminative, reminiscent, anecdotal; they are concerned with his own novels and tales—but they are also profound and considered reflections on the whole art of fiction, written firmly from his own idiosyncratic point of view, but considering other points of view with judicious and expansive calm. They have been collected as *The Art of the Novel* (ed. R. P. Blackmur, New York, 1934). More may be found in his letters, especially in his correspondence with H. G. Wells—see *James and H. G. Wells: a Record* (ed. Leon Edel and Gordon N. Ray, Urbana, Ill., 1958). This large body of writing forms a majestic survey of the problems of prose fiction.

James is not much of an abstract theorist. He has a theory, but he prefers to express it through concrete and particular cases. This means that his critical thinking has many facets, and it is almost impossible to give a proper account of it in summary form. James's thinking about the novel moves between two poles; one is 'realism', the true representation of life as it is lived; the other is form, the scrupulous ordering of material, the exact choice of treatment. He often discusses them separately, but in his most deeply felt passages he sees these two problems as one. The right form of the novel is simply the arrangement and treatment that allows most truth to be told. There is nothing predetermined about it—no neo-neo-classical rules. Each subject makes its own demands, and in his own writing James was always varying his technical methods. What is constant is his insistence that subjects *do* make inexorable demands; slapdash or reach-me-down methods of narration can never do justice to the subtlety and complexity of life. And this means an unremitting warfare against the easy-going view, which he attributes with some justice to the English, 'that a novel is a novel, as a pudding is a pudding, and that our only business with it could be to swallow it'. His allies in this more strenuous approach to the novel—allies with whom he was nevertheless not entirely comfortable—were the French.

One side of James's novel criticism belongs with the realist controversy of the 1880s. Like George Moore he is impatient with the subjugation of English taste to the young-lady public, its confinement to what could be safely read aloud in the family circle. His personal tastes were genteel upper-bourgeois, and he was extremely uneasy in the more grisly social and moral areas that French fiction liked to explore. And he argues seriously, not as a matter of taste but of fact and principle, that common experience includes more kindliness, decency, and decorum than, say, Maupassant and Zola would allow. But he is absolutely firm in his conviction that the artist in fiction must be allowed his own *donnée*, his own choice of material, and that the prime purpose of the novel is to be a truthful and honest representation. 'The only reason for the existence of a novel is that it does attempt to represent life.' In the preface to his novel *The American* he accepts Nathaniel Hawthorne's distinction between the novel, conceived in these terms, and the romance, which sits more loosely to actuality; and though he extends a tender indulgence to the romance his most serious allegiance is to the other side, fidelity to things as they are. His reflections on this subject are scattered through dozens of individual discussions; collected together they form one of the most reasonable, temperate, and untendentious presentations of the realist case. Those who think of James as the great formalist critic of the novel forget how firmly his formal concerns were based on the primacy of truthful representation.

This is obscured for us by the fact that his own choice of subjects was very different from that which we commonly associate with the idea of 'realism'. Here his formal interests come in. He did not value a subject either for its harshness and violence, or for its innocuous sweetness; he valued it for its capability of treatment in a complete and organic way. The vast panoramic novels, 'loose and baggy monsters', as he called them, were not much of his taste. The ideal of the novel to him was the complete and rounded development of a single situation, and 'form' was not a superadded elegance, but simply the procedure by which the given situation could be most richly and completely worked out. He disliked the prefabricated plot, and preferred to start from a character or group of characters in a particular set of circumstances. Many of his best discussions are about the genesis of individual works of his own, where he considers, selects, and rejects alternative modes of treatment. He pays much attention to the point of view from which the story should be told, working gradually towards the elimination of the external narrator, and the centring of the work in the consciousness of one or more of the characters. It is therefore important to him that the central character should have a finely developed consciousness. He has his reservations about Flaubert's *Madame Bovary*, because of the meanness and imperceptiveness of Emma Bovary herself. Equally he deplores the dissipation of interest caused by artless switching about from one consciousness to another. Ultimately he comes to see analogies between the novel and the drama, and to prefer the novel constructed by means of relatively few perfectly developed scenes.

James's conception of the novel is a special one, and much of what he says applies particularly to his own kind of fiction. But however specialized the discussion he is always opening up the central technical questions of prose narrative; and by the time he has finished with them they have ceased to be merely technical and have become passionate inquiries into the fundamentals of the art. No one before him in England had seriously considered the novel as an art at all, and I believe that no one in England or elsewhere has made it the subject of such prolonged and scrupulous study. The importance of his critical writing was not realized at the time. It is only in our own day that the full value of this pre-1918 criticism has been felt.

III

The most widely influential achievement of English criticism in this period is the formal academic study of English literature. It dates only from the later years of Queen Victoria's reign, and even then was slow in getting under way. The Cambridge English School, for instance, was begun only in 1917. Traditional literary education had been in the classics, and the study of English literature was a matter for undirected private enterprise. In the early years of this century it becomes increasingly the subject of organized scholarship. Scholarly editions of most of the major English poets were produced in these years, many of them at the Oxford University Press. For the first time reliable and easily accessible texts became available, and what had formerly been a matter for antiquarianism and research became a general possession. The outlines of English literary history were firmly sketched in. George Saintsbury's *Short History of English Literature* dates from 1898, his monumental *History of Criticism and Literary Taste in Europe* appeared from 1900 to 1914, his *History of English Prosody* from 1900 to 1910; and these are only the peaks of his huge output of literary history and criticism. Saintsbury (1845–1933) was an omnivorous and genial reader; his range extended from the classics through English and all the principal modern European languages, up to the work of his own time; and wherever he went he left his records and compilations behind him. Himself an old-fashioned high Tory, with crotchets and prejudices that he did not trouble to conceal, his literary criticism is remarkably free from ideological prepossessions. He was not unaffected by the art-for-art's-sake theory of the later nineteenth century (he appears, rather surprisingly, as a contributor to *The Yellow Book*); and he regarded literature as a vast enchanted kingdom with its own boundaries and its own laws. His criticism is for the most part of a summary and descriptive kind; he was not primarily an evaluator or an analyst. But anyone of literary interests who was growing up in the early part of this century naturally went to him for information on an immense range of periods, kinds, and languages.

On a more restricted scale, and with more detailed criticism, Oliver Elton (1861–1945) performed similar services. His *Survey of English Literature 1780–1830* appeared in 1912, and the companion volumes extending to 1880 in 1928. They are scholarly, temperate, and informative, and they are still probably the standard general histories of their period. Walter Raleigh (1861–1922) wrote studies of Milton (1900), Wordsworth (1903), Shakespeare (1907), and Johnson (1910). He is somewhat easy-going and commonplace in tone, consciously unacademic in a way that itself became an academic mannerism. This has called down upon him the disapproval of a later generation, but probably more than he deserves. He provided agreeable and unstrenuous introductions to much great literature for students and general readers of the pre-Eliot, pre-Leavis period; and I do not know that he did them any harm.

The massive work of E. K. Chambers (1866–1954) on the history of English drama is scholarship of a severer kind. His *Medieval Stage* came out in 1903, and its continuation *The Elizabethan Stage* falls just outside the confines of our period, in 1923. They are theatrical history rather than criticism, but they are works of great and enduring importance. They have had a lasting influence on the study of our early dramatic literature. His *William Shakespeare: A Study of Facts and Problems* is much later (1930). It can be described as the first scientific life of Shakespeare, without legend or bardolatry. It includes a complete collection of all the relevant documents, an authoritative survey of such biographical facts as there are, and of stage and editorial history. Chambers's books may serve as early examples of a kind of work that has been of growing importance in this century—the exact historical study of literary matters. Much of it is not in itself literary; but it provides the background of authenticated information without which literary and critical studies would go far astray.

The work of A. C. Bradley (1851–1935) is of a different kind. His *Shakespearean Tragedy* (1904) is more than a work of information and an aid to study. It is a critical classic in its own right. It is the first philosophic interpretation of Shakespeare's tragedies since Coleridge, as profound as all but the best of Coleridge and far more systematic. It has a strong philosophical foundation, partly Hegelian and partly Aristotelian, but it rarely loses sight of the text. Bradley's approach is through character and action rather than symbol and image, and for a time there was a reaction against his kind of character-criticism. By now the controversy has died down, and *Shakespearean Tragedy* stands as one of the perennial and fundamental studies. His *Oxford Lectures on Poetry* (1909) are also notable. The lecture on 'Poetry for Poetry's Sake' is the clearest and most thoughtful exposition of the art-for-art's-sake doctrine that exists.

This rather dull catalogue of what many will regard as academic textbooks is nevertheless of great significance. It would be hard to overestimate the difference to literary study and literary appreciation made by this organized scholarly approach. It is not 'creative criticism' and it has little connection with the active literary life of its time. But it lays the foundations of a new literary period in two respects. First by the wide dissemination of straightforward information on the literature of the past. Earlier men of letters had formed themselves on the independent study of the classics of English literature, and the selection and emphasis was largely determined by their personal taste or by that of their age. From this time on there is a background of received, documented literary history, largely factual and indisputable, and of literary opinion that had at least a formidable body of authority behind it. Secondly, the writers we have been speaking of were not amateurs or independent men of letters; all except Chambers were professors of literature, situated in the universities, with a body of students formally taught and formally examined. From this time on the greater part of criticism, quantitatively speaking, goes on within the universities, in an academic context, and the greater part of those who are reasonably informed about literature are so because they have studied it as part of their regular education. The result is a higher level of competence and a lower level of talent, enterprise, and originality. It is possible to look forward with dismay to a time when there are readers' guides to everything, and nothing is ever read without the inevitable scholastic mentor at the elbow. The critic has never at any time been *persona grata* to creative writers, but in this century a further split has become evident between the academic critic and the critic who is himself an original writer, or at least closely connected with the practice of the arts. Often there is little connection between the two worlds. The more acute symptoms of this division appear later, from the thirties onwards; but it is in the pre-war years, with the establishment of English literature as an academic discipline, that they are first to be observed.

FOR FURTHER READING

The last thing to be recommended is too much criticism of criticism. David Lodge's essay, 'Literary Criticism in England in the Twentieth Century', in *The Sphere History of Literature in the English Language: Vol. 7. The Twentieth Century*, ed. B. Bergonzi (1970) provides a competent narrative.

Henry James's Prefaces to the New York Edition have been collected in *The Art of the Novel: Critical Prefaces*, ed. R. P. Blackmur (1934). These form a classic treatise, and have enormously influenced subsequent thinking about the novel. The other great classic of the period, of course, is A. C. Bradley, *Shakespearean Tragedy* (1904).

15

The Other Arts

EDWARD LUCIE-SMITH

During the period 1900–18, the visual arts, architecture, and music are the servants of a common impulse. Paradoxically, however, this impulse took two contradictory forms. On the one hand, the significant artists, architects, and musicians were nearly all of them the servants of the 'modernist' idea. In fact, modernism was more truly international in the decade and a half which preceded the First World War than it was ever again to be afterwards. The opening years of the century saw the coming together of two worlds, one of which was soon to destroy the other. The 'old' world, in this sense, was the Europe of cultivated people, which still retained much of the unity which it had enjoyed during the eighteenth century. Throughout these early years of modernism, we find an extraordinary openness to new ideas, and a rapid transmission of these ideas from one country to another. The prophet of Futurism, Filippo Tommaso Marinetti (1876–1944), travelled extensively, preaching his doctrines to the Russians, the English, and the French as much as to his fellow-Italians. The first Futurist Manifesto, indeed, appeared in French in a Parisian newspaper (*Le Figaro*, 20 February 1909). But this manifesto contained more than one disturbing note. Besides the demand that the past be rejected, the celebrated coat-trailing statement that a racing automobile is 'more beautiful than the Victory of Samothrace', Marinetti put forward some new ideals, among them fearlessness, rebelliousness, aggressiveness, patriotism, and the glorification of war. 'We want to pull down the museums,' he said, 'and the libraries, to fight against moralism, and opportunistic and utilitarian baseness.' Marinetti was a nationalist, and the 'new' world of the arts was a world of nationalism, which linked primitivism and primitive emotions to a worship of the machine. The frenetic energy which possessed the arts before the catastrophe is something which has been much admired and commented upon by later historians. But it was also part of the mood which brought the catastrophe about.

Marinetti, however, was merely a man who arrived in the midst of an already established scene. He did not create it single-handed. Something very like the 'avant-gardism' we know today had already established itself in Paris before the turn of the century. Perhaps it is to be dated back as far as the first Impressionist Exhibition of 1874. Impressionism had been followed by the Neo-Impressionism of Georges Seurat (1859–1891), and the Post-Impressionism of Van Gogh, Cézanne, and Gauguin. In the work produced by the painters connected with these three movements, the forms of modern art were already being created. Towards the end of his long life, Claude Monet (1840–1926), the acknowledged leader of the Impressionists, was to produce pictures which many people now regard as the precursors of the Abstract Expressionism which was to triumph in New York after 1945.

More significant for the immediate future, however, was the work of Paul Cézanne (1839–1906) and Paul Gauguin (1848–1903). They both began their careers as artists in the circle of the Impressionists, and Cézanne showed at the first Impressionist Exhibition. But, in both cases, their development led them away from the Impressionist ideal. Cézanne became more and more involved with a search for the very structure of things, and of the way in which reality could be put upon canvas without compromise with the medium. For him, he found, the truly satisfactory representation in two dimensions must also be a completely structured surface, end to end and corner to corner. For him, therefore, art was 'a harmony parallel to nature'. It was this insight which opened the door to modernism.

Gauguin's significance is somewhat different. With his disciples of the Pont-Aven Group he reacted against Impressionism. It was Maurice Denis (1870–1943) who, in 1890, defined a painting as 'essentially a flat surface covered by colours arranged in a certain order'. In putting forward this definition, he was basing himself on the work and ideas of Gauguin. But Gauguin had a broader significance than his influence over Denis and the painters who called themselves the Nabis. Gauguin, said the admiring Denis, was 'a kind of Poussin without classical culture, who, instead of serenely studying antiquity in Rome, sought stubbornly to discover a tradition underlying the crude archaism of Breton Calvaries and Maori idols'. The voyage the painter made to the South Seas was due to much more than a superficial attraction towards the exotic. It was prompted by the desire to find new roots. He might well have cried, with Rimbaud, in his prophetic poem Le Bateau Ivre:

J'ai vu des archipels sidéraux! et des îles
Dont les cieux délirants sont ouverts au vogueur:
—Est-ce en ces nuits sans fonds que tu dors et t'exiles,
Million d'oiseaux d'or, ô future Vigueur?*

Gauguin, through his young followers, was allied to the Symbolists. Symbolist art critics, such as Félix Fénéon and Albert Aurier, fought the good fight for Gauguin's work in the 1880s and 1890s. But more than any other of the painters with whom the Symbolists identified themselves—Gustave Moreau, Puvis de Chavannes, Odilon Redon—Gauguin pointed the way to the future. And the artists of the future were often to be violently anti-Symbolist. Marinetti, for example, regarded Symbolism and Futurism as entirely opposed to one another, and refused to acknowledge the debt he owed to these predecessors. It was the savage, or consciously primitive, side of Gauguin's work which was to have spectacular results, and, in painting at least, Symbolist subtleties were to be mocked and forgotten.

If any single date must be chosen to mark the birth of modern painting, it must surely be 1905, when the artists who were immediately labelled the 'Fauves', or 'wild beasts', showed in Room 7 of the Salon d'Automne. Among them were Matisse, Derain, Vlaminck, and Marquet. Of all these, Henri Matisse (1869–1954) was infinitely the most important—the acknowledged leader of the group even then. Matisse's influences, as he matured as a painter, were almost copybook. They included Cézanne, Gustave Moreau (with whom he studied for three years), the Neo-Impressionists, and Gauguin. But these influences were by no means uncritically accepted. Matisse criticized Gauguin, for example, on the grounds that he did not 'construct space by means of colour, which he uses excessively as an expression of feelings'. 'Composition,' he remarked, 'is the art of arranging in a decorative manner the various elements at the painter's disposal for the expression of his feelings.' This marked a still further stage in the liberation of the painter from the duty to represent what was before him. By giving a special twist to the idea of representation—which he defined as 'recreation' —Cézanne had already prepared the way for this. But all the same, the work of the Fauves, with its violent, dazzling colours, its often deliberately crude and simplified drawing, came as a considerable shock to the Parisian public.

* I have seen sidereal archipelagos! and islands / Whose delirious skies are open to the sea-wanderer: / —Is it in these bottomless nights that you sleep and exile yourself, / Million golden birds, O future Vigour?

Yet, curiously enough, Matisse's career, unlike that of Picasso, was never that of a deliberate innovator. Rather, he was an artist who came to certain decisions, and then pursued them with tranquil logic. Matisse said, later, that 'Fauvism came from the fact that we completely abandoned imitative colour, and that with pure colours we obtained stronger, more evident simultaneous reactions; equally important was the luminosity of the colours.' This is very much the remark of a decorative painter, and Matisse remained a great decorator all his life. The ten years following 1905 were very fruitful ones for Matisse, and during them he painted some of the most satisfying large compositions in twentieth-century art, among them, 'The Joy of Living' of 1905-6, now in the collection of the Barnes Foundation, and 'The Dance', of 1910, now in Moscow. It is significant, as we shall see later, that the latter was commissioned by a Russian patron. The hallmark of these compositions is the simplicity—though a very subtle simplicity—of the compositions, the bold colour, and the suave fluency of line.

But if Matisse was the original herald of modernism, the most controversial of its prophets was undoubtedly the young Spaniard, Pablo Picasso (b. 1881). Picasso was born in Barcelona, the son of an artist, and early established a reputation as something of an infant prodigy. He paid his first visit to Paris in 1900, where he immediately began to assimilate the new ideas which were in the air. After repeated visits during the next few years, he finally settled in France for good in 1904. After a period during which he was heavily influenced by Toulouse-Lautrec, Picasso embarked on the paintings of the 'Blue Period' in 1901. This was followed by the 'Rose Period' in 1904. The paintings of these years are a curious amalgam—social criticism of the fiercest kind rubs shoulders with the mannerisms of Art Nouveau. In 1905, Picasso felt the impact of the Fauves, though it was not until 1906 that he met Matisse at the house of Leo and Gertrude Stein. During the winter of 1906-7 he painted 'Les Demoiselles d'Avignon'.

It is not often that a single work of art deserves all the historic and symbolic importance which critics and gallery-goers afterwards attribute to it. But in the case of this large picture of a group of nudes (jokingly named by the poet André Salmon for their supposed resemblance to the inmates of a brothel in Barcelona) the tribute is deserved. 'Les Demoiselles' is, however, far from being a constructive work like 'The Joy of Living', which tries to build a new tradition to replace the old. Rather, it is a kind of bomb-explosion, and has the formal disarray which this description implies. Nothing about it is consistent—neither the modelling nor the treatment of space. Though it belongs to Picasso's so-called 'Negro Period', the resemblances to the Negro sculpture which Picasso had begun to admire are only superficial. What it does seem to express is a kind of will to barbarism, the feeling that the ground must be cleared with great sweeps of the axe if painting is to begin anew.

The strange thing is that this expressionist picture leads straight into one of the most classical periods of painting to be found in the history of Western art. The short-lived Cubist movement, whose chief protagonists were Picasso and his friend Georges Braque (1882–1963), has been awarded an importance by historians of twentieth-century painting which is both deserved and misleading: deserved because of the perfection of its principal masterpieces, misleading because, the longer one examines its precepts, the less they seem to relate to anything that followed afterwards. The German Expressionists, the Russian and Italian Futurists—all of these pointed the path towards the future. Cubism, on the other hand, seems a last-minute effort to save what could be saved from the wreckage of traditional painting.

Guillaume Apollinaire (1880–1918), in his account of the birth of the Cubist movement, attributes the label to Matisse. He explains that 'the young painters adopted it at once, because it representing *conceived* reality the artist can give the appearance of three dimensions'. And this is essentially what Cubism was about—a new and still more radical way of applying the gospel preached by Cézanne. The way in which 'Les Demoiselles d'Avignon' contributed to this new development was in its break with the convention of the single viewpoint. In 1908 Braque (who had been introduced to Picasso by Apollinaire towards the end of 1907) and Picasso each began to paint severely Cézannean landscapes and still-lifes, where the compositions were broken into emphatic planes and facets. By early 1910, Analytical Cubism had begun, and the two artists, 'roped together like mountaineers' as Braque put it, were busy exploring this new frontier of the visible. Analytical Cubism has been given this label because its main concern lies in the analysis of appearances. The artist attempts to encompass the subject in every part. 'I paint objects as I know them, not as I see them', said Picasso at this time. The spectator, looking at the picture, is in front of, beside, above, and behind what is depicted, all at the same time. The extreme complexity which this entailed serves to explain both the simplicity of the subject-matter (mostly single figures and still-life) and the restricted palette of grey and ochre which makes such a marked contrast to the Fauves.

The ever-increasing complexity of treatment meant that the subject-matter eventually seemed to disappear altogether. The attempt to reintroduce reality led from Analytical Cubism to Synthetic Cubism, chiefly via the newly invented technique of *papier collé*. Newspaper, wallpaper, and other scraps of ready-made material were added to the composition, so that this literal reality was played off against the 'real' things which the painter was trying to show. Pictures made by these heterogeneous means acquired an identity as objects which was stronger than the identity of what they depicted. With this further discovery, Cubism began at last to lose its impetus, though it persisted long enough for Picasso to paint the Synthetic Cubist masterpiece, 'The Three Musicians', as late as 1921. Braque's work was to show the impress of the style for the rest of his life.

Picasso and Braque were not, of course, the only Cubists; nor was Cubism the only style competing for the attention of the Parisian public in the years immediately preceding the war. Perhaps the most important of the other Cubists were Fernand Léger (1881–1955) and Juan Gris (1887–1927). A related, but competing, movement was the Orphism (sometimes called Orphic Cubism) of Robert Delaunay (1885–1941). He and his followers wished to combine Fauve colour and Cubist form, and Apollinaire acted as their apologist, much as he had originally done for Cubism itself. By 1912 Delaunay had moved towards a lyrical art which relied on colour alone, and which was entirely abstract—a matter of whirling discs and interpenetrating forms. 'We no longer want apples in a fruit bowl,' he cried, 'we want the heartbeat of man himself.' This development had its parallels elsewhere.

The Paris which produced Fauvism, Cubism, and Orphism was an infinitely complex cultural organism, and it is impossible to keep the various spheres of cultural activity entirely separate from one another. Foreign artists came to Paris to cry their wares—like Marinetti and the Futurists. And writers and musicians remained in close contact with the milieux of the painters. For example, Apollinaire not only acted as the most important cultural impresario of the time, but made experiments in his poetry which seem to reflect what the artists were doing. The simultaneity of Cubist painting turns up in Apollinaire's verse as a kind of rapid, cinematic cutting from image to image which is something new:

La mère de la concierge et la concierge laisseront tout passer
Si tu es un homme tu m'accompagneras ce soir
Il suffirait qu'un type maintînt la porte cochère
Pendant que l'autre monterait *

Nor was Apollinaire the only poet working in this manner. The link between his work and the two early long poems by Blaise Cendrars (1887–1961), *Pâques à New York* (1912) and *Transsibérien* (1913), has often been pointed out. Meanwhile, though frequenting a slightly different circle, the German poet who was perhaps the greatest of his generation, Rainer Maria Rilke (1875–1926), was briefly resident in Paris. He acted as secretary to the sculptor Rodin during the winter of 1905–6. His verse, too, was deeply influenced by his interest in the visual arts.

Germany itself was almost as much a cultural crossroads as France, but it lacked the point of focus which was supplied by Paris. Different centres tended to give their allegiance to different things. In Berlin, as the new century began, Impressionism reigned, under the leadership of Max Liebermann and Lovis Corinth. In Vienna, the Vienna Secession practised a version of Art Nouveau, under the leadership of Gustav Klimt. It soon became apparent, however, that the main current of development was towards Expressionism— a movement which had much in common with the Fauves, but which, because it was fundamentally nordic, did not achieve the extreme detachment of Matisse. Emil Nolde (1867–1956), perhaps the most important of all the North German Expressionists, was interested from the very beginning not so much in decoration as in the expression of psychic traits. His original heroes were Goya, Rembrandt, and Daumier. Later he was to be influenced by Van Gogh, the Norwegian Edvard Munch, and the Belgian James Ensor. All of them drew him towards the ecstatic, the demonic, the apparently uncontrolled. German Expressionism is the very opposite of Cubism—its characteristic concerns are with emotion rather than form. Paul Klee described Nolde as 'the demon of the lower realm'.

The artists most closely linked to Nolde were the three painters who founded 'Die Brücke' in 1905: Ernst Ludwig Kirchner (1880–1938), Erich Heckel (b. 1883), and Karl Schmidt-Rottluff (b. 1884).

---

* The concierge's mother and the concierge will let anyone in/If you're a man you'll come with me this evening/It will be OK if someone looks after the carriage entrance/While the other guy goes up

('Lundi Rue Christine')

They had met each other while studying architecture in Dresden, and the purpose of the new group was, as Schmidt-Rottluff said to Nolde, in a letter inviting him to join, 'to attract all revolutionary and fermenting elements. Nolde joined early in 1906. Of the founder-members, Kirchner was clearly the most talented, and, when he went to Berlin in 1911, he discovered a gift for expressing the evil and sinister nature of the modern metropolis which produced some memorable images. Of all the 'founding fathers' of modernism, however, the reputation of the artists of Die Brücke remains the most uncertain. The modern spectator still finds it difficult to come to terms with the apparent clumsiness and the unrestrained violence of much of their work.

A later, and, it seems to me, more important development in German painting came with the formation of the 'Blaue Reiter' group in Munich, in December 1911. This crystallized around the person of a Russian expatriate, Wassily Kandinsky (1866–1944). Kandinsky had first come to Munich in 1896—his painting at this time harked back to his recollections of Russia, both Russian folk-tales and Russian popular arts. But Kandinsky, as well as being a gifted painter, was a brilliant theoretician, and his theories gradually drew him towards a new kind of painting. In particular, he moved steadily towards idealism. In an exhibition preface of 1910 he speaks of 'the spiritual vibrations of the artist' which 'must . . . find a material form capable of being understood'. He also remarks that 'the principle of inner necessity is the sole unalterable law of art in its essence. . . .' In a way, these are particularly traditional attitudes for a Russian artist to take. Something very like them inspired the art of the icon-painter. But now the consequences were different. The direction which Kandinsky took was towards a purely abstract art. In 1910 he painted the first wholly abstract picture.

The Blaue Reiter was preceded in Munich by a group called the 'Neue Künstlervereinigung', founded in 1909. When this split on the rock of Kandinsky's obstinacy, the new and more important association was formed. Among the membership were Franz Marc (1880–1916), August Macke (1887–1914), and Paul Klee (1879–1940). What attracted all of these artists was the idea of a new culture, which shed the complex trappings of contemporary civilization and returned to the freshness of the primitive. Kandinsky, for instance, was attracted to the work of the French primitive painter Henri Rousseau (1884–1910) because of its literalism. For him, Rousseau represented the 'Greater Realism' which was the balancing force of the 'Greater Abstraction'. The artists of the Blaue Reiter were mystical and spiritual. They knew about and were interested by the Futurists and by the Orphism of Delaunay. Klee, speaking of a crucial visit he paid to North Africa in the company of Macke, uses the phrase 'Matter and dream at once, and wholly embedded in them a third factor, myself'. It is perhaps significant that Klee was an accomplished musician, and that the yearbook which the Blaue Reiter issued in 1912 contained a discussion of Scriabin's *Prometheus*. Arnold Schoenberg (who contributed some paintings to the first Blaue Reiter exhibition) was closely associated with the group.

From Kandinsky and the Blaue Reiter, it is an easy step to Russia itself. With the coming of Stalinism, the collapse of modernism in Russia was to be both sudden and complete. In consequence, modern art in Russia is not too well documented. The result has been an inveterate tendency, especially in France and in England, to neglect the importance of a school of artists who were arguably as important in the history of painting as the École de Paris itself. Certainly, it seems easier to trace back a good number of the more 'extreme' post-Second World War developments to Russian rather than to French sources.

Russian art, like Russia itself, has two principal centres, St. Petersburg and Moscow. Thanks to Diaghilev and the Ballets Russes it was the Petersburg artists who were the first to make their impact in the West. Among the dominant figures in St. Petersburg were the artists who were to create Diaghilev's early décors, Alexandre Benois and Léon Bakst. Benois cannot be described as a modernist in any real sense of the term; Bakst (1866–1924) did, at least, with his superb décors in dazzling colours, feed the contemporary taste for the 'primitive' and the exotic. Far more important were two artists who were to do work for Diaghilev at a slightly later date, Mikhail Larionov (1881–1964) and Natalia Gontcharova (1881–1962). These came not from St. Petersburg but from Moscow, and by 1909 they had evolved a primitivism which was far more radical than anything which Bakst could offer.

Basing themselves on the rich Russian folk tradition, and on children's art, Larionov produced a high-spirited, splendidly irreverent kind of painting in tune with the political and social restlessness to be found in the Russia of the time. Larionov's deliberate irreverence anticipated many of the devices of the Russian Futurist poets, among them Vladimir Mayakovsky (1893–1930) and the two brothers David and Vladimir Burliuk. David Burliuk was also to be well known as a painter, and the link between the arts is once again clearly present. An important part of Futurist activity in Moscow at this time lay in the organization of discussions and cabarets (the line was not always very clearly drawn between the two). Strange clothes and extraordinary behaviour—much of it a malicious parody of the aesthetic poses of the Symbolists—were among the hallmarks of the new art.

By 1911 Larionov was already moving towards abstraction, and in 1913 he was ready to give his new style a formal launching with the help of a 'Rayonnist manifesto'. This contains some significant phrases:

> We deny that individuality has any value in a work of art. One should only call attention to a work of art and look at it according to the means and laws by which it was created.
> Hail beautiful Orient! We unite ourselves with contemporary Oriental artists for communal work.
> Hail nationalism!—we go hand in hand with house painters.
> Hail our rayonnist style of painting independent of real forms, existing and developing according to the laws of painting. (Rayonnism is a synthesis of Cubism. Futurism and Orphism.)

The ideas of Kandinsky mingle strangely here with the voice of the coming Revolution.

Gontcharova and Larionov are better known in the West than the artists I shall now mention, both because of their connection with Diaghilev and because of the fact that they both eventually emigrated and settled in the West. But people such as Kasimir Malevich (1878–1935), Alexander Rodchenko (1891–1956), and Vladimir Tatlin (1885–1953) played an equally significant role. Malevich, the oldest of the three, began under the influence of Larionov's primitivism, but then moved towards a personal interpretation of Cubism—first a version of the style with Futurist overtones, and then one more directly related to the Synthetic Cubism of Braque and Picasso. This was the point he had reached by 1913, when he began to move towards a yet newer manner which he labelled Suprematism. The first Suprematist works by Malevich were exhibited in St. Petersburg in December 1915. The new creed was thus defined by its prophet: 'Suprematism is not concerned with objects, themes, and so on, but is simply "abstract" in general, without any qualification. Suprematism is a definite system through which colour passes in the long journey of its culture.'

In fact, Malevich's thought seems to have gone through two quite distinct phases. To begin with, he produced the earliest examples of 'reductionist' art—the black square, the black cross, the black circle.

Because they were so resolutely doctrinaire, these works made a considerable impression at the time, but that impression was later dissipated by the general collapse of Russian modernism. It was only after the Second World War that they could be seen as astonishing anticipations of a newly important tendency. The later Suprematist works are more complex formally, more concerned with mystical ideas about space and infinity. It was concerning these that Malevich said: 'At the present moment man's path lies through space. Suprematism is the semaphore of colour in this endlessness.'

Later still, with the 'White on White' series painted in 1917–18, Malevich was to return to a new kind of reductionism, more transcendental than the first. This series formed the climax of his career as a painter. After 1918, he gave up painting almost entirely, and began to devote himself to elaborating his theories on art.

Tatlin also began his career as an artist under the influence of Larionov and Gontcharova. But the turning point appears to have been a visit which he made to Paris in 1913, chiefly in order to see Picasso. Picasso was working on his Cubist constructions, and these influenced Tatlin deeply. When he returned to Moscow he himself began to make constructions and 'Painting Reliefs'. These experimented with the use of real materials in real (rather than illusionist) space in a way which pushed Cubist collage techniques much farther than they had so far been taken. Many anticipate the 'assemblages' and 'junk-sculptures' which were to be made by American artists in the 1950s and 1960s. The lack of finish only served to emphasize the revolutionary spatial concepts that Tatlin was interested in exploring.

Both Malevich and Tatlin (deadly rivals in most other ways) united to recognize in the Revolution of 1917 an event which had already been foreshadowed by the 'revolutionary' nature of their own art. And not only they, but others. 'We do not need a dead mausoleum of art where dead works are worshipped, but a living factory of the human spirit—in the streets, in the tramways, in the factories, workshops, and workers' homes,' declared Mayakovsky, in a discussion held at the requisitioned Winter Palace in November 1918. The easel painting was dismissed as a bourgeois anachronism, and the artists put themselves ardently at the service of the Revolution. They concerned themselves with such things as the Agit-prop trains, which were designed to carry the new doctrines out to the mass of the Russian people. Tatlin's ideas were taken by himself and his young disciple Rodchenko towards a fully developed Constructivism—the characteristic style of the 'heroic years' of the Revolution.

Though the geographical distances (and eventually the ideological ones) between the Italian Futurists and the Russian ones were vast, the two movements had at one point a great deal of sympathy for one another—a sympathy which was cemented by the visit which the Futurist prophet Marinetti paid to Russia late in 1909 or early in 1910. The Italian Futurists, though perhaps less important artistically than any of the painters and movements in art which I have so far discussed, did have one unfailing gift—that of seizing the attention of the public. In part, this was because Futurism was a political as well as an aesthetic creed. Marinetti and his followers were hot for war against Austria. They were also fierce critics of the apathy into which Italian culture had been allowed to sink. Because Futurism was a 'total' creed (Marinetti later became an admirer of Mussolini) it is perhaps not surprising to find the Futurist painters trying to express the totality of experience. The principal members of the movement were Giacomo Balla (1871–1958), Umberto Boccioni (1882–1916), and Gino Severini (1883–1966). What they chiefly sought means to express were sensations of movement and speed, and the simultaneity of sensory impressions. These were set up as the 'absolute of modernity'. They believed that 'Movement and light destroy the materiality of bodies'.

The result was a kind of painting which had perhaps too few inner resources to survive for very long. One of the best known of all Futurist works is Balla's 'Leash in Motion' of 1912, in which a small dog patters along beside its mistress, while the lead which links them swings in catenary curves. The device is based on experiments which had already been made in photography, where various movements (a man running, a horse galloping) appeared in a single image. Not that all Futurist painting was quite so simplistic. Boccioni speaks, in the preface to the catalogue of the First Exhibition of Futurist Painting, of creating 'an emotional environment, by searching for in an intuitive fashion, the sympathies and links between the external (concrete) scene and the internal (abstract) emotion'. To exemplify this he painted a series of canvasses entitled 'States of Mind'. These date from 1911.

Futurism was not the only modernist style produced by Italy during this period. The other was the *Pittura Metafisica* of Giorgio de Chirico (b. 1888) and Carlo Carrà (b. 1881). Since De Chirico and Carra did not encounter one another until January 1917, the movement itself only appears at the very end of the period I am now discussing. Nor was it very long-lived. Its interest lies in the personality of De Chirico himself, and in his anticipations of things which were to be very important to the post-war Surrealists. Desolate and empty, De Chirico's 'Piazze d'Italia' foreshadow, in a genera¹ way, the desert landscapes of Dali and Tanguy. In 1913, the *manichini* (faceless idols, automata, dressmaker's dummies) began to make their appearance in the artist's work, and these enigmatic creatures point the way to a whole new development in painting. De Chirico knew how to create 'an emotional environment' with greater effectiveness than his Futurist rivals.

However, it was not here that Surrealism got its real start. Its truest ancestor is the Dada movement which began in Zürich during the First World War. All the styles I have so far discussed were deeply rooted in the pre-war context. They represent the exuberance, the fierce aggressiveness and nationalism, even the will to destruction, of those dizzying years. The ferocity and daring of much of the painting I have discussed may be thought of as a kind of pre-echo of political events. Dada was directly the product of the war—an expression of weariness at the waste and futility of it, and at the same time an explosion of high spirits and defiance, a criticism of the stupidity of the world which was now crumbling into ruin. It sprang into being in Zürich, where, on 10 February 1916, the poet Hugo Ball (1886–1927) founded the Cabaret Voltaire 'which has as its sole purpose to draw attention, across the barriers of war and nationalism, to the few independent spirits who live for other ideals'. Many Dada techniques—including the whole idea of an outrageous cabaret—derived from Futurism. The importance of Zürich Dada was that it grouped together for the first time a good many people who were to have a big influence on how things went post-war: the Rumanian poet and *provocateur* Tristan Tzara (1896–1963) and the Alsatian painter Hans Arp (1885–1967) notable among them. Arp was later to say of this period: 'We were seeking an art based on fundamentals, to cure the madness of the age'.

The point about Dada, though, was its essential heterogeneity. For this led to more and more emphasis being placed on the idea, not only of the primitive, but of the absurd, the irrational, the deliberately paradoxical. In the midst of the world's madness, the Dadaists tried to set the psyche free, having come to the conclusion that fools were better guides than wise men. They relied to some extent on the already established French tradition of the *voyant* (Rimbaud) which often went hand in hand with a taste for black farce (as in Apollinaire's *Les Mamelles de Tirésias*, or the *Ubu* plays of Jarry). It was Dada, aided by the war, that broke the rule of reason in art.

It flourished not only in Zürich, but also in New York, where an equivalent 'anti-art' movement had begun to flourish quite independently. The group of participants here was centred upon the photographer Alfred Stieglitz (1864–1946). Among his associates there were Marcel Duchamp (1887–1968) and Francis Picabia (1878–1953). It was Duchamp who arrived in New York in 1915, bearing with him a glass ball containing Paris air, as a present for the collector Walter Arensberg and his wife. It was also Duchamp who invented the concept of the 'ready-made'—the object selected from the environment, and presented to the public as a work of art. The most famous of these ready-mades is the urinal signed 'R. Mutt' which was submitted to the first New York Salon des Indépendants.

As soon as the war was over, Dada spread like wildfire—to Berlin, to Paris, to Cologne, to Hanover. In Berlin, Dada seemed to sum up the despairing post-war mood; in Paris, it led towards the establishment of Surrealism. But above all, Dada was the culmination of much which had originally been triggered off by the Fauves.

Yet it is worth remembering that it was only one of two poles. I can best demonstrate this by turning very briefly to another art movement which grew up on the fringes of the war—De Stijl in Holland. De Stijl was all of those things which Dada was not—clear, orderly, logical, concerned with an almost clinical neatness and impersonality. The genius of the movement was undoubtedly Piet Mondrian (1872–1944). Mondrian had settled in Paris in 1910, but returned to Holland in 1914 for a holiday, and was kept there by the war. Mondrian had begun by making abstractions based on things seen in nature. He now began to investigate elementary pictorial relationships, unconnected with a motif. At this point (1916/17) he met Bart van der Leck (1876–1958) and Theo van Doesburg (1883–1931). Van der Leck was a painter who had been experimenting along lines somewhat similar to these which Mondrian had been pursuing. Van Doesburg was a talented organizer and entrepreneur, who had collaborated with the architects Oud and Wils, and who was later to put De Stijl in contact with the Bauhaus, and also to collaborate with some of the Dadaists.

But basically De Stijl stood for a total integration which was opposed to Dada's preference for disintegration; for discipline in the place of unruliness, and Mondrian's work was the perfect expression of its aims. Mondrian was to emerge from the movement ready to establish his mature style, where the rectangles of colour (a theme he had begun to explore in 1917) were kept firmly in place by a tracery of black lines.

The year 1918 is in many respects an excellent vantage point from which to survey the development of modern art. The huge proliferation of movements and ideas which took place in the decade and a half which divided the appearance of the Fauves from the end of the war did in fact anticipate nearly everything which has happened in the half-century which followed. The major themes are already present—primitivism going hand in hand with the worship of the future; the urge to simplify (both the forms of art, and, as with Duchamp, the ideas which related to those forms); the deliberate search for self-consistent systems and for unity of style, and the opposing desire to cultivate disorder, paradox, and unreason; the worship of logic and the desire to free the psyche from its trammels. Especially persistent have been certain notions which generation after generation of critics have tried to dispose of as at best barren and at worst ridiculous or even dishonest—among them reductionism and the idea of anti-art.

The period also saw the gradual growth, not merely of communities of modern artists, but of an *avant-garde* society-within-society. The advanced ideas put into currency from 1905 onwards failed to conquer culture as a whole, but they established a powerful bridgehead. Indeed, modernism lost ground rather than gaining it during the twenty years between the wars.

II

If it is logical to begin a description of the situation in the visual arts by speaking of what went on in Paris, it seems equally so to begin an account of twentieth-century architecture by speaking of developments in the United States. Of all the arts, architecture is most bound to, and most influenced by, new developments in technology. Architects, too, are even more directly affected by social change than painters and sculptors. The drive of social and technological change was what overcame historicist inertia.

One of the most significant developments in the United States was the development of the skyscraper. As a completely new sort of building, the skyscraper inexorably drew architects towards a new sort of architecture. The logic of skyscraper-construction was accepted earlier in Chicago than it was even in New York, and in buildings such as that for the Guaranty Trust (1895) by Louis Sullivan (1856–1924) one sees the first stirrings of the new architecture. One reason why it came to birth in the Midwest lay not only in the fact that Chicago was a 'new' city, and rather proud of it, but also in the further fact that iron-frame construction, which was originally used for factories, was here first applied to solving another problem—that presented by the high office building. In fact, the first iron-frame office building in Chicago went up in the 1880s.

Sullivan's most important pupil was Frank Lloyd Wright (1869–1959), who joined his office in 1887. Wright's career spans the whole history of modernism, and he is one of the great 'maverick' figures of the twentieth century arts—not the leader of a school, but a seminal influence in many schools. The so-called 'Prairie' houses which Wright built around Chicago in the first decade of the twentieth century are immensely original in their use of inter-locking spaces, and their openness to the world outside. The Robie House of 1909 is more than a decade ahead of its time, at least in European terms, with its low-slung roofs and simple horizontal lines. Nor did Wright confine himself to domestic architecture. One of his best-known early buildings, Unity Church in Oak Park, Illinois, anticipates by a decade many of the ideas of De Stijl. The Larkin Company office building, which Wright built in Buffalo in 1904, was equally original in its treatment of space, and in the way in which it seemed to base itself on the industrial, 'anti-architectural' vernacular of grain towers and silos. Very early, Wright sensed the potentialities which were offered to architects by reinforced concrete, but this was something which he was to exploit chiefly in the years that followed the war. All the same, his early buildings show that he had progressed further than any other architect of the period.

In Europe, the 'new' architectural style in 1900 was still Art Nouveau, and it produced some remarkable buildings, such as those designed by Victor Horta (1861–1947) in Brussels, and Antoni Gaudi (1852–1926) in Barcelona. Gaudi embarked on some of his most important late projects in the first decade of the century, including the Guël Park.

But it was not so much a new concept of 'style' as technology itself which impelled European architecture into the twentieth century. It is not for nothing that Paxton's Crystal Palace of 1851, often spoken of as the first really 'modern' building, was an achievement in engineering rather than in the field traditionally given to archi-tecture. As one surveys the most important buildings to be put up in Europe during the first two decades of the century, one becomes more and more aware that what makes them memorable is their technological achievement. In 1902, for example, Auguste Perret (1874–1954) was the first to use a concrete skeleton for a domestic building—a block of flats in the rue Franklin in Paris. Still more original, from a constructional point of view, is the concrete-framed Théâtre des Champs Elysées in Paris. An equally new and original use of concrete was made by the Swiss engineer Robert Maillart (1872–1940). In 1910, Maillart built a bridge over the Rhine at Tavanesa which was the first such structure to be made of reinforced concrete. Maillart's bridges are among the most graceful ever built. A comparable figure is Max Berg (1870–1940), the architect to the city of Breslau, who in 1913 designed and built for the town a Centenary Hall spanned by a concrete dome which shows a soaring lightness that up to that point had seemed impossible to achieve.

At the same period, equal thought was being given to questions of town-planning, and the social use of architecture. One of the most impressive break-throughs of the time was Tony Garnier's (1869–1948) plan for a Cité Industrielle of 35,000 inhabitants. Garnier first began to elaborate this plan in the years 1899–1904, though it was not finally complete until 1917. The originality of Garnier's plan was that it was based strictly on the functions and services of the city itself. Considerations of symmetry were discarded. There were to be plenty of green spaces, and concrete was to be used throughout. Houses were to be simple blocks. Ambitious projects were also made by the Futurist architect Antonio Sant 'Elia (1880–1916) who died too young to realize them.

New building methods and new planning techniques were, in the long run, to have more significance for the twentieth century than 'architecture' itself. If there is one tendency which can be traced in the development of contemporary building, it is the steady movement away from the monument. In a way, it is a pity that histories of architecture are still so commonly written from the point of view of the Renaissance, to which the idea of the monument was so important.

Nevertheless, the International Modern which was to dominate architecture from the 1920s almost to the end of the 1950s was a perfectly coherent architectural style, which had its roots in the pre-war years, though the real development was to come later. The first stirrings are perhaps visible in some of the work done by prominent Art Nouveau architects, notably in the School of Art built by Charles Rennie Mackintosh (1868–1928) in Glasgow in 1897–8. But the real roots of the style are in Germany and Austria —in the late work of Otto Wagner (1841–1918), in that of Wagner's pupils Adolf Loos (1870–1933) and Josef Hoffmann (1870–1956), and in that of Peter Behrens (1868–1940). Their progress can be charted in certain key buildings—Wagner's design for the hall in the Vienna Postal Savings Bank (1905) in which he broke free of Art Nouveau, Loos's uncompromisingly stripped and cubic Steiner House, built in Vienna in 1910 (Nikolaus Pevsner has said of this that 'here for the first time the layman would find it hard to decide whether this might not be of 1930'), and Hoffmann's luxurious Palais Stoclet in Brussels (1910). Behrens was more than just an architect. He was chief designer for the Allgemeine Elektrizitätsgesellschaft, and designed not only the firm's buildings, but their products and even their stationery. In all there is logic and a finely controlled simplicity.

Behrens's pupil was Walter Gropius (1883–1969), who in 1919 was to convert the art school at Weimar into the Bauhaus, which was perhaps the most important centre from which the International Modern style radiated. Even before the war broke out, Gropius had created at least one building entirely in the new idiom —the Fagus factory at Alfeld, built in 1910. In modern architecture logic and reason were to triumph.

III

The development of music in the first two decades of the century was also to be less convulsive than that of painting. It was a period of the very highest musical achievement, but these achievements were of strangely different kinds. 'Traditional music' had managed to remain alive in a way that 'traditional painting' had not. In Vienna, for instance, the tradition of the German symphony continued to flourish. Gustav Mahler (1860–1911) wrote his Fifth Symphony in 1902, and his Ninth, and last, in 1909. But, in its highest expressions, his was a melancholy art. 'Das Abschied', the last song in the ambitious cycle *Das Lied von der Erde*, shifts in mood from the brooding to the radiant, but it is still in essence a tragic farewell, not only to life (Mahler knew he was dying when he composed it), but to a whole way of thinking and feeling.

The most interesting pre-war work of Richard Strauss (1864–1949), Mahler's much longer-lived contemporary, reflects the same mood. Strauss was an opera composer, rather than a symphonist, and he made an immense reputation for himself with three operas *Salome*, *Elektra*, and *Der Rosenkavalier*, all of which continue to hold the stage fifty years later. In the first two, Strauss is an Expressionist—*Salome* is based on the play by Oscar Wilde, *Elektra* on a play by the Austrian poet, Hugo von Hofmannsthal (1874–1929). Hofmannsthal also wrote the libretto for *Der Rosenkavalier*, and for the other operas which followed until the poet's death. *Rosenkavalier* is a marvellously subtle piece of nostalgia. Without surrendering anything that Strauss had learned from Wagner, it harks back tenderly to the Vienna of Maria Theresa, and the central character, the tender and beautiful, but ageing, Marschallin, takes an autumnal farewell of youth and love. The interesting thing is that the characters in this opera—the Marschallin herself, her young lover Octavian, the boorish Baron Ochs, are far more convincingly alive than the frenzied Elektra or Salome, who, superficially at least, fit the world of the Fauves so much better.

Also Viennese, and, to begin with, equally under the spell of Wagner, was a man who was to play a very different part in the history of modern music. Arnold Schoenberg (1874–1951) has so convincingly maintained his reputation as a revolutionary that it is sometimes forgotten how much of his music was composed before the First World War. From the beginning, Schoenberg was a controversial figure. A performance of some of his songs in Vienna in 1900 provoked boos and catcalls. But at this early stage Schoenberg was still a post-romantic composer—indeed, in the broad sense, he remained a romantic all his life. His frequently enunciated principle of 'unity' also meant unity with the natural world. Schoenberg spoke of the work of art as 'the perfect organism'. He said 'In an apple tree's blossoms, even in the bud, the whole future apple is present in all its details.' The culmination of Schoenberg's romantic phase was the work with which he finally stormed the Viennese public, the *Gurrelieder*, whose composition occupied him from 1900 to 1911. An immense cantata, which requires about four hundred performers, the *Gurrelieder* push the late-romantic tradition about as far as Schoenberg or anyone else could hope to carry it.

But already a change had overtaken his music. In 1909, Schoenberg moved towards atonality. Consonance and dissonance were now to be the same, and there was no home key. His work became much more concentrated and intense, and at the same time atonal procedures intensified the expressionism of his music. Characteristic is *Erwartung* of 1909—a work for the theatre which is yet not an opera, but rather a monodrama, as there is only one soloist to contend with the huge orchestral forces. The plot is typical of the time: a woman searches through a wood at night, looking for a faithless lover. At last she stumbles over his dead body. Even more interesting is a less ambitious semi-dramatic piece—the famous

Pierrot Lunaire of 1912. Scored for female reciter and five instruments, this makes use of *Sprechstimme*, a form of declamation midway between song and speech. *Pierrot Lunaire* remains one of the most striking products of German Expressionism, on a par with the heart-rending poems of Georg Trakl.

The full impact of Schoenberg's influence was only to be felt after the war, though he had already begun to gather disciples around him, such as the young Alban Berg (1885–1935) and Anton Webern (1883–1945), both of whom were producing their earliest compositions. But it seems best to leave a discussion of their work, and of the dodecaphonic method which Schoenberg evolved after 1923, for a chapter in the subsequent volume.

Besides Vienna, there was one other, and perhaps even more important centre for new music—Paris. Here the musical world was dominated by the influence of Claude Debussy (1862–1918). Debussy is usually classified as an 'impressionist'—a term which irritated him. In fact, he seems to stand in much the same relationship to the main nineteenth-century tradition of romantic music as the symbolist poets stood to their romantic predecessors. Despite the fact that Debussy once described music as 'an open-air art, an art boundless as the elements, the wind, the sky, the sea!', his was essentially a talent that revelled in subtleties and nuances. His opera *Pelléas et Mélisande*, based on the play by Maeterlinck, was ten years in the making before it received its premiere in 1902. It created a sensation. Here was a new kind of opera, with the unity of Wagner, but with quite a different emotional tone: muted, lyrical, discreet. Debussy was already known to a small circle of important admirers —he frequented the 'Tuesdays' of the poet Stéphane Mallarmé— but *Pelléas* made him an influence on a European scale. And this influence persisted. If Debussy's effect on the course of twentieth-century music cannot be so precisely charted as that of Schoenberg, or even Stravinsky, it has still been pervasive. Especially important was the passive, almost static quality of Debussy's music, and the composer's obsession with sonorities. Both of these remind one vividly of the work which was later to be done by composers such as John Cage. The emphasis on the 'sound-value' was also to have an influence upon the new electronic music.

Other 'impressionist' composers seem less relevant today, though one must recognize the technical perfection of much of the music of Maurice Ravel (1875–1937), and the rather cloying sensitivity of that of Frederick Delius (1862–1934).

To me a far more interesting figure than either of these is the eccentric Erik Satie (1866–1925). Satie was a key-figure in the pre-war Paris *avant-garde*, and many of his musical ideas (and indeed his musical jokes) have passed as common currency ever since. Long before the Dadaists arrived on the scene, Satie understood the essence of Dada humour. The '3 Morceaux en forme de poire' (*poire* is French slang for 'idiot') of 1903 were written as a kind of retort courteous to Debussy, who told Satie that his works were not sufficiently strict in form. Satie's later works are pervaded with a strange combination of poetry and facetiousness. He pioneered a sly use of musical cliché, experimented with the aesthetics of bore-dom, in the aptly titled 'Véxations', which were designed to be played over and over again. But he also stood for the utmost strict-ness and purity of style, as can be seen from one of the masterpieces of his late period, *Socrate* (1918), which is a symphonic drama in four parts based on the dialogues of Plato. Equally important is the ballet he wrote for Diaghilev, *Parade* (1917), but to this I shall revert in a moment.

French and German music formed, so to speak, the two main-stream traditions. The powerful influence of nationalism, however, was felt especially strongly in music. Here it had established itself early in the nineteenth century as an essential part of romantic picturesqueness, and by 1900 it was much more fully established among musicians than elsewhere. The result was that the musical world of the first two decades of the century was adorned with a whole group of 'nationalist' composers who now seem, though much of their music has survived, oddly irrelevant to the development of the modern arts as a whole. Among them were the Finn Jean Sibelius, the Czech Leos Janaček, the Spaniard Manuel de Falla, the Italian Giacomo Puccini, and the American Charles Ives. But one national tradition in particular was to have a powerful influence on the development of modern music as a whole, and that was the Russian.

In the early years of the century Russian music was in any case fashionable in western Europe, thanks, for example to the concert tours of Alexander Scriabin (1872–1915) and the success of such compositions by him as the *Poem of Ecstasy* (1908) and the *Poem of Fire* (1910). The season of Russian music arranged by Diaghilev in Paris also had a certain impact. But it was another of Diaghilev's enterprises, the Ballets Russes, which brought the music of the young Igor Stravinsky (1882–1971) before the Parisian public. Stravinsky was a pupil of Rimsky-Korsakov, and his first com-mission from Diaghilev was *L'Oiseau de Feu* (1910). This was followed by *Petrouchka* (1911), *The Rite of Spring* (1913), and the opera *Le Rossignol* (1914). In these works one sees Stravinsky gradually freeing himself from specifically 'nationalist' influences, and then moving through a phase of primitivism with *The Rite of Spring*. This last, which was the cause of a famous scandal, is also the beginning of the specifically 'modernist' phase of Stravinsky's career—a phase which, with many modifications, lasted until his death in 1971. The violence and percussive dissonance of the music are precisely in line with the kind of thing which the Fauves had been trying to achieve a few years earlier—and Stravinsky resembles Matisse in the firm foundation of objectivity and classicism which underlies the appearance of Dionysiac ferocity.

The war put Stravinsky in an especially unenviable position. Cut off from his country, in want of money, he was forced to abandon the large-scale works which he had hitherto composed and limit himself to smaller forces. The result was the burlesque *Reynard* (1917) and *L'Histoire du Soldat* (1918). *L'Histoire* is an entertainment written for six instruments and percussion, and has four characters—the Soldier, the Devil, and Princess (who does not speak), and the Narrator. The tale tells, with Brechtian irony (and a number of dramatic devices that foreshadow Brecht), how the Soldier loses his soul to the Devil and is carried off by him. The whole thing forms a kind of concluding gesture or summary for two decades of music. *L'Histoire du Soldat* and *Rosenkavalier*, for instance, are utterly opposed to one another. *Rosenkavalier* relies upon the existence of a rich and stable world. *L'Histoire* is a parable for a world where everything has become uncertain. Essentially the process of stripping down which we see at work in Stravinsky and Satie (and even to some extent in Debussy and post-1909 Schoenberg) was a reaction which was essential if music was to survive. The tradition had become too rich; the resources open to post-Wagnerian composers were too ample. For a moment, it looked as if kinaesthetic experiments, such as those made by Scriabin, would lead music to a new realm. But they proved abortive. Music was already moving rapidly towards the austerity which the war eventually enforced.

Nevertheless, the old pre-war world, before it died in the holocaust, performed great services for the *avant-garde* arts. It is now sometimes said that one of the troubles which afflicts the 'advanced' artist is his inability to induce real shock in the bourgeois public—that he is constantly pursued and flattered by those whose susceptibilities he most wishes to wound. The implication is that this is a new phenomenon, post-1945. An examination of the facts will prove that things were quite otherwise. Nowhere is the traditional alliance between the world of fashion and the *avant-garde* more strikingly exemplified than in the history of the Ballets Russes. These were the creation of the most remarkable impresario of the period, Serge Diaghilev (1872–1929).

Diaghilev had had considerable experience as an *animateur* before the Ballets Russes came into being in 1909. His first venture was the '*Mir Iskustva*' (The World of Art) group, and the magazine of the same name. The group came into being in 1898. Diaghilev was responsible for organizing exhibitions which showed the newest Russian painting. He also had a quarrel with the management of the Imperial Russian Theatres (where he had briefly been employed) which resulted in a humiliating dismissal. This was one of the things which turned his attention towards the West. In 1906 he organized a Russian section at the Salon d'Automne in Paris. In 1907 there was a series of concerts of Russian music at the Paris Opéra, in 1908 he returned to the Opéra with a series of performances of *Boris Godunov* in which Chaliapin sang the title role. In 1909 he decided to take a mixed programme of opera and ballet to Russia. The performances were wildly successful and it was the ballets in particular which delighted the Parisian public.

It was not until the second season of the Ballets Russes, in 1910, that the characteristic style of its first phase was established. *Scheherazade* in particular, with music by Rimsky-Korsakov, choreography by Fokine, and costumes and décor by Bakst, took the town by storm and established a whole series of new fashions overnight. Fashionable clothes (such as those designed by Paul Poiret) and fashionable interior decoration all followed the same exotic genre. But Diaghilev was not content merely to establish an image of passion, luxury, and exoticism. He was determined to ally himself to the whole European *avant-garde*, and to harness its energies to his own purposes. His young protégé Nijinsky, who was also the principal star of the company, was set to work to provide a ballet to fit Debussy's prelude *L'Après-Midi d'un Faune*. *Daphnis and Chloë* was commissioned from Ravel, and *The Legend of Joseph* from Richard Strauss. The young Jean Cocteau was roped in to provide librettos. Larionov and Gontcharova were summoned to do décors. By May 1917, when *Parade* was given its first performance, the marriage between the Ballet Russes and the international *avant-garde* was complete: the book of that ballet was by Cocteau, the music by Satie, and the scenery by Picasso. Diaghilev was already set on the course he would pursue for the remaining twelve years of his life, a period during which his company of dancers remained cut off from their original base by the Russian revolution.

The thing which made *Parade* a memorable event was the fact that it showed the *avant-garde* arts not merely in isolation, but at work together, supporting one another to make an event with its own wholeness. In one sense, *Parade* was merely an extension of the goings-on at various Futurist cabarets, or even at the Café Voltaire in Zürich. In a different sense it was epoch-making, because it showed that rigid aesthetic principles could be applied to all these nose-thumbing antics, and, furthermore, hinted at an entirely new realm of aesthetic experience. Diaghilev's taste, his appetite for the 'new', were invaluable. No one need doubt that his celebrated remark to Cocteau—'*Étonne-moi!*'—was meant to be taken very seriously.

Finally, I must mention an entirely new art—that of the cinema—though most of its triumphs were still to come. 'Moving pictures', as such, began with Thomas Edison's Kinetoscope in 1889. The images here could only be viewed by one person at a time, looking through a peephole. By 1895, Thomas Arnat had perfected a workable projector, and the cinema was more or less in being. By 1897 it was possible to show a film eleven thousand feet in length—the record of a boxing match. Trick-effects began about the same time, with the work of the Frenchman Georges Méliès. The first proper attempt to tell a story did not happen until 1903, with *The Great Train Robbery*. One-reel melodramas such as this were duly succeeded by longer historical films, of a kind which we should now call 'epics'. One of the most successful of these was *Queen Elizabeth*, starring Sarah Bernhardt. Despite the participation of this great actress, the film up to this point remained very much a popular entertainment, with few pretensions to be anything more. But in 1914 D. W. Griffith made *Birth of a Nation*, and it began to be realized that the film could be something in its own right, a medium with its own very particular rules. Griffith's next film, *Intolerance*, made in 1915, confirmed its potentiality. In 1918 the film was ready to offer a challenge to the theatre, which could no longer be thought of as the only 'total' art form. Through the film, an artist could hope to reach more people, and to command their imaginations more absolutely, than he could through any other medium. And this was to have enormous consequences for the future.

IV

The birth of the cinema may not be the least of the reasons for regarding the period 1900–18 as perhaps the most important in the history of the arts for several centuries. Even the Italian Renaissance did not present so vast an upheaval, compressed within so small a space of time. One can look at this upheaval from several different points of view. For example, the violence of the Futurists can, as I've said, be regarded as an expression of the mood which led to the outbreak of the First World War. Marinetti's open worship of war is significant here. The continuing cult of violence in the *avant-garde* arts of the twentieth century, even after the harsh experience of two world wars, casts a somewhat ironic light upon our epoch. Yet there is another way of regarding this violence, and that is in connection with the idea of the 'alienated' artist. The phenomenon of alienation is not new, though the label perhaps is contemporary. Early Mannerists, such as Pontormo, or Baroque artists, such as Michelangelo Caravaggio, Annibale Carracci, or Salvator Rosa, were equally capable of displaying the symptoms which we now think of as characteristic of alienation. The writers and musicians and artists of the *Sturm und Drang* displayed them more plainly still. What was new was the alienation of whole communities of artists—the kind of thing we find with the Russian Futurists and with Dada. Equally new is the way in which society begins to accept the alienated artist as inescapably part of itself.

If the peace and prosperity of the nineteenth century bred restlessness among artists, so did the vast technological changes which had come about in the course of it, and technology was certainly one reason for the alienation which I have been talking about. Yet technology could not fail to excite the artistic imagination, and the cultural explosion of the first two decades of the century was in part motivated by the attempt to get to grips with it, to align the arts with the new skills which man had discovered for himself. Again as I have already pointed out, there is the greatest possible contrast between the rationalism of De Stijl in Holland and the irrationality of Dada, though the two movements are precisely contemporary. Similarly, in a musician such as Schoenberg, we find a temperamental urge towards the most violent forms of expressionism which goes hand in hand with an increasingly rigorous technical discipline. A similar comparison can be drawn between the 'orgiastic' Stravinsky of *The Rite of Spring* and the neo-classical Stravinsky of the years immediately following the First World War. Some traces of the dichotomy can even be found in modern architecture, though architecture is, by its very nature, the most rational of the arts. The primitivism which plays so great a part in the birth of modern painting may even be regarded as a direct reaction to technological advance, the necessary counterweight to developments elsewhere.

In considering the period 1900–18 from the standpoint of today, two things seem to me to be especially striking. One of them is the false emphasis which the historians of the modern arts have tended to place upon France, and especially upon French painting. Modernism was a movement in which most of the European powers participated almost equally—the exceptions seem to have been England and Spain. Britain, having given an important impulse to modernism through the work of the Art Nouveau architects and designers, and especially Mackintosh, was content to play a comparatively minor part. The Vorticism of Wyndham Lewis (1882–1957) was a pale reflection of developments on the Continent, and especially of Italian Futurism. The best English modernist painting—for example the Futurist war pictures painted by C. R. W. Nevinson (1889–1946)—hardly stands comparison with the work that was being done elsewhere. On the other hand, critics such as Roger Fry (1866–1937) and Clive Bell (1881–1964) were, for English-speaking readers, the prophets of modern art, and the country which these critics looked towards was France. Fry's saint was Cézanne. As a result, there has been a persistent tendency to interpret the history of modern painting in a strictly Cézannean sense—an interpretation which involves the exaltation of Cubism over all other modernist styles. In my view, this involves an important distortion of the facts. It is perhaps possible to grant that the Cubists achieved a statement which has a completeness denied to their rivals, but it was at the price of making Cubism a closed system. It is easy enough to point out what Cubist painting derives from; it is far more difficult to show that it prompted new developments or that it remains a vital force within the art of our own day. In fact, I can only repeat that Cubism seems to me a brilliant dead end, a final heroic effort to force the ideas and standards of the past into some kind of relationship with the world which the artists saw and sensed around them.

One need not strain to discover Futurist, Dada, and Expressionist ideas at work in our own day. And this is equally true of the work of the pioneer abstractionists, such as Kandinsky, Malevich, and

Mondrian. Indeed, any close study of the modern arts is bound to leave one with the feeling that in many important respects they have not been able to go beyond their own beginnings, that the pioneers provided their successors with a rich stock of forms and attitudes, and that these are still only gradually being explored. Dada, for instance—so frequently written off, so ephemeral by its very intentions—has shown astonishing powers of survival. The whole spectrum of Futurist techniques and notions crops up in every new *avant-garde* declaration of the sixties. What this suggests is that we need a new historical framework—that the whole idea of the regular progression of styles is no longer a useful instrument of interpretation. What one needs, in fact, is a means of explaining why what was 'new' in 1900–18 remains so perpetually new, and why the limits of the advances which were made then have set up barriers which it is still difficult to surmount half a century later.

FOR FURTHER READING

The *Encyclopaedia of Modern Architecture*, ed. G. Hatje (1963) and *Twentieth Century Music*, ed. Rollo Myers (1960) are essential reference books. Other invaluable general books are Werner Haftmann, *Painting in the Twentieth Century* (new ed., 1965), Nikolaus Pevsner, *The Sources of Modern Architecture and Design* (1968), and Paul Rotha, *The Film Till Now* (1949).

Theory is usefully dealt with in John Willett, *Expressionism* (1971) and Marianne W. Martin, *Futurist Art and Theory* (Oxford, 1968). Camilla Gray, *The Russian Experiment in Art* (1971) is excellent. For a flavour of the whole period, see Roger Shattuck, *The Banquet Years* (1959).

Major books on individual artists are Francis Steegmuller, *Apollinaire* (1964), Arnold Haskell, *Diaghileff* (1935), Alfred H. Barr, *Matisse* (New York, 1951) and *Picasso* (New York, 1946), and Eric W. White, *Stravinsky* (1966). James Joll, *Intellectuals in Politics* (1960), includes a useful essay on F. T. Marinetti.

INDEX

Abbey Theatre, Dublin, 389–90, 464
Act of Union (1800), 34
Action Française, 150, 155
Acton, Lord, ix, 102ff., 111
Addison, Christopher, 8
Adler, Alfred, 237
alchemy, 312ff.
alcohol, consumption of, 44, 75, 87
Alexander, Samuel, 177, 207ff., 244, 245
algebra, Boolean, 188
Allport, Gordon, 232
American Journal of Psychology, 225
American Naturalist, 351–2
American Psychological Association, 225
American Viscose Company, 62
amino-acids, 328
anaesthetics, synthetic, 325
Angell, Norman, 121
Anglo-Saxon, literary influence of, 380, 385
Anti-Corn Law League, 17
anti-Semitism, 116, 117
Antoine, André, 448
Apollinaire, Guillaume, 489, 490, 497
architecture, 499–502, 509
Arensberg, Walter, 498
Aristotle, 175, 185, 186, 227
Army Act (annual), 37
Arnat, Thomas, 508
Arnold, Matthew, xi, 114, 215, 478
Arp, Hans, 497
Art Nouveau, 491, 500, 501–2, 510
Asquith, H. H.: Boer War, 16; career, 5ff., 89; and female suffrage, 33; Ireland, 35ff.; reforms, 20, 22, 24, 26ff.; war, 41ff.
Ashton, F. W., 302
atom, structure of, 253, 260, 289, 301ff., 313ff., 337ff.
Attlee, C. R., 45
Auden, W. H., 397, 406

Aurier, Albert, 487
Austen, Jane, 417, 420
Austin, Herbert, 57, 67
Avogadro, Amedeo, 314

Babbitt, Irving, 406
Bacon, Francis, 313
Bacon, Roger, 313
Badische Aniline und Sodafabrik, 333, 334
Bagehot, Walter, 132
Bain, Alexander, 182
Bakeland, Leo, 330
Bakst, Léon, 493, 507
Balfour, A. J.: career, 5, 6, 12, 14; education, 16; and female suffrage, 33; Ireland, 20; Liberal budget, 25ff.; social measures, 21
Ball, Hugo, 497
Balla, Giacomo, 496
Ballets Russes, 493, 505, 507–8
Balmer, J. J., 307
Bank of England, 84
Barkla, Charles, 338
Barnes, William, 376
Barrès, Maurice, 154
Barrie, J. M., 28
Bateson, William, 346ff.
Bauhaus, 498, 502
Beard, Charles A., 109, 110
Beardsley, Aubrey, 475
Bebel, August, 137, 141, 142
behaviourism, 233, 239, 243
Behrens, Peter, 502
Bell, Clive, 510
Bell, Lady, 77
Belloc, Hilaire, 117, 129, 395, 475
Benn, Gottfried, 373
Bennett, Arnold, 403, 421, 422, 431, 440, 444
Benois, Alexandre, 493
Bentham, Jeremy, 113, 118, 122, 125, 133, 177, 182, 212ff.